CHRONICLE OF THE FIRST WORLD WAR

VOLUME II: 1917 - 1921

CHRONICLE OF THE FIRST WORLD WAR

VOLUME II: 1917 - 1921

Randal Gray

with Christopher Argyle

Facts On File
Oxford • New York

CHRONICLE OF THE FIRST WORLD WAR 1917-1921

Facts On File Limited
Collins Street
Oxford OX4 1XJ
UK

or

Facts On File Inc.
460 Park Avenue South
New York NY10016
USA

A British CIP catalogue record for this book is available from the British Library.

A United States of America CIP catalogue record for this book is available from the Library of Congress.

ISBN 0-8160-2139-2 Vol. I
ISBN 0-8160-2595-9 Vol. II
ISBN 0-8160-2597-5 Two-vol. set

Facts On File books are available at special discounts when purchased in bulk quantities for businesses, associations, institutions or sales promotions. Please contact the Special Sales Department of our Oxford office on 0865 728399 or our New York office on 212/683-2244 (dial 800/322-8755 except in NY, AK, or HI).

Produced by Curtis Garratt Limited,
The Old Vicarage, Horton cum Studley, Oxford OX9 1BT

Index by D F Harding

Maps by Neil Hyslop

Printed and bound in Great Britain by
Butler & Tanner Ltd, Frome and London

10 9 8 7 6 5 4 3 2 1

This book is printed on acid-free paper

CONTENTS

To Captain G. G. P. Hewett CBE, RN (1880-1966)
who served with the Grand Fleet in the bleakest years.

INTRODUCTION

This reference work was conceived in January 1986 on it being discovered that no general English-language chronology of 1914-18 had appeared since the Committee of Imperial Defence's *Principal Events* was published in 1922, the immediate aftermath of the Great War. The very detailed but specialist and unindexed *Economic Chronicle of the Great War for Great Britain & Ireland 1914-19* (with Supplement on 1920-22) by N B Dearle appeared at the start of the Great Depression — 1929. In other languages the gap of years scarcely lessened, Major Amedeo Tosti's *Chronologia della guerra mondiale* was published in 1932, and Félix Debyser's 263-page *Chronologie de la guerre mondiale* came out in that ominous year 1938.

So far as the authors can discover, no more modern chronologies exist in any language. No new German-language coverage seems to have been attempted after the course of the war itself. The date of Debyser's diplomacy-emphasized effort perhaps partially explains why nothing more recent has been published. The Second World War was imminent and there was no desire or leisure to rechronicle the horrors of the First. Even in 1920 Major-General Lord Gleichen, a 1914 BEF brigade commander and Director of the British Ministry of Information's Intelligence Bureau, had to seek funds from His Majesty King George V and other patrons to complete the third and final volume of his authoritative *Chronology of the War* (Constable, London 1918-20). This was the case even though a commercial publishing house was involved.

Furthermore a similar time-lag followed for the chronicling of the Second World War. Between the Royal Institute of International Affairs' 1947 chronology and Christopher Argyle's *Chronology of World War II* (Marshall Cavendish, London 1980) nearly a third of a century elapsed without a new general English-language book devoted to day-by-day events.

Perhaps chronologies are off-putting to modern historians and publishers as well as to readers. Yet chronology is the backbone of history, and can be popular as the recent phenomenal success of the Longman *Chronicle* series attests. All too often today it is treated both in general and particular works of scholarship with infuriating vagueness. Even official histories and sources can disagree on the dates of the most crucial and recent events.

This book is an attempt to chronicle the day-by-day events and mood of the First World War from the perspective of the late 1980s, more than 70 years after the Armistice and as its living veterans dwindle to ever fewer thousands. It says much for the current revival of interest in the first, shorter yet more important global conflict that over 30 per cent of our principal sources have been published in that decade. All three of the main English-language official or *The Times* chronologies, published between 1918 and 1922, have been reprinted in facsimile since 1985, further testimony to the curiosity of those who research their ancestors' experiences of the trenches and home privations.

No chronology can be omniscient or, however many help write it, trawl all that has gone before. It is a humbling thought that a 1987 Belgian bibliography of 1914-18 contains over 12,000 works. This chronology and its supporting features has aimed to be as international and detailed as possible within the inevitable limits of space, selection and time.

HOW TO USE THIS BOOK: THE CHRONOLOGIES

The nine parallel columns facilitate a coherent thematic approach. References to other dates are almost always forward looking. It is important to note that linked events, not just military operations over several days, in the same month are often consolidated into a single day's entry. Portentous events such as revolutions, invasions and declarations of war are emphasized in capital letters. Lesser but still important events and appointments are in bold type.

The arrangement of the nine columns or strands is as follows, across a double page.

WESTERN FRONT
Subheadings: **Flanders, Somme, Verdun, Vosges,** etc.

EASTERN FRONT
Subheadings in North to South geographical order: E Prussia, Poland, Galicia, Bukovina, Rumania, etc excluding Caucasus. From April 1918 this strand becomes simply Russia which was no longer formally at war with Germany and in revolutionary turmoil.

SOUTHERN FRONTS
Subheadings include: Serbia, Italian Front, Isonzo, Trentino, Bulgaria, Albania and Salonika/Greece, Macedonia.

TURKISH FRONTS
Subheadings: Mesopotamia, Palestine, Egypt, Gallipoli, Persia, Aden, Arabia, Armenia and The Yemen; includes Allied Pacific and Far East operations against German colonies in 1914 and India NW Frontier fighting.

AFRICAN OPERATIONS
Subheadings include: German SW Africa, E Africa, S Africa (esp 1914-15 rebellion), Cameroons, Tripolitania and Cyrenaica and W Desert for the Senussi Revolt, Morocco, Somaliland.

SEA WAR
Subheadings: North Sea, Atlantic, Channel, Baltic/White Sea, Mediterranean, Black Sea, Indian Ocean, Red Sea, Caspian, Pacific and Far East, Aegean and Adriatic.

AIR WAR
Subheadings: relevant front, sea or country.

INTERNATIONAL EVENTS
Subheadings include: Occupied countries, Diplomacy,

Neutrals, Secret War; coverage includes the Americas, PoW events and declarations of war.

HOME FRONTS

Subheadings include domestic events of all combatant nations.

Subheadings are not used for single entries on a day where the location is clear.

The Chronicle does not cover the internal events of the contemporary Portuguese, Mexican and Chinese Revolutions, all well under way by 1914; deaths of people essentially uninvolved in the war are not mentioned, nor are births, polar exploration, cultural or sporting events unconnected with it. Events in neutral countries unattributable to 1914-18 are similarly ignored.

NOMENCLATURE

Some mostly common abbreviations have been used and are explained in the glossary. Imperial measurements have been used as they were by the English-speaking world at the time. An important distinction should be made here between 'capture', 'take' and 'occupy' which historians often use interchangeably for the act of possessing hostile territory. We have tried to use the first two verbs when significant fighting was involved for the objective, with 'capture' implying the heaviest form of struggle. 'Occupy' means little or no resistance. 'Seize' implies a degree of surprise and rapidity in the operation. 'Storm' means a sudden costly seizure. 'Enter' means just that, no total occupation of a point or town, the opposing side may still be present. An 'action' is obviously a smaller engagement than a battle. Place names are the ones used at the time, hence Lemberg not Lvov. Eastern European place names in particular have undergone many baffling changes since 1914-18, not to mention many variations in their spelling then and now.

The term 'British' has often been used to denote any forces of the British Empire especially when several of its nation-alities were involved. This was practice at the time and no disrespect is intended to what were then the Dominions and the Colonies. In the case of Dual Monarchy of Austria-Hungary, the term 'Austria' has been used for the whole Habsburg Empire and 'Hungary' only mentioned when specifically meant.

Russia did not adopt the New Style Gregorian calendar until 31 January 1918 but we have applied it before for uniformity. The reader therefore should be aware that the Old Style Julian Calendar meant Russia was 13 days behind the rest of Europe excluding Bulgaria (changed 1915); Turkey (1918); Rumania and Yugoslavia (1919); and Greece (1923). This discrepancy is inevitably a fertile source of confusion. However, the most common variation is 24 hours either side of a given date even in the most impressive sources. An event may happen overnight or only become general news in the next day's newspapers. We have tried to be right but often the choice can be little more than guesswork.

We hope our chronology and its supporting features will be of assistance to all those wanting precise and accurate reference on the Great War of 1914-18 and its turbulent aftermath.

OTHER FEATURES

The Chronicle is not simply a chronology, though that is its main purpose. Succinct background narrative can be found in the annual focus on the fronts essays as well as for the causes and consequences of the war. The map section covers all the main campaigns. The make-up of Europe before and after hostilities is compared in map form.

Tables provide statistics for all the important military operations, forces engaged and losses incurred. Annual losses on the fronts are also recorded or at least estimated. The symbol + means that they were certainly higher but available figures only add up to the one given. Numbers of guns and prisoners lost are stressed as they are traditional yardsticks of military success and the Western Front, in particular, often offered little else.

Overall war statistics are also given, though the reader will do well to remember that apparently precise figures are not necessarily the truth, and in such an appallingly wasteful conflict can never be exactly known.

The glossary provides listing of wartime terminology and abbreviations with entries also giving the strengths of military formations and units, and some of the weaponry used.

Sources are arranged by chronological strand and are the actual ones used to compile this work. The index is by date not page and non-chronological features are named.

LOOKING UP AN EVENT

Taking the great naval Battle of Jutland as an example. The reader will find it under SEA WAR on 31 May 1916. Ship types engaged will be detailed under 1916 Sea War Tables. The opposing commanders Jellicoe, Beatty and Scheer are each profiled. A map of the North Sea will locate the fight-ing. The battle is set in context under Focus on the Fronts 1916. Naval terms such as battlecruiser and flotilla are explained in the glossary. Other references to Jutland can be found in the index and particular sources are given under 'Sea War, North Sea and Grand Fleet'. If this apparatus is borne in mind, much more information can be acquired than just the original factual chronological entry.

ACKNOWLEDGEMENTS

The authors would like to record their debt to the London Library; the British Library; Westminster libraries notably Maida Vale's superb military and naval history reserve collection; Leicester University Library; the Royal United Services Institute for Defence Studies' Library; and the Library of RMA Sandhurst. Without Mary Gray's unflagging word processing skills, and the book production expertise of Curtis Garratt, this superdreadnought of a project might never have entered the water.

JANUARY 1917	WESTERN FRONT 1	EASTERN FRONT 2	SOUTHERN FRONTS 3	TURKISH FRONTS 4
Mon 1 January 1917	Public announcement of Haig's promotion to FM. (Jan) 50 German inf gun btys formed for AT use on top of 28 already formed. BEF joined by 62nd (3) and 58th Divs (20). BEF est strength 1,591,745 incl 125,517 Anzacs & 104,538 Canadians.	(Jan) STAVKA orders 12-bn divs instead of 16 bn (exc Guard & Armenian Front) to form 62 new divs by mid-Mar. Russian Army has c16,300 MGs, STAVKA wants 133,000; also requires 20,530 guns with 18,376 trench guns (37mm) and mortars.	**Salonika** — Milne promoted Lt-Gen. Army Anti-Gas School formed. (Jan) French 30th Div arrives, Gen Grossetti i/c French Army of the Orient. Allied armies 30,000 under strength.	Now 300,000 Turk deserters, some in 150-strong bands. **Persia** — Baratov probing ops (-3) ended by snow after 300 cas (*see* 21).
Tue 2	Haig issues orders for 8 Apr Arras offensive (*see* 8). **Lorraine** — Mudra (from E Front) takes over German Army Det A (-18 June 1918) from Gen d'Elsa (i/c since 15 Apr 1916).	**Galicia** — *Südarmee* attack nr Zloczow repulsed. **Dobruja** — Mackensen's Bulgars take Macin & Jijila. **Baltic Provinces** — Gen Scholtz takes over Eighth Army (-22 Apr) from Mudra (i/c since 22 Oct 1916). Gen Hutier replaces Scholtz i/c Army Det D.		**Arabia** — Lawrence & 35 camel men ambush Turk camp SE of Yanbo. Feisal's 10,400 men, 4 guns & 10 MGs march (3) to Owais wells, 15 miles N of Yanbo for 185-mile advance on Wejh (*see* 18).
Wed 3		**Baltic Provinces** — Germans take Dvina I nr Glandau NW of Dvinsk but Russians recover (8). **Bukovina** — Lechitski attack succeeds nr Mt Botosul, 2218 German PoWs taken between Kimpolung & Jakobeny (27 & 30); 3 German night attacks fail (31). **Rumania** — Cossack Div leaves Rumanian III Corps for Russian one causing gap that Falkenhayn exploits (6).		
Thu 4	Nivelle visits & impresses K Albert, tells him 'We must gain our objectives in the first two days.' Nivelle also forms a Gen Staff 4e bureau to handle all logistics at army level.	**Rumania** — Mackensen takes Gurgueti & Romanul, piercing Braila bridgehead which Russians evacuate. Falkenhayn begins Battle of the Putna (-8).		**Sinai** — British railway reaches El Arish (*see* 9).
Fri 5	**Somme** — British capture 2 German posts nr Beaumont Hamel.	**Baltic Provinces** — Battle of the Aa (-3 Feb): Surprise Russian Twelfth Army (Radko) offensive with 2 Lett bdes (3 other regts refuse to attack, 94 shot), without prelim shelling, between L Babit & Tirul Marsh W of Riga. It gains 4 miles, 8000 PoWs & 36 guns by 11 despite German counter attacks (11-13,*see* 23).	**Allied Rome Conference** (-7): 5th Meeting of Allied military & political heads: Cadorna asks for 8 divs & 300 heavy guns (later 10 & 400) to capture Laibach & Trieste and so eliminate Austria. Anglo-French only willing to lend guns till Apr (W Front offensive), first month when Italian large-scale ops possible (*see* INT'L EVENTS & 17). Conference also acts to improve communications to Salonika via S Italy. **Salonika** — Sarrail & Milne attend Rome Conference, but Italians decline to reinforce them although former impresses Lloyd George. Gen Sir H Wilson temporarily i/c Salonika Army (3-10). British 65th Bde raid on Akinjali village only takes 4 PoWs.	
Sat 6	French *GQG* moves from Chantilly to Beauvais. Gen Rucquoi becomes Belgian CoS (on †Wielemans).	**Dobruja** — **Clear of Russians & Rumanians** after Sakharov's defeat at Vacareni (*see* 22).		
Sun 7				**Mesopotamia** — Maude's

AFRICAN OPERATIONS 5	SEA WAR 6	AIR WAR 7	INTERNATIONAL EVENTS 8	HOME FRONTS 9
(E Africa unless indicated) British ration strength 54,910 incl 28,763 whites & 16,943 Indians. KAR total 15,734 (8 bns, *see* 1 July), 4 more bns formed in Jan. Smuts takes German lines nr Kisaki in Mgeta valley (Nigerians clear N bank & cross) & pursues towards Kibambawe on R Rufiji. **W Africa** — French ops v Tuareg (-15 May).	(Jan) HMS *Muskerry*, world's first fleet minesweeper enters service, 19 sisters follow by Aug 1917. Beatty proposes 157-mile minefield with 80,000 mines (only 1100 in stock) to encircle Heligoland Bight, officially announced (23). **E Med** — Egypt-bound British troop transport *Ivernia* sunk by *UB47* off Cape Matapan (120 lost). **N Sea** — (Jan) Lt battlecruisers *Courageous* & *Glorious* join Grand Fleet (*see* 17 Nov). **Caribbean** — (Jan) US Atlantic Fleet manoeuvres (- Anr)	**W Front** — (Jan) After his Albatros D III's lower wing cracks in combat, Richthofen switches temporarily to a more conventional Halberstadt. Despite modifications wing failures continue to plague the 'Vee-strutter' Albatros D III & D V/Va. No 53 (BE2) Sqn arrives in France (No 43 Sqn Sopwith 2-seater 17; No 35 Sqn Armstrong-Whitworths 24). **Secret War: Salonika** — Lt W S Scott of RFC 17 Sqn lands second agent behind Bulgar lines (1st 17 Dec 1916). Capt G Murlio Green (17 Sqn) forces down 2 Albatros 2-seaters behind British lines (4 & 14, *see* 12 Feb).	**Neutrals: USA** — (Jan) German film *Germany and its Armies of Today* shown in New York. Kaiser says K Albert must not be allowed to return 'and the coast of Flanders must be ours'.	**Britain** — RFP 87% (up 3%). (Jan) Wheeldon family arrested for farcical plot to murder PM on golf course with air rifle poison dart (charged at Derby 31, jailed Mar). Official film *Battle of the Ancre & the Advance of the Tanks* released. Rail fares up 50%. **Turkey** — Bank of National Credit formed.
Action of Beho-Beho (-4) continues German retreat, but big game hunter Capt Selous DSO killed aged 65 (4). Beves' SA advance guard crosses R Rufiji in 4 Berthon boats.				**Russia** — Imperial family buries Rasputin at Tsarskoe Selo by night. His murderers exiled (6).
	E Med — Russian predreadnought *Peresviet* sinks on U-boat (probably *U73*) mine off Port Said; ship a Russo-Japanese War prize bought back from Japan.	**Turkey** — RNAS bomb & hit Maritza rail bridge at Kuleli Burgas, S of Adrianople (already damaged 14 Dec).	**Neutrals: USA** — Wilson speech 'There will be no war ... it would be a crime against civilisation for us to go in'. **Diplomacy** — London and Berlin agree to swap all internees over 45.	
Sheppard occupies Kibambawe on R Rufiji & crosses it (night 5/6) despite hippos sinking some boats. Smuts visits Kibambawe (6) & orders new night crossing by 30th Punjabis, who gain bridgehead (-8).	**Biscay** — French steamer escapes twice only to be caught after 15-hr chase (-6) during *U48* patrol claiming 11 ships worth 27,000t. **Black Sea** — 4 Russian predreadnoughts, 1 cruiser and 3 destroyers sink 39 Turk sailing coasters off Anatolia (-9).		Allied Rome Conference forms (Ship) Chartering Ctee (6, 1st meets 15); Lloyd George vainly proposes Julian Alps Allied offensive.	**Britain** — Lloyd George war aims speech to TU delegates at Central Hall, Westminster (*see* 5 Jan 1918). WAAC formed (*see* 13 Mar).
	RN orders 6 *Anchusa*-type 'Flower'-class convoy sloops for June & Sept completion (2 more, 13, & remaining 20,21 Feb), enter service June 1917-June 1918.		**Neutrals: USA** — Serb Legation opens.	
Action at Ft Kibata (-9): KAR	Final consultations between	**W Front** — Sgt Mottershead of		**Germany** — **Pless Crown**

JANUARY 1917	WESTERN FRONT 1	EASTERN FRONT 2	SOUTHERN FRONTS 3	TURKISH FRONTS 4
Sun 7 contd				feints begin with shelling of the Hai & Sannaiyat (7th Div trench raids). **Secret War** — Arab Bureau reports Baron Oppenheim's mission at Medina.
Mon 8	BEF GHQ sets 2 officers to work on plans for Flanders breakout & coast clearance (*see* 11 Feb).	**Rumania** — Falkenhayn captures Focsani with 5500 PoWs, crosses R Putna N & SE (9) only to be repelled (10).		**Mesopotamia** — Khalil Pasha moves Sixth Army HQ from Baghdad to 20 miles W of Kut but refuses to evacuate S bank.
Tue 9	**Somme** — British capture trenches E of Beaumont Hamel.	Hoffmann diary on Russian Spring offensive '... we have enough reserves to be able to face it with equanimity'.	Greek Athens govt agrees to move Army from N Greece to Peloponnese (*see* 18), but false rumour of German intervention at Larissa same day (19,*see* 25).	**Mesopotamia** — **Battle of Kut** (-24 Feb): 3rd Indian Div (700 cas) & 70 guns storms Turk front line in Khadairi Bend & holds v counter-attacks. **Sinai** — Action of Rafa: Chetwode's Desert Column (486 cas) storms Turk border defences, Turk losses inc 1635 PoWs & 4 guns. **Egypt now clear of Turks**; 8 British tanks land at Alexandria (*see* 17 Apr).
Wed 10	**Somme** — British attack takes trenches on ³/₄-mile front NE of Beaumont Hamel, Fifth Army ops on Ancre (-13 Mar) involve Anzac & 3 other corps (11 divs).	**Rumania** — Austrians storm 2 heights in Oituz valley. Rumanian Casin valley success (11).		
Thu 11				**Mesopotamia** — Turk 45th Div breaks through British line (650+ cas) but gradually forced back to Tigris S bank (-night 18/19). British Cav Div occupies Hai town, but inhabitants attack it retiring (14). **Sinai** — War Cabinet cables Murray to defer large-scale ops in Palestine till later in yr. **Arabia** — K Hussein finally declines British troops.
Fri 12	Foch forwards 'Plan H' — to counter a possible German outflanking movement against Italy or Lyons through Switzerland with 30 divs within 10 days — to Nivelle who approves (*see* 22).	**Rumania** — Mackensen's Turks take Mihalea on R Sereth NW of Braila, he takes Vadeni 10 miles NW (14) but driven out (16).		**Yemen** — 5 British ships land force at Salif, capture 100 Turks & recover British rock salt works after 3hr action. Britain recognizes Farson Is as Idrisi territory (22).
Sat 13		**Rumania** — Battle of Pralea (-18): Rumanians hold Susitza valley.		**Arabia** — Abdulla's 5000 Arabs capture Mecca-bound Turk convoy (much gold), reach Wadi Ais, 50 miles NW of Medina (19).
Sun 14	Nivelle study paper boasts: 'We shall break the German front when we wish, on condition that we do not attack the strongest point and that we execute the operation by surprise and abrupt attack in 24 or 48 hours.' Frost temporarily hardens the ground.	Russian Army 6,900,000 men. **Rumania** — Falkenhayn repulsed NE of Focsani (13-14), but takes Nanesti (19) & Fundeni (20).		
Mon 15	Nivelle in London (-16) expands his plan & wins British cabinet support despite War Office	RN Armoured Car Unit awarded 46 Russian decorations.		

AFRICAN OPERATIONS 5	SEA WAR 6	AIR WAR 7	INTERNATIONAL EVENTS 8	HOME FRONTS 9
capture 6 hills as Lettow raises siege.	German Foreign Minister Zimmermann & Ambassador Bernstorff on unrestricted U-boat warfare (*see* 20).	No 20 Sqn RFC wins (posthumous) VC for landing in his burning FE2 that saves his observer Lt W Gower, only NCO on 1914-18 air ops to win VC (12 Feb), dies of first-degree burns (12).		**Council backs unlimited U-boat war**. Kaiser's civilian cabinet chief diary entry: *'Finis Germaniae'*. **Rumania** — Michael the Brave War Order created (3 classes).
	Britain — †Adm Sir G Warrender (ex-2nd Battle Sqn, Grand Fleet 1914-15) aged 56 in London having resigned as C-in-C Plymouth due to ill-health (6 Dec 1916).		Müller diary 'The general war situation demands our ultimate weapon' (unlimited U-boat war). Kaiser so orders Naval Staff (9). Allied ultimatum to Greece demands acceptance of 31 Dec terms. Greece accepts (10).	**Russia** — PM Trepov resigns. Prince Golitsin succeeds. **Britain** — 1st major munitionette strike (-9, 2000 at Leeds) v girl's dismissal for striking forewoman. **Germany** — Effective agricultural war economy bureaux & agencies formed in every province & district
Gol Dobbs to Smuts, 'I honestly cannot see how we are going to feed the troops', advises reducing forward units (*see* 30).	After final council of war (at Pless) a Kaiser order is issued: 'I command that UNRE-STRICTED U-BOAT WAR-FARE BE INSTITUTED WITH THE UTMOST ENERGY ON FEBRUARY 1.' Bethmann says 'U-boat warfare is the last card'. (Austria backs decision 20,*see* 27). **C Med** — British battleship *Cornwallis* (13 lost) sunk by 3 torpedoes from *U32* (Hartwig) 60 miles SE of Malta. **E Atlantic** — Raider *Seeadler* sinks first victim & another British ship (10) S of the Azores.	**Palestine** — 6 RFC aircraft bomb Beersheba airfield (1st of 5 raids -16, Germans move to Ramleh by 29) while support for Rafa action incl 2 radio aircraft with 4 RHA sand-sleigh mtd wirelesses (*see* Turkish Fronts).		
	Channel — **First Anglo-French collier convoy sails** (up to 45 colliers with 3 or 4 trawler escorts) only 5 of 2600 lost by 30 Apr.		Allies reply to Wilson's peace note with special message from Belgium. **Neutrals: USA** — German San Francisco Consul-Gen & 4 employees found guilty of conspiracy to sink arms ships. Bernstorff cables Zimmermann war inevitable if U-boats unleashed.	**France** — Mlle Francillard shot at Vincennes for acting as German lover's courier. **Austria** — Expects 12m quintal grain deficit, appeals to Germany for more aid (*see* 27 Feb). **Britain** — Food Controller given greater powers. Sir Sam Fay made Director of Military Train Movements.
	E Med — Seaplane carrier *HMS Ben-my-Chree* sunk in Kastelorizo I harbour by Turk guns off SW Asia Minor (more shelling of French island base 27 Feb). British implement dispersal & coasting system in E Med to try & cut shipping losses, causes friction with French (*see* 23).		Turco-German Settlement Treaty signed at Berlin (*see* 10 Apr 1918). Austro-German note to neutrals & Vatican disclaims blame for war's continuation. **Montenegro** — 2nd proposal for union with Serbia; Gen Martinovic succeeds Radovic as PM (*see* 5 June).	**Britain** — 3rd War Loan (-16 Feb) launched at Guildhall by PM & Bonar Law; raises £1.1bn. from c8m subscribers. Sir L Macassey made Controller of Shipbuilding Labour. Admiralty i/c shipbuilding (from 15).
Lyautey creates temporary command covering Algeria, Tunisia & W Africa (Gen Laperrine arrives Algiers 22 *see* 13 Feb).			Count Czernin tells Austrian Common Ministers Council compromise peace must be sought. Allied Rome Note pledges to work for liberation of all Habsburg subject peoples.	**Russia** — HM Ambassador vainly begs Tsar to change policy. **France** — Butter prices fixed.
			US & Dutch Ministers leave Rumania. **Neutrals: USA** — Trotsky lands in NY (*see* 3 Apr).	
Nigerians cross R Rufiji at 2 points (-18) inc swing bridge, take Mkindu Hill (17).	**Channel** — Q-ship *Penshurst* makes her 2nd kill, *UB37*. **N Sea** — (c) Beatty concentrates Grand Fleet for wide sweep & exercises especially in night shooting.		**Occupied Poland** — Provisional Council of State 1st meets; Prince Niemoyovski appointed Regent by Kaiser (18, *see* 1 Feb).	
			Italy signs 1914 Anglo-French Naval Convention. British War Cabinet confers with Haig &	

JANUARY 1917	WESTERN FRONT 1	EASTERN FRONT 2	SOUTHERN FRONTS 3	TURKISH FRONTS 4
Mon 15 contd	misgivings.			
Tue 16	**Flanders** — British daylight trench raid W of Lens (& 17).			
Wed 17	**Somme** — British capture German posts on 600-yd front N of Beaucourt-sur-Ancre, repulse 4 counter-attacks (4 Feb).	**Emperor Charles moves Austrian GHQ from Teschen to Baden nr Vienna** despite Conrad's protests (*see* 1 Mar).	Cadorna report to PM Boselli stresses 'Allied co-operation on the Isonzo Front would have most important consequences in the general interest of the coalition.' If Anglo-French troops obtained they should move in mid-Feb. Despite Lloyd George's interest, strategy not adopted as Nivelle Offensive wins his backing instead.	
Thu 18			**Greece** — British Military Attaché & Chief Control Officer reports 8948 Greek troops; 3132 animals, 78 guns, 62 MGs have transferred to Peloponnese in past month.	**Arabia** — Feisal begins final march on Wejh (*see* 24).
Fri 19				**Mesopotamia** — 3rd Indian Div has cleared Khadairi Bend (S bank of Tigris below Kut) for 1639 cas since 9.
Sat 20		**Rumania** — Germans decide to halt offensive at R Sereth.		**Mesopotamia** — British armoured cars reach front. **Secret War: Palestine** — Jewish spy Lichansky reaches Australian patrols (*see* 21 Feb).
Sun 21	**Verdun** — French repulse attacks N of Bois de Caurières.			**Persia** — Ali Ihsan ordered to move troops to Baghdad, 44th Regt leaves Kermanshah (*see* 20 & 24 Feb).
Mon 22	Foch assumes temporary command of E Army Gp (-28 Mar) E for Castelnau (on Allied mission to Russia). Foch's CoS Weygand goes to Berne for secret talks with Swiss Gen Staff on steps v any German invasion of Switzerland.	**Dobruja** — 2 Bulgar bns cross S arm of Danube nr Tulcea but thrown back (23) losing 337 PoWs.		
Tue 23		**Baltic Provinces** — German Eighth Army counter-offensive regains most ground lost between L Babit & Tirul Marsh (-25), taking 900 PoWs (30).	**Italian Front** — Conrad suggests Austro-German offensive from around Caporetto and Tolmino (*see* 29 Aug).	

AFRICAN OPERATIONS 5	SEA WAR 6	AIR WAR 7	INTERNATIONAL EVENTS 8	HOME FRONTS 9
			Nivelle (-16, *see* W FRONT).	
NRFF takes Malawis bridge over R Ruhudje. Kilwa Force occupies Mohoro & takes *Königsberg* gun. **Tripolitania** — Gen Latini's 5 bns defeat Senussi nr Zuara (-17, *see* 12 Mar).		**W Front** — Richthofen awarded *Pour le Mérite*.	**Neutrals: USA** — †Adm Dewey, 1898 victor of Manila Bay and serving as first Chm of Navy's General Board, aged 79.	**Germany** — **A7V tank prototype ordered** (*see* 14 May). **Italy** — Food Commission appointed.
		E Front — German air raid on Dvinsk.	**Secret War** — **RN's Room 40 partially deciphers Zimmermann Telegram** 2 days before Bernstorff receives it in Washington.	**Austria** — Croat representatives declare Habsburg allegiance (Rumanian Club 24). **Russia** — War Minister Gen Shuvaev resigns, Gen Bielaev succeeds. **Germany** — Imports forbidden save by Chancellor's leave. **Portugal** — Gen Alorn made C-in-C W Front Exped Force. **France** — Minimum wage ends Paris area munition strikes.
	S Atlantic — Raider *Wolf* lays 29 mines off Cape Agulhas, S Africa; 2 ships sunk & only 7 mines swept in 1917 (*see* 18 Feb). **Channel** — *UC18* torpedoes RN destroyer *Ferret*, but latter survives to be converted to a minelayer. **Black Sea** — Russian submarine *Narval* sinks 3000t steamer, 440 mines added to fields off Bosphorus (18).			**Canada** — Parlt votes first Dominion income tax & $100m loan (*see* 29 Aug). **Britain** — Bar's AGM refuses to admit women. **Britain** — **Silvertown** (E London) **munitions factory explosion** (69k, 400 injured), heard in Salisbury, Wilts.
Hoskins succeeds Smuts as C-in-C (*see* 30 May). Main & Kilwa Forces only 40 miles apart. Hoskins flies from Kilwa to GHQ in a BE2c; only c15,000 fit troops v 8400 Germans, 20 guns & 73 MGs. Smuts sails from Dar-es-Salaam for London (*see* 26).	**E Med** — French Salonika-bound transport *Admiral Magon* (5566t) sunk by *U39* (Forstmann).	**Mesopotamia** — 3 RFC pilots bomb & hit Baghdad citadel (2 unexploded 100lb bombs). Maj J Tennant becomes W/Cdr i/c RFC in theatre, Capt de Havilland takes over No 30 Sqn.	Austrian Baden Crown Council just endorses German U-boat war decision. **Rumania** — National Ctee of Rumanian emigrants formed at Jassy, declares war v Dual Monarchy.	**Russia** — Col Knox writes '... all classes in opposition to the Govt...if there is a revolution, little blood will be spilt'. **France** — Supply Ministry closes bakeries for 2 days pw. **Britain** — No exemptions from military service for men under 31.
150 Germans repel 125 KAR from Mpotora W of Kilwa.		**E Front** — Airship *LZ97* raids Kishinev, Rumania.	Pres Wilson's 'Peace without Victory' speech to Senate (*see* 30).	
	N Sea — A Room 40-warned Harwich Force (3 cruisers & 14 destroyers) engages German 6th Torpedo Boat Flotilla (8 ships) & damages destroyers *G41* & *S50* in icy small hours bound for Zeebrugge. British destroyer *Simoom* sunk by *S50* torpedo. German flotilla leader *V69* driven damaged into Ymuiden (Holland) but not interned. **Allied London Naval Conference** (-24) opened by Lloyd George who stresses its importance & appeals for unity. It agrees to withdraw 4 RN battleships from Med, Adriatic Sqn to use crews in smaller ships, likewise only *Lord Nelson* & *Agamemnon* to stay in E Med; Anglo-French compromise on dispersed or fixed shipping routes in Med, to try both until next conference; British cmdre to be i/c Otranto Barrage under Italian C-in-C.	**Germany** — 10 RNAS Sopwiths bomb Burbach blast furnaces nr Saarbrücken (1 other raid Feb, repeated twice Mar). **W Front** — French ace Guynemer destroys 5 German aircraft (-26, *see* 16 Mar).	Bernstorff asks Berlin for $50,000 to sway Congress (US discloses 21 Sept). Anglo-Swiss & German-Norwegian trade agreements.	**Germany** — War & Munitions Procurement Agency 'Germany can never achieve the full Hindenburg Programme' (*see* 6 Feb).

JANUARY 1917	WESTERN FRONT 1	EASTERN FRONT 2	SOUTHERN FRONTS 3	TURKISH FRONTS 4
Tue 23 contd				
Wed 24				**Arabia** — 400 of Feisal's regulars & 200 sailors (3 British ships) capture Wejh from 200 Turks (-25) as Feisal & Lawrence (in Cairo 28) approach by land (see 31, 20 Feb).
Thu 25	**Verdun** — German success at Hill 304; mile-long stretch of French trenches stormed, but French regain most of them (26).		Sarrail requests permission to occupy Greek port of Volos to relieve Salonika congestion, but refused.	**Mesopotamia** — Maude attacks Hai salient SW of Kut on a mile front with 13th Div (1135 cas inc 3 bn COs & 2 VCs) & 114 guns; only half captured trenches held v counter-attacks.
Fri 26				**Mesopotamia** — 14th Indian Div retakes Hai W bank sector, creeping advances (-31).
Sat 27	**Somme** — British take position nr Le Transloy & capture 350-strong garrison.			
Sun 28	**Somme** — Severe British Jan pressure on the Ancre prompts Rupprecht to demand a voluntary retirement to *Siegfried Stellung* (*OHL* vetoes 29, *see* 4 Feb).			
Mon 29				
Tue 30	**Lorraine** — Destructive French trench raid S of Leintrey; penetrates to German 2nd line taking PoWs.			
Wed 31	**Somme** — British repulse counter-attacks on the Ancre. BEF takes 1228 PoWs in Jan.			**Arabia** — Col Brémond visits Feisal at Wejh; latter, warned by Lawrence, says he can take Aqaba without Allied help.

AFRICAN OPERATIONS 5	SEA WAR 6	AIR WAR 7	INTERNATIONAL EVENTS 8	HOME FRONTS 9
	Non-essential imports to be restricted. Standing International Shipping Ctee formed. Britain to send Italy as much coal as possible.			
Maj Grawert's 289 Germans surrender at Likuju in S. Maj Otto's 600 (46 cas) beat Nigerians (64 cas) at Ngwembe (-25) S of Rufiji.			**Neutrals: Greece** — Govt formally apologizes for 1 Dec events.	**Germany** — **Railway chaos in winter freeze** prevents all extra traffic (-5 Feb) despite mobile unloading teams.
V heavy rains begin (-May), worst in living memory.	White Star liner & AMC *Laurentic* (350 die) mined off Ireland, her gold cargo partially salvaged after Armistice. **N Sea** — German destroyer raid on Southwold, Suffolk. **Austria** — Grand Adm Haus argues to Emperor Charles for unrestricted U-boat war (*see* INT'L EVENTS 22). Charles then sees German Adm Holzendorff (promises 42 U-boats in Med, *see* May) & Zimmermann.		German Wolff Bureau in Constantinople falsely claims Abd-el-Malek's capture of Fez & Casablanca.	**France** — Restaurants restricted to 2 courses. **Japan** — Emperor dissolves Diet following attack on Govt (*see* 20 Apr).
In S Africa Smuts claims back of German resistance broken (*see* 12 Mar).	At Pless Austro-German naval chiefs draft note declaring Med prohibited zone to Allied shipping, Austrian U-boats to operate beyond Adriatic (*see* 31). **Arctic** — Minelaying *U76* rammed by Russian trawlers; she founders off Hammerfest.	**Britain** — Beatty forms Grand Fleet Aircraft Ctee, reports (5 Feb) that 40 aircraft needed with it (only 24 currently in 3 carriers). **Canada** — RFC training begins at Toronto (*see* 26 Jan 1918).	Tsar backs Pres Wilson's call for a free Poland with Baltic access. Dixie Jazz Band of New Orleans opens in Chicago (*see* 7 Mar).	**Canada** — National Steel Factory estab at Toronto. **Austria** — *Ausgleich* Agreement (1867) with Hungary changed & renewed in latter's favour for 20 yrs. **Germany** — War spending to date est at £5 bn.
Kaiser's birthday message refers to Lettow's 'small band of heroes'.	U-boat leader Bauer orders his cdrs '... unrestricted U-boat warfare is to force England to make peace and thereby decide the whole war. Energetic action is required and above all rapidity of action...expend only one torpedo on each ship stopped...'. Dover Straits route now compulsory to maximize time on stn.		Japan asks Britain to approve her assuming German rights in China (done 16 Feb).	
	Black Sea — 2 Russian destroyers sink or capture 22 Turk sailing craft between Ordu and Sinope (-31).		*U53* sinks Spanish SS *Nueva Montana* (ore for Newcastle) off Ushant & similar ship (29). **Secret War** — RN Room 40 intercepts Bernstorff's 2nd protest v unlimited U-boat war. **Mexico** — Pershing ordered home (*see* 5 Feb).	
160 KAR besiege Ft Utete on R Rufiji; c200 Germans escape on rainy night (30/31) & maul pursuit (2 Feb).	RN submarine *K13* sinks on acceptance trials in Clyde, 47 men survive after 57hr ordeal (*see* 16 Nov).		Allied delegation (Lord Milner, Gens Wilson & Castelnau) arrives at Petrograd (-21 Feb, *see* 3 Feb). **Neutrals: Switzerland** — **Prince Sixtus of Bourbon receives Emperor Charles' peace letter** from his mother (also Empress Zita's, *see* 13 Feb).	**Britain** — 1st fish rations issued to Home Army. **Germany** — National Ctee for Women's War Work unites all female organizations.
Nigerians on half rations (*see* 14 Feb).		**E Front** — Airship *LZ98* raids Petrograd.	Germany replies to Wilson's 22 Jan message, will do her best to protect US interests.	**Britain** — Call up minimum now 18+7 mths (formerly 18).
	Germany informs US Govt it will not 'leave any means whatever unturned [ie U-boat terror] to hasten the end of the war. Since the Allies have rebuffed Germany's attempt to reach an understanding by negotiation...The Imperial German Government must therefore abandon the limitations...imposed upon itself...'. **Germany announces zone in which all shipping liable to be sunk** as from	**Britain** — Cmdre Godfrey Paine Fifth Sea Lord & Director of Air Services (succeeding Rear-Adm Vaughan-Lee). **W Front** — (Jan) 4 *Jagdstaffeln* formed, another 6 in Feb.	**GERMANY DECLARES UNRESTRICTED U-BOAT WAR** & threatens cross-Channel hospital ships (alleged munition cargoes). Bernstorff orders sabotage of German ships in US ports.	**Britain** — Lowest mthly loss of working days (24,500). (Jan) Tractor imports from US begin (4000 in 1917). (Jan) 1,748,602 troops (34,703 in munition work) at home, 1917 total never falls below 1,685,537 of which max 830,749 trained & 581,756 available for service overseas.

JANUARY 1917	WESTERN FRONT 1	EASTERN FRONT 2	SOUTHERN FRONTS 3	TURKISH FRONTS 4
Wed 31 contd				
Thu 1 February 1917	(Feb) German Army now has 15 assault bns and 2 coys of *Stosstruppen* (given title of Grenadier, and Gd insignia, Mar). Each German inf coy to have 3 Bergmann LMGs. BEF forms 1st Tank Bde (2nd, 15; 3rd, 24 Apr), Central Work-shops & Stores begun 7 Jan. (Feb) 57th (6) and 59th Divs (21) join BEF. **Flanders** — German inf wearing winter white battle dress unsuccess-fully raid British positions nr Wytschaete. Severe frost on this & several succeeding nights. This week temperature falls below zero °F. **Somme** — Unsuccessful German trench raid nr Grandcourt. British trench raiders seize 56 PoWs nr Gueudecourt. **Occupied France** — (Feb) German senior cdrs & staffs, attend tactical School at Solesmes to learn new defence methods (school at Sedan opens Mar).	(Feb) Two Russian army censors destroy 18,075 letters from Front. (Feb) Each Russian cav regt (excl Cossacks) loses 2 of its 6 sqns to start a 3000-strong inf regt for each cav div. **Galicia** — White-clad Germans break through 15 miles S of Halicz but are repulsed, also cross Dniester ice but driven back (11).	**Occupied Serbia** — (Feb) Bulgars declare conscription for all men of military age in their zone (Timok, Nis, Uskub & Macedonia),*see* 1 Mar. **Italian Front** — Nivelle visits Cadorna at Udine (-2); Cadorna doubts being ready to attack by 1 Apr (*see* 8 Apr).	**Mesopotamia** — 14th Indian Div assault on W Hai salient fails (but succeeds 3). RFC shoot down Fokker & guns sink 2 Turk ferries nr Kut.
Fri 2		**Baltic Provinces** — German attacks E of Kalutsem Highroad (W of Riga) repulsed (also 4)		
Sat 3	**Portuguese Expeditionary Corps arrives in France** (first of 55,084 men *see* 17 June) under Gen Tamagnini de Abreu. **Somme** — British advance 500yds E of Beaucourt, taking over 100 PoWs.	**Baltic Provinces** — Battle of the Aa ends (Russian cas 23,000).	**Albania** — Austrian bde has occupied Pogradec on SW shore of L Ochrid & pushes patrol to within 5 miles of Koritza; Sarrail concentrates new French 76th Div there by 15 (*see* 17).	
Sun 4	KAISER SIGNS ORDER FOR			**Mesopotamia** — Turks

AFRICAN OPERATIONS 5	SEA WAR 6	AIR WAR 7	INTERNATIONAL EVENTS 8	HOME FRONTS 9
	Terschelling (Holland) N to Udsive (Norway) then NW to Faroe Is & down longitude 20° W 350 miles W of Ireland to Cape Finisterre. Zone also includes whole Med excl Balearic Is & Seas E of Gibraltar as far as Spain's heel. A 20-mile channel left for ships sailing to Greece until 11 Jan 1918 (qv). Archangel added to barred zone (Mar 1917). Scheer Order of Day says whole Navy must support U-boats. (Jan) U-boats have sunk 180 ships (51 British, 63 Allied, 66 neutral incl 34 Norwegian) worth 328,391t (British 109,954t), 2 U-boats lost. U-boat toll in Med is 75,541t.			
	GERMANY BEGINS FINAL UNRESTRICTED SUBMARINE WARFARE CAMPAIGN: 105 U-boats in service (42 under repair, 51 lost to date). (High Seas Fleet 49, Flanders 23, Baltic 2, Adriatic 24 incl Austrian, Constantinople 3). 51 more U-boats ordered. Max of 44 at sea on any one day. RN C-in-C Ireland has 10 Q-ships operational in home waters & Bermuda. **Britain** — 4 new seaplane stns cover SW Approaches (*see* Apr). **Over 600 neutral ships refuse to sail. N Sea** — HM Special Service Smack *I'll Try* (ex- G & E) scores 2 hits on U-boats (*see* 14 Aug). (Feb) Superdreadnought *Queen Elizabeth* becomes Beatty's Grand Fleet flagship. **Aegean** — (Feb) RNAS forms 4-seaplane base at Suda Bay, Crete, to patrol v U-boats.	**Germany** — Daylight bomber offensive v England (*Turkenkreuz* /Turk's Cross) scheduled to begin 1 Feb with planned availability of 30 Gotha bombers, but material shortages, production & technical problems plus realistic training impose 3-months delay (*see* 7 Mar).	UNRESTRICTED U-BOAT WAR BEGINS. **Diplomacy** — Constantinople University proposes Kaiser for Nobel Peace Prize. **Neutrals: Norway** — Forbids foreign submarines in her waters. **USA** — Newspaper *Fatherland* retitled *American Weekly* .	**Germany** — (Feb) Steel prod 252,000t below Hindenburg Programme target; only 6400t gunpowder (7500t target), influences W Front withdrawal.
Rhodesia — 2nd Native Regt formed, leaves for E Africa 16 Sept.	**N Sea** — RNAS bomb Bruges harbour (& 14, 16) where 20 torpedo boats & 3 U-boats frozen up.		**Neutrals: USA** — Wilson tells Cabinet he wants neither side to win.	**Britain** — **Food Controller appeals for voluntary weekly rationing** (London Feb meat consumption falls 15%). **Germany** — U-boat workers, railwaymen (12) & other key sectors put under Auxiliary Service Law due to widespread job changing. Coal use restricted (3, *see* 24).
	E Atlantic — *U53* sinks US grainship *Housatonic* off Scilly Is, British ship rescues crew (*see* INT'L EVENTS). **Adriatic** — Duke of **Abruzzi ceases to be Italian C-in-C**, Adm Cutinelli succeeds (-23 June). Vice-Adm Thaon di **Revel again becomes CNS & overall Navy C-in-C** (16). Italy creates inspectorate for Defence of the National Maritime Traffic (27) — against U-boats with Traffic Defence Commands. Night voyages, use of neutral waters & coast hugging, arming of merchant ships & daylight escorting stressed; 3 experi-mental 3-ship convoys run from Gibraltar (27). By end of war 392 escorts, 103 aircraft (60 attacks on U-boats), 7 airships, 702 coast guns employed (latter fire 167 times v U-boats) (*see* 8 Mar).		**US severs relations with Germany** after *U53* sinks US SS *Housatonic* off Scilly Is. **Diplomacy** — Allied delegation dines with Tsar at Tsarskoe Selo. Portuguese troops land in France.	
W Desert — Brig-Gen H	**Philippines** — German crews		US note to neutrals suggests	**Turkey** — **Grand Vizier Said**

FEBRUARY 1917	WESTERN FRONT 1	EASTERN FRONT 2	SOUTHERN FRONTS 3	TURKISH FRONTS 4
Sun 4 contd	RETIREMENT TO SIEGFRIED STELLUNG (Op *Alberich*). Whole zone between existing fighting front & pillbox-studded new line (65 miles from nr Soissons to Arras, av depth 19 miles) is given rigorous scorched earth treatment (*see* 9). New line will shorten W Front by 25 miles & release 13 divs into res. British not accurately aware of Hindenburg Line until 25.			evacuate Hai triangle E of Canal for new line in Dahra Bend, inc Kut S bank liquorice factory. British losses since 13 Dec 8524 but higher Turk ones, inc 2006 buried & 578 PoWs.
Mon 5		**Pripet** — German attacks repulsed 10 miles S of Kieselin.	**Italian Front** — Austrian attacks beaten off in several sectors.	
Tue 6	**Somme** — British occupy 1000-yd section of German trench near Grandcourt, S of R Ancre. Germans evacuate village, British occupy (7).	**Rumania** — R Sereth, SE of Focsani, freezing over, light German attacks repelled (*see* 18).		
Wed 7				
Thu 8	**Somme** — British capture Sailly-Saillisel ridge (Hill 153) with 78 PoWs, German counter-attacks (9), & advance from Grandcourt astride the Ancre.			**Yemen** — Cruiser HMS *Fox* causes Loheia's surrender to Idrisi's Arabs.
Fri 9	**Meuse** — French repulse German attacks. **Somme** — Op *Alberich* : Germans begin demolitions with programmed removal of material and civilians (*see* 22).		**Italian Front** — Austrians claim 1000 PoWs in attack E of Gorizia, but Italians regain trenches taking 100 PoWs (11). (c) Italian Intelligence reports new Austrian arty & troops on Asiago & in Upper Adige.	**Mesopotamia** — British 13th & 14th Divs storm liquorice factory (-10).
Sat 10	**Somme** — British capture 1250-yd wide trench system S of Serre Hill (Ancre), taking 215 PoWs. German counter-attack fails (11).		**Salonika** — c600 British trench raid (158 cas) on Petit Couronne W of L Doiran, gains 27 PoWs. Smaller raid on German 59th Regt E of Vardar (21).	**Mesopotamia** — 60pdr battery severs Turk Shumran Bridge at 9600yds range & forces it W.

AFRICAN OPERATIONS 5	SEA WAR 6	AIR WAR 7	INTERNATIONAL EVENTS 8	HOME FRONTS 9
Hodgson's armoured cars (among 146 vehicles) defeat 1200 Senussi & 2 guns at Girba, occupy Siwa Oasis & capture Munasib Pass, forcing dispersal to S (-5, *see* 8).	wreck engine-rooms of 9 interned steamers at Manila.		they follow her example (Switzerland declines 5, also Scandinavia 7). US Navy interns 17 German ships. **Occupied Belgium** — Separatists form 50-member 'Council of Flanders' (*see* 3 Mar).	**Halim resigns**, Young Turk **Talaat Bey succeeds**, made Pasha (*see* 15). Law fixes universal military service 20-45 yrs.
			Germany refers to US break 'The struggle is for our existence. For us there can be no retreat.' **Neutrals: Mexico** — Pershing & last 10,000 US cav leave. **Secret War** — DNI Capt Hall RN sees Foreign Office about publishing Zimmermann Telegram (*see* 8 & 19). **Neutrals: USA** — Pres Wilson forbids sale, lease or charter of American vessels to foreign flags.	**Britain** — **National Service volunteer scheme begins** enrolling 18-61 yr olds (100,000 by 3 Mar inc 15,000 women in 3 days, allowed to be taxi drivers 13). **Turkey** — 1st drug profiteers punished (100s arrested May). **Italy** — 4th War Loan opens. **NZ** — Sheepskins commandeered.
E Africa — Germans inflict 30 cas on Gold Coast Regt & 40th Pathans at Njimbwe but evacuate Kipandamoyo on flooding R Kinyani.		**Britain** — RFC Hospital opens in London. New Air Board formed (Lord Cowdray Chm).	Zimmermann cables Vienna Ambassador 'We can carry through even our moderate demands only as victors.'	**Germany** — Ludendorff orders halt on all new factories (exc nitrate plants) not completable by May.
			Brazil & Argentina threaten to sever relations if Germany attacks their shipping. **Germany** — All US citizens held as govt hostages (- 17).	**Russia** — 125,000 in Moscow & Petrograd political strikes (20 leaders arrested 10-11, *see* 18). **Britain** — King opens Parlt. Petrol licence issues suspended, **private motoring virtually eliminated** (331,897 licences 1916).
W Desert — **British ops v Senussi end** (*see* 17 Apr). **W Africa : Sahara** — Nearly 3000 French & 16 MGs in 4 cols ready to relieve Agades; main col (828) leaves Zinder (*see* 21).	**Adriatic** — Grand Adm Baron Anton von Haus, C-in-C **Austrian Fleet dies** of lung disease aboard flagship *Viribus Unitis* aged 65; Emperor Charles attends funeral. Senior Vice-Adm **Njegovan** (1st Sqn) **succeeds**, also made Admiralty Chief (30 Apr). **N Sea** — Destroyer HMS *Thrasher* sinks *UC39* with depth charges off Flamborough Head. **Channel** — Dover Strait minefield completed by RN minelayers, but has to be swept & relaid (June-July). HM Destroyer *Gurkha* mined & sunk. *UC46* rammed & sunk by destroyer *Liberty* SE of Goodwin Sands. **Britain** — War Cabinet decide only to continue with building battlecruiser *Hood* (*see* 22 Aug 1918), 3 sisters suspended 9 Mar as Germans known to have stopped work on capital ships.	**W Front** — Guynemer shares shooting down of Freiburg-based Gotha bomber nr Bouconville; this 32nd victim goes on display in Paris.	Wilson proposes to Britain that Allies declare v Austro-Hungary's total break up but Lloyd George declines (11). **Secret War** — Zimmermann telegram (RN Room 40 decipher) '... you are desired ... to broach ... an alliance to the President [Carranza].... The President might, even now ... sound Japan'.	
		Neutrals: Denmark — 1st rationing (sugar).		**Austria** — Col Gen Baron Hazai i/c Troop Replacement Branch reports direct to Emperor. **Britain** — Govt Employees Conciliation & Arbitration Board appointed (*see* 2 May). **John Buchan made Director of new Dept of Information.**
Secret War — Turk & German Madrid Ambassadors write to Moroccan Pretender El Hiba congratulating him on his victory over pro-French Pasha of Taroudant (*see* 16 Mar).	**Med** — 10 German & 1 Austrian U-boat at sea (*see* 2 Apr).	**Albania** — Italian airmen capture 2 of 3 Austrian seaplanes off Valona.	Peru & China protest to Berlin. Chile refuses to recognize blockade. US Ambassador Gerard leaves Berlin after some delay. **Britain** — Weizmann meets HMG reps to discuss Jewish colony in Palestine.	

FEBRUARY 1917	WESTERN FRONT 1	EASTERN FRONT 2	SOUTHERN FRONTS 3	TURKISH FRONTS 4
Sun 11	K Albert's war diary deplores Anglo-French Flanders landing schemes. **Somme** — British take 600-yd stretch of trenches nr Beaucourt-Puisieux road.			
Mon 12	**Somme** — Successful British trench raid S of Souchez.	**Bukovina** — Germans take Russian positions nr Jakobeny with over 1200 PoWs but Russians defeat attack (21,*see* 27).	**Serbia** — In Crna bend German surprise flamethrower attack recaptures Hill 1050 with 92 Italian PoWs & 5 MGs. Italians retake some lost trenches (27) & c70 PoWs but fail to regain summit; 400 cas in all.	
Tue 13	**Artois** — British trench raid NE of Arras (40 PoWs).			
Wed 14	**Aisne** — French trench raid 12 miles NW of Compiègne.	**Galicia** — Germans report successful raid between Zloczow & Tarnopol (281 PoWs).		
Thu 15	**Flanders** — German trench raids nr Loos, W of Messines & NE of Ypres. **Champagne** — Nivelle's instructions issued for general offensive. German attack gains them, 858 PoWs & trenches from French salient W of Maisons de Champagne (*see* 8 Mar).			**Mesopotamia** — British clear Dahra Bend (-16), take 1995 PoWs for 503 cas. Heavy rain (-17) prevents further S bank ops. **Arabia** — Lawrence secret despatch on 'Feisal's Table Talk' appears in *Arab Bulletin*.
Fri 16	Nivelle visits Haig at Montreuil (*see* 26), latter unaware that Lloyd George dealing with Nivelle direct. Nivelle reviews British 7th Div (17).	Hoffmann diary 'There is very encouraging news from the interior of Russia. It would seem that she cannot hold out longer than the autumn'.		
Sat 17	**Somme** — 3 BEF Fifth Army divs (3800 cas) gain 500-1000yds & 773 PoWs in 2 attacks at Miraumont N & S of the Ancre (night 17/18). **Alsace** — French raid on German salient NE of Altkirch causes heavy loss.	**Baltic Provinces** — White-clad Germans take 50 PoWs on R Lavkassa SW of Dvinsk.	**Albania** — **French & Italians link up at Herseg making 240-mile Allied front from Adriatic to Aegean.**	**Mesopotamia** — 7th Indian Div (500+ cas) fails & panics in attack on Turk Sannaiyat N bank position (3000 Turks, *see* 22).
Sun 18	**Somme** — British repulse attack on their new positions above Baillescourt Farm (N of the Ancre).	**Rumania** — Russian surprise attack takes German Trotus valley hill position.		
Mon 19	**Flanders** — British take 114 PoWs in raid E of Ypres. **Somme** — Germans with flamethrowers capture British post & 30 PoWs S of Le Transloy.			
Tue 20	**Nivelle postpones final deployment for Aisne offensive from 15 Mar to 10 Apr.**			**Arabia** — **First major raid on Hejaz Railway:** Capt Garland's 50 Arabs from Wejh blow up engine & bridge at Toweira (*see* 3 Mar). **Sinai** — British surprise and take Turk posts at Nakhl & Bir-el-Hassana.

AFRICAN OPERATIONS 5	SEA WAR 6	AIR WAR 7	INTERNATIONAL EVENTS 8	HOME FRONTS 9
E Africa — Kraut attacks British outposts at Johannesbrücke & Nyamasi on Songea-L Nyasa supply line to cover his retreat towards Portuguese frontier. **Ethiopia** — Judith (Zawditu) crowned Empress in Addis Ababa (Central Powers reps not invited).		**W Front** — **First successful night aircraft v aircraft combat**: Germans Peter & Frohwein in DFW CV destroy 2 French bombers on landing approach to Malzeville (night 11/12).	Germany attempts to re-open talks with USA via Swiss Minister. Wilson declines (13) unless 1 Feb measure lifted. **Secret War** — Prince Sixtus meets Jules Cambon re Austrian peace offer & returns to Switzerland, meeting Emperor's envoy Ct Erdödy at Neuchatel (13 & 21).	
		Macedonia — Lt J C F Owen burns his BE12 beside Bulgar airfield of Drama when forced down by a Fokker, Capt Murlis Green bombs airfield pm (*see* 26).	**Emperor Charles meets Kaiser at Vienna & refuses to break relations with USA.**	**Britain** — Commons votes £200m war credit; war costing £5.7m pd. 4lb loaf of bread now costs 11d.
S Algeria: Sahara — 150 rebels repulsed from Ain El Hadjadj S of Ft Flatters (*see* 9 May).				**France** — Mata Hari arrested in Paris (*see* 24 July).
E Africa — Nigerian convoy repels ambush nr Mkindu. (Feb) 80 Gold Coast Regt men hospitalized with starvation.	**Black Sea** — 2 Russian destroyers and a minelayer from Batumi sink 15 Turk schooners between Amasra and Sinope.		Ct Bernstorff sails from Hoboken NJ (home 14 Mar). British Commons pledge that Alsace-Lorraine's return a war objective. Secret Russo-French Treaty signed at Petrograd on territorial aims. **Neutrals: USA** — Congress votes funds for fortifications & $3.6m for airships.	**Britain** — RN voted 40,000 men, making 400,000.
	E Med — *U39* (Forstmann) sinks unescorted Italian Salonika-bound transport *Minas* (870 of 1000 die) W of Cape Matapan. French transport *Athos* also sunk (17) by *U65* (Fischel) 200 miles E of Malta. **Germany** — Lt cruiser *Nürnberg II* completed at Kiel, last of 4-strong class finished since 12 Aug 1916 to serve with High Seas Fleet Scouting Forces.			**Turkey** — New Grand Vizier's 1st speech to Chamber proclaims equality for all Ottoman peoples; violent Senate food debate (19, *see* 10 Mar). **Britain** — 1st RN special leave train departs Euston for Thurso (-30 Apr 1919, 717 miles). **Australia** — Hughes new PM.
		W Front — Airship *LZ 107* bombs Calais & overflies Deal — causing false alarm in London (night 16/17).		**Britain** — 30,000 troops available for spring farmwork. **S Africa** — Parlt opens.
	Torpedoed Q-ship *Farnborough* (Campbell wins VC) sinks *U83* (Hoppe), 2 survivors, off SW Ireland with 25 shots at 300yds (*see* 12 May).		**Neutrals: Greece** — Allies call Govt's attention to hostile Greek press; arms searches yield weapons.	
	Indian Ocean — Raider *Wolf* lays 58 mines off Ceylon (*see* 15 Mar), swept by 6 trawlers for loss of 2 large ships.	**Palestine** — Lt F McNamara of No 1 Sqn AFC in BE2 bombs German airfield at Ramleh (drops note suggesting that defenders improve camouflage measures) (*see* 20 Mar).		**Russia** — Gen Khabalov of Petrograd MD given special powers to maintain order.
E Africa — NRFF engages Kraut's rearguard nr Litembo & Capt Wintgens' 500 men, 3 guns & 13 MGs nr Tandala, saving that post (**Wintgens heading N on own solo raid - 2 Oct**).			**RN Room 40 deciphers Zimmermann Telegram full text**, shows it to US Embassy, Balfour gives Hall free hand (20, *see* 24).	**Britain** — (c)Sir A H Lee appointed DG Food Production. **Germany** — GHQ moves from Pless to Kreuznach.
	W Med — French cruiser-minelayer *Cassini* sinks on *UC35* mine in Bonifacio Straits.		**Neutrals: USA** — Wilson asks for powers from Congress. **Secret War** — Austrian note invites Prince Sixtus to Vienna for peace talks. Emperor Charles hints at separate peace (*see* 20 Mar).	**Britain** — Fuel Research Board appointed. *The Times* price doubled to 2d.

FEBRUARY 1917	WESTERN FRONT 1	EASTERN FRONT 2	SOUTHERN FRONTS 3	TURKISH FRONTS 4
Wed 21			**Trentino** — Italian guns destroy Austrian railhead at Tarvis. **Macedonia** — Gen Lyautey approves Sarrail's spring offensive plan submitted 8 (*see* 11 Mar) whose final objective is Sofia. Sarrail finally consults Milne (28) & they agree on L Doiran sector British attack (*see* 5 & 11 Mar).	**Secret War: Palestine** — HMY *Managam* visits Athlit, contacts NILI Jewish spy ring and delivers funds (*see* 15 Apr).
Thu 22	**Somme** — Due to continued British pressure on German First Army, *Alberich* programme for retirement to *Siegfried Stellung* is accelerated; prelim withdrawal of 3 miles on a 15-mile frontage (*see* 14 March).		**Isonzo** — **Cp Mussolini w** on Carso (Sector 144) in grenade or mortar shell accident, 4k out of 20 soldiers, has 44 pieces removed from his body. Visited by King at Ronchi hospital, moved to Milan, on crutches in Aug.	**Mesopotamia** — 7th Indian Div (1332 cas) storms & holds first 2 Sannaiyat lines v 7 Turk counter-attacks as diversion to pin reserves; 88 Punjabis (in 11 pontoons) raid across Tigris, 4 miles E of Kut.
Fri 23		**Rumania** — Russians lose Magyaros Heights & 1000 PoWs NW of Okna.		**Mesopotamia** — **Main Tigris crossing**: 14th Indian Div (350 cas) makes dawn crossing into Shumran Peninsula 7 miles W of Kut, builds a pontoon bridge & takes 544 Turk PoWs. Kiazim Karbekir evacuates Sannaiyat (night 23/24).
Sat 24	**Somme** — Germans retreat from Serre salient, evacuating Serre, Miraumont, Petit Miraumont, Pys & Warlencourt.			**Mesopotamia** — **Turks abandon Kut**, retreat W on Baghdad losing 1730 PoWs & 4 guns but British Cav Div fails to pursue vigorously although 2 armoured cars do damage (-25). RN gunboat *Mantis* re-hoists Union flag at Kut. **Persia** — **Turk 6th Div falls back from Hamadan** to Kermanshah, 2nd Div follows (26, *see* 28).
Sun 25	French PM Briand proposes that: 'In order to ensure unity of command on the Western Front, the French General-in-Chief will from the 1 March 1917 have authority over the British Forces...in all that concerns...operations...dispositions...allotment of material and resources...to the Armies'. Haig & Robertson object (plan modified 27 qv). **Somme** — BEF 2nd Div & Anzac Corps fight for the Thilloys (-2 Mar) SW of Bapaume. **Flanders** — Gen Sixt von Arnim takes over Fourth Army from Duke Albrecht of Württemberg who now commands his own Flanders Army Gp; both i/c for duration.	**Baltic Provinces** — 100 RND PoWs arrive at Reiskatte Reprisal Camp (c3 miles from Front) to dig trenches, often under Russian fire (-10 June); another 500 PoWs join them.		
Mon 26				**Mesopotamia** — British 13th Div belatedly drives Turk rearguard from Sheikh Ja'ad, but 3 RN gunboats (2 hit) destroy Turk flotilla (4 ships, 1500 PoWs) & recapture HMS *Firefly* .
Tue 27	**Calais Agreement**: Lloyd George and French War Ctee (Briand & Lyautey) agree on Nivelle/Haig plan of ops. British agree (Haig reluctantly) that general conduct of imminent campaign should only be in	**Bukovina** — Russians lose several high positions & 1300 PoWs to Austro-Germans nr Jakobeny but counter-attack a partial success (28).	At Anglo-French Calais Conference CIGS Robertson argues for reducing Salonika campaign to holding port perimeter & switching British troops to Palestine (*see* 6 Apr).	**Mesopotamia** — British cav recce Aziziyeh (-28) 50 miles W of Kut but supply shortage forces them back to river. Turk losses since 23 inc 4300 PoWs, 39 guns, 22 mortars & 11 MGs. Maude cables C-in-C India

AFRICAN OPERATIONS 5	SEA WAR 6	AIR WAR 7	INTERNATIONAL EVENTS 8	HOME FRONTS 9
W Africa: Sahara — French Agades relief col's camel section ambushed, loses 35 cas (-22, *see* 3 Mar).			New British blockade orders insist ships sailing to neutrals with access to enemy enter a British port for examination.	
	Channel — *U21* (Hersing) homeward bound from Med sinks 6 of 8 Dutch steamers (incl Holt liner *Perseus*)in convoy off Falmouth, unaware these 'easy kills' have been granted 'safe passage' by Berlin (*see* INT'L EVENTS).		Turkey backs unrestricted U-boat war. **Neutrals: Holland** — *U21* torpedoes 7 Dutch ships (4 sunk off Falmouth), *see* 9 Mar. Britain requisitions Dutch ships in her ports (26).	**France** — 150 Renault light tanks ordered (*see* 1 Mar).
E Africa — Brig-Gen O'Grady lands at Lindi to take command.	**N Sea** — U-boat sinks a Norwegian & 4 British steamers. **Black Sea** — 30 landing ships ordered for Russian Fleet, 3 completed by Apr 1918.			**Ireland** — 28 Sinn Fein agitators arrested & exiled for alleged plotting with Germans (*see* 7 Mar). **Britain** — PM's speech warns of more import restrictions (14th list issued), announces minimum wheat & oat prices till 1922 & 25s pw minimum wage in farming. **Russia** — Duma Pres Rodzianko in last report urges Tsar to appoint new ministry, also sees CoS Gen Gourko (24-25) (Duma re-opens 27).
		Mesopotamia — RFC flies 19 bombing sorties v retreating Turks (-25), having protected Tigris crossing.	US London Ambassador Page, having received Zimmermann Telegram from Balfour cables Wilson with news, received with 'much indignation' but awaits Sec of State's return (*see* 1 Mar).	**Belgium** — Contraband lists follow British. **Germany** — **Imperial Coal Commissar** appointed but coal supply disorder (-Apr). **Turkey** — Civil marriage established, polygamy conditional on 1st wife's written consent. **Britain** — Lloyd George gets War Cabinet agreement (War Minister & CIGS absent) to Nivelle's Anglo-French W Front command.
E Africa — British occupy Rupiage.	**Channel** — 11 German destroyers (Tillessen) raid, (night 25/26), Dover barrage incl 10-min shelling of Margate & Broadstairs (4 civ cas) (*see* 17 Mar). **E Atlantic** — The **'Overt Act'**: Cunard liner *Laconia* sunk by U-boat off Fastnet (12 dead incl 4 Americans). US Pres Wilson chooses to regard this latest outrage as conclusive proof of Imperial Germany's perfidy & bad faith (*see* INT'L EVENTS 27).	**Rumania** — Airship *LZ101* raids Jassy, Rumania's temporary capital.		
E Africa — Wintgens reaches Magoje.		**Macedonia** — 20 aircraft of *KG 1* (transferred from Bucharest) surprise bomb French Gorgop airfield; 8 French aircraft destroyed, 4 damaged. *KG 1* later bombs Yanesh airfield (RFC), British dumps & camps (28 cas).	Allied Calais War Conference (-27) fixes next W Front offensive. **Neutrals: USA** — Wilson asks Congress for power to arm merchant ships (Bill introduced 28 but filibustered in Senate to session's end, 3 Mar).	**Russia** — Petrograd: crowds of up to 500 protest in streets (*see* 3 Mar).
	Ludendorff asks German Navy to answer Enver Pasha's request for U-boats in E Med to cover Palestine front & Syria, *UB42* & *U63* sent, but waters too empty & shallow for targets.	**Salonika** — *KG 1* bombs British Summerhill camp N of Salonika (376 cas). Raiders intercepted by fighters of Nos 17 & 47 Sqns; 1 Halberstadt escort forced down (pilot taken PoW). Most of 47 Sqn's fighters	Bethmann hails U-boat success & justifies breaking agreement with USA. **Neutrals: USA** — John M Browning demonstrates his new short recoil, watercooled MG. Wilson says *Laconia* sinking (25, 4	**Austria** — Imperial decree establishes Gen Pragenau's joint food inspection (31 districts), but Hungarians reluctant. **Germany** — Kaiser note to military cabinet chief that Hindenburg & Ludendorff +

FEBRUARY 1917	WESTERN FRONT 1	EASTERN FRONT 2	SOUTHERN FRONTS 3	TURKISH FRONTS 4
Tue 27 contd	hands of the French C-in-C subject to Haig's usual right of appeal to London (*see* 13 Mar). **Somme** — On 26 & 27 British capture villages of Le Barque, SW of Bapaume, & Ligny; in past week gains on 11-mile front (S of Gommecourt to E of Gueudecourt) to max depth of 3 miles. **Flanders** — Successful British trench raid E of Armentières.			asking further advance approval after necessary supply pause till 5 Mar.
Wed 28	Nivelle letter to govt warns of 'pacifist propaganda' reaching troops. **Somme** — British have captured 11 villages & 2133 PoWs during Feb. **Secret War** — (end Feb) British make first pigeon drops by balloon (after 3 agents so sent), 40% return rate by end of war.	Brusilov deadline for individual army offensive plans. II Siberian Corps (N Front) report arty units selling bread to inf at extortionate prices.	**Italian Front** — Austrian attacks N of Gorizia & on Asiago repulsed.	**Mesopotamia** — War Cabinet telegram approves advance to Baghdad (Maude receives 2 Mar). **Persia** - Baratov reoccupies Bijar.
Thu 1 March 1917	Reorganization of German Armies: Fourth Army (Arnim) on Belgian coast goes into Rupprecht's Army Group; Army dets on Rupprecht's left flank formed into new Army Group (Archduke Albrecht) formed 25 Feb; Seventh Army (*see* 11) from Rupprecht's Group to Crown Prince's Group. Now 1422 bns on front v 1289 in Sept 1916 although bn strength reduced from 1080 estab to 750 (not universally). (Mar) 66th Div, last (TF) formation from Britain, joins BEF.	**Arz succeeds Conrad as Austrian CoS**. Col Hentsch (Marne decision) made CoS German Rumania military occupation.	**Occupied Serbia** — (early Mar) 8000 Serbs rebel W of Nis but suppressed by Austro-Bulgar forces (incl 1st Bulgar Div from Rumania) after fierce fighting & over 2000 executions.	**Mesopotamia** — Turks begin fortifying R Diyala line, E of Baghdad (8 miles completed by 6); also begin line S of Baghdad (2) but cannot agree which till 4. RN Tigris Flotilla reaches Aziziyeh. MEF ration strength 149,531 (70,472 British).
Fri 2	**Somme** — British gains NW of Puisieux & N of Warlencourt, German counter-attacks nr Bapaume, but the Thilloys lost.	**Baltic Provinces** — Fighting nr Riga. **Galicia** — Germans claim success on R Narajowka, attack SW of Brzezany (3); Russian night attack to S fails (6). **Bukovina** — Fighting continues in S.		**Persia** — Baratov reoccupies Hamadan, Kangavar & Sehna (5,*see* 9).
Sat 3	**Somme** — British advance E of Gommecourt (-5). **Aisne** — German 51st Res Div raid S of Ripont captures Nivelle 16 Dec 1916 memo on general offensive.	**W Russia** — Russian gas attacks N of L Naroch nr Krevo (4). **Pripet** — German 1st *Landwehr* Div (400 field guns & mortars support) attack W of Lutsk nets 9000 PoWs, 15 guns, 200 MGs & mortars.		**Arabia** — Capt Newcombe & Arabs wreck Hejaz Railway at Dar-el-Hamra Stn. (c) Cairo intercepts Djemal Pasha cable to Medina indicating evacuation plan, Lawrence urges Feisal to act (*see* 13).
Sun 4	Gen d'Esperey (N Army Gp) vainly asks Nivelle to let him attack retreating Germans (& 6), asks for tanks (9, *see* 15).	Hoffmann diary 'The Russian Army is deteriorating.' **Rumania** — Rumanians bombard nr Calieni, but lose Magyaros	**Isonzo** — Italians form Gorizia Defence Command (3 corps) for Mt Kuk-Mt Santo sector under Gen Capello, Second	**Mesopotamia** — First of 13 fresh Indian bns arrive at Basra. **Sinai** — British 74th Div forms at El Arish from 18 dismtd

AFRICAN OPERATIONS 5	SEA WAR 6	AIR WAR 7	INTERNATIONAL EVENTS 8	HOME FRONTS 9
		damaged (*see* 4 Mar).	Americans drowned) 'overt act for which he was waiting'. **Secret War** — Wilson thanks Balfour for 'information of such inestimable value'.	industry a 'revolutionary undermining of Crown rights ... that flies in the face of all Prussian tradition'. **Britain** — Plan announced for employing women on lt duties behind W Front.
	(Feb) British 10th (Minesweeping) Sloop Flotilla transferred from Immingham on E Coast (Humber) to Queenstown to meet mine threat off S Ireland, loses 2 ships in Mar. 7 *Arethusa*-class cruisers (Harwich Force & Grand Fleet) converted to lay 70-74 mines each (Feb-Nov); carry out 35 ops (2553 mines laid by Nov 1918). Allied Feb shipping losses 254 ships of 500,573t (German fig 520,412t) incl record 105 British ships worth 313,486t. Med toll is 105,670t.		Allied memo to China backs her attitude v Germany, promises to suspend 1900 Boxer Rebellion indemnity payments (*see* 4 Mar). **Neutrals: USA** — Munitions Standard Board created. US Marines land at Guantanamo Bay, Cuba (*see* 8 Mar).	**Germany** — **Only 60,000 Auxiliary Service Law Volunteers** (mainly women) **instead of 200,000 hoped for.** **Russia** — Duma member Kerensky calls for end to 'medieval regime'. **India** — Act forms Indian Defence Force (all British European subjects).
E Africa — **Rain all month.** (Mar) Compulsory Service Act in British E Africa and Uganda (*see* 17).	(Mar) Av of 40 U-boats at sea pd, max 57. **Shipping entering British ports** (Feb & Mar) **only 25% of Feb-Mar 1916 levels.** 16 British oilers (Fleet tankers) sunk Mar-Sept. Germany announces end of safe period for sailing ships in Atlantic. **Channel** — British hospital ship *Glenart Castle* (*see* 26 Feb 1918) damaged by mine between Le Havre & South-ampton. Further mine or torpedo disasters to hospital ships (*see* 19) on 20 (*Asturias*), (14k); 30 (*Gloucester Castle*, no lives lost); 10 Apr (*Salta*, 52k); 17 (*Lanfranc*, 35k incl 20 German patients) & ambulance-transport (red crosses & distinctive marks dropped) *Donegal*, (41k). Germans convinced hospital ships carrying munitions & radioing U-boat positions. From mid-Apr in Med British ones zigzag & get 2 destroyer escorts (*see* 26 May). French embark 70 German officer PoWs (15 Apr-c15 Aug) in 5 hospital ships & notify Berlin (which sends 200 French officer PoWs to W Front areas shelled by Allies).	**Occupied Belgium** — (Mar) Gotha IV deliveries to *Kagohl 3* 'England Squadron'. **Britain** — Hit-&-run single raid on Broadstairs by German floatplane from Zeebrugge; 6 w (similar raid on Westgate coastal shipping 16). (Mar) **K Albert makes his first flight**, in a Belgian aircraft over Nieuport & Dixmude coming under AA fire. **Rumania** — (Mar) 37 French aircrew helping Rumanians (92 French aircraft supplied).	**Neutrals: USA** — **Wilson hands press Zimmermann Telegram.** (Mar) DW Griffith sails for Europe to make 2 British-funded films (W Front). **Switzerland** — Rice & sugar rationing cards issued (2 meatless days pw since 12 Feb).	**Britain** — RFP up 3% to 92%. 600,000t import reduction pm to end 1917. Canals taken over for essential traffic. **France** — Sugar rationing. (Mar) Mlle Dufays, munitions worker, shot for selling secrets to Germans. (Mar) Renault not using ⅓ of its machinery due to lack of workers (*see* 9).
			Zimmermann tells press his telegram true (*see* 12).	**France** — 1918 recruits called up. **Austria** — Charles' Army reforms.
W Africa: Sahara — French relieve Agades after heavy fighting; turning point v Senussi, Khoassen flees 75 miles N, is again defeated (13 Apr, *see* 13 July).			Japan & Mexico deny receiving Zimmermann proposals. **Occupied Belgium** — Council of Flanders group in Germany (sees Kaiser) to petition independence (*see* 21). **Neutrals: USA** — Special Preparedness Fund & 1st Excess Profits Acts passed.	**Russia** — Petrograd Putilov Works strike begins. **Britain** — *Nation* newspaper claims BEF outmanoeuvred by German retreat, Govt bans further articles after Germans reprint first.
		Salonika — Despite 18-aircraft RFC dawn bombing, *KG 1* bombs camps & dumps & field hospital at Dudular (64 cas).		**Russia** — Bread riots, Petrograd (& 6, 7). **France** — Tubercular Ex-Soldiers Flag Day. **Britain** — War Office

MARCH 1917	WESTERN FRONT 1	EASTERN FRONT 2	SOUTHERN FRONTS 3	TURKISH FRONTS 4
Sun 4 contd	**Aisne** — French advance between the Oise & the Aisne, S of Mouvron. **Somme** — British 8th Div (1137 cas) captures Bouchavesnes with 217 PoWs & repels 6 counter-attacks (-5). **Verdun** — German 28th Div penetrates Caurières Wood.	Ridge (8) & fail to regain it (10 & 28).	Army reduced to IV Corps (*see* 5 Apr). Austrian attack E of Gorizia repulsed. Italians occupy heights in Costabella Mts. Fighting in the Dolomites (5, *see* 16).	Yeomanry regts.
Mon 5	**Lorraine** — German attack W of Pont-à-Mousson.	Rumanian Austrian PoWs in Darnitsa Camp nr Kiev sign oath to fight Dual Monarchy (*see* 16 Apr).	**Salonika** — Milne letter to CIGS 'This is impossible country to fight in, too cold in winter, too hot in summer, one gets almost two months in spring and two in autumn...'	**Mesopotamia** — Maude resumes advance: 13th Hussars' charge foiled by 2nd trench line. **Palestine** — Kress evacuates Wadi Sheikh Nuran for Gaza-Beersheba line (*see* 26)
Tue 6	BEF line now extends from Ypres Salient to near Roye, twice length of Mar 1916.			**Mesopotamia** — British occupy Lajj & Ctesiphon.
Wed 7				**Mesopotamia** — British fail to cross R Diyala but cross Tigris to S bank by steamer (bridged 8).
Thu 8	Cdn PM visits BEF, Haig and Nivelle (-12). **Champagne** — French regain most of salient lost on 15 Feb (Butte de Mesnil-Maisons de Champagne), (more gains in E sector 12). **Flanders** — 5 raids on British trenches N of Wulverghem (Messines).	**Baltic Provinces** — Germans repulsed nr Mitau; Russian gas attack to E (11).		**Arabia** — Wingate orders Rabegh's evacuation to transfer Arabs N to Wejh.
Fri 9			**Salonika** — British 26th Div advances line 1000yds fortifying 3 mounds in No Man's Land. Two small raids E of R Struma (15).	**Mesopotamia** — Gertrude Bell letter to father 'That's the end of the German dream of domination in the Near East ... their place is not going to be in the sun'. Capt Reid's 100 men cross R Diyala, repel 6 Turk attacks (Reid gains VC). S of Tigris Turks forced back to inner line. **Persia** — Turk XIII Corps reaches Karind. Russians invite Persian Govt to repossess reoccupied towns, Baratov reoccupies Kermanshah (11) & Karind (17, *see* 31).
Sat 10	**Somme** — Irles & Grévillers Trench captured by British 2nd & 18th Divs with 292 PoWs.			**Mesopotamia** — British bridge R Diyala & turn Turk W flank 3 miles from Baghdad. **Khalil Pasha grudgingly lets subordinates evacuate city & leaves by train.** 9500 Turks & 48 guns retreat before 45,343 British & 174 guns. German radio stn blown up.

AFRICAN OPERATIONS 5	SEA WAR 6	AIR WAR 7	INTERNATIONAL EVENTS 8	HOME FRONTS 9
		Germany — RNAS bomb Brebach (Saarbrücken).		decides to form 9 tank bns (total 1000 tanks).
E Africa — 1/2nd KAR Bn lands at Lindi; KAR cross Lukuledi Estuary from Lindi & put post on Nyanda Hill to S (9). British take Shaeffer's Farm W of Lindi but Germans retake.		**Mesopotamia** — 2 Martinsydes crash in dust storms (*see* 11, 3 Apr). **Palestine** — 30 RFC aircraft drop 2³/₄t bombs on Beersheba, its rail jctn & Turk camps (-8) but fail to disrupt limited Turk withdrawal (*see* 20 & 26). **Arabia** — RFC aircraft first flies over Medina, photographs Turk defences.	Austrian reply to USA backs U-boat war. **Neutrals: USA** — Wilson's 2nd term inaugural address 'We stand fast on an armed neutrality.' London Ambassador Page cables US 'France & England must have ... enough credit in the US to prevent collapse of world trade'. **Diplomacy** — Lord Milner returns from Petrograd saying 'it is quite wrong to suppose that in Russia there is any controversy about the waging of the war'.	
		W Front — **First DH4** fast, high-flying S/E **bombers** with first Constantinesco cc MG synchronizing gear (6000 issued to Dec) join No 55 Sqn RFC.		**Germany** — 250 British PoWs entrain at Minden to work in Ruhr coalmines (2000 Allied PoWs there already). **Britain** — Controller of Potatoes appointed. Army Demobiliza-tion Trades Register begun.
	Austria — C-in-C Njegovan urges hastened U-boat & MTB construction. **N Sea** — RN CMBs torpedo German destroyer leaving Zeebrugge during air raid. **Black Sea** — Russian submarine *Kashalot* sinks 8 Turk sailing coasters and 3 tugs E of Bosphorus.	**Occupied Belgium** — New German Gotha bomber base of Scheldewindeke operational S of Ghent. **Britain** — 11 home air defence sqns have 147 aircraft instead of 222 estab & 113 pilots of 198. FM French orders no AA firing at hostile aircraft (-7 June) except in specific coastal defences; crews reduced to send men to France.	**Neutral: USA** — First jazz recording released by Victor Co, 'The Dixieland Jazz Band One-Step'.	**Russia** — First Petrograd factory lockouts. **Austria** — 1920 recruits called up.
	Italy — Rear-Adm Mortola First Inspector of Shipping Defence. **N Sea** — Norwegian relief ships *Storstad* torpedoed, *Lars Fostenes* (13).	**Germany** — †Count Ferdinand von **Zeppelin** aged 79, pioneer of giant metal-framed rigid airships (civil & military) since 1891 *and* of giant LR biplane aircraft.	**Secret War** — Prince Sixtus reports to Poincaré on Austrian peace talks (*see* 20). **Neutrals: USA** — Radio contact between US & Germany suspended. **Cuba** — 400 US Marines land at Govt's request (*see* 7 Apr). **Diplomacy** — HMG accepts Nizam of Hyderabad's £100,000 for ASW.	**Russia** — Demo & red flags in Nevski Prospekt, Petrograd, 90,000 on strike. **Britain** — First Lord of **Admiralty warns of food crisis**, 500,000t sunk in Feb. Dardanells Ctee interim report partly blames Kitchener (*see* 20.)
		W Front — Richthofen (petrol tank & engine hit) leads fighters that shoot down 4 of 9 No 40 Sqn FE8s.	£40m British loan to Rumania. **Neutrals: Holland** — Germany guarantees Dutch shipping in N Sea, Holland-Norway zone after apologies (1 Mar) for 22 Feb sinkings (*see* 21).	**Germany** — Ludendorff warns War Minister & Chancellor home front having an 'un-healthy influence upon the morale of the Army'. **France** — GQG, persuaded by Estienne, orders 1000 Renault light tanks. Prototype tested (14), order approved 10 Apr (*see* 9 Apr & W FRONT 1 May).
	E Atlantic — **Epic action between** NZ Shipping Co *SS Otaki* (4.7in gun) (A Bisset Smith, posthumous VC) & German raider *Möwe* (15 cas), 350 miles E of Azores. *Otaki* sinks after c30 hits but hits *Möwe* 7 times. **N Sea** — RN submarine *G13* sinks *UC43* off Shetlands (*see* 1 May). **W Med** — In tragic error troopship-escorting sloop HMS *Cyclamen*			**Russia** — **Martial law declared in Petrograd** as general strike begins (-19). Petrograd Soviet elected. **Turkey** — Talaat Pasha obtains Chamber T3.5m food board credit, promises radical solutions (24, *see* 6 July).

MARCH 1917	WESTERN FRONT 1	EASTERN FRONT 2	SOUTHERN FRONTS 3	TURKISH FRONTS 4
Sat 10 contd				
Sun 11	French First Army reports 40 villages in flames, explosions in & S of Noyon. **Aisne** — Gen Boehn takes over Seventh Army (-6 Aug 1918) from Schubert (i/c since 28 Aug 1916). **Meuse** — Fuchs replaces Boehn (since 2 Feb) i/c Army Det C at St Mihiel.	Lechitski (Ninth Army) promoted C-in-C W Front (*see* 7 May).	**Albania** — Spring campaign in Macedonia begins (-21 May): French 76th Div advances from Koritza on Resna but blizzard & Austrian-paid irregulars force suspension (19). Snow continues into Apr. **Salonika** — Sarrail and Venizelos at a review.	FALL OF BAGHDAD (pop 150,000+) : British enter before 0900, find 600 sick & wounded. Maude lands from steamer at 1530. His troops have marched 110 miles in 15 days.
Mon 12	**Aisne** — German incendiary shelling of Soissons. **Somme** — Germans evacuate sector nr & incl Péronne, leaving only small parties to hold it. British 46th Div attacks Rettemoy Graben.	Tsar leaves STAVKA for Petrograd. By now Alexeiev convinced no offensive to support Nivelle possible, only end July. **Galicia** — Successful German raids nr Zloczow-Tarnopol railway, Brzezany & on R Narajowka.		
Tue 13	In London Haig & Nivelle sign clarifications of command spheres. **Somme** — British advance guard now 1½ miles from Bapaume. Further gains E & NE of Gommecourt. **Aisne** — Germans repulsed at Hill 185. **Meuse** — Fighting nr St Mihiel.	**Rumania** — Bulgars shell Galatz from Danube.		**Arabia** — A dysentery-wracked Lawrence reaches Abdulla (stays -23, while ill formulates guerrilla war theory for Arab Revolt) with message to attack Medina (unheeded); French also fail to persuade him (20,*see* 26).
Wed 14	**Somme** — MAIN GERMAN RETREAT TO THE HINDENBURG LINE begins (-5 Apr): Second & First Armies involved. BEF Fifth Army follows cautiously incl 4th (1st Indian) Cav Div.	**Petrograd Soviet Order No 1 demoralizes Army**, orders elected ctees to control weaponry & 1 rep per coy to Soviet; saluting off duty abolished. Tsar's train stopped at Pskov.		**Mesopotamia** — **Battle of Mushahida Stn** (20 miles N of Baghdad, W of Tigris): Cobbe's 7th Div (518 cas) & 46 guns smashes Turk rearguard (800-1000 cas) after night march from Baghdad (returns 17). British 40th Bde occupies Kasirin (28 miles N of Baghdad, E of Tigris).
Thu 15	**Somme** — British advance on 1½-mile front between St Pierre Vaast Wood & Saillisel. French finally begin advance in S.			
Fri 16	**Somme** — British occupy St Pierre Vaast Wood, dominating Péronne. **First marching day of Op Alberich**: 35 German divs begin synchronized retreat to Hindenburg Line.		**Serbia** — Gen Grossetti's 3 French divs capture Hill 1248 NW & Svegovo N of Monastir (-18) & 2000 PoWs v tough resistance. Fighting peters out after 27. **Dolomites** — Austrians destroy Italian defences in San Pellegrino Valley.	

AFRICAN OPERATIONS 5	SEA WAR 6	AIR WAR 7	INTERNATIONAL EVENTS 8	HOME FRONTS 9
	rams & sinks Italian submarine *Guglielmotti* (14 die) off Capraia I (*see* 9 Jan 1918). **Med** — Q-ship *Wonganella* (damaged) saves British SS *Springwell* from *U38*.	**Mesopotamia** — No 30 Sqn RFC lands at former German Baghdad airfield, finds wrecked Albatros & 13 engines (6 ex-RFC from Kut).		
E Africa — Smuts on arrival in London calls campaign 'practically over'. **Tripolitania** — Italians occupy Bukamez W of Tripoli (*see* 27; 5 Apr).	US State Dept announces that all US merchant ships sailing through war zones to be armed. Q-ship *Privet* (Petz) off Start Point nr Plymouth (*UC68* blows up on own mines there 13). US *SS Algonquin* torpedoed without warning (*US Healdton* 22).	**Macedonia** — *KG 1* bombs Vertekop on Salonika-Monastir railway (field hospital hit by spillage, 2 British nurses k) & Yanesh airfield. 13 RFC aircraft (1 FTR) bomb German base (*see* 18).	FIRST RUSSIAN REVOLUTION (-15). Anglo-French London Conference (-13) reconciles W Front C-in-Cs & PoW use in fighting zone. **Secret War** — Dr Göppert reports on German diplomatic code security (Eckhardt cleared 4 Apr). **Neutrals: USA** — Wilson authorizes merchant ship arming, U-boat sinks US SS *Algonquin* without warning (3 more sinkings by 16).	RUSSIAN REVOLUTION (-15): Whole 17,000 Petrograd garrison joins crowds. Temperature 0°F. Duma prorogued but forms Prov Govt at Tauride Palace. No bread or transport. Only 2 regts & police loyal to Tsar in sporadic street fighting. **Canada** — 3rd War Loan opens. **Britain** — Bread order makes sale by weight compulsory.
E Africa — Action nr Nambanje: 80 KAR lose 1 MG to Lettow's flanking det. **Morocco** — 1st Mtd Coy, 1st Foreign Legion Regt fights out of a trap at Timalou (-18).	**US** Navy Dept authorizes **armed merchant ships to take action against U-boats**. **France** — Parlt *Commission de la marine de guerre* urges anti-U-boat directorate & priority to patrol craft (*see* 18 June). **Baltic** — Petrograd: Revolutionaries murder captain of refitting cruiser *Aurora*, crew elect first ship ctee. **Mutiny at Kronstadt naval base** (-14) kills c40 officers & NCOs, 162 officers arrested. Fleet C-in-C first main one to accept Prov Govt (14, *see* 16).			**Britain** — Govt takes over all quarries & mines (non-coal). **First WAAC enrolled**, mainly ex-Women's Legion (*see* 31). **Russia** — *Izvesteya* (Petrograd Soviet formed 12) paper first published. Crowd storms military Hotel Astoria but British present save many Russian officers.
			China severs relations with Germany (Parlt votes so 11), seizes 10 German ships & trade posts. Anglo-French Ambassadors recognize Russian Prov Govt as *de facto* .	**Russia** — **Prov Govt proclaimed**, meets Petrograd Soviet. Strikes & 30,000-strong march at Reval (-15). **France** — War Minister Lyautey resigns v Socialist hostility.
E Africa — Lettow reaches Mpotora N of R Matandu, unknown to British till c29.	**Channel** — Dover Patrol destroyers *Foyle* mined, *Laforey* (23), *Myrmidon* (26). **Red Sea** — HM Sloop *Odin* intercepts *Wolf* prize minelayer *Iltis* (26 German PoWs) in Gulf of Aden where she laid 25 mines (swept by Somali-manned tugs within 2 months for 1 ship lost,*see* June).		TSAR ABDICATES. Miliukov new Russian Foreign Minister (*see* 16 May). **Neutrals: Switzerland** — Lenin gets news of Revolution, envisages train journey through Germany (19), publicly opposes new Prov Govt (27, *see* 25).	**Russia** — TSAR ABDICATES at Pskov. Prince Lvov PM; Kerensky Justice Minister; Guchkov War & Marine Minister. Political & religious amnesty declared plus widespread freedoms. Immediate preparations for Constituent Assembly (universal suffrage) announced. Ukrainian National Rada formed at Kiev (*see* 19 May). **Germany** — 6th War Loan opens. **France** — Army has received 160 tanks (208 by 1 Apr).
S Morocco — Gen Lamothe (4 bns + 5500 Moroccan allies) storms El Hiba's defences (6000) S of Tiznit (-17), killing 1200 (*see* 5 Apr).	**E Atlantic** — German disguised raider *Leopard* (ex-British SS *Yarrowdale*) sunk 200 miles NE of Faroes during attempted breakout into Atlantic by RN cruiser *Achilles* & armed boarding steamer *Dundee*. **Black Sea** — Russian Fleet shells Derkos (*see* 13 Apr). **Baltic** — Russian 2nd Battleship Bde (4 ships) leads revolution at Helsinki (night 16/17, c50 officers & NCOs k) but no bloodshed at Reval (15) or	**Britain** — Abortive Navy airship op v London; adverse weather. First sortie by 4 R-class 'height climber' Zeppelins at 17,000-19,000ft. *L39* shot down by French AA fire nr Compiègne (night 16/17). **W Front** — Guynemer achieves first French ace's triple victory & receives Russian Order of St George (4th class) from Pres Poincaré (*see* 25 May).	Count Czernin tells Bethmann in Berlin to talk peace '... the Monarchy stood at the end of its strength'. Turk Sheikh-al Islam again proclaims Jihad. **Neutrals: Greece** — British Athens legation announces arrival of 3300t wheat to prevent starvation. **USA** — Ex-Berlin Ambassador Gerard tells Pres Wilson only U-boat failure can improve peace prospects.	**Russia** — Kerensky Duma speech thanks workers & soldiers delegates. Winter Palace declared state property. **Turkey** — General mobilization ordered. **Britain** — Sugar supplies limited to 40% 1915 level. Cabinet asks for another invasion threat assessment.

MARCH 1917	WESTERN FRONT 1	EASTERN FRONT 2	SOUTHERN FRONTS 3	TURKISH FRONTS 4
Fri 16 contd				
Sat 17	**Somme** — French occupy Roye, **2nd Australian Div occupies Bapaume**. Germans blow up all public & commercial buildings & leave secret huge mine under the *mairie* (explodes, 27, killing 2 French deputies & British staff). BEF occupies 13 villages. British Lucknow Cav Bde ordered forward. **Aisne** — German Seventh Army evacuates Crouy for position 5 miles to N; French can enter Lassigny.	**W Russia** — Russian 1st (Sumski) Hussars (500 strong), summoned & riding 50 miles from R Dvina trenches, suppress revolution without bloodshed in Rejitza (-18) until unit recognizes Prov Govt and returns to Front.	**Salonika** — **First use of gas in theatre**: Bulgars gas shell (-18) British Doiran front (103 gas cas) but defenders receive box respirators. Milne asks for 65,000 gas shells (25) receives only 20,000 after Apr attack (*see* AIR WAR 18).	
Sun 18	**Somme** — BEF GHQ Intelligence summary reports wells at Barleux SW of Péronne poisoned with arsenic. French reoccupy Noyon (pop 12,000; streets mined & booby-trapped, explosions till mid-Apr). British 48th Div occupies Péronne & BEF Chaulnes. Allies enter Nesle together. **Verdun** — German attacks in Avocourt-Mort Homme sector repulsed (-19).			**Armenia** — Kemal C-in-C Turk Second Army (Deputy 5) in new Army Gp Caucaus (Ahmed Izzet Pasha), only 40,000 strong, and still typhus-ridden. Russians reoccupy Van. **Mesopotamia** — British occupy Baquba (35 miles NE of Baghdad) after 240 lorried inf & 4 armoured cars fail to seize bridge there (14).
Mon 19	Haig & Nivelle meet at Beauvais (*GQG*), latter explains minor changes to his plan due to German retreat, which 29 divs have completed.	**Petrograd Soviet Exec Cttee appoints commissars to all units.**	**Italian Front** — Activity in Trentino, Carso, & E of Gorizia.	**Mesopotamia** — **Maude's proclamation to Baghdad promises Arab freedom**. British take Falluja (W of Baghdad) ending Turk control of Euphrates sluice gates.
Tue 20	**Aisne** — Germans demolish irreplaceable medieval castle of Coucy-le-Château, 10 miles N of Soissons, to remove potential OP. **Artois** — BEF preparatory bombardment for Arras offensive opens (*see* 4 April).	Ex-Tsar reviews troops at STAVKA, urges loyalty to Prov Govt & war's continuation. **Rumania** — (c) CoS Gen Iliesca blames Russia for autumn 1916 disasters.		
Wed 21	**Oise** — French Third Army occupies Tergnier on Crozat Canal, fights its way across (22).	**W Russia** — Germans take trenches nr Lida (nr Vilna). Russians retake (22).		
Thu 22	Heavy snowstorms.			
Fri 23	Germans flood Oise valley & La Fère (French nr suburbs 24). Nivelle confesses to K Albert that 'many people are against the offensive'.	German proclamation to Russian soldiers blames English for war & Tsar's abdication. **Baltic Provinces** — Germans mass on Riga-Dvinsk front. **Rumania** — Russians lose trenches W of Moinesci nr R Trotus.		

AFRICAN OPERATIONS 5	SEA WAR 6	AIR WAR 7	INTERNATIONAL EVENTS 8	HOME FRONTS 9
	elsewhere. Fleet has over 89,000 all ranks.			
E Africa — Hoskins asks for 15,000 carriers pm to replace wastage + 500 American light lorries (200 promised for mid-May), orders 300 new KAR (mainly ex-German askaris) to leave Morogoro by rail for Tabora. They leave there for S (23).	HM sloops *Migonette* & *Alyssm* (18) mined & sunk off SW Ireland (-18). **Channel** — 16 German destroyers raid Ramsgate & Broadstairs (night 17/18) also sink destroyer HMS *Paragon* (10 survivors) & torpedo destroyer *Llewellyn*. **Baltic** — **C-in-C Nepenin** resigns, is shot & **murdered** by lone sailor. Vice-Adm **Maksimov elected** in his place; restores order with 2 Prov Govt envoys.	**W Front** — Fonck fights off 5 Albatrosses, destroying 1 (2nd kill). **Britain** — German aircraft drops 4 bombs nr Dover submarine pens. **Arabia** — RFC Flt moves from Rabegh up coast to Wejh.		**France** — **Briand Govt resigns** due to Lyautey crisis (*see* 19). **Russia** — Bolshevik CEC declare working with Prov Govt impossible; *Pravda* ('Truth') newspaper first published (18).
		Salonika — 2 attempted /(O1 raids broken up by RFC fighters; Capt Murlis Green in BE12 shoots down 1 bomber, damages another (*see* 28).		
	Kaiser approves announcement that Allied hospital ships in Med no longer to be spared except in neutral corridor under strict conditions (*see* 21 Apr, 26 May & 10 Sept). **W Med** — *U64* sinks modern French battleship *Danton* (296 lost) SW of Sardinia.		Allies raise Greek blockade.	**Russia** — Finnish autonomy proclaimed. Petrograd Soviet votes for Tsar's arrest. **France** — **Ribot new PM** (wins confidence vote 21) & Foreign Minister; Painlevé War Minister. Supply Ministry created (- 20 Jan 1920). **Britain** — TNT safety rules in force. Bonar Law gives National Debt as £3.9bn, Allies & Dominions owe £964m.
	Raider *Möwe* returns to Kiel. **China** — Chinese Navy takes over 2 interned German river gunboats before declaration of war (*see* 14 Aug); 20 interned steamers (21,000t) already seized (14).	**Palestine** — Lt F McNamara of No 1 Sqn AFC in Martinsyde wins VC (only Australian 1914-18 air VC) for rescuing BE 2 bomber pilot Capt Rutherford from attacking Turk COW aircraft despite serious shrapnel wound. **France** — Daniel Vincent, ex-Flanders air observer, appointed Under Sec of Aviation (-13 Sept), soon boosts aircraft production.	**Secret War** — Princes Sixtus & Xavier in Vienna (-25, *see* 24). **British Imperial War Cabinet first meets** (14 meetings -17 May). **Neutrals: USA** — US Cabinet agree war inevitable, Wilson summons Congress for 2 Apr.	**Britain** — Asquith defends Kitchener in Dardanelles debate.
		W Front — First dedicated RFC night bombing sqn (No 100) crosses to France, receives first of 12 FE2bs (28, *see* 5 Apr).	US tanker *Healdton* sunk (20 die) by U-boat in Holland safety zone. French Military Mission sails for New York. **Occupied Belgium** — **German decree partitions country** with centres at Brussels & Namur; Flemish official language in W, French in Walloon districts.	**Russia** — **Ex-Tsar arrested** at Mogilev (joins Tsarina at Tsarskoe Selo 22). **Austria** — Govt empowered to seize all supplies & fix prices (likewise in Hungary 23).
	Adriatic — RN monitor *Picton* joins 6 Italian monitors to support land ops (*see* 24 May).	**E Front** — German aircraft shoots down Russian Morane Parasol (No 317) into German wire SW of Dünaburg.	USA (1st), Allies & Switzerland recognize Russian Prov Govt.	**Germany** — Interior Minister *Reichstag* speech praises Auxiliary Service Law, food restrictions not serious, health surprisingly good, infant mortality lower than peace-time. **France** — Decree forbids imports except essential foods.
		Aegean — Zeppelin bombs Mudros.	Lloyd George cables Russian PM Prince Lvov Revolution a portent for Prussian military autocracy. **Secret War: Austria** — Emperor Charles & Count Czernin meet Princes Sixtus & Xavier at Laxenburg Castle, drafts letter to Poincaré (24, *see* 31).	**Russia** — Council of United Nobility supports Prov Govt.

MARCH 1917	WESTERN FRONT 1	EASTERN FRONT 2	SOUTHERN FRONTS 3	TURKISH FRONTS 4
Sat 24	British occupy Roisel E of Péronne.	**Russian Army proclaims loyalty to Prov Govt**: Junior officer writes 'There was a gulf between the troops and the officers which could not be bridged'.		
Sun 25	Germans shell Reims (395rnds).	**Gen Alexeiev made C-in-C by Prov Govt** (-4 June) instead of Grand Duke Nicholas, Tsar's choice (arrived from Caucasus 23) . **W Russia** — German gas attack in Dvinsk area repulsed, but attack (26) SW of Baranovichi gains E bank of R Shchara & 300 PoWs.		**Mesopotamia — Battle of Jebel Hamrin**: having bridged 2 canals (24), Keary GOC 3rd Indian Div's 4600 men (1165 cas) & 26 guns repulsed by 5650 Turks & 24 guns (Ali Ihsan's XIII Corps from Persia who cross to Diyala W bank 29).
Mon 26	Heavy snow & rain (plus hail 27). **Somme** — Australians capture Lagnicourt (c50 PoWs), 6 miles NE of Bapaume. **Aisne** — French Third Army push back Germans beyond Barisis-Servais line & recapture Coucy-le-Château.		**Isonzo** — Austrians occupy Italian trenches S of Vipacco (Carso) but attack unsuccessfully (28-29).	**Palestine — First Battle of Gaza** (-27): Dobell's British E Force (39,000 men & 136 guns v 16,000 Turks & 74 guns) cuts off Gaza with 8500 cav & belatedly captures Ali Muntar Ridge above city, but ceases battle at nightfall (3967 cas inc 246 PoWs, 2 planes). Turk 2447 cas (837 PoWs) inc 48 Austro/Germans, 2 guns, 1 aircraft (*see* AIR WAR).
Tue 27	A French soldier writes 'Victory is smiling on our arms.' **Aisne** — French reach Aisne-Oise Canal N of Soissons.			
Wed 28	Foch hands back command of E Army Gp to Castelnau. **Verdun** — French recapture Hill 304.	Germans report spring thaw prevents large-scale fighting.		
Thu 29				**Mesopotamia** — Action of Duqma ('the burning Marl'): Caley's 13th Div (514 cas inc 2/ Lt Slim w) defeats but fails to trap 3000-strong Turk 52nd Div (380+ cas) against Tigris.
Fri 30	Heavy rain. British occupy 8 villages (4 more 31) towards Cambrai.		**Salonika** — Due to investigations into Black Hand & internment of 180 suspect officers at Bizerta (Tunisia), Gen Bojovic abolishes Serb Third Army & splits its formations between the other two armies.	**Mesopotamia** — British Cav Div occupies Delli Abbas, Keary occupies Jebel Hamrin (31). **Palestine** — War Cabinet telegram makes Jerusalem Murray's objective.
Sat 31	German Army ration strength 7,630,456. (Mar) French order 150 Renault lt tanks (*see* 9 Apr).			**Persia** — Russian Gen Radatz (c2500 men & 4 guns) reoccupies Kasr-i-Shirin (*see* 2 Apr).

AFRICAN OPERATIONS 5	SEA WAR 6	AIR WAR 7	INTERNATIONAL EVENTS 8	HOME FRONTS 9
	Irish Sea — Mines reported off Liverpool (*see* 9 Apr).		France protests to neutrals v German devastation in newly evacuated French territory. **Neutrals: Greece** — Greek Govt demands Italian troops' withdrawal from Epirus. Allied Ministers return to Athens. **USA** — Council of National Defense creates Commercial Economy, & Gen Munitions Boards (31) **Diplomacy** — Tsar Ferdinand of Bulgaria advises German Minister not to exploit Russia's weakness by offensive (none planned 27).	**Britain** — National Service Week (-30); National Service Ministry formed (28).
		W Front — **Bishop gains 1st of 72 victories**. Only 1 of 6 Sopwith 2-seaters (No 70 Sqn) survive recon to Valenciennes (2 lost 24).	US Brussels Legation moves to Le Havre, other neutrals to undertake Belgian relief work. **Secret War** — *OHL* approves sending Bolsheviks in Switzerland home in special train (Lenin accepts 31, *see* 4 Apr). **Neutrals: USA** — USN to be increased by 26,000 to 87,000.	**Russia** — Death penalty abolished & medals except St George Cross. All Tsar's property & income transferred to State. **Italy** — National Board for War Invalids authorized. **Britain** — Commons votes £60m war credit.
		Palestine — Germans (8 Rumplers & a few Halberstadt fighters) outperform RFC (21 serviceable aircraft) in vital recon role during First Battle of Gaza (-28).	Bethmann & Count Czernin sign Berlin Document giving Austria Rumania after final victory & Germany gains in E.	**Germany** — War Office bureaus to mediate in strikes & ease food supply. **Britain** — Women's Land Army Training Scheme begun. Commons statement on PoWs (55,397 Germans held). Bread rising to 1s for 4lb loaf.
Cyrenaica — Senussi-Italian PoW exchange (*see* 17 Apr).	**Germany** — **Long-range ocean U-cruiser Flotilla formed** with *U155* (*see* 24 May); 5 boats by 22 Sept. In or outside prohibited zones ships without lights to be sunk without warning.		Petrograd Soviet appeals to peoples of the world for peace. **Neutrals: USA** — Wilson tells E House war decided 'What else can I do?'.	**Russia** — Grand Dukes & Princes renounce hereditary rights. **Britain** — Commons blockade debate.
Uganda — KAR coy recovers 97 stock from Turkana raiders (70 more KAR reinforce early Apr, *see* 17 May).		**Macedonia** — 10 *KG 1* bombers attempt raid on Snievche airfield (No 47 Sqn RFC) but are intercepted by 4 1½-strutters, 1 Sopwith triplane & a BE 12 (Murlis Green) & chased all the way back to their Hudova base (*see* 5 Apr). **W Front** — 5 Halberstadt fighters shoot down 3 FE2bs (No 25 Sqn) covering BE arty aircraft.	Britain reaffirms that Falklands her dependencies. **Neutrals: Greece** — HM Ambassador details method of subsidising 7+ Greek newspapers at £650 pm.	**Russia** — All Romanovs have taken oath of loyalty to Prov Govt. **Germany** — Hindenburg & Ludendorff in Berlin food talks with Austrians. **Britain** — Asquith announces conversion to female suffrage (Lloyd George announces bill 29). **India** — Viceroy asked if 100,000 troops could be raised to relieve British.
		W Front — Richthofen scores 4 victories (10 in Mar).	Bethmann declares no German intention of meddling in Russian home affairs nor to be blamed for Sino-US hostility. **Russian Prov Govt acknowledges Poland's independence.**	**Germany** — *Reichstag* Socialists vote v Emergency Budget.
			Neutrals: USA — Wilson & Cabinet discuss German-American subversion.	**Russia** — Duma electoral reform debate. All imperial & monastic lands confiscated. **Britain** — Cabinet thinks public should be educated about victorious campaigns, especially Mesopotamia & Palestine.
	Allied shipping losses 556,775t or 310 ships (German official fig 564,497t or 281 Allied ships incl 61,917t in Med). Of 1200 British collier March sailings (convoyed) to France only 3 ships lost. 3 U-boats lost.	**W Front** — (Mar) RFC losses 120 aircraft. German fighters claim 60 Allied aircraft (Feb & Mar) for loss of 7.	**Secret War** — Prince Sixtus hands Emperor Charles' letter to Poincaré, it mentions France's 'just claims' to Alsace-Lorraine (*see* 13 Apr). **Neutrals: USA** — takes formal possession of 3 Danish W Indies Virgin Is.	**Britain** — **Only 9 wks supply of wheat & grain in country**. Now 300 War Pensions Ctees (68,269 widows pensions granted). First WAAC draft arrives in France (6023 by 12 Mar 1918). **Russia** — Pig iron production down 17.6% on 1st quarter 1916. **Italy** — War costing £30m pm (£730m so far).

APRIL 1917	WESTERN FRONT 1	EASTERN FRONT 2	SOUTHERN FRONTS 3	TURKISH FRONTS 4
Sun 1 April 1917	BEF est strength 1,893,874 (139,353 Anzacs & 130,255 Canadians). **Somme** — British Fourth Army capture Savy & Savy Wood 4 miles W of St Quentin. Pres Poincaré visits liberated area. **Aisne** — French push back Germans to Vauxaillon NE of Soissons. **Champagne** — Germans shell Reims (25,000rnds in wk, *see* 8).	(Apr) 27 Russian corps & 5 army cdrs retired. Shcherbachev new Russian C-in-C in Rumania.	**Italian Front** — (Apr) 96 British 6in howitzers & 35 French heavy guns arrive (*see* 7, 8 & 19); Gen Diaz i/c new XXII Corps. **Salonika** — (Apr) Turk 46th Div withdrawn home (*see* June), Bulgar 10th Div replaces it on Struma sector. **Macedonia** — Bulgar-German gas shelling of Monastir.	(Apr) Enver appeals to Ludendorff for help to retake Baghdad, offers to put 90,000-strong *Yilderim* Army Gp under German command (*see* 7 May). **Palestine** — 3 British bns recce E of Wadi Ghazze. Dobell submits plan for 2nd Gaza (3), modified 10 (*see* 17).
Mon 2	**Aisne** — French rangefinding & counter bty work begins for 4544 guns (3m shells) but hampered by weather & German air opposition. **Artois** — BEF capture 9 villages (6 fall to 7th Div & 4th Australian Div with 700k & 240 PoWs for 1000 cas) between Arras & St Quentin. **France** — Pétain meets PM Ribot for first time at dinner (*see* 6).		Serb 'Salonika Trial' opens for 81 sessions with 100-plus witnesses; all 10 accused found guilty (*see* 26 June).	**Mesopotamia** — **British & Russians meet** at Kizil Ribat. Lt-Col Tennant lands nr Pai Taq Pass in BE2c from Baghdad with Maude's letter to Gen Pavlov (*see* 22).
Tue 3	French *GQG* moves N from Beauvais to Compiègne. **Somme** — French occupy 7 villages S & SW of St Quentin (-4).	**Pripet** — Linsingen's Germans cross R Stokhod, take 10,000 PoWs in Russian Tobol bridgehead.		
Wed 4	**Artois** — BEF 2000-gun Arras barrage begins incl gas shells, wreaks great destruction on 12-mile front. **Aisne** — German raiding party captures copy of div order at Mt Sapigneul giving movements of 3 corps on right of French Fifth Army. Nivelle told (7).			
Thu 5	**Somme** — Allied pursuit of retiring Germans has been impeded by bad weather, collapse of roads, demolitions, booby traps & rearguards. But now most German outposts have been driven in & Allies face Hindenburg Line.	New War Minister Guchkov's manifesto to Army to do its duty; all men over 43 released; amnesty for all deserters returning by 28 May (*see* 21).	**Italian Front** — Cadorna forms 10-div strategic reserve.	**Mesopotamia** — 2 British div cols concentrate astride Tigris for limited offensive. **Palestine** — EEF railhead now at Deir-el-Balah (E Force HQ since 30 Mar).

AFRICAN OPERATIONS 5	SEA WAR 6	AIR WAR 7	INTERNATIONAL EVENTS 8	HOME FRONTS 9
	BRITISH APRIL SHIPPING LOSSES (373 Allied ships) REACH RECORD MONTHLY TOTAL OF 545,200t (world losses 873,754t). Now 120 U-boats. 600,000t German merchant shipping (interned since 1914/15) seized by USA. **Med** — (Apr) Japanese 2nd Detached Sqn (Rear-Adm K Sato), cruiser *Akashi* & 8 wartime-built destroyers (*see* 4 May & 11 June) arrive (c 17 Apr), based at Malta. (made public by Lord R Cecil 24 May). Cruiser *Idzumo* arrives with 4 more destroyers (Aug), 2 RN destroyers turned over (June). **Secret War: France** — Langevin tests his first quartz transmitter in laboratory tanks, it kills fish in its path (*see* Feb 1918). **Adriatic** — Austrian *U30* lost by unknown cause in Otranto Straits (or 2). **Britain** — (Apr) Aircraft join seaplanes on anti-U-boat patrols (*see* Sept). **Baltic** — (Apr) Bolsheviks claim 1400 members aboard 22 ships.	**W Front** — (Apr) 'BLOODY APRIL': Richthofen's 'Flying Circus' rules the skies. Only the exploits of Collishaw, Dallas, Little & the Sopwith Triplanes of RNAS 'Black Flight' hold promise the tide will eventually turn. RFC has 754 aircraft (41 sqns) in France.	Armed US steamer *Aztec* torpedoed nr Brest (28 lost). **Neutrals: China** — Hentig Mission sails from Shanghai in US ship.	**Britain** — **Century's coldest April**, mean temp 37.7°F (snow 10). RFP 94% (up 2%).
	Med — 13 German & 2 Austrian U-boats at sea.		Pres Wilson's war message to Congress **'The world must be made safe for democracy'** (*see* 6). **Britain** — US & British flags fly from Victoria Tower, Westminster.	**Russia** — **Equal rights for women.** Legal & religious curbs and capital punishment abolished, 8hr day for workers (6).
KAR from Tabora reach Kitunda, 130 miles to S (*see* 14).		**Mesopotamia** — RFC BE2c damaged by German Fokker (9 aircraft newly arrived). Another BE2c (flown since Nov 1915) shot down by Halberstadt over Samarra (15), but RFC new Bristol Scout destroys a Halberstadt (22, *see* 30).	Kaiser (after hernia op) meets Emperor Charles at Homburg but refuses Count Czernin's suggestion to cede Alsace-Lorraine for Poland & Galicia. Czernin says 'Unless the war ends within 3 months the people will end it without their govts.' **Canada** — Trotsky arrested at Halifax, moved to U-boat PoW camp at Amherst (-29), *see* HOME FRONTS 16 May).	**Russia** — Prov Govt forms War Ctee & repeals anti-Jewish legislation. *Pravda* publishes Lenin's 'Letters from Afar' (-4). **Britain** — In Commons Churchill criticises misuse of wounded men. **Germany** — OHL letter to Chancellor, only War Office not Interior Ministry i/c postwar demobilization & transition, Bethmann rejects as unconstitutional (17, *see* 5 May).
	RN decides to convoy Scandinavian ships carrying imported wood pulp (*see* 17 Oct). **W Med** — British liner *City of Paris* (122 lives lost) sunk by *UC35* S off Nice.	**W Front** — **RFC Arras offensive begins** despite low clouds & rain. **N Sea** — RNAS Short seaplanes attack Zeebrugge Mole (nights 4/5, 7/8, *see* SEA WAR 7).	**Neutrals: USA** — Senate votes war resolution 82-6. **Secret War** — Lenin and Zurich councillor Platten negotiate with German Berne Ambassador Romberg (*see* 8).	**Britain** — Food Order fixes weekly meatless day for hotels & restaurants from 15, *see* 15). CIGS tells TUC Army needs 500,000 more men by July, Jellicoe stresses food economy.
Morocco — **Lyautey again Resident-General** (*see* 29 May). **Tripolitania** — Gen Cassini's 9919 men (6 bns+ & 16 guns) from Zuara defeat 4000 rebels at El Agelat Oasis (*see* 4 Sept).		**W Front** — RFC Arras bombing starts with attacks v kite balloons (only 5 destroyed -8). No 100 Sqn RFC bombs Douai airfield ('Richthofen Circus' base), 4 hangars damaged (night 5/6) repeated twice (7/8) with new 1dpr pom-pom strafing; Frankl in Albatros of *Jasta 4* shoots down a BE2c in first planned night interception. RFC loses 75 aircraft (105 crew, -9), another 56 crashed or written off. Bristol Fighter 2-seater flies first offensive patrol, 4 of 6 shot down by Richthofen's 5 Albatros DIIIs. **British airman's Apr life expectancy 23 days.** **Macedonia** — *KG 1* bombs &	Britain informs Russia of her support for an independent, united Poland. U-boat sinks Brazilian coffee ship *Parana* (3 lost) off N France (*see* 11).	**Britain** — Rejected & some disabled men to be re-examined for military service. Asst Chief Commissioner Thomson finds 'a good deal of ignorant alarmism [about industrial unrest], especially among the generals present'. **Rumania** — **K Ferdinand proclamation promises land & civic rights to peasants** (& Army order, 6 May).

APRIL 1917	WESTERN FRONT 1	EASTERN FRONT 2	SOUTHERN FRONTS 3	TURKISH FRONTS 4
Thu 5 contd				
Fri 6	Poincaré & generals meet in train at Compiègne to reconsider offensive. Nivelle threatens to resign, but given approval provided attack called off after 48hrs if expected gains not forthcoming. 5350 guns now bombarding.		Robertson canvasses Jellicoe about Salonika withdrawal or reduction to save scarce shipping for 1918. Jellicoe agrees (17) but Allies take no decision at St Jean de Maurienne (19, *see* INT'L EVENTS and *see* 5 May).	CIGS cable to Gen Alexeiev appeals for Russian offensive to Mosul.
Sat 7			British send 40 6-in howitzers to Italian Front, deployed on Carso (another 24 sent July).	
Sun 8	Reims' civil population evacuated (city shelled again 15-24, cathedral damaged).		Foch meets Cadorna at Vicenza, latter worried about German intervention, former's staff prepare Allied reinforcement route details (*see* 7 May).	**Mesopotamia** — British capture Balad Stn & 200 PoWs.
Mon 9	Easter Monday: **Artois** — BATTLES OF ARRAS (-16 May) begin at 0530 in bitter cold & sleet on 12-mile front. Allenby breaches Hindenburg Line 3rd line, taking 5600 PoWs & 36 guns in 2000-6000 yd advance, but 4-mile gap open for 7hrs not fully exploited as cav too slow (-10). BATTLE OF VIMY RIDGE (-14): After 3-min 1203-gun shelling (383 heavies) and with 150 Vickers MGs' barrage, 30,000 men of **Cdn Corps** (Byng) **storm the Ridge** on 2-mile front with 5 villages & 4000 PoWs & 54 guns. N end of Ridge remains in German hands. **France**— Renault lt tank trials begin (*see* May).			**Palestine** — Djemal Pasha evacuates Jaffa's civilians (inc 9000 Jews on Passover) to Syria (*see* 15 & 19). **Mesopotamia** — 7th Cav Bde (600+ & 10 guns) delaying action v Turk XIII Corps (6250 & 32 guns) for 10 miles S of Delli Abbas.
Tue 10	**Artois** — Canadians (7707 cas, 9-10) clear Vimy Ridge with fall of tough Hill 145. German reserves begin to seal off Arras gap. **Champagne** — French shell Moronvilliers massif E of Reims (-17).			
Wed 11	**Artois** — British 3rd Cav Div & 2 divs of Third Army, with 11 tanks, capture Monchy-le-Preux & Wancourt, but German line stiffening. Allenby has inflicted 21,000 cas (7000 PoWs), taken 112 guns for 8238 cas. British 62nd Div & 4th Australian Div with 11 tanks (2 knocked out by German AT rifles & captured) make first attack on Bullecourt, a fiasco costing 3052 cas (1170 PoWs) (*see* 15).	Gen A M Dragomirov report to Gen Ruzski (N Front C-in-C) 'The mood in the Army is becoming more tense with every passing day .... Arrests of officers and commanders have not ceased .... All thoughts are turned towards the rear.'		**Mesopotamia** — British 13th Div (4300 & 48 guns) & Cav Div check Ali Ihsan's corps on Khalis Canal in great heat & mirages.

AFRICAN OPERATIONS 5	SEA WAR 6	AIR WAR 7	INTERNATIONAL EVENTS 8	HOME FRONTS 9
		destroys munition train & dump at Karasuli by L Ardjan N of Salonika.		
		W Front — Mannock posted to No 40 Sqn (*see* 7 June). 5 Sopwith Pups of No 3 (Naval) Sqn destroy all of 4 Halberstadts.	USA DECLARES WAR ON GERMANY at 1300, (House so votes 373-50) seizes 87 German ships in her ports (14 Austrian ships seized 9).	**Britain** — 1st Govt farm for ex-soldiers opens at Turk I, Yorks. **USA** — All 234 ship launch ways have a vessel building (*see* 16).
	N Sea — 4 British CMBs raid on Zeebrugge (night 7/8); *CMB8* torpedoes & sinks German destroyer *G88* (8).	**W Front** — 2/Lt Ball returns (to 56 Sqn, *see* 22) after teaching pilots in England. Richthofen's 5 Albatros DIIIs shoots down 2 of 6 Nieuports (No 60 Sqn), latter lose 4 of 6 (16).	**Cuba & Panama declare war on Germany** (4 German ships seized Havana).	**Germany** — Kaiser's Imperial Easter message promises full postwar secret ballot in **Prussia**. Jubilation in Hesse. **Russia** — Govt orders grain monopoly.
	E Atlantic — The **Torrington Massacre**: *U55* (Werner) sinks British steamer off Scilly Is, destroys 1 lifeboat (14k) & drowns 20 passengers by deliberately submerging while they are on outer casing.	**Macedonia** — *KG 1* bombs Yanesh railhead; 2 Sopwiths force down an already AA-riddled Friedrichshafen G-type bomber, 3 crew taken PoW (*see* 22). **W Front** — Lt Gen Hoeppner & CoS Lt Col Thomsen both awarded *Pour le Mérite* for reorganizing German Army Air Service since 12 Nov 1916.	**Austria severs relations with US** (Bulgaria 10, *see* 7 Dec). **Secret War** — Lenin & **19-20 Bolsheviks begin 'sealed train' journey** from Switzerland to Petrograd (- 16) via Berlin (11, Kaiser told).	American Federation of Labor pledges support for war effort. **Germany** — Kaiserin & military entourage motto 'Only soldiers help against democrats'.
	Irish Sea — US liner *New York* mined (by *UC65*) off Liverpool with **Rear-Adm Sims USN arriving to confer with British naval authorities**. Jellicoe apparently tells him (10) no solution now to U-boats (*see* 26).	**W Front** — Cmndt de Peuty note to Trenchard 'Victory in the air must precede victory on land.' RFC 754 (385 single-seater fighters) v German 264 (114 single-seater fighters). RFC (incl Lt 'Billy' Bishop) give strafing close support to ground advance.	Russia tells Allies she supports self-determination of peoples & lasting peace. Foreign Office decide to give British propaganda films to K of Siam.	**Canada** — 407,302 overseas enlistments to date. **France** — 1st official Renault light tank trials. **Britain** — Food Hoarding Order. Munitionettes' pay raised to 24-27s pw. **USA** — General Munitions Board created. Eddystone Ammo Corp plant at Chester, Pa blows up (122k).
	N Sea — Each Lowestoft Q-ship to receive 50 Mills grenades & 3 MGs (*see* 28).	**W Front** — RFC No 60 Sqn single-seater Nieuports first sent on photo-recon.	Argentina approves US action, decides on benevolent neutrality towards her (11). Emperor Charles/Czernin letter to Kaiser, 'Five monarchs have been dethroned in this war ...' warns of Russian Revolution impact (*see* 11 & 14). **Germany** — Berlin *Lokal Anzeiger's* corpse conversion factory story (1st appears in Belgian newspaper) becomes war's most notorious atrocity story (not exposed till 1925). Balfour writes (26) that it might be true. **Occupied Poland** — Austria transfers Polish Legions to German control (*see* 2 July).	**Germany** — *OHL* agrees to War Office request for 40,000 miners' return from front.
Lt Kinley's 75 Gold Coast Regt (12 cas) ambush Germans at Makangaga, causing 48+ cas.		**W Front** — Richthofen equals Boelcke's score of 40 with a BE2c of No 13 Sqn (wing lost but crew only bruised) on day RFC loses 13 aircraft to 5 German.	**Brazil breaks relations with Germany** (*see* 15; 2 June, **Bolivia likewise** 13) but neutral in US-German war. German Ambassador only leaves (27). Berlin rejects Czernin's joint peace approach to Russia (*see* 14). Lloyd George & Ribot discuss Emperor Charles' peace letter at Folkestone, agree Italy must be consulted (*see* 18).	**USA** — Reported many single men marrying to avoid draft (*see* 28). **Germany** — Independent Labour Party founded. **Britain** — Army requests 1000 doctors by end May (*see* 21). **Russia** — Soviets' Conference in Petrograd (-17).

APRIL 1917	WESTERN FRONT 1	EASTERN FRONT 2	SOUTHERN FRONTS 3	TURKISH FRONTS 4
Thu 12	**Artois** — Canadians storm Pimple hill N of Vimy Ridge, but 2 German 'counter-attack' divs now holding Méricourt-Arleux line v breakout.			**Mesopotamia** — British armoured cars raid Istabulat's rear (12 miles SE of Samarra).
Fri 13	**Artois** — Canadians capture Vimy village & Petit Vimy. British 50th Div attacks Wancourt Ridge, captures it by 15. **Somme/Oise** — French Third Army attack (-14) soon called off despite aid of 390 heavy guns.			**Mesopotamia** — Ali Ihsan disengages & retreats to Delli Abbas & Jebel Hamrin foothills (-15, *see* 26).
Sat 14	**Artois** — **Battle of Vimy Ridge & First Battle of the Scarpe 1917 end** (*see* 23). 10 men of R Newfoundland Regt (485 cas) hold Monchy v 3rd Bav Div for 5hrs until reinforced. Canadian losses 10,602 for a 4500 yd advance capturing 4000+ & PoWs, 54 guns, 104 mortars & 124 MGs. .	7688 deserters from Russian N & W Fronts (-21) considerable underestimate.		**S Persia** — c1000 Indian troops (left Bandar Abbas 27 Feb) reach Shiraz (& 18).
Sun 15	**Artois** — Anzac Corps & 62nd Div (Fifth Army) repulse major German 4-div attack on Lagnicourt (7-mile front).	(c)W Front reports to STAVKA offensive possible in 1 or 2 months once revolutionary excitement abated.		**Secret War: Palestine** — HMY *Managam* fetches 2 Jewish agents from Athlit (*see* 15 June)
Mon 16	**Aisne** — NIVELLE OFFENSIVE OR SECOND BATTLE OF THE AISNE on 25-mile front (-20): Despite long preparatory bombardment & **first French tank attack**, from 0630 to nightfall 20 French divs (6731 inf cas in 3 divs alone) have advanced c600yds v 15 German divs instead of 6 miles anticipated. Decimated by MG fire, Senegalese troops break & flee. Fifth Army's 128 Schneider tanks bog down (32 knocked out), only few reach German 3rd line. **French losses up to c100,000 instead of 15,000 planned for.** Nivelle belatedly confines effort to either flank of Chemin des Dames. Forewarned, Germans have inserted new First Army (F Below) from Somme between Third & Seventh Armies on the front of attack (*see* AIR WAR). **Artois** — Haig & his army cdrs meet to plan next assault (*see* 23).	Russian Prov Govt agrees to 30,000 Rumanian PoWs forming volunteer corps. Kiev Ctee calls on all Rumanian PoWs to help liberate their provinces (26,*see* 9 June).		
Tue 17	**Champagne** — Battle of the Hills (Moronvillers) begins (-20 May) in worsening weather: French Fourth Army (7 divs) fails to break through on E flank taking 1st line only in up to 1½-mile push. **Aisne** — Germans evacuate & burn 4 villages S of Chemin des Dames. Foch visited by Gen H Wilson at Senlis; (Foch clear, notes Wilson 'that Nivelle was done, owing chiefly to the failure of the Sixth Army ...Foch said he knew ... positions which this army were ... to attack were impossible... He thinks... Nivelle will be *degommé* (dismissed) and Pétain, put in his place, who will play a waiting game			**Palestine** — **Second Battle of Gaza** (-19): 40,000 British, 170 guns, 8 tanks v 19,500 Turks, 101 guns & 86 MGs. British storm Samson's Ridge but tanks & gas shells too few to retain gains. Dobell loses 6444 cas (272 PoWs) & 3 tanks to 2013 Turks (200 PoWs).

AFRICAN OPERATIONS 5	SEA WAR 6	AIR WAR 7	INTERNATIONAL EVENTS 8	HOME FRONTS 9
		Palestine — German planes twice bomb Rafa. RFC drop 2000lb bombs on Huj & Kh-el Bir (*see* 4 May).	Spain protests to Berlin re *San Fulgencio* torpedoing (9). Costa Rica places her waters & ports at US disposal. **Neutrals: Switzerland** — Bulgar and Austrian envoys make peace-feelers to Allies.	**Austria** — Gen Stöger-Steiner succeeds Gen Krobatin as War Minister. **Britain** — London meetings celebrate US entry into war, US Ambassador says aim 'to save the earth as a place worth living in'. **Russia** — Law enlarges Estonia and permits it a Diet.
1/3rd KAR reaches Utete II waterhole, 22 miles SW of Ft Utete (lose sentry to lion), takes Kiawe Bridge on R Lugonya thanks to home-made coracle (29).	**Baltic & Black Sea** — Many Russian battleships & cruisers renamed by Prov Govt to sound more democratic (& 29), often return to pre-1905 Mutiny names.	**W Front** — Richthofen scores twice more incl 1 of 6 RE8s destroyed as not met by escort. 21 RFC bombers (4 lost to Richthofen's unit, 1 lost) +17 escorts strike Henin-Lietard rail stn.	Allied Washington Naval Conference. Kerensky receives Anglo-French Socialist delegations. **Secret War** — Prince Sixtus meets Poincaré & Ribot at Elysée Palace (*see* 18).	**Britain** — Labour Ministry announces demobilization will be by trades not regts.
Capt Wintgens forces out-numbered KAR to retreat on Sikonge (*see* 1 May).	**Britain** — Lloyd George & Carson, First Lord, visit Beatty at Rosyth (-15); latter visits London & backs convoy introduction (17).	**Germany** — 21 French & British aircraft bomb Freiburg in reprisal for Allied hospital ship losses (*see* SEA WAR 1 Mar). RNAS 3rd Wing withdrawn mid-May from Luxeuil.	Emperor Charles draft letter to Czernin 'A smashing German victory would be ruin'. **Russia spurns Austrian peace-feeler.**	**Turkey** — Newspapers complain 'butter' 75% water. **USA** — Wilson appoints ministerial Ctee on Public Information (= censorship). **Britain** — Admiralty empowered to install radio & train operators in any British ship. **France** — 2 meatless days pw decreed.
	E Med — British transports *Cameronian* (22 lives lost) sunk despite 2-destroyer escort, by *U33* (Siess) 150 miles E of Malta & Egypt-bound *Arcadian* (279 lost) sunk off Milo, Aegean by *UC74*.		**Neutrals: Brazil** — 1000 rioters burn c300 German buildings in Porto Alegre (17); 7400 troops sent there & elsewhere.	**USA** — Wilson appeals for aid to Allies. **Britain** — Horses Rationing Order. Labour Ministry to prepare weekly statement on labour disputes for War Cabinet.
	E Med — Convoyed French transport *Sontay* (45 lost incl heroic skipper) sunk by *U33*.	**Aisne** — **131 French aircraft** (200 on paper) **support Nivelle Offensive**, 153 by 21, but **German fighters drive off French arty & contact patrols.** Bad weather also hampers.		**Germany** — **Strikes** (-23) in Berlin (217,000 workers) & Leipzig **v bread ration cut** (15). **Russia** — **Lenin arrives at Petrograd** makes 'April Theses' (17) speech to Petrograd Soviet. **USA** — Shipping Board's Emergency Fleet chartered, 280,000 shipyard workers enrolled by 20.
Cyrenaica — Italians reach *modus vivendi* with Senussi leader Sayyid Idris at Acroma, W of Tobruk (British agreement 14 inc PoW & Turco-German surrender); Idris gets 2000 rifles & 4 guns to use v Tripolitanian rebels.	**British Thorneycroft depth charge thrower designed in 10 days** (by Sir J Thorneycroft, marine engineer); 2760 made & 28 U-boats sunk by it (6 in 1917). Jellicoe urges Salonika withdrawal to save shipping for 1918.	**W Front** — Weather virtually precludes flying (-20). **Palestine** — 31 RFC aircraft (max) help engage 63 arty targets (-19) & 4 aircraft scatter 2800 Turks about to counter-attack (20). **Britain** — King visits Sopwith Aviation Co.		

APRIL 1917	WESTERN FRONT 1	EASTERN FRONT 2	SOUTHERN FRONTS 3	TURKISH FRONTS 4
Tue 17 contd	until the USA come ..., say a year hence. I asked about a central organization of the Allies to really take hold and he was all in favour...would love to be the French representative'. FRENCH ARMY MUTINIES BEGIN with 17 men of 108th Inf Regt abandoning posts before an attack (*see* 29). (By end Aug: 46 divs seriously affected (c35,000 mutineers who call themselves strikers); 2873 court-martialled and sentenced, many suspended; 629 receive death sentences (only 43 certainly suffer ultimate penalty).			
Wed 18	**Somme** — British Fifth Army captures Villers Guislain (12 miles S of Cambrai) & Gonnelieu (20, 8 miles SW). **Aisne** — German counter-attack repulsed nr Juvincourt.			**Mesopotamia** — Marshall's 4000 men & 40 guns force & bridge Shatt-el-Adhaim (E of Tigris), take 1250 PoWs & 6 MGs in 14-mile pursuit for 73 cas.
Thu 19	**Aisne** — French capture Ft Condé & secure Chemin des Dames rd on Craonne plateau. **Champagne** — Legion RMLE (²/₃ cas) storms Aubérive, German legionnaire Sgt-Maj Mader captures 6 Saxon heavy guns with grenades (21).	Knox diary, Riga 'The officers have lost heart and the Army therefore will do no good'. 13 all ranks of 109th Div vainly (20) demand immediate peace at Twelfth Army (Riga) assembly.	Nivelle calls on Cadorna to attack, but Italian date already fixed (12) at 7 May.	**Mesopotamia** — British bridge Tigris at Sinija (275 yds). **Palestine** — Djemal announces Jerusalem's intended evacuation, but Zimmermann intervenes (26) and Enver countermands.
Fri 20	**Aisne** — SECOND BATTLE OF THE AISNE ENDS. Battle of the Hills ends. After 5 days Nivelle's main achievement is Sixth Army's (Mangin) capture of 4-mile deep salient on W flank. This pyrrhic victory gives Germans a straighter line to defend. Captures include 16,300 PoWs, 140 guns & 300 MGs. The ludicrously sanguine Nivelle now forced to cease breakthrough attempts, having sacrificed 134,000 men (by 25) now proposes to revert to local attacks. Lloyd George at Paris conference.			
Sat 21	**Somme** — British 40th Div (Fourth Army) captures 3 local objectives (24 & 25). **Aisne** — Mangin protests at offensive continuing, ammo supply critical. Tenth Army (Duchêne) committed between Hurtebise and Berry-au-Bac.	Russian War Minister's Decree: Election of officers forbidden and deserters to return by 14 May (*see* 29).		**Mesopotamia** — **Battle of Istabulat** (-22): Gen Cobbe with 7th Div (2228 cas) & 76 guns twice attacks Shefhet's 7000 Turks (c2200 cas inc 700 PoWs) & 31 guns astride railway, taking position & 1 gun. Lt Graham (MG Corps) wins 23rd & last VC of campaign. **Palestine** — Chetwode replaces Dobell as GOC E Force, Chauvel takes over Desert Col.
Sun 22	**Artois** — Falkenhausen removed from Sixth Army probably for poor defensive tactics, replaced by O Below (-9 Sept), Col Lossberg already able new CoS, since 11.	**Baltic Provinces** — Hutier made C-in-C German Eighth Army (-12 Dec), replaces Scholtz. Count Kirchbach takes over Army Det D (-12 Dec).	**Macedonia** — Gen Scholtz (from Eighth Army, E Front) replaces Below (*see* W FRONT) i/c German Eleventh & Bulgar First Armies (Army Gp Scholtz) for duration.	**Mesopotamia** — Maude meets Gens Pavlov & Radatz at Baghdad (-23) to plan joint offensive (*see* 11 May). **Palestine** — Murray cables CIGS asking for 2 more divs & extra arty.
Mon 23	**Artois** — **Second Battle of the Scarpe** (-24): 9 British divs (Third Army) with 2685 guns (v 1329 German pieces), 20 tanks (5 disabled) attack on 9-mile front gaining 1-2 miles N & S of R Scarpe; 63rd (RN) Div repulses 5 counter-attacks at Gavrelle; 15th Div captures Guémappe. British capture 2500 PoWs but lose 10,000 cas. **Aisne** — Poincaré urges			

AFRICAN OPERATIONS 5	SEA WAR 6	AIR WAR 7	INTERNATIONAL EVENTS 8	HOME FRONTS 9
450 British beaten at Rumbo, W of Kilwa in heavy rain, lose 4 MGs.	War Minister Lord Derby writes to Haig '... we have lost command of the sea'. **E Med** — French battleship *Requin*, 2 RN monitors & 3 French destroyers bombard Gaza.	**USA** — Pacific Aero Products Co becomes Boeing Airplane Co.	Prince Sixtus-Lloyd George Paris meeting re Austrian peace offer (& 20, *see* 22). **Occupied Belgium** — †Gov-Gen Bissing (73), Gen Baron Falkenhausen succeeds (*see* 29 May).	**Germany** — Leipzig strike ends for wage rise & 52hr week. War Minister orders military region cdrs to ban flight from land if local food shortages.
	First US shot of the war: *SS Mongolia* repels U-boat.	**Channel** — 3 Gotha torpedo-floatplanes of *SFA 1* from Zeebrugge attack British shipping in Dover Straits. Poor visibility, no hits (*see* SEA WAR 1 May).	Anglo-French PMs meet Baron Sonnino at St de Maurienne, he hints at Italy's defection if peace with Austria pursued (*see* 22). **Italy offered Smyrna & Aydin Province** (in Turkey) subject to Russia's agreement. Final British refusal to offer Tsar asylum.	**Germany** — Troops militarize 2 Berlin factories. Hindenburg appeal published. All still striking by 21 to be drafted into Army. **Britain** — More frequent or new publications banned (to save paper). **USA** — Cotton price highest since Civil War.
	Channel — British Antarctic explorer Capt Evans (later Lord Mountevans) with Dover Patrol destroyers *Broke* (57 cas) & *Swift* (5 cas) **defeat 6 German 2nd Flotilla destroyers** (night 20/21) in complete darkness off Belgian coast. Evans sinks *G42* by ramming & there is hand-to-hand fighting on *Broke's* decks. *G85* also sunk (*see* 23 & 25), 140 of 180 Germans rescued.		**Turkey severs relations with US** (Young Turks badly split over this).	**Japan** — Govt wins elections.
	Hindenburg informed that Austrian U-boats will not attack hospital ships, nor can German ones flying Austrian flag. **Adriatic** — 4 Austrian MTBs & 3 destroyers raid Otranto Barrage, causing slight damage (night 21/22, rpt 25/26 & 5/6 May, *see* 14 May). **Germany** — Battlecruiser *Mackensen* launched at Hamburg by Blohm & Voss but never completed.	**W Front** — RFC destroy 2 German balloons (3 British lost) & damage 3 more. Arras bombardment renewed. 2 new Sopwith Triplanes of RNAS No 1 Sqn disperse 14 German DFW CVs & shoot 3 down at 16,000ft before they can recon BEF lines.	US announces Allies have food priority over neutrals. Argentina protests v *Monte Protegido* U-boat sinking (13, *see* 4 July).	**Britain** — All doctors of military age called up (rescinded 25) but 100 pw still to be supplied. **Russia** — **Prov Govt proclaims Cossack historic rights to lands.**
3500 Sierra Leone carriers sail from Freetown for E Africa.		**Macedonia** — *KG 1* bombs British bivouacs nr Yanesh. **W Front** — No 56 Sqn (SE5s) destroys 4 Albatroses (1 to Ball) on its 1st patrol.	Balfour's British Mission arrives in Washington (French Mission arrives New York 24). **Allies reject Prince Sixtus approach.**	**Russia** — Lenin *Pravda* article claims 2nd govt already (Soviets). Prov Govt cannot be overthrown 'immediately' (*see* 23).
c500 British take Yangwani NW of Lindi after night march but repulsed (62 cas) by c400 Germans & 6 MGs from Lutende (25). War Cabinet on Smuts' advice asks Deventer to be C-in-C (*see* 3 May).	**Atlantic** — Battleship *New Mexico* (BB49) launched at NY Navy Yd, first dreadnought with turbo-electric drive (completed 20 May 1918). **N Sea** — 3 RNAS seaplanes bomb 5 German destroyers off Zeebrugge, sink 1.	**W Front** — 68 RFC fighters on offensive patrol for ground attack's renewal. An hour-long massive 'dogfight' without any fatal cas. Ball makes 2 kills. Richthofen's *Jasta 11* scores its 100th victory (of 350 in war, top German unit score).	Hindenburg & Ludendorff list enlarged war aims at Kreuznach Conference, Chancellor bitterly acquiesces 'If we are able to dictate the peace.'	**Britain** — National Service Ministry appeals to schoolboys to work on land; 3m acres of grassland to be converted for 1918 sowing. **Japan** — Trading with enemy forbidden. **Russia** — Lenin pamphlet says 'We must call ourselves the Communist Party' (*see* 27). **Germany** — Unions warn their officials v independent socialists & Spartacists &

APRIL 1917	WESTERN FRONT 1	EASTERN FRONT 2	SOUTHERN FRONTS 3	TURKISH FRONTS 4
Mon 23 contd	postponing offensive.			
Tue 24			**Salonika — Battle of L Doiran** (-25): British 22nd & 26th Divs attack on 2½-mile front at 2145 but, under 147 Bulgar guns (incl German 5.9in naval gun bty) & 33 searchlights, never penetrate beyond first line of concrete defences on steep round hills. British losses 3163; Bulgar/German 835+ (22 PoWs) incl 7 counter-attacks (*see* AIR WAR 25).	**Mesopotamia** — Gen Cobbe occupies Samarra (60 miles N of Baghdad, railway stn occupied 23), takes 340 sick & wounded. Marshall drives 2000 Turks E over Adhaim taking 160 PoWs but heat halts ops.
Wed 25				
Thu 26	Haig sees Painlevé & Ribot in Paris, told that offensive will be maintained.		**Salonika** — Continued Bulgar attacks & shelling of Hill 380 (their old front line) & 28. Sarrail postpones offensive to W due to bad weather (*see* 5 May).	**Mesopotamia** — Marshall recces Ali Ihsan's Band-i-Adhaim position (dug since 23). Dust storms & great heat (110°F+) prevent much shelling (-29).
Fri 27		Russian officers' servants at Pskov decide to agitate for 8hr day & not to be sent to front.		
Sat 28	PÉTAIN APPOINTED CHIEF OF FRENCH GEN STAFF; Paris anxious to restore confidence & apply a brake to Aisne offensive without sacking Nivelle (Haig still supports); Fayolle to command Centre Army Gp. **Artois** — Battle of Arleux (-29): Cdn 1st Div (c1000 cas) capture village & 450 PoWs from German 111th Div in 2-hr, 1000-yd advance despite numerous MG nests in 3 sunken roads, but, to S, 3 British divs fail with heavy losses incl 475 PoWs.		**Italian Front** — Italo Balbo, future Fascist aviator, posted to 8th *Alpini* Regt as 20-yr-old res 2/Lt after 5 months' training at Modena.	
Sun 29	**Artois** — British 2nd Div capture trenches S of Oppy. **Aisne — Nivelle abandons Mangin** (replaced 2 May by Maistre). **Marne/Champagne** — 200 men of French 20th Regt flee to woods from Châlons barracks rather than return to front.	Alexeiev to War Minister 'The situation in the Army grows worse every day; information ... from all sides indicate that the Army is systematically falling apart'. War Minister's order No 213 gives all punishment powers to disciplinary courts (officer as pres, 2 soldiers elected for 6 months) except in action but each army differs.		
Mon 30	Haig again meets army cdrs. BEF Apr losses 120,070, heaviest since July 1916.	Hoffmann diary 'We are showering newspapers and leaflets on the Russians and trying to get at them in various ways ... the Russian Revolution is a godsend to us'.		**Mesopotamia — Battle of Band-i-Adhaim:** Marshall's 5200 men (692 cas) & 64 guns v 6270 Turks (565 cas inc 365 PoWs) & 39 guns (1 lost). British storm Turk 2nd line & beyond but lose gains to 6 -1 counter-attack in dust storm

AFRICAN OPERATIONS 5	SEA WAR 6	AIR WAR 7	INTERNATIONAL EVENTS 8	HOME FRONTS 9
		W Front — 5 of Richthofen's fighters survive attacks by 20 RFC fighters. First **German** *Kampfstaffel* or 'Battle Flight' **special ground attack** with MGs & hand grenades **in support of inf** attack.		prevent May Day strikes. **Russia** — Ukraine demands autonomy (*see* 19 May). USA — Liberty Loan Act: $7bn ($3bn for Allies). **France** — 155mm GPF gun first test fired (at Paris).
	UB18 (Steinbrinck) sinks RN sub *E22* after latter tries to ram. **Channel** — German destroyers shell Dunkirk, (night 21/26), French destroyer *Etendard* sunk with all hands, but Anglo-French patrols repel them. Others shell Ramsgate (5 civ cas) (night 26/27).	**Macedonia** — 6 British fighters & 8 bombers encounter *KG 1* bomber formation; latter is dispersed (each side loses 1 plane). British bombers proceed to attack designated objective (dumps at Bogdanci) (*see* 1 May).	**Chile breaks relations with Germany**. US loans Britain $200m. **Neutrals: China** — Provincial military governors meet in Peking & agree war should be declared v Germany (*see* 14 Aug).	**Britain** — **Food Ministry warns supplies may not last till harvest** if no bread economy. Gen Hamilton unveils 29th Div memorial chapel at First Gallipoli Service of Remembrance.
	Admiralty Anti-Submarine Div director urges general convoy system, **Jellicoe approves trial convoy** from Gibraltar (27,*see* 30, 10 & 17 May). Schooner Q-ship (NZ skipper Sanders wins VC) *Prize* (first German ship *Else* captured 1914) damages *U93* (11 ships sunk on her first cruise) & captures her captain Spiegel plus 2 others, but boat gets home (sunk 7 Jan 1918 by *SS Braeneil* ramming). *Prize* sunk with all hands by *U48* 14 Aug 1917.		French Socialists refuse to send delegation to 15 May Stockholm Conference.	**Britain** — Lloyds Weekly Index of Shipping Movements suspended due to U-boats.
NRFF occupies Capt Lincke's evacuated camp at Likuyu, having crossed that river (23).			**Guatemala severs relations with Germany** (*see* 23 Apr 1918). US London Ambassador wires Washington urging 30 more destroyers for European waters (Navy Secretary orders 32, 20 June).	**Britain** — Lloyd George speech on U-boat menace. **Russia** — Lenin chairs Petrograd City Bolshevik Conference (-5 May). Kronstadt Soviet declares itself virtual republic in support (29).
	Ionian Sea — Allied Corfu naval conference aboard battleship *Provence* (-1 May) decides no return to 1916 patrolled fixed routes, instead urges night navigation only & some convoy, eg Bizerta to E; more use of Italian railways & Cape route; more fixed barrages & hunting groups, also votes to form international Malta-based *Direction Générale*.	**W Front** — RFC loses 12 aircraft incl 10 on contact patrols.		**USA** — Conscription decided: Congress passes Army draft Bill to raise 500,000 men (*see* 18 May). **Germany** — Interior Minister *Reichstag* speech claims over 1.6mt Allied shipping sunk in first 2 months, urges Germans to hold out.
		W Front — Richthofen scores 3 victories (50th-52nd) in 3 sorties, incl one Spad with one by brother Lothar before lunch in mess with father Maj Baron Albrecht von Richthofen.	Anglo-French Missions visit Washington's tomb.	**Italy** — Munition Workers insurance compulsory.
	ALLIED AND NEUTRAL APRIL SHIPPING LOSSES WORST MONTH OF BOTH WORLD WARS 873,754t (373 ships). German U-boat history figure 860,334t of which 278,038t (23,037 to Austrians) in Med; another 113,000t shipping	**Mesopotamia** — (Apr) RFC fly record 335hrs. **Britain** — RNAS Airship *SL 9* destroyed in storm. **W Front** — Clashes over front line as German 2-seaters strafe British lines. *Jasta 11* combined with *2* , *3* & *33* into *Jagdgruppe* 1 of 20		**Britain** — (Apr) Under 10 days sugar supply, 1916 potato crop almost finished by 23. Daily munition factory hrs reduced 12-10. Record wages increase. **Russia** — Coal output 22.2% down on Apr 1916. **USA** — All Reserve Corps officers called

APRIL 1917	WESTERN FRONT 1	EASTERN FRONT 2	SOUTHERN FRONTS 3	TURKISH FRONTS 4
Mon 30 contd				
Tue 1 May 1917	(early May) Nivelle insists 1000 Renault lt tanks top priority order (*see* 20 June). **Champagne** — French repulse 2 counter-attacks S of Moronvilliers & raids (2). (May) Germans give each inf coy 2 Bergmann LMGs (another 2 in Sept). **Artois** — Since 9 Apr BEF has advanced 2-5 miles on 20-mile front, fired 6,466,239 shells, engaged 32 German divs (16 forced into res), taken 18,128 PoWs & 230 guns; 227 mortars; 470 MGs (*see* 16) for 83,970 cas.			**Turkey** — (May) Allied agent network uncovered & executed by Vali of Smyrna who refuses Compton Mackenzie's £1m bribe for city's surrender, but releases last & chief agent to HMY *Aulis*. **India: NW Frontier** — British convoy (115 cas) repulses Mahsuds in Gwalerai Pass (& 16,*see* 9).
Wed 2		Alexeiev & Front commanders tell Prov Govt & Petrograd Soviet 'The Army is on the very brink of ruin' (*see* 22). 2M DESERTERS IN MARCH & APRIL.		**Mesopotamia** — Marshall's col disperses to summer quarters.
Thu 3	**Artois** — **Third Battle of the Scarpe** (-4): British attack on 16-mile front E of Arras with 14 divs, 2685 guns (v 1429 German pieces) & 16 tanks before dawn at 0345 with few Third Army gains although Canadians (1259 cas) storm Fresnoy, capturing 500 PoWs (*see* 8). **Artois** — **Battle of Bullecourt** (-17): 6 British-Australian divs with 12 tanks of Fifth Army break into strongly fortified village 14 miles W of Cambrai and break through Hindenburg Line switch at Quéant. **Aisne** — Colonial div & 2 French inf regts (21st Div)			**Arabia** — Lt-Col Leachman ('OC Desert' Mesopotamia) meets Feisal and Lawrence at Wejh, no love lost (*see* 9).

AFRICAN OPERATIONS 5	SEA WAR 6	AIR WAR 7	INTERNATIONAL EVENTS 8	HOME FRONTS 9
	damaged. PROJECTED SINCE 17, 50% RISK OF DESTRUCTION TO HOMEWARD BOUND SHIPS 2 IN 11, ANNUAL LOSS RATE. ONE IN 4 SHIPS LEAVING BRITAIN BEING SUNK. ONLY 1 U-BOAT LOST. British mine-sweepers (almost 1pd lost) sweep record 5l5 mines. U-BOATS HAVE ATTACKED 781 SHIPS SINCE 1 FEB, 526 SUNK, 37 DAMAGED FOR LOSS OF 10 U-BOATS (record 802t per U-boat day sunk in Med), 13 NEW ONES COMMISSIONED. Lloyd George visits Admiralty & reinforces convoy decision. **Secret War** — (Apr) RN orders 136 Nash Fish towed hydrophones after successful trials (on N Sea patrols 1918, used in 54 patrol vessel v U-boat encounters).	single-seaters which RFC dub 'Richthofen's Circus' (renamed *Jagdgeschwader 1*, 24 July). Richthofen goes on leave 1 May after 21 Apr victories. RFC Apr losses 316 aircrew & 151 planes (88 to *Jasta 11*) of which 82 to 5 pilots; German 119 aircrew & 66 aircraft. German Apr victories: Kurt Wolff 21; Karl Wolff & Lothar von Richthofen 15 each; Otto Bernert 11 & Sebastian Festner 10.		up.
British form Edforce (1700 & 14 MGs) v Wintgens.	**Med** — (May) 28 U-boats in Pola-Cattaro Flotilla. Allies have 858 patrol vessels (89 destroyers) of which 387 available to protect shipping, but only 201 to protect c3000 ships pd at sea at any one time. (May) British Admiralty orders 1108 new ASW vessels incl 97 destroyers 60 submarines. 47 U-boats at sea pd (av). **E Atlantic** — HM submarine *E54* sinks *U81* off W Ireland (*see* 12 Sept). **N Sea** — German seaplane sinks British SS *Gena* off Suffolk, but latter shoots down escorting seaplane. **Channel** — (May) 4 Dover Barrage drifters damaged by its mines. (May) **Record 13 German mine-sweepers mined & sunk** (only 12 so lost Nov 1916-Apr 1917). **Secret War** — (May) Transport U-boat *UC20* takes 7 Germans to set up radio stn (-Aug) at Misurata (Tripolitania) with Senussi rebels.	**W Front** — (May) 'B' or Black Flight of RNAS No 10 Sqn destroys 87 German aircraft (-July, *see* 6 June). RFC flies 39,500hrs in May (record till Mar 1918). **N Sea** — (May) Germans have 47 seaplanes at Zeebrugge & Ostend, shoot down 6 French flying boats; RNAS send extra 9 seaplanes. **Macedonia** — (early May) After ineffective (& increasingly more costly) bomber ops *KG 1* is withdrawn from Hudova & railed to W Front (RFC belatedly discovers 10). **France** — The 'Ribot Cable': French PM asks US to send 4500 combat aircraft to W Front during 1918; with trainers, grand total required by 30 June 1918 is 22,625.	US Senate receives Marshal Joffre & ex-PM Viviani. British Cabinet minutes 'If Russia collapsed it would be beyond our power to beat Germany.' **Occupied Poland** — Council of State presents demands for independence to Central Powers.	**Britain** — RFP 98%, up 4%. *Punch* describes England as 'no longer merry though not downhearted'. National War Museum announced in Commons (funded 25 July and called Imperial by 31 Jan 1918). **Russia** — **Over 50,000 wounded & maimed demonstrate for war to continue. France** — Police disperse 5000 workers anti-war demo, Paris (*see* 11). **USA** — (May) Pulitzer Prizes first awarded.
	'Then called on Carson at Admiralty...still deeply depressed about submarine war' C P Scott, Editor *Manchester Guardian* (*see* 14). **Austria** — At breakfast German Adm Holtzendorff assures Emperor Charles that Apr U-boat sinkings will be 1mt, Empress Zita deplores U-boat war. **Channel** — RN destroyer *Derwent* sunk by mine (52 lives lost).	**W Front** — From behind BEF barrage hedge-hopping Nieuports destroy 4 German balloons (7 destroyed similarly 7 for 2 Nieuports lost). 40-aircraft dogfight E of Arras in which Capt Ball makes only kill.	Talaat Pasha visits Kaiser. **Neutrals: Greece** — PM Lambros resigns, Zaimis (again) succeeds. **Argentina** — Germany pays reparation for sinking *Monteprotegido* .	**USA** — **1st Liberty Loan** of $2bn raises $3bn (-15 June) from 4m people (*see* 31). **Britain** — Budget, no new taxes but tobacco duties & entertainment tax increased. Total war bill so far £4318m, (only 26% from revenue). **Royal proclamation urges 25% cut in bread eating** (*see* 31), read in churches for 4 Sundays beginning 6.
British C-in-C Hoskins told he will be replaced (*see* 29).			Anglo-French Paris War Conference (-5, *see* S FRONTS 5). US loans Italy $100m, France also (8) Russia (16). **Neutrals: Brazil** — Foreign Minister Müller resigns as German name hampers his neutral policy (*see* 1 June).	**Russia** — 1st demonstration v Prov Govt, Foreign Minister Miliukov defends policy to Petrograd crowds. Prov Govt just wins Petrograd Soviet confidence vote (4).

MAY 1917	WESTERN FRONT 1	EASTERN FRONT 2	SOUTHERN FRONTS 3	TURKISH FRONTS 4
Thu 3 contd	affected by mutinies (-4).			
Fri 4	All 52 German res divs of 1 Apr have been engaged, Allies still have 30. **Aisne** — French XVIII Corps captures Craonne & trenches on 3-mile front NW of Reims. Inter-Allied conference in Paris (-5): **Haig & French cdrs unanimously agree to continue offensive** with limited objectives to prevent Germans recovering from their heavy second Aisne & Arras losses and to prevent them striking at Russia & Italy, but **BEF will make main attack.**			
Sat 5	**Aisne** — With 48 Saint Chamond tanks (combat debut) in support (6 lost) French take crest of Craonne Ridge incl Chemin des Dames, Laffaux Mill & 6000 PoWs (De Lattre's 3rd Bn, 93rd Inf has 300 cas but takes 500 PoWs & Cerny underground works); French repulse counter-attacks (6).		**Italian Front** — Italians repulse Austrian attacks on Carso. **Macedonia** — Allied arty preparation begins, French 122nd & Greek Seres Divs take Bulgar Vardar sector trenches nr Gevgeli (Bulgar frontier), repulse counter-attack (7). At Paris conference British announce 1 div & 2 cav bdes will be withdrawn from Salonika (*see* 22 & 30 June); Jellicoe says force will starve unless reduced.	**Armenia** — Russians withdraw from around Ognot.
Sun 6	**Aisne** — French Res Army Gp dissolved, Micheler takes over Fifth Army from Mazel. **Artois** — British repulse counter-attack nr R Souchez.		**Italian Front** — Arty duels on Trentino & Isonzo sectors.	
Mon 7	Haig tells army cdrs at Doullens current ops will be ended, utmost arty fire & economy of inf prior to summer offensive in Flanders. **Artois** — Australians advance between Bullecourt & Quéant.	**Russia** — Lechitski relieved of W Front command at own request, Gourko succeeds (*see* 28).	Bad weather postpones Italian offensive to 12. Anglo-Italian convention for contingency British reinforcement signed.	**Falkenhayn reaches Constantinople** (& leaves 13) **to discuss Baghdad's re-conquest** (*see* 3 June). **Palestine** — Imperial Camel Corps blow up wells S of Beersheba (-14,*see* 23).
Tue 8	**Artois** — 5th Bav Div (176+ guns supporting) recaptures Fresnoy at 2nd attempt (-9). **Aisne** — French storm & hold trenches nr Chevreux (NE of Craonne) despite counter-attacks.		**Salonika** — **Battle of Doiran** (-9) contd: British night attack from 2200 again fails under Bulgar searchlights between lake & Petit Couronne but gains 500yds on 2-mile front to W. British losses 1861; Bulgar guns fire 28,874 shells.	
Wed 9	**Aisne** — NIVELLE OFFENSIVE ENDS: German counter-attacks fail at Chemin des Dames, Craonne & Corbény.		**Serbia** — **Allied attack in Crna loop & in Moglena Mts** (Serb Second Army captures Hill 1824): in former, Russian 2nd Bde capture Orle village a mile into Bulgar lines but forced out with 50% losses, & French 16th Col Div seizes the Mamelon only to be driven back by German attacks; French losses 1579. Italians reach 1st line but retreat at night.	Lloyd George urges Palestine Campaign on War Cabinet to gain bargaining territory. **Arabia** — Lawrence & 27 others leave Wejh with £20,000 in gold to recruit Howeitat tribe in Syrian Desert (*see* 20). **India: NW Frontier** — c500 Mahsuds force back 370 Gurkhas & militia (172 cas) in Kharkhwasta Pass (-10) back to Ft Sarwekai (*see* 13).
Thu 10	PERSHING APPOINTED C-IN-C AMERICAN EXPEDITIONARY FORCE (AEF). Ribot cabinet decide to make Pétain C-in-C but Nivelle refuses to go (11,*see* 15). **Somme** — British advance on S bank of R Scarpe.	Gen Kornilov resigns after Govt fails to back him v Petrograd Soviet (*see* 25). **Baltic Provinces** — Prov Govt relieves Gen Ruzski of N Front command.	**Serbia** — Renewed but badly arranged Allied attacks fail (-11,*see* 14 & 17).	

AFRICAN OPERATIONS 5	SEA WAR 6	AIR WAR 7	INTERNATIONAL EVENTS 8	HOME FRONTS 9
	6 **US destroyers** (Cdr Taussig) **arrive at Queenstown** (S Ireland). **W Med** — *U63* sinks Egypt-bound British transport *Transylvania* (413 lost) in Gulf of Genoa, but rest of c3000 troops saved by escorting Japanese destroyer *Matsu*.	**Palestine** — 5 German aircraft bomb EEF Deir-el-Balah HQ (30 cas). RFC bomb Beersheba (10).		**Germany** — Double guard on Crefeld PoW Camp to stop locals raiding Red Cross food parcels (*see* 23).
	N Sea — German CNS Adm Bachmann forbids 'any participation in meeting and assemblies regardless of political orientation without obtaining special official sanction'. Ban extended to 'socialist lectures' 4 June (*see* 22 June).	Austrians bomb Gorizia.	**Balfour first non-American to address Congress**. Liberia severs relations with Germany. Foreign Minister Miliukov tells Petrograd Soviet 'Russia will never agree to a separate peace.' Dumas Pres says same 10, (*see* 19).	**Germany** — 2nd Hindenburg letter to Chancellor wants economy militarily subordinate for next war preparations. Bethmann rejects (6 June). Italy — Kipling arrives in Rome for visit at HM Ambassador's request, writes 5 newspaper accounts of Italian Front (-20 June).
		Britain — **First night aeroplane raid on London**: Albatros C VII (Klimke & Leon) on own initiative drops 5 x 22lb bombs between Holloway & Hackney (night 6/7, 3 cas).	Austrian Common Ministers Council agrees to reopen *Mitteleuropa* talks with Germany (Berlin owed RM6bn). Emperor says 'I do not agree at all' (14). **Neutrals: Greece — Salonika mass meeting of 30,000 demands King's deposition** (*see* 28). Salonika plot to murder Venizelos discovered (10). **Russia —** Kiev Czech congress recognises Masaryk & Czech National Council.	
		W Front — Capt Albert Ball RFC (44 victories, last 2 on 5) k aged 20 in an SE5 inverted from low cloud behind German lines; cause perhaps vertigo. Only 5 of No 60 Sqn's 11 Scouts he was among return from evening patrol. Posthumous VC.		**Russia** — 1st post-Revolution Bolshevik Party Conference (-12), 80,000 members, Lenin elected to Central Ctee.
	N Sea — Destroyer HMS *Milne* rams & sinks *UC26* in Thames estuary.		France refuses Socialist deputies Stockholm passports (USA likewise 24)	
Sahara: S Algeria — Ft Flatters repels 250 Senussi regulars, but they take convoy (12).	**N Sea** — *U19* sinks ship in British Scandinavian convoy E of Shetlands.			**Russia** — **Act abolishes exile to Siberia. Britain —** Commons votes record £500m credit (war cost £7.5m pd since early Apr, *see* 11 June).
	First Allied general trade convoy (trial) **sails** (16 ships in 3 cols at 6½ kts from Gibraltar with 5 escorts, *see* 17 & 24), reaches Plymouth unscathed (20) after 8 destroyers meet it 200 miles from Channel (18). **N Sea** — German battlecruiser *Hindenburg* (launched 1 Aug 1915) joins High Seas Fleet.			**Britain** — Commons secret session on U-boat menace (-11). Unofficial strikes involve 160,000 engineers (incl London bus drivers 13) v dilution on private work (-24). 8 strike leaders arrested (released 23 after Munitions Minister meets shop stewards 19).

MAY 1917	WESTERN FRONT 1	EASTERN FRONT 2	SOUTHERN FRONTS 3	TURKISH FRONTS 4
Fri 11	**Artois** — Cdn 44th Bri regains 300 yds of trenches W of Avion and holds v repeated German 80th Res Div counter-attacks. British attack astride Scarpe captures Roeux (German div fails to retake -14), Cavalry Farm & Chemical Works.	**W Russia** — German officers visit Gen Dragomirov's N Front HQ at Dvinsk at his soldiers' request but with little result. Prince Leopold's follow-up letter suggesting armistice made a German leaflet (29) (*see* INT'L EVENTS).		**Mesopotamia** — Gen Radatz forces 3 Diyala fords (-13) but Ali Ihsan retakes 2 (17) and Russians break off to reassemble at Kasr-i-Shirin (*see* 26); 2 small British cols in contact with Turks (12-14).
Sat 12	**Artois** — British capture most of Bullecourt.		**Tenth Battle of the Isonzo** (-4 June) 2-day Italian barrage begins at dawn on 25-mile front with 1058 heavy & 1320 field guns v 1400 Austrian pieces. Gen Capello gives Badoglio, aged 45, II Corps due to previous cdr's inadequate arty preparation.	
Sun 13	**Flanders** — Gen Sir H Gough to command key N wing of Ypres offensive. **Somme** — British gains on 'Greenland Hill'. **Champagne** — German counter-attacks N of Reims & in Maisons de Champagne repulsed.	War Minister Guchkov resigns, points out 'There is a limit [to Army democratization] beyond which disintegration is bound to begin'.		C-in-C India wires CIGS that situation worse than in past year, 5 bdes needed v Mahsuds, 10 bns for Egypt & E Africa being retained (*see* 20 June).
Mon 14	German trench raids on Aisne & in Champagne. **Artois** — British advance N of Gavrelle.	**Petrograd Soviet proclamation appeals for end to fraternization.** At STAVKA C-in-Cs discuss resigning *en masse,* decide to visit Petrograd.	**Isonzo** — Italian Gorizia Command & Third Army (28 divs) v Austrian Fifth Army (11 divs). Italians attack at noon with main thrust N of Gorizia E of Plava, capturing Hill 383, & Zagora & Mt Santo. E of Gorizia *Messina* Bde takes Hills 174 & 126 but forced out by heavy counter-attacks. Badoglio promoted Lt -Gen (confirmed 23 Aug). **Serbia** — Serb Sumadija Div captures 2 spurs a mile from Mt Dobropolje.	
Tue 15	NIVELLE DISMISSED AND REPLACED BY PÉTAIN (who assumes command 17). FOCH APPOINTED COGS in Paris. **Artois** — Heavy fighting round Bullecourt (British secure 17, advance NE 19,*see* 20). **Aisne** — Heavy fighting on Chemin des Dames. **Meuse** — French trench raids in the Woëvre & in Lorraine.		**Isonzo** — Badoglio's II Corps storms Mt Kuk (2004ft) & Vodice ridge. Italians claim 4021 PoWs so far, Austrians 2000 on Carso. **Salonika** — British 10th & 28th Divs capture 3 villages in 3¹/₂ mile advance E of Struma on 9-mile front (-16), taking 89 PoWs from Bulgar 7th Div, but prepare to withdraw to summer line from 26 (*see* 14 June).	(c) Capt Newcombe & Arabs make several breaks in Hejaz Railway
Wed 16	**Artois** — **Battles of Arras end:** BEF has regained 61 sq miles, taken 20,834 PoWs & 252 guns in 38 days. British repulse counter-attacks N of Gavrelle.	**Kerensky War Minister;** he is visited at Petrograd by all the C-in-Cs. Austrian CoS Arz (to Czernin) believes Russian Army collapse will obviate need for armistice talks.		
Thu 17	Belgian K Albert tours British-Somme, Aisne and Arras battlefields (*see* 25). Pétain's Directive No.1 rejects breakthrough aim 'for the moment'.	All Front C-in-Cs ask for abolition of committees, detailing of duties as well as rights, Kerensky refuses.	**Isonzo** — Italians hold gains with British 6in howitzer help despite repeated Austrian counter-attacks. Cadorna orders medium & heavy arty fire only for attacks or enemy counter-attacks due to shell shortage, guns being moved S to Carso (*see* 23). **Serbia** — Last French attacks in Crna bend & N of Monastir fail v German counter-attacks with	

AFRICAN OPERATIONS 5	SEA WAR 6	AIR WAR 7	INTERNATIONAL EVENTS 8	HOME FRONTS 9
Half-hearted German attempt to retake Kiawe Bridge as they retreat S.	**Black Sea** — Successful Russian submarine *Morzh* sails on last patrol, mined or sunk by air attack off Bosphorus. **Baltic** — Russian Baltic Fleet Central Ctee meets as Centrobalt at Helsinki.	**W Front** — 12 FE2bs & Nieuports of Nos 11 & 16 Sqns strafe German inf ahead of Third Army barrage (likewise 20 with 2 x 20lb bombs as well).	5 Russian officers try to join British Army at Petrograd Embassy. Col Knox advises Foreign Office to make more military aid conditional on discipline being restored.	**USA** — Only 125 aliens arrested since 6 April. **France** — 10,000 Paris clothing workers strike (-23) v living costs. **Britain** — Appeal for men of 41-50 to volunteer, also coal economy.
	N Sea — 3 Dover Patrol monitors (total 6 15in guns), & with air cover among 41 ships, shell Zeebrugge for 73 min from 28,000yds (*see* 5 June), for 1hr but vital locks not hit although 19 of 250 shells land within 15yds. **Med** — 6 Australian destroyers (3 from Singapore) being sent to Med.	**W Front** — French ace Nungesser shoots down 2 of 6 Albatroses over Douai.	Viviani addresses Canadian Parlt (Balfour 29). *Pravda* says all Tsarist treaties with Allies should be repudiated.	**Portugal** — Food riots in Lisbon area (-22) due to bakers closing. Martial law declared (200+ k). **Germany** — Kaiser cables Bethmann v wartime social reform (*see* 7 July).
	U-boat sinks Spanish *SS Carmen*.		Bethmann visits Vienna to stiffen alliance, told of Italian peace offer (14). Socialist Conference opens at Stockholm.	
	N Sea — Sir E Geddes appointed Controller at Admiralty, post of First Sea Lord & CNS combined.	**N Sea** — RNAS 'Large America' H12 flying boat shoots down Zeppelin *L22* nr Terschelling Light Vessel (*see* 20).	Russian papers beg Austro-German Socialists to stop their armies fighting.	**Britain** — King tours industrial North. Merchant shipbuilding control reverts to Admiralty. **Germany** — **Ist German tank** (A7V) **on trial** at Mainz.
	Adriatic — **Otranto Action** (largest in Straits): 3 Austrian cruisers (incl Horthy's flagship *Novara*) & 2 destroyers with 13 aircraft's & 3 U-boats' support sink 2 destroyers (Italian *Borea* & French *Boutefeu*); 14 RN armed trawlers (72 PoWs) & damage 4 out of 47; 2 merchantmen plus 1 seaplane ouf of 13 aircraft. Vainly & chaotically pursued by Allies (21 ships) incl cruisers *Bristol* & *Dartmouth* (latter torpedoed by *UC25* but eventually reaches Malta). New Italian flotilla leader *Aquila* disabled by shot through steam pipe. Horthy w & *Novara* taken in tow but op in 8 days. Brindisi Rear-Adm Bollo superseded. **Otranto Barrage restricted to daylight use.**	**W Front** — Lt Gontermann wins *Pour le Mérite* (16 victories 6 Apr-11 May).	**Rumania** — French Munitions Minister Albert Thomas visits Rumanian temporary capital Jassy (*see* 21).	**Germany** — Socialists refused passports for Stockholm. **USA** — Officers' training camps open (1st class passes out Aug). **Britain** — Russian Flag Day: 'People refused to buy'. **Canada** — PM Sir R Borden arrives home from imperial conferences in Britain & W Front visit, announces conscription proposals (18, *see* 11 June).
	Adriatic — Austrian *U5* mined & sunk off Pola but raised & re-used.		**Bethmann offers immediate peace to Russia** in *Reichstag* (Emperor Charles repeats 31). Tereshchenko succeeds Miliukov (resigned 15) as Russian Foreign Minister. US loans Belgium $45m.	**Russia** — **Trotsky arrives in Petrograd** (from 3 Apr internment in Canada). Cabinet reshuffle admits 6 Petrograd Soviet Menshevik members. **USA** — Aircraft Production Board set up.
Uganda: Turkana — Action at Nakot Pass: Capt Rayne & 22 KAR (12 cas) form square & repel 250 Turkana & Ethiopians (38k, *see* 17 Oct).	British Admiralty appoints convoy research ctee (draft scheme approved 14 June).		**Honduras severs relations with Germany** (Nicaragua 19). Austro-German Kreuznach Agreement (-18): Austria to get Balkans territory for letting Germany have Poland & Baltic gains (Czernin's peace effort thwarted).	**Serbia** — †Marshal Putnik at Nice (aged 70). **Russia** — Peasant Deputies' Soviet established (*see* 7 June).

MAY 1917	WESTERN FRONT 1	EASTERN FRONT 2	SOUTHERN FRONTS 3	TURKISH FRONTS 4
Thu 17 contd			1113 cas (*see* 21). Sarrail fails to get Serb First Army (Misic) into action (*see* 21).	
Fri 18	Haig meets Pétain at Amiens, latter says British Flanders plans too ambitious (*see* 2 June), former's diary finds Pétain 'businesslike, knowledgeable and brief of speech'. **Aisne** — French easily repulse attacks on Chemin des Dames California plateau (-19). Germans regain 200yds (20).		**Macedonia** — Gen Dietrichs asks for & gets 6 wks rest for Russian 2nd Bde (*see* 30 June).	**Mesopotamia** — 918 British river craft + 148 on order from India. **Palestine** — EEF begins offensive patrols in Gaza sector.
Sat 19	**Several mutinies a day now reported in French Army** (*see* 27).	Kerensky orders that no senior officer can retire, all unreturned deserters will be severely punished; **Pripet** — Intense German fire on trenches nr Kukhary (Kovel).	**Isonzo** — Italians evacuate temporary Bodrez Isonzo bridgehead & repulse Austrian night attack on Vodice (night 19/20).	**Palestine** — 455 Italian troops land at Pt Said (sailed Naples 6), leave for Rafa 13 June. 3000 French (3bns + under Col de Piépape) also leave port for Rafa (25). **Arabia** — K Hussein admits need for European advisers in Syria & Mesopotamia.
Sun 20	**Champagne** — French take 500 PoWs in Moronvilliers sector (other successes 21, 25). **Artois** — BEF Fifth Army actions on Hindenburg Line (-31), British 33rd Div captures whole first line N of Bullecourt.	**Kerensky begins visiting units** (*sees* 8). Brawl between Russian & RN armoured car unit at Tiraspol (Bessarabia), 1 killed on each side.	**Isonzo** — Austrian Carso attacks beaten off.	**Arabia** — Lawrence crosses Hejaz Railway nr Dizad, dynamiting line, reaches Howeitat camp (28).
Mon 21	**Artois** — British now hold advanced line of Hindenburg Line from Bullecourt to 1 mile E of Arras (with a 2000-yd gap) & make gains on Fontaine-les-Croisilles. **Flanders** — British Messines Ridge bombardment begins with 144,000t of shells brought up since Mar, 2250 guns fire 3,258,000 shells (-7 June).		**Trentino** — Italians foil Austrian Tavignolo valley attacks. **Macedonia** — At Serb request **Sarrail ends Allied spring offensive** after 14,000 cas for minimal gains.	
Tue 22	**Artois** — Skirmishing; arty duels. **Aisne** — Successful French raids.	**Kerensky demands Alexeiev resignation, replaces him with Brusilov** (*see* 4-6 June).		
Wed 23	**Aisne** — French repulse dawn raid on Vauclère Plateau (Craonne); make slight gains round Craonne (24) and Mt Cornillet (Moronvilliers), 25.		**Isonzo** — **Italian offensive on Carso** from Kostanjevica to sea aided by 60 British guns & RN monitors (*see* SEA WAR 24) begins with 6-hr barrage from 0600, attack at 1600 with **130 aircraft in close support** (*see* AIR WAR). Four hills stormed. Austrian attacks beaten off (24).	**Palestine** — ALH and Camel Corps destroy 13 miles of (and 6 bridges along) Turk Beersheba-Auja railway.
Thu 24		**Kerensky's Declaration of the Rights of Soldiers** (published 27).		Lt-Col Meinertzhagen arrives in Cairo to head GHQ Intelligence.

AFRICAN OPERATIONS 5	SEA WAR 6	AIR WAR 7	INTERNATIONAL EVENTS 8	HOME FRONTS 9
			Britain — VIP letters in *Jewish Exponent* argue v need for national homeland.	**USA** — Selective Conscription Act for men aged 21-31 (*see 5 June*). **US Base Hospital** No 4 (243 staff) **reaches Britain** (1st US soldiers to do so). **Britain** — John Buchan reports on poor 'public feeling', urges more domestic propaganda. Cabinet agrees (22) to a campaign to 'counter-attack the pacifist movement' (*see 4 Aug*).
Action at Schaeffer's Farm: 475-strong 1/2nd KAR (59 cas) checked W of Lindi & 2 other cols forced back.	**Baltic** — 4 Russian submarines sail from Reval on year's 1st patrol, *Bars* sunk (28) either mined or depth charged off Norrköping, Sweden. Second group also has no success (June, *see* 11 June & 8 Aug). Kerensky speaks at Helsinki naval base (23).		**Russia repudiates separate peace**, but general one to be without annexations or sanctions. US announces regular div going to France.	**Russia** — Ukrainian Army Congress declares for autonomy (*see* 12 June). **USA** — Hoover Food Controller.
	Kaiser finally orders **German Navy to regard US warships in blockaded zone as hostile** (U-boats told to stay 4 miles off Spanish coast 29). **W Med** — Italian-built Russian submarine *Svyatoi Georgi* commissioned at Spezia, sails 5000 miles (June-Sept) to join Arctic Ocean Flotilla.	**N Sea** — **First U-boat thought to be sunk by aircraft**: *UC36* by RNAS H12 America flying boat (Flt Sub-Lt Morrish) from Felixstowe, 2 other May attacks, also 24 and 29 July (*see* 22 Sept). UC36 actually lost 17/18 May off Isle of Wight, probably to mine.	Prince Sixtus (in Vienna 5-11) gives Emperor Charles' second peace letter to Poincaré & Ribot, but it remains unanswered (*see* 23). Serb Govt moves from Corfu to Salonika.	**Canada** — Conscription announced, & well-received.
Wintgens (typhus, captured by Belgian 6th Bn & allowed to keep sword 23) **hands over to Lt Naumann** 469 troops, 2 guns & 12 MGs. They cross Central Railway W of Malongwe 2 miles from 4th Nigerian Bn (26).			French Munitions Minister Thomas speaks tellingly in Moscow (visit - 23 June).	**Britain** — **Imperial War Graves Commission chartered. USA** — Capt Rintelen & 2 other German agents fined & imprisoned. Navy Secretary says a USMC regt will go to France (Congress authorizes Corps strength of 31,323, 22).
	E Med — British Malta-Alexandria convoys begin (4 ships with 4 escort trawlers, only 2 ships lost -16 July).			**Hungary** — **PM Count Tisza resigns** at Emperor's bidding (*see* 8 June). **Britain** — Postwar shortage of 500,000 houses estimated. Brig-Gen Nash succeeds Sir E Geddes as Insp-Gen Transportation.
		Britain — 6 Navy airships fly v London but nearest 40 miles away; (1 fatal cas to 60 scattered bombs) (night 23/24). 76 defence sorties (1 RNAS FTR) only sight 1 Zeppelin. **Italian Front** — D'Annunzio flies in aircraft over Carso, wins 3rd Silver Medal, promoted Maj 29 Sept.	Prince Sixtus sees K George V & Lloyd George (& 30, 5 June).	**Germany** — 3 British officers escape Schwarmstedt PoW camp (N of Hanover; 3 more, June).
	First homeward-bound British transatlantic convoy sails from Hampton Roads, Va, USA, arrives safely despite fog & rough seas, 1 straggler lost to U-boat (4 convoys follow in June with 60 ships, no losses,*see* July). **First U-cruiser patrol** (2 5.9in guns & 18 torpedoes) begins: *U155* (Meusel) sinks 10 steamers & 7 sailing ships in 104 days or 52,000t (-4 Sept) on **10,220-mile voyage, longest yet**. **Adriatic** — French submarine *Circe* torpedoes & sinks *UC24* off Cattaro. 2 RN monitors shell Prosecco crossroads & airfield nr Trieste despite Austrian		Prince Udine's Italian War Mission sees Wilson (landed New York 9-10).	**Britain** — Bonar Law tells Commons German national debt similar but HMG has raised £400m extra revenue to German £85m. Central Billeting Board formed to quarter civil war workers. **Turkey** — Anti-Profiteering Law & Commission cuts prices drastically; gradually loses impact (*see* 14 Feb 1918).

MAY 1917	WESTERN FRONT 1	EASTERN FRONT 2	SOUTHERN FRONTS 3	TURKISH FRONTS 4
Thu 24 contd				
Fri 25	Haig sees K Albert who has declined to command 6 French divs as well in Flanders. **Aisne** — German Chemin des Dames success nr Braye, N of Soissons.	**Kerensky's Order for the Offensive** of the Army and Fleet declares exhorts 'Without discipline there can be no safety'. **Bukovina** — Kornilov takes over Eighth Army from Kaledin (*see* HOME FRONTS 30 June).	**Isonzo** — Italians take 2 villages & clear Hudi Log salient with 2000 PoWs.	
Sat 26	FIRST US TROOPS DISEMBARK IN FRANCE (1308 by 31). **Champagne** — 3 German counter-attacks fail.	Hoffmann diary 'The Russians are making violent counter propaganda against our efforts to paralyse their Army by suggestions of peace.'	**Isonzo** — Italian 4th Div occupies ruins of Kostanjevica village but Austrian guns force evacuation. Italians capture 10 guns & reach R Timavo taking 800 PoWs but Hill 28 (Maj Randaccio dies in poet D'Annunzio's arms) not secured (-27).	
Sun 27	Skirmishing on Champagne, Verdun & Alsace fronts. French 18th Inf Regt's 2nd Bn (844 cas, 4-8) mutinies at Villers sur Fère (-28), 12 court-martialled, 5 sentenced to death, 3 executed. **Worst disorders at Fère-en-Tardenois rail stn (-28) as mutineers try to reach Paris.**	Reported that 30,000 deserters pass through Kiev daily.		
Mon 28	**Aisne** — Unsuccessful German attack nr Hurtebise.	Gourko resigns as C-in-C W Front v Kerensky's 24 May Declaration (*see* 8 June).	Italian guns within 10 miles of Trieste. Cadorna orders preparations for summer Isonzo offensive (*see* 18 Aug). Austrian counter-stroke on Carso regains little (*see* 4 June).	
Tue 29	**Somme** — Arty duels & skirmishing nr St Quentin. **Champagne** — Arty actions & patrol activity. **France** — 80 mutinous incidents (-10 June).		Isonzo fighting diminishing after max 4500yd Italian advance on Carso gains 16,000 PoWs + 6000 in Gorizia zone.	
Wed 30	**Champagne** — Heavy German attacks on Moronvilliers Massif fail (-31)			
Thu 31	**Flanders** — Arty duels round Ypres & Wytschaete (daily -5 June). **Aisne** — Mutiny in French 77th Inf Div (-6 June): 150 men of 157th Light Inf Bde & 97th Inf Regt detained & disarmed. In almost unique incident light inf of 60th Bde refuse to move into line to support Moroccan Div, disciplinary measures taken.			

AFRICAN OPERATIONS 5	SEA WAR 6	AIR WAR 7	INTERNATIONAL EVENTS 8	HOME FRONTS 9
	seaplane attacks (1 bomb hit, 1 shot down). **Atlantic** — U-boat sinks AMC *Hilary* (4 lost).	**Britain** — GOTHA BOMBING CAMPAIGN BEGINS: 21 of 23 Gotha bombers of *Kagohl 3* (Brandenburg) fail to reach London due to clouds & 1 FTR (shot down by RNAS Dunkirk) attack Folkestone & Shorncliffe army camp with 5.1t bombs in 10min (171 civ cas, 116 service cas — more than in any Zeppelin raid). Home Defence Gp allotted 20 extra fighters (28, *see* 31; 5 June). **W Front** — Guynemer achieves 4 kills in 1 day (total 45).		**Britain** — Lloyd George speech claims more success v U-boats than ever before. **France** — Chamber secret session on U-boat war.
German property vested in British custodian (*see* 1 June).	**W Med** — British hospital ship *Dover Castle* (7 lost) sunk by *UC67* (Neumann) off Algeria, but destroyer escort gets wounded off. [Neumann acquitted at June 1921 Leipzig War Crimes Trial on higher orders defence.]	**Channel** — Heinkel designed Brandenburg seaplane fighters shoot down a formation of 4 French Navy FBA flying boats.		**USA** — 2000 Germans now interned (mainly sailors).
		Macedonia — 10 RNAS & RFC aircraft destroyed in hangar explosion at Marian airfield, 9 cas. Disaster kept secret for many weeks.		**Turkey** — War Ministry private society to look after crippled soldiers (a few sent to Germany). **Germany** — 600 daily papers reported to have closed. **France** — Local 'Social Duty' Flag Day.
	CNS Adm Bon in London concedes to Jellicoe that a British Med C-in-C should handle shipping protection under supervision of French Allied C-in-C (Gauchet) (*see* 1 Aug).		**Anglo-French London Conference** (-29) **discusses K Constantine's deposition** (*see* 6 June).	
Deventer reaches Dar-es-Salaam from S Africa, **becomes C-in-C** (30). **Morocco** — Lyautey returns to Casablanca after Gouraud bloodlessly executed his plan to split hostile 8200ft Middle Atlas with 3 new garrisons, new road by summer 1918.	**Black Sea** — Russo-Rumanian naval coastal raid (2 cruisers, 2 torpedo boats and 1 sub-chaser) on Anatolia, sinks or captures 50+ sailing craft during shelling of 4 ports incl Samsun and Sinope (-30).		Philippines Act provides 1 destroyer & 1 submarine for USA. Henderson (Labour MP) leaves with deputation for Russia. **Occupied Belgium** — New 10m franc tax brings German total to 720m fr.	**Britain** — May 1916 Clyde Deportees allowed to return to Glasgow. *War Office Topical News* weekly newsreel first released (-23 Feb 1918).
	Allied & neutral shipping losses 285 ships of 589,603t (German U-boat official hist fig 616,316t incl 170,626t in Med). **Record 7 U-boats lost**, only 5 commissioned. *UC65* (O Steinbrinck) has sunk 72,311t & damaged 51,452t since 1 Feb. 63 Q-ships operating in Home Waters. **Secret War** — (May) **Room 40 finally incorporated into Admiralty Naval Intelligence Div** as Section 25 under Cdr William 'Bubbles' James (*see* 25 June).			**Austria** — *Reichsrat* meets for 1st time since March 1914; Polish reps declare for independence, Serbs, Croats & Slovenes form 'Yugoslav Parliamentary Club'.
		W Front — RFC cas since 27 Apr 361. **Britain** — CIGS chairs home air defence conference, 24 trained AA observers to be transferred from France to serve in lightships, but FM French writes to War Office that too few aircraft (5 June).	British Cabinet make Northcliffe Head of British War Mission (after Balfour) to USA (made public 6 June).	**Austria** — Emperor Charles promises more liberal post-war constitution. **Germany** — 118,000 (79,000 women, youths or old men) civilians now in military agencies but still 260,000 troops at home or in occupied territories. **Britain** — May bread consumption reported 10% below Feb. **USA** — Wilson subscribes $10,000 to Liberty Loan.

JUNE 1917	WESTERN FRONT 1	EASTERN FRONT 2	SOUTHERN FRONTS 3	TURKISH FRONTS 4
Fri 1 June 1917	BEF has taken 76,067 PoWs to date. (June) Rupprecht transfers 10 divs from Lens-Lille sector to Flanders. **Aisne** — Up to 2000 men of French 23rd & 133rd Inf Regts (43rd Div) mutiny (-2) at Ville-en-Tardenois & Chambrecy (Sw of Reims), display red flag. German 4-coy local dawn attack preluded by 3-min mortar shelling and indirect MG fire behind French first line.	Hoffmann diary 'An armistice is...in being at many points ...at other points firing is going on — it is indeed a strange war'.	**Isonzo** — Italian attacks succeed S of Kostanjevica. **Salonika** — Peak British ration strength (incl sick) 231,564.	**S Persia** — S Persia Rifles 4450 strong + 1496 Indian troops (*see* 5 July).
Sat 2	New French C-in-C Pétain's CoS Debeney informs Haig that, due to mutinies, French Army can give only minimal support in planned Allied offensive. Haig decides to attack a key sector immediately & so distract Germans from French; Messines offensive already scheduled for 7 June fits the bill.			
Sun 3	**Artois** — After 600-projector gas barrage Cdn 10th Bde (550+ cas) captures 100 PoWs but cannot hold La Coulette S of R Souchez (-25) & Lens. **Flanders** — British arty at Messines begin feint creeping barrage (& 5), drawing German guns for counter-bty retaliation. **Aisne** — 5 German Chemin des Dames attacks repelled, another nr Hurtebise fails (5).			Falkenhayn reports offensive v Baghdad feasible (*see* 20). **Arabia** — Lawrence leaves Nebk (with 2 local guides) to sound Syrian tribes (-16), blows bridge on Aleppo-Damascus railway nr Baalbek, apparently meets Turk Damascus commandant (highest -ranking Arab Gen Ali Riza Rikabi) outside city (*see* 19).
Mon 4	**Aisne** — War Minister Painlevé estimates **only 2 reliable French divs between Germans and Paris** (70 miles away): 1500 mutineers march on Villers-Cotterelts to try and reach Paris (-5).	Brusilov spends 4hrs trying to get an ensign to release a div cdr. Denikin addresses Officers' Congress for Alexeiev, stresses officers' need for support.	**Isonzo** — **Austrian counter-offensive on Carso** under Gen Wurm with fresh 3 divs (from E Front) to relieve pressure on Trieste. Italian Third Army driven off lower slopes of Mt Hermada with loss of many PoWs although Diaz's XXIII Corps holds to N (-5).	
Tue 5	**Somme** — British attack N of the Scarpe, captures positions on Greenland Hill (6).	Brusilov farewell to SW Front (200,000 men short) 'I carry luck everywhere with me....now I will lead all the armies of Russia to victory'. **Occupied Rumania** — Gen Eben i/c German Ninth Army (-18 June 1918) replacing Falkenhayn.	**Macedonia** — Gen Steuben replaces Winckler i/c German Eleventh Army for duration.	
Wed 6	**Only cas of French mutinies** when 1k & 3w by 42nd Regt MG (*see* 8).	Gen Gutor new C-in-C SW Front (with Dukhonin as CoS who tells Italian officer, 5, that future offensive 'could not go far, horses half-starved') as Brusilov leaves for STAVKA after 3 speeches.	**Isonzo** — Austrians claim 10,000 PoWs since 4.	

AFRICAN OPERATIONS 5	SEA WAR 6	AIR WAR 7	INTERNATIONAL EVENTS 8	HOME FRONTS 9
British civil postal service begins. British ration strength 45,011 incl 14,559 whites & 13,639 Indians (lowest total since 1 May 1916) with 38 guns (2) & 61,950 porters.	**(June) Convoys being regularly run**, 113 destroyers available for escort in Home Waters, 37 in Med, av of 55 U-boats at sea pd (*see* 30). **Med** — 18 German & 3-4 Austrian U-boats on ops(-15).	**W Front** — Significant nos of SE5, Camel Triplane, Bristol Fighter & Spad S 13 enable Allies to regain air superiority (*see* 21). **USA/Europe** — (June) Maj Raynal C Bolling Mission leaves USA for 2-month tour of Allied aircraft manufacturing & remit to conclude licence production agreements. **Adriatic** — (June) No 6 Wing RNAS begins anti-U-boat patrols from Otranto (*see* 2 Sept).	Brazil revokes neutrality in US-German war & seizes 46 German ships (but revokes decree 28). **Occupied Belgium** — Belgians repatriated from Germany but have to work in German-run factories. **Neutrals: China** — Military governors demand war declaration v Germany. **Switzerland** (June) — Police arrest British agents with 60,000 leaflets for Germany. **Turkey** (June) — Germans form own Arab Bureau in Damascus, publish *Der Neue Orient* . (June) British Press Bureau finally established in Paris	**Russia** — Bolshevik Kronstadt revolt v Prov Govt fails (-6). **Britain** — RFP 102%, up 2%. Food Controller Lord Devonport resigns, Lord Rhondda succeeds (15). Lord Milner writes to PM for 'strong steps to stop the "rot"..., unless we wish to"follow Russia"'.
W col of Edforce (702) leaves Tabora to join Belgians in cutting off Naumann from W; vain pursuit handed over to Belgians.	**E Med** — British transport *Cameronian* (63 lost) sunk 50 miles off Alexandria.	**W Front** — Cdn ace Capt Bishop flies dawn raid on German airfield nr Cambrai, destroying 3 Albatroses that rise to engage; returns to base in bullet-riddled Nieuport (VC award 11 Aug). **Flanders** — RFC Second Army aircraft destroy 32 aircraft for loss of 18 (-7).		**Russia** — Grand Duke Nicholas arrested at Tiflis on plotting charge. **Britain** — United Socialist Party Conference at Leeds (1150 delegates) to honour Russian Revolution, also Leeds anti-Jewish rioting (3-4) for alleged call-up evasion. King confers 351 medals in Hyde Park.
			Italy proclaims protectorate over Albania. U-boat sinks Uruguayan ship *Rosario* (*see* 7 Oct).	
		N Sea — **Sopwith Camel first in action** with RNAS No 4 Sqn (Dunkirk) scores 1st victory (5) of 2500 (*see* 27).	**France authorizes Polish Army's formation on W Front** (*see* 15 Aug). Noulens new French Ambassador to Petrograd (Paléologue resigns due to ill health).	**France** — PM Ribot wins confidence vote (453-53). **Britain** — Carson speech says US entry helps tighter control of neutral imports to Germany. **Britain** — OBE founded (public warrant 21).
	('Leader of U-boats') Cmdre Bauer relieved of cmnd. Bauer has advocated mass 'wolf-pack' tactics, ie using cargo submarine *Deutschland* as radio/fuel vessel for U-boat flotilla; *U66* is used (5-10) to try radio-location equipment but U-boats only work in pairs radioing convoy reports. Capt Andreas Michelsen replaces Bauer. **N Sea** — Harwich Force (8 cruisers & 17 destroyers) covers Dover Patrol bombardment of Ostend by 2 monitors (20 of 115 shells land in or nr dockyard damaging several craft), sinks German destroyer *S20* (9 survivors) & damages another; *UC70* also sunk, but raised to sink more ships (*see* 28 Aug 1918). RNAS bomb Ostend & Zeebrugge (1 & 3).	**Britain** — 22 Gothas (1 FTR) attack Sheerness & Shoeburyness (47 cas). Only 5 out of 68 British fighters get within range (*see* 12 July), although 10 RNAS Dunkirk fighters attack formation on its way home after German fighters meet it.	Montenegrin PM Gen Martovinic resigns after urging union with Serbia, Popovic succeeds (*see* 20 July).	**USA** — **Draft Registration Day** for nearly 10m men aged 21-31; 56,830 exemptions recognized inc Quakers; 3000 'slackers' fled to Mexico.
		W Front — RNAS fighter ace Collishaw in Sopwith Triplane 'Black Maria' destroys 3 Albatroses in 1 action, among 16 victories in 27 days of June (awarded DSC).	**Neutrals: Greece** — High Commissioner for the Protecting Powers Jonnart arrives (*see* 12).	**Russia** — Council elections, 140 Petrograd factories put on 6hr day (coal shortage). **Britain** — Appeal to farmers to use more women workers.

JUNE 1917	WESTERN FRONT 1	EASTERN FRONT 2	SOUTHERN FRONTS 3	TURKISH FRONTS 4
Thu 7	**Flanders** — BATTLE OF MESSINES RIDGE (-14): 9 divs of British Second Army (Plumer) attack on 9-mile front & capture Messines-Wytschaete ridge. Attack preceded at 0310 by devastating, 500t **largest non-nuclear explosion** of 19 mines (1 still unexploded); causes panic in Lille 15 miles distant. British take 6400 PoWs. German *Gruppe Wytschaete* cdr Laffert sacked (16). **Belgium** — Pétain impresses K Albert at first meeting, tells him 'The French Army is no longer what it was', Belgians to join Anglo-French Flanders advance at certain stage.			
Fri 8	Foch meets CIGS Robertson at Abbeville. Pétain given right to order immediate executions, only orders 7 (-13 July). Wilson tells British War Cabinet offensive necessary to keep France in war. **Flanders** — British repulse counter-attacks E of Messines Ridge; advance (10); Germans withdraw to new line running through Warneton (11). **Artois** — 6 Cdn bns (709 cas) make powerful raid W of Avion, bomb 150+ dugouts, inflict 836+ cas (136 PoWs), night 8/9.	Kerensky degrades Gen Gourko to div cmd in Kazan MD, he actually leaves (21) for Caucasus and addresses Don Cossacks (25, *see* HOME FRONTS 4 Aug).	**Greece** — Without warning Allies, Italians from Albania occupy Jannina in Epirus (*see* INT'L EVENTS 3) & port of Preveza (10)	
Sat 9	**Byng replaces Allenby as GOC BEF Third Army** (*see* TURK FRONTS 27). Cdn Lt-Gen Sir A Currie becomes GOC Cdn Corps for duration.	**Prov Govt refuses German C-in-C's unlimited armistice offer** (made by radio). **Rumania** — First 2 Transylvanian volunteer bns arrive in Jassy.	**Isonzo** — Italian losses 157,000 since 14 May incl 27,000 PoWs; Austrian nearly 75,700 (23,400 PoWs). **Trentino** — Italian Mt Zebio mine explodes prematurely causing 122 cas.	
Sun 10	**First 2 French mutineers executed, outbreaks already receding** (7), only 20 (-2 July). Pétain speaks to an ex-mutinous regt (19) and brings tears to the soldiers' eyes, visits almost 90 divs (June/July), *see* HOME FRONTS.		**Trentino** — **Italian Offensive N of Asiago** with 12 divs, 1500 guns & mortars on 9-mile front but signals & deserters have alerted Austrian Eleventh Army. Barrage (incl gas shell) from 0515 in near zero visibility (mist) till 1100. *Alpini* assault from 1100 captures Agnello Pass & Peak 2101 (6794ft) of Mt Ortigaro with 500 PoWs but Austrians retain Height 2105 (6906ft). Attacks by 5 other divs on 5 other peaks to S fail. Italian Sixth Army C-in-C Mambretti fails to persuade Cadorna to call off offensive, he allows only 48-hr pause. **Greece** — French regt & guns land at Corinth & French (mainly cav) div enters Thessaly, takes Larissa for 6k, captures 300 royalists in only bloodshed (12)	
Mon 11	Haig's memo: 'Present situation and future plans'; Germany may suddenly weaken under Allies offensive 'within 4 to 6 months...she will be unable to maintain the strength of her units in the field...may well be forced to conclude a peace on our terms before the end of the year'.	**Bukovina** — Kornilov tells Col Knox 'If Russia stops fighting, I hope you will take me as a private soldier in the British Army, for I will never make peace with the Germans'.	**Trentino** — Austrians reinforce front line (-13) & send 4 bns forward for counter-attack on 15.	**Palestine** — Murray told he will be replaced (leaves 16, *see* 27). British 52nd Div trench raid causes 62+ Turk cas nr Gaza.

AFRICAN OPERATIONS 5	SEA WAR 6	AIR WAR 7	INTERNATIONAL EVENTS 8	HOME FRONTS 9
	U-boats begin offensive off US E Coast (*see* 22). Q-ship *Pargust* (Campbell, crew win 2 VCs) sinks *UC29* (Rose) off SE Ireland. **Baltic** — 1st Congress of the Baltic Fleet (-28) at Helsinki tries to clarify C-in-C's authority (*see* 15).	**W Front** — Mannock scores his 1st victory (*see* 12 July).		**Russia** — Peasant Deputies Congress votes to transfer all land to peasants without compensation. **Britain** — Messines Ridge mines explosion audible in London, 1st wounded arrive Charing Cross 1415. **USA** — Announced that 25,000 planes will be built.
			Lloyd George argues for separate peace with Austria, war policy ctee set up. **Occupied Poland** — Austro-German Emperors agree that Germany to control Polish forces (*see* 2 July). (June) Warsaw University shut due to students' strike.	**Britain** — Lord Curzon writes to PM against Churchill's rumoured recall (*see* 18). **USA** — Film *Pershing's Crusaders* opens in New York. **Hungary** — Count Esterházy new PM (-9 Aug), Parlt debut (21).
	Cmdre Tyrwhitt writes to his wife after visiting Beatty at Rosyth 'There's no doubt that he is the right man in the right place.' **Med** — Capt Pullen appt 'Leader of U-boats' with rank of Cmdre.		K George V meets & tells Gen Pershing 'It has always been my dream that the two English speaking nations should some day be united in a great cause' (*see* W FRONT 13). Anglo-French reply to Russian Prov Govt's 9 April war aims declaration. London meeting on 'Muslim interests in Palestine' (watched by MI5). US loans $3m to Serbia.	
O'Grady's Linforce advances to W (-12): c800 British & 8 MGs land by night at Mkwaya from lighters 10 miles up R Lukuledi to capture *Königsberg* gun, but are forced back to boats minus 2 MGs after Capt Looff's 2 attacks (11).		**Italian Front** — 141 Italian aircraft support Trentino attack (145 on 19).		**Britain** — Labour Trafalgar Sq demo for world's industrial workers. **Ireland** — Sinn Fein riots in Dublin (*see* 15). **France** — Interior Minister cables 83 prefects for morale reports, 44 say 'poor' or 'indifferent', 36 towns 'contaminated'.
	Channel — British drifter destroys 2 German seaplanes. **E Med** — Austrian *U27* torpedoes Japanese destroyer *Sakaki* (68 die) off Crete, ship saved & repaired. **Baltic** — Russian submarive *Lvitsa* sunk off Gotland (probably by mine), sister *Pantera* damaged by Zeppelin (14) & forced back to base.		Pres Wilson's message to Russia published: no people to be 'forced under a sovereignty under which it does not wish to live'. **Santo Domingo severs relations with Germany** (**Haiti follows**, 15).	**Britain** — Sailors & Firemens Union prevent Ramsay Macdonald sailing for Russia. **Britain** — Apr-May cost of war £7,884,000pd. **Canada** — PM introduces his Military Service Bill to conscript 20-45 yr-old men in 10 classes (*see* 6 July).

JUNE 1917	WESTERN FRONT 1	EASTERN FRONT 2	SOUTHERN FRONTS 3	TURKISH FRONTS 4
Tue 12	Pétain asks *Troisième Bureau* to study Russian defection consequences.		**Salonika** — British withdraw back across Struma (-14) to avoid summer malaria.	**Armenia** — **Gen Prjewalski replaces Yudenich as C-in-C.**
Wed 13	**AEF C-in-C Pershing** in 177-strong party **lands at Boulogne**, arrives in Paris, met by Foch & Joffre (26, *see* 22 & 28).			
Thu 14	**Flanders** — 3rd Australian Div attack Infantry Hill (lose ground 18, regain it 20).	Knox diary '...whole units on this Front (SW)...only read the *Pravda*, printed and distributed with German money'.	**Greece** — British det lands at Piraeus after c9500 French (*see* INT'L EVENTS 12), 500 reinforce French at Larissa (16) also to gain grain supplies.	**Palestine** — 60th (London) Div begins arriving from Salonika.
Fri 15	**Flanders** — German counter-attack SE of Ypres repulsed. **Artois** — Small British advance nr Bullecourt.		**Trentino** — Austrian attack in Mt Ortigara sector at 0230 eventually fails (1000 PoWs lost). **Salonika** — (c) Turk 50th Div withdrawn from E of Struma home, to Aleppo; 1 Turk regt left in theatre (*see* 28 June 1918).	**Secret War: Palestine** — HMY *Managam* returns 2 Jewish agents to Athlit via Cyprus where given training in explosives for use on Damascus railway.
Sat 16			**Trentino** — Italians vainly attack Austrian Mt Ortigara positions all day, losses over 6000.	
Sun 17	**Flanders** — **Portuguese Expeditionary Corps first in action**. **Champagne** — French Fourth Army advance between 'Mts' Cornillet & Blond, repulse attack on Mt Le Téton (21).		**Isonzo** — Italian advance nr Jamiano.	
Mon 18			**Trentino** — Italian guns begin 20hr shelling of Mt Ortigara-Lepozze Austrian positions.	

AFRICAN OPERATIONS 5	SEA WAR 6	AIR WAR 7	INTERNATIONAL EVENTS 8	HOME FRONTS 9
British N Linforce col occupies 3 villages & Schaedel's Lower Farm forcing local pullback by Wahle (-13).			**K Constantine abdicates** in favour of 2nd son Alexander following 24hr Allied ultimatum (11) & leaves country (14). Allied blockade raised (16, *see* 21).	**Austria** — German Ambassador Wedel writes of 'pale, emaciated, even half-starved figures' in Vienna (*see* 18 July). **Britain** — Industrial Unrest Ctee of Inquiry set up. **USA** — Bureau of the Census finds 5m aliens from the 4 Central Powers.
		Britain — 'Diamond' formation of Brandenburg's 14 GOTHAS (20 sent) ATTACK LONDON from 15,000ft at 1130; Central Telegraph Office set on fire, Liverpool Street rail terminus & Royal Mint hit; 3 others bomb downriver. Total of 4.3t bombs (72) dropped causing **worst civ cas of war**: 158k, 425w incl 46 children in Poplar school (Service cas 21). Gothas on return repel Bristol Fighter (observer mortally w), one of 94 defence sorties. Brandenburg awarded *Pour le Mérite* but injured in crash (19) returning from Kreuznach (*see* 4 July). No 56 Fighter (SE5) Sqn temporarily withdrawn from France as a result (21 June-5 July).	US & railroad missions arrive in Petrograd.	**France** — 5000 women workers strike with red flags in Toulouse ammunition factory (-18), win 30-50% pay rise. 32 die in Renault Paris factory collapse. **Britain** — Munitions factory explosion at Ashton-under-Lyne, Lancs (41 die). War Depts authorized to alter contracts where profits excessive.
	N Atlantic — U-boat sinks AMC HMS *Avenger*. **N Sea** — Harwich Force destroys Zeppelin *L43*.			**Russia** — Women admitted to the Bar. **USA** — Wilson Flag Day speech warns of German-American subversion (7m copies distributed).
	N Atlantic — 35 RN destroyers & 15 submarines on special hunting op (-24) N of Scotland sight U-boats 61 times, make 12 attacks, but inflict no damage. **Baltic** — Rear-Adm Dmitri N Verderevski made C-in-C by Kerensky (Maksimov becomes STAVKA (CNS) aged 44, but some crews press for elected cdrs.	**Mesopotamia** — RFC 31st Wing formed, No 63 Sqn joins No 30 (July).	Italian PM tells Chamber that Germany had asked for separate peace, Baron Sonnino on war aims (20). US Congress votes embargo on exports to the 4 N European neutrals (& 6 Oct).	**Germany** — Hindenburg note to Bethmann blames inflation on 'The monstrous increase of worker wages'. **USA** — **Espionage Act** inc fines up to $10,000 & up to 20 yrs jail; 2 anarchists arrested for disrupting registration. Congress votes $3281m for Army & Navy.
	Med — **Allied blockade of Greece lifted**, frees small craft for ASW.	**Britain** — Strasser (new 'Leader of German Navy Airships') rashly attempts London raid on nearly shortest night of year with 4 Zeppelins (2 return early). *L42* (Dietrich) fortuitously detonates a Ramsgate naval ammo store, but *L48* (Schütze, Strasser's deputy) hounded to death from c13,000ft over Suffolk by 3 RFC aircraft after suffering double engine failure (night 17/18, 3 survivors).	Russian Prov Govt proposes Allied conference to revise war aims. German Socialist peace terms published at Stockholm inc independence for Poland & Belgium, free trade & limited armaments.	**Russia** — 1st Congress of Workers & Soldiers Soviets opens in Petrograd (-22), 781 deputies inc 100 Bolsheviks (Lenin speaks twice). **Austria** — Govt repeals civil powers from military cdrs bordering on fronts & relaxes activities of War Surveillance Office. **Germany** — 200 die in northern smallpox epidemic. **Ireland** — 120 remaining Easter Rising prisoners released incl de Valera (see 10 July) after Dublin demo for them (10).
		W Front — RFC resumes bombing after pauses since 9.	**France** — **1st US serviceman buried**, at Pauillac (sailor, drowned 12). Paris economic conference on future.	**Italy** — Gen Giardino War Minister & Adm Triangi Marine Minister after Albanian policy crisis ends. **Russia** — Prov Govt declares *Zemstvo* self-govt for Siberia & Far East. **USA** — Charlie Chaplin film *The Immigrant* released.
	French *Direction Générale de la Marine des Guerre Sous-Marin* set up under Rear-Adm Vignaux, made independent of Naval Staff (Sept).	**E Front** — German air raid on Dvinsk.	Pres Wilson sees Belgian Mission. **Neutrals: Switzerland** — Foreign Minister Hoffmann resigns after aiding German peace overtures to Russia, anti-German Ador succeeds.	**Britain** — Pensioners in special hardships get supplementary allowance (up to 10s pw). Board of Trade appeals for retention of glass bottles. Churchill declines Chancellorship of the Duchy of Lancaster. **USA** — Red Cross Week.

JUNE 1917	WESTERN FRONT 1	EASTERN FRONT 2	SOUTHERN FRONTS 3	TURKISH FRONTS 4
Tue 19	Haig and CIGS present Flanders offensive plan to PM's special Cabinet Ctee (-21), preparations continue.		**Trentino** — From 0600 *Alpini* (15 bns) storm Mt Ortigara summit (6906ft) taking 1000 PoWs (incl *Kaiserjäger*) but Austrians hold 6729ft peak & Mt Camigoletti although 9 bns v 35; Austrians bring up 2 bns & Conrad's requests for more reserves finally answered.	**Arabia** — Lawrence & 500 Arabs begin march on Aqaba but then execute 100-strong N sabotage diversion v Amman-Deraa railway before 27 (*see* 28).
Wed 20	**Pétain orders 3500 Renault lt tanks**. **Artois** — British repulse attacks on R Souchez after making gains (19). **Aisne** — German attack nr Vauxaillon takes ground mainly lost again (21), likewise SE of Filain (22, lost 24).		**Carnia** — Italians capture Piccolo Lagaznoi.	At Aleppo Enver Pasha & 4 Army cdrs discuss *Yilderim* project for Baghdad's recapture. **India: NW Frontier** — Shahur Valley ops (-24) inc RFC bombing (-27) force Mahsud submission 2 July (formal peace 12 Aug).
Thu 21	**Flanders** — British Fourth Army (Rawlinson) begins ops on Flanders coast (-18 Nov,*see* 6 July); they involve 8 divs.	Kerensky reviews newly formed (19) Women's 'Death Battalion' at Petrograd. Denikin arrives at Minsk to take over W Front.		**Mesopotamia/Persia** — Turks by now reoccupy Kizil Ribat & Kasr-i-Shirin.
Fri 22	Pétain tells Pershing French morale v low.		**Salonika** — British 7th Mtd Bde (c2100 men) begins to embark for Egypt (8th Mtd Bde embarked from 31 May) *see* 30.	
Sat 23		**Galicia** — Preparatory orders for Russian offensive stress destroying captured drink.		
Sun 24	**Artois** — BEF First Army advances astride R Souchez as Germans retreat before 46th Div's attacks (night 24/25), *see* 28.			**Mesopotamia** — Maude cables CIGS that Arab help of little value, only small raids not guerrilla warfare desirable, levies not worthwhile.
Mon 25	**Aisne** — French capture 'Dragons's cave' nr Hurtebise.		**Trentino** — At 0230 surprise Austrian attack by 7 bns with 103 guns & mortars in close support recaptures all 3 Mt Ortigara heights & repulses 7 *Alpini* bns in evening (& 26). Italian losses 5633 (c1800 PoWs).	**Sinai** — British 75th Div begins forming at El Arish.

AFRICAN OPERATIONS 5	SEA WAR 6	AIR WAR 7	INTERNATIONAL EVENTS 8	HOME FRONTS 9
c950 British & 12 MGs of NRFF leave Iringa to advance on Ifakara (*see* 30).	Vice-Adm **Kolchak, C-in-C Russian Black Sea Fleet, deposed** by delegate assembly of sailors' councils & replaced by Vice-Adm Lukin. Russian Navy pay rise backdated to 13 May (*see* 26). **Channel** — French submarine *Ariane* torpedoed & sunk on trials by *UC22*.		Hindenburg letter to Bethmann, U-boats will win peace but not sure when.	**Britain** — King abolishes **Royal Family's enemy titles**, British peerages for Tecks & Battenbergs. Commons 330 majority to give wives over 30 the vote.
	Germany — Food supervisory ctees (*Menage-kommissions*) allowed in all German warships to give ratings a say in food selection & preparation (*see* 5 July). For many months they have eaten boiled or dried turnips & a 'nauseous' ersatz meat & veg stew dubbed *Drahtverhau* (literally, 'wire entanglement!'). Last German dreadnought *Württemberg* launched at Hamburg by Vulcan but never completed (broken up 1921).	**Italian Front** — 145 Italian aircraft drop 5¹/₂t bombs on S Tyrol, only 26 Austrian aircraft oppose.	**Secret War** — (c) Somerset Maugham accepts mission to Russia (*see* 28 July). German *OHL* Intelligence Branch becomes Foreign Armies Branch.	
2 KAR coys take German trenches at Schaedel's Upper Farm. Wahle bombards Mingoyo forcing camp's move.		**W Front** — **First operational Fokker Dr I triplane fighters delivered** to Richthofen's *Jasta 11* at Courtrai.	Lloyd George argues in War Cabinet for Italian Front offensive to draw Germans. Rumanian Mission arrives in Washington (left home 18 Apr). **Neutrals: Greece** — Venizelos arrives off Athens in French warship (*see* 26).	**Canada** — Food Controller appointed (Fuel Controller 12 July). **Britain** — S Wales coal owners agree all miners must be trade unionists for duration. 'Triple Alliance' demands conscription of wealth.
	Atlantic — U-boats unsuccessfully attack US troop transports. **N Sea** — Adm Krosigk of Wilhelmshaven naval base orders careful watch kept on Indep Socialists ('dangerous agitators',*see* 2 Aug).		1st Armenian Refugee Congress in Tiflis cables Wilson with thanks to US.	
	N Sea — German torpedo boat escorts 4 steamers from Rotterdam (part of German coastal trade revival since Apr,*see* 16 July). K George V goes to sea for 5th Battle Sqn practice firing (visits Rosyth & Invergordon 24). **Indian Ocean** — P & O liner *Mongolia* (23 lives lost) sunk by *Wolf* mine off Bombay, but vessels based there sweep (June) 51 of 68 mines laid off port (*see* 4 Sept).	**Germany** — *Amerikaprogramm* submitted to *OHL* to double fighter units by 1 Mar 1918 & produce new high-performance fighter. **Palestine** — RNAS (3 Shorts from carrier *Empress*) & RFC (7 aircraft) simultaneously bomb Tulkarm stn & El Ramle airfield; 8 RFC aircraft (5 FTR) hit Turk Mount of Olives HQ (26).		**Austria** — Dr Seidler new PM after Count Clam-Martinitz resigns (21) over budget impasse.
		W Front — Germans shoot down 3 BEF Second Army balloons, 2 more subsequently. **Independent** *Jagdeschwader 1* of *Jasta 4, 6, 10 & 11* **formed under Richthofen** (returned from 6wk leave 14) with c50 fighters.	**Austria** — Count Czernin 'We could have a separate peace with England in 8 days . It would be a momentary salvation, but ... the certain ruin of the dynasty.' **Neutrals: Greece** — PM Zaimis resigns, will not recall Venizelist-dominated Chamber of 13 June 1915.	**Serbia** — PM Pǎsić forms new Cabinet. **Russia** — Ukraine Rada proclaims autonomy after Prov Govt postpones decision (16) until Constituent Assembly.
	Black Sea — German cruiser *Breslau* destroys Russian radio stn & lighthouse on Fidonisi I. **Adriatic** — Vice-Adm Cerni becomes Italian Fleet C-in-C under Revel's supervision. **Secret War** — Admiralty forms Convoy Section to provide escorts & organize 'evasive routeing' based on Room 40 intelligence. Room 40 now sending 66 special telegrams pm based on German codes or signals, especially from radio-happy U-boats via 40 British Isles intercept stns (11 later in Med) which often fix their bearings.		**Neutrals: Norway** — German Minister Dr Michaelis recalled over bomb plot.	

JUNE 1917	WESTERN FRONT 1	EASTERN FRONT 2	SOUTHERN FRONTS 3	TURKISH FRONTS 4
Tue 26	**Artois** — British occupy La Coulotte. In thunderstorm Cdn Corps begins capture of Avion S of Lens (-29). Advance guard of US 1st Div ('Big Red One') lands at St Nazaire, France.		**Salonika** — Col Dimitrievic & 2 other officers shot at dawn.	**Mesopotamia** — **Commission Report blames India & India Office most for 1915-16 setbacks** (Vincent-Bingley Medical Report, 27). **Persia** — Russians take Serdesht.
Wed 27	**Flanders** — German 'Long Max' 15-in gun at Luegenboom fires 55 shells at Dunkirk (24-mile range).		**Trentino** — Austrian attack on Agnello Pass fails.	**Gen Allenby becomes C-in-C EEF** replacing Murray at Cairo.
Thu 28	**14,000 US regulars & marines (2/3 recruits) land at St Nazaire** (*see* 4 July). **Verdun** — Fierce fighting W of Hill 304 (& Mort Homme 30) Germans capture some trenches (-2 July). **Artois** — BEF First Army in 2 attacks advances on 2-mile front S of R Souchez: Canadians secure most of Avion; 46th Div clears Hill 65; 15th Inf Bde (5th Div) captures position on edge of Oppy Wood under cover of smoke, previous assaults without failed bloodily. **Verdun** — Germans capture trenches on Hill 304, more fighting W of Mort Homme (30).	**Galicia** — Preliminary Russian shelling (inc RNAS-manned trench mortars) from 0400, bridge behind Brzezany blown up.		**Arabia** — Lawrence's force leaves for El Jefer wells (-1 July).
Fri 29	**Aisne** — German attacks on Chemin des Dames (-1 July) around Cerny (*see* 3 July).	**Galicia** — Kerensky order 'Your C-in-C [Brusilov], beloved through victory, is convinced that each day of delay merely helps the enemy ....I call on the Army, fortified by the strength and spirit of the Revolution, to take the offensive'. II Cav Corps forces surrender of 1500 mutineers (19th Siberian Div) at Kolomea.	**Trentino** — Austrian coy retakes Height 6585 (Porta Maora) by surprise descent (night 29/30). **Dolomites** — Austrian attack repulsed.	
Sat 30	Gen Anthoine i/c French First Army in Flanders delivers signal from Pétain to Haig: 'The [BEF] offensive in Flanders must be an unqualified success particularly because of the present state of [French] morale.' **Ludendorff only now learns of French mutinies when worst is over.**	**Galicia** — Heavy artillery action, German reply includes gas. Cdr Locker-Lampson sees Kerensky in SW Front HQ train 'Prodigious effort speaking...and making up by personality for ... discipline had worn him out'.	**Trentino** — Italian Sixth Army losses (since 10) 23,736 (12,735 *Alpini*); Austrian 8828. **'Ortigara Tragedy' demoralizes Italian line troops.** **Salonika** — British 60th Div sails for Egypt. French have to force some of 2500 Russians after leave at Athens to re-embark for Salonika (*see* 16 & 23 July).	**Mesopotamia** — Over 20,000 British troops on leave.
Sun 1 July 1917	**Artois** — British 46th Div (First Army) attacks Liévin. **Verdun** — French counter-attack NW of Mort Homme.	**Galicia** — KERENSKY OR SECOND BRUSILOV (SUMMER) OFFENSIVE (-18) on 50-mile front astride Brzezany with 31 inf divs & 1328 guns, objective Lemberg. Seventh Army gains little ground and loses it all to Germans by 6, but Eleventh Army drives 3-mile wedge between opposing armies at Koniuchy. Russians take 10,429 PoWs & 5 guns for 17,339 cas.		**Arabia** — Lawrence leaves El Jefer wells, blows bridge on the Hejaz Railway S of Maan (2).

AFRICAN OPERATIONS 5	SEA WAR 6	AIR WAR 7	INTERNATIONAL EVENTS 8	HOME FRONTS 9
	Russia — Kerensky appoints his comrade Vladimir I Lebedev acting Director of Navy Dept.		**Neutrals: Greece — Venizelos appointed PM** (*see* 30). **Secret War** — Bethmann discusses peace chances with new Papal Nuncio Eugenio Pacelli (later Pope Pius XII) who sees Kaiser (29); Chancellor ready to recognize Belgium under certain conditions.	**USA** — Orville Wright asserts aircraft can win war for Allies.
	Biscay — French cruiser *Kléber* (42 lost) sunk off Brest by mines from *UC61* (*see* 26 July). German Admiralty orders U-boats to act off France & Italy as well as severing Salonika transport route, neutral ships in British convoys to be treated as hostile (30).	**W Front** — First Sopwith Camel RFC victory (with No 70 Sqn first RFC unit to receive fighter, 3 more sqns receive it July).	**Neutrals: Spain** — Martial law declared.	**Germany** — Hindenburg letter to Kaiser on morale decline, says it seems beyond Chancellor. **Russia** — Prov Govt sets 13 Oct for Constituent Assembly's opening. **France** — Chamber's Army Ctee protests v light treatment of Gens Nivelle & Mangin. Chamber secret session on Nivelle Offensive & mutinies (29 June-6 July).
		Russia — Ukraine declares independence.		**Britain** — Lloyd George Glasgow speech optimistic, no honourable peace attainable yet. **Russia** — Income tax increased to 30% on salaries over $200,000 eqvt.
33 KAR led by 3 African NCOs rout German coy (with 2 MGs) attack on ration escort nr Lindi. British Iringa col advances from Boma Mzinga.	Allied & neutral shipping losses 286 ships at 674,458t (U-boat official history fig 696,725t incl 164,299t in Med); 2 U-boats lost, 8 commissioned (**record 61 U-boats at sea during June**). Shipping forecasts for Controller Sir J Maclay indicate not enough British shipping for import of necessities by 1 Dec if 300,000t pm lost, but neutral shipping entrances only 20% down on normal thanks to US entry & much diplomacy. British merchant fleet has lost 2¼mt not 3½mt Adm Holtzendorff hoped. **N Sea** — (June) RN lay 1120 mines in S half. US Shipping Board recruits 41,977 officers & sailors (-30 June 1920, *see* 3 July).	**Macedonia** — German *Jasta 38* fighter unit formed.	**Greece severs relations with Central Powers** (*see* 2 July).	**Germany** — 'Union Demands for the Transition from a Wartime to a Peacetime Economy' presented to *Bundesrat* & *Reichstag*. (June) 50,000 troops demobilized for mining. **Russia** — Gen Kaledin elected Don Cossack Ataman. **USA** — War Dept invites 'How to Win War' ideas. **Britain** — PM gets freedom of Dundee. Glasgow shop steward J Maclean released.
KAR strength now 23,978 (16 bns). c120,000 porters on strength (31) (*see* 8 Aug).	3000 British merchant ships have guns, 2180 guns mounted in 1917 only 190 under 12pdr (3in) calibre (*see* 31). **ASW depth charge issue doubled** to 4, 6 by Aug. 100-300 used pm during 1917 (prod 1678pm) v U-boats. Bomb or howitzer thrower (most common 7.5in how) begins to equip 542 warships & 735 merchantmen, able to fire 111-113-lb bombs 650-2600yds astern or broadside on. **First regular eastbound transatlantic convoy sails** from Hampton Roads Va, codelettered HH1.		**Secret War** — (July) Sir Basil Zahroff meets Enver Pasha & Abdal Karim (Col Frobenius) in Switzerland & offers $1.5m for Turkey to sign separate peace, but refused (*see* 9 Jan 1918). **Occupied Belgium** (July) — Capt Landau (MI1c) takes over 129-strong La Dame Blanche train watching network & crucially expands it by end-Sept (*see* W FRONT 23 Sept). **Germany** — Emperor Charles state visit to Bavaria and Württemberg.	**Britain** — RFP 1%, up 2%. Voluntary Tea Control Scheme (compulsory 17 Oct). **Russia** — Bolsheviks dominate Petrograd peace demo (others in Helsinski & 4). **Germany** — (July) Army Signals Service reorganized as Branch. **USA** — (July) *Atlantic Monthly* magazine on 'Disloyalty of the German-American Press'.

JULY 1917	WESTERN FRONT 1	EASTERN FRONT 2	SOUTHERN FRONTS 3	TURKISH FRONTS 4
Sun 1 contd				
Mon 2		**Galicia** — Eleventh Army's Czechoslovak Bde triggers Austrian 19th (Czech) Div's desertion.		German c6500-strong Asia Corps (3 bns, 3 cav troops, 18 guns, 18 MGs, 12 mortars, 4 air sqns) formed, as elite help under Col Frankenburg for Turks (*see* 7 & 20).
Tue 3	**Aisne** — Larger scale German attacks on 11-mile front N of the Aisne.	**Galicia** — Eleventh Army has taken 14,000 PoWs & 30+ guns so far, but slow reserves prevent exploitation.		**Arabia** — Lawrence's 450 Arabs destroy Turk bn (460 cas) at Abu-el-Lissal; 120 Turks at Guweira surrender to Sheikh Ibn Jad.
Wed 4				**Palestine** — Turk cav recce from Beersheba shelled into retreat (& 19). **Arabia** — Lawrence takes 120 Turk PoWs at Kethira post in surprise attack during eclipse. **Mesopotamia** — Maude tells CIGS he can meet any attack.
Thu 5	**Flanders** — Slight British advance S of Ypres. Arty duels on the Aisne & in Champagne.	Denikin new Russian W Front C-in-C, Klembovski N Front.		**Arabia** — Lawrence confronts 300 Turks from Aqaba who reject 2 surrender summons. **S Persia** — Action at Kafta (N of Shiraz): 250 British defeat 500 tribesmen & storm fort.
Fri 6	**Pershing tells Washington that a million men must be sent to France by May 1918. Flanders** — Germans fire 300,000 shells of HE & gas at new British Yser bridgeheads taken over from French (-10).	**Galicia** — Kornilov's Eighth Army attacks S of Dniester at 0700 v Austrian Third Army, takes 7000 PoWs, 48 guns & Jutrena Gora summit by 8, only German reserves stem rout.		**Arabia** — **Fall of Aqaba**: 300 Turks surrender to Lawrence's 2500 Arabs, 130 miles from Allenby's front. Lawrence leaves with 8 camel riders to cross Sinai & get food ship from Suez (arrives 8,*see* 10).
Sat 7	Minor French gains on the Aisne (German attacks repulsed 8 & 9) & at Verdun. **Flanders** — 2174 British guns concentrated (*see* 17).			Falkenhayn given command of *Yilderim* Army Group (HQ staff 65 Germans and 9 Turks).

AFRICAN OPERATIONS 5	SEA WAR 6	AIR WAR 7	INTERNATIONAL EVENTS 8	HOME FRONTS 9
	Other regular convoys from Canadian Sydney (Cape Breton), Gibraltar & New York (*see* 31). U-boat attack on US troop convoy defeated (4). Av of U-boats at sea falls to 41pd. **N Sea** — (July) Grand Fleet has 32 battleships to German 21 as in Mar, but only 34 destroyers (46 on ASW work, 29 refitting).			
			GREECE DECLARES WAR ON CENTRAL POWERS. Anglo-German PoW Agreement signed at The Hague (Franco-German one, 26). Kaiser (told first US troops landed in France) & Ludendorff in Vienna War Council (*see* 25). **Occupied Poland** — Pilsudski resigns & refuses loyalty oath to Germany (arrested 22; **Polish Legions broken up** & 5000 interned for refusing oath 9).	**Austria** — **Emperor grants amnesty to all condemned by emergency military courts** (2593 freed by 31). **Britain** — King & Queen at 1867 Canadian Federation Jubilee Service, Westminster Abbey. **USA** — 37 negroes killed in E St Louis (Ill) race riots during strike; 15,000 New York blacks stage silent protest march.
Hawthorn's NRFF col advances from Likuyu driving Capt Lincke N on Mahenge.	US Pres suspends regulation that watch officers in American ships must be US citizens.	**Dardanelles** — 9 RNAS aircraft open night bombing offensive from Mudros v Gallipoli (raids 8, 11, 15, *see* 9).	**Neutrals: Holland** — Riots in Amsterdam.	**Russia** — Kerensky cables PM Lvov to crush any further demos. **Britain** — Munitions Ministry limits summer hols to 1 wk.
	N Sea — Redesigned lt battlecruiser HMS *Furious* joins Grand Fleet (rebuilt since 19 Mar) as carrier with 10 aircraft (*see* AIR WAR 2 Aug). **Baltic** — Dreadnought *Petropavlosk* at Helsinki issues anti-govt ultimatum threatening to sail & shell Petrograd (*see* 17).	**Britain** — 18 of 25 Gotha bombers (Capt Kleine) sent to attack Harwich & Felixstowe (RNAS Stn damaged, 4 civ cas, 43 service cas (*see* 22). 5 Sopwith Camels from Dunkirk attack homeward-bound Gothas without success. 21 Gothas (1 lost to Bristol fighter off Ostend) repeat, raid (22) when 122 fighters ascend to no avail, 1 Gotha crashes on landing. **USA** — Liberty air engine sent to Washington tests (publicly passed 12 Sept).	Argentina protests v U-boat torpedoing of 2 ships. German Ambassador Count Luxburg using Swedish Legation to contact Berlin (since at least 3, *see* 8 Sept). **France** — **Pershing leads 14,500 US troops through Paris**; Capt Charles E Stanton says at Piépus Cemetery **'Lafayette, we are here!'** *see* W FRONT 14).	**France** — Maritime Transport Secretariat created to control all vessels over 100t.
	N Sea — Hunger & coaling strike by ratings beginning with High Seas Fleet flagship secures estab of food supervisory ctees aboard most ships (July, *see* 2 Aug).			**France** — *Bonnet Rouge* editor arrested, paper suspended (12, *see* 5 Sept). **Russia** — Reval naval base 'Death Battalion' leaves for front.
Action at Mnindi involves 3 Kilwa Force cols & 1st use of mortars, causes German retreat to Mchakama.		**W Front** — Guynemer scores first victory with his new 37mm *Puteaux* cannon-armed Spad S12, DFW downed with a single shot (Fonck achieves 6 kills with this powerful but dangerous recoil weapon). Germans bomb RNAS Bray Dunes airfield, damage 12 aircraft (night 6/7). **Richthofen w in air combat** by FE26 of No 20 Sq RFC, out of action for 6 wks, but *JG1* scores 9 victories without loss (7) under Capt W Reinhard. .	British Bureau of Information (96 staff) opens in New York, branches in Chicago & San Francisco. *Reichstag* Catholic Deputy Erzberger proposes Germany renounces territorial gains for peace (*see* 19).	**Germany** — *Reichstag* (recalled 5 to vote RM15bn war credit) demands reforms & peace without annexations. 50,000 Cologne metal workers strike for pay rise and 51hr wk. **Canada** — Conscription Bill passed. **Turkey** — Govt tries to take over meat distribution (*see* 5 Sept). **Russia** — Kronstadt Soviet condemns Kerensky offensive (*see* 17).
		Britain — 22 **Gotha bombers** (2 FTR incl 1 shot down, 3 written off in crash landings on return) **attack London** with 4.3t bombs on City & E End (roof of St Martin's-le-Grand GPO hit + Ironmongers' Hall — £200,000+ damage). 108 defence sorties (20 or so engage, 145 civ cas, 5 service cas). Anti-foreigner riots in E End, shops smashed. Cabinet meets pm (again 9, *see* HOME FRONTS 9), sanctions 3 more home defence sqns, No 46 withdrawn from France, 24 Camels not sent (-30 Aug).		**Germany** — Kaiser in Berlin approves Prussian Parlt voting on equal francise, orders bill's preparation (11, *see* 9).

JULY 1917	WESTERN FRONT 1	EASTERN FRONT 2	SOUTHERN FRONTS 3	TURKISH FRONTS 4
Sat 7 contd				
Sun 8				**Mesopotamia** — British occupy Dhibban on Euphrates during hottest summer in memory (122°F in shade at Baghdad).
Mon 9	German military propaganda service entrusted with 'enlightenment' of the front-line troops (*see* 25). **Flanders** — Slight British advance on Messines sector. **Aisne** — French counter-attacks at Braye-en-Launnois.	**Galicia** — Austrian Third Army retreats to R Lomnica, losing 1000 PoWs. Its C-in-C Tersztyanzky replaced by Kritek by 16.	**Isonzo** — Austrian attacks W of Tolmino fail. (July) *Catanzaro* Bde mutiny suppressed by force (*see* 17).	
Tue 10	**Flanders** — **German dusk 15 bn attack on Nieuport:** Fierce arty duels. German marines advance nr Lombaertzyde on 1400-yd front E of Yser mouth & **take 1000+ PoWs;** 2 British platoons surrounded, fight to last man. 1st & 32nd Divs otherwise hold. More German attacks repulsed (14,*see* 19).	**Galicia** — Kornilov takes Halicz with 2000 PoWs, Kalusz (11), crosses R Lomnica (12). By 13 total Russian PoW haul 36,643.		**Egypt — Lawrence meets Allenby at Cairo,** gains £200,000 monthly subsidy for Arabs (later £500,000) apart from £16,000 in gold for Aqaba. **Mesopotamia** — British occupy Madhij Defile 18 miles W of Falluja on Euphrates; 2 German airmen surrender on foot at Samarra.
Wed 11			Health statistics of British Salonika Army published.	**Mesopotamia** — c2500 British, 4 armoured cars, 14 guns with 127 vans & lorries (600 inf carried) attack 820 Turks & 6 guns at Ramadi but foiled by terrain, dust & burning heat (321/566 cas to heat). British beat off 1500 Arabs in retreat to Dhibban (13-14).
Thu 12	**Flanders** — FIRST USE OF MUSTARD GAS: Germans fire 50,000 rnds (125t) at British nr Ypres (Allies dub it Yperite), 2490 gassed (87 deaths), mainly in 15th Div (*see* 17).			Allenby cables War Office for reinforcements to reach Jaffa-Jerusalem line (*see* 10 Aug).
Fri 13				
Sat 14	**Flanders** — Between 14 July and 4 Aug German arty fire 1m rnds (2500t) of mustard gas shell at British between Nieuport & Armentières; 14,726 gassed (500 deaths). **Champagne** — French capture trenches on Moronvilliers Massif; counter-attacks repulsed (15 & 16). **Aisne** — Germans make small gains on Chemin des Dames & at Cerny. **Artois** — First AEF cas, Lt Louis I Genella suffers shell w with BEF SW of Arras (*see* 4 Sept). **France** — Gen Estienne reviews his Schneider tanks at Champlieu camp nr Compiègne.			
Sun 15		**Galicia** — Litzmann's 4 new German divs block Kornilov after 18-mile advance, he	**Isonzo** — Italian Carso raid gains 275 PoWs.	

AFRICAN OPERATIONS 5	SEA WAR 6	AIR WAR 7	INTERNATIONAL EVENTS 8	HOME FRONTS 9
		Germany — French raid Essen & other towns in reprisal for bombing of Nancy & Épernay.		
Deventer visits Lindi.	RNAS bomb Constantinople War Ministry & *Goeben*. Ludendorff warns German Navy that British may try landings behind Turks in Palestine, U-boat always to be in E Med (16) & Port Said-Gaza route to be mined, 3 U-boats assigned (29 Sept). **N Sea** — Battleship *Vanguard* sunk by internal explosion (unstable cordite) at Scapa (804 dead, 3 survivors).	**Britain** — Gen Wilson to Haig on Gotha London raid 'one would have thought the world was coming to an end'. **Turkey** — An RNAS Handley Page (flown out to Mudros May) bombs (8 x 112lb) Constantinople (Golden Horn area) & Turco-German Fleet for 35min after 7hr flight; destroyer damaged & Turk War Office stables hit.	Kaiser rejects Bethmann's peace policy without annexation (*see* HOME FRONTS 9, 10, 12).	**USA** — **Food, metal & fuel export embargo. Britain** — Commons Secret Session on London air raids (PM receives air defences' deputation 13). **Germany** — Ludendorff tells Kaiser that Bethmann must go, ordered back to *OHL*.
				Britain — 117,772 PoWs & 759 guns taken to date. War bread to be officially tasted after public complaints. **Germany** — Kaiser refuses Bethmann resignation (*see* 12). **Ireland** — De Valera wins E Clare by election for Sinn Fein (*see* 25 Oct).
		Britain — Cabinet decides to set up ctee incl Smuts on air defence & organization (*see* 19, 5 Aug). **W Front** — After bad weather delay, **RFC Flanders pre-Third Ypres offensive begins**, incl night bombing. **Mesopotamia** — 121°F heat evaporates water in 3 RFC aircraft trying to support Ramadi attack (2 German aircraft similarly lost 9).		**Russia** — Overworked & insomniac Lenin travels to Finland for rest (-17). **Britain** — **India Secretary Austen Chamberlain resigns in Mesopotamia Debate**, his PUS Montagu succeeds (17). Kipling's poem 'Mesopotamia' published in *Morning Post*.
	N Sea — Destroyer HMS *Patriot* depth charges & sinks *U69* E of Shetlands.	**W Front** — Mannock scores 4 victories (-13). Record air activity to date incl 30 Anglo-French fighters v 30 German (2 lost) on day that costs 9 British & 14 German aircraft. **Palestine** — Allenby asks for 3 more RFC sqns, gets 2 by Sept.		**Germany** — Hindenburg & Ludendorff cable resignation from Kreuznach but called to Berlin (13). Crown Prince receives party leaders there. **USA** — 1186 IWW members deported from Arizona to Columbia, N Mexico, for allegedly aiding miners to strike for Germany (*see* 5 Sept).
Sahara — 960 French & Allies from Agades defeat Senussi Khoassen & take his gun at Amzet but he raids Dammerghou killing 20 French (30 Aug, *see* 14 Feb 1918).

Kilwa Force (Beves) surprises & drives Germans from Mtandawala. Shorthose's NRFF col (700+ & 2 guns) gets air-dropped orders to occupy Tunduru 100 miles to N, rafts across R Rovuma (31, *see* 23 Aug). **Morocco** — Lyautey commemorates 10th anniversary of French landing at Casablanca. | | | **Bethmann resigns as Imperial German Chancellor, Dr Michaelis** (not known to Kaiser) **succeeds** (14). Foreign Minister Zimmermann resigns (15, *see* 5 Aug).

Finland declares independence from Russia. | **France** — General Petroleum Ctee formed. **Germany** — **Bethmann resigns**, Michaelis from Prussian Food Office succeeds as first non-aristocrat Chancellor (14).

Germany — Upper Silesia strikes have cost 500,000t coal; end early Aug after military repression. **France** — First Bastille Day parade since 1914, Foreign Legion participates. |
| | Cmdre Tyrwhitt of Harwich Force knighted. (c) U-boats switch main attack to | **S Turkey** — 4 RNAS Short seaplanes from HMS *Empress* report hits on cotton factories nr | | **Germany** — Exempted workers total 1.9m (1.2m Sept 1916). **Russia** — Kadet ministers |

JULY 1917	WESTERN FRONT 1	EASTERN FRONT 2	SOUTHERN FRONTS 3	TURKISH FRONTS 4
Sun 15 contd		evacuates Kalusz (16) but then holds, gaining & then losing Nowica (18).		
Mon 16	**Artois** — Cdn Corps relieves British 1 Corps in sector opposite Lens and Hill 70 (*see* 15 Aug).		**Salonika** — **Mutinies in French 57th Div & 2nd Zouaves** over lack of leave; Gen Grossetti dissuades 300 men & 90 others arrested. From Aug leave parties use new shorter trans-Greece railroad route to Itea (Gulf of Corinth) & Taranto then train to Marseilles.	
Tue 17	**Third Ypres bombardment** (-30) **begins**: British fire 4,283,550 shells (cost £22,211,389 14s 4d) incl 100,000 rounds (250t) of chlorpicrin gas shells at Germans (-31), 1250 gassed (75 deaths). British trench raids. **Verdun** — French regain positions NW of Mort Homme lost during previous 18 days. Unsuccessful German trench raids NW of Verdun (18).		**Italian Front** — *Alpini* officer writes '... certain bad elements who have got into the units, worry me a good deal...'.	
Wed 18	**Somme** — British repulse trench raids SW of St Quentin.	**W Russia** — Battle of Dvinsk (-25): *Armeeabteilung D* (Kirchbach) repels Denikin's W Front.		
Thu 19	German attacks in Nieuport, St Quentin & N Aisne sectors.	**W Russia** — Battle of Smorgon-Krevo (-27): German Tenth Army repulses assault after 2-mile Russian penetration (22). **Galicia** — **Hoffmann's counter-offensive** with Eben's 9 divs (8 from W Front) makes 12-mile wide breach E of Zloczow helped by Bruchmüller hurricane barrage. Russian Eleventh Army flees en masse, losing 6000 PoWs & 70 guns by 21.		**India: NW Frontier** — Mohmand blockade ends.
Fri 20	British Cabinet sanctions Haig's Ypres offensive, provided it is called off if progress is unsatisfactory (*see* 25).			Army Group Kommando F formed to control German troops. **Palestine** — British 54th Div (100+ cas) trench raids SW of Umbrella Hill causing 118+ cas (MG & mortar taken).
Sat 21	**Flanders** — Arty duels (-22).	**Baltic Provinces** — Russian N Front 'offensive' (-23): only 2 of 6 divs allocated participate (182nd Div at gunpoint). **Galicia** — Germans near Tarnopol despite heroic RNAS armoured car action (5 cars lost).		

AFRICAN OPERATIONS 5	SEA WAR 6	AIR WAR 7	INTERNATIONAL EVENTS 8	HOME FRONTS 9
	outwardbound unescorted shipping, twice as risky for latter as homeward bound by Aug (*see* 7 Aug).	Adana (*Empress* aircraft starts fires in Beirut quay warehouses Aug & 27 Sept, *see* 9 Oct).		resign from Prov Govt over Ukrainian autonomy.
	N Sea — Harwich Force (8 cruisers & 17 destroyers) capture 4 German steamers from Rotterdam in neutral waters & drive 2 more ashore on Dutch coast (24 German merchant ships sunk on this route in 1917). **Britain** — (c) New Admiralty Planning Section formed under Capt Dudley Pound.	**Arabia** — 3 RFC aircraft damaged by storm at Gayadah airstrip after 3 raids on Hejaz Railway (11, 12, 16); unit recalled to Egypt from Wejh by 31.	British Cabinet agree to postpone war aims discussion for as long as possible (*see* HOME FRONTS 4 Aug).	**Russian 'July Days' Rising** (-19): abortive part-Trotsky inspired revolt in Petrograd, Lenin returns (17) & calls it off.
			British Royal Family change name from Saxe-Coburg-Gotha to Windsor.	**Russia** — Justice Ministry documents allege Lenin a German agent (-18) as do other sources (*see* INT'L EVENTS 18 Aug). Kronstadt sailors (6000) join Red rising but Cossacks begin charges as troops arrive from Front. **USA** — Presidential order drafts 678,000 of 5 June registrees. War Secretary draws 1st no for draft (20). **Britain** — Govt reshuffle makes **Churchill Munitions Minister** (Addison becomes new Reconstruction Minister), Carson joins War Cabinet.
German rearguard stands 5 times N of Narungombe.	French tell Greek Minister of Marine, Fleet to be returned in batches, first cruiser *Helle* , 4 destroyers & torpedo boat by 13 Aug (*see* 30). **Italy** — Vice-Adm Del Bono Minister of Marine for duration. **Baltic** — 2 destroyers sail from Helsinki with 100-strong delegations supporting 'July Days Rising'; both arrested. Kerensky condemns Fleet's disloyalty (20) and appoints Destroyer Div Cdr, Capt Alexander V Razvozov, Rear-Adm & C-in-C, aged 38 (20) after cashiering the hapless Verderevski. Centrobalt dissolved (23) temporarily.		Baron Rothschild writes to Balfour 'At last I am able to bring you the formula you asked me for' (*see* 2 Nov).	**Russia** — Officer Cadets smash *Pravda* offices, Lenin goes into hiding & fears assassination (*see* 23). **Austria** — Arz memo says only Rumanian food imports sustaining Monarchy till new harvest (*see* INT'L EVENTS 3 Aug).
Battle of Narungombe: 1700 British (363 cas) & 20 MGs attack Capt Liebermann's c800 men, 2 guns & 48 MGs in waterhole hill positions. Narungombe occupied (20) as Germans retreat S to Mihambia, minus 1 MG.	**Carson, First Lord of the Admiralty, resigns, succeeded by Sir E Geddes** (20,*see* HOME FRONTS 17; 7 Aug)	**Britain** — FM French tells Smuts 'Air should be separate service' (*see* 5 Aug).	*Reichstag* **Peace Resolution** on war aims by 212-126 vote 'strives for a peace by agreement and a permanent reconciliation'. New Chancellor Michaelis says Germany will not again offer peace (*see* 27).	**Russia** — **Kerensky succeeds Prince Lvov as PM** after news of German breakthrough. Petrograd: last 500 rebels surrender to Gen Polovtsev. Finnish *Scim* proclaims Finland's autonomy (*see* 3 Aug). **Germany** — Crown Prince Rupprecht letter to Interior Minister bemoans Bavaria's plight v Berlin heavy industry.
			Corfu Declaration, signed by PM Pašić, Dr Trumbic & Montenegro Ctee for National Union, seeks union of Serbs, Croats & Slovenes.	**Britain** — Govt decides to lower bread & meat prices inc a 9d loaf (24, *see* 17 Sept).
		France — RNAS seaplane stn (3 aircraft) opens at Cherbourg.	Lloyd George says new German Chancellor's speech means military have won, speech of 23 says peace only achievable with German people.	**Russia** — Kerensky orders arrest of only 6 Bolsheviks (exc Trotsky) & allows only voluntary disarming. **Britain** — Lloyd George says 1917/18 food supplies already secured. Churchill speech at Dundee 'We are the heart, the centre of the League of Nations. If we fail, all fail.' (*see* 29).

JULY 1917	WESTERN FRONT 1	EASTERN FRONT 2	SOUTHERN FRONTS 3	TURKISH FRONTS 4
Sun 22	**Aisne** — German attacks in N Aisne sector; fierce fighting, French recover lost ground (24). **Verdun** — German trench raids.	**Galicia** — Emperor Charles visits HQ at Zloczow.	**Salonika** — British 27th Div trench raid on Homondas village takes 35 PoWs & destroys 2 mtn guns.	
Mon 23	**Flanders/Artois** — British-Canadian trench raids (& 28); Cdn 116th Bn (74 cas) captures 53 PoWs from German 36th Res Div W of Lens.	**Galicia** — **Russian retreat on 150-mile front**, Stanislau & Halicz given up as Austrian Third Army (Kritek) recrosses R Lomnica. **Rumania** — **Battle of Marasesti** (-1 Aug): Averescu's Rumanian Second Army advances 12½ miles on 20-mile front, takes 30 villages, 2977 PoWs, 57 guns from German Ninth Army (Kosch), but Russian Fourth Army refuses help.	**Salonika** — British 27th Div horse show (-25) under air cover; Sarrail & Milne visit it (25). (c)18,000 Russian troops return to front as a div but Gen Dietrichs recalled to Petrograd (Aug,*see* Oct).	
Tue 24				
Wed 25	**British Cabinet assures Haig of its approval and whole-hearted support for his offensive**. Ludendorff confidential instruction warns v spread of 'political propaganda' in German Army, ordering minute examination of all letters for the front (*see* 29). **Aisne** — German attacks repulsed N of river (-27). **Champagne** — German attacks at Mt Haut (& 27) repulsed.	**Russian Govt restores death penalty & courst-martial.** **Galicia** — German 1st Gd Div takes Tarnopol & crosses R Sereth (26) watched by Kaiser. Austrian Third Army retakes Kolomea (26).	At Paris Conference (-26) British insist on moving another Salonika div & heavy arty to Palestine despite Allied & Serb diplomatic protests (*see* 3 & 7 Aug).	
Thu 26				
Fri 27	British Heavy Branch MG Corps becomes Tank Corps. **Flanders** — British Gds Div occupies 3000yds of German evacuated front-line trenches & beats off counter-attack.			
Sat 28		**Galicia** — Austro-Germans reach Russian frontier at Gusiatyn (Wild Cossack Div confronts 40,000 deserters there, 25-27) on R Zbruch. Kaiser leaves for Vilna.		
Sun 29	Ludendorff issues detailed prog for patriotic propaganda in German Army. **Flanders** — Arty duels. Allenby's only son, an RHA Lt, k by shell splinter.	**Galicia** — Russian resistance S of Dniester stiffens, but Bukovina retreat continues.		
Mon 30	**Aisne** — Arty in action.	**Galicia** — Austrian Third Army retakes Zaleszczycki & Sniatyn. *Südarmee* Austrians & Turk div	**Salonika** — British hospital cases c12,500 (mainly malaria,*see* 31 Aug).	

AFRICAN OPERATIONS 5	SEA WAR 6	AIR WAR 7	INTERNATIONAL EVENTS 8	HOME FRONTS 9
	N Atlantic — U-boat sinks AMC *Otway* (10 lost).		SIAM DECLARES WAR ON GERMANY & AUSTRIA. German Vienna Ambassador reports that plebiscite in Austria alone would find majority for joining Allies & fighting Germany.	**Britain** — National Baby Week (-28) to nurture infant life. Churchill writes to PM to 'limit the consequences' of any W Front offensive. **France** — Clemenceau attacks Interior Minister Malvy for defeatism. **Russia** — Lenin leaves Petrograd to hide with Zinoviev on L Razliv, 16 miles NW (*see* 21 Aug).
	Naval part of Allied Paris conference (-26) agrees that Otranto Barrage come under new British Med C-in-C (*see* 1 Aug).		Kühlmann retires as German Constantinople Ambassador (*see* 5 Aug).	**Britain** — Commons votes record £650m war credit. Recruiting transferred from War Office to Local Govt Bd. **France** — **Mata Hari's trial** opens in public, death sentence (25), 2 appeals rejected (*see* 15 Oct). **USA** — Congress votes $640m for military aviation.
		N Sea — 5-7 RNAS Sopwith Pups or Camels cover Belgian coast net barrage laying (-27) & destroy 3 German aircraft.	Allied Balkan Conference in Paris (-26). Czernin meets Kaiser & appeals for more moderate war aims, also to help Austrian home position.	**USA** — 10,000 attend anti-draft rally at New Ulm (Minn).
	Channel — Minelayer cruiser *HMS Ariadne* (38 lost) sunk by *UC65* off Beachy Head. *UC61* beached on Cap Gris Nez & surrounded by Belgian cav; RN recover documents showing British minesweeping report code broken (*see* 4 Aug). **Black Sea** — Russian motorboat approaches Bosphorus, comes under German/Turk coastal gunfire, drops bottles with revolutionary anti-German proclamation to Turks (night 26/27).	**Flanders** — **Major air battle over Polygon Wood** involving 94 British & German aircraft, repeated (27) when c20+ Albatros Scouts lose 9 aircraft to 2 British after Allied trap (59 RFC single-fighters + French) sprung over the wood. Haig congratulates Trenchard (28).		**Britain** — Labour pledges lm new houses after war.
Kilwa No 2 Col occupies Nanganachi 12 miles SW of Narungombe, then Mssindye (29-30).		**Germany** — Ludendorff suggests that naval Zeppelin building cease to save materials for aircraft (*see* 31).	Ramsay Macdonald's Commons motion to approve *Reichstag* Peace Resolution defeated 148-19. **Secret Franco-Italian Agreement on Asia Minor spheres of influence** (Britain joins 18 Aug).	**Britain** — 8000 (inc soldiers) break up London E End Soviet meeting after Special Branch tip to *Daily Express*.
			Secret War — Somerset Maugham sails for Vladivostok (*see* 20 June).	**Britain** — Royal Warrant authorizes Tank Corps.
	N Sea — HM gunboat *Halcyon* rams & sinks *UB27* off Smith's Knoll (Harwich).	**Flanders** — Stormy weather prevents air combat (-30).		Churchill gets PM's agreement to Munitions Ministry reform & discusses poor US programme; he is re-elected (5266 majority, Dundee).
	Med — Venizelos accepts return of British Naval Mission (Capt C Brown with Hellenic	**E Front** — RNAS armoured car shoots down strafing German plane on R Zbruch, Galicia.	Lloyd George tells press Russia will recover to be as formidable as ever. **Occupied Belgium** —	

JULY 1917	WESTERN FRONT 1	EASTERN FRONT 2	SOUTHERN FRONTS 3	TURKISH FRONTS 4
Mon 30 contd		force R Zbruch & beat off Siberian regt & RNAS armoured cars (31).		
Tue 31	THIRD BATTLE OF YPRES ('PASSCHENDAELE') (-18 Nov): 9 British & 6 French divs attack at 0350 (sunrise) on 15-mile front from R Lys to R Yser after 3091-gun barrage (British record). Objective to drive Germans from Pilckem Ridge commanding Ypres from S to NE. **Battle of Pilckem Ridge** (-2 Aug): German Fourth Army, with counter-attack divs, restricts Allied advance (15,000 BEF cas, 12 VCs won, 19 tanks knocked out) **as rain begins** but it penetrates 1$^{1}/_{4}$ -2$^{1}/_{2}$ miles capturing 12 villages & parts of German 2nd trench line. German losses are heavy, incl 5000 PoWs. French gain most. **Aisne** — French make small gains W of Chevregny ridge. 2 German bns attack Cerney Plateau *after 5-min bombard-ment*. Mangin put on res list following Nivelle Offensive inquiry (*see* 15 Dec).	**Bukovina** — Russians retreat in Czernowitz region.		**Mesopotamia** — Kut-Baghdad, Baghdad-Baquba & Sumaiha-Sadiya railways completed. **Persia** — (July) Baratov's Russian forces begin withdrawing (-Mar 1918).
Wed 1 August 1917	**BEF at peak est strength** of 2,044,627 (1,721,056 British). **Ypres** — Germans recapture St Julien (British recapture 3) & make gains nr Ypres-Roulers rail line (British recapture 2). French gains on W bank of Yser Canal.	KORNILOV, aged 47, REPLACES BRUSILOV AS C-IN-C. His order of the day condemns treachery of 'certain units'. **Galicia** — Russians drive *Südarmee* back across R Zbruch at Gusiatyn. **Rumania** — Battle of Marasesti 1st phase ends.	**Greece** — (Aug-Sept) French Military Mission (Gen Braquet) of about 150 officers arrives to train Greek Army, 2 classes of conscripts called up (Aug).	
Thu 2	**Ypres** — Battle of Pilckem Ridge ends after max advance of 3000yds by 9 British divs costs 31,850 cas. **Waterlogged shellholes begin to appear. Artois** — Germans storm some trenches on Infantry Hill (Monchy-Arras).	Hoffmann diary 'Propaganda & guns must work together'.		**Mesopotamia** — CIGS telegram agrees with Maude Russian co-operation cannot be relied on. Maude (5) cables he can deal with 81,500 Turks & 370 guns by end Sept.
Fri 3	**Artois** — British success on Infantry Hill. Unsuccessful Allied attack astride the Scarpe (9). **Ypres** — German 2nd Gd Res Div reduced to 2208 men incl 600 sick. British 39th Div captures St Julien after 3861 cas.	**Bukovina** — Kövess' (made FM by 9 & Baron) Austro-German Third Army's XIII Corps (42nd Honved Inf Div & 5th Inf Div) reoccupies capital Czernowitz, then 10 miles E & regains Vama (5), Cheremissov's Eighth Army having evacuated Kimpolung (2). **Rumania** — 600 Russo-Rumanian guns begin 3-day	**Salonika** — Milne ordered to send 18 6in & 60pdr guns to Egypt, then an inf div (9), 10th Div relieved from 19 (*see* 15, TURK FRONTS 10,*see* Sept).	

AFRICAN OPERATIONS 5	SEA WAR 6	AIR WAR 7	INTERNATIONAL EVENTS 8	HOME FRONTS 9
	rank of Rear Adm).		German sappers restore Canal du Centre nr Mons.	
	2750 British ships now have hydrophone sets (for U-boat detection, *see* 31 Dec); 21 Atlantic convoys have escorted 354 ships for loss of only 2. **Only 27 ships lost since 1 May in grand total of 8894 ships convoyed**, 18:1 advantage over independent sailings, 354 lost from c3000. **Channel** — British Dover Strait mine barrage now relaid. **Atlantic** — U-boat sinks British SS *Belgian Prince*, 3 crew survive to tell of other 36 men's murder. Allied & neutral July shipping losses 224 ships worth 545,021t; German fig 555,514t (incl 90,334 in Med + 16,969 to Austrians; 6 U-boats sunk (1 by depth charges after ramming) but 11 commissioned & 95 ordered for completion by 1 Jan 1919.	**Germany — Army Airship Service dissolved** (*see* 17 Aug), 3 Zeppelins transferred to Naval Airship Div. Army has lost 26 airships & flown 232 bombing missions.	British War Cabinet discusses possibility of Russian collapse. Germany tells Bulgaria & Turkey she will meet all their 1917/18 campaign costs.	**France** — Income tax to rise 12 % (from 1 Jan 1918), tax on all profits but door & window tax to end. **Britain** — Army told available medical manpower exhausted. Postponed wartime 'New Derby' horse race held.
	Med — (Aug) Vice-Adm Sir S **Gough-Calthorpe** new C-in-C (HQ Malta, *see* 14). RN has 72 Q-ships (12 at Queenstown, Ireland 3), convoy sloops & PC boats in service or fitting out.	**Ypres** — Guynemer, with *Esc SPA 3*, makes 3 Aug kills (*see* 11 Sept). **France** — (Aug) First flight of Spad S13 fighter (220hp Hispano-Suiza engine). **Lorraine** — (Aug) US racing driver Rickenbacker transfers to AEF Aviation Section from being Gen Pershing's chauffeur (*see* 13).	**Papal peace note to combatants** (sent 9, published 14), Kaiser supports (17), but Allies very critical. Britain replies (23) & Wilson rejects (27), new German Govt required (*see* 30, 19 Sept). **Secret War** — (Aug) Compton Mackenzie recalled from Aegean.	**Britain** — RFP 102%, falls 2%. (Aug) Last death sentence on German spy passed (commuted). **Austria** — (Aug) War Minister warns Emperor Army only has replacements till May 1918.
	N Sea — At Wilhelmshaven 600 men of German battleship *Prinzregent Luitpold* (after over 9mths idle in harbour) led by anarchist stokers Johann Beckers & Albin Kobis strike & stage mass walkout v draconian discipline & meagre rations, march back to ship. Kobis shouts 'Down with the war! We no longer want to fight this war !' **Mutiny in German Fleet is crushed** (temporarily), 18 arrested, 100s of men with 'bad political attitudes' transferred to shore stns or Flanders naval inf bde; 5 court-martialled for mutiny. Kobis & Seaman Reichpietsch of flagship *Friedrich der Grosse* sentenced to death (25) by firing-squad, carried out 5 Sept, (*see* 14, 15, 18; HOME FRONTS 9 & 12). **Pacific** — German sailing ship raider *Seeadler* wrecked on Lord Howe I, having sunk 16 (6 British) ships or 30,099t in S Atlantic (45 PoWs). Capt Luckner & 5 crew captured in motor boat, Chilean schooner rescues rest.	**N Sea — First aircraft landing on a ship steaming**: RNAS Sqn-Cdr Dunning's Sopwith Pup side-slips onto HMS *Furious* (repeat attempt in stronger headwind kills him 7). **Austria** — 20/36 Capronis (10 damaged by AA) reach Pola, drop 8t bombs on naval base (night 2/3); 28 repeat (night 8/9, *see* 18; 4 Oct).		**Russia** — Kerensky resigns (*see* 6). **France** — Marine Minister Adm Lacaze & Blockade Under Secretary resign (replaced 10 & 17 by Chaumet - 16 Nov). **Britain** — Kentish PoWs Flag Day.
Linforce action at Tandamuti: 3 British cols repulsed by Lettow's concealed positions but Germans retreat W (-4) to Narunyu. KAR Signal Coy formed. **Ethiopia** — Lij Yasu escapes from fall of Dessie (Wollo Province's capital), but no more resistance.	**USA** — Pres Wilson requisitions all ships over 2500t building for national service, 431 ships of 3,056,000t.	**W Front** — Pétain appoints Col Duval as first Air CoS at *GQG*.	Austro-German talks on Rumanian grain quotas, former to get over half. Baron de Broqueville new Belgian Foreign Minister, Gen Ceuninck War Minister.	**USA** — Emergency Fleet Corp requisitions all steel ships of over 2500t building. **Britain** — Ship Repairing directorate formed. **Russia** — **Petrograd Soviet indicts Lenin for treason**. Prov Govt decree dissolves Finnish Diet (*see* 2 Oct).

AUGUST 1917	WESTERN FRONT 1	EASTERN FRONT 2	SOUTHERN FRONTS 3	TURKISH FRONTS 4
Fri 3 contd		bombardment (170,000 shells) for offensive on 7 (cancelled).		
Sat 4				
Sun 5	**Ypres** — German success nr Hollebeke, but later pushed back.			**Armenia** — **Russian troops being withdrawn to Europe**. (Aug) British estimate 123,500 effective inf v 64,000 Turks. Nihad Pasha takes over Turk Second Army for duration. **Palestine** — German airman lands & damages pipeline nr Salmana. **Arabia** — Lawrence returns to Aqaba in RIMS *Hardinge* , restores Howeitat tribes' loyalty with £1000 (*see* 23).
Mon 6		**Rumania** — **Battle of Marasesti** 2nd phase begins (-3 Sept): Mackensen (12 divs & 865 guns) storms positions N of Focsani, as Russian Fourth Army (Ragoza) flees, advances 8 miles & takes 3000 PoWs (-7).		
Tue 7			British War Cabinet agree not to withdraw more Salonika troops after Allies allow 10th Div to go 'unless unexpected events occurred' (*see* 15). **Italian Front** — In London conference Baron Sonnino asks for 400 heavy guns (-8, *see* 7 Sept).	
Wed 8	**Ypres** — Heavy rain. French gain ground NW of Bixschoote.	**Galicia** — Turk 20th Div hands over to German 24th Res Div (night 8/9) before leaving for Constantinople (11Sept). **Rumania** — Third Battle of Oituz (-22): 2 Austro-German divs attack & force Allied retreat in Trotus valley SW of Okna. Rumanians counter-attack (12 - 13).		
Thu 9		**Rumania** — Mackensen beyond R Susitza threatens Allied rear. Lt Rommel wounded in left arm but carries on for 2 wks.	**Salonika** — 3 Bulgar howitzers at 5-mile range destroy or damage 3 RFC aircraft on Struma sector airfield, 6 surviving planes fly to safer field (*see* AIR WAR 11 & 31). British patrol (21 men) W of L Doiran on 'P' ridge bayonets 14 Bulgars & takes 1 PoW for 1 man missing.	
Fri 10	**Ypres** — **Second Allied attack of 'Third Ypres'** Battle: British advance on 2-mile front E of			**Palestine** — Allenby told he will get div from Salonika, must 'strike the Turks as hard as

AFRICAN OPERATIONS 5	SEA WAR 6	AIR WAR 7	INTERNATIONAL EVENTS 8	HOME FRONTS 9
	Irish Sea — *UC44* sunk on *UC42* mines off Waterford after Room 40 sends bogus signal in code Germans discovered to be breaking. New FFB signal book recovered from wreck by diver-shipwright E C Miller. **Britain** — Last 2 of 51 wartime-built R-class destroyers launched (since 14 May 1916), 11 modified R-class also built in 1917. First of 25 V-class destroyers (ordered June-Aug 1916) come into service (Aug 1917-June 1918).		**Liberia declares war on Germany.** French accept formation of Czech Army on W Front (talks since 20 June), 2000 vols by Nov, *see* 7 Feb 1918. **Neutrals** — Norway & Holland offer shipping to Allies in return for food.	**Britain** — 3000 Russian troops for W Front land at Invergordon. King and Queen attend Westminster Abbey 3rd War Anniversary Service. National War Aims Ctee launched (3192 constituency meetings by Oct). **Russia** — Gen Gourko arrested at his Petrograd home, kept in Fortress of SS Peter & Paul (-19 Sept) until allowed to sail for England.
Kilwa Force fights at Nanyata, 9 miles from Mssindye camp. Naumann breaks through Chenene Gap (night 4/5, *see* 28).	**Med** — French sloop *Antares* rams & damages *U39*, sister *Aldebaran* damages *U23* (8).	**Britain** — Brig-Gen **Ashmore made cdr new London Air Defence Area**, takes over (8).	**Kühlmann new German Foreign Minister.** Argentina demands German indemnity for ship losses (agreed 28, *see* 8 Sept).	**Germany** — 4 new Ministers announced inc Imperial Economic Office. **USA** — National Guard drafted into US Army.
			French PM Painlevé & Lloyd George in London (-8, *see* S FRONTS 7) discuss separate peace with Austria (*see* 22). Tereshchenko new Russian Foreign Minister, tells Col Knox that Russia will fight through winter (12, Knox leaves for London 18, having seen Kerensky 16).	**Russia** — Kerensky as PM forms 'Save the Revolution National Ministry'.
	Vice-Adm Sir R Weymss succeeds Adm Sir C Burney as Second Sea Lord.			**Britain** — Churchill sees Clyde deportee Kirkwood, makes him Mile-End London shell factory manager (10) by late Sept highest production in country.
British mass porter levy called off for fear of unrest in occupied districts.	**Convoys extended to outward-bound shipping**, 18 convoys run from Milford, Falmouth, Queenstown, Buncrana (Scotland) & Devonport, only 2 of 219 ships sunk (*see* 30 Nov). **Biscay** — Q-ship *Dunraven* (Campbell) fights *UC71* for 4hrs, but sinks (9) in tow back to Plymouth. U-boat sinks Q-ship *Bergamot* (13,see 20). **Baltic** — First 1917 Russian submarine success: *Vepr* sinks German iron ore steamer in Gulf of Bothnia. RN submarines move base from Reval to Hangö, Finland (end Aug, *see* 12 Sept).	**Germany** — First Allied night bomber shot down by fighters nr Frankfurt-am-Main.		**Russia** — 6th Bolshevik Congress opens in Petrograd (-16), membership c140,000. RC Church & Jesuit Order restrictions lifted.
		Artois — 7 RFC aircraft strafe before & during British 12th Div local attack, tactics repeated (19 & 26).	**Occupied Belgium** — German decree makes Flemish Flanders' official language.	**Hungary** — PM Count Esterhazy resigns, pro-German Dr Wekerle succeeds (20).
Linforce recces Lettow's Narunyu position. First Belgians reinforce Iringa Force which			British Labour Party decides to send delegates to Stockholm but Bonar Law refuses	**Germany** — Hindenburg memo to new Chancellor lists *OHL* Home Front demands. **Britain**

AUGUST 1917	WESTERN FRONT 1	EASTERN FRONT 2	SOUTHERN FRONTS 3	TURKISH FRONTS 4
Fri 10 contd	Ypres, capturing Westhoek & Glencorse Wood; 18th Div captures Inverness Copse, but Gheluvelt Plateau as a whole not taken. French advance E & N of Bixschoote.			possible'; he moves GHQ from Cairo 200 miles to Kelab nr Front (11), forms DMC, XX & XXI Corps (12).
Sat 11	**Ypres** — German counter-attacks E of Ypres, part of Glencorse Wood recaptured (*see* 22).	**Rumania** — Mackensen forces R Sereth at 1 point, claims 7000 PoWs. Rumanian Royal Family leaves Jassy.		
Sun 12		British CIGS cables encouraging reply to Kornilov telegram of 10.		
Mon 13	**French 2400-gun Verdun bombardment** (1100 heavy) **begins** on 12½-mile front (-20); German arty fire 1m rnds (2500t) mustard gas shells at French nr Verdun (-24 Sept); 13,158 gassed (143 deaths),*see* 20.	Kornilov shows British Gen Barter his written request to Prov Govt for military powers in interior. **Rumania** — German Maj E Buchner (1907 Nobel Prize for Chemistry) k aged 57.		
Tue 14	**Ypres** — Heavy rain postpones BEF attack to 16.	**Rumania** — German *Alpenkorps* storms Height 334 as Russian VIII Corps flees.		
Wed 15	**Artois** — **Battle of Hill 70** (-25): Cdn Corps (9198 cas), supported by c326 guns & 160 MGs, captures important height N of Lens + 5 nearby villages despite c24 German counter-attacks in which 5 German divs mauled (incl 1170+ PoWs).	**Rumania** — Austro-Germans retake Soveja as Allies retreat S towards R Sereth.	**Salonika** — Sarrail refuses to shorten British line despite War Ministry orders (19,*see* 19 Oct); Milne cables CIGS (18) that 4 divs not enough to hold v determined Bulgar attack (*see* 23).	**Mesopotamia** — Maude estimates Turk Sixth Army at 33,560 men (6 divs) & 124 MGs, actually 164+ MGs with 160 guns.
Thu 16	**Flanders** — **Battle of Langemarck** (-18): British advance on 9-mile front N of Ypres-Menin road, capture Langemarck & cross R Steenbeek. Furious German counter-attacks only push back British line a short distance, though depleted 16th Irish & 36th Ulster Divs driven back to start. French marine bn captures Drie Grachten bridgehead on Yser canal. **Aisne** — French advance on Craonne Plateau. **Meuse** — Germans capture some trenches on E bank, but French recapture (18).	Kornilov sees Kerensky in Petrograd (-17, & 23) but latter demurs over military powers. **Rumania** — Mackensen takes Baltareta bridgehead on Sereth but held up in Okna & Susitza valleys.		

AFRICAN OPERATIONS 5	SEA WAR 6	AIR WAR 7	INTERNATIONAL EVENTS 8	HOME FRONTS 9
crosses R Idete (26) after indecisive action there (12).			passports (13), as does US Govt (11).	— OAPs get 2s 6d pw increase. Pension rises for officers, nurses & war dependents. **USA** — USMC now 33,075, double 6 April strength, recruiting halted. **France** — Mourier Law directs all 1903-17 conscript classes to fighting units unless a year already served.
	Sierra Leone convoys start. **S Atlantic** — British liner *City of Athens* (21 lost) sunk by raider *Wolf* mine nr Cape Town. **N Sea** — Destroyer HMS *Oracle* rams & sinks *U44* off S Norway coast. **Biscay** — 2 French destroyers escort in first Brest-bound US troop convoy.	**Bulgaria** — 15 RFC & RNAS aircraft from Thasos drop 3374lb bombs on Livunoro & Gereviz airfields in retaliation for German raid on Thasos (4). **Britain** — 11 (13 sent) Gotha bombers (1 shot down by RNAS, 3 crash) attack Southend with 21t bombs. 139 defence sorties (Gotha shot down by RNAS Pup Flt pilot Sub-Lt H S Kerby), 44 civ cas, 3 service cas.		**Britain** — Henderson resigns from War Cabinet over Stockholm issue, ex-docker G Barnes succeeds. **Rumania** — 1st newsreels shown, Jassy. Ex-Tsar & family moved to Abalak Monastery, Tobolsk, Siberia.
		USA — 1st Aero Sqn sails for France (arrives 3 Sept). **W Front** — RFC bombing E of Lens (night 13/14), 2 German airfields bombed (14), 4 Sopwith 2-seaters attack & help disperse 1600 German inf (15). **Mesopotamia** — No 63 Sqn (RE8s) from W Front arrives at Basra, but 154 out of 230 all ranks soon stricken with fevers & heatstroke, deployment delayed (*see* 25 Sept).	Japanese Viscount Ishii arrives US W Coast, speaks to Senate (30, *see* 2 Nov).	**Germany** — Military region cdrs given free hand to suppress strikes. **Italy** — 40,000 march v war at Turin (Petrograd Soviet delegation, *see* 22).
4/4th KAR reach Korogwe to garrison it v Naumann.	**Germany** — Scheer writes to Navy Minister Capelle urging a 'political prosecution' of the USPD (Indep Social Democratic Party) to expose 'the roots of the evil' in the Navy (*see* 18). **N Sea** — HM Special Service smack *Nelson* (Crisp posthum VC) & trawlers *Ethel* & *Millie* sunk in gun duel with U-boat on Jim Hove Bank. **Med** — Allied naval conference at Malta extends Calthorpe's command to Red Sea & Cape St Vincent. Cmdre Heneage replaces Kerr i/c Adriatic Force. Rear-Adm Fremantle replaces Thursby i/c Aegean Sea (*see* 22).		CHINA DECLARES WAR ON GERMANY & AUSTRIA. At Berlin Conference Germans reject Czernin's peace offer of Poland & Galicia for concessions in West.	**Britain** — Maximum cereal prices fixed to June 1918.
Belgian col (Maj Batille) advances from Kilosa towards R Ruaha, beats Germans at Kidodi 50 miles S (18), drives them from Tepe (19) & crosses R Ruaha (21).	**N Sea** — Adm Meurer of German Fleet's 4th Battleship Sqn orders senior officers to lecture the men on special responsibility & political conformity.		**US troops pass through London**. War Cabinet decides to send 8 guns to Russia (none sent since Mar, & 150 promised). Dmowski's Polish National Ctee set up in Paris.	**France** — Gen Staff Intelligence briefing: 'the nation's patriotism seems to have revived'.
		Ypres — Weather hampers RFC effort for Battle of Langemarck, 22 air combats cost 3 German aircraft; 9 German airfields attacked.		**Germany** — OHL remove Gen Gröner from War Office (to 33rd Div, Verdun), Gen Scheuch succeeds, but put under War Minister (22). **Britain** — PM speech on shipping losses, appeals for canal use instead of railways.

AUGUST 1917	WESTERN FRONT 1	EASTERN FRONT 2	SOUTHERN FRONTS 3	TURKISH FRONTS 4
Fri 17	**Ypres** — French success E of Bixschoote.			
Sat 18		**Rumania** — Gen Eben tells Mackensen his divs down to 340-1000 effectives as Rumanians retreat towards Marasesti.	**Salonika** — **Great fire begins** in wooden old quarter with oil spilling from stove, brought under control (21) but 80,000 made homeless & nearly half city destroyed; British base HQ gutted on waterfront, but port not affected (*see* 25). **Italian Front** — ELEVENTH BATTLE OF THE ISONZO (the Bainsizza) (-12 Sept): After barrage from 0600 Italian Second & Third Armies (44 divs, 3566 guns, 1760 mortars) on 30-mile front night attack Austrian Fifth Army (18 divs with 248 bns incl 3 divs from E Front, 6 transferring) capture 1st line & 7500 PoWs but only across 6 of 14 Isonzo bridges (more built night 19/20) planned due to Austrian resistance.	
Sun 19	**Ypres** — Slight advance by British on Ypres-Poelcapelle road in which 12 tanks (1 ditched) capture pillboxes at St Julien for 26 cas; Germans retake briefly (25).	Germans claim 22,000 PoWs in recent Galicia & Bukovina fighting. **Rumania** — Mackensen attacks at Marasesti (-20) with 4 divs & 3hr shelling but Averescu regains lost ground when Gen Popescu's 47th & 51st Regts (13th Div) bayonet charge through Razoave Forest, lull till 28.	**Isonzo** — 12 Italian bns across river; Hill 300 taken by Badoglio's II Corps & many advances uphill. Italian Third Army attacks on Carso (-23) but ops suspended after minimal gains (except to Diaz's XXIII Corps) for heavy losses.	
Mon 20	**Ypres** — Since 31 July, 17 German divs 'used up' (*verbraucht*) according to Gen Kuhl, CoS to Rupprecht. British attack profitably with 7 tanks. **Verdun** — **Second Offensive Battle of Verdun** (-9 Sept): Guillaumat's French Second Army, with 18 divs v 12, takes German defences N of Verdun on 11-mile front to depth of 1¼ miles incl Avocourt Wood, Mort Homme, Hill 240 & 5000 PoWs (-23). German Fifth Army (forewarned) previously evacuated Talou ridge & other positions.	Kornilov orders Cossack concentration within rail distance of Petrograd or Moscow (or 19). **Baltic Provinces** — Russians evacuate some positions SW of Riga (-22) 3-8 miles to shorten line, plus stores & sick from city itself. German Eighth Army begins approach march for Riga op (22,*see* 1 Sept).		**Mesopotamia** — Gen Thomson's bde group occupies Sharaban (garrison retreats to Jebel Hamrin). **Egypt** — *Arab Bulletin* publishes Lawrence's '27 Articles' on bedouin intelligence work.
Tue 21	**Artois** — Canadians (1154 cas) advance on 200-yd front W & NW of Lens. **Verdun** — French recapture Côte de l'Oie (Moroccan Div incl the Legion), Regnéville & Samogneux either side of R Meuse, watched by Pétain & Pershing.	**Bukovina** — Kövess attacks Sereth town & takes hill defences nearby; renews attacks E of Czernowitz, (26) captures Dolzok height (27).	**Isonzo** — *Bersaglieri* storm Ossoinica & Osedrih (lost). *Tortona* Bde takes Mt Kuk (2004ft); Mt Jelinck taken from 3 sides (22), breakthrough nr Auzza on 2000-yd front shakes Austrians.	
Wed 22	**Ypres** — 4 British divs & 16 tanks engaged before St Julien, 2 more with 18 tanks S of Fortuin while 3 more with tanks battle along Menin Road (-23). 500-880-yd gains for heavy losses (3000 cas). 2 British bns capture & hold Glencorse Wood (-24).		Emperor Charles & Arz visit Boroevic, tell him of planned Tolmino-Caporetto offensive with 14 divs (6 German) *see* 26 & 29.	

AFRICAN OPERATIONS 5	SEA WAR 6	AIR WAR 7	INTERNATIONAL EVENTS 8	HOME FRONTS 9
		Germany — Kaiser decides Navy will be limited to 25 Zeppelins & only build replacements every 2 months instead of 2 pm. **Macedonia** — Anglo-French aircraft bomb various targets (-20) despite high winds.	Balfour speech on Balkans. Ramsay Macdonald letter to Wilson & E House says US neutrality would have been better for peace.	**Britain** — Brig-Gen A Geddes succeeds Neville Chamberlain as DG National Service. **Austria** — Emperor's 30th birthday.
Linforce forms square entrenched camp v Narunye. Brig-Gen O'Grady reinforces it (19) to hold v spasmodic attacks from 3 sides. **Cameroons** — French forbid female slavery.	**N Sea** — During Wilhelmshaven visit by Kaiser & Capelle, Scheer calls recent mutiny a 'socialist plot' that necessitates a 'few death sentences'; demands implicated USPD deputies be tried for treason. Capelle demurs, saying deputies enjoy parliamentary immunity. Kaiser has first sea voyage of war in new flagship *Baden* from Wilhelmshaven to Heligoland. **W Med** — Scout cruiser USS *Birmingham* (Rear Adm Wilson) arrives at Gibraltar as flagship US Patrol Force, 2 others & 7 gunboats to work on Atlantic side of straits (*see* 24 Sept).	**Occupied Belgium** — The *Hollandflug*: abortive Gotha bomber mission v London. 28 aircraft sent (8/9 FTR) but recalled due to gale-force winds; 2 shot down in neutral Holland, 6 or 7 crash in Belgium, others ditch in sea. **Italian Front** — 85 Caproni bombers hit Austrian supply/ relief cols, ammo dumps & HQs (*see* 28 & S FRONTS).	German Under State Secretary Bussche to German Copenhagen Minister: 'The suspicion that Lenin is a German agent has been energetically countered in Switzerland & Sweden at our instigation.'	**Britain** — Govt proclamation forbids threatened rail engineers strike. Churchill replaces 50 Munitions Ministry Depts with 11-man Council (meeting weekly) & secretariat, his Munitions Bill passed (21). **USA** — Forces total 943,141. Food Administrator Hoover asks each family to save 1lb of flour pw.
	Atlantic — **Penultimate British Q-ship success:** *Acton* sinks *UC72* (damaged Q-ship *Penshurst* 19, *see* 25 Dec).		**Swiss-German Agreement** for former to export 200,000t coal & 19,000t iron & steel pm. Swiss-Allied Economic Agreements (30 & 29 Sept) for wood exports. Emperor Charles' letter to German Crown Prince stresses Austria's plight. Wingate sends Balfour Aaronsohn's long report on Palestine & Zionists.	**Hungary** — Food shortages cause release of all civil prisoners serving under 2 yrs (*see* 19 Sept).
	Caribbean — Cuba transfers 4 large German steamers (seized 7 Apr) to US.	**Britain** — 8 Navy Zeppelins fly v the Midlands; unsuccessful, only 10% of 24,000lb bombs dropped recorded (1w, night 21/ 22).	British War Cabinet declines to give Kornilov decoration before Moscow Conference.	**Russia** — Lenin, beardless & wearing wig, moves to Finland (-22, or 3-4 Sept). **Britain** — **Reconstruction Ministry formed**. Corn Production Act fixes minimum prices to 1922. National minimum farmhands wage 25s pw.
	Calthorpe sees Revel in Rome & secures 4 destroyers to escort Genoa-bound colliers from Gibraltar, but Revel warns no naval ops possible if British coal shipments suspended (*see* 14 Sept).	**Britain** — LAST DAYLIGHT ATTACK ON ENGLAND: 10 (15 sent) Gotha bombers (3 FTR) attack Margate, Ramsgate & Dover. 138 defence sorties, 2 bombers shot down by RNAS fighters, 1 by AA fire (total cas 39 incl 16 servicemen).	**Secret War** — Count Armand presents French terms to Austrian Count Revertera in Switzerland (having met 7): Germany must return Alsace-Lorraine & Belgium, Austria to evacuate Balkans & Trentino for link with Bavaria & Prussian Silesia. No reply ever sent.	Now 102,218 German PoWs to 43,000 British. **Russia** — Constituent Assembly elections put back to 12 Nov from 17 Sept. **Italy** — **Turin strikes & riots** (-28): Bread shortage leads to factory close down & shop sacking, 2 churches burnt down. Army uses tanks & MGs to clear barricades (23) & repulse worker cols. Order restored (24) after 50k (3 soldiers) & 800 arrests. Turin not imitated by rest of Italy.

AUGUST 1917	WESTERN FRONT 1	EASTERN FRONT 2	SOUTHERN FRONTS 3	TURKISH FRONTS 4
Thu 23	Slight British successes in Flanders & Artois.		Macedonia — Allied lengths of front: British 90 miles; French & Greeks 50 miles; Serbs 34 miles; Russians 22 miles; Italians 9.3 miles. Isonzo — Italians take 5 mountain peaks on 12½ mile front as Austrian fires & demolitions signal their retreat (night 23/24) to new defence line.	Arabia — Feisal arrives at Aqaba with last 400 of his 1800 regulars + Egyptian detach-ment.
Fri 24	Verdun — French advance 1½ miles on 2000-yd front taking Hill 304 & Camard Wood & reach S bank of Forges Brook, gains N of Mort Homme.		Isonzo — Italians have advanced 6 miles on a 10-mile front, taken 20,000 PoWs & 125 guns but no water or roads for pursuit over Bainsizza plateau & over 2m of 3.5m medium/heavy shells used. Austrian counter-attack loses 1000 PoWs (28).	
Sat 25	Ypres — Second phase of Third Ypres ends. Haig decides to transfer battle from Gough to Plumer who submits plans 29. BEF losses 68,010 since 31 July. Artois — Battle of Hill 70 ends. Verdun — French advancing N of Hill 304, only 14,470 cas since 20, but have taken 9100 PoWs, 30 guns, 22 mortars & 13+ MGs (see 4 Sept).		Salonika — K Alexander of Greece visits '... very frank and bitter against Venizelos and French'.	Mesopotamia — 71,670 animals with MEF.
Sun 26	Verdun — French XXXII Corps on E bank of Meuse reaches Beaumont outskirts, repulses counter-attack (27). Somme — British III Corps captures ½ mile of position E of Hargicourt NW of St Quentin. Ypres — 4 British divs and 12 tanks fight N of St Julien; sea of mud restricts progress to 2000yds.		Emperor Charles' letter to Kaiser: 'The experience of our eleventh battle convinces me that the twelfth will be very hard...it is best to overcome the difficulties with an offensive' asks for Austrian E Front divs & German guns. 'My entire army considers the war against Italy as "our war".' (see 29).	
Mon 27			Salonika — British arty shelling (-30) & small raids on L Doiran sector.	
Tue 28	Verdun — French now stand on virtually same line as before German onslaught of 21 Feb 1916.	Kornilov appeals at Moscow National Conference for restoration of Army's discipline & supply (Kerensky tells Gen Barter that troops will winter in trenches & regain discipline 27). Rumania — Mackensen attacks in Marasesti & Okna sectors; Russian div defects but Rumanians hold heroically at Varnita-Muncelu (-3 Sept).		
Wed 29			Isonzo — Cadorna orders Bainsizza ops suspended except for blow N & E of Gorizia. Italian Front — Gen Waldstatten submits Austrian offensive plan to Gen Arz for offensive with 13 divs (incl German) from Tolmino bridgehead N of Bainsizza Plateau towards Cividale. Hindenburg & Ludendorff eventually approve what becomes Caporetto offensive after Bavarian mtn warfare expert Gen Krafft inspects front (see 9 & 15 Sept).	
Thu 30	Artois — British repulse night raid on trenches SE of Lens.			
Fri 31	Ypres — Desultory British shelling of Menin Road Ridge defences begins. Germans capture some British advanced		Salonika — British hospital cases c18,000 (see 16 Oct). Italian Front — Italians claim 27,000 PoWs since 19. Heavy	S Persia Rifles nearly 6000 with c154 British officers & NCOs.

AFRICAN OPERATIONS 5	SEA WAR 6	AIR WAR 7	INTERNATIONAL EVENTS 8	HOME FRONTS 9
Shorthose's NRFF col (700) occupies Tunduru (*see* 28 Sept).				**Britain** — Churchill meets Cumberland miners over their anti-recruiting strike (6-11). **Russia** — Ex-Tsarist War Minister Sukhomlinov's treason trial in Petrograd (-26), sentenced to hard labour for life. **USA** — Garfield made Fuel Administrator.
Belgians drive Germans from R Sansa & press them v L Nyasa (27).		**Britain** — War Cabinet in principle accept Smuts' report on unified air service.	$100m US loan to Russia announced. Salvador allows all US ships to use her ports.	**Britain** — King & Queen visit Canadian wounded at Taplow. **USA** — 17 die in black soldiers' riot at Camp Logan, Houston after white policeman hits black woman.
			Polish State Council resigns v Germans (*see* 12 Sept).	**Russia** — Kerensky opens Moscow National Conference (-29), Bolsheviks boycott (*see* 28).
				Turkey — 'Armenian Conspiracies' Report published.
Naumann reaches Arusha Chini; 50 of his men loot trains & burn stores at Kahe (29). Iringa Force enters Ifakara, joined by 13th Belgian Bn (*see* 2 Sept).	**Baltic** — German aircraft drop 90 bombs on Russian shipping in Gulfs of Finland & Riga (*see* 12 & 27 Sept); destroyer *Stroini* crippled by 130lb seaplane bomb (21).	**Arabia** — 4 RFC aircraft from Kuntilla in Sinai (40 miles NW of Aqaba) drop 32 bombs (4 hits) on Maan engine shed & barracks (c100 Turk cas); 3 aircraft bomb Turk Abu-el-Lisal camp & Maan again (29). **Italian Front** — 1474 Italian sorties flown since 19, av of 225 aircraft pd, 81 aircrew k.		**Russia** — Kornilov claims in Moscow that munitions output has fallen 60%.
				Canada — **Conscription Act signed**, 5000 demonstrate against in Montreal (*see* 10 Nov). **Britain** — Churchill writes to union leaders on necessity for increased aircraft production. **Germany** — Industrialists tell Chancellor 'they are ready to fight 10 more years' to keep the mineral-rich Longwy-Briey basin.
		France agrees to supply US with 5000 aircraft & 8500 engines (Spad & Breguet).	Papal Nuncio Pacelli in Munich sends German Chancellor Anglo-French note to Vatican on Belgium (evasive German reply 24 Sept, *see* 19 Sept).	
	N Sea — RNAS raid Belgian coast airfields. Allied & neutral Aug shipping losses to U-boats, 186 (84 British) ships worth	**Salonika** — Peak of 229 RFC aircraft serviceable, strength falls to 154 by year's end and is 31-58 in 1918.		**France** — **Interior Minister Malvy resigns after Clemenceau attack in Senate.** **Britain** — Month's imports

AUGUST 1917	WESTERN FRONT 1	EASTERN FRONT 2	SOUTHERN FRONTS 3	TURKISH FRONTS 4
Fri 31 contd	posts N of St Julien-Poelcapelle road. **Aisne** — French gains nr Hurtebise.		fighting at key Mt San Gabriele NE of Gorizia. **Secret War** (Aug) — Italian *Comando Supremo Crittografico* unit first completely reads Austrian radio signals.	
Sat 1 September 1917	**Most BEF divs 2000 men under strength**. Pershing opens AEF GHQ at Chaumont on upper Marne (*see* 4). **Somme** — Germans briefly capture & occupy positions at Havrincourt SW of Cambrai, but are repulsed (3). **Aisne** — Unsuccessful German counter-attack NE of Craonne, 4 attacks fail (2).	**Baltic Provinces** — HUTIER'S GERMAN RIGA OFFENSIVE (-5) begins with 2hr Bruchmüller gas shelling (116,400 gas shells inflict 1000+ Russian cas) causing panic. By 0840 3 bridges being built & 2 islands stormed 18 miles E of Riga. 3 divs cross Dvina in 225 pontoons covered by low-flying aircraft, carve out 7-mile bridgehead by 1035 but then halt. Klembovski evacuates Riga bridgehead & Riga (-2).	**Isonzo** — Slight Italian advance gains 340 PoWs. **Salonika** — British ration strength 201,269 men with 76,731 horses & mules.	**Palestine** — EEF total ration strength 225,176 incl 20,207 Anzacs & 19,141 Indians with 117,449 animals (25 Aug) incl 44,502 camels. **Egypt** — (Sept) NACB takes over 41 canteens. **Mesopotamia** — Turk railway has only reached Nisibis. (Sept) US Persian Famine Relief Commission arrives in Baghdad (also oil interests).
Sun 2	British military-political conference in London reviews Flanders situation (-4): Haig urges Ypres ops be continued, rather than transfer of all reserves to Italy, Pétain still imploring him to keep Germans away from French Army — only continuing major offensive can achieve this. He wins Cabinet majority approval. **Somme** — British repulse attacks on advanced posts nr Havrincourt.			
Mon 3	**Ypres** — Slight British advance nr St Julien. **Champagne** — French raid on suspected poison gas storage site on Souain-Somme Py road.	**Baltic Provinces** — **German** 2nd Gd & 1st Res **Divs enter Riga**, claim many thousand PoWs & 150 guns, but still held S of highway & railway. **Rumania** — **Battle of Marasesti ends**: Germans gain only 5 miles on 18-mile front, taking 18,000 PoWs & 22 guns. Gen Morgen reports 61 Rumanian counter-attacks; they claim 65,000 German cas since 19 Aug.		
Tue 4	**First US fatal land cas, 13 (4k) in air raid** on British base hospital. **Verdun** — Legion RMLE relieved having captured 680 PoWs, 15 guns & 13 MGs since 20 Aug (Pétain decorates its colours, 27).	**Baltic Provinces** — II Siberian Corps (incl women's 'Death's Battalions') counter-attack SW in Hinzenberg area; Prussian 1st Guard Div later reaches coast, but Russians 30 miles E.	**Salonika** — 200-300 Bulgars (15+ cas) on rare raid into British L Doiran sector but soon driven out. **Isonzo** — Austrian offensive in Mt Hermada seaward sector claiming 6000 PoWs there & NE of Gorizia. Italians inland take 1600 PoWs pushing for Mt San Gabriele (*see* 11).	**Palestine** — Djemal's gendarmerie raid Jewish Athlit NILI spy base, having found 1 carrier pigeon, get 1 member to talk (*see* 23).
Wed 5	**Cambrai** — First 2 US soldiers k by shellfire, 11th Engineers repairing railway nr Gouzeacourt.			**Falkenhayn decides to deploy Kemal's Seventh Army for Palestine** *Yilderim* **offensive** (*see* 30). He inspects Front 9-10.

AFRICAN OPERATIONS 5	SEA WAR 6	AIR WAR 7	INTERNATIONAL EVENTS 8	HOME FRONTS 9
	509,142t (U-boat fig 472,372t incl 79,549t in Med); 5 U-boats sunk. **Best month of war for Austrian U-boats'** merchant ship sinkings, 38,823t claimed, more than in 1914-16 altogether.			exceed £100m for 1st time. E Morel, anti-war Union of Democratic Control secretary, arrested (6 months jail) for sending pamphlets to Switzerland.
Highest British ration strength since 1 Dec 1916 and for duration, 58,317 (incl 22,052 whites, 16,853 Indians) with 38 guns, 140,590 porters, 16,606 animals (31 Aug, incl 6033 oxen).	(Sept) **RN at last has the efficient H2 mine** (copy of German Herzhorn contact mine) in volume prod, 12,450 of 100,000 ordered by end 1917, sink 9, possibly up to 16, U-boats. **Atlantic** — 300 ships sailing weekly in convoys (inward & outward, *see* 30). **Britain** — (Sept) 31 air stns have 190 aircraft & 50 airships for anti U-boat work (*see* 22). **N Sea** — Grand Fleet's 4th Lt Cruiser Sqn & 15th Destroyer Flotilla raid Horn's Reef, drive 4 German minesweepers ashore at Ringkiobing Fjord (Jutland).	**W Front** — (Sept) RFC makes 226 bombing raids (7886 bombs worth 135t to German 969 bombs) ranges 9539 targets, issues 930 new aircraft, only surpassed Mar & May 1918; takes 14,678 photos; 214 RFC k & missing, 2nd worst 1917 month. (Sept) 2 German night raids destroy 85 French aircraft in Verdun area. (Sept) US air training school opens at Issoudon.	**Occupied Belgium** — (Sept) Allied Biscops train-watching courier service betrayed (*see* I Nov).	**Britain** — RFP 106%, up 5% (1917 highest). Subsistence allowance paid to all volunteer munition workers away from home. Free Govt air-raid damage compensation scheme up to £500. **Turkey** — Food & fuel prices now double or treble Jan (*see* 5).
German losses 500 since 30 Aug esp in retreat to Mahenge before Belgians (*see* 7).	**N Sea** — RNAS bomb Bruges docks.(3k), Zeebrugge mole & shipping off Ostend (15). **Arctic** — *U28* destroyed in explosion of British munitions ship *Olive Branch* torpedoed off N Cape.	**Britain** — Three consecutive moonlight raids by **Gothas** on SE England (London on 4) **begin** 19 **night raids** (-20 May 1918). Total cas 326 incl 130 naval recruits k & 88w at Chatham drill hall. First operational trials of Sopwith Camel night fighters by No 44 Sqn, CO 22yr-old Capt Murlis Green (4½ Salonika victories 1916-17) *see* 18 Dec (3 on nights 2/3, 3/4 & 4/5). **Adriatic** — Pola bombed by 148 Caproni bombers & 11 flying boats; Austrians bomb Venice (7) which has balloon barrage defence. Gales abort RNAS attempt to attack Cattaro naval base with 6 Short torpedo seaplanes (*see* 27). **Occupied Belgium** — RNAS drops 18t bombs on Bruges docks (-5). **W Front** — Germans bomb St Omer (night 3/4).	Czernin informs Berlin he is willing to meet French PM in Switzerland but Kühlmann sabotages plan.	**Germany** — *OHL* found & fund Tirpitz's new **Fatherland Party** (he addresses 1st meeting in Berlin 25; 1.25m members by July 1918).
Nigerian Bde reassembles nr Kilwa (+1000 replacements 12).	**Channel** — Armed boarding steamer HMS *Dundee* sunk by U-boat. **Baltic** — **Last 2 Russian destroyers leave Riga** (until 1940), *see* E FRONT. They mine gulf entrance (*see* 12).		British Cabinet debate Jewish homeland & reject French idea of using Ibn Saud land on Persian Gulf.	**Britain** — Munitionettes get 2s 6d advance pw. **Italy** — By now coal shortage (although Britain supplied 690,000t in Aug) has made 75% of trains idle, remainder burn wood & naval stocks; sailing coasters used to distribute goods (*see* SEA WAR 14).
Tripolitania — Gen Cassini's 6 bns & 16 guns from Zuara defeat 4000 rebels, 2 guns & 1 MG at Bu Agela (again 7) & meets force from Tripoli (8, *see* 20).	Allied Naval Conference (-5) incl US Atlantic Fleet C-in-C Adm Mayo, fixes 9 Med convoy routes & their priority. **N Sea** - U-boat (30rnds) shells Scarborough, 3k, 6w. **Indian Ocean** — *Wolf* lays her last 110 mines NW of the Andamans, not found in 1917.	**Britain** — 5 of 11 Gothas sent (1 FTR due to AA fire) bomb London (night 4/5, 90 civ cas, Cleopatra's Needle scarred). British think 26 raiders bombed, only 2 fighters see them.	Anglo-French Conference in London on help for Italy.	**USA** — Wilson 30 Aug letter published, wishes he could be in trenches too. **Russia** — †Ex-PM Stürmer, from disease, aged 68, imprisoned by Prov Govt.
	N Sea — *U88* sunk by RN Heligoland Bight mines off Terschelling, with her cdr Schwieger, having sunk *Lusitania* among 49 ships worth 183,838t.		Industrialist Putilov tells British Ambassador of imminent Kornilov coup, latter begs him to await another Bolshevik rising (*see* E FRONT 8).	**Russia** — Grand Dukes Michael & Paul arrested. **USA** — Federal agents raid IWW offices in 23 cities (168 arrests). 687,000 draftees begin assembling by rail. **Turkey** — Army Commissariat put i/c civilian food. Farmers ordered to till c7 acres for each yoke of oxen & work 8hrs pd (27).

SEPTEMBER 1917	WESTERN FRONT 1	EASTERN FRONT 2	SOUTHERN FRONTS 3	TURKISH FRONTS 4
Wed 5 contd				
Thu 6	Flanders — Slight British reverse nr Frezenberg.	**Prov Govt decree restores death penalty in interior** & **Kerensky Army Order praises** officers' role since Revolution. **Baltic Provinces — Kaiser reviews troops in Riga**. Kornilov puts Gen Krymov i/c new 'Detached Petrograd Army' incl Kronstadt, Baltic Fleet & XLII Corps (Finland), *see* 12.		Munitions explosion at Haidar Pasha Station (Constantinople-Asian rail terminus) dislocates *Yilderim* .
Fri 7	Haig & Pétain meet amicably, agree 100 French heavy guns can go to Italy (*see* S FRONTS).		**Albania** — Gen Jacquemot's mixed French div begins advance on Austrian-held Pogradec (*see* 10), having been joined by Essad Pasha's 500 Albanians from Salonika (6). **France** — Pétain ordered to send 72 medium guns to Italy, they detrain (10) and are used nr Gorizia and Plava.	
Sat 8	Verdun — French capture Fosses, Caurières & Chaume Woods & 800 PoWs.	ABORTIVE KORNILOV PETROGRAD COUP (-11), Forces begin to move (9).		
Sun 9	**Somme** — British capture 600yds of German trenches at Villeret, NW of St Quentin, 400yds more captured (10). **Verdun** — Second Offensive Battle of Verdun ends. French repulse German counter-attack on E bank of Meuse. **France** — **c2000 British troops mutiny** at Étaples Infantry Base Depot (-14) due to poor conditions & Third Ypres reinforcement system, 3 sentenced to death after GHQ dets restore order.	**Kerensky sacks Kornilov & issues arms to Petrograd Soviet**. 3000 Kronstadt sailors reinforce capital (10). Revolutionaries then Cossacks seize C-in-C W Front Gen Denikin.	**Italian Front — Gen O Below takes cmd of new German Fourteenth Army for projected offensive**, plans drafted by 10 (*see* 15); 7 German & 8 Austrian divs with 1000 guns (800 German) pass through Trentino onto Drave/ Sava valleys 60 miles E of Caporetto, all marches at night.	
Mon 10			**Albania** — French enter Pogradec, on SW side of L Ochrid.	
Tue 11		Kornilov issues final Order No 900 & appeal to the people. **Rumania** — Battle of Ciresoaia (-12): Russo-Rumanian attack fails, **last major fighting in sector**.	British War Minister Lord Derby visits Cadorna at Udine, promises 160 British heavy guns (200 Anglo-French guns sent 18, but *see* 20). **Isonzo** — After shelling of record intensity Italian 11th Div captures Mt San Gabriele with 2000 PoWs but Austrian fire forces it 100ft below summit; Lt-Col Sauer of Austrian 14th Regt 'Who could fully describe this San Gabriele, this sort of Moloch which swallows up a regiment every three or four days...'.	
Wed 12	*GQG* estimates German losses to end July at 4m.	Gen Krymov shoots himself after seeing Kerensky.	**Albania** — French advance ends after 414 Austro-Bulgar PoWs & 4 guns taken for 175 cas in 20-mile advance; only real Allied 1917 Balkans success. Essad's Albanians return from Skumbi valley raid with 156 Austrian PoWs (20).	

AFRICAN OPERATIONS 5	SEA WAR 6	AIR WAR 7	INTERNATIONAL EVENTS 8	HOME FRONTS 9
				Large landowners exempted from military service (*see* 1 Nov).
		W Front — 6 sqns of newish German Halberstadt CLII ground-attack aircraft decimate British div reserves crossing Somme bridges.		**Britain** — Press Bureau tries to stem long air raid press accounts (& 28). **Australia** — £80m war loan bill (War Profiteering Act 22). **France** — PM Ribot at Fère-Champenoise for 3rd anniversary celebrations of Marne victory.
Belgians force R Kilimbro, attack & take Madege-Kalimoto positions (-16).		**W Front** — Germans bomb Allied hospitals, dead incl Americans.	Col Knox briefs British War Cabinet (minus PM & Curzon) on Russia's plight (*see* 10). Serb PM Pašić in Rome.	**Britain** — PM confident of future in Birkenhead speech.
			US Secretary of State publishes 3 Count Luxburg messages, 1 urges 2 Argentine vessels be sunk without trace (*'spurlos versenkt'*) (*see* 12).	
			French PM & Foreign Minister Ribot resigns (*see* 12). **Neutrals: Spain** — *UB49* interned at Cadiz after damaged by Allied escort ('escapes' to Cattaro 7 Oct).	**Germany** — Adm Capelle reveals 2 Aug navy mutiny to *Reichstag* (*see* 12). **Russia** — Rail workers prevent Kornilov's advance as Soviets mobilize 25,000 workers (*see* 11). **Britain** — King's special decoration for 1914 campaign announced.
Deventer joins Kilwa Force (Hannyngton) for combined offensive.	**Med** — German U-boats ordered not to attack unescorted Allied hospital ships (Spanish naval officer commissioners now placed aboard to ensure neutrality, *see* 17 Oct). **N Sea** — US Atlantic Fleet C-in-C Adm Mayo visits Grand Fleet (since 9). **Baltic** — 2 destroyers sent from Reval to protect Petrograd v Kornilov; most officers sign loyalty oath to Prov Govt but 4 shot for refusing. Revolutionary Exec created (*see* E FRONT 8 & 9).		British War Cabinet talks of using Japanese troops to stiffen Kornilov, but CIGS dissuades them.	**Germany** — Hindenburg-Ludendorff note to Chancellor & War Minister: many exempted workers to be called up by spring without cutting munitions production (*see* 3 Oct).
	E Atlantic — *U49* (Hartmann) rammed & sunk by SS *British Transport* W of Biscay, having claimed 38 ships worth 86,433t.	**Ypres** — Legendary French ace **Guynemer** (54 victories) **missing** over Poelcapelle aged 22, first revealed in London (27)' on day Germans claim 6 Allied single-seaters.	Ludendorff opposes restoring Belgium at Berlin Crown Council (*see* 19).	Petrograd: Putilov Works on fire, British airmen & gunners protect British Embassy. **Britain** — 1st PoWs from Switzerland arrive. Est 200,000 women working on the land.
	Baltic — Germans prepare to capture Gulf of Riga Is by amphibious op (*OHL* approve 18): High Seas Fleet detaches 2 battle sqns (10 ships, *see* 24), battlecruiser *Moltke*, 2nd Scouting Gp (lt cruisers, *see* 9 Oct) & 5 destroyer flotillas (47		**Painlevé new French PM** with Ribot Foreign Minister. **Neutrals : Argentina** — Count Luxburg handed passports. Argentine Parlt votes to sever relations (19 & 25) despite German apology (17) but President disagrees (*see* 1 Feb	**Germany** — Able Seaman Köbes due to be shot by Army at Cologne for mutiny, writes to parents: 'I die with a curse on the German-militarist state'.

SEPTEMBER 1917	WESTERN FRONT 1	EASTERN FRONT 2	SOUTHERN FRONTS 3	TURKISH FRONTS 4
Wed 12 contd			Italian Front — Italian losses since 18 Aug a record 166,000 (18,000 PoWs) so far (see 30; 31 Oct); Austrian c85,000 (29,000 PoWs).	
Thu 13	Flanders — German raid nr Langemarck repulsed. Verdun — German counter-attack penetrates French advanced trenches N of Caurières Wood (French recapture 14, see 24).	Hoffmann diary 'A German advance on Petersburg now would bring about the complete collapse of Russia'. Galicia — Germans evacuate Gusiatyn on border. Kornilov surrenders to Alexeiev at Mogilev & is moved to Bykhov monastery (see 2 Dec).		
Fri 14	Flanders — Capt Chavasse VC & bar of RAMC DoW.		Austrians close Swiss frontier, but Italians warned from Berne of imminent attack, possibly on Middle Isonzo.	
Sat 15	Flanders — British capture strongpoint N of Inverness Copse. Portuguese repulse attack at Neuve Chapelle. Aisne — Pétain adopts plan for limited attack (see 16 Oct).	Kerensky proclaims himself C-in-C with Alexeiev as CoS, all 3 Front cdrs changed.	Isonzo — 4 Austrian attacks across Bainsizza Plateau fail. Sassari Bde captures Hills 895 & 862 on its E edge. Gen Below & his CoS Krafft visit Archduke Eugene to concert offensive plans.	Mesopotamia — Maude orders Gen Brooking to attack Ramadi; 410 vans & lorries for his move to Falluja (-22, see 26).
Sun 16	Haig approves Byng's Cambrai tank attack scheme (see 13 Oct). Meuse — French repulse attack on Apremont Forest (St Mihiel). France — The La Courtine 'Massacre': Loyal Russian troops (3rd Bde) with 75mm bty storm La Courtine internment camp to suppress mutinous Bolshevik 1st Bde (Globa), 200 miles S of Paris.			Arabia — Lawrence leads 100 Arabs v Mudauwara Station on Hejaz Railway, blows up & captures Turk train (180+ cas inc Austrian gunners) to S (19) & returns to Aqaba (21). Palestine — Maj-Gen Bols succeeds Lynden-Bell (appt 27 Oct 1915) as Allenby's EEF CoS.
Mon 17				
Tue 18		Lithuanian Conference at Vilna (-23) elects National Council & demands independence (see 11 Dec).	Cadorna cancels 12th offensive & starts defensive preparations, tells Allies (20) who halt guns (25). Trentino — 5 Italian bns take 200 PoWs in Val Sugana but fail in dash for Trento inspired by Czech officer deserters (night 18/19) at Carzano.	
Wed 19		Lett Bde repulses Germans from Lemberg E of Riga.		
Thu 20	Battle of the Menin Road Ridge (-25): 3rd Allied attack of 'Third Ypres', directed by Plumer begun in mist. Main weight of attack — 11 divs & 52 tanks — thrusts v Passchendaele-Gheluvelt line in attempt to win high ground between Ypres & Roulers-	Gen Alexeiev resigns, Dukhonin becomes effective C-in-C.		Armenia — Independent Republic of Transcaucasia declared. Russians defeat Turks nr Ortobo (Bitlis, 25).

AFRICAN OPERATIONS 5	SEA WAR 6	AIR WAR 7	INTERNATIONAL EVENTS 8	HOME FRONTS 9
	ships). Russian warships shell German guns on Courland coast . 19 German trawlers hunt RN submarine *E9* off Pomerania after latter misses 2 merchant ships (another miss 13). **Med** — Fiction now ended that *U35*, *U38* & *U39* Austrian flag warships at Austrian request. **N Atlantic** — HM Submarine *D7* sinks *U45* N of Ireland (*see* 19 Oct).		1918). **Occupied Poland** — Central Powers grant temporary constitution inc Regency Council (courts already transferred 1).	
				Portugal — Martial law declared v general strike.
	British conference aims to supply Italy with 700,00t coal pm (incl 60,000-70,000t US) on Gibraltar-Genoa route if Italy spares 11 destroyers for escort (conditionally accepted after long wrangle & Caporetto 23 Nov, *see* 5 Dec).			**Russia** — **Kerensky proclaims Republic** & Council of Five, but power really passing to Petrograd Soviet. **USA** — $2bn naval spending in last yr. **Canada** — War-Times Election Act enfranchises close women relatives of servicemen for duration & demobilization.
	Germany — Last battlecruiser *Graf Spee* launched at Danzig by Schichau but never completed despite 1500 workers' efforts.		China offers Allies 300,000 soldiers for W FRONT.	**Britain** — **Sugar rationing begins**. **USA** — Food Administrator Hoover takes control of sugar industry.
		Germany — Allied air raids on Stuttgart & Colmar (*see* 22).		
			Churchill meets French Munitions Minister Loucheur in Paris, latter urges Allied Munitions Council.	**Britain** — **Bread subsidy with 9d loaf**. BST ends 2am. Coalminers flat wage up 1s 6d pd. **Russia** — Trotsky released from Kresty prison. **Germany** — Govt asks 15yr-olds to volunteer for Army.
	Channel — U-boat sinks destroyer HMS *Contest* (50 survivors). **Med** — British patrol instructions advise limit of 12 ships per convoy with 4 escorts (*see* 3 Oct).		Painlevé redefines French war aims as Alsace-Lorraine & reparations.	
Kilwa Force action at Mihambia (-20) costs 145 cas & fails to cut off 1100+ Germans retreat behind burning grass. British advance resumes (24) after thirst quenched.	**Baltic** — 20 Russian warships at Helsinki raise Red Flag (*see* 2 Oct).	**Ypres** — Sopwith Camels first used as light bombers (4 x 20/ 25lb).	German Chancellor replies to Papal peace note without mentioning Belgium (*see* 21).	**Hungary** — Count Karoly, leader of Independence Party, launches peace campaign.
Tripolitania — Cassini defeats Nuri Pasha's 4000 rebels (1600 cas) at Zanzur, W of Tripoli.		**Ypres** — RFC RE8s plus balloons report and/or direct fire at 208 German btys. 112 air combats, 11 British & 7 German aircraft lost.	British Petrograd Ambassador asks for money & agents to counter German espionage. **Transcaucasian Republic proclaimed.**	**Canada** — War servicewomen get vote. **Britain** — Aircraft Operations Ctee to report on priorities. Sir A Yapp Food Economy Director. **USA** — Lord Northcliffe addresses National War Convention of US Chambers of Commerce.

SEPTEMBER 1917	WESTERN FRONT 1	EASTERN FRONT 2	SOUTHERN FRONTS 3	TURKISH FRONTS 4
Thu 20 contd	Menin railway. Under unprecedented fire-layered 8-hr creeping barrage with gun to every 5.2yds, British capture Inverness Copse, Glencorse Wood, Veldhoek, Hollebeke & part of Polygon Wood in average 1500yd advance despite 11 counter-attacks. Sgt W Burman of 16th Rifle Bde uses sword to kill 11 Germans in an MG post, wins VC. GOC 19th Div T Bridges severely w, loses leg. Letter from Capt Patton, US Cav, to wife: 'The Germans shoot a gas which makes people vomit and when they take off the masks to spit they shoot the deadly gas at them. It is a smart idea is it not ?' (*see* 19 Nov).			
Fri 21	**Ypres** — British take 3243 PoWs on 20 & 21, repulse attacks on 'Tower Hamlets' ridge.	**Baltic Provinces** — Russian XXVIII Corps evacuates Dvina bridgehead at Jakobstadt, held since Oct 1915. German Eighth Army (700 cas) takes it with 4000 PoWs & 50 guns. Courland proclaims independence & requests German protection (*see* 16 Nov).		**Mesopotamia** — Maude finally rules out Russian help.
Sat 22			**Carnia** — Slight Italian advance in Marmolada region, more fighting (28).	
Sun 23	BEF Ypres losses 20,000 since 20 (*see* SEA WAR). **US Tank Corps founded** (*see* 29; 19 Nov).			**Palestine** — HMY *Managam* visits Athlit for last time, told NILI must cease work for time being (*see* 1 Oct).
Mon 24	**Verdun** — Unsuccessful German attack N of Bezonvaux, Fosses & Chaume Woods.		**Salonika** — Gen Grossetti leaves with poisoning complaint (†7 Jan 1918 aged 56), Gen Regnault temp C-in-C French Army of the Orient (*see* Dec).	
Tue 25	At Boulogne Conference (*see* INT'L EVENTS) British agree in principle to extending BEF front (*see* 13 Oct). **Ypres** — Battle of the Menin Road Ridge ends: Germans penetrate between Tower Hamlets & Polygon Wood, but later retire.			**Arabia** — Hejaz Army CoS ex-Turk Army Aziz Ali al-Masri resigns after rows with Hussein & sons, goes to Cairo.
Wed 26	**Ypres** — **Battle of Polygon Wood** (-3 Oct): British 0550 thrust (15,000 cas) incl 15 tanks & Anzacs, gains almost all			**Mesopotamia** — Brooking secretly masses 6000 men & 32 guns 8 miles from Ramadi.

AFRICAN OPERATIONS 5	SEA WAR 6	AIR WAR 7	INTERNATIONAL EVENTS 8	HOME FRONTS 9
		Ypres — RFC Nos 100 & 101 Sqns continue night bombing of Menin & Roulers v arriving German troops, using parachute flares (repeated 25/ 26, 26/27).	**Costa Rica severs relations with Germany**. Bernstorff papers on bribing US Congress published. Austria welcomes Papal peace plan, wants arbitration, disarmament and freedom of the seas.	
Battle of Bweho Chini: 1100+ Germans & 20+ MGs (est 340+ cas) just fail to storm sur- rounded Nigerian Bde camp (134 cas). Kilwa Force reunited (24). Belgians fight at Hyka on R M'kaha.	Convoys from Dakar start. **N Sea** — Dover Patrol monitor *Terror* shells Ostend (35 shells), sinks floating dock (& 25). **N Sea** — **Only British air kill of a U-boat**: RNAS H12 America flying boat (Flt sub-lt N Magor) bombs *UB32*.	**N Sea** — 3 RNAS Sopwith Camels over Dover Patrol destroy, force down or capture 4 German seaplanes from Ostend & Zeebrugge (& 25). **Germany** — French raid Stuttgart, Trier, Koblenz & Frankfurt.		**Germany** — **War Office orders factory shutdowns to meet 20m ton coal shortage** despite S German protests, last to Armistice. **USA** — Maj-Gen Bliss Army CoS (Scott retired). **Finland** — Bolsheviks dominate 3rd Finnish Regional Congress (-25). **Australia** — War Profiteering Act.
	Flanders — Haig calls off long- planned & prepared amphibious landing by 24,000 troops nr Westende, because Third Ypres battle bogged down.	**W Front** — †Lt **Werner Voss** (48 victories since 27 Nov 1916), leader of *Jasta 10* **kia**, aged 20 in Fokker triplane by Lt Rhys-David (kia 27 Oct) among McCudden's 6 SE5s of No 56 Sqn RFC (unit destroys 2 more German fighters 30, making total of 200 since 23 Apr).		
Linforce (Beves) resumes ops v Narunyu (*see* 28).	**Med** — (c) 5 old US destroyers arrive at Port Said from Philippines, go on to Gibraltar for escort work. **Secret War: Baltic** — (c) Russian Baltic staff learn from Room 40 that German battleships coming E.	**Britain** — 11 Navy Zeppelins dispatched: 5 wander E & N counties; only 3 civ cas but 5 defence fighters crash (night 24/25); 3 of 16 Gothas reach London, 1 bomb causes 39 cas (of 91) in Southampton Row; 30 defence sorties incl first from Biggin Hill. **France** — Germans bomb RNAS St Pol depot nr Dunkirk (-1 Oct), destroy 140 engines (*see* 2 Oct).	Britain apologizes to Denmark for Jutland 1 Sept violation (*see* SEA WAR), offers indemnity.	**USA** — Socialist Party abolishes itself.
		Britain — 15 Gothas (1 FTR) dispatched, 4 reach London. **Mesopotamia** — RFC No 63 Sqn loses 2 RE8s on 1st recon from Baghdad to German aircraft nr Tikrit (*see* 16 Oct). **Ypres** — RFC claims 19 German aircraft for loss of 1 missing. **Occupied Belgium** — RNAS & RFC attack St Denis Westrem & Gontrode Gotha bases (-10 Oct) forcing bombers to disperse & use 2 other airfields. **Adriatic** — Italians bomb Pola & Olivi Rock submarine base.	Anglo-French PM-level Boulogne Conference on W Front, decides to withdraw 100 French heavy guns from Italy (British War Cabinet told 1917 Italian offensive called off 21, *see* S FRONTS 11 & 20).	**Russia** — Lenin writes to Central Ctee (-27) that armed uprising necessary. **Ireland** — †Easter Rising rebel T Ashe (rearrested 14 Aug) after forcible feeding in prison (*see* 25 Oct).
British surround Naumann with 25-mile ring (*see* 30).	**Irish Sea** — RN *PC61* rams & sinks *UC33* in St George's Channel.	**Ypres** — RFC reports or ranges 260 German btys. Both sides make low-flying attacks on troops (MGs bring down 5 of	*Reichstag* President Kaempf denounces Pres Wilson for trying to split Kaiser & German people.	**Greece** — Venizelos resigns War Ministry. **Canada** — **Conscription in force** (*see* 13 Oct). **Britain** — 75 strikes

SEPTEMBER 1917	WESTERN FRONT 1	EASTERN FRONT 2	SOUTHERN FRONTS 3	TURKISH FRONTS 4
Wed 26 contd	1200yds planned, smashes 3 *Eingreif* divs (12½% cas) in 4 counter-attacks & takes 1600 PoWs. 'A day of heavy fighting, accompanied by every circumstance that could cause us loss.' (Ludendorff).			
Thu 27	**Flanders** — British repulse 7 counter-attacks E of Ypres; 5th Australian Div completes recapture of Polygon Wood.			
Fri 28	English poet & philosopher T E Hulme, commissioned from ranks into RMA, k by shell nr Nieuport. Haig amazes Gough & Plumer by wishing for breakthrough in Oct, his diary records '... the enemy is tottering'.			**Mesopotamia** — **Battle of Ramadi** (-29): Brooking (995 cas) annihilates 4100 Turks & 10 guns (3456 PoWs), takes 4 small craft on Euphrates.
Sat 29	**First German tank unit formed**, 113 men with 5 A7Vs (delivered Dec, 8 more units created).		**Isonzo** — Italian 44th Div captures Na Kobil (2552ft) with 1400 PoWs on Bainsizza Plateau (600 more, 30), but victorious Gen Papa k there 5 Oct.	**Mesopotamia** — Maude's strength 166,450 (58,887 British) excluding 130,241 followers (10 Oct). (Sept) 17th Indian Div formed. 7th Cav Bde & 4 armoured cars evict Turks from Mandali (Jebel Hamrin sector).
Sun 30	AEF personnel in Europe total 61,927 (*see* 30 Nov). **Flanders** — British take 5296 PoWs & 11 guns during Sept. 3 German flamethrower attacks between Tower Hamlets and Polygon Wood. **Aisne** — Brief German advance at Berry-au-Bac.	(Sept) Gen Niessel replaces Gen Janin i/c 200-strong French Military mission to STAVKA.	**Italian Front** — 56,000 Italian deserters (Cadorna's report of 3 Nov), monthly desertion rate 5500 (July-Sept) v 650 in 1915.	**Kemal protest letter to Enver & resignation as Seventh Army Cdr at Aleppo**. He urges defensive strategy & independence from Germany; best divs lose 50% before reaching Front; 'Public life is in full anarchy'. Fevzi Pasha replaces him.
Mon 1 October 1917	(Oct) German Army reaches 238 divs (147 in W) & 18,416 guns, max till May 1918. It has 12,432 guns in W v 6000 BEF & 10,000 French. French Army combatant strength 1,142,000 inf; 71,000 cav; 522,000 gunners; 121,000 engrs; 35,000 airmen. **Ypres** — 5 German counter-attacks in the Salient. British take 4446 PoWs 1-5 Oct (K George cables congratulations 5). **Verdun** — German advance between Chaume Wood & Bezonvaux. French launch repeated counter-attacks (2) between Samogneux & Hill 344 (repulse small attack 4), but fail to dislodge attackers. Arty duels (3).		**Italian Front** — More than 70,000 Italian deserters. **Isonzo** — Austrian attack on Bainsizza Plateau defeated. Others on Mt San Gabriele fail (2-3). Arty active (7 & 13). **Macedonia** — Peak Italian strength 57,874.	**Palestine** — Turk police smash NILI Jewish spy ring, arrest Sarah Aaronson who commits suicide (5) after 4 days' torture.

AFRICAN OPERATIONS 5	SEA WAR 6	AIR WAR 7	INTERNATIONAL EVENTS 8	HOME FRONTS 9
		11 German aircraft lost in day).		reported since 19. **Russia** — Central Georgian Council formed (*see* 30).
Kilwa Force action at Nahungu Hill (-28): another 3 col assault met by dusk counter-attack cover to German retreat; hospital & food store abandoned.	**Baltic** — **First air-dropped mining success**: Russian destroyer *Okhotnik* sinks on German aircraft-laid mine (one of 70 since 1 July) off Zerel (Oesel I). **Britain** — Order-in-Council improves RN pay & pensions, abolishes 'hospital stoppages'.			**Russia** — National War Bonds started.
Linforce (99 cas) drives Wahle from Mtua (-29), 3rd Nigerian Bn loses 110 cas to Wahle at Nyengedi (30). NRFF col 66 miles SW of Liwale.		**Britain** — 2 'Giant' bombers for first time among 25 German aircraft sent (3 FTR), 16 Gothas turn back due to dense low cloud, only 9 manage to scatter bombs over Essex and Kent, 6 crash on return landing. **Ypres** — RFC makes 20 bombing raids on a fine day, at least 8 German aircraft shot down.	German Chancellor refuses to state war aims. Levantine financier Bolo Pasha arrested in Paris & charged with being German agent.	**Britain** — London Underground says stns only refuges *after* air raid warnings; no pets.
		W Front — 2 RNAS Camels fly special night bombing op v kite balloon shed nr Quiery-la-Motte, W of Douai. **Occupied Belgium** — RNAS Handley Pages bomb Zeebrugge (nights -2 Oct) but 220 bombs fail to hit lock gates. **Britain** — 7 Gothas (1 crash lands in Holland) & 3 Giants dispatched, 3 & 1 (1 lost to Dover AA fire) respectively bomb London, Waterloo Stn damaged (127 civ cas). **Palestine** — 'The mastery of the air has ... passed over to the British', Turco-Germans estimate RFC strength at 30-40 (*see* 5 Oct).	Kühlmann to Ludendorff 'The Bolshevik movement could never have attained the scale or the influence which it has today without our continual support .... also ... the Finnish & Ukrainian independence movements.'	**Italy** — King returns from W Front visit. **Britain** — Army & Navy NCO pay increases (-1 Oct). **Austria** — Council of Ministers meet on Czech-German Parliamentary clash. **USA** — *Rasputin*: *The Black Monk* New York film premiere a sell-out.
Kilwa Force action at Kihende Hill (-1 Oct): R Mbemkuru crossed under fire to within 500 yds of German position. Naumann requests conference (*see* 2 Oct).	(Sept) Rear Adm Souchon returns to Germany from Turkey to command High Seas Fleet 4th Battle Sqn, Vice-Adm Rebeur-Paschwitz i/c Turk Navy (*see* 20 Jan 1918). Allied & neutral **shipping loss** to U-boats 159 ships (68 British with 293 lives) **lowest since Jan** or 338,242t (German fig 353,602 incl 111,241t in Med). **Record 11 U-boats lost**. Only 6 ships lost over 50 miles from land (Sept-Dec), ie **convoys forcing U-boats inshore**.	**Britain** — 6 of 11 Gothas sent (no losses) bomb London, most damage to E End houses (52 civ cas). **Turkey** — RNAS Handley Page (Flt Cdr J Alcock) forced to ditch in Gulf of Xeros by Turk AA fire, 3 crew PoWs. **USA** — (c) RFC Advanced HQ opens at Fort Worth, Texas, helps train 10 American sqns on 3 airfields for RFC (-Apr 1918, *see* 6 Feb 1918).		**Russia** — Non-Slav Kiev Conference demands autonomy for all nationalities. **Britain** — War cost to date nearly £5bn, increasing national debt £3bn. Trade union unemployment exceeds 1% for 1st time since June 1915.
Nigerians bring in 600 German foodstuff loads to Nahungu.	Admiralty staff now has Director of Minesweeping under ACNS. More efficient British 'Nash Fish' hydrophone comes into service (effective towed slowly, giving limited directionals); **54.2% U-boat attacks on British home waters shipping at night** (-31 Dec) now moving inshore to areas before convoys assemble or after they disperse eg N Channel, St Catherine's Point & the Smalls (Bristol Channel), 82% sinkings (Aug-Dec) under 50 miles from land (58% under 10 miles). (Oct) - **Peak of 140 U-boats operational but German deadline for U-boat victory over Britain passes. Med** — (Oct) Record 52,500t Italian steamers (ie 16) sunk by	**Britain** — 6 of 18 Gothas sent bomb London; 6 others bomb Kent, Essex & Suffolk (53 cas). British first use 15ft spherical sound locator nr Dover to detect German aircraft 12-15 miles out in Channel. (Oct) **First London balloon barrage operational**, 10 by June 1918 despite 1st trial in Richmond Park (21 Sept) killing 2 air mechanics. **Baltic Provinces** — German aircraft bomb Oesel I (& 9).	Montenegrins in Paris declare v ex-PM Radovic & for union with Serbia.	**Britain** — RFP 97% (9% fall, mainly bread subsidy). **USA** — 2nd Liberty loan ($3bn), 50% oversubscribed by 7. Congress creates Air Board.

OCTOBER 1917	WESTERN FRONT 1	EASTERN FRONT 2	SOUTHERN FRONTS 3	TURKISH FRONTS 4
Mon 1 contd				
Tue 2	Fierce Flanders arty duels (& 13). **Champagne** — Germans gain foothold nr Beaumont.			**Mesopotamia** — 389 motorized British inc 4 armoured cars fail (poor road, heavy sand) to surprise Hit, 32 miles NW of Ramadi. **Palestine** — 10th Irish Div (from Salonika) arrives at Rafa (-16).
Wed 3	**Ypres** — Battle of Polygon Wood ends. **Champagne** — French guns disrupt German reserves massing for attacks E of Reims.	**Baltic Provinces** — Intense artillery duel in Jakobstadt area. **Bukovina** — Russian guns foil attack 7 miles N of Rumanian border. **Rumania** — Bulgars attack Rumanians N of R Buzeu mouth.		**Mesopotamia** — Russians take Nereman village 50 miles N of Mosul.
Thu 4	**Ypres** — **Battle of Broodseinde**: British pre-emptive (without prelim bombardment) attack (incl 12 tanks which help capture Poelcapelle) ridge on 8-mile front in drizzle, but gain on av only 700yds. Heavy German losses compel Ludendorff to modify his latest tactic of packing more inf into front line. He recommends Fourth Army form an 'advanced zone' of mobile troops in 'No Man's Land' to slow down advancing Allied inf so as to provide easier targets for arty. British Second Army reaches crest of Ypres Ridge. Intermittent rain (-7).	**Germans withdraw 5 divs from Riga sector to W Front (-18)**. German attack 28 miles ENE of Riga repulsed (7).		
Fri 5	**Ypres** — In 67 days' fighting BEF has taken 36 sq miles, 20,564 PoWs & 55 guns for 162,768 cas.			Falkenhayn meets Khalil Pasha between Mosul & Ras-al-Ain, Diyala sector to be held (*see* 16).
Sat 6	Pershing & Bliss promoted first full US generals (*see* 21). **Ypres** — British repulse dusk attack on Polygon Wood, take 380 PoWs. **Verdun** — Transient penetration of French trenches at Hill 344.	**Bukovina** — Heavy fighting 25 miles S of Czernowitz, Russians take 750 PoWs. **Russia** — Georgia starts a separate army.	**Italian Front** — Italians have identified 43 Austro-German divs. Intelligence warns of offensive for 16-20 (*see* 20).	**Arabia** — Lawrence & 150 Arabs blow up Turk supply train N of Maan. Lawrence sees Allenby (15,*see* 24) who asks for Arab support of his imminent offensive.
Sun 7	**Ypres** — German attack nr Reutel. Steady rain falling. Haig refuses Plumer & Gough's request to close down Ypres offensive. **Champagne** — French repulse big raiding party. **Aisne** — French (Maistre) attack Chemin des Dames & clear Germans from road after month-long series of		**Trentino** — Austrian attack on Mt Costabella repulsed (& 12). Cadorna visits Mt Grappa defences (begun 1916) between Piave & Brenta. **Salonika** — Brig-Gen Corkran arrives to be CIGS rep with Serb Army.	

AFRICAN OPERATIONS 5	SEA WAR 6	AIR WAR 7	INTERNATIONAL EVENTS 8	HOME FRONTS 9
	enemy action. RN has 18 destroyers, 33 sloops, 69 armed trawlers, 5 yachts & 1 gunboat but not all free for convoy escort (*see* 3). **Flanders** — U-boat Flotilla made into 2 with 43 boats. **N Sea** — Battlecruiser *Repulse* first capital ship to receive turret flying-off platform, Sqn Ldr Rutland flies off Sopwith Pup.			
Naumann Force (189 troops & 350 porters) **surrenders** to Edforce.	Cruiser HMS *Drake* (19k) sunk by *U79* (Rohrbeck) in shallow water N of Ireland. **E Atlantic** — Q-ship *Q10* (ex-sloop *Begonia*) sinks in collision with *U151* off Casablanca. **Baltic** — **Russian Fleet refuses to obey Govt's orders** (Bolsheviks dominate Centrobalt by 30, *see* 12).	**France** — 22 Gothas & 2 other bombers drop c10t of bombs on RNAS St Pol depot, destroy 23 aircraft being erected, damage 30. RNAS builds new depot nr Calais. **W Front** — 9 Sopwith Pups bomb Cruyshautem & Waereghem airfields (night 2/3).	Britain declares trade embargo with Scandinavia & Holland to stop re-exporting to Germany (*see* 11, 18, 19). Czernin Budapest speech stresses Wilsonian international ideas. **Secret War** — Berne British MI2 reports Turco-German Berlin meeting planning counter to British Zionist support (*see* 16).	**Russia** — Finnish Diet elections return non-Socialist Govt for independent republic within Russia (7, *see* 1 Nov). **Germany** — Hindenburg's 70th birthday. **Britain** — 5% National War Bonds issued. (c) PM asks press for more restrained air reporting, 62,504 London traffic accidents Jan 1915-Aug 1917 v 1506 air raid cas.
Nigerian Bde (1750) begins gruelling 80-mile advance S to join Linforce.	**Med** — **Local convoys start, through convoys by 30**, up to 3pw from 15. Indian Cape trade diverted to Port Said for through Med convoy (first 2 lose 5 ships, but next 4 unscathed). Japanese mainly escort troopships.			**Russia** — Democratic Conference: Kerensky threatens to resign if no coalition govt, Bolsheviks walk out (4, *see* 20). **Germany** — 30,000 exempted workers to return to Front by 31 Dec. **France** — Sugar ration reduced to 18oz pm. (Oct) Bread rationing in towns over 20,000 (*see* 7). **USA** — **War** Revenue Act **doubles** 2% 1916 **income tax**.
Kilwa Force blocked by German position on Mbemba road (-6) until it outflanks it & occupies Mbemba (8).		**Ypres** — Despite rain, low clouds & high winds RFC manages 17 sorties & 49 with fire calls (similar 9). **Adriatic** — 12 **Capronis** (moved from Milan to heel of Italy 25 Sept) cross Adriatic, **bomb Cattaro U-boat base**, torpedo store & seaplane hangars (night 4/5) in 280-mile round trip (*see* 24).	Bulgar PM Radoslavov speaks on peace.	**Britain** — War Cabinet discuss pacifist propaganda & possibility of German funding (*see* 13 Nov).
	Adriatic — Austrian torpedo boat *Tb11* mutinies & deserts to Italians. **N Sea** — UB41 mined & sunk off Flamborough Head.	**Palestine** — RFC Palestine Bde formed for Allenby's offensive under Brig-Gen W Salmond, 5 new Bristol fighters fly first sortie (7) & destroy 2 German fighters (8 & 18, *see* 27).	**Peru (Uruguay 7) breaks relations with Germany** (*see* 17). (8 German ships interned at Callao, seized 14 June 1918). Sweden protests v British seizure of ships in British ports (4 taken over 11 as mainly British-owned).	**Britain** — Merchant Navy pay increases (-6). Sir A Lee gives Chequers to nation as PM's country residence. **USA** — Britain promised 1m 6in howitzer shells (Haig asks 3).
				Germany — Socialist *Reichstag* deputies complain v Pan-German propaganda in Army. **USA** — Trading With the Enemy Act.
	N Sea — In secret Fleet order Adm Scheer demands that rumour-mongers be tracked down; orders officer corps to watch for signs of continuing revolutionary activity by USPD.		Kühlmann 'Our policy hopes for a penetration of Austria-Hungary.' Ludendorff insists on 24 guarantees if Austria to have Poland (*see* 22). Bolshevik Central Committee records refusal of money from German agent Karl Rosa.	**France** — Scantiest harvest for 50yrs announced.

OCTOBER 1917	WESTERN FRONT 1	EASTERN FRONT 2	SOUTHERN FRONTS 3	TURKISH FRONTS 4
Sun 7 contd	bloody localized actions. Attack & counter-attack fail round Craonne (8).			
Mon 8	Haig letter to CIGS Robertson reports 'good progress' at Ypres & assures Robertson that BEF can fight German Army with minimal Allied (ie French or Russian) assistance until arrival of US armies in 1918. Haig deplores 'interference' by Allies or PM (Lloyd George). **Champagne** — French attack SW of Beaumont.			
Tue 9	**Flanders** — **Battle of Poelcapelle**: Severe fighting. On 6-mile front 3 British divs (nearly 7000 cas) gain crest of Broodseinde Ridge & reach S edge of Houthulst Forest; 2000 PoWs. German counter-attack on 2000-yd front S of Ypres-Staden rail line. Rain breaks drainage system on Passchendaele 'heights'. Haig orders Cdn Corps (4 divs) to Ypres (see 20). **Verdun** — Arty duels N of Chaume Wood. Germans penetrate 1st line trenches N of it (10).	**Pripet** — Emperor Charles reviews troops in Kovel.		
Wed 10	**Flanders** — French advancing up Corverbeck valley. Pétain again appeals to Haig for continued BEF attacks to divert German attention away from still recovering French Army. BEF Intelligence Chief Charteris concedes in diary '...now no chance of complete success here this year'.		**Isonzo** — Rain (-20).	**Palestine** — Col Meinertzhagen leaves bloodstained haversack (plans) to be captured by Turks, as successful ruse for forthcoming Gaza attack (see 17 & 31).
Thu 11	**Flanders** — French First Army repulse counter-attack E of Dreibank. Rupprecht reports to *OHL*: 'In order to save material and men it may become necessary to withdraw the [Flanders] front so far from the enemy that he will be compelled to make a fresh deployment of his artillery.' **Verdun** — Germans briefly penetrate advanced trenches N of Hill 344; those of hill itself (17).	Germans gain ground ENE of Segewold & try to fraternize in Riga area.		**Armenia** — Turk attack repulsed 16 miles SW of Erzincan.
Fri 12	**Flanders** — FIRST BATTLE OF PASSCHENDAELE: II Anzac Corps attack NE of Ypres on 6-mile front but heavy rain & deep mud impede ops; severe fighting. German manpower wastage compels Ludendorff to divert 12 divs, already moving from E Front to Italy, to Flanders.	**Baltic Provinces — German landings on Gulf of Riga Islands**: Operation *Albion* with Gen Kathen's 23,000 men (42nd Inf Div), 5000 horses, 1400 vehicles & 54 guns in 19 transports from Libau, troops ashore in 5 hrs (see SEA WAR).		
Sat 13	French incl Foch (at Chequers, England) demand BEF front extension before 1 Nov, but matter left to C-in-Cs (see 18). **Flanders** — Haig cancels attacks until weather improves but approves Cambrai thrust for 20 Nov (Byng briefs corps cdrs at Albert 26) for which tank/inf training starts.	Germans occupy Arensburg (capital) on Oesel I but fail to land on Dagö I (see 17).		

AFRICAN OPERATIONS 5	SEA WAR 6	AIR WAR 7	INTERNATIONAL EVENTS 8	HOME FRONTS 9
		Germany — Navy airship *L57* destroyed in accidental explosion.	Allied Parliamentary Ctee Conference (-10).	**Russia** — Kerensky forms 3rd Coalition Govt to rule until Constituent Assembly meets. Trotsky now Petrograd Soviet chm denounces it as a govt of civil war. 1.2m rail workers on strike since 6.
Belgians occupy Mahenge (old German highlands HQ) & make 260 PoWs, but Capt Tafel escapes. Belgians repel German attack to SE (13) & join British 12 miles S (16) **British Somaliland** — Camel Corps (250 & 5 MGs, 10 cas) kills 70+ of 300 dervishes at Endow Pass.	**N Sea** — Speaking in *Reichstag*, Adm Capelle asserts he has written proof 'main architect' of Aug mutiny, Reichpietsh, had presented plans to 3 USPD deputies & had received 'full support' in organizing same. There is uproar & German Navy's efforts to outlaw USPD soon collapses (*see* 23). **Baltic** — Germans embark troops for Op *Albion* (*see* 12), sail from Libau (11); 11 German motorboats recce Gulf of Riga. **Atlantic** — U-boat sinks AMC HMS *Champagne* (56 lost).	**Ypres** — RFC No 1 Sqn (1 Nieuport hit) destroys at least 3 fighters, score 200 since 1 Feb.	**Egypt** — †Sultan Hussein Kamel, youngest brother Ahmed Fuad succeeds. **Russia** — Allied ambassadors see Kerensky, hint at withdrawing support if 'anarchy' not dealt with (*see* 16 & 31).	**USA** — All-black div authorized.
Kilwa Force No 1 Col takes Ruponda road & supply centre. Linforce (3200) resumes advance on Mtama. Portuguese take Mauta 26 miles N of R Rovuma.	**Baltic** — *Kurland* U-boat Flotilla disbanded (*see* Dec). **Britain** — Beatty meets new Deputy First Sea Lord Weymss to discuss possible intervention in Holland, also argues for dawn 120 torpedo-plane strike (from 8 carriers) v High Seas Fleet, but Admiralty discouraging (20).		Kühlmann in *Reichstag* says Germany will never return Alsace-Lorraine.	**Germany** — Chancellor & War Minister criticized in *Reichstag* Law of Siege debate. **USA** — Army urged to convert conscientious objectors (non-combatant service undefined till 20 Mar 1918).
		France — RFC's 41st Wing (DH4s, FE2bs & 8 RNAS HPs) formed, LAUNCHES 13-MONTH day/night STRATEGIC BOMBING campaign V INDUSTRIAL TARGETS IN W GERMANY & Alsace-Lorraine up to 125 miles from W Front front line (*see* 17).	Britain stops cables to Holland until Dutch barge sand & scrap iron traffic from Germany into Belgium ceases (Dutch ask for war-use proof 17). To reassure Germany's allies, Kaiser visits Sofia (Bulgaria), goes on to Constantinople (*see* 17).	
Nigerian Bde evacuates 283 sick, captures 120 foodstuff loads & 9 whites (14).	**Baltic** — German landings on **Oesel** (anchor in Tagg Bay), **Dagö & Moon in Gulf of Riga** (12-20): battlecruiser *Moltke* (Vice-Adm Schmidt), 10 battleships (2 mined but carry on); 9 cruisers; 52 destroyers & light warships; 19 troop transports; 6 U-boats; 6 Zeppelins; 101 aircraft (*see* E FRONT) v Vice-Adm Mikhail K Bakhirev's 2 battleships, 1 cruiser, c24 destroyers, 13 minesweepers (1 op), 6 submarines (4 British). **Baltic** — German minesweepers (1 lost) partially clear Soelo Sound between Oesel & Dagö Is. Russian minelayer *Pripiat* refuses to lay mines in it (night 13/14) and blockship runs aground.		**Neutrals: Argentina** — Count Luxburg interned. **USA** — Polish-American Army begins recruiting.	**Belgium** — Postwar Reconstruction Ministry formed. **USA** — Censorship & War Trades Boards created. **Britain** — Police tell DH Lawrence to move from Cornwall (German wife). Japanese offer of 2000 doctors rejected .**Canada** — Sir R Borden forms Coalition Union Govt (*see* 17 Dec). **Britain** — Munitions Ministry 12½% bonus to 250,000 engineers & moulders (*see* 9 Nov). Geddes presents manpower budget to War Cabinet, 450,000 can be spared, estimates 1918 'wastage' at 820,000 so Army shortfall 320,000.

OCTOBER 1917	WESTERN FRONT 1	EASTERN FRONT 2	SOUTHERN FRONTS 3	TURKISH FRONTS 4
Sun 14		**Oesel I** — Russians cut off in SW Svorbe peninsula. Germans advance along it & bar escape to Moon I (15), secure island (16) with 10,000 PoWs & 50 guns.	**Salonika** — British 27th Div (47 cas) recaptures Homondos (night 13/14, *see* 22 July) village with 153 Bulgars (79k) & 3 MGs & occupies 2 villages to cover taking up of 'winter line' in Struma valley (-17, *see* 25). **Isonzo** — Badoglio moved to XXVII Corps in path of imminent Austro-German offensive.	
Mon 15	**Aisne** — German guns fire 90,000 rnds phosgene gas shell (-22) at French in Ailette Basin nr Laffaux; 1200 gassed (110 deaths). Arty duels NE of Soissons (17).			
Tue 16	**Aisne** — French attack W of Craonne fails. 1800 French guns & 460 mortars prepare way for limited offensive (-22) on 7½-mile front, ie max of 1 gun to 6yds with 120,000t of shells.	**Baltic Provinces** — Russian civilians evacuate Reval (Estonia). **N Russia** — Main body RNAS Armoured Car Sqn sails from Archangel (most land Newcastle 29).	**Salonika** — Record 21,434 British in hospital (mainly malaria, *see* 30 Dec).	**Mesopotamia** — Marshall masses 16,000 men & 78 guns (3 cols) to clear Jebel Hamrin & R Diyala, done by 20 without serious opposition.
Wed 17	**Ypres** — Eqvt of 14 BEF engineer/pioneer bns repairing and extending plank roads in Salient.	**Baltic Provinces** — German landing on Dagö I repulsed but Marines succeed (19) & secure (20) with Schildau I.		**S Persia** — Shiraz col destroys 3 forts (-19); Sykes Mission has c1700 Indian troops (31).
Thu 18	Haig & Pétain meet at Amiens, former agrees by 2 Nov to extend BEF line to Oise (*see* 17 Dec). **Aisne** — French repulse attack on Vauclere Plateau, W of Craonne.	Russian War Minister proposes 2.5m reduction in Army to improve morale; all politics to cease after 15 Nov elections. 43,000/ 210,000 officers unemployed but still 121 Austro-German divs on Front. **Baltic Provinces** — Russians evacuate Moon I; Germans claim 5000 PoWs.	**Italian Front** — Local fighting on Trentino & Carnia sectors.	German War Minister Stein & Enver Pasha sign Turco-German military convention (inc postwar co-operation).
Fri 19			**Salonika** — Sarrail finally announces relief of a British bde in sector E of Vardar, completed 9 Nov.	

AFRICAN OPERATIONS 5	SEA WAR 6	AIR WAR 7	INTERNATIONAL EVENTS 8	HOME FRONTS 9
	Baltic — 4 German battleships silence Zorel bty on S point of Oesel (Russians blow up the 4 12-in guns). 13 German destroyers enter Soelo Sound and, covered by battleship, sink Russian destroyer *Grom* (of 4 and gunboat engaged).			
Battle of Nyangao/Mahiwa (-18): 'An equatorial Gettysburg' (largest battle of the war), c4950 British, 12 guns, 4 mortars, 147 MGs v 3000 Germans & c3 guns. Wahle evacuates Mtana due to Nigerian Bde & fights it N of Mahiwa.	**E Atlantic** — RN Q-sloop *Tamarisk* tows U-boat torpedoed destroyer USS *Cassin* into harbour (*see* 17 Nov).		Warsaw Polish Regency Council appointed, but Allies recognize Polish National Ctee (20).	**France** — **Mata Hari shot as spy** at Vincennes, aged 41. **USA** — Shipping Board takes over private ocean-going ships. **Germany** — Ludendorff reports to War Office on *OHL* meetings with unions.
Wahle evacuates Nyangao, but Lettow's 1000 men & 2 guns reinforce him to surround Nigerian Bde in 2 groups, which lose 300 cas & 1 gun.	**Baltic** — German fleet inside Gulf of Riga before Avensburg & facing Moon Sound. RN submarine *C27* (Sealy) torpedoes the minesweeper tender *Indianola*, only success of numerous attacks (*see* 24 & 29). **Adriatic** — 2 Austrian battleships & 10 torpedo boats shell Italian coast nr Cortellazzo (Piave); 2 Italian MAS boats attack.	**Mesopotamia** — 3 RFC No 30 Sqn Martinsydes (1 forced down) bomb Kifri airfield (& 31, 4 aircraft lost).	Wilson approves Balfour's draft pro-Jewish homeland statement (*see* 2 Nov). **Secret War: Russia** — Somerset Maugham cable urges Allied $500,000 pa propaganda campaign (*see* 31).	**Britain** — **Air raid shelters for 1m people in London area.** **France** — Secret Chamber Session on Briand-Lancken affair (German diplomat's peace move reported 12 Oct).
O'Grady's Linforce a mile from Nigerian Bde as both sides retreat after ferocious, confused, close-quarter fighting. British lose 2348 cas (528 Nigerians), 1 gun & 9 MGs plus 352+ carriers (*see* 6 Nov). Lettow loses 519 & abandons *Königsberg* gun (*see* 11 Nov). British claim 918 PoWs alone (15-18).	**N Sea** — **Fast German cruiser-minelayers** *Bremse* & *Brummer* **surprise & destroy British-escorted** Bergen-Lerwick-Britain **convoy** 65 miles E of Shetlands. Destroyers *Mary Rose* (Fox) & *Strongbow* fight suicidal delaying action (135 lost, survivors fired on) while 3 British merchant ships escape; 9 Scandinavian ships sunk in 2 hrs 20 mins. No radio warning got off (*see* INT'L EVENTS 25 & 1 Nov), 30 RN cruisers & 54 destroyers at sea, but powerless (*see* 12 Dec). **Atlantic** — US transport *Antilles* (67 lost) sunk by U-boat. **Baltic** — **Gulf of Riga 27-min battleship action**: Russian battleship *Slava* damaged (3 hits) by *König* & *Kronprinz*, goes aground & later scuttled W of Papilad I (*see* 29). Battleship *Grashdanin* (ex-*Tsesarevich*) retires N damaged (2 hits). **E Med** — British hospital ship *Goorkha* damaged by mine off Alexandria.	**Germany** — 8 DH4s of No 55 Sqn (41st Wing) RFC bomb Burbach works, nr Saarbrücken (& 25), works & houses damaged (14 cas). **E Med** — Turk air recon finds no Cyprus preparations for British landing in Gulf of Alexandretta (*see* 8 Nov).	Colombian Congress resolution v U-boat campaign. Kaiser visits Gallipoli battlefields.	**Germany** — 2 RFC lts receive 10yr prison sentence for insulting leaflet dropping (*see* AIR WAR 28 Jan 1918). **Britain** — Max tea prices compulsory (July-Oct consumption 1/3 normal). Cabinet told air raids upset worker travel.
Hanforce KAR & Gold Coast Regt with 2 armoured cars just hold Maj Kraut's counter-attack at Lukuledi Mission & occupy it (19).	**N Sea** — Some German sailors refuse to sail in U-boats from Ostend.		USA to use Dutch shipping in her ports outside war zone in return for food & raw materials.	**USA** — Navy Sec Daniels calls Liberty loan U-boat (on display NY) 'this stiletto of modern warfare'; 58 enemy aliens arrested at Hoboken Docks NJ. Hoover launches lower food price campaign. **Russia** — Kerensky decides to move capital to Moscow. **Kuban Cossack Rada declares republic.**
Deventer cancels another attack, replaces Beves with Cunliffe as GOC Linforce. Lettow gains respite (*see* 6 Nov).		**Britain** — **The 'Silent Raid'**: 11 German naval Zeppelins (5 FTR) fly disastrous high-altitude mission v N England industrial centres (78 defence sorties cost 4 wrecked aircraft). *L45* by chance bombs London (83 of 91 cas total), 660lb bomb hits	US embargo on trade with N Neutrals. **Neutrals: Spain** — British films not allowed public screening.	**France** — Govt wins confidence vote (346-74), *see* 13 Nov.

OCTOBER 1917	WESTERN FRONT 1	EASTERN FRONT 2	SOUTHERN FRONTS 3	TURKISH FRONTS 4
Fri 19 contd				
Sat 20	**Ypres** — Canadians relieve undaunted Anzacs.		**Albania** — 3 French cols advance W of L Ochrid but Paris War Ministry, after Italian pressure, halts progress (21) 5 miles N of Pogradec. **Italian Front — Czech officer deserter warns Italians of offensive** on 26 between Plezzo & sea; 2 Rumanian deserters warn of breakthrough to come at Tolmino. Gen **Capello (flu) hands Second Army to newcomer Gen Montuori;** returns from Padua (22) when attack imminent, but illness again forces relinquishment (*see* 26). Austro-German attack postponed from 20 to 24, their guns begin to register.	
Sun 21	**Lorraine** — US TROOPS ENTER LINE: US 1st Div joins French in Lunéville sector. Each American unit is attached to a French unit (*see* 23).	**Baltic Provinces — Germans land on mainland Estonia** at Verder opposite Moon I, but repulsed 8 miles N & 8 miles S (23); claim 20,130 PoWs & 141 guns since 12 for 54k. **Russian SW Front** — 84,948 officers & men on ctees.	**Serbia** — Bulgars & Germans again shell Monastir. **Italian Front** — Cadorna cables British DMO Maj-Gen Maurice 'The attack is coming but I am confident of being able to meet it.'	**Palestine** — Allenby's DMC & XX Corps begin pre-battle advance (-30), orders issued (22).
Mon 22	**Flanders** — Anglo-French advance astride Ypres-Staden railway on 2½-mile front, 200 PoWs from S end of Houthulst Forest (Germans regain part 23, but repulsed 24).		**Dolomites** — Italians repulse strong Austro-German attack. **Isonzo** — German Fourteenth Army now in start positions. Tapped telephone warns Italians of arty barrage from 0200 (24).	**Mesopotamia** — Falkenhayn orders Turk XVIII Corps (4000-6000) S from Tikrit W of Tigris but soon retreats before Gen Cobbe (23) whom Maude orders (28) to attack Turk position 12 miles S of Tikrit (*see* 2 Nov).
Tue 23	*OHL* appreciation : 'The guiding principle of our general military situation remains...that the decision lies in the Western theatre of war'; Maj Wetzell of ops section submits proposals for a spring 1918 offensive on W Front (*see* 11 Nov). **Flanders** — Seventh German counter-attack in Ypres Salient since 22. **Verdun** — Germans gain temporary foothold NE of Hill 344. **Aisne — Battle of La Malmaison** ('Laffaux Corner') (- 1 Nov): A second 1917 triumph for Pétain's carefully planned limited attack strategy. Maistre's Sixth Army attacks with 8 divs at 0515 in fog & cold, aided later by c80 tanks, captures 3 villages & Ft Malmaison, 8000 PoWs & 70 guns in 2-mile advance. A German div is heavily gassed & routed. French advance on Chavignon in Laffaux salient; Germans withdraw behind Oise-Aisne Canal. **Lorraine — First American shot fired in a land theatre of active ops**: At 0605 by Sgt Alex L Arch's French-made 75mm gun of Bty C, 6th Field Arty, 1st Inf Div nr Xanrey (*see* 3 Nov). First American w with AEF (a 2nd Lt).	Germans have retired 20 miles since night 21/22 from NE of Riga, destroying bridges to shorten line. Russians follow up (24).		

AFRICAN OPERATIONS 5	SEA WAR 6	AIR WAR 7	INTERNATIONAL EVENTS 8	HOME FRONTS 9
		Piccadilly Circus, remainder dispersed by unpredicted 60mph northerly gales; 4 airships blown across to France, *L50* disappears over Med; *L44* shot down by French AA fire from 19,000ft, *L45* crash lands & burnt by crew W of Sisteron (Provence); *L49* falls into French hands at Bourbonne-les-Bains nr Langres (night 19/20).		
		Flanders — 45 RFC Camels & Spads (2 lost) attack Rumbeke airfield SE of Roulers from 400ft, also claim 7 German aircraft in air combats.	Japanese Foreign Minister tells Russian Ambassador no change over not sending troops to Europe.	**Russia** — **Lenin returns to Petrograd from Finland** (by now est 240,000 Bolsheviks). **Greece** — Athens Archbishop degraded for 25 Dec 1916 Anathema ceremony.
Hanforce saves Lukuledi garrison & pushes Kraut 2 miles S towards Ndanda, but retires N back to Ruponda (22 Oct -7 Nov).	**N Sea** — Dover Patrol shells Ostend; monitors *Erebus* & *Terror* (off Dunkirk) survive total of 4 torpedo hits (from 3 German torpedo boats) thanks to bulge protection.	**USA** — First flight trials of Packard Liberty aero engine.	Petrograd Soviet's peace terms issued.	**Germany** — Imperial Economic Office established. Treasury Minister tells War Office financial decline makes 'continuation of the war impossible'. **Russia** — Duma dissolved till 25 Nov elections.
		Ypres — 2 No 45 Sqn Sopwith Camels scatter 2 German bns on Staden-Houthulst rd.	Austro-German Foreign Ministers' personal war aims agreement: Austria to have Poland, Germany to have Rumania (*see* 5 Nov).	**Britain** — PM, Bonar Law & Gen Smuts launch Economy Campaign at Albert Hall. **Russia** — Trotsky accuses Kerensky of treason at Petrograd Soviet. **USA** — Custodian of Enemy Property begins work.
	German Navy ban on all newspapers (15), pamphlets & meetings connected with USPD.		Barthou succeeds Ribot as French Foreign Minister. British War Cabinet discuss volunteer Russian army movement.	**Russia** — **Bolshevik Central Ctee votes 10-2 for Lenin's armed uprising**; Trotsky to organize 20,000-strong Red Guard (Petrograd armoured car unit defects to Reds 24). **USA** — NY Police thwart Sinn Fein Easter 1918 Rising plot.

OCTOBER 1917	WESTERN FRONT 1	EASTERN FRONT 2	SOUTHERN FRONTS 3	TURKISH FRONTS 4
Wed 24			**Italian Front** — BATTLE OF CAPORETTO (TWELFTH ISONZO -9 Nov) begins on misty, rainy day with 0200 hurricane bombardment of 4hrs (incl 2hrs of gas shells that Italian gas masks unable to cope with so guns fall silent). Austro-German assault (10 divs) at 0800 on 20-mile front penetrates along valleys up to 14 miles isolating, panicking & destroying 3 Italian divs (18,000 PoWs & 100 guns) E of Upper Isonzo, although flanking armies' attacks fail. German 12th (Silesian) Div takes Caporetto at 1530. Cadorna belatedly calls up 9 res divs & orders Tagliamento defences (*see* 29). Austrian Jewish-born lyric poet Lt Franz Janowitz (2nd Tyrol Sharpshooter Regt) mortally w by MG in assault on Mt Rombon, dies 4 Nov aged 25.	**Arabia** — Lawrence leaves Aqaba for Yarmuk Valley (*see* 6 Nov).
Thu 25	**Aisne** — French capture Filain in closing up to R Aillette & Oise Canal; they take 11,157 PoWs; 200 guns; 222 mortars; 720 MGs by 26 for 12,000 cas (*see* 1 Nov).		**Isonzo** — Austro-German pincers close behind Mt Nero. Lt Rommel's Württemberg Mtn Bn (*Alpenkorps*) seizes Mts Kuk & Cragonza on Kolovrat Ridge with 3600 Italian PoWs incl 4th *Bersaglieri* Bde. Austrian 22nd Div seizes Stol Ridge (night 25/26). Fourteenth Army now has 30,000 PoWs & 300 guns and Second Isonzo Army (1000+ cas) div takes c4000 PoWs & 60 guns on Bainsizza. Cadorna refuses Capello's advice to retreat to R Torre & possibly Tagliamento after Gen Montuori says attack can be held (2100). **Salonika** — British 27th Div (77 cas) captures 3 villages E of R Struma taking 106 PoWs & 1 MG but main garrisons escape.	
Fri 26	**Flanders** — SECOND BATTLE OF PASSCHENDAELE (-10 Nov): 'The enemy charged like a wild bull against the iron wall which kept him from our U-boat bases' (Ludendorff). Main thrusts v Houthulst Forest (French), Poelcapelle, Cdn Corps (426 guns, 1558 cas) attacks (at 0530, in rain) and gains 1000 yds on 2800-yd front towards Passchendaele, Bercelaere, Gheluvelt (c3500 British cas), & Zandvorde. Canadians gain rising ground SW of Passchendaele on 2 spurs (*see* 28 & 30).		**Isonzo** — Krauss' 3 Austrian divs cross Stol Ridge (6467ft) & capture Mt Maggiore. After 12-mile advance Rommel captures Mts Mrzli & Matajur (5414ft) with 2700 *Salerno* Bde PoWs who defy officers to surrender; 2 German divs 5 miles from Cividale (HQ Italian Second Army). Austrian Second Isonzo Army penetrates Italian Bainsizza 2nd line & First Isonzo Army reports Italian retreat on Carso. Germans claim 60,000 PoWs & 500 guns. **Lloyd George orders** CIGS to send **2 British W Front divs to Italy** (*see* 5 & 6 Nov, *see also* W FRONT 31 Oct, 9 Nov).	
Sat 27	**Flanders** — French & Belgians penetrate up to 1¾ miles astride Ypres-Dixmude Road.	Local & Railway militia formed from Russian wounded. Germans try to fraternize with N & W Fronts (& 31). They evacuate Verder. **Rumania** — Transylvanian Volunteer Corps to be enlarged (*see* 17 Nov).	**Isonzo** — **Cadorna orders general retreat** at 0230, already widely happening on jammed roads. German *Alpenkorps* & 2 other divs reach R Torre beyond Cividale. Cadorna accepts Foch's offer (26) of 4 French divs (*see* 30).	**Palestine** — 218 British guns shell Gaza (-31, Allied naval bombardment from 29); 8th Mtd Bde holds Turk 3rd Cav Div recce in force N of El Baqqar. **Arabia** — Maulud's 550 Arabs nr Petra repel 4 Turk bns, cav regt & 10 guns from Maan.

AFRICAN OPERATIONS 5	SEA WAR 6	AIR WAR 7	INTERNATIONAL EVENTS 8	HOME FRONTS 9
German Gov of Chiwata Province asks Lettow to surrender but he replies 'We are fighting for the future.'	**Brazil seizes 43 interned German merchant ships. N Sea** — Harwich Force flagship cruiser *Centaur* badly damaged by own depth charges washed overboard after vain night sortie to catch German destroyers. **Baltic** — RN submarine *C32*, trapped in Gulf of Riga, beaches in Vaist Bay W of Pernau. (Russian submarine *Gepard* probably mined 28), but trapped *C26* (Downie) reaches Hangö (Finland) at 3rd attempt (13 Dec).	**Germany** — 9 HPs (2 FTR) of RNAS 'A' Sqn & 14 FE 2bs (2 FTR) raid industrial & rail targets in Saarbrücken area. **Italian Front** — Capronis make 18 raids on Austro-German troops (-c14 Nov) but forced to move bases behind Piave.		
	Baltic — German warships from Moon Sound shell Kuno I nr Pernau (Gulf of Riga), Khainash, 40 miles to S bombarded (26).		**Italy** — **PM Boselli & Cabinet resign** (Orlando succeeds 29). **Diplomacy** — Anglo-French Military Service Convention. **Neutrals: Norway** — Polar explorer Amundsen returns his 3 German decorations because of 17 Norwegian sailors' deaths in N Sea (*see* SEA WAR 17).	**Russia** — Kerensky tells HM Ambassador Bolsheviks will revolt in next few weeks. **Ireland** — Sinn Fein Dublin Conference (-27) elects De Valera Pres & announces Irish Republic constitution.
S Tunisia — French Dehibat garrison skirmishes with Senussi (-9 Nov, convoy attacked 19 Aug 1918).			BRAZIL DECLARES WAR ON GERMANY: Pres Braz announces Germans caught in plot to invade (*see* HOME FRONTS 16 Nov).	
		Ypres — RFC & balloons help engage 116 German btys & 200+ other targets. 2 German airfields bombed. Night bombers strike 7 more & 3 stns + other targets (night 27/28). **Palestine** — RFC aircraft patrol in pairs to cover Allenby's concentration, Bristol Fighter destroys German 2-seater before it can return with vital photos (30). Air photography has plotted 131 Turk btys (*see* TURK FRONTS).		**USA** — 20,000 women in NY suffrage parade (*see* 6 Nov).

OCTOBER 1917	WESTERN FRONT 1	EASTERN FRONT 2	SOUTHERN FRONTS 3	TURKISH FRONTS 4
Sun 28	**Flanders** — Canadian losses since 26 — 2481, but 370 German PoWs taken. **Aisne** — Attack & counter-attack on Oise-Aisne Canal. **Verdun** — Germans advancing at Chaume Wood & Bezonvaux. **France** — US 26th (National Guard) Div (*see* 1 Nov) is second to land.		**Isonzo** — Despite rain & snowstorms German 200th Div crosses R Torre at 0400 & occupies Udine 20hrs after *Comando Supremo* & Second Army HQ evacuate, latter formation split in two. Germans claim 100,000 PoWs. Austrians reoccupy Gorizia & advance 8 miles W.	
Mon 29		**Baltic Provinces** — German attack in Janinzen-Skuli sector repulsed.	**Isonzo** — Below orders Tagliamento bridges' seizure; Italians blow Codroipo bridges prematurely leaving 12,000 men on wrong side, but XXIV Corps holds off pursuit to cross flooding river lower down. Third Army crosses Isonzo. Cadorna issues preliminary orders for retreat to Piave. 3 Italian cav bdes charge Austro-German advanced guards W of Udine (-30). Cadorna communiqué blames Second Army for collapse.	
Tue 30	**Flanders** — Cdn Corps (2321 cas) enters Passchendaele but later driven back to outskirts; 5 German counter-attacks.	Kerensky puts Finland, Petrograd & Moscow under N Front. Knox's diary: 'There is evidently not the slightest hope that the Russian Army will ever fight again.' Hoffmann promoted Maj-Gen.	Foch visits Cadorna's new Treviso HQ and tells him 'You've lost only one army, fight hard with the others!', as **first French troops arrive in Italy**. Gen Duchêne & Tenth Army HQ to command 4 divs (120,000 men), *see* 3 Nov. **Isonzo** — Italian Navy complete Grado's evacuation (SW of river mouth). German 26th Div reaches Tagliamento taking Dignano & 20,000 PoWs.	
Wed 31	Total of 700 Mk IV tanks delivered to BEF by end Oct. BEF Oct monthly loss of 119,808 second worst of 1917. **Flanders** — Haig inspects 23rd Div, about to leave for Italy (*see* S FRONTS 6 Nov).		**Isonzo** — By 0100 **Italians behind Tagliamento** via 8 bridges. British CIGS Robertson arrives at Cadorna's Treviso HQ, agrees with Foch that Italians can hold river lines. Archduke Eugene claims 180,000 PoWs & 1500 guns.	**Palestine** — THIRD BATTLE OF GAZA (-7 Nov): after 24-30 mile march, **DMC** (11,000 & 28 guns) **captures Beersheba** from 5400 Turks & 28 guns. XX Corps (17,000 engaged) storms W defences, (Cp Collins, 25th Welch Fus), wins VC for carrying wounded & bayoneting 15 Turks). Col Newcombe's 70 British camelry cut Hebron-Jerusalem telegraph in diversion. Allenby gains 1947 PoWs, 15 guns & 4+ MGs for 1348 cas.
Thu 1 November 1917	**Aisne** — **Battle of La Malmaison ends: outflanked German Seventh Army retreats from Chemin des Dames** (-2): French reoccupy 4 villages on heights. **Flanders** — Australian Corps of 5 divs formed.	STAVKA counts 5,925,606 all ranks but only 2,143,500 combatants & 9276 guns.	Italians hold R Tagliamento (up to 3000yds wide) line (-2) to allow time for Carnia & dilatory Fourth Army retreat plus Piave preparations. Austrian 10th Div reaches lower Tagliamento at Latisana. Foch & Robertson visit King at Padua.	**Palestine** — Bulfin's XXI Corps (11,000 men, 148 guns) captures Gaza's outer defences night 1/2 (1000+ Turks k, 550 PoWs, 3 guns & 30 MGs for 2696 cas, -4). (Nov) First 2000 of 8000 donkeys (4 coys) begin to help supply the EEF front line.

AFRICAN OPERATIONS 5	SEA WAR 6	AIR WAR 7	INTERNATIONAL EVENTS 8	HOME FRONTS 9
		W Front — Lt Gontermann, top-scoring German 'balloon-buster' (39 victories since 8 Apr), dow when his *Jasta 15* Fokker Dr I breaks up in flight; shortly after all German triplanes temporarily grounded. First 5 of 12 fighter *Jagdgruppen* (36-75 aircraft each) made permanent.		
250 NRFF occupy Liwale (*see* 16 Nov).	**Baltic** — German battleship *Markgraf* mined in Irben Strait, Gulf of Riga. Capital ships subsequently withdrawn back to High Seas Fleet due to mine & British submarine threat (3 battleships attacked) (30). (Oct) **E Med** — Anglo-French naval bombard-ment of Gaza resumes (av 1 cruiser, 4 monitors, 2 gunboats, 2 destroyers) (*see* 11 Nov).	**Britain** — 1 of 3 Gothas (2 attack Calais) sent drops 8 bombs between Burnham & Southend. Hit & run raid (11 bombs) v Dover (night 30/31). **Salonika** — 8 German fighters shoot down 2 of 5 RFC aircraft after they bomb Cestovo dump (also bombed 5).		**Russia** — 8hr day decreed.
		Ypres — c100 RFC offensive patrols mainly unopposed.	**Bavarian PM Count Hertling** (aged 73) **succeeds Michaelis** (resigned 28) **as Chancellor.** Balfour speech on the Balkans.	**Britain** — Commons votes £400m war credit.
Monthly reported British cas of 1923 (inc 237 deaths from disease) worst of war.	**Baltic** — Russian admirals declare 'the fate of Finland and the approaches ot the capital depend primarily on the will of the enemy'; C-in-C Razvozov told his post will be elective soon (30). (Oct) Allied & neutral shipping losses to U-boats, 159 ships (68 British with 293 lives) worth 448,923t. German fig 466,542t incl 144,603t in Med. 99 homeward convoys have sailed since May. 1502 steamers (10 lost in convoy, *see* 30 Nov); 6 U-boats lost, all to mines). **N Sea/ Channel** — 10,400 RN mines laid in Heligoland Bight & Dover Straits (-31 Dec).	**Britain** — First German Gotha incendiary raid: 22 Gothas bomb (183 dropped in Kent), 10 reaching London (83 bombs) cause only 32 civ cas as 10lb incendiaries often fail to ignite. 50 defence sorties (2 crash landings) achieve 6 brief sightings; 5 Gothas crash on return (night 31/1 Nov).	Kerensky sees Somerset Maugham, urges immediate Allied peace offer, only its refusal will persuade Russians to fight in self-defence; requests more regular Allied aid but Lloyd George only gets report 18 Nov despite Maugham's immediate departure.	**Britain** — Military enlistments now 4,421,694. **Germany** — 400th Anniversary of Lutheran Reformation celebrated.
Jubaland — 2 KAR coys occupy Garba Harre v Aulyehan tribe (*see* 20 Dec).	(Nov) 139 Allied destroyers on convoy duty (*see* 18) incl 40 in Med (11 British ships lost). 381 ships sail in Med convoys (only 9 lost, or 2.35%). USN has 40+ ships at Brest under Adm Wilson for convoy escort. **Channel** — (Nov) 14 British ships lost. Geddes forms Channel Barrage Ctee under Rear-Adm Keyes, Director of Plans, (*see* 18 Dec). **Baltic** — (Nov) Thousands of mutinous **sailors from Russian Baltic Fleet act as shock troops of the Bolshevik** (October) **Revolution** at Petrograd (*see* 7). German U-boat & auxiliary *Equity* land supplies in Finland for nationalists. **N Sea** — British submarine *E52* sinks *UC63* S of Goodwins (*see* 3). (Nov) RN lays 960 mines off Flamborough Head (E Coast) v Flanders U-boats (*see* 18). **Britain** — First Lord Geddes	**Med** — (Nov) First of 17 flying boats built at Malta dockyard.	Balfour tells War Cabinet Russia will make peace in 2 months if no US/Japanese divs sent. **Occupied Belgium** — (Nov) Germans arrest Abbé Buelens, head of Allied Lux network. **Neutrals: Norway** — Oslo protests to Berlin over sinking of neutrals.	**Britain** — RFP 106%, up 9%. National Service Ministry takes over recruiting from War Office. **Coal rationing in force.** Taxi fares up 75% for 1st mile. (Nov) Films released on Women's Land Army, Chinese & S African Native Labour contingents. Prisoners' bread ration cut to 11½ oz pd. **France** — 1st of 311 British Munitions Ministry locomotives arrives. **Turkey** — (Nov) 3 meatless days pw in Constantinople; bread over double Jan price. **Russia** — Finnish Diet meets, declares its supreme power (15); elects 11-man Senate (28, *see* 14). **USA** — (Nov) Union Carbide & Carbon Corporation formed & swamped with war orders. Farm prices 31% up on 1916. **Germany** — (Nov) Belgian PoW Lt Bastin escapes to Holland from Ingolstadt Ft 1X, a 10th escape attempt.

NOVEMBER 1917	WESTERN FRONT 1	EASTERN FRONT 2	SOUTHERN FRONTS 3	TURKISH FRONTS 4
Thu 1 contd				
Fri 2		**Petrograd** — Expected Bolshevik demo does not happen.	**Isonzo** — Austrian 55th (Bosnian) & German 12th (Silesian) Divs cross Tagliamento via damaged rail bridge at Cornino & a footbridge at Pinzano (night 2/3).	**Mesopotamia** — Battle of Daur on Tigris 85 miles N of Baghdad: Cobbe's 14,500 men (224 cas) & 58 guns storm Turk 51st Div's 2 lines (c260 cas) after 19-24-mile night advance. **Palestine** — 6 Turk bns compel Newcombe's surrender. Turk Seventh Army counter-attacks DMC 10 miles N of Beersheba (-7).
Sat 3	**First 3 AEF US troops killed & 11 made PoWs in German storm coy trench raid** (*see* 20). **Aisne** — French patrols reach S bank of R Ailette.	**Baltic Provinces/W Russia** — Fraternization.	Cadorna informs Rome he will retreat behind R Piave & hints at separate peace. **French 64th & 65th Divs begin arriving W of L Garda** (-5, *see* 12). **Germans refuse any more divs for Italy.**	
Sun 4	**Flanders** — Trench raids. **Verdun** — Arty in action N of Chaume Wood. German attack there (7), repulsed (10), French success there (19,*see* 25).	**Petrograd** — Bolshevik Military Revolutionary Ctee tells garrison (155,000) to ignore orders to go to Front.	Austrians take 10,000 PoWs & 24 guns cut off S of Tolmezzo from Italian XII Corps (Tassoni) (-5) retreating from Carnia. Italians begin retreat from Tagliamento to Piave (night 4/5), after Austrian Isonzo armies force crossings.	**Mesopotamia** — Maude orders attack on Tikrit as Turk radio reveals evacuation.
Mon 5		**Petrograd** — Kerensky calls loyal troops from suburbs, closes 2 Bolshevik newspapers, portrayed as 'counter revolution'.	At Rapallo conference Italians ask for 15 Allied divs, but settle for 11 (*see* INT'L EVENTS 7). Temporary British C-in-C Italy Lt-Gen Lord Cavan arrives at Pavia with ADC Prince of Wales, sees Cadorna (6) & agrees to concentrate around Mantua not Milan (*see* 13). Most Italian troops stand behind R Livenza to let Fourth Army come down from N.	**Mesopotamia** — **Battle of Tikrit:** Cobbe (1801 cas) storms 6-mile Turk line aided by 13th Hussars' 2 charges. 6000 Turks lose est 1500 (137 PoWs) & retreat (-6) destroying SS *Julnar*. **Palestine** — Kress begins Gaza's evacuation. Falkenhayn reaches Jerusalem.
Tue 6	**Flanders** — **Canadians** (2238 cas) **capture Passchendaele** after 0600 assault by 0900; also Goudberg & Mosselmarkts with 464 PoWs. French I Corps captures Merckem.	**Petrograd** — 3 Don Cossack regts decide not to back Kerensky. Bolsheviks seize railway stns, bridges, state bank & telephone exchange. Lenin arrives at Smolny Institute HQ.	Gen Giorgio's Special Corps' rearguard action at Sacile. British 23rd & 41st Divs entrain for Italy (-17, *see* 11), 4 divs by 25.	**Palestine** — 17,000-strong XX Corps (1300 cas) storms central Turk Sheria position (c4000 men + c40 guns) without prelim barrage, takes 600+ PoWs & 12 guns. **Hejaz Railway** — Lawrence & c100 Arabs cross S of Deraa but lose explosives for Tell-el-Shehab rail bridge (*see* 12).
Wed 7		**Petrograd** — Kerensky leaves by car to find loyal troops, other ministers in Winter Palace (1000 troops) surrounded by 18,000 Reds. Red cruiser *Aurora* signals bombardment from 2210.	Cadorna issues final Order of the Day 'We have taken the inflexible decision to defend here...from the Piave to the Stelvio [Pass]...To die and not to yield !'.	**Palestine** — **Allenby occupies Gaza** & pursues 8 miles N, (already has 4255 PoWs, 59 guns & 84+ MGs for 9650 cas).
Thu 8	Arty actions in many sectors. Successful British trench raids nr Fresnoy & Armentières.	BOLSHEVIK REVOLUTION: Red Guards overrun Winter Palace at 0100. c1800 Red sailors arrive by train from Helsinki.Military Revolutionary Ctee cables all fronts to accept revolution or face arrest. **Lenin elected Chm, Council of**	At Peschiera British & French urge Cadorna's removal, King replies already decided & that Piave line will be held. Bulk of Italian Fourth Army (9 divs) from Dolomites joins First & Third Armies (21 divs) on Piave line. Austrians occupy Vittorio	**Palestine** — Action at Huj: 158 Yeomanry (66 cas) charge & overrun Turk rearguard taking 11 guns. 52nd Div (702 cas) storms Sausage Ridge at 5th attempt.

AFRICAN OPERATIONS 5	SEA WAR 6	AIR WAR 7	INTERNATIONAL EVENTS 8	HOME FRONTS 9
	says in Parlt 4500 ships convoyed safely to & from Norway since Apr. (Nov) HMS *Wakeful* first of 23 W-class destroyers (ordered Dec 1916) completed (-Oct 1918), 16 modified W-class launched Jan 1918-11 Nov 1919.			
	N Sea — RN light force covered by battlecruisers *Glorious* & *Repulse* sweeps into the Kattegat (*see* 17); destroyers sink German decoy ship *Kronprinz Wilhelm* off Kullen Light (*see* 17).		BALFOUR DECLARATION. Jewish-Arab London Rally welcomes (30). Lansing-Ishii Agreement: **US recognizes Japan's special interests in China.**	
	Channel — British submarine *C15* sinks *UC65* (top 1917 sinker with 103 ships worth 112,859t) off Dartmouth, last of 6 RN submarine 1917 U-boat kills.		Anglo-French-Italian Agreement pools tonnage for food programme (*see* 5 Jan 1917).	
			Ludendorff vetoes Austro-German Foreign Minister Agreement, insists on German slices of Poland (-6). British White Paper on Anglo-German exchange over alleged misuse of British hospital ships.	**Britain** — Fixed butter prices extended to all brands (6 & 13). Railway wage increases.
Linforce resumes advance & occupies Mahiwa. Kilwa Force resumes advance (7).		**W Front** — 4 RFC Camels get lost & come down nr Namur & Rheims (1 pilot escapes into Holland after burning plane).		**Britain** — Churchill memo to War Cabinet on 'Duplication & Waste of Effort' especially on home defence. **USA** — New York 1st E Coast State to grant women vote.
	Baltic — Bolshevik cruiser *Aurora* (retained 5) lands some of her 522 sailors to seize Nikolai Bridge in Petrograd. Revolution at Petrograd climaxes with searchlight assisted (but inaccurate) shelling of Winter Palace (*see* E FRONT). Minelayer *Amur*, 2 minesweepers, 2 steamers, and 5 small craft arrive from Kronstadt with 3800 sailors (c9700 in capital) & 950 soldiers. 4 destroyers sail from Helsinki to back Lenin (2 arrive 7) despite C-in-C's protest.		**Allied Rapallo Conference** (-9, Anglo-French PMs left for Italy 4) **agrees on Supreme Allied War Council** (9, *see* 27).	
Linforce Nigerians (150 cas) drive Wahle rearguard from Mkwera Hill & take 1 MG, more skirmishes (-10).	**Adriatic** — Italians request 20 Allied destroyers to counter feared post-Caporetto Austrian naval offensive, Jellicoe & French can spare none (*see* 13, 16 & 21). **Germany** — Scheer report to Capelle argues only more U-boats can redress	**Palestine** — RFC destroy 9 German planes in airfield attacks (-9), have ranged 126 targets (1-7), drop c700 bombs (7-14) on other targets (*see* 28).	BOLSHEVIKS SEIZE POWER IN PETROGRAD. Trotsky Commissar for Foreign Affairs. E House US Mission arrives in London (sees War Cabinet 20).	**Russia** — Congress of Soviets approves Commissars of the People inc Rykov (Interior) & Stalin (National Minorities). Civil Service strike v Reds (strikers arrested & drafted 27). Reds seize Yaroslavl, Kazan & Samara on Volga & Vladimir.

NOVEMBER 1917	WESTERN FRONT 1	EASTERN FRONT 2	SOUTHERN FRONTS 3	TURKISH FRONTS 4
Thu 8 contd		**People's Commissars**. Reds occupy Kremlin but Cossacks retake Minsk (*see* 19).	Veneto & make it HQ Fourteenth Army (9). **Fayolle made French C-in-C** in place of Duchêne, arrives (21).	
Fri 9	**Flanders** — British Second Army HQ moves to Italy (*see* S FRONTS 6), Rawlinson replaces Plumer i/c Flanders sector (*see* 20 Dec).	4m copies of Bolshevik Peace Decree sent to Front. Kerensky occupies Gatchina (28 miles S of capital) with 600 wavering Cossacks, having reached Gen Krasnov's III Cav Corps HQ at Ostrov (8).	**Gen Diaz succeeds Cadorna as C-in-C**, with Badoglio senior of 2 sub CoS. **Piave** — Rommel fords upper river & with help captures 8000 Italians & 20 guns at Longarone (night 9/10, *see* 18 Dec). Italian front 75 miles (180 miles on 24 Oct) but only 33 divs not 59. Last 3 Italian divs cross river (-10) & bridges blown. Conscript class of 1899 arriving. **Trentino** — Austrians reoccupy Asiago.	**Palestine** — Panic in Turk Eighth Army HQ & rear but thirst slows British pursuit. Anzac Mtd Div bde takes 984 PoWs & 210 wagons in 16-mile ride that meets XXI Corps from Gaza.
Sat 10	**Flanders** — **Second Battle of Passchendaele ends**: 1st Cdn Div (1094 cas) advances 500yds N along main ridge E of Passchendaele-Westroosebeke highway despite 3 German counter-attacks, over 500 guns opposing and air attacks. Allied advance since 31 July 4½ miles.	Kerensky occupies Tsarskoe Selo. Street fighting in Moscow (-15). Arthur Ransome reports in *Daily News*, 'It is folly to deny ... that the Bolsheviks do hold a majority of the politically active population.'	**Trentino** — Conrad attacks but Italian First Army in skilful withdrawal retains key ground (-14). Krauss' Austrians occupy Belluno, reach Feltre (12).	
Sun 11	MONS CONFERENCE between Ludendorff, Wetzell (principal *OHL* strategist), Kuhl (CoS Army Gp Rupprecht), & Schulenberg (CoS Army Gp Crown Prince). **Ludendorff proposes great offensive on W Front** in 'New Year' (*see* 20). **Flanders** — Cdn cas since 26 Oct 12,924 (22 PoWs & 1171 gassed). **Alsace** — French repulse raid at Harmannsweilerkopf.	**Bolsheviks crush Cadet 'Bloody Sunday' rising in Petrograd** & take Krasnoyarsk.	**Piave** — FIRST BATTLE OF THE PIAVE (-30 Dec). Austrians gain small bridge-head at Zenson (night 12/13, *see* 15) 17 miles from river mouth, 20 miles NE of Venice & occupy islands in river (13). Archduke Eugene moves HQ from Klagenfurt to Udine. First 2 British divs (23rd & 41st) begin arriving in Mantua area (-21).	
Mon 12		12,000 Bolsheviks (esp sailors) halt Kerensky's 700 Cossacks & 1 armoured train nr Pulkovo Observatory; they retreat to Gatchina.	**Italy** — 3 French divs move from Brescia to Vicenza nearer front, 46th & 47th Divs of *Chasseurs d'Alpin* arrive (since 5); *see* AIR WAR.	**Palestine** — Falkenhayn drives back Australian Mtd Div 4 miles with 5000 Turks (10,000 rallied at Ramleh 10). **Hejaz Railway** — Lawrence mines troop train at Minifer, captures 60 rifles (*see* 23).
Tue 13	**Flanders** — German bombardment & inf assault on Ypres Salient fail. Belgian trench raid SE of Nieuport. **Champagne** — German trench raids nr Reims.		**Italy** — Gen **Plumer** arrives at Mantua to take over as **British C-in-C** (appt 10) 423 Italian bns (33 divs) & 3500 guns v 736 Austro-German bns (55 divs) & 4500 guns (*see* 25). **Trentino** — Austrian 1st Mtn Bde enters Primolano, Brenta valley, takes Mt Tonderica (15). Italians forced off Gallio heights but hold Mt Sisemol.	**Palestine** — Allenby attacks towards Jctn Stn (Jerusalem railway) with 25,000 men & 136 guns v 9000 Turks & c60 guns. 800 Yeomanry (130 cas) charge & storm El Mughar Ridge & village, take 1000+ PoWs, 2 guns & 14 MGs.
Wed 14	**Flanders** — British consolidate NW of Passchendaele. German attacks N of Menin Road & NE of Passchendaele (15). Relief of Cdn Corps begins (-20) after 15,654 battle cas since c18 Oct.	Kerensky's troops change sides, but he escapes disguised as sailor, hides in forest cottage nr Luga for 40 days.	**Salonika** — British begin 50-mile Stavros light railway, with 4000 Turk PoWs in batches from Cyprus, to replace uncertain shipping service from Salonika (completed May 1918). **Trentino** — Conrad & Krauss' Austrians link up at Fonzaso.	**Palestine** — British 75th Div & armoured cars occupy Jctn Stn. NZ Mtd Bde beats 1500 Turks at Ayun Kara. **Falkenhayn orders general retreat, his 2 armies split.**
Thu 15		**S Russia** — Alexeiev arrives at Don Cossack capital Novocherkask, but Kaledin says Cossacks unwilling to fight so he moves to Kuban Cossack capital Ekaterinodar.	**Piave** — German 117th Div gets 4 bns across nr Ponte di Piave (night 15/16) but wiped out by 3 Italian bdes who take 600 PoWs (-16); **first Italian success since Caporetto**. Below & Boroevic cease crossing attempts, although 41st Hungarian Div crosses river delta & captures Cava Zuccherina, 16 miles of lagoon	**Palestine** — Anzac Mtd Div occupies Ramleh & Ludd. Yeomanry charge v Turk rearguard at entry to Judean Hills.

AFRICAN OPERATIONS 5	SEA WAR 6	AIR WAR 7	INTERNATIONAL EVENTS 8	HOME FRONTS 9
	setbacks.			
			Petrograd Telegraph Agency broadcasts Bolshevik peace conditions (Germany refuses to publish but press do, 12). **Neutrals** — Uruguay seizes 8 German ships at Montevideo. **Austria** — Tsar Ferdinand of Bulgaria visits Trieste.	**Britain** — 500,000 unskilled munition workers demand 12% bonus (granted 22).
Kilwa Force takes Ndanda Mission Stn (62 German civilians).			Austria's Count Czernin urges Kühlmann to accept Bolshevik offer publicly but he declines (11, *see* 17). **Secret War** — German Treasury agrees to provide RM15m to Bolsheviks via Stockholm (*see* 16).	**France** — Central Foodstuffs Office established. **Canada** — 21,568 have reported for military service & 310,376 applied for exemptions since 13 Oct call-up.
Linforce occupies Nangoo, takes last *Königsberg* gun & meets Kilwa Force.	**E Med** — *UC38* (Wendlandt), 1 of 3 U-boats sent to help Turks since 31 Oct, sinks British monitor *M15* (26 dead) & destroyer *Staunch* off Gaza, rest of sqn retire to Port Said. **USA — First of 247 fast flushdeck, four-funnel destroyers launched** (-11 Apr 1921) USS *Little* (serves at Queenstown, Ireland 1918).			**Russia** — 8hr working day declared. Reds control Saratov on Volga.
	Adriatic — Kaiser visits Pola & Med U-boat Flotilla (5 UB boats en route). Austrian sorties v Italian Brindisi-Valona route foiled by bad weather (& 22).	**Italy — Allied air reinforcements**: RFC Nos 28 (Camel) & 34 (RE8) Sqns reach Milan (& 14, left France 7, No 66 Sqn follows 17), No 42 Sqn leaves 26/27, No 45 11-12 Dec (*see* 29). They become operational 28 Nov-21 Dec.	Lloyd George speaks in Paris, Supreme War Council vital (& in Commons 14 &19) 'We have won great victories. When I look at the appalling casualty lists I sometimes wish it had not been necessary to win so many.'	**Britain** — New voluntary ration scale issued. **Canada** — 4th War Loan. **Russia** — Lenin's 1st radio broadcast.
	Med — Adm Calthorpe reports to Admiralty on maritime implications of Italy making separate peace: Anglo-French must seize her 35 destroyers; Otranto Barrage to be maintained from Corfu & Albania. Contingency planning & organization continues incl approach to French 10 Dec (-11 Apr 1918).	**France** — Germans bomb Calais (earlier raids 20, 21 & 24 Oct).	Venizelos in London.	**Russia — Lenin appeals to Party to seize whole country**. Reds control Smolensk after defeating Cossacks (also capture Tashkent 14). **Britain** — Thomson reassures War Cabinet no German link with pacifists, boredom main motivation (*see* 22). **France** — Painlevé Ministry defeated 186-279, resigns (14, *see* INT'L EVENTS 16).
1/3rd KAR (Kilwa Force) captures Mwiti Ridge.			French PM Painlevé & Foreign Minister Barthou resign after losing vote (*see* 16).	**Finland** — Workers General Council declares general strike & Red Guards (mobilized 10) run amok (-21).
Giffard's 1/2nd KAR takes Chiwata with 606 PoWs & liberate 67 British PoWs after Lettow's evacuation.		Japan declines British request for 2 battlecruisers to join Grand Fleet.		**Russia** — Reds win fight for Kremlin. **France** — Morale report on soldiers on leave 'All signs of despondency have disappeared'. **Ireland** — 102 hunger strikers released (-21). **USA** — Fuel Administrator bans electric signs on Sundays & Thursdays.

NOVEMBER 1917	WESTERN FRONT 1	EASTERN FRONT 2	SOUTHERN FRONTS 3	TURKISH FRONTS 4
Thu 15 contd			from Venice (*see* SEA WAR 16).	
Fri 16	**Flanders** — Arty duels round Passchendaele.	**Baltic Provinces** — Courland National Council declares itself autonomous Latvia (*see* 27 Dec).		**Palestine — NZ Mtd Bde occupies Jaffa** & Australian Mtd Div Latrun. Turk Eighth Army behind R Auja to N.
Sat 17	Anglo-French trench raids on Flanders, Somme & Champagne fronts.	Gen Dukhonin orders no more troops be sent to Petrograd. 54,000 now in W Front ctees alone. **Rumania** — Enlarged Transylvanian Corps formed at Hirlau.		
Sun 18	Arty duels on various fronts. Pétain tells war ctee 'The situation...remains complex and imprecise'. **Somme** — German raids NW of St Quentin.		Krauss' Austrians & German *Jäger* Div attack Mt Grappa sector (-22) between R Brenta & Piave, take 1286 PoWs (18). **Albania** — Austrians attack in S & try to cross R Voyusa 12 miles N of Valona, attack Italians (22) & force R Osum (night 25/26).	**Mesopotamia** — †**Maude of cholera in Baghdad** aged 53. Lt-Gen Marshall succeeds, has 69,500 men & 302 guns nr Baghdad (total MEF 254,924 + 158,428 followers). **Palestine — Allenby resumes ops v Jerusalem** (-24) with 14,500 men & 18 guns v c5900 Turks & 50 guns. British enter Judean Hills as winter rains begin (19, Falkenhayn moves HQ from Jerusalem to Nablus).
Mon 19	**Flanders** — German trench raids on British sector. **Cambrai** — British Tank Corps, moved up by train, begins to move to start line (night 19/20). **Lorraine** — Capt Patton joins US Tank Corps (*see* 8 Jan 1918).	HM Ambassador Buchanan's diary 'At the moment force alone counts'. **W Russia** — Bolshevik armoured train retakes Minsk.		
Tue 20	Kuhl memo to Ludendorff on an offensive in Flanders. **Cambrai** — BATTLE OF CAMBRAI (-3 Dec). FIRST MASSED TANK ATTACK: Reinforced British Third Army (Byng) with 19 divs & entire Tank Corps led by Brig-Gen Elles in 'Hilda' launch surprise attack without prelim shelling on Hindenburg Line. 389 tanks (179 lost, 65 to gunfire) debouch from assembly points at 0620, flatten German wire, rout front line inf **& open breach nearly 6 miles wide & up to 4000yds deep.** They **capture 4200 PoWs, 123 guns & 281 MGs for 4000 cas.**	**Bolsheviks declare Ukrainian People's Republic.**	**Piave** — Austrians take Mt Fontanasecca at start of week-long fighting. **Italy** — Two last French divs (23rd & 24th) arrive (-22). Foch leaves for Paris (23).	**Palestine** — 75th Div storms 3 ridges aided by mist, gets 5 miles N of Jerusalem (21), but Yeomanry Div expelled from Zeitun Ridge.

AFRICAN OPERATIONS 5	SEA WAR 6	AIR WAR 7	INTERNATIONAL EVENTS 8	HOME FRONTS 9
Belgians engage Tafel's rearguard at Lukundi, S of Linwale, in last action.	**N Sea** — RN *K1* steam submarine has to be sunk after colliding with *K4* in Grand Fleet sweep (*see* 31 Jan 1918). **France** — **Clemenceau appoints Georges Leygues Marine Minister** (for duration). **Adriatic** — 2 old Austrian battleships & 14 torpedo-boats shell Italian Cortellazzo coast guns nr Piave mouth (*see* 28; 10 & 19 Dec). Italian 15-in gun monitor *Alfredo Cappellini* wrecked off Ancona.		**Secret War** — Bolshevik Vorovski in Stockholm telegrams Berlin 'Please fulfill your promise immediately' (ie more funds for peace talks). **Clemenceau new French PM & War Minister**, Pichon Foreign Minister.	**Brazil** — War law especially v domestic German interests. State of siege in capital & 6 states, c700 aliens (mainly German reservists) arrested. **Britain** — Chm of Air Board Lord Cowdray resigns, Lord Rothermere succeeds (26). **USA** — **Enemy alien registration required**, 600,000 affected, expelled from Washington & barred from military places (over 200,000 investigated).
KAR & Nigerians (last 38 cas) win fight at Lutshemi despite 2 disabled guns. Lettow at Newala picks his force to invade Portuguese E Africa.	**N Sea — Last cruiser action off Heligoland**: Vice-Adm T Napier's battlecruisers *Glorious, Courageous* & *Repulse*, 8 cruisers & 10 destroyers chase 4 German lt cruisers (covering & smokescreening minesweepers) for 2hrs firing 147 15in shells until battleships *Kaiser* & *Kaiserin* appear & dense fog intervenes. Germans suffer 7 hits, Adm Reuter's flagship cruiser *Königsberg II* (31 cas) hit by *Repulse*; *Pillau* hit by *Courageous*. RN ships suffer 5 hits incl cruisers *Caledon* & *Calypso* hit (Capt H L Edwards k) (*see* 12 Dec). **E Atlantic — First US Navy U-boat kill**: convoy escort destroyers *Fanning* & *Nicholson* sink *U58* off Milford Haven (*see* 6 Dec). **Russia** — Pro-Soviet Capt Modest V Ivanov made Asst Navy Minister (Lenin sees him 14). Supreme Naval Board formed 20.		Kühlmann complains that Czernin discussing Bolshevik proposals with Turks & Bulgars (*see* 19 & 29). Rumanian King cables London for Allied help to take Army through S Russia to Mesopotamia, otherwise terms possible with Central Powers (*see* 21).	**Russia** — 5 Pro-Socialist Co-operation Bolshevik leaders leave Central Ctee after Lenin speech. Trotsky takes over empty Foreign Ministry. Tsaritsyn goes Bolshevik. **USA** — Film *The Zeppelin's Last Raid* showing.
Nigerians take hospital with 959 PoWs & liberate 32 Allies 18 miles SE of Chiwata.	**Med** — U-boat sinks sloop/Q-ship *Candytuft* (9k). **Baltic** — Russian Gulf of Finland mine sinks *UC57*. **Britain** — Jellicoe memo to War Cabinet '...our naval policy is necessarily governed by the adequacy of our destroyer forces'. **N Sea** — RN *P57* rams & sinks *UC47* (sank 52 ships worth 65,884t in 1917) off Flamborough Head.		Churchill leaves for Paris to meet French & Italian Munition Ministers (-21 & 29 Nov-4 Dec).	**Turkey** — Parlt debates Civil Service pay plight, it gets special tax exemption.
			Bolsheviks call for immediate armistice on all fronts (*see* 29 & 30). Italy successfully asks Britain & France for 300,000 rifles, 4000 MGs, 640 guns & 40 tanks.	**Britain** — Cement exports to Holland stopped (*see* INT'L EVENTS 11 Oct).
Giffard's 1/2nd KAR takes 127 PoWs at another camp. 900 Portuguese arrive at Ngomano. Lettow dismantles Newala radio stn & begins march S to R Rovuma.		**Cambrai** — RFC concentrates 289 aircraft in 15 sqns to support Third Army and first mass tank thrust v only 78 German planes; 4 sqns (13 aircraft FTR or wrecked, 13 damaged by ground fire) fly ground attack 45 min after assault & 20 Camels (4 FTR) & Pups attack 4 of 6 targeted airfields. Air observers fail to report German btys at Flesquières, one pilot in error reports village captured before 1100.	Clemenceau's 'War, nothing but war' speech in Chamber (Churchill watches).	**France** — Clemenceau wins Chamber vote (418-65). **Britain — Commons disenfranchizes conscientious objectors.** Food position serious due to French & Italian harvest failures.

NOVEMBER 1917	WESTERN FRONT 1	EASTERN FRONT 2	SOUTHERN FRONTS 3	TURKISH FRONTS 4
Tue 20 contd	Tank Battle Drill with 4 of 5 inf assault divs works as trained, but 51st Highland Div halt before key central Flesquières sector (39 tanks lost, *Unteroffizier* Krüger's gun knocks out 7) & cav fail to get up in time. 107th Inf Div (from E Front) is detraining at Cambrai when British attack. Germans blow up St Quentin Canal crossings. **Lorraine** — US 1st Div relieved from first trench stint (83 cas).			
Wed 21	**Cambrai** — British advance to Cambrai resumed and with 12 tanks captures Cantaing (300 PoWs) & Tadpole Copse; 2 tanks & 6th Div recapture Noyelles. At Fontaine-Notre-Dame they are only 2½ miles from Cambrai, but tiredness, fuel & ammo shortages telling. German 20th Div recaptures Moeuvres on N flank. **Aisne** — French storm salient on Craonne Plateau S of Juvincourt, beat off counter-attack (22).	Bolsheviks radio C-in-C Gen Dukhonin to negotiate armistice. Trotsky tells Petrograd Soviet 'We make a formal offer to commence peace negotiations and to conclude an armistice'.		
Thu 22	**Cambrai** — Germans recapture Fontaine-Notre-Dame.	**Lenin sacks Dukhonin for refusing to negotiate & makes Ensign Kirilenko C-in-C.** He leaves for N Front, his Order No1 ends 'Long live immediate peace!'.	**Piave** — **Crisis day in key Mt Grappa sector** as Austro-Germans storm onto Mt Tomba (3176ft), but Laderchi's IX Corps' final effort drives them off (1 Italian regt reduced to 400) & reserves consolidate (23). **Trentino** — Austrian mtn troops storm Mt Pertica from Monte Baldo *Alpini* Bn, but *Alpenkorps* & Austrian 50th Div fail to hold gains to E (-23). **Salonika** — 150 Bulgars raid British line at the Mamelon (night 23/24), L Doiran sector, causing 27 cas.	**Palestine** — Turks fail 3 times to regain Nebi Samwil Hill (2942ft) from 75th Div but it & 52nd Div fail at El Jib Height (-24). **Aden** — British take Turk post at Jabir, 15 miles N of Aden (British strength 7137-10,278 1 Oct 1917-1 Nov 1918).
Fri 23	**Cambrai** — **Battle of Bourlon Wood** (-28): British 40th Div attack, with 62 tanks (16 lost, 5 to German flak guns) & 432 guns v 200 German guns, reaches crest but fails to reach village. Byng promoted general.			**Syria** — Lawrence leaves Azrak after brief but traumatic arrest by Turks at Deraa, reaches Aqaba 26.
Sat 24	**Cambrai** — British fail to storm Bourlon Hill (Col Wade & party hold part of village (-26) & recover Fontaine-Notre-Dame; renewed attacks on 25-27 fruitless. Haig letter laments severe shortage of inf.		**Trentino** — Emperor Charles ends attacks in Asiago sector, Conrad's losses 15,030 (nearly 7000 sick) since 10.	**Palestine** — Anzac Mtd Div gains but loses 2 bridgeheads N of R Auja (-25, Turk loss 437, *see* 20 Dec).
Sun 25	**Cambrai** — German counter-attacks at Bourlon, British 40th Div loss now 4000 since 23, only 12 tanks in action. **Verdun** — French take 800 PoWs in Samogneux sector, success nr Hill 344 (27).	**W Russia** — Fraternization nr Baranovichi. Orsha railway jctn stops anti-Bolshevik troops going to Moscow.	**Italian Front** — Italian strength up 114 bns & 964 guns since 13 (*see* 2 Dec).	
Mon 26	**Flanders** — Arty duels round Ypres. **Cambrai** — 7 German divs & 500 guns now engaged.	Kirilenko sacks Gens Cherimisov (N Front) & Boldirev (Fifth Army, whose XIX Corps sends 3 armistice delegates to German lines.	**Trentino** — Austrian *Edelweiss* Div (only 2000 strong by 27) fails to capture Col della Berretta (*see* 12 & 14 Dec) v 2 Italian bdes, *Alpini* Val Brenta Bn & 60th *Bersaglieri*. Mt Pertica changes hands 7 times & is left fire-swept with both sides below summit. **Piave** —	

AFRICAN OPERATIONS 5	SEA WAR 6	AIR WAR 7	INTERNATIONAL EVENTS 8	HOME FRONTS 9
	Channel — Dover Straits deep minefield (Varne-Cap Gris Nez) **partially laid** with night illumination & 80-100 patrol vessels, but 21 U-boats get through (-8 Dec, *see* 19 Dec). **Med** — Allied naval conference in Rome (Weymss, Bon, Calthorpe, Revel): British offer 1200 mines & minelayers; French offer to send submarines to Upper Adriatic; Otranto Barrage to be reinforced.	**Cambrai** — German aircraft strafe BEF 62nd Div as it advances on Bourlon Wood (& 22). **Salonika** — Top German fighter pilot Lt Eschwege (20 victories), 'Eagle of the Aegean" k by explosive-packed balloon (3 British ones attacked since 28 Oct).	British War Cabinet decides to seek Cossack aid for Rumanians who are cabled to appeal direct (*see* 7 Dec).	
		Cambrai — 19 RFC pilots (8 aircraft lost or wrecked) attack German cols & positions; 3 German fighters shot down.	**Neutrals: Holland** — Protests v extension of German U-boat zone.	**Britain** — Navy voted 50,000 men (now 450,000). Thomson (Special Branch) promises National War Aims Ctee notice of all pacifist activities.
Zeppelin *L59* (left Jamboli, Bulgaria 21 with 15t supplies incl 30 MGs after vain attempts 13 & 16) turns back W of Khartoum during 95hr non-stop flight due to British message in German cipher from Newala radio stn. Returns to base after record 4200-mile flight (*see* AIR WAR 9 Mar 1918).		**Cambrai** — German lorry-mounted flak guns stiffen defence of Fontaine. 50 RFC aircraft (15 wrecked) support BEF ground attack, but Richthofen now i/c sector & shoots down DH5 in Bourlon Wood. 3 RFC day bomber sqns attack 6 targets.	Trotsky begins publishing Allied secret treaties in *Izvestia*.

US propaganda delegation sails for Europe. | **Russia — All class distinctions & civil ranks abolished. Britain** — Ship-building Council appointed. Church bells ring for Cambrai victory. |
| **Lettow crosses R Rovuma at Ngomano into Portuguese E Africa** 1 mile from Portuguese fort with 2000 troops, 3000 porters & 1 gun (-26). His attack takes fort, 700 Portuguese, 6 MGs, 30 horses & 6 days' rations. | **Germany extends U-boat barred zone** to 720 miles from Irish coast & area around Azores & Cape Verde Is (effective 11 Jan 1918). In Med 20-mile wide neutral corridor to Greece closed. | **Cambrai** — 12 No 49 Sqn DH4s fly first W Front raid on railhead E of Cambrai, but other units switched to routine strategic targets (-29). | | **Russia — Constituent Assembly elections** (-27): Bolsheviks win only 25% of vote, ie 9.8m of 36m with 225 delegates to 420 Socialists (20.75m votes, *see* 11 Dec). (**Last free elections till 1989**.) **Hungary** — 100,000 workers march in Budapest for peace & Russian Revolution.

Britain — Army pay raised to min 1s 6d pd (from 29 Sept); Navy by 2d to 6d pd. Successful Coventry strike by 50,000 aircraft workers for shop stewards' recognition (-3 Dec). King confers 20 VCs. **France** — 3rd War Loan opens, raises Fr10.2bn. |

NOVEMBER 1917	WESTERN FRONT 1	EASTERN FRONT 2	SOUTHERN FRONTS 3	TURKISH FRONTS 4
Mon 26 contd			Austrians secretly withdraw Zenson bridgehead (-2 Dec).	
Tue 27	**Cambrai** — Exhausted British disengage at Cambrai after Gds Div (with 32 tanks) driven back in Bourlon & Fontaine sectors. Ludendorff & Rupprecht confer at Le Cateau as 20 fresh German divs mass under Marwitz nr Cambrai: 'There never has been such an opportunity for a smashing counterstrike', says Ludendorff who insists all must be ready before 30 Nov as Cambrai a vital rail centre. **Britain** — War Office sanctions doubled Tank Corps estab of 18,462 (originally requested 13 Apr).	**Armistice delegates return with German consent in principle.** Next meeting 1 Dec.		**Palestine** — 15,800 Turks & c120 guns gain ground from Yeomanry & 54th Divs until reserves stabilize line (30).
Wed 28	**Cambrai** — 16,000 German gas & HE shells rain down on Bourlon Wood. **France** — AEF US First Army Staff College opens at Langres (3-month course).	Lenin/Trotsky radio telegram proclamation 'The Russian Army and the Russian people cannot and will not, wait any longer.' ESTONIA DECLARES INDEPENDENCE.	Austrians pause to renew offensive (-30, *see* 2 Dec). **Piave** — Italians shell Austrian boats on lower river.	**Palestine** — British railway now 7 miles N of Gaza.
Thu 29	**Cambrai** — British success W of Bourlon Wood.	**Rumania** — Russian guns foil German Trotus Valley ops.		
Fri 30	**Flanders** — Total German cas since 31 July: c400,000. **Cambrai** — GERMAN SURPRISE COUNTER-ATTACK BEGINS with 0830 barrage incl much gas shell: Second Army, reinforced to 20 divs, employs infiltration tactics & close air support, tested at Riga & Caporetto; 11 divs attack on 12-mile front in 2 sections salient Vendhuille-Bourlon Wood-Moeuvres and penetrate to La Vacquerie & Gouzeaucourt **capturing 6000 PoWs & 158 guns in advances up to 3 miles**; British Gds Div recapture latter, then 36 tanks arrive. British Army's youngest gen, Brig-Gen 'Boy' Bradford VC (GOC 186th Bde, 62nd Div) k by shell outside his HQ, aged 25. **France** — 129,623 AEF personnel in Europe. **Transfer of 42 German divs** (over 500,000 trops) from E Front and elsewhere to W **begins** (-21 Mar 1918).		**Macedonia** — Anglo-French arty destroy ammo dumps in Doiran sector & N of Monastir. **Piave** — British 41st Div begins relieving Italian 1st Div in Montello sector (*see* 2 Dec).	**Palestine** — 80 men of 74th Div bluff 450 Turks into surrender 10 miles NW of Jerusalem.
Sat 1 December 1917	**Cambrai** — British Gds Div & dismtd cav with 19 tanks recapture Gonnelieu SW of Cambrai & most of Gauche Wood but British 29th Div withdraws from Masnières salient. Heavy German attacks at Bourlon Wood. **Verdun** — German attack N of Fosses Wood, others fail to reach Avocourt & Forges (4, arty duels NE of city, (8).	Ex-C-in-C Dukhonin surrenders STAVKA to Second Army Bolsheviks. (Dec) Still 62 German divs on E Front.	Allied Versailles Conference includes Serb, Italian, Greek & British complaints v Sarrail (*see* 10). Franchet d'Esperey declines to replace him (2) so Pétain & Foch select Guillaumat (*see* 22). Italian strength in Italy, Macedonia & Albania (110,000) 1,859,500.	**Palestine** — Turk 19th Div's German-style storm bn destroyed attacking ALH & 52nd Div at El Burj. Kress hands over Eighth Army to Djevad Pasha. 2 Australian armoured cars liberate Hebron in 210-mile round trip (-2) looking for Turk agent (*see* 5).

AFRICAN OPERATIONS 5	SEA WAR 6	AIR WAR 7	INTERNATIONAL EVENTS 8	HOME FRONTS 9
215 Germans & 1100 followers of Tafel's foodless force from Mahenge surrender at Luatala to 120 Baluchis who beat off their attack (26) thanks to 25th Cav charge. Capt Otto & 25 men break through to Lettow.	**Baltic** — Russian destroyer *Bditelni* mined & sunk off Aaland Is by *UC78* minefield.	**W Front** — US Brig-Gen Foulois becomes chief of AEF Air Service succeeding Brig-Gen Kenly.	**Supreme Allied War Council appointed** (Gens Wilson, Foch, Cadorna & Bliss, Versailles). Trotsky warns Russia may be driven to separate armistice if Allies do not negotiate. Buchanan to Foreign Office 'Every day that we keep Russia in the war against her will does but embitter her people against us.' Franco-Brazilian Agreement to use 30 interned German ships for Allied food.	**Russia** — Lenin addresses Soviets Congress (23-28). Bolshevik decree on workers' control & agreement with SR. **Britain** — Buying foreign shares or currency forbidden. Trading With Enemy Act extended to enemy aliens interned in neutral countries. † Scottish woman Dr Inglis at Newcastle, heroic field hospital organizer on Serb and Russian fronts. **France** — Loire Dept strikes involve 25,000 by 30 (*see* 3 Dec). **USA** — Beer alcohol content reduced to 3%.
Tafel's main body of 1312 troops & c2200 porters surrender. GERMAN E AFRICA ALL IN BRITISH HANDS. K George V's telegram congratulates Deventer (30).	**Home Waters** — U-boat sinks British Elder-Dempster liner *Apapa* (77 lost). **Adriatic** — Austrian destroyers & torpedo boats shell coast railway nr Senigallia. **Britain** — WRNS founded (*see* HOME FRONTS 29).	**Palestine** — RFC drop 100 bombs on new German Tulkarm airfield (-29).		**Turkey** — All-female Constantinople robber band (destitute) discovered.
		Italian Front — First British flight over Italian lines (Montello area) shoots down 1 Austrian single-seater but fighter attacks prevent RE8 photo-recon. 500 US trainee pilots begin course at Foggia (28).	Allied Paris Conference (-3 Dec). **Lord Lansdowne *Daily Telegraph* letter urges compromise peace with Germany.** War Cabinet bars Bolshevik propaganda & suspends all warlike aid. **German Chancellor's speech welcomes Bolshevik peace offer.** Kaiser wires Kühlmann to try for Russian alliance 'in spite of everything' (*see* 3 Dec).	**Britain** — **WRNS for shore service begun** with *The Times* ad; no uniform till Jan 1918; 7000 recruited.
	Allied (standing) **Naval Conference formed** in London, creates co-ordinating Allied Naval Council incl politicians for first time (*see* 1 Dec). (Nov) **Allied & neutral shipping losses** to U-boats **lowest of 1917**, 126 ships (56 British with 376 lives) worth 289,095t (U-boat fig 302,599t incl 104,479t in Med; 8 U-boats lost. **90% of British ocean-going shipping now in convoy.**	**Cambrai** — At least 30 low-flying 'battle' aircraft support German advance in S, more in N. 10 Australian DH5s of No 68 Sqn assist British pm counter-attack. c50 RFC aircraft & as many German over Bourlon Wood, both sides strafe. 11 German aircraft lost, 7 British. **Macedonia** — French bomb Vardar valley & N of Monastir (*see* 16 Dec). **Britain** — Vickers Vimy T/E heavy bomber first flies. **Mesopotamia** — RFC bomb German Kifri airfield (night 30 Nov/1 Dec), but fail to check recon for Turks. **W Front** — *OHL* has 144 twin-engine bombers in 7 *Bogohl* (36 in *Bogohl 3* v England).	Austria accepts Bolshevik armistice offer as basis for peace proposals (*see* 3 Dec).	**Britain** — Nearly 1m working days lost, most since May. PoWs (all fronts) taken in Nov given as 26,869 with 221 guns. **Italy** — (Nov) Lira at record low of 43 to £, 47% devalued since 1914 but recovers.
	US CNO Benson promises Italian Marine Minister in London 5 5000t merchant ships & 2-3 tankers, minesweepers, tugs, small escorts & 5in guns. (Dec) **All U-boats withdrawn from Baltic** (last sinkings Oct). **US dreadnought div** of 4 battleships (Rear-Adm Rodman in *New York*) **joins Grand Fleet. W Med** — (Dec) 751 merchant ships arrive at Gibraltar, 252 coal, 56 handle cargo, 107 repaired.	**W Front — Record 4338 RFC aircraft serviceable. Egypt/ Palestine** — Record 692 RFC aircraft serviceable. **Cambrai** — RFC more active than Germans, 5 air combats cost 3 German & 1 British aircraft with 2 balloons. Greece — (Dec) First all-Greek recon/bomber escadrille (French-trained) formed, 3 other units created by Armistice.	**Allied Supreme War Council begins work** at Versailles (presents 1918 plans 13). Allied PMs decide no more supplies for Russia, but guarantee Rumania's monarchy & prewar territory & defer Polish question. Austrian *Neue Freie Presse* prints Ludendorff interview. Russian Revolution '... is the outcome of our victory .... we can conclude an armistice with Russia only when we are certain it will be	**Britain** — Women's Land Army now 7000. (Dec) Air raid film *London: British Fact and German Fiction* released. **Canada** — £70m subscribed to victory loan. **India** — NE Frontier Chin Hills punitive ops begin. **Turkey** — (Dec) temporary 20% price fall at illusory hopes of benefit from Russian peace. **Germany** — *Reichstag* votes RM15bn war credit.

DECEMBER 1917	WESTERN FRONT 1	EASTERN FRONT 2	SOUTHERN FRONTS 3	TURKISH FRONTS 4
Sat 1 contd				
Sun 2	**Cambrai** — Fierce fighting for high ground about La Vacquerie. Haig visits, orders Byng to choose 'good winter line'.	CEASEFIRE begins on dates fixed by local army cdrs. **Russian Armistice Commission crosses German lines** at Dvinsk & continues to Brest-Litovsk welcomed by German C-in-C Prince Leopold. Kornilov & 5 fellow generals (incl Denikin) escape from prison in Bykhov, head for Don by train (*see* 9).	**Piave** — Italian strength 552 bns + 86 Anglo-French as **3 British divs take over Montello sector** (-4, *see* 19) and 3 French Mt Tomba area (*see* 30), but not attacked as expected. **3 German divs ordered back to Germany**, 4 remain (*see* 11). **Emperor Charles suspends main offensive** though Trentino attack to go on.	**Gen Seeckt appointed CoS & adviser to Enver** at Constantinople.
Mon 3	**Cambrai** — British withdraw from La Vacquerie & bridgehead over canal E of Marcoing. **Ypres** — British gains SW of Polygon Wood. Haig warns his army cdrs: '... situation on the Russian and Italian fronts...the paucity of reinforcements which we are likely to receive will in all probability necessitate adopting a defensive attitude for the next few months. We must be prepared to meet a strong and sustained hostile offensive' (*see* 7).	Bolshevik mob murders Gen Dukhonin at Mogilev Stn. (Mannerheim passes through to Finland hrs later.) **Brest-Litovsk talks begin between Russia & all Central Powers** (-6*see* 13). CIGS cables Gen Ballard (Liaison Officer with Rumanian Army) to finance Kaledin 'up to any figure necessary'. **Rumania** — Russian C-in-C Gen Shcherbachev informs K Ferdinand of Mackensen's ceasefire approaches (*see* 9).	**Trentino** — 213 Austrian guns & mortars heavily bombard (mainly gas shell) Mt Sisemol-Mt Badenecche (-4).	**Mesopotamia** — 3rd Action of Jebel Hamrin: Egerton's 20,000 men & 116 guns + Col Bicharakov's 1000 Cossacks advance v 4400 Turks & 34 guns, occupy Sakaltutan Pass (4), take Kara Tepe (5), inflict 542 Turk cas for 219. **Palestine** — British 74th Div bn (286 cas) takes but loses Beit-Ur-el Foka. **Armenia** — War Cabinet decide to meet 'Any reasonable demands for money from Russian Caucasus Army.'
Tue 4	**Cambrai** — **Battle of Bourlon Wood ends**; British obliged to evacuate salient (night 4/5-7) by threat of renewed German attacks, and loathsome conditions created by unburied corpses, clouds of poison gases & pools of stagnant water.		**Trentino** — **Scheuchenstuel's Eleventh Army** (35 bns) **eliminates Mts Meletta-Badenecche salient** NE of Asiago (in 4hrs), taking 16,000 PoWs, 90 guns & 200 MGs (-5) helped by inadequate Italian gas masks & incompetent Gen Armani (later sacked); Italian 29th Div destroyed.	**Mesopotamia** — 7th Indian Div to leave for Palestine (-31). **Palestine** — Chetwode's XX Corps (10,500 & 142 guns) prepare new push for Jerusalem (-7, *see* 8).
Wed 5			**Trentino** — Conrad drives towards Foza, but delayed by *Bersaglieri-Alpini* rearguard.	**Palestine** — 1st British trains reach Ramleh. Mott's Detachment occupies Hebron, 17 miles S of Jerusalem.
Thu 6	**Cambrai** — German attacks round La Vacquerie.	RUMANIAN CEASEFIRE WITH CENTRAL POWERS (*see* 9 & 10). **Ukraine** - Antonov forms Red S Front (*see* 21). **Don** — French capt from Rumania meets Kaledin at Novocherkask and other White leaders later, reports hopes of new anti-German front exaggerated (*see* 9).	**Trentino** — Austrian 21st Rifle Div storms Mt Sisemol (2000 PoWs). **Italians consolidate new line farther S across Valstagna & Frenzela valleys** (*see* AIR WAR 8, 23).	
Fri 7	**BEF GHQ Intelligence predict German 1918 offensive** no later than Mar (*see* 17 Jan 1918). **Battle of Cambrai ends**: British 2-2½ miles in advance of 20 Nov line in N but have lost almost equal own ground in S (*see* HOME FRONTS 12). **France** — US 42nd 'Rainbow' Div arrives (from 26 states).	Official truce between Russia & Central Powers (-17).		
Sat 8	Germans make 225 trench raids v BEF (-21 Mar 1918), gain 62 unit identifications.	All hostilities suspended.		**Palestine** — **Advance on Jerusalem begins** despite heavy rain, 60th Div takes 2 villages, 297 PoWs, 3 guns & 12 MGs. Turk XX Corps (12,000 & c50 guns) evacuates Jerusalem (-9).

AFRICAN OPERATIONS 5	SEA WAR 6	AIR WAR 7	INTERNATIONAL EVENTS 8	HOME FRONTS 9
			observed'.	
Lettow captures Portuguese Ft Nanguari (food & ammo) in Ukula Hills on R Lugenda, has already split force into cols under Wahle & Göring.	**Channel** — *UB81* (1 survivor) mined & sunk off the Owers nr Portsmouth.	**Cambrai** — Only limited air ops (-6), 3 German aircraft shot down (2 by McCudden), 3 British with 2 missing.		
	N Sea — Adm Krosigk refuses to accept more unreliable sailors on shore at Wilhelmshaven...'the effort to strengthen and maintain morale on the ships must not lead to the collection of all the worst elements...(at) Wilhelmshaven. They cannot be either employed, supervised or segregated from shipboard crews'.	**W Front** — Spad-equipped Spa 125, aka *Esc Lafayette* , to be taken under AEF command from Feb 1910. **Italian Front** — No 34 Sqn moves to Istrana airfield W of Treviso, No 42 Sqn joins (7, begins ops 9, bombs Austrian San Felice airfield 15 & 16, *see* 26).	Allied Maritime Transport Council formed (Council for War Purchases & Finance 14). Trotsky threatens British arrests if Chicherin (un-recognized Soviet Ambassador) & Petrov not set free for Clyde agitation. Kühlmann replies to Kaiser that Russian alliance desirable after separate peace.	**USA** — War Savings & Thrift stamps go on sale. **Italy** — **Compulsory food rationing begins in Rome**. **Britain** — Voluntary food ration scale issued for all under 18. **France** — 7000 strikers close Saint-Etienne munitions factory (-5). **Britain** — 4 German PoWs briefly escape from Farnborough.
			Wilson message to Congress says peace will come when German people agree to a settlement of justice & reparation. **French Foreign Minister Pichon signs decree forming independent Czech Army**. US War Trade Board blacklists 1600 German firms in Latin America.	**Austria** — Emperor Charles Vienna Crown Council on Army split into Austrian & Hungarian forces, majority v & decision deferred till war ends. **Germany** — Ludendorff demands 10% production increase, blames decrease on high wages (*see* 8).
Lettow sends Capt Köhl's 5 coys & gun E from Nanguari to Mwalia-Medo district, keeping in touch by relay.	**Atlantic** — 23-ship convoy leaves Hampton Roads for Italy, arrives Gibraltar (c23) & met by 8 Italian destroyers.		Trotsky claims Russia wants general peace without secret diplomacy. **Neutrals** — Swiss-US Agreement for latter to supply 240,000t food till next harvest. **Austria** — Emperor Charles says ready for any peace retaining Dual Monarchy's integrity (*see* 7).	**Portugal** — Maj Paes & 1500 men overthrow Democrat Govt (-8) after 1350 cas. Paes PM, War & Foreign Minister (11) & Prov Pres of New Republic (28, *see* 8 Jan 1918). **Germany** — U-boat office opens in Berlin.
	US destroyer *Jacob Jones* torpedoed & sunk by *U53* off Scillies, 37 survivors (*see* 19). **Channel** — *U96* collides with *UC69* (sunk) off Cape Barfleur, latter sank 50 ships worth 88,138t in 1917.	**Britain** — 19 of 21 German (2 Giant) aircraft (2 shot down by AA fire, 1 missing) raid London, Kent & Essex in small hrs (36 cas incl 2 servicemen).	FINLAND DECLARES INDEPENDENCE (seeks Swedish recognition 29, Bolsheviks recognize 31). Count Czernin tells Hungarian delegation 'I see no difference between Strassburg & Trieste.' Djemal Pasha at Beirut reveals Sykes-Picot Agreement & 'taunts Hussein'. Anglo-Spanish Commercial Agreement.	**Canada** — **Halifax wrecked** by French munition ship explosion (4000t TNT), 2682 cas, 2 sq miles levelled, 25,000 homeless, est cost $40m. **USA** — Manacling of conscientious objectors ends but 142 get life imprisonment (last 31 set free Dec 1923). **France** — Loire Dept strikes end with union officials reinstatement & promise of negotiated wage rises (*see* 25 Jan 1918).
	N Atlantic — British 10th Cruiser Sqn paid off, its AMCs now too vulnerable to U-boat attack.		US DECLARES WAR ON AUSTRIA (Panama 10, Cuba 16). Austrian Ministers agree on peace with Russia without gains.	
		Italian Front — 150 Allied aircraft over Frenzela valley fighting, Trentino (*see* 26). Italian ace Baracca scores 3 victories, winning Gold Medal.	British Ambassador in Petrograd disclaims wish to interfere in internal affairs. **Ecuador breaks relations with Germany**	**Germany** — Ludendorff note to Govt calls industrial profits 'in the main, high beyond any justifiable measure' & praises British methods.

DECEMBER 1917	WESTERN FRONT 1	EASTERN FRONT 2	SOUTHERN FRONTS 3	TURKISH FRONTS 4
Sun 9		**Armistice** (Truce of Focsani) **between Rumania** (Gen Lupescu) **& Central Powers** (German Gen Morgan). **S Russia** — Soviet Commissars declare war v Cossack chiefs. Escaped generals, excl Kornilov, sent on to Kuban (see 20). First White Volunteer Army units, organized by Gen Alexeiev, parade at Novocherkask (see 12). **Finland** — Removal of Russian troops demanded.	**Piave** — Italians contain Austrian bridgehead on Lower Piave delta, more fighting (19 & see SEA WAR). Plumer tells Diaz British will not retreat even if Italians do.	FALL OF JERUSALEM: Mayor hands keys to Ptes Church & Andrewes (mess cooks), then to GOC 60th Div which storms Mt Scopus. Mott's Det occupies Bethlehem.
Mon 10	Pétain visits K Albert, 'deplores the inefficiency of the British Command. The troops are excellent but they have been clumsily used. The Americans lack discipline and experience' (see 13). **Cambrai** — British capture post E of Boursies (on Bapaume-Cambrai road). **Verdun** — Unsuccessful German attack on Chaume Wood (& 15).	Lenin drafts outline peace programme for negotiations. **Ukraine** - Red railway detachments defeat Kornilov N of Kharkov & nr Belgorod (13).	**Salonika** — **Clemenceau recalls Sarrail** who leaves 22.	**Egypt** — Port Said Italians form volunteer 1st Coy *Cacciatori di Palestina*.
Tue 11		**National Council proclaims Lithuanian independence** (see 16 Feb 1918). Russian Front forces sent v Don Cossacks. Commissar for Polish Affairs appointed.	**Piave** — Krauss (4 divs & 460 guns) attacks Mt Grappa ('Sacred Mountain') sector; German 5th Div storms Mt Spinoncia but can get no farther despite repeated attacks. Austrian 4th Div (from E Front) captures Col della Berretta (see 14).	**Allenby enters Jerusalem** on foot via Jaffa Gate with Allied parties inc Maj TE Lawrence & Lt-Col Wavell (film released at home Feb 1918).
Wed 12	Wetzell's Appreciation: 'the [German] offensive in the West and its Prospects of Success' (ie in spring 1918). **Somme** — Germans take out small salient between Bullecourt & Queant.	Bolsheviks fight Cossacks at Rostov, occupy it (14). Gen Kaledin retakes (15) with Alexeiev's Volunteer Army forcing local Reds to flee to Black Sea Fleet. Baltic-German Estonian nobility appeal for German help. Gen Count Kirchbach takes over German Eighth Army (Hutier to W Front).		**Djemal Pasha resigns as Gov-Gen of Syria & Arabia & as C-in-C Fourth Army** (see 25 Jan), returns to Constantinople.
Thu 13	Skirmishing on Flanders, Cambrai & Verdun fronts (& 23). Pétain persuaded not to resign after French council criticism of his defensive tactics (see 20 & 29).	Brest-Litovsk armistice negotiations resume.	After Austrian Czernin *status quo* peace hint (5), PM Orlando tells deputies in secret session Italy will fight on even if armies have to fall back to Sicily.	
Fri 14	BEF GHQ memo details defence in depth system to meet German 1918 offensive. **Flanders** — Germans capture part of British front trench nr Polderhoek Chateau.		**Piave** — Austrian 4th Div takes Col Captile on Brenta valley side but shell shortage postpones exploitation (see 18).	Allenby cables War Cabinet only minor early 1918 advances possible.
Sat 15	Kuhl memo to Ludendorff urges his *St George* scheme for a Flanders offensive since now fairly certain BEF unable to launch offensive until numerous US troops arrive. **Flanders** — Snow hampers ops. Since 15 June 77 German divs have	BREST-LITOVSK 28-DAY ARMISTICE (-14 Jan 1918) signed between Russia & Central Powers to begin noon (17). Fraternization centres fixed, week's notice of termination. Germans given police powers in Baltic		Allenby Order of the Day praises 60-mile advance on 30-mile front in 40 days. EEF losses 18,928 to 25,000 Turk (12,036 PoWs), 100 guns & 132+ MGs, 20+ aircraft. **Persia** — (c) Mutinies among Baratov's troops at Hamadan.

AFRICAN OPERATIONS 5	SEA WAR 6	AIR WAR 7	INTERNATIONAL EVENTS 8	HOME FRONTS 9
	Channel — Convoy escort trawler *Ben Lawer* rams & sinks *UB18* (sinker of 126 ships worth 128,555t, 1916-17).	**Palestine** — RFC No 14 Sqn (BE2cs) flies 50hrs despite rain & drops 100 bombs on retreating Turks. More ground attacks (-12).		
	Adriatic — 2 **Italian MAS boats** penetrate Trieste, *MAS9* (Lt Rizzo) **sinks Austrian battleship** *Wien*, worst Austrian warship loss so far (*see* 19, also 10 June 1918). **N Sea** — RNAS seaplanes bomb Bruges docks & airfields nr Ghent (& 24).		British War Cabinet decides CIGS will advise on Russian areas which 'showed a disposition not to accept Bolshevik rule' (*see* 14). **Neutrals: Sweden** — International Red Cross awarded Nobel Peace prize.	**Italy** — National Institution of Ex-Soldiers founded.
	E Atlantic — *U155* shells Funchal, Madeira (Portuguese I).		Balfour announces receiving German Sept peace proposals; no reply to Allied acknowledge-ment. **Neutrals: Sweden** — Bolshevik envoy Vorovski recognized at German request. **Switzerland** — (c) HM Berne Legation reports ex-Khedive of Egypt Abbas Hilmi in Constanti-nople canvassing Arab chiefs.	**Russia** — **Constituent Assembly meets at Petrograd** (-13) **till broken up by Bolsheviks. France** — Clemenceau demands removal of parlt immunity from ex-PM Caillaux (arrested 12) & 2 other deputies (done 22-23).
	N Sea — 4 German destroyers annihilate British Norwegian convoy, sink destroyer *Partridge*, damage consort *Pellew*, 6 merchant ships & 4 trawlers in 45mins (75 PoWs); 3 covering British cruisers arrive too late. 4 other German destroyers sink 3 convoy stragglers off the Tyne. Admiralty sails Norwegian convoys at longer intervals with stronger escorts (*see* 26).	**Ypres** — Gotha *Bogohl 3* unit loses CO Capt R Kleine shot down & k in daylight attack on Allied troops, Lt R Walter replaces.		**France** — **Worst civil railway disaster in history**, 543 k at Modane when train jumps tracks. **Britain** — Inquiry into Cambrai reverse ordered; *The Times* calls it 'One of the most ghastly stories in English history' (*see* W FRONT 15 Jan 1918). Commons votes £550m war credit (1917-18 total £2450m). **Russia** — Lenin proposes Stalin, Sokolnikov & Trotsky for *Pravda* editorial board.
	N Sea — *U75* sunk in mine nets off Terschelling (she had mined HMS *Hampshire* & drowned Lord Kitchener). **Adriatic** — 3 Austrian destroyers sortie v Valona-Otranto route but sight 4 Allied ones & retire (night 13/14). **E Med** — French ship *Paris II* sunk at Adalia (Anatolia).			**Britain** — First Lord of the Admiralty Geddes says U-boat menace held, shipbuilding improving but not yet replacing losses. **Italy** — Chamber secret session on war (Senate likewise 29).
	Naval Allied Council to be formed (ministers & CNSs). **Ionian Sea** — *UC38* (Wendlandt) sinks French cruiser *Chateaurenault* (10 lives lost, 1162 saved incl 985 troops for Salonika) in Gulf of Patras off Cephalonia. *UC38* (also sinker of 36 merchant ships worth 52,525t) then depth charged & sunk by convoy escort destroyers *Mameluk* & *Lansquenet*.		Lloyd George London speech 'No halfway house between victory and defeat' (*see* 17). British War Cabinet agrees to pay any sums required to Russians resisting Central Powers.	**Turkey** — Single members of 'Society for Finding Employ-ment for Women' (c15,000 members) must marry or lose job (those eligible listed in press *see* 9 Feb 1918). **Britain** — Home Office & MI5 decide not to prosecute in 41 subversion cases. **Local butter and margarine rationing begins** (*see* 14 July 1918). (Dec) **Local tea rationing begins** (1¹/₂-2oz per head pw), affects 17.5m.
		Macedonia — 29 Allied aircraft drop 1848lb of bombs on Bulgar Cestovo depots.	Turk Crown Prince Vahiddin (party inc Kemal) state visit to Germany (-5 Jan 1918). New Portuguese Govt backs Allies.	

DECEMBER 1917	WESTERN FRONT 1	EASTERN FRONT 2	SOUTHERN FRONTS 3	TURKISH FRONTS 4
Sat 15 contd	been transported to Fourth Army front (from Lille-Armentières road to coast) & 63 transferred elsewhere. **Verdun** — (Dec) Mangin restored to duty i/c French IX Corps.	Provinces.		Turks & Russians to evacuate according to Brest-Litovsk Armistice demarcation agreed at Mosul.
Sun 16	**Artois** — British success E of Avion.			
Mon 17	Haig & Pétain meet, latter accepts BEF extension to R Oise by end Jan 1918 (*see* 10 Jan), former sees GHQ-*GQG* relations as best he has known. Fighting nr Ypres-Comines Canal.	ARMISTICE FROM NOON.		**Arabia** — HMG give King of Hejaz written assurance of future Arab independence.
Tue 18		Kaiser in Kreuznach Crown Council approves Armistice terms. **Ukraine** — Ukrainian Rada rejects Red transit demands (Lenin ultimatum 17) mobilizes 19, cuts telegraph links (*see* 24).	**Piave** — Austrian 4th Div captures Mt Asolone (5315ft) with 2000 PoWs & view of plains below, **farthest Austrian advance**. Rommel's Württemberg Mtn Bn withdrawn from final but local & costly success (after German failure to take Mt Solarolo); he & CO receive *Pour le Mérite*.	
Wed 19			**Piave** — British arty in action (Montello). Italian counter-attacks v Mts Rertica & Asolone fail to gain ground (-21) until fog & thick snow end ops (*see* 14 Jan 1918).	**Palestine** — Heavy rain (-20).
Thu 20	Pétain Directive urges defence in depth (& 22) but not all generals comply. **Flanders** — Germans capture fog-shrouded British advanced post W of Messines.	**Don** — Kornilov arrives at Novocherkask, is made White C-in-C.	**Salonika** — British bn (13 cas) raids village NW of L Butkovo, taking 55 Bulgar PoWs (& c30k).	**Palestine** — Battle of Jaffa (-22): XXI Corps' 8100 men & 88 guns surprise cross R Auja (-21), take 259 PoWs & 5 MGs from 6200 Turks & 60 guns. 6 RN ships & 36 RFC planes aid 52nd Div 5-mile coast advance to Arsuf (22), Jaffa put out of Turk gun-range. 54th Div captures Bald Hill & 2 villages inland.
Fri 21	**Alsace** — Fierce clashes at Harmannsweilerkopf, Germans ejected.	Antonov, People's Commissar for War, made C-in-C 'for the struggle with counter-revolution'.		**Mesopotamia** — British Baghdad-Falluja (Euphrates) railway completed.
Sat 22	Lt-Gen Sir R Maxwell BEF QMG since Jan 1915 resigns; succeeded by Lt-Gen Sir T Clarke. Gen Debeney i/c French First Army (for duration). **Flanders** — Germans storm some British advanced posts on Ypres-Staden rail line, trench raid nr (29).	**Brest-Litovsk peace negotiations begin**. Rumanian troops occupy Bessarabia (*see* 10 Jan 1918). Independent Moldavian Republic proclaimed there (23).	**Salonika** — New Allied C-in-C Gen Guillaumat (aged 54) arrives, reads Milne his instructions (30) to protect Greece, then use her army in offensive (*see* 3 Jan).	
Sun 23		**Crimea** — Tartars appoint Regional Govt.	French Tenth Army C-in-C Fayolle informs Foch that Italians 'had recovered their	

AFRICAN OPERATIONS 5	SEA WAR 6	AIR WAR 7	INTERNATIONAL EVENTS 8	HOME FRONTS 9
	Bristol Channel — Sloop HMS *Arbutus* sunk by U-boat.			Britain — Lt-Col Freyberg VC condemns Sassoon's anti-war attitude to Lady Cynthia Asquith.
Lettow & HQ arrive at Chirumba (Mtarika), Portuguese Nyasa Co's stn.	**Med — Italian Navy ordered to economize stringently on coal & oil fuel** (c50,000t used pm & national stocks only c360,000t). **Pacific** — 2 US submarines collide in fog; *Carp* (F1) sinks with 19 crew.	**Mesopotamia** — RFC attack German Tigris airfield at Humr (& 27, 28, 2 German aircraft bomb Samarra RFC airfield 31/ 1 Jan 1918).	Count Hertling replies to PM's speech of 14 'It is not Mr Lloyd George who is the world judge, but history.'	**Russia — All Church property to be confiscated, religious teaching abolished**. Britain — Lord Rhondda says 'Food queues must be stopped', rationing probably inevitable. No post to neutrals, except to PoWs or under permit. Canada — Unionist Govt wins General Election.
	Baltic — C-in-C Razvozov & many officers leave Fleet during Armistice as Soviets intensify control (*see* 29).	**Britain** — 14 of 16 German bombers (1 Giant) attack SE England, 6 reach London. Total of 11,300lb bombs cause 97 cas & £238,861 property damage, worst since 8/9 Sept 1915 Zeppelin Raid. No 44 Sqn CO Capt Murlis Green MC achieves **first night fighter success v aircraft over Britain** in Sopwith Camel with 4 attacks over E London, forcing Gotha to ditch off Folkestone (armed trawler *Highlander* rescues 2 survivors); 2 other Gothas burnt after crash landing.	Trotsky appeals to Europe's 'oppressed peoples' after Brest-Litovsk armistice signing. **Secret War** — Smuts meets Austrian Mensdorff (ex-Ambassador to London) on separate peace chances (-19). At Geneva Lloyd George's Sec Philip Kerr meets Dr Parodi (Turkey).	**USA** — Congress approves 18th Amendment (Prohibition), submitted to 36 states & ratified by 16 Jan 1919. **Russia** — Only civil marriages recognized. Supreme Soviet of National Economy founded.
	Channel — New Dover Straits minefield claims first victim, *UB56* after Vice-Adm Bacon advised to start flare & searchlight surface patrol along it. **Adriatic** — 2 old Austrian battleships, 1 cruiser, 6 destroyers shell Italian Cortellazzo btys again, but big ships withdrawn to Pola (20), 3 old battleships mothballed after 28 to obtain personnel.	**Britain** — Air defences finally told of Giant bomber, codenamed Bertie, after its 8th raid.		
Jubaland — 1436 British & tribal levies resume ops v the Aulyehan (*see* 26).			Tentative German peace proposals through neutral legation in Washington. Serb Mission arrives in US.	**Austria** — Lower House adopts peace resolution. **Australia** — 2nd referendum again defeats conscription 1,181,747 v 1,015,159 votes; 1918 recruiting falls to c2500 pm (*see* 8 Jan 1918). **Russia — Bolshevik Cheka Secret Police founded** under Pole Dzerzhinski to 'fight counter-revolutionaries & saboteurs'.
			Lenin meets Col Robins of US Mission. Lockhart (ex-Cons-Gen Moscow) & other British propagandists for Russia meet Lloyd George.	**Italy** — 3500 munition plants v 125 in 1915. **Britain** — PM calls for higher food prod. Local rationing schemes authorized. Munitions Ministry empowered to restrict lighting.
	Britain — Jellicoe visits Beatty at Rosyth (latter meets Geddes at Edinburgh 27, *see* 26).	**Britain** — Several Gothas thwarted in raid on SE by bad weather (1 Gotha emergency lands S of Margate, burnt by crew), 3 Giants (1 diverts to Boulogne) merely drop bombs in sea off Kent.	Russian peace proposals (Czernin rejects most 25). **Occupied Belgium — Flanders proclaimed independent**.	**Italy** — Chamber approves Orlando's 'Resistance, nothing but resistance policy'. Told Italy has food for 13 days. **USA** — Ford receives order for 5000 Liberty air engines, only reached planned 50 pd prod in Nov 1918.
N Africa — Nivelle C-in-C French forces outside Morocco (confirmed 14 Oct 1918).	**Irish Sea** — Armed boarding steamer HMS *Stephen Furness* (101 lost) sunk by U-boat. **N**		Kaiser, visiting Second Army on W Front, says 1917 proof that God an ally of German people.	

DECEMBER 1917	WESTERN FRONT 1	EASTERN FRONT 2	SOUTHERN FRONTS 3	TURKISH FRONTS 4
Sun 23 contd			spirit and wanted to fight'. **Trentino — Conrad's final attempt to break through before winter snows,** promises soldiers winter at Bassano in plains below & Christmas Mass in Venice: After hurricane shelling incl gas (by 550 guns) Austrian Eleventh Army captures Col del Rosso (4183ft), Mt Melago & 3 other features in 2-mile advance, claims 9000 PoWs (-24).	
Mon 24		Austrians row with Bulgars at Brest-Litovsk. **Ukraine** — Battles at Tamarovka Stn & Oboyan (W of Kharkov), Sievers' Reds capture Lyubotin (25).	**Trentino** — Italian counter-stroke recaptures Mt Melago & Col del Rosso save summit. First heavy snow, a month late.	**Palestine** — Heavy rain & mud delay Allenby's advance N of Jerusalem, railways cut or flooded (-25), EEF animals on half-rations.
Tue 25		**Ukraine** — RNAS Armoured Car Sqn rear party disable remaining cars & guns after ugly confrontation with local Reds (*see* 16 Jan 1918).	**Trentino** — *Toscana* Bde & 5th *Bersaglieri* etc stiffen Italian line & repulse final Austrian attack.	
Wed 26	**Verdun** — German setback in Caurières Woods.	Bolsheviks break off Brest-Litovsk talks when Germans say Poland & Baltic States will become independent.		CIGS doubts Turkey can surrender due to German grip.
Thu 27	2nd conference between Ludendorff & army gp staff chiefs on 1918 offensive in the W. Gen Hutier, from E Front, takes over new Eighteenth Army at St Quentin.	**Baltic Provinces** — Riga Council declares Latvian independence from Russia & requests Kaiser's protection.		**Palestine — Turk counter-attack towards Jerusalem** fails 3 miles N astride Nablus road despite fresh 1st Div. Deciphered radio message warns Allenby & Chetwode before 24; 60th Div repels 8 Turk attacks; 10th & 74th Divs capture Zeitun Ridge & village in 4000yd advance. 33,000 British & 180 guns advance up to 6 miles v strong but flagging resistance by 20,000 Turks & c100 guns (28-30).
Fri 28	**Somme** — Both sides conduct raids N of St Quentin.	**Lenin attends Demobilization Congress which votes for Army's dissolution;** he requests 'revolutionary units' to hold front line.	Arz replies to Ludendorff (23), agrees his W Front 1918 spring offensive will be decisive & Austrian troops will be sent, once no longer needed in Russia.	
Sat 29	French V Corps cdr Gen Pellé writes to Thomas (ex-munitions minister) that only way to stop Germans is by pre-emptive Allied offensive & deplores 'awaiting' (30). Micheler also lobbies Poincaré (Dec).	**Old Russian Army ranks abolished**; decision in principle to organize new Red Army (*see* 2 Jan & 14 Feb 1918). Adm Kaiserling & German Military Mission arrive in Petrograd to discuss Armistice technical details. **Ukraine** — Red Guards capture Lozoyova & Pavlograd on Kharkov-Crimea railway, occupy Kharkov (31).		**Mesopotamia** — 18th Indian Div forming at Baghdad.
Sun 30	**Somme** — British 63rd Div recaptures parts of Welch Ridge (S of Marcoing), repulses counter-attacks (31).		**Piave** — French 47th Div (259 cas) recaptures Mt Tomba in 25min with nearly 1564 PoWs. Austrians forced to evacuate Zenso bend bridgehead, Lower Piave. **Salonika** — Sir R Ross urges min of 15,000 British malaria cases be sent home, 9000 repatriated by 30 Apr.	**Palestine** — Turk cas since 27: 1558+ (558 PoWs) & 9 MGs; EEF 1360, 1 armoured car & 2 MGs. Total Turk 1917 loss since 31 Oct : 28,443.

AFRICAN OPERATIONS 5	SEA WAR 6	AIR WAR 7	INTERNATIONAL EVENTS 8	HOME FRONTS 9
	Sea — 3 Harwich Force destroyers on Dutch convoy duty (*Torrent, Surprise* & *Tornado*) **sink on German minefield** N of Maas Light Buoy, 252 lives lost. Flotilla leader *Valkyri* egets home with broken back. Surviving destroyer *Radiant* rescues survivors (*see* 31).		**Secret War** — Anglo-French Paris Convention on spheres of influence in S Russia (British War Cabinet approve 26).	
Uganda — Coy of 1/6 KAR (ex-German askaris) recover much stock from Turkana raiders (-26, *see* 29 Apr 1918).	**Jellicoe resigns as First Sea Lord** at Geddes' request (made public 26). **Adm Sir W Wemyss succeeds**, Adm Sir S Fremantle replaces Oliver as DCNS; Bacon recalled from Dover Patrol (28, *see* 1 Jan 1918).		K Albert replies to Papal peace note. Czernin (Red delegate Joffe at Brest-Litovsk assures him over Tsar 26) to Emperor Charles 'Your Majesty must therefore get Poland in order to maintain parity [with Germany]'.	
British patrols pursue Germans 40 miles S of R Rovuma. Lettow receives Christmas dinner from his officers.	**Irish Sea** — RN sloop *Buttercup* & *PC56* (convoy escorts) ram & sink *U87*. Twice-victorious Q-ship *Penshurst* sunk by U-boat.		K George V to Lloyd George '... we must pray 1918 may bring us an honourable peace'.	**Germany** — British officer PoWs at Holtzminden raise £2289 for Red Cross. **Russia** — 1st All-Ukraine Soviet Congress elects ctee in Kharkov to take over. **France** — *774,000* conscripts in the factories and farms.
Jubaland — 502 KAR & levies disperse Aulyehan at Hagagabli, capture 1233 camels. By 20 Feb 1918 fines, 402 rifles & chiefs collected excl the leader.		**Italy** — Large air battle 18 miles N of Venice, 9 of 30-40 Austrian aircraft shot down bombing Istrana airfield (RFC hangars suffer minor damage, 2 Italian aircraft destroyed). Raids repeated nights 29/30, 30/31.	Ukraine tells Berlin she wants separate status at Brest-Litovsk peace talks.	US Shipping Board promises 5m tons in 1918.
Germans capture Portuguese Mt M'Kula Post.			Sir F E Smith emphasizes British solidarity in New York. Japan secretly decides v Vladivostok intervention, though her warships arrive (30).	**Russia** — Banks nationalized & search for hoarded gold ordered. **Germany** — *Simplicissimus* magazine cartoon hails Hindenburg as the German Balance. Kaiser and Ludendorff row in Berlin over Polish frontier details. Latter leaks resignation rumour to reinforce his position. **Brazil** — Conscription law for 21-30s only doubles Army to 60,000.
		Italy — Austrians bomb Padua (-30), cause 79 cas, bomb Treviso, Bassano, Vicenza & Castelfranco (31). **W Front** — RFC ace McCudden shoots down 3 LVGs in 20 min (4 kills 23).	French Foreign Minister Pichon outlines war aims (Italian PM likewise 31).	**USA** — Pres Wilson takes over railroads, McAdoo to be DG.
	Adm Kaiserling's German naval mission arrives in Petrograd.		**Neutrals: Holland** — 1st British PoW trainload arrives for internment.	**Britain** — National Labour Convention demands general rationing. Churchill letter 'I am strongly pressing that the cavalry shd be put by regiments into the Tanks'. Masterman of War Propaganda Bureau 'As a result of the double propaganda, 19 countries have declared war against Germany & 10 have broken off relationships with her'.
	E Med — British destroyer *Attack* mined & sunk off Alexandria by *UC34* while rescuing survivors of torpedoed troopship *Aragon* (610 lost). Fleet auxiliary *Osmanieh* sinks on another mine (31, 198 lives lost).		Trotsky appeals to Allied Govts to open peace talks.	Churchill declines French request for 200 of latest tanks by March 1918.

DECEMBER 1917	WESTERN FRONT 1	EASTERN FRONT 2	SOUTHERN FRONTS 3	TURKISH FRONTS 4
Mon 31	British took 1018 PoWs & 4 guns. 183,896 AEF personnel now in Europe.			**Secret War: Arabia** — Philby arrives at Jeddah from Kuwait in vain bid to reconcile Hussein with Ibn Saud.
Tue 1 January 1918	BEF strength 1,907,906 (cf 1,192,668, 3 Jan 1917). British 4th Tank Bde formed. German raids nr Loos & Mericourt fail. **Verdun** — French repulse raid at Beaumont, & Chaume Wood flamethrower attack (12 & 13), make successful raid to SE (16). Gallwitz i/c Army Gp for duration.	Allied Supreme War Council decides to supply Ukraine/ Rumania via Persia & Siberia & take over Trans-Siberian Railway via Vladivostok if Germans reopen offensive.	**Piave** — British cross-river raid succeeds (109,103 British troops in Italy). **Salonika** — British receive 8in gun bty & 12 6in Newton mortars & 2 sound-ranging sections. **Macedonia** — (Jan) Russian div withdrawn from front (see 8) & disarmed due to Soviet disaffection, some join French Foreign Legion, at least 14,979 (15 Apr) join Allies as labour force (see 12 Mar) but 10,000 Serbs from Russian-Rumanian front corps arrive (via Archangel, Cherbourg, Orange & Taranto). Greek Army has 36,242 troops (3 divs) & 14,717 animals at front (15) + 18,260 in interior (15 Mar, see 1 Feb).	**Armenia** — National Armenian Corps 21,000 strong (see 14). **Persia** — Early in Jan Bicharakov's Cossacks & 2 guns leave Kasr-i-Shirin (small British det occupies 8) to rally loyal Russian troops at Kermanshah but fail by 24. **E Persia** — British cordon extended to Birjand by 15, complete 31. **Hejaz Railway** — Lawrence attacks Turk Mudauwara post with British armoured cars (see 22). **Mesopotamia** — (Jan) RN hands over 8 'Fly' class gunboats to Army (& last 8 Mar). Film *With the Forces in Mesopotamia* released at home.
Wed 2	**Flanders** — German trench raid repulsed nr La Bassée.	**Brest-Litovsk** — Bolsheviks denounce terms as 'annexationist'. All-Russian Board formed for organizing Red Army (see 16). Kaiser in Berlin discusses new Russian frontier with Hindenburg & Ludendorff.		
Thu 3	**Artois** — Slight British advance S of Lens. **Alsace** — French heavily repulse attack nr Anspach.	**Brest-Litovsk** — Ukrainian delegation arrives (see 10). Bolsheviks propose moving talks to Stockholm (Central Powers refuse 9). HM Ambassador Buchanan recalled (departs 7).	**Salonika** — New C-in-C Gen Guillaumat visits British Army (& 9), soon inspires confidence of all Allies, organizes gen arty res (see 15).	
Fri 4	**Cambrai** — German attacks compel withdrawal of 4 British outposts nr Canal du Nord.	**France & Sweden recognize Finland's independence** (Norway & Denmark 10).		Allenby telegram insists on consolidation & capturing Jericho as EEF advances another mile N of Jerusalem. Britain notifies Hussein that Palestine must have special regime (see 4 Feb).
Sat 5	**Cambrai** — German attacks on British E of Bullecourt repulsed (& 8), trench raid nr Bullecourt (8). 2 German raids nr Hollebeke. Germans raid British post nr Flesquières, both sides raid in sector (19). **Ypres** — German raid repulsed.		**Piave** — Arty action from Asiago to sea. Patrol actions on Brenta-Piave sector (6).	Lloyd George says no intention of molesting Turk homelands, Straits to be internationalized. **Aden** — Strong British recce on Hatum & Jabir destroys former post (300 British cas Aug 1917-Feb 1918, Turk more).

AFRICAN OPERATIONS 5	SEA WAR 6	AIR WAR 7	INTERNATIONAL EVENTS 8	HOME FRONTS 9
	Allied & neutral Dec shipping losses to U-boats, 160 ships (76 British, 520 lives lost) worth 382,060t (U-boat figure 411,766 incl 148,331t in Med; 8 U-boats lost (only 2 in Med). 3680 portable hydrophone sets now in British service. **N Sea** — British 1917 Dutch convoys (1031 ships) lose only 6 ships, but escorts lose 5 destroyers, 9 damaged, & 1 cruiser, damaged in collision (520 lives lost). **Baltic** — Russians have laid annual record of 13,418 mines.		British Foreign Office forms Russia Ctee under Lord Cecil. Lenin demands 'intensified agitation against the annexation policy of the Germans'. Anglo-Turk PoW exchange agreement signed at Berne.	**Britain** — Lowest working days lost since April. Now 217,000 allotments in urban areas. **France** — Elections postponed for duration. Stamp duty on purchases over 10 francs. **USA** — Army 485,250; Nat Guard 416,031; Nat Army 480,000; Reserve 157,225.
(Jan) British planes shower German askaris with leaflets in Swahili (few could read), induce desertions but some return.	Depth charge prod up to 4647pm, escorts armed with 30-40 each, use 1745pm from June. Now 21 German MTBs in service, 14 in Flanders. **Channel** — Vice-Adm **Keyes takes over Dover Patrol** from Adm Bacon (see 24 Feb). **Biscay** — Acting on Room 40 intercepts, armed boarding steamer HMS *Duke of Clarence* captures Spanish ship *Erro Berro* (sinks in tow) before she transfers wolfram (ore-producing tungsten) to 2 U-boats which are ambushed unsuccessfully. **Med** — 2 U-boat Flotillas formed, 1st at Pola, 2nd at Cattaro, 7-8 boats on ops in Jan (see 22), incl *UB49* & *UB48* together. **Baltic** — Est 40,000 sailors have left Russian Fleet for home or interior land fighting.	**Germany** — (Jan) Fokker wins first competition to find obsolescent Albatros fighter replacement. **W Front** — (Jan) RFC No 19 Sqn first to receive Sopwith Dolphin high-altitude fighter, No 141 Sqn at Rochford, Essex gets & crashes one but used only as day fighter. **Italy** — Austrians bomb Bassano (& 4), Treviso (& 26) & Mestre (& 4, 26), Castelfranco (4). **Britain** — Total air defences have 376 aircraft, 469 AA guns, 622 searchlights, 258 height-finders & 10 sound locators (see 17).	Hyams succeeds PM Baron de Broqueville as Belgian Foreign Minister (latter has to resign for backing K Albert's compromise peace ideas). **Neutrals: Switzerland** — Bread allowance ³/₅ litre per person (see 1 Mar). **Occupied France** — Germans start to exact 92m francs from Lille from this day.	**Austria** — (Jan) Door locks & latches being removed for metal. **Germany** — (Jan) 2.3m exempted workers, half Field Army eligible. **Turkey** — 40,594 non-military 1918 deaths in capital (22,244 in 1914). **Britain** — RFP 106%, up 10% during 1917. **Sugar rationing** (1/2lb per person pw) + compulsory meatless day (2 from 25). Local lard rationing of 2oz per person pw for 1.5m (see 14 July 1918). **France** — (Jan) Seine freezes over for first time in 120 yrs. **Occupied France** — Germans exact 92m francs from Lille (-17 Oct).
		Britain — **Air Ministry established**. (Jan) RFC stops enlisting American citizens (see 6 Feb).	US War Mission in Europe urges speedy troop dispatch & merchant ship building; first 100 of 1500 US farm tractors en route to France.	**USA** — *Outlook* magazine article denounces anti-German hysteria esp forced flag kissing. **Britain** — King gives Haig his FM's baton at Buckingham Palace, latter urges clear war aims be announced to BEF. **Germany** — Ludendorff and Hoffmann (effective E Front cdr as CoS) part company over latter's plan to retain only small part of Poland.
		Britain — Air Council replaces Air Board, analogous to Army Council & Board of Admiralty. Lord Rothermere first Sec of State for Air. **Trenchard first Chief of Air Staff**. **Palestine** — RFC bomb airfields at El Afule & Jenin (-4). **Germany** — Allied air raids on Metz area, RFC repeat (4, 16 & 21). **W Front** — S African ace Lt Beauchamp-Proctor scores 1st of 54 victories.		
	Bristol Channel — British hospital ship *Rewa* (4 lives lost) from Med sunk by *U55*. **N Sea** — RNAS aircraft raid Ghistelles airfield nr Ghent. Flanders U-boat Flotilla has 29 boats (loses 24 in 1918).		Churchill urges War Cabinet that US bns be incorporated in British bdes.	
		Germany — 5 Navy airships (*L46, L47, L59, L58* & *SL20*) destroyed by explosions & fire at Ahlhorn (petrol fire under *L59* rear gondola likely, or sabotage), 15 dead. **Italy** — 74 RFC aircraft serviceable, later 1918 strength varies from 65 to 91.	**Lloyd George war aims speech** to TUC Manpower London Conference envisages peace based on moral principle & League of Nations war alternative.	**France** — Nantes & Bordeaux-Brest Atlantic Coast put under military control.

JANUARY 1918	WESTERN FRONT 1	EASTERN FRONT 2	SOUTHERN FRONTS 3	TURKISH FRONTS 4
Sun 6		**Germany recognizes Finland's independence. Secret War** — British Maj Banting reports 'On all sides German agents are appearing... buying up existing stocks'.	**Albania** — Italians repel Austrian dets on R Osum.	**Hejaz Railway** — Nasir's 300 Arabs & 1 gun capture Jurf-ed-Derawish Stn & 200+ Turks 30 miles N of Maan (Maulud's Arabs advance near 7).
Mon 7	BEF GHQ Intelligence analysis 'If Germany attacks and fails, she will be ruined.' (*see* 21).			
Tue 8	Haig's 4th Dispatch on Battles of Arras, 'Lens', Messines & Third Ypres in previous summer, claims 131 German divs defeated. Pétain writes to Clemenceau 'In reality, the 1918 battle will be defensive ...' He & Haig present strategy together (24 &30), only choice until US arrives in strength. **Upper Marne** — Patton's US Tank School opens at Langres (*see* 21 Feb). **Meuse** — Major French trench raid nr Seicheprey (Woëvre): Legion (141 cas) bring back 188 PoWs, 16 MGs & 9 mortars.	**Brest-Litovsk** — Bolsheviks resume talks under Trotsky (arrived 7); Talaat Pasha arrives.	**Serbia** — Small Bulgar raid on old Russian trenches.	
Wed 9	Canadian raid S of Lens succeeds (& one to N, 18).	Trotsky appeals for volunteers to march v 'Bourgeoisie of the world' (*see* 18). **S Russia** — White Volunteer Army manifesto by Kornilov & Alexeiev pledges resistance to Reds & Germans.		
Thu 10	Supreme War Council recommend BEF take over more of French sector, and creation of general Allied reserve (23,*see* 2 Feb). **British War Office orders reduction in bns per div** from 12 to 9 thus disbanding 141 bns & 2 cav divs (-10 Mar) to compensate for insufficient reinforcements (200,000 instead of 615,000 requested). **Somme** — British Fifth Army relieves French in St Quentin sector (completed 14, *see* 2 Feb). **Ypres** — British trench raid.	Britain assures Bolsheviks she supports an independent Poland. **Central Powers & Bolsheviks recognize Ukraine** as separate state (*see* 16). **Don** — Independent Republic declared under Gen Kaledin. **Rumania** — After request (6) 3 Rumanian divs cross R Pruth into Bessarabia, enter capital Kishinev (26, *see* 13 & 27).		
Fri 11	French raids in Argonne, Vosges & Champagne, German one fails S of Armentières.			
Sat 12	British raid at Loos, disperse 4 German ones S of Lens & E of Monchy.	LATVIA DECLARES INDE-PENDENCE. 1st of 3 Japanese warships arrives at Vladivostok (RN cruiser *Suffolk* from Hong Kong 14) to protect 600,000t of Allied supplies.		
Sun 13		Reds imprison Rumanian Ambassador Diamandi (released 15 after diplomatic corps protest) & seize Rumanian gold in retaliation for Bessarabia takeover, also order K of Rumania's arrest (15, *see* 27).	Italians have received 300,000 British gas masks.	
Mon 14	**Artois** — British raid N of Lens, German ones repulsed nr	Lenin receives diplomatic corps, speaks at departure of	**Piave** — Italian 22nd Inf Div reaches Mt Asolone summit,	**Armenia** — Turk Army Gp Caucasus C-in-C Vehip Pasha

AFRICAN OPERATIONS 5	SEA WAR 6	AIR WAR 7	INTERNATIONAL EVENTS 8	HOME FRONTS 9
	N Sea — At Beatty's urging first Flag Officer, Seaplane Carriers, Grand Fleet appointed.			**Russia** — Lenin takes Finland holiday (-11). **Austria** — Czech Prague Convention demands sovereign state (*see* 22).
Main body **Gold Coast Regt** (500 + 300 carriers) **lands at Port Amelia**. British col from Ft Johnston drives German force N in Mwembe area.	**Channel** — *U95* (Prinz) rammed & sunk by steamer after sinking 14 ships (37,930t) since mid-1917.		Lord Reading High Commissioner & Ambassador Extraordinary to USA (*see* 14 Feb).	**Britain** — 12½% munitions bonus extended to all time-work metal workers + 7% for piecework. **USA** — Supreme Court upholds Selective Service Act.
			WILSON'S FOURTEEN POINTS MESSAGE TO CONGRESS outlines peace programme. Office of Public Information distributes all over Europe. French Parlt adopts (11), *see* 24.	**Australia** — PM Hughes resigns & forms new Govt (9). **Britain** — Nearly 1500 OBEs published. 2m trees to be planted to alleviate home timber shortage. **Portugal** — Lisbon naval revolt put down.
Hawthorn's 3 KAR bns drive Göring Det (3 coys) to E bank of R Lugenda & take Luambala from it (15).	Destroyer HMS *Racoon* lost with all hands in storm off Ireland, RN destroyers *Opal* & *Narbrough* wrecked on rocky Pentland Skerries off Scotland (12, 1 survivor from 180). **W Med** — Convoy escort sloop HMS *Cyclamen* sinks *UB69* with high-speed paravane off Bizerta. **N Sea** — Beatty memo establishes new Grand Fleet strategy of containing Scheer in his bases rather than fighting at any cost (Cabinet approves 18).		**Secret War** — Lloyd George sends terms to Zahroff in Monte Carlo for next talks with Enver ($10m for gaining Turk Straits 16, *see* 27).	
		W Front — RFC bomb ammo dump nr Courtrai.		**Britain** — Balfour Edinburgh speech 'the horrors of war ...are nothing to...a German peace'. House of Lords adopts women's suffrage clause.
				Russia — Sovnarkom orders all interest & divident payments to cease.
				Britain — Officers pay put up to 10s 6d pd + child allowances. Workers loot closed food shops in Leytonstone & Wembley. **USA** — Employment Service organizes women's div. Army DSC and DSM instituted.
			Lenin & Stalin's Decree No 13 in *Pravda* backs Armenian self-determination. **Neutrals: Norway** — Sugar, coffee, corn & meal rationing.	
Gold Coast Regt patrol skirmish 44 miles W of Port Amelia (&	**N Sea** — German destroyer raid on Gt Yarmouth (12 cas	**Germany** — 12 DH4s of No 55 Sqn RFC damage workshops at	Allied Wheat Convention with Argentina. Serb industrial	**Britain** — Geddes introduces Manpower Bill to reassembled

JANUARY 1918	WESTERN FRONT 1	EASTERN FRONT 2	SOUTHERN FRONTS 3	TURKISH FRONTS 4
Mon 14 contd	Neuve Chapelle (18).	'first volunteers of the Socialist army' & escapes shots fired at his car.	taking 400 PoWs, but forced off (-16, *see* 27). Some Italian advance in Piave Delta.	proposes peace with independent Transcaucasia (*see* 12 Feb). **Arabia** — Nasir forces Tafila's surrender (150 Turks) 15 miles SE of Dead Sea despite snow & hail (*see* 25).
Tue 15	**Cambrai Inquiry (Bryce) Report**: British War Cabinet satisfied German counter-stroke did not surprise BEF cdrs, but admits 'breakdown'. **Lorraine** — US I Corps formed (Gen Hunter Liggett) at Neuf Chateau — 1st, 2nd, 26th & 42nd Divs.	**Brest-Litovsk** — Czernin receives Vienna's appeals to make early 'bread peace' (*see* 22). British War Cabinet cables Gen Poole to destroy Allied military stores (*see* 23).		
Wed 16		Central Powers & Ukraine reach settlement in principle (announced 21). CEC adopts decree forming Red Army (*see* 14 & 28 Feb).	**Piave** — Austrian attack on Capo Sile (lower river) fails bloodily, Italians occupy Austrian advance post (24) & repulse attack (26).	
Thu 17		**Ukraine** — Red Guard drive on Kiev begins, takes Poltava (18.)		
Fri 18		**Brest-Litovsk** — Trotsky breaks off talks, envoys leave to confer at home 20. **Finland** — **Mannerheim, Army C-in-C** since Pres Svinhufvud's promise of no Swedish intervention (16), takes night train from Helsinki to W coast port of Vaasa.	**Trentino** — Austrian patrols active on Asiago Plateau.	**Mesopotamia** — Maj-Gen Dunsterville arrives at Baghdad (left Karachi 6) to head British Mission to Caucasus (*see* 27). **Palestine** — British advance on 4-mile front nr Durah 12 miles N of Jerusalem. **Arabia** — Arab raids damage Hejaz Railway (70 miles NW of Medina — 60 miles S of Maan -28).
Sat 19				
Sun 20		**Ukraine** — French Gen Tabouis vainly orders Czech Corps to cover Mogilev-Vinnitsa rail line v Germans (*see* 8 Feb).		

AFRICAN OPERATIONS 5	SEA WAR 6	AIR WAR 7	INTERNATIONAL EVENTS 8	HOME FRONTS 9
17). **W Africa** — French decrees authorize universal conscription & native medical school at Dakar.	incl 3 military), Harwich Force (Tyrwhitt promoted Rear-Adm today above 48 captains) sails within 90mins of shelling starting but unable to intercept (-15).	Karlsruhe in daylight raid (*see* 27).	delegation visits Britain to promote postwar trade (-16 Feb).	Commons, 420,000-450,000 men needed immediately. **France** — Ex-PM Caillaux arrested on treason charge of peace intrigue with Germans during 1915 Argentina visit (*see* 21). Convicted on lesser grounds Feb 1920 and soon released.
			Neutrals: Mexico — After 15 US agent captures German spy Lothar Witzke (alias Russian Pablo Waberski) in Nogales. Sentenced to death in Texas, but commuted & freed 1923.	**USA** — War Labor Administrator appointed & draft compulsory ration scheme issued. **Britain** — Russian PoW Help Ctee ceases work.
	Aegean — Battleship *Lord Nelson* (Rear-Adm Hayes Sadler) leaves Mudros (returns 21) & sister *Agamemnon* for Salonika. French battleship *Republique* in dock. RN submarine *E12* has defective propellor (*see* 20 & 28 Jan).	**W Front** — BEF GHQ (Trenchard) document insists RFC continue air offensive despite defensive ground situation.	Prussian Finance Minister Hergt says sufficient US troops cannot reach Europe (*see* 28).	**Austria** — **Gen strikes** (-21) **over daily bread ration cut** (7^1/2 oz to under 6oz) & Brest-Litovsk impasse involve nearly 100,000 workers in Lower Austria alone & Govt taken by surprise. Spreads to Hungary (18). **USA** — Fuel Administrator closes all non-war industry E of Mississippi for 5 days (18-22) +9 Mondays to save moving coal (*see* 26). **Germany** — Hindenburg letter removes Kaiser's radical Civil Cabinet chief (for past 10yrs) Valentini (who protests to Crown Prince). **Britain** — Board of Trade & Munitions Ministry allowed to drill for oil.
	Germany — Lt cruiser *Cöln II* completed at Hamburg, first of projected 10-ship class, only 5 launched and one other, *Rostock II* completed (28 Mar).	**Britain** — London Air Defence Area has c100 op fighters (*see* 28; 8 Feb).	Rumanian nationalist weekly *La Roumanie* launched in Paris (- 11 June 1919).	**Austria** — Emperor Charles cables Czernin 'If peace is not made at Brest it will be revolution here, no matter how much there is to eat'.
		W Front — Maj-Gen Sir **J Salmond i/c RFC**, succeeding Trenchard.		**Italy** — War Cross of Merit instituted. (Jan) Anti-war Socialist Party Sec Luzzatti arrested. (Jan) New Ministry of Pensions & Army Welfare headed by Bissolati. **Hungary** — Bad strikes in Budapest. **Russia** — CEC dissolve Constituent Assembly in Petrograd (-19, *see* 23), aided by Anarchist-led guard at Tauride Palace. Red sailors murder 2 ex-Prov Govt ministers in hospital beds (night 19/20).
				Hungary — 86th Inf Regt mutinies at Szabadka, 2 other regts likewise (11 & 14 Feb).
	Aegean — **Action off Imbros**: *Goeben* & *Breslau* (Vice-Adm Rebeur-Paschwitz) **sortie** against British monitors nr Dardanelles, sinking *Raglan* (127 dead) & *M28*. *Breslau* sunk by 5 mines, *Goeben* also mined 3 times & runs aground at Nagara Point, Dardanelles. After 65 RNAS raids drop 180 bombs (2 hits) refloated (*see* 31 Mar) & towed into Constantinople. Adm Calthorpe arrives at Mudros to direct ops (25, *see* 28; 16 Mar). **N Sea** — U-boat sinks armed boarding steamer HMS *Louvain* (224 lives lost). 2 German destroyers sunk by mines.			

JANUARY 1918	WESTERN FRONT 1	EASTERN FRONT 2	SOUTHERN FRONTS 3	TURKISH FRONTS 4
Mon 21	LUDENDORFF MAKES FINAL DECISION TO LAUNCH GREAT SPRING OFFENSIVE, D-Day to be 14 Mar. **Lorraine** — US 1st Div takes over 8 miles of trenches NW of Nancy (first cas 30). **Flanders** — Smuts and Hankey visit GHQ (-26), find no alternative to Haig.	Lenin discusses German peace terms with 63 Red leaders, 32 vote for 'revolutionary war' (*see* 24).		Allied Supreme War Council urges 'a decisive offensive against Turkey'. War Cabinet sending Smuts to Allenby (28, *see* 15 Feb).
Tue 22	German raids nr St Quentin & La Bassée, another E of Loos (25).	Czernin back in Vienna asks permission to make separate peace if necessary, Austria has only 2 months grain.		**Hejaz Railway** — Arabs repulsed from Mudauwara Stn despite 3 RFC attacks by 3 planes.
Wed 23	Germans storm French trenches E of Nieuport but then lose them. **Champagne** — French raid E of Auberive.	**Brest-Litovsk** — Trotsky suspends talks calling German policy 'a most monstrous annexation' (*see* 30). British form Allied Petrograd Trade Barter Co to stop supplies falling to Germans. Kerensky reaches Helsinki from Petrograd.	**Italian Front** — Below's German Fourteenth Army HQ closes (*see* W FRONT 1 Feb).	
Thu 24	Lt-Gen Sir H Lawrence appointed BEF CoS, replaces Lt-Gen Sir L Kiggell. French repulse raids N of Aisne & at Caurières Wood (Verdun). Last French Army mutiny cases (minor).	Lenin's immediate peace policy rejected 9-7 for Trotsky's 'no war no peace'. **Crimea** — Red Guards take Feodosia & Yalta, suppress Tartar revolt.	**Salonika** — At Compiègne (France) Haig suggests withdrawal of all Anglo-French forces to W Front.	**Mesopotamia** — Turk air raids on Baghdad cause slight damage (-25). **Arabia** — Fakhri Bey's 1000 troops from Amman & Kerak surprise Arabs E of Tafila: **S Persia** — Burma Mtd Rifles sqn cause c105 cas to robbers at Gumun NE of Shiraz (& 27).
Fri 25		German *Südarmee* disbanded. Rumanians fight Reds at Galatz on Danube. **Russia** — Red Commissar of Military Affairs orders sailors to stiffen all dets sent to the interior.	**Piave** — British 5th Div relieves Italian VIII Corps (-27).	**Arabia** — Battle of Tafila: Lawrence's 600 Arabs (c100 cas) destroy Fakhri Bey's force (200+ PoWs, 2 guns, 27 MGs). Turks evacuate Kerak & retreat to Amman, Lawrence later awarded DSO. Turk Fourth Army (Djemal Kuchuk) put under Falkenhayn with German CoS Maj Papen.
Sat 26	*OHL* publishes *The Attack in Position Warfare* , bible of 1918 offensives, stresses attack in depth with air support. **Somme** — British Fifth Army relieves French Third Army from St Quentin S to Barisis, S of R Oise (-30). **Flanders** — Haig dines with Asquith (visiting surviving son).	UKRAINE DECLARES INDEPENDENCE. **Siberia** — Prov Socialist Govt elected at Tomsk. **Finland** — Red Guards mobilize at midnight.		**Persia** — Bolshevik rep Bravin arrives in Tehran.
Sun 27		**Bolsheviks sever relations with Rumania**, latter's legation leaves Petrograd (28).	**Trentino** — (Asiago) *Sassari* Bde & 4 *Alpini* bns surprise attack & recapture Cols del Rosso & d'Echele with Mt Corone (-29) provoking 4-div counter-attacks that yield 2500 PoWs, 6 guns & 100 MGs for 5240 cas.	**Mesopotamia** — Dunsterville Mission (20 men + 41 vehicles) leaves Baghdad for Kermanshah (*see* 3 Feb).
Mon 28	2 small French attacks in	CIVIL WAR IN FINLAND (-15	**Trentino** — 4th *Bersaglieri* Bde	**Palestine** — Railway to

AFRICAN OPERATIONS 5	SEA WAR 6	AIR WAR 7	INTERNATIONAL EVENTS 8	HOME FRONTS 9
Deventer's dispatch 'An equally arduous campaign ...will still be necessary.'		**W Front** — RFC bomb German Flanders airfields (& 23), Roulers (& 28), Menin, & Coutrai bombed (22). **Salonika** — 3 RFC aircraft fly to Mudros to share in bombing of *Goeben* (*see* SEA WAR 20); 7 more aircraft sent (22 & 28), return 29. **Mesopotamia** — 12 RFC DH4s (1 lost to flak) bomb German Kifri airfield. 2 German aircraft retaliate v Baghdad (24), RFC respond v Humr & Kifri airfields (night 25/26, *see* 31).		**Austria** — Strikes over, but **7 divs permanently recalled from fronts** & news leaks to Germany (*see* 28). Factory workers to get extra bread rations, at Army's expense (*see* 25). **Britain** — Sir E Carson resigns from War Cabinet on Irish question. *Daily Mail* attacks Gen Staff for squandering Britain's manpower. **France** — Ex-Interior Minister Malvy's Senate trial (-6 Aug).
	Allied Naval Council first meets in London (-23) incl Adms Bon, Revel & agenda incl neutral waters & potential fear of Germans seizing Russian Black Sea Fleet (*see* 3 Mar). **Adriatic** — German & arsenal workers at Pola strike (-27) worsening U-boat repair situation (up to 17 pd), although leaders sacked.			**Austria** — PM Seidler resignation refused. Germans in Bohemia demand own province. **Britain** — Thomson (Special Branch) reports 'a decided increase in letters for an immediate peace' (*see* 10 Apr).
	RN convoy sloops & 20 PC patrol boats (based Pembroke) no longer to be used as Q-ships (had sailed regularly with convoys but as Q-ships since Oct 1917).		Italian PM Orlando visits London (-29). Hindenburg on risk to food reserves in helping Austria 'Compared with this, a collapse of Austria-Hungary would not play a decisive role'.	**Russia** — 3rd Soviets Congress (-31).
			Counts Hertling & Czernin reject Allied Fourteen Points.	**Germany** — *Reichstag* debate on war aims (-26); Hertling refuses any Alsace-Lorraine discussion.
Gold Coast Regt captures German post at Pumome (5t of food). Heavy rains continue.				**France** — Frequent union peace meetings start in Loire Dept, up to 7000 attend (*see* 5 Feb). **Hungary** — 'Red Prince' Windischgraetz becomes Food Minister.
	U-boats' costliest day of the war: Irish Sea — U-boats sink Dublin steam packet *Cork* & Spanish *SS Giralda* (50th victim). **Channel** — Returning *U109* blown up in Dover Barrage (only 5 High Seas Fleet boats try it outwardbound in Jan). Destroyer *HMS Leven* depth charges & sinks *UB35* N of Calais. **St George's Channel** — RN *PC62* rams & sinks *U84*.	**France** — Germans bomb Dunkirk, Calais & Boulogne. **Canada** — 4036 RFC airmen trained in past year (34 fatal accidents); 200 trained pilots pm sent to Britain in 1918.	Balfour proposes Japan acts as Allied protector of Trans-Siberian Railway (France agrees 30). Proposal repeated 8 Feb (*see* 13 Feb).	**USA** — Food Administrator asks for 2 voluntary wheatless days pw & 3 meatless days pw + use of Victory bread. *New York Times* reviews *The Eagle's Eye* , 20-part Govt-approved exposé of German espionage.
	Atlantic — Cunard liner *Andania* sunk (7 lives lost) by *U46* off N Ireland. **N Sea** — RNAS bomb Aertrycke & Engel (-28), Coolkerhe (Bruges) airfield bombed (29).	**France** — 6 of 12 DH4s (No 55 Sqn) raid Trier (barracks & railways). French bomb Conflans (RFC bombed 5) & Metz. **Germany** — RFC 2/Lts Scholtz & Wookey (PoWs on 17 Oct 1917 nr Cambrai when shot down in Bristol Fighters) sentenced to 10yrs penal servitude for dropping anti-war leaflets behind German lines on W Front (*see* 28; INT'L EVENTS 6 Feb).	Russia denounces Anglo-Russian 1907 Persian Treaty. **Secret War** — Zahroff arrives in Geneva, Enver Pasha arrives 28 (*see* 29).	**Britain** — Home Army rations reduced to civilian level by 6 Feb. **Germany** — Kaiser leaves Berlin on 59th birthday for Homburg spa till 11 Mar (*see* 10 Feb).
KAR Mtd Inf occupy Ankuabe	**Dardanelles** — HM Submarine	**Britain** — 233 cas in moonlight	US Army Sec Baker says	**Germany** — Great 400,000-

JANUARY 1918	WESTERN FRONT 1	EASTERN FRONT 2	SOUTHERN FRONTS 3	TURKISH FRONTS 4
Mon 28 contd	Champagne & Alsace. †Canadian war poet Lt-Col John McCrae of pneumonia & meningitis at Wimereux.	May): 9 Red Guard bns take Helsinki but Mannerheim seizes Vaasa & Russian garrisons (5000 PoWs, 37 guns, 34 MGs, 8000 rifles for 20 cas -31). Sovnarkom decrees formation of Worker-Peasant Red Army (*see* 14 Feb). **S Russia** — Reds fight Ukrainians at Lutsk. Don Cossacks mutiny & depose Kaledin. **Baltic Provinces** — Baron Dellinghausen invites Germans to occupy Estonia (*see* 25 Feb).	driven off Mt Valbella but retake it (29), British guns assisting.	Jerusalem restored (Allenby's Ludd railhead opens 4 Feb). Abdulla-el-Feer's 70 Arab horsemen capture & destroy Turk Dead Sea supply flotilla (7 boats, 60 PoWs) at El Mezra.
Tue 29		**Ukraine** — Red troops take Kiev & Odessa.		
Wed 30	BEF now deployed from Houthulst Forest, NE of Ypres, to Barisis, NW of Laon.	**Brest-Litovsk** — Talks resume on Trotsky's return. White politicians form Constitutional Council at Rostov. Lenin orders 25,000 rifles & 30 MGs for Russian troops in Finland. RNAS Armoured Car Sqn rear party sail from Murmansk (& 1 Feb).		
Thu 31	BEF takes 171 PoWs during Jan. (Jan) 1000 Portuguese reinforcements arrive.	USSR PROCLAIMED. Austrian Col-Gen Böhm-Ermolli made FM (*see* 16 May). Red 1st Northern Flying Column (incl 400 sailors) takes Orenburg (Urals) from Ataman Dutov.	**Italy** — (Jan) Italian War Ministry agrees to French request for unarmed soldier labour on W Front in return for food and coal, 60,000 eventually sent, some fight v German March Offensive (*see* 18 Apr).	
Fri 1 February 1918	(Feb) French Army adopts lighter, more comfortable ARS gas mask (5m made). **Artois** — New German Seventeenth Army formed under O Below.	**Central Powers recognize independent Ukraine Republic** (*see* 9). Yeremeyev forms Soviet I Corps at Petrograd (*see* 14). (Feb) 5	**Greece** — Greek troops mutiny at Lamia v being sent to Salonika: K Alexander visits, refuses clemency to ring-leaders & orders shooting of 2	**Mesopotamia** — Turk 52nd Div being broken up. MEF at peak ration strength of 280,665 incl 126,078 British, 399 Anzacs (first time), 154,188 Indians;

AFRICAN OPERATIONS 5	SEA WAR 6	AIR WAR 7	INTERNATIONAL EVENTS 8	HOME FRONTS 9
camp site.	*E14* (11 survivors PoWs) mined & sunk off Kum Kale in vain attempt to torpedo *Goeben*. (Lt-Cdr G S White posthumous VC in only RN vessel to have 2 captains with VC).	raid on London (night 28/29) by 3 of 13 Gothas sent (7 attack, 1 FTR) & 1 Giant of 2, 8100lb bombs dropped. Record 103 defence sorties (1 Bristol Fighter lost to Giant R12, 1 Camel shot down by AA fire); Hackwill & Banks of No 44 Sqn in Camels shoot down Gotha GV at Wickford, Essex; Banks' Camel is special (3-gun) model with illuminated Neame ring-sight. 660lb bomb from R12 hits London Odhams Press, Long Acre (118 cas of night's total 233). **W Front — All British aircraft leaflet-dropping stopped** (-31 Oct); balloons instead.	500,000 troops in France soon, 1.5m by end 1918. **Neutrals: Spain** — U-boat torpedoes SS *Giralda*, Spain protests 6 Feb.	**strong peace strike in Berlin** (-4 Feb). **Russia** — Lenin orders 'Send grain, grain & again grain!! Otherwise Petrograd will starve to death...for God's sake!' **Rumania** — Bratianu Cabinet resigns.
Wahle driven down R Lugenda towards Mtarika (*see* 3 Feb).		**Britain** — Moonlight raid on London (20 cas) by 3 of 4 Giants sent; defences misidentify them as 15 Gothas). Maj Murlis Green (No 44 Sqn CO) attacks R25 (hit 88 times) from close range but discovers new RTS ammo explodes prematurely; 4 other fighters (out of 73 sent up) also attack without success (night 29/30).	**Secret War: Switzerland** — Enver & Zahroff hold fruitless talks, former says Kaiser has told him 'the future of Mesopotamia & Palestine would be decided on the French front'.	
		France — First of 31 Gotha raids on Paris (259 cas), 267 bombs (14t) dropped by 30 Gothas in 30min (1 shot down) (*see* HOME FRONTS 31).	3rd Allied Supreme War Council meeting at Versailles (-2 Feb). **Brazil** — Adm Bronti to command Brazilian Fleet in European waters (*see* SEA WAR 1 May).	**Germany** — Strikes spread to 6 major cities, but leadership divided.
	N Sea — U-boat minelayers attempt (-late Sept) to seal off Forth to Grand Fleet & Norwegian convoys with batches of 36 mines at 10-mile intervals in a semi-circle, but after 3rd batch British locate & sweep without Germans realizing. 'Battle of May Island': In sortie with 5 battlecruisers from Rosyth 2 K-class submarine flotillas suffer record disastrous night collisions in which *K4* & *K17* are lost (103 die); 2 others damaged along with battlecruiser *Inflexible* & cruiser *Fearless* (night 31 Jan/1 Feb). Adm Sturdee leaves Grand Fleet to be C-in-C the Nore, Vice-Adm Sir M Browning takes over 4th Battle Sqn. Allied & neutral shipping lost to U-boats 123 ships (57 British with 291 lives) worth 302,088t (British 179,973). U-boat fig 160 ships worth 295,630t incl 61 ships of 141,166t in Med (7 of 26,020t to Austrians); 10 U-boats sunk (3 unknown cause). **Germany** — World's largest destroyer *S113* launched at Elbing (Baltic) by Schichau, 2415t & 347ft overall with 4-5.9in guns, 4 torp tubes & 40 mines. Top speed 36 kts but poor seakeeping prevents her & 6 others launched by Armistice from being operational.	**W Front** — (Jan) Record 18 *Jastas* (incl *48-63*) formed (*see* 1 Feb) after 7 in Dec 1917; 14 new airfields opposite BEF Fifth Army. **Germany** — (Jan) Monthly aviation fuel delivery 6000t only 50% of target. **Britain** — (Jan) 3 National Aircraft Factories begin production (5 more by July). **Mesopotamia** — 2 RFC Spads shoot down German 2-seater nr Falluja but crew escape. RFC loses 4 aircraft to engine failure in month.		**Germany** — Martial law in Berlin & Hamburg, factories militarized, many workers drafted. *OHL* prepares div for home use (*see* 3 Feb). **Russia** — 3rd Soviet **Congress adopts** 'Fundamental Law of Land Socialisation' (decree published 19 Feb) & replaces Julian with **Gregorian Calendar**. **France** — Gare de Lyons ticket offices 'besieged' following German air raid on Paris (*see* AIR WAR 30).
	N Sea — RN minelayers lay a deep minefield off the Skaw (Kattegat, *see* 15 Apr) (*see* 24). **Adriatic — Austrian naval mutiny at Cattaro**, sailors	**Italian Front** — (Feb) New high-speed Italian Ansaldo SVA3 2-seater introduced (1200 built), improves long-range & photo recon work (*see*	**Secret War: Switzerland** — New Franco-Austrian (Armand-Revertera) talks at Freiburg (& 3, final 23 & 25, *see* 2 Apr). **Neutrals** — Argentina recalls	**Britain** — RFP 108% (up 2%). Est 2,5,000 acres growing wheat (45% up on 1 Feb 1917). Fit 23s & under removed from protected occupations.

FEBRUARY 1918	WESTERN FRONT 1	EASTERN FRONT 2	SOUTHERN FRONTS 3	TURKISH FRONTS 4
Fri 1 contd	**Occupied Belgium** — (Feb) At Charleroi Bavarian Capt Bornschlegel restores 30 British Cambrai Mk IV tanks to an operational state for German use (*see* 27).	German divs transfer to W Front.	who plunder village (*see* 7; 12 Mar). **Italian Front** — 3 ex-Second Army (Caporetto) corps now reorganized as Fifth Army (Capello) operational though partly with French guns & rifles. **Italy** — (Feb) Caporetto inquiry commission recalls Cadorna from Allied Supreme War Council.	plus 166,951 followers.
Sat 2	Supreme War Council sanctions Allied General Reserve for W, Italian & Balkan Fronts. Foch submits plan (6) for 17 divs behind W Front & 13 on Italian. Pétain (12) & Haig (*see* 24; 11 Mar) oppose then compromise on a 12-mile extension of BEF line.			
Sun 3		**Finland** — 1600 White Guards capture Oulu in N & clear up to Swedish border (-6). In centre, Reds vainly assault White line (2-12 *see* 25).		**Persia** — Dunsterville reaches Kermanshah (*see* 15)
Mon 4	More US units assigned to front-line. **Lorraine** — Count Bothmer (ex-E Front *Südarmee*) i/c new German Nineteenth Army for duration.	**Don** — Alexeiev's 3500-officer Volunteer 'Army' begins 'Ice March' (*see* 13).		
Tue 5		Ludendorff to Austro-German Brest-Litovsk delegates in Berlin 'If Germany makes peace without profit, then Germany has lost the war'.		
Wed 6		**Mackensen 4-day peace talks ultimatum to Rumania** (*see* 23). Rumanian PM Bratianu resigns, Gen Averescu forms new Cabinet (9). (c) German-language Red broadcast from Tsarkoe Selo calls for military revolt and Kaiser's murder.		Allenby approves EEF newspaper *The Palestine News*. EEF Railhead Ordnance Post opens at Jerusalem. **Mesopotamia** — British form Directorate of Irrigation.
Thu 7		**Brest-Litovsk** — Kaiser orders Kühlmann to end talks & demand Baltic States. **Rumania** — C-in-C Averescu	**Salonika** — K Alexander visits British incl Struma front (9). **Italian Front** — K Albert of the Belgians visits (-9), 'I thought	

AFRICAN OPERATIONS 5	SEA WAR 6	AIR WAR 7	INTERNATIONAL EVENTS 8	HOME FRONTS 9
	demand peace without annexation, demobilization, better living conditions, but fail to win army garrison or German U-boats. Mutiny collapses on ultimatum & arrival of 3 battleships from Pola. 3 leaders flee to Italy in seaplane, c800 men removed from ships, 40 tried & 4 executed (*see* 28). Emperor Charles sends Archduke Adm Stephen to conduct inquiry. **Channel** — (Feb) High Seas Fleet U-boat flotillas abandon Dover Straits route due to mine barrage (*see* 15 & 18) but 29 Flanders boats use route in Feb. **Secret War** — (Feb) French physicist Langevin begins sea test of quartz transducer off Toulon, **detects submarine for first time** at up to 5 miles (*see* Mar). **Baltic** — British Foreign Office rejects Centrobalt idea of Britain paying Russian fleet (*see* 11).	9 Aug). **France** — (Feb) 3 Italian Caproni bomber sqns arrive (19), fly 68 ops for 22 cas by Armistice. RFC 41st Wing becomes 8th Bde (*see* 6 June). 4 Gotha sqns raid Paris, 45 die. **Britain** — Prince Albert (future K George VI) joins RNAS HMS *Daedalus* at Cranwell, Lincs, becomes OC No 4 Sqn Boy Wing (Capt in RAF 1 Apr). RFC fighter sqn aircraft estab increased from 18 to 24, 7 Camel sqns thus by 21 Mar. **Germany** — *JG3* (Capt Tutschek) formed from *Jastas* (each 14 aircraft) *12, 13, 15* & *19* & *JG3* (Capt Bruno Lorzer) from *Jastas 2, 26, 27* (Göring) & *36*. Another 12 *Jastas* incl Nos *68-75* formed in Feb. **Salonika** — (Feb) RFC now have up to 8 SE5as enabling it to destroy up to 4 German aircraft (31 Jan & 5 Feb). **N Sea** — US Air Service takes over Dunkirk seaplane stn. **E Africa** — Last 6 RFC planes withdrawn by 9.	Naval & Military Attachés from Germany. **Britain** — Sir E Geddes says U-boats being sunk as fast as Germany can build them. **France** — (Feb) Clemenceau's offer of licensed brothels for US Army declined.	Prestwich By-election: Lt Cawley elected (5688 maj). **France** — Bread ration cards, Paris. **Canada** — Soldier Re-settlement Board founded (+ Minister 21). **Greece** — Army mutiny at Lamia. Ex-PMs Lambros & Skouloudis arrested (*see* S FRONTS). **USA** — (Feb) Senate investigates National German-American Alliance (-13 Apr). **Russia** — **Patriarch anathematizes Bolsheviks (Church & State separated). Turkey** -(Feb) *Vakit* newspaper cites 1970% cost of living rise since July 1914, only 24% in Germany. **Hungary** — Franz Lehar's *Where the Lark Sings* opera opens in Budapest (*see* 24 May). **Germany** — (Feb) Ludendorff tells Prince Max of Baden if his spring offensive fails 'then Germany will just have to suffer annihilation'. **France** — National Office of Disabled & Discharged Soldiers formed.
Cape Corps occupies Mtarika; Lettow has already marched E, using 3 canoes to ferry main body over R Lugenda to Mtende.		**Italy** — Austrians bomb Venice (& 5, 25) & with Padua (20).	Allied Supreme War Council's enlarged powers announced at Versailles. Finn Stockholm Minister on own initiative requests Swedish intervention, PM refuses, suggests mediation (-4). Finn cables Berlin (*see* 21). **Secret War** — American George D Herron meets Austrian Imperial adviser Lammasch in low-level abortive peace feelers (Switzerland). HMG renew pledge to King of Hejaz for freeing Arab peoples (*see* 7 May).	**Germany** — Berlin garrison cdr tells strikers return to work or be shot (*see* 17). **France** — Bolo Pasha court martial, death sentence (14, executed Vincennes 17 Apr), had received German funds to corrupt press (*see* 18). **USA** — German Aliens registration week.
	Atlantic — **First US troops killed in transit**: British troopship *Tuscania* sunk by U-boat (166 US soldiers, 44 crew dead) off Ireland.	**W Front** — Lt Thompson of 103rd Aero Sqn (mainly Lafayette Esc veterans) **first American fighter pilot serving in US forces to score in air combat** (*see* 18 & 26). AEF has 225 aircraft (9 sqns) 1 Feb.		**Britain** — Food Ministry offers amnesty to food hoarders. **USA** — Capt Rintelen & 10 other Germans fined & imprisoned for trying to sink British SS *Kirk Oswald* . Ctee on Public Information appeals to public not to shoot US Signal Corps carrier pigeons. **France** — 3000 in Roanne (Loire Dept) protest v bread shortage, burn cotton magnate's house, looting (-6) but ends by 26 (*see* 25 Mar).
		W Front — First US RFC sqn (No 17) arrives (left Texas 19 Dec 1917), 9 follow (-Mar, *see* 13 Aug).	Britain threatens reprisals if her leaflet-dropping air-men badly treated. 2 officers released 13 Mar.	**Britain** — Electoral Reform Act passed, 6m WOMEN OVER 30 RECEIVE VOTE, Commons enlarged by 37 members to 707.
			British Foreign Office cables Jassy urging no separate Rumanian peace. French decree creates Czech Army	

FEBRUARY 1918	WESTERN FRONT 1	EASTERN FRONT 2	SOUTHERN FRONTS 3	TURKISH FRONTS 4
Thu 7 contd		promises Gen Ballard to try & stop munitions going to Central Powers.	that the Italian Army was more disciplined than ours'.	
Fri 8	German trench raids on the Aisne & Meuse. AEF weekly newspaper *Stars and Stripes* launched (-13 June 1919).	**Ukraine** — Czech Corps made part of Czech Army in France. **Finland** — Mannerheim moves HQ inland to Seinajoki rail jctn, first 5 Swedish officers join him (10).		
Sat 9	**Somme** — GHQ allows Gough (Fifth Army) to conduct fighting withdrawal before expected spring offensive (*see* 17).	**Central Powers sign separate peace with Ukraine** inc 1m t food for Polish Kholm land.		**Palestine** — Chetwode submits plan for advance to Jordan as soon as weather allows (*see* 14). **Mesopotamia** — Marshall cables that little hope of keeping Russian forces, advance on Mosul preferable.
Sun 10	**Flanders** — Australian 3rd Div 204-man trench raid on Warneton (Messines) (48 cas) secures 33 PoWs.	**Brest-Litovsk** — **Trotsky** (before leaving talks for 4th time) **announces 'no peace, no war'** v Central Powers though demobilization ordered (*see* 18). **Finland** — Unarmed Finn Civil Guards land in Aland Is but forced out by Sweden (*see* 2 Mar).	**Trentino** — Austrian activity on Asiago sector, but Italians gain advantage (11).	
Mon 11				Bicharakov arrives in Baghdad by plane (-13) from Kermanshah to fetch remaining followers.
Tue 12	Skirmishing nr Passchendaele. **Artois** — Canadian trench raids nr Hagnicourt-Lens.	**S Russia** — Reds capture 2 points on Novorossiisk-Tsaritsyn railway & defeat Polish Corps at Rogachev.		**Armenia** — **Turk Offensive** (45,000-50,000 in 8 divs, 160 guns) begins with taking Cardakli on Zara-Sivas road & advance to Erzincan (14). Col Morel's 2000 Armenians & 6 guns make epic retreat to Erzerum (14-25, *see* 24).
Wed 13	Ludendorff promises Kaiser victory in proposed spring offensive. **Champagne** — French finally eliminate Tahure-Butte du Mesnil Salient, US guns give fire support, 177 PoWs. German counter-attack (18), *see* 1 Mar.	Bad Homburg Crown Council decides on further advance into Russia, Kaiser demands Bolsheviks be 'beaten to death'. **Don** — Kaledin commits suicide at Novocherkassk, having raised only 147 Cossack vols (*see* 24), Nazarov elected Ataman (-25).	**Piave** — British line extended.	
Thu 14		RED ARMY FORMED (Decree published 23): Volunteer force, cdrs to get 4 months basic training at 4 cities (10, *see* 8	**Salonika** — Milne diary: 'Greek, Serb and Russian New Year Day spend the morning calling, and am fairly lucky in	**Palestine** — British XX Corps prelim 2-mile advance on 6-mile front occupies 2 villages NE of Jerusalem (*see* 19).

AFRICAN OPERATIONS 5	SEA WAR 6	AIR WAR 7	INTERNATIONAL EVENTS 8	HOME FRONTS 9
			(see 29 June).	
	Channel — Destroyer HMS *Boxer* lost by collision with SS *St Patrick*. **Irish Sea** — Only 3 Q-ships now based at Queenstown. **Med** — Revel memo detailing Italy's weak maritime situation shocks Allies in Rome conference (-9) which concentrates on Otranto Barrage, (British mobile concept approved). US Adm Sims presents plan for Adriatic offensive involving 30,000 troops, 25,000 mines & 5 US battleships to seize Curzola I & attack Cattaro (*see* 12 Mar); First Lord Geddes goes on to tour Med bases, urging end to shipping delays (-17).	**Britain** — London Air Defence Area has 200 aircraft, 323 searchlights, 249 AA guns. **Germany** — French bombers attack Saarbrücken.	British War Cabinet rejects Lockhart's plea for Bolshevik recognition. Red envoy Litvinov in London protests v British Army's recruiting of Russian subjects. Gen Giardina replaces Gen Cadorna on Supreme War Council.	**Britain** — Skilled Aircraft Woodworkers wages rise order backdated to 1 Nov 1917. **Russia** — Merchant Navy nationalized. **Canada** — War Trade Board created.
			Allied Economic Council sits in London. Allies provisionally raise embargo on commercial cables to Holland.	**Turkey** — 1st Women's Labour Bn (male officers initially) attached to First Army.
Gov of Uganda H R Wallls retired for opposing porter recruitment.	**Adriatic** — Poet D'Annunzio goes on failed raid by 3 MAS boats to attack 4 steamers nr Fiume (night 10/11, *see* 4 Apr).	**Britain** — Beaverbrook, new British Information Minister, will promote propaganda leaflet raids on W & Italian fronts (by both aeroplanes & small unmanned balloons).		**Britain** — **Information Ministry founded,** Beaverbrook Minister (Ministry formally estab 4 Mar 'To direct the thought of most of the world'). (c)4500 motor vehicles using coal gas. **Turkey** — †Ex-Sultan Abdul Hamid II (75, deposed 1909) at Manisa, Asia Minor. **Germany** — Kaiser addresses Homburgers 'War is a disciplinary action by God to educate mankind ... Our Lord God means us to have peace'.
Italian Somaliland — 300 Italians from Buloburti take 50 dervishes, 25 rifles & 260 camels (-18).	**Soviet 'Red Fleet' founded** on volunteer basis, 5 commissars (Sovnarkom) to run Baltic Fleet (12). **Adriatic** — British Adriatic Force reorganized. Franco-Italian net barraged completed between Fano I & Corfu (*see* 15 Apr).		**Wilson adds 4 war aims points** in Congress address, says no general peace obtainable by separate negotiation. **Occupied Belgium** — Great Brussels demo v separate Flanders (*see* 7 Apr).	**Germany** — Berlin papers prematurely hail peace with Russia.
	E Atlantic — *U89* rammed & sunk off Malin Head (N Ireland) with all hands by British cruiser *Roxburgh* (night 12/13).	**Germany** — 12 DH4s of No 55 Sqn bomb railways & barracks at Offenburg (Baden, *see* 17). **Salonika** — 20 RFC bombers burn out Cestovo ammo dump.	Lloyd George indicates change on W Front due to massive German reinforcements. Kaiser speech 'We desire to live in friendship with neighbouring peoples, but the victory of German arms must first be recognized. Our troops under the great Hindenburg will continue to win it . Then peace will come'.	**France** — Decree fixes Fr20 meal. Confectionary sale or manufacture forbidden. **USA** — All Broadway theatres closed to save coal (-14).
	Adriatic — (c) French submarine *Bernouilli* probably lost to mines.		US Sec of State Lansing informs Allies America cannot approve Japanese action in Siberia (*see* 25). At Homburg Kaiser demands war be continued v international Jewry & freemasons, Ludendorff promises victory in coming offensive.	**Russia** — Gen Poole letter from Petrograd 'Highway robbery is very frequent even in frequented thoroughfares'. **Britain** — Lloyd George invites Northcliffe to direct independent Dept of Enemy Propaganda (*see* 21). Commons Pacifist Group defeated. Reported that 65% vital food from N America. **Italy** — Deputy reads secret 1915 Treaty of London to Chamber, starts bitter wrangle.
Sahara — French Agades col smashes Senussi Khoassen at Tamaclak (-19).	**Secret War: W Med** — *U35* lands 2 agents & 12 cases of anthrax germs (immediately seized) off Cartagena, Spain.		†British Ambassador to Washington Sir Cecil Spring-Rice at Ottawa. Lord Reading (arrived 11) succeeds.	**USA** — Al Jolson sings 'My Mammy' in *Sinbad*, NY. **Turkey** — Chamber attacks Anti-Profiteering Commission as

FEBRUARY 1918	WESTERN FRONT 1	EASTERN FRONT 2	SOUTHERN FRONTS 3	TURKISH FRONTS 4
Thu 14 contd		May).	finding people out'.	
Fri 15		British special envoy Lockhart first meets Trotsky who asks for Allied forces & trade in return for propaganda in Germany.		**Palestine** — Smuts cables that Allenby should have 2 divs from Mesopotamia for 1918 offensive. **Persia** — Dunsterville & armoured car leave Hamadan for Enzeli on Caspian (arrives 17 *see* 20). Last Russians evacuate Meshed in E, 176 British replace 14 Mar.
Sat 16	British Intelligence appreciation on imminence of German offensive. Foch aiming at Pétain's removal (Fayolle diary & 26). US Army Supply Services open at Tours.	LITHUANIA DECLARES INDEPENDENCE (*see* 23 Mar). Germans declare Armistice will end noon 18.		
Sun 17	BEF army cdrs' conference complains '... 'defence in depth' is not generally understood by the troops'.	Hoffmann diary: 'The whole of Russia is...a vast heap of maggots'. Ukrainian Rada appeals for German help v Red invasion. CEC rejects Lenin's proposal to accept German peace terms. **Finland** — 80 Finn *Jägers* land from Germany with 44,000 rifles, 65 MGs & some guns; 1130 more *Jägers* land (25).		
Mon 18	Wilson succedds Robertson as CIGS; Rawlinson replaces Wilson as British rep on Supreme War Council (19). **Flanders** — British trench raid in Houthulst Forest (& 27).	GERMANS RESUME WAR (-2 Mar): Op *Faustschlag* with 52 divs, which take Dvinsk & Lutsk, advancing down railways 30 miles pd. Lenin radio message accepts peace conditions.	**Italian Front** — Plumer ordered to return 2 divs to BEF (Haig prefers them to 4 Italian divs 15), but Italians provide no facilities until 22 after PM Orlando cables his protest (21, *see* 1 Mar).	**Mesopotamia** — Euphrates: British advance 14 miles from Ramadi to occupy Khan Abu Rayan & position 10 miles S of Hit.
Tue 19		7 Germans 'capture' 600 Cossacks. Hoffmann radios Trotsky that acceptance must be in writing.		**Palestine** — XX Corps + Anzac Mtd Div (6800 men & 54 guns) gain 2 miles on 15-mile front E of Jerusalem (-21) from Turk 53rd Div (3000).
Wed 20	**Lorraine** — French trench raid E of Nancy nets 525 PoWs.	**Germans march into Minsk** & Hapsal (Estonia, via G of Riga ice), have now taken 1500+ guns & 9000 PoWs.		**Persia** — Dunsterville leaves Enzeli for Hamadan just before 3000 Reds land from Baku to arrest him. He cables CIGS that a bde will secure British interests (26, *see* 23 Mar).
Thu 21	Patton writes from Langres '... I get requests...to transfer into tanks nearly daily'.	Lenin asks Sverdlov to form Revolutionary Defence Ctee v Germans who take Rechitsa W of Gomel. **Don** — Kornilov's 3000-strong Volunteer Army		**Palestine** — **Fall of Jericho**: Wellington NZ Regt sqn rides to Dead Sea. British cas 510 for 144 PoWs & 8 MGs.

AFRICAN OPERATIONS 5	SEA WAR 6	AIR WAR 7	INTERNATIONAL EVENTS 8	HOME FRONTS 9
				valueless (*see* 18 Mar).
Portuguese re-occupy Maloktera on upper Lurio. Rosecol from Port Amelia nearing Maza.	**Channel** — 11 German destroyers (2nd Flotilla) raid Dover Straits Barrage (night 15/16), sink trawler & 7 drifters (4 more vessels damaged) in 3hrs without any retaliation (*see* 21 Mar) due to RN misreading of Dover Patrol signals. U-boat shells Dover (16, 8 cas). *U55* last High Seas Fleet U-boat to use Dover Straits (18).		Allies form Allied Maritime Transport (*see* 11 Mar). **Occupied Poland** — Gen Haller & 5000 men escape to Russia (*see* 18).	**USA** — Govt takes control of foreign trade (from 16). **Britain** — Russian exchange rates no longer published. **Russia** — Sovnarkom creates Food & Transport Extraordinary Commission. **France** — Govt empowered to regulate economy by decree and requisition merchant fleet.
		Britain — Moonlight raid on London (18 cas): Giant R12 (Seydlitz-Gerstenburg) rams balloon apron 10,000ft over Woolwich & plunges 1000ft, inadvertently dropping 2 x 660lb bombs & injuring air mechanic; remaining bombs jettisoned at Beckenham, & before return to Belgian base. R39 drops **first 2204lb bomb** (largest of war) delivered to England, destroys N Pavilion of Chelsea Hospital. 1 (or 2) Giants ineffectually raid Dover (night 16/17); 60 defence sorties (3 brief attacks). **W Front** — RFC No 101 Sqn (FE2bs) begin night bombing of German airfields & rest billets (19, 21, 24 & 25). McCudden again scores 4 victories.		German Industrial Council formed.
		Germany — Solid cloud cover with rain forces 12 DH4s of No 55 Sqn to end mission v Mannheim chemical works. **Britain** — Giant R25 bombs St Pancras Stn & Hotel (42 cas from total 53) in solo London raid (night 17/18), engaged by only 3 of 69 defence sorties (1 fatal crash).	Kaiser's retort to Emperor Charles' telephone call on Bucharest peace talks 'Who does this young man think he is? Who conquered Rumania?'	Hindenburg memo to Chancellor: no more strikes, SDP & unions must condemn or be judged traitors.
		Germany — 8 FE2s (1 FTR) of No 100 Sqn start fire at Trier central stn; town receives 3 British raids (18-19, 2 day, 1 night). Damaging FE2 raid on Thionville blast furnaces & gasworks. **France** — Germans bomb Calais causing false alert in SE England, 55 sorties (night 18/19) & 2599 AA shells. **W Front** — **95th Aero (Pursuit) Sqn arrives in France: 1st 'homegrown' US fighter unit**, begins patrols 14 Mar (*see* 11 Apr).	**Occupied Poland** — Strikes in Warsaw (PM Kucharzewski resigned 11), demo (14) v territory transfer to Ukraine.	**Finland** — For Mannerheim Senate makes military training compulsory for men of 21-40 (effective 28). **Britain** — **CIGS Robertson resigns, Wilson succeeds**. Labour Ministry announces demobilization arrangements. Churchill attributes munitions increase to 12% bonus. Road Transport Control Board founded. **France** — Ex-Senator Humbert arrested for Bolo Pasha complicity.
		W Front — RFC issues concentration plan v expected German offensive. **Italian Front** — 11 RFC Camels bomb Casarsa (ex-Italian) airfield.	Gen Rawlinson appointed British rep to Supreme War Council. PM defends latter in Commons. **Secret War** — Emperor Charles sends peace message for Wilson to King of Spain via Madrid Ambassador (RN Room 40 intercept 20 & K Alfonso receives 21, handed to Pres Wilson 25, *see* 6 Mar).	**Russia** — **Land Nationalization decree published. Britain** — Prince of Wales takes his seat in the Lords.
	Baltic — Germans form task force at Kiel of 3 battleships, 3 cruisers & 4 torpedo boats (Rear-Adm Meurer) to support Finland intervention (-31 May; *see* E FRONT 2 Mar on).			**Britain** — Labour situation report suggests Brest-Litovsk main reason for industrial quiet.
	N Sea — K George V visits Harwich Force (new flagship cruiser *Curacoa*). **Adriatic** — Austrian *U23* sunk by Italian torpedo boat *Airone* off Valona.		Germany accepts Finn request for intervention (*see* E FRONT 26).	*Morning Post* editor & military correspondent fined £100 each for publishing without lawful authority. A Chamberlain attacks PM's press baron

FEBRUARY 1918	WESTERN FRONT 1	EASTERN FRONT 2	SOUTHERN FRONTS 3	TURKISH FRONTS 4
Thu 21 contd		evacuates Rostov (night 21/22) as several Red cols converge on it.		
Fri 22	**Flanders** — German trench raid on Ypres-Staden line.	French Gen Niessel has Russian defence plan ready but Trotsky (24) says no use.		
Sat 23	**Aisne** — Franco-American raid over R Ailette.	German peace terms become stiffer. Kühlmann & Czernin arrive at Bucharest to negotiate with Rumania. **Finland** — Mannerheim's 'Karellan' order of the day v Lenin. Bolsheviks agree to evacuate all Russian forces.		
Sun 24	Clemenceau visits Haig, former promises to deflect Foch's res scheme (done at Paris meeting 28, *see* 14 Mar).	**Soviets accept German terms** after CEC votes 116-85 for Lenin after he threatens resignation. Germans take Borisov & Dorpat (Estonia) with 3000 PoWs. Estonian Prov Govt forms in Reval, proclaims independent republic. **Don** — Reds occupy Rostov & Novocherkassk (25), Ataman Nazarov shot; 1500 Cossacks follow Whites.		**Armenia** — Turk II Caucasian Corps reoccupies Trebizond & Gümüsane, Turk 36th Div nearing Erzerum (25, *see* 10 Mar).
Mon 25		Seckendorff's N Corps takes Pernau, Reval with 626 guns, (Estonia, *see* SEA WAR) & Pskov. **Ukraine** — Linsingen reaches Zhitomir. Polish-German Military Convention signed at Bobruisk SE of Minsk. **Finland** — Mannerheim has 14,000 troops as 20,000 Reds attack towards Haapamaki & in Karelia (2000 Whites).		**Palestine** — Liman replaces Falkenhayn as Turk C-in-C (*see* 1 Mar).
Tue 26		**Soviet delegates return to Brest-Litovsk**. Maj-Gen Count Goltz put i/c 12th *Landwehr* or Baltic Div for projected German/Finland intervention (*see* 7 Mar).		
Wed 27	**Ludendorff & Kaiser first see the A7V German tank** (crew 16) & captured British Mk IVs (*see* 21 Mar).	German peace terms' ultimatum sent to Rumanian Govt at Jassy (*see* 5 Mar).		
Thu 28	(Feb) BEF take 312 PoWs. German general preparation period incl training for 56 divs over, now 180 divs in W (6 arrive in Feb). French order first (970) SP guns (Renault 75mm). **Aisne** — German attack nr Chavignon repulsed.	**Ukraine** — Austrians (incl Polish Legion) enter N of R Prut. Germans capture Russian Army Pripet Marshes Flotilla and reach R Dnieper nr Mosyr.		Allenby & Lawrence (visited GHQ 21) agree Arab Army (+700 supply camels) should take Maan while British cross Jordan, take Es Salt & destroy Hejaz Railway S of Amman.
Fri 1 March 1918	(Mar) French Army receives first Renault lt tanks (*see* 31 May). BEF strength 1,886,073 (incl 293,264 Empire troops) plus 118,427 labourers & non-combatants. **Flanders** — German trench raids, especially on Portuguese Sector nr Neuve Chapelle (Portuguese counter-attack succeeds 9). **Artois-Somme** — German final preparations (-14) begin with	Lockhart first sees Lenin, says Allied help acceptable v more German aggression. Trotsky cables Murmansk to accept 'any and all [Allied] assistance' (*see* 5). Peace and Amity Treaty between Red Finnish Social Republic & Russian FSR. Germans occupy Polotsk, Bobruisk, Gomel and Mohilev (old STAVKA). (Mar) 11 German divs leave for W Front	**Macedonia** — Gen Guillaumat reports to Foch no offensive possible till W Front or Italian Front Allied success, but probing attacks possible (*see* 14 Apr). **Italy** — British 41st Div entrains for France at Padua (-3, all back with BEF by 13); British 5th Div follows (16-1 Apr). Peak British ration strength 139,415 (under 90,000 from 1 May for duration) with	Turk Field Army (all fronts) only 200,000. German Ambassador Count Bernstorff writes 'Only Liman can pull off victory'. **Palestine** — Liman orders XX Corps to recross R Jordan (3-4) + 11th Div (from Armenia) down from Damascus. 38th Jewish Bn lands in Egypt. **Mesopotamia** — Ex-RNAS Armoured Car Sqn lands at Basra to be Duncars (24 Austins, *see* 5

AFRICAN OPERATIONS 5	SEA WAR 6	AIR WAR 7	INTERNATIONAL EVENTS 8	HOME FRONTS 9
				appointments.
Hawthorn NRFF col fights Capt Göring's 5 coys at Mtende (75 miles E of Luambala). Lettow now at Nanungu.		**Yemen** — 4 RNAS seaplanes from carrier *City of Oxford* scout, photo & bomb Turk positions nr Loheia (-28) giving the Idris's men footing in the hills; more air ops over Maidi (19-22 Mar).		
		Mesopotamia — 3-10 RFC aircraft bomb Turk camps & airfield in Hit area (-27) forcing German air unit back to Haditha.	United Socialist Republic of Transcaucasia established.	**Britain** — 3 Moscow Bolshe-viks inc Kamenev arrive in Aberdeen; go on to London. **Germany** — 2 PoW privates escape from Westerholt Camp, reach Holland 27.
	Adriatic — German raider *Wolf* returns to Pola having sunk 11 ships (33,000t) in 15 months. **Channel** — Keyes submits Zeebrugge Raid plan, Admiralty approves (*see* 22 Apr).		Count Motono says Japan will take adequate measures if Russia makes separate peace. Northcliffe asks Balfour's permission to focus propaganda on Austria's dissolution, Balfour refuses (26, but *see* 5 Mar).	**Russia** — Lenin *Pravda* article 'An Unfortunate Peace'. **Britain** — Police raid Communist club in Soho (37 arrests).
	Baltic — Russians scuttle 11 submarines at Reval to avoid capture, cruiser *Admiral Makarov* last ship to leave after German cyclists ride in. Red evacuation (5 cruisers, 8 submarines, 12 minesweepers & 31 auxiliaries take 4000 refugees) despite thick ice.	**Italy** — Austrians bomb Venice, Castelfranco & Mestre.	British War Cabinet discuss Siberian intervention. PM approves encouraging telegram to Japan (26, *see* 1 Mar). Britain recognizes Estonian Prov Govt.	**Britain** — Meat (2oz per adult pw) **bacon/ham** (4 oz per head pw), **butter & margarine** (5 or 6oz per head pw) **rationing for London & Home Counties** affects 10m people (*see* 7 Apr); German PoWs inc (26); queues vanish.
Rosecol occupies Meza after skirmish	**Bristol Channel** — Outward-bound British hospital ship *Glenart Castle* (95 lost) sunk by U-boat off Lundy I.	**Germany** — RFC night bombers destroy 100yd-long hangar at Frescaty airfield nr Metz (night 26/27). **S Fronts** — Austrian Gothas fly damaging 8-hr raid over Venice (night 26/27, *see* 4 Mar). **W Front** — 2nd Balloon Coy first US Air Service unit to give direct support to US front-line troops (*see* 4 Mar).		**Ireland** — Extra troops sent v lawlessness (carrying of arms forbidden 20).
		Britain — War Cabinet agree aircraft priority for W Front, but AA guns first to home defence.	US, British & other embassies leave Petrograd for Vologda & re-open there (by 13 Mar, -25 July).	British *Pictorial News* Official weekly newsreel replaces *War Office Topical Budget* (-7 Nov).
	Adriatic — Adm **Njegovan resigns as Austrian C-in-C** to facilitate 'rejuvenation' of command (*see* 10 Mar). Allied & neutral shipping losses to U-boats, 115 ships (68 British with 697 lives) worth 318,174t (British 226,896t). U-boat fig 138 ships worth 335,202t incl 37 ships of 84,118t in Med or 574t per U-boat day, highest since May 1917.			**Britain** — Lady Maude granted £25,000 (*see* TURK FRONTS 18 Nov 1917). **Serbia** — Pašić Cabinet resigns. **Canada** — Women's Ottawa War Conference (-2 Mar). **Hungary** — Army food supply in critical state, Govt orders more requisitioning.
British civil admin extended (i/c telegraphs in N from 1 June).	(Mar) **Top all-time U-boat ace Arnauld recalled** from Med to command new U-cruiser *U139* in which he sinks another 6 ships worth 7208t. **Secret War** — Canadian physicist R W Boyle obtains echoes from Harwich submarine at 500yds (inboard sets achieve up to 300yds by Armistice). U-boat sinks AMC HMS *Calgarian* (67 lives lost) off Ireland.	**Palestine** — RFC makeshift hydroplane 'Mimi' breaks down in attempt to destroy Turk boats on Dead Sea. **Germany** — Aero engine production 1400pm instead of 2500pm target under *Amerikaprogramm*; 1800 aircraft deliveries pm instead of 200. **W Front** — French form 2 mobile air reserves, *Aviation Res* with N Army Gp & *Escadre No 11*	Wilson approves Japanese action in Siberia, will send separate invitation (-2) but rethinks (5). **Germany refuses to supply Bulgar Army with munitions & clothing. Neutrals: Switzerland** — Fat & butter rationing cards.	**Britain** — RFP 107%, down 1%. Import limits to save 7-8mt in next yr. **Germany** — Pay cuts in Army-run plants. **France** — 35m rnds of 75mm field gun ammo available.

MARCH 1918	WESTERN FRONT 1	EASTERN FRONT 2	SOUTHERN FRONTS 3	TURKISH FRONTS 4
Fri 1 contd	advance parties moving up (-5). **Champagne** — Slight German advance at Butte du Mesnil, French recover 14.	(*see* 21).	457 guns & 180 mortars.	May).
Sat 2		Trotsky orders old Army's demobilization. **Linsingen captures Kiev. Finland** — 900 Germans occupy Aaland Is (sailed Danzig 28 Feb) & ready to intervene to Mannerheim's fury (*see* 5) but dissuaded from resignation.		**Palestine** — 53rd Welsh Div night advances 3000yds astride Jerusalem-Nablus road (& night 6, *see* 9).
Sun 3	BEF forms 5th Tank Bde. German trench raids in Flanders (& 8) & on Somme.	RUSSO-GERMAN PEACE OF BREST-LITOVSK: Russia renounces Baltic States, Poland, Belorussia, Finland & 3 Armenian districts to Turkey; 630,000 Austrian PoWs to come home. **S Russia** — Terek Cossack Soviet Republic declared. **Finland** — Red Guard offensive fixed for 9. **Estonia** — German Eighth Army occupies Narva (c85 miles W of Petrograd, *see* 12) after routing 1600 Red Guards & sailors, have captured 17,000 Russians & 1500 guns for 109 cas since 18 Feb. Hoffmann orders advance to halt except in the Ukraine.		
Mon 4	**Artois** — Cdn 21st Bn ejects 240-280 German raiders from Aloof Trench, W of Lens.	Germans claim 63,000 PoWs, 2600 guns, 5000 MGs & 500 planes since 18 Feb. Supreme Military Soviet formed at Petrograd. **Finland** — Order of the Cross of Liberty instituted at Mannerheim's suggestion.		
Tue 5	Germans introduce new ultrasecure 5-letter field cipher for Ludendorff Offensive, but French (Painvin) first solve c4 Apr, break 26; by 29 May only 2-day delay in reading it. **Flanders** — Belgian counter-attack N of Pervyse.	RUMANIAN-CENTRAL POWERS PRELIM PEACE signed at Buftea (*see* 22, 7 May: Dobruja ceded; Hungarian frontier to be 'rectified'; 8 divs to demobilize at once; Rumania to help Central Powers' march on to Odessa and grant German trade privileges. **Finland** — Mannerheim cables Ludendorff, thanks Kaiser for weapons & insists on Finn command of German troops & non-interference (Hindenburg agrees 10). **N Russia** — 130 Royal Marines land at Murmansk (French cruiser *Amiral Aube* arrives at RN request 19). **Latvia** — Falkenhayn (from Palestine) takes command of German Tenth Army for duration.	**Italian Front** — Lt-Gen Earl **Cavan succeeds** Gen **Plumer as British C-in-C** (*see* 12 Apr) despite Italian request that latter remain.	
Wed 6	**France** — YMCA takes over US Army canteens. **Yser** — Belgians repulse German night raid nr Ramscapelle (*see* 18).	**7th Bolshevik Congress renames Party Communist**, majority vote for peace (8). **Finland** — Peace Treaty signed with Germany (Berlin).		**Arabia** — Turks (inc 703rd German Bn) retake Tafila from Zeid & drive him on to Shobek (7), but Arabs re-occupy Tafila (20).
Thu 7	Haig & Pétain agree mutual reinforcement arrangements.	Hindenburg persuades Kaiser invading Finland 'healthy pressure' on Reds (*see* 1 Apr). Hoffman diary 'Our Bolshevik friends are now beginning to destroy the railways'.		

AFRICAN OPERATIONS 5	SEA WAR 6	AIR WAR 7	INTERNATIONAL EVENTS 8	HOME FRONTS 9
	Med — (Mar) Av of 10 U-boats at sea. **Channel** — (Mar) 29 U-boats transit through Dover Barrage (*UB54* lost 19).	(c250 aircraft) for ops E of Verdun, former becomes 1st Air Div (*see* 16 May).		
	Baltic — German landings in Aaland Is; 900 *Jägers* transported from Danzig (*see* E FRONT).		Lockhart cables Balfour after seeing Trotsky, urging Japan's restraint (*see* 4).	**Austria** — 2nd Pan-Slavic Conference at Agram (Zagreb) includes calls for independence.
	Central Powers' *Diktat* at Brest-Litovsk strips Russia of all Baltic naval bases except Kronstadt; also Odessa & Nikolayev (*see* E FRONT 12, 17; 17, 21 & 31) stipulates disarmament & detention of Russian warships in these ports pending general peace (*see* 12 May). **N Sea** — **First mine of Northern Barrage laid** in Area B up to 50 miles from Orkney (*see* 22, 26 May).	**W Front** — RNAS Dunkirk sqns put under Haig's orders prior to 1 Apr amalgamation (*see* 4 June).	'Sykes'(?) British letter to Feisal urges him not to oppose Jewish settlement (*see* 7 May).	**Germany** — R Göring's play *Seeschlacht* opens at Berlin. Kaiser orders flags in every city and day off school to celebrate peace with Russia. **Turkey** — Muslims of Samsun massacre all Armenians.
	Atlantic — Mysterious disappearance of ocean-going collier USS *Cyclops* en route Barbados-Baltimore with 10,800t Brazilian manganese (309 dead).	**Britain** — DH10 ('Amiens') heavy bomber first flies. 8403 women employed in RFC. **W Front** — US 94th Aero (Pursuit) Sqn arrives (flies first US recon petrol over German lines 19), is joined by future top ace Rickenbacker. **Italy** — Austrians bomb Venice for 8hrs (300 bombs) but lose 13 aircraft, also attack Padua, Mestre & Treviso; (early Mar) German *Jastas* 1, *31* & *39* return to W Front (for Ludendorff Offensive).	Balfour cables Tokyo to invite Siberian intervention (repeated 9, *see* 7, 13, 14, 22, 26); War Cabinet authorizes limited landing at Murmansk (*see* E FRONT 5).	**Britain** — 'Businessmen's Week' (-9) sells £138m of national war bonds, half in London at 'tank' banks. Louise Smith sentenced 10 yrs for spying. **USA** — Gen Peyton C March Acting CoS (appt 5 Feb & recalled from France), full CoS 24 May.
	Arctic — Allied naval ops begin (*see* E FRONT).	**W Front** — 1st US kite balloon coy in action.	Lloyd George asks for study of Bolshevik guerrilla warfare potential v Germans. Cabinet approves Austrian focus of Northcliffe's Enemy Propaganda Dept (*see* 18 Apr). US-Spanish Trade Agreement: former receives mules & blankets for cotton & oil.	Churchill War Cabinet memo 'How are we going to win the war in 1919?'; promises Lloyd George 4000 tanks by Apr 1919 (8). First Lord Geddes criticizes shipbuilding output, in Commons.
	British War Cabinet gives 1917 Allied & neutral shipping losses, a 2,632,297t deficit.	**W Front** — RFC night bombing of railways, airfields & ammo dump on 7 nights (-20).	Wilson reply to Emperor Charles asks for full territorial details before reps meet. Austrian reply sent via Japan never received. Allied Ctee for Chemical Warfare Supplies formed.	**Britain** — †Irish Nationalist leader J Redmond MP (62), Dr J Dillon succeeds (30). **USA** — Baruch Chm, War Industries Board. Navy Sec declares 5-mile alcohol-prohibited zones round naval training stns.
	Japan declines to send more destroyers to European waters.	**Britain** — 3 of 6 'Giant' bombers sent attack London (63 cas, 25 houses destroyed, night 7/8) in moonless conditions; 2nd 2204lb bomb employed. 42 defence sorties k	Japan tells Britain Siberian intervention impossible without US approval. Yugoslav Ctee & Italian deputies sign co-operation agreement in London (*see* 10 Apr).	**Britain** — Commons votes record £600m war credit. Est daily cost pd £6.75m. **USA** — Wilson authorizes bronze Army medal DSM.

MARCH 1918	WESTERN FRONT 1	EASTERN FRONT 2	SOUTHERN FRONTS 3	TURKISH FRONTS 4
Thu 7 contd				
Fri 8		**Trotsky appointed People's Commissar for War**. Baltic Duchy of Courland's throne offered to Kaiser; Germans declare protectorate (15).		
Sat 9	German gas bombardment for Somme offensive (Ypres-St Quentin): 500,000rds mustard gas & phosgene (1000t) directed at British (esp Flesquières salient opposite Cambrai) & French positions; 7223 gassed (87 deaths) (-19).	Russo-Rumanian Peace Treaty. Berthelot's French Military Mission leaves Rumania (3 trains to Murmansk). **Finland** — 15,000 Red Guards attack & fail v 7350 Whites in central region (-14). Red C-in-C sacked (15).		**Mesopotamia** — Euphrates: Brooking's 15th Indian Div occupies Hit (valuable bitumen fields), Turks retreat 22 miles to Khan Baghdadi (*see* 26). **Palestine** — Actions of Tell 'Asur or Battle of Termus Aya: Chetwode's XX Corps (21,500 & 325 guns) crosses Wadi Auja, captures Tell 'Asur (2958ft) despite 5 Turk counter-attacks (8800 & c150 guns), advancing 2-5 miles on 13-mile front (-12) for 1313 cas, only 169 Turk PoWs.
Sun 10	BEF GHQ Weekly Intelligence Summary: '... the imminence of the [German] offensive in the Arras-St Quentin area has been confirmed ...'. **Hindenburg orders Op Michael** (*see* 16). Germans begin diversionary ops & feints in various sectors incl Champagne & Verdun.			**Armenia** — Fighting round Ilica & Tekedere (-11).
Mon 11		Lenin article stresses Russia's might will be restored. Wilson sympathy message to Congress of Soviets on peace treaty.		
Tue 12	**Champagne** — German attack at Vaudesincourt E of Reims.	**Soviet Govt moves from vulnerable Petrograd to Moscow** (Lenin arrives 11). **Rumania** — PM Gen Averescu resigns (*see* 20). **Finland** — Red offensive in Karelia ends, Whites 11,700-strong. **Ukraine** — **Linsingen occupies Odessa**, Austro-German row over precedence. Austrians capture Russian midget submarine (3) at Reni, R Duna. **Siberia** — Sino-Japanese vols fight Reds at Blagoveschensk.	**Macedonia** — 3000 Russians riot at internment camp nr Vertikop, French cav unit restores order with sabres. Greek 1st (Larissa) Div (12,000 & 16 guns) begins move to Struma valley, enters British sector line from 26 (*see* 14 Apr); 13th (Chalcis) Div replaces 1st in Naresh training area.	**Palestine** — Bulfin's XXI Corps (104 cas) advances 3 miles on 7-miles of coastal sector, taking 5 villages & 112 PoWs. **Armenia** — **Turks retake Erzerum** (Armenian military cas 600), reach Olti (26).

AFRICAN OPERATIONS 5	SEA WAR 6	AIR WAR 7	INTERNATIONAL EVENTS 8	HOME FRONTS 9
		2 pilots in collision, no sightings. **Occupied Belgium** — Scheldewindeke Giant bomber base opens S of Ghent, probably first airfield with paved runways.	**Neutrals: Holland** — Allied note demands unconditional use of Dutch ships in Allied ports (*see* 18).	
	Irish Sea — German U-boat mine found off Walney I (Lancashire). Mersey-laid mines found (9) & cleared by paddle-steamers in 48hrs.	**France** — 60 Gothas (1 lost) drop 92 bombs on Paris (59 cas). **Mesopotamia** — RFC bombs & strafes Turks retreating from Hit (-10), 225 bombs dropped (*see* 25).		**France** — Clemenceau speech wins confidence vote. **USA** — Soldiers & Sailors Civil Relief Act; war cost $30m pd.
		W Front — DH9 operational debut: controversial DH4 replacement aircraft of No 6 (Naval) Sqn attack St Pierre Capelle. 53 RFC aircraft attack 3 German airfields W of Le Cateau, hits on all three (repeated on Busigny 17 & 18 qv). Ludendorff's *Michael* offensive, air units fly in (-12, *see* 21). **Germany** — British raid to Mainz. **Italy** — Germany Navy airship *L59* (Bockholt) attacks Naples naval base & steel plant (50 cas); raid attributed to Austrians (their seaplanes do raid 11). RFC claim 64 kills since 10 Nov 1917 for only 12 losses.	**Last peace feelers till Sept:** Smuts meets Austrian diplomat Skrzynski in Switzerland (-14) & Lloyd George's Private Sec Kerr also has meeting (15). Czernin cables Vienna (19) that Franco-Italian annexation demands destroy any continued talks.	**Turkey** — Chamber attacks on Govt food policy, latter proposes (30) doubling produce tax in kind to feed Army & officials & forms Supreme Food Commission (but *see* 21 July).
	Adriatic — Emperor Charles makes 49yr-old Capt **Horthy** Rear-Adm & **Austrian C-in-C**, 4 cruisers & 2 old battleships soon taken out of service to redeploy crews. (c) Younger Vice-Adm Cusani (ex-CNS) appt Italian Fleet cdr. **Bristol Channel** — Hospital ship *Guilford Castle* torpedoed in by U-boat but makes port.	**Germany** — 11 DH4s (1 FTR, crew taken PoW) of No 55 Sqn attack Stuttgart Daimler motor works; formation attacked after bombing (1 fighter driven down). Same sequel after 9 DH4s hit Koblenz barracks (70 cas, 12).	US War Sec Baker arrives in France, visits US 2nd Div 20.	**France** — **Bombing causes mainly orderly 200,000-strong rail exodus from Paris** (-6 Apr, *see* AIR WAR 8 & 11). **USA** — Film *The Kaiser, the Beast of Berlin* opens.
HQ Pamforce estab at Meza.		**France** — 60 Gotha bombers (4 FTR) attack Paris (night 11/ 12, 141 cas incl 101k when War Ministry hit). Another 66 die in panic rush for Metro shelters. AA guns fire 10,000 rnds. Single bomber attacks (24). (*see* HOME FRONTS 10.) **Russia** — Austrians launch **first ever scheduled international airmail service** (-Nov) between Vienna & Kiev using modified Hansa-Brandenburg C I 2-seater recon aircraft (-Nov).	Kühlmann visits Bucharest, **Secret War** — DMI cables Adm Kolchak at Singapore, asks him to go to Manchuria via Peking.	**Portugal** — Universal suffrage for over-21s (*see* 26 Apr). **Britain** — British Industries Fair, London (-22). *The Times* now 3d.
Germans driven from Poluvu.	Allied Naval Council, 2nd meeting in London (-14) discusses Adriatic offensive but Allied generals lukewarm. **Baltic** — 4 Russian dread-noughts & 3 cruisers leave Helsinki for safer Kronstadt, arrive (17) after icebreakers clear way (*see* 4 Apr).	**Britain** — Woman dies of shock, another w when Navy Zeppelins *L61* , *L62* & *L63* bomb Hull; dense cloud prevents attack on Midlands objectives, 2 of 3 Giants divert to Boulogne; *L42* (Dietrich) drops 21 bombs on W Hartlepool docks (47 cas, night 13/14). **W Front** — Richthofen's 64th victory in *Jasta 11*, clash with 9 Bristol Fighters of No 62 Sqn (4 lost). Next day (13) Richthofen's c35 fighters destroy 4 aircraft but lose 3 Fokkers & 1 Albatros (incl Lothar von Richthofen w in crash) (*see* 18). **Salonika** — RFC derail Bulgar train nr Porna, shoot German plane into L Tahinos (13), bomb Drama airfield hitting 4 hangars (22, more raids follow).	**Rumania** — Gen Berthelot seen off by King & Queen at Socola Stn.	**Austria** — Report on Govt wartime measures (-1 July 1917) published. Strikes resume on railways & in 2 munition factories. **Britain** — Labour Ministry forms Resettlement Ctee.

MARCH 1918	WESTERN FRONT 1	EASTERN FRONT 2	SOUTHERN FRONTS 3	TURKISH FRONTS 4
Wed 13	**Flanders** — Australian raid nr Ypres-Comines Canal. British capture strong point SE of Polygon Wood.			
Thu 14	Allied Supreme War Council (Lloyd George & Clemenceau) in London backs Haig-Pétain partnership despite Foch's protest, Allied reserve only when AEF present in force.	Soviets 4th Congress ratifies Brest-Litovsk Treaty at Moscow. Reds occupy Ekaterinodar (Kuban Cossack capital), *see* 9 Apr.		Retreating Armenians on old Russian frontier. Turco-Transcaucasian Trebizond Conference opens (*see* 30).
Fri 15	French Reserve Army Gp reformed under Fayolle.	Allies in London discuss Japanese intervention v Germans but Americans object. Sovnarkom allows Czech Legion evacuation to Omsk (*see* 18). **Finland** — Mannerheim Offensive (12,000) towards Tampere (-19), takes 700 PoWs & 10 guns (*see* 20). 2nd phase (20-25) cuts off town (-25), he cables for speedy German arrival (20).		
Sat 16	Most German Op *Michael* arty now in position, inf begins night approach marches (-18). **Verdun** — Raid & counter-raiding, French take 160 PoWs, Germans 200.			**Arabia** — Arabs disperse Turk camel corps NW of Medina. Hejaz Railway nr Bowat damaged, train derailed (19-20).
Sun 17	2 German deserters tell BEF XVIII Corps to expect 6hr barrage, but no date.	**Ukraine** — Kosch's German LII Corps (from Dobruja) occupies Nikolayev, hold all W of Dnieper incl Kherson (20), advance continues (-29).		
Mon 18	Hindenburg & Ludendorff moved forward from Spa to Avesnes. British & Portuguese trench raids. Churchill visits front (-22). **Yser** — Belgians (1800 cas) repulse heavy local attacks at 3 points & one E of Nieuport (30).	**Allies refuse to recognize Brest-Litovsk Treaty**. Czech Legion begins rail journey E but stopped at Penza by Soviet (22,*see* 26).		
Tue 19	German attacks in Champagne & on Meuse. **Somme** — Gen Gough writes home predicting German offensive on Thu 21. Germans issued with special gasmask filters, 20 AT bullets, & grenades. British pre-emptive gas bombardment nr St Quentin: 5649 projectors fire 85t phosgene; 1100 gassed (250 deaths).			
Wed 20	Final council of war on Op *Michael* at German GHQ Avesnes. Record (so far) 190 German divs in theatre.	**Rumania** — Maghiloman new PM, Arian Foreign Minister. Bucharest talks with Central Powers from 21.		
Thu 21	**Somme** — SECOND BATTLE OF THE SOMME AND GERMAN SPRING OFFENSIVE begins: German Michael Offensive (or 'Kaiser Battle') (-5 Apr) against BEF. Ludendorff aims to cut off British from French between Rs Oise & Scarpe. Battle of St Quentin (-	German Army strength 698,883 men (42 divs); 176,688 horses; 2739 guns; 232 mortars; 9645 MGs. Lockhart wires Balfour Trotsky wants British instructors for Red Army. **Rumania** — Col Drozdovski (ex-CO Russian 14th Inf Div) leads 900 men in 61-day, 900-mile march to	**Macedonia** — German strength 60,481 men, 18,769 horses, 293 guns, 36 mortars, 336 MGs.	**Palestine** — German strength 4 bns, 4 MG coys, 72 guns (18 flak), 86 MGs. **Mesopotamia** — Nejef Political Officer Capt Marshall murdered.

AFRICAN OPERATIONS 5	SEA WAR 6	AIR WAR 7	INTERNATIONAL EVENTS 8	HOME FRONTS 9
			War Cabinet told of RN Petrograd Attaché's warning that Japanese action may drive Russia into German arms.	**Germany** — Interior Minister Waldow decides to cut farmers' rations not workers to save 140,000t before Ukraine grain arrives.
		Italy — RFC No 42 Sqn leaves to rejoin BEF. **N Sea** — Floatplane clash: 2 RNAS attack 5 German (1 FTR, 1 damaged, 1 observer k).	Balfour defends proposed Japanese Siberian intervention in Commons (*see* 22). 4th Supreme War Council meeting in London (*see* 18).	**Britain** — Haig at No.10 'They did their best to get me to say that the Germans would not attack'. **France** — Social Insurance law inc worker/ employer/state contributions.
	E Atlantic — Destroyer HMS *Michael* depth charges & sinks *U110* off N Ireland.	**W Front** — French ace Fonck (20 victories to date) kills German ace & fighter leader Tutshek (27 victories) over Champagne (*see* 9 May).	Prince Lichnowsky's Aug 1916 memo justifying British pre-war diplomacy appears in German press, he is retired for it (26 Apr).	**France** — Explosion in Courneuve district nr Paris (30k, 1500w). **Britain** — Haig's son (present Earl Haig) born.
Nigerian Bde (3 transports) returns to Lagos & great reception (*see* 11 June).	**Aegean** — Rear-Adm C Lambert replaces disgraced Hayes-Sadler i/c RN Sqn.			**Secret War** — Haig tells King he can smash any attack. Churchill memo envisages mine-clearing tanks. **Austria** — Vienna police report '... great and rather widespread resentment against Germany'.
	Black Sea — German occupation of Nikolayev gains ships building incl 1 dread- nought, 3 cruisers, 4 destroy- ers, 2 gunboats & 3 submarines (*see* 21 & 31).			**Ireland** — De Valera tries to hold public meeting v military proclamation in Belfast.
L Nyasa — Ex-German gunboat *Hermann von Wissmann's* maiden voyage as British transport *King George*.		**W Front** — Air 'Battle of Le Cateau': Richthofen leads 30 fighters (among up to 50 German) v 29 RFC aircraft, destroying 9 for 1 Albatros. Germans claim total of 28 Allied aircraft for loss of 7.	**Allies refuse to recognize German treaties with Russia & Rumania. Neutrals: Holland** — Govt accepts Allied ultimatum with reservations. Allies repeat 19 & USN seizes 40 Dutch ships in her ports (20, full compensation to be given; 3000 sailors repatriated July). Britain does likewise (21).	**Canada** — Parlt (-24 May) votes $500m war spending.
	N Sea — Harwich Force (Capt St John *vice* Tyrwhitt on leave) with 3 French destroyers from Dunkirk tows 6 barges with seaplanes to make dawn recon off Terschelling I shooting down 1 German seaplane (repeated 21).		Austrian ex-Foreign Minister Burian diary 'No one will now listen to the word "peace". Everything is based on the forthcoming offensive as if everyone were entrusting himself without a tremor to the decision of fate' (*see* 29).	**Britain** — House of Lords debates League of Nations principle. **USA** — Daylight Saving Act for 31 May-27 Oct.
	E Med — Allied convoy loses 4 ships to U-boat N of Alexandria, warning of its presence not received. **Britain** — Lord Pirrie made DG of Merchant Shipbuilding, soon improves repair procedure for damaged ships.	**Germany** — **Iron Cross markings ordered changed** to *Balkankreuze* (Greek Cross) as from 15 April. **Britain** — Trenchard tenders resignation but retained till 15 Apr. **W Front** — French capture German observation balloon with (bogus) documents revealing *Roland* offensive for 26 in Champagne.	Allied Blockade Ctee formed & first meets in London. Henderson declares Labour cannot accept Brest-Litovsk. France recognizes Polish National Ctee as head of Polish Army on W Front. *Reichstag* ratifies Russian & Rumanian treaties.	**Germany** — *Reichstag* debates Army seizure of Daimler (Stuttgart). **Britain** — Sir E Geddes says world shipping tonnage fell 8% in 1917, Britain's by 20%; Lord Pirrie made Controller-Gen, Merchant Shipbuilding. COAL, GAS AND ELECTRICITY RATIONING INTRODUCED; theatres to close at 10.30pm, restaurants at 10pm (*see* 26).
	N Sea — Destroyer action: HMS *Botha* (from Dunkirk) rams & sinks German coastal torpedo boat *A7*, one of 2 and 5 destroyers shelling Dunkirk. HMS *Morris* sinks disabled *A19* after pursuing remainder back to Ostend which Dover Patrol monitors shell.	**W Front** — On *Michael* sector of attack: 720 German aircraft (326 fighters) v 579 RFC (261 fighters) in 31 sqns. Udet designated CO *Jasta 11* succeeding Lothar von Richthofen. Total German front line strength 3668 aircraft. **Fog hinders early air ops** but 36		**Britain** — **Miners under 25 lose military service exemption** (to recruit 50,000). **USA** — Railroad Control Act gives Federal control until 21 months after peace ratification.

MARCH 1918	WESTERN FRONT 1	EASTERN FRONT 2	SOUTHERN FRONTS 3	TURKISH FRONTS 4
Thu 21 contd	23): **German main attack v British Fifth Army** (Gough) on 42-mile S sect from Gouzeaucourt to Barisis, S of La Fère. German N attack on British Third Army (Byng) by 25 divs of Seventeenth (Below) & Second Armies. 5hr German bombardment by record 6473 guns & 3532 mortars on 43-mile front v 2500 British begins at 0440, shelling 20 miles behind, causing up to 7500-8000 cas. Lavish use of Blue & Green Cross gas shells is expected to paralyse British arty (2m gas shells expended by 6 Apr). German stormtroops attack in dense mist at various points between 0700 & 0930 & advance up to 4^{1}/$_{2}$ miles; meet fierce battle zone resistance. Germans advance to Crozat Canal SW of St Quentin. First of Gough's res divs in evening action. First 9 German tanks in action. **For 39,929 cas Germans inflict 38,512 cas (21,000 PoWs), take 532 guns, 46 ruined villages & 98.5sq miles of ground more than Allied 1916 Somme offensive in 141 days. Artois** — British gas attack at Lens: 3728 projectors fire 57t phosgene; 700 gassed (150 deaths). **Champagne** — German attack between Maisons de Champagne & Navarin; hand-to-hand fighting in French forward trenches. Mustard gas attack on US 42nd Div.	escape Germans, reach Rostov (4 May), and join White Volunteer Army. German strength 156, 672 men (8 divs); 38,307 horses; 563 guns; 130 mortars; 1073 MGs.		
Fri 22	**Somme** — GERMANS OVERRUN MOST OF BEF BATTLE ZONE. Masses of inf advance; Germans 'leapfrog' fresh divs through tired troops. British slowly pushed back, 25 tanks (16 lost) & 19th Div counter-attack well at Beugny. Germans capture Epéhy & Roisel, cross Crozat Canal & reach Vaux. 2nd of Gough's res divs enters battle am. Gough decides to fall back on positions E of Somme. Germans claim 16,000 PoWs & 200 guns.		British CIGS advises that 5 more Allied divs be sent from Italy to W Front incl 2 Italian (*see* 18 Apr).	**1st Trans-Jordan 'Raid':** Shea's Force (85 cas) cross swollen river at Hijla v 1000 Turks & 6 guns for raid on Amman.
Sat 23	**Somme** — **Battle of St Quentin ends.** British lose line of Crozat Canal: Gough decides to continue retreat to W bank of Somme. Germans enter Ham & Péronne (evacuated) & pursue to there; some bridges lost more or less intact. French inf (5 divs ordered) begin to arrive by lorry to take over front S of Péronne, 1 regt in action. Byng's Third Army abandons Flesquières (Cambrai) Salient. **Paris Gun**: 3 special 8.26in Krupp guns (misnamed 'Big Berthas') begin daily shelling (303rds) of Paris (-9 Aug) with 23 shots at range of 74 miles (256k, 620w). First bombardment 183 shells (-1 May), *see* HOME FRONTS 29.	Hoffmann agrees to make Crimea a German colony. German recognizes Lithuania (*see* 14 May).	British War Cabinet decide not to send any of the 4 Salonika divs to France, too malaria-ridden (*see* 21 Apr). **Salonika** — 16,000 watch (incl Milne & Guillaumat) British Salonika Army's boxing championship. **Italian Front** — Conrad ordered to prepare Austrian Asiago offensive, but Piave one added by 21 Apr (*see* 31).	**Persia** — Dunsterforce begins famine relief incl road improvements. First inf join Dunsterforce as last Russians leave Hamadan (29). British E Persia Cordon field force 1514 + 1474 local levies (31).
Sun 24	**Somme** — **First Battle of Bapaume** (-25). Separation of BEF & French Armies threatened. Germans destroy 500-strong SA Bde, cross Somme between Ham &	Reds seize Vladivostok telegraph office, causing strike, Red Guards arrive (26, *see* 28).	**Italian Front** — 3 French divs recalled to W Front (-26); Corsican Graziani replaces Maistre as C-in-C.	Anzac Mtd Div & Camel Bde across Jordan, ride 9 miles on Amman in rain & mud; 60th Div captures El Haud Hill & 3 guns. Now 9600 British & 82 guns v 5500 (max) Turks & Germans &

AFRICAN OPERATIONS 5	SEA WAR 6	AIR WAR 7	INTERNATIONAL EVENTS 8	HOME FRONTS 9
	Secret War — French naval attaché in Jassy (Rumania) cables that 7 trainloads of German sailors reported in Kiev bound for Black Sea (*see* 31).	RFC sqns see action by end of day losing 16 planes for 14 claimed crashed kills (Germans admit 11 & claim 21 Allied planes). British lose 3 observation balloons. 27 German *Schlachtstaffeln* (168 planes) attack British Third & Fifth Armies.		
	N Sea — British minesweeping sloop *Gaillardia* (68 lives;lost) mined & sunk due to too shallow-laid Northern Barrage mines. Laying not resumed until 20 Apr. Destroyer HMS *Kale* mined & sunk (27).	**W Front** — **17 RFC sqns move bases back**; ops almost all ground attack (RFC lose 30 to German 11). RFC night bombers destroy 2 ammo dumps.	France asks Japan for ships to evacuate Czechs from Vladivostok, but none immediately available (*see* 26).	**Britain** — Call for 3-month volunteer doctors gains only 27 (*see* 18 Apr).
	N Sea — 4 British echo-ranging E Coast stns accurately fix Dover Patrol monitors bombarding Zeebrugge. **W Med** — Italian minelayer *Partenope* sunk by *UC67* off Tunisia after firing her last shell.	**W Front** — French fighters reinforce RFC (38 planes lost incl 6 in Flanders; Germans claim 29 Allied aircraft for loss of 14) between the Oise & Somme (-24) who claim 36 German aircraft as weather improves.	Wingate chairs Residency/Arab Bureau Cairo meeting on 'The Future of Arabia', it agrees Ibn Saud not going to accept Hussein as overlord.	**Britain** — War Cabinet crisis meeting after which FM French urges that Plumer replace Haig. 1st general govt dried fruit distribution. **Germany** — Kaiser returns to Berlin, shouting that English beaten.
		W Front — Waves of 20-80 French bombers intervene in BEF's Somme battle, *Gp Féquant* from Soissons & Fère-en-Tardenois, & *Gp Manard* from Châlons (25), effort		**Britain** — Churchill dines with PM & CIGS: 'I never remember in the whole ... war a more anxious evening', PM 'unshaken'.

MARCH 1918	WESTERN FRONT 1	EASTERN FRONT 2	SOUTHERN FRONTS 3	TURKISH FRONTS 4
Sun 24 contd	Péronne; farther S they push back Allies & capture Chauny rail jctn. At Villeselve 150 British cav (73 cas) charge & inflict 195 cas, take 3 MGs. A shaken Pétain orders Fayolle above all to keep 'the solid connection of the French armies and then, if possible, to preserve contact with the British Forces'. At 2300 Pétain visits Haig & refuses further reserves as he expects main German blow in Champagne at any moment. Haig enquires if he means to abandon BEF right flank & allow Germans to penetrate; Pétain nods assent! Haig cables War Office for Wilson & War Minister Milner to come to France at once, emphasizing 'unless General Foch or some other determined general is given supreme command of the operations...there will be a disaster'.			c26 guns.
Mon 25	**Somme — A gap opens between BEF & French Armies. Germans capture Bapaume, Nesle & Noyon.** Gough's Fifth Army pushed back c4 miles on 23-mile front. Haig fears Allied armies' separation only a question of time, asks for 20 French divs to fight astride Somme & cover Amiens (under heavy bombardment). Gen Fayolle takes command S of Somme; 7 French inf divs & 1 cav div now engaged. *OHL* now claims 45,000 PoWs. Germans oust Third Army from Bapaume. Noyon falls to night assault despite British 18th Div counter-attack. Gaps opening between BEF & French armies & between British XIX Corps (Watts) & XVIII Corps (Maxse). **Crisis of the battle:** Gough summons his chief engineer Maj-Gen Grant & directs him to form scratch force (Carey's Force -2 Apr) of 3000 with 92 MGs incl 500 US rail engineers & hold line E of Amiens. Pershing offers Pétain 4 US divs at 2200; 2 relieve French divs in quiet sectors. Haig, Wilson & Weygand meet at Abbeville.	**Finland** — Mannerheim attacks Tampere (-28) v bitter resistance (*see* 3 Apr). Karelian Finn ski troops raid into Russia & cut railway to Petrograd (-26). Last Red attack on Ahvola (Karelia) just fails (26).		**Palestine** — 3rd ALH occupy Es Salt.
Tue 26	DOULLENS CONFERENCE between Clemenceau, Lord Milner, Haig, Pétain & Foch (all but Haig met at Compiègne 1700, 25). At Haig's proposal FOCH APPOINTED TO CO-ORDINATE ALLIED MOVE-MENTS (Pres Wilson approves 29). Foch immediately switches Debeney's First French Army from St Mihiel sector towards Amiens & asks both Haig & Pétain to maintain a united front. Pétain makes a pessimistic report on his plans to fortify & defend Amiens 20 miles behind front. Foch retorts: 'We must fight in front of Amiens. We must stop where we are now. As we have not been able to stop the Germans on the Somme, we must not retire a single centimetre!' **Somme — German 3rd**	Soviet-Czech agreement for Czech Legion's evacuation (Stalin cables Paris).		**Mesopotamia — Battle of Khan Baghdadi** (-27): Brooking's c11,000 men, 48 guns, 16 planes, 13 armoured cars & 300 Ford vans storm 2 Turk trench lines & cut Aleppo rd trapping 5254 PoWs (inc Nazim Bey, CO 50th Div), 12 guns & 47 MGs for 159 cas.

AFRICAN OPERATIONS 5	SEA WAR 6	AIR WAR 7	INTERNATIONAL EVENTS 8	HOME FRONTS 9
		especially v German convoys continues (26-29). Capt J L Trollope in Camel of No 43 Sqn RFC scores 6 victories. **RFC lose 65 aircraft** to claim of 42 German (17 in Flanders). German claim is 35 Allied for 14 lost. Germans night bomb Albert & Amiens (10hr interruption to rail traffic). **Germany** — Handley Page makes first raid on Cologne since 1914 (night 24/25). **India, NW Frontier** — 3 bombs kill 14 armed tribesmen at Marri district capital (submits 19 Apr). **Palestine** — 8 RFC aircraft bomb Amman.		
		W Front — Over 100 RFC aircraft ground attack to support BEF Third Army. **Mesopotamia** — RFC CO Col Tennant shot down & captured in DH4 at Khan Baghdadi by Euphrates (8 armoured cars rescue 28). RFC air liaison essential in British Khan Baghdadi victory, also make 32 ground attacks dropping 6344lb of bombs (26-27).	Sino-Japanese Agreement to resist hostile influences. **British War Cabinet discuss possibility of BEF retreat to Channel ports.**	**France** — May Day Saint Etienne strike only voted 35-19 (*see* 1 May). **USA** — Boston Symphony Orchestra Director K Muck arrested as enemy alien (actually Swiss).
	St George's Channel — RN *PC51* depth charges & sinks *U61*, sinker of 36 ships (90,770t) since 1916.	**W Front** — British Third Army uses 27 of its 34 RFC sqns or over 250 aircraft for close support, total 29t (c1437) bombs & 228,000rnds by formations of up to 60 aircraft. RFC lose 50 planes (Germans claim 12 for loss of 5) for 10 German claimed. Both sides night bomb. RFC drop record 1326 bombs.	Japanese PM says Siberian crisis may soon compel action. Allied Paris Food Supplies Conference (-27).	**Britain** — **Churchill cables all factories for increased output** & Easter holidays' deferment (1500+ firms do); assures War Cabinet 2000 guns ready for BEF by 6 Apr. Light, Heating & Power Order, no lighting in public places after 10.30pm.

MARCH 1918	WESTERN FRONT 1	EASTERN FRONT 2	SOUTHERN FRONTS 3	TURKISH FRONTS 4
Tue 26 contd	**Marine & 54th Res Divs enter Albert**. British Whippet light tanks first in action: 12 rout 2 German bns, helping Anzacs plug Hébuterne-Colincamps gap in Third Army front after 22-mile retreat in 5 days. Germans capture Roye from the French.			
Wed 27	BEF weekly officer cas record 6325 since 21. **Somme — Turning point in great offensive** (Rupprecht). French ousted from Montdidier (c50 miles from Paris), key railhead for reinforcements to Amiens, by Hutier's Germans, but checked by Fayolle between Lassigny & Noyon. **Battle of Rosières**: British XIX Corps takes 800 PoWs and holds firm by the Somme. In Allied centre Germans capture Proyart, Morcourt & Lamotte-Warfuseé & are 12 miles E of Amiens. Still a 10-mile gap between the British & French. Foch orders 'lose not another metre of ground!' Dismounted cav halt key German thrust 11 miles E of Amiens as 3rd Australian Div (Monash) comes up.	**S Russia** — Kornilov joins Kuban volunteers (*see* 9 Apr).	**Salonika** — Heavy snowstorm.	**Palestine — Allenby warned to stay on defensive & spare troops for France** (9 Yeo regts, 26). Anzac Mtd Div attacks & temporarily isolates Amman, but 2nd attack fails (28) as Turk Fourth Army C-in-C Djemal Kuchuk takes over German-stiffened defence.
Thu 28	**Pershing places AEF units at Foch's disposal** (*see* 2 Apr). **Artois** — FOURTH BATTLE OF ARRAS: Ludendorff's Op *Mars* fails bloodily with 9 divs v 4 to clear N flank of his 'bulge' against British Third Army & Arras itself. Local German attacks towards Amiens gain 3 miles; Germans take Hamel, Mézières & Démuin, but fail to cut off XIX Corps' retreat from Rosières. At 1630 **Rawlinson replaces Gough (recalled)**. French counter-attacks recapture 3 villages. Ludendorff orders completion of preparations for reduced Flanders Op *Georgette*. In the est 8-10 days before (actually 12 days) he orders all efforts be made to secure Amiens. King visits BEF (-30).	Lockhart says Reds willing to rejoin Allies. Lenin ensures Red Army has central non-elective command (inc ex-Tsarist officers *see* 1 Apr & 8 May). **Siberia** — US Adm Knight (cruiser *Brooklyn*) reports Reds moving 40 rail cars pd of Allied munitions.		**Mesopotamia** — British armoured cars capture Ana, its radio stn & drive 73 miles beyond (-29).
Fri 29	**Somme** — German offensive slackens, along Ancre N of Somme, quiet phase begins (-3 Apr). Kaiser briefed at Mons. Lüttwitz's III Corps drives Anglo-French back up to 2 miles on 7-mile front between the Avre & Luce.	**Ukraine** — German 2nd Cav Div occupies Poltava.		**Palestine** — R Jordan again rises (9ft), *see* AIR WAR.
Sat 30	**Somme** — British, Australian & Canadians (1400 cav) counter-attack, recapture most of Moreuil Wood & 3 other woods. Marwitz's 8 divs gain only a mile, now 11 miles E of Amiens. French heavily engaged on 25-mile front between Moreuil & Lassigny as 14 Germans divs gain 2 miles on av, capturing 6 villages & doubling Avre bridgehead.	Lenin urges revolutionary court to be 'mercilessly severe in dealing with counter-revolution-aries, hooligans, idlers & disorganizers'.	**Albania** — Austrian attempt v Italian Avlona bridgehead fails.	**Palestine** — 3rd attack on Amman fails v citadel, night retreat ordered. NZ Bde covers (31). **Armenia** — Turk I Caucasian Corps takes old Karaurgan frontier post, patrols penetrate c8 miles.
Sun 31	Easter Day: Germans claim 75,000 PoWs & c1000 guns since 21 Mar. German Army peak ration strength 7,917,170. **Somme** — Indecisive fighting. Hofacker's LI Corps recaptures woods lost on 30. Ludendorff orders 4 Apr thrust for Amiens	Germans form new Army Group Eichhorn (18 divs) at Kiev for Ukraine occupation, CoS Gröner to organise railways; Linsingen removed & *Bugarmee* dissolved.	**Italian Front** — Announced that British troops now on Asiago Plateau (transferred 11-31) instead of Montello. They carry out frequent trench raids (-9 June). (c) Arz to Hindenburg 'I am confident as a result of our [forthcoming spring]	

AFRICAN OPERATIONS 5	SEA WAR 6	AIR WAR 7	INTERNATIONAL EVENTS 8	HOME FRONTS 9
Part of Pamforce advances 18 miles W through Natovi & Namarika (-28).	**N Sea** — 5 minelaying British destroyers sink 3 German armed trawlers (72 PoWs) 70 miles NW of Heligoland Bight.	**W Front** — *JG1* shoots down 13 RFC planes (39 lost in all) over Albert (3 to Richthofen) without loss. *Schlachtstaffeln* attack 4 villages on Somme & Ancre. **RFC drops record 50t bombs & fires 313,345 MG rnds**. On whole front Germans admit 6 losses for 34 Allied victims. Can 2/Lt A McLeod wins posthumous VC for repelling 3 Fokker Triplanes & his saving his w observer.		
	Atlantic — UA cruiser *U157* investigates Spanish liner *Infanta Isabel de Bourbon*.	**W Front** — RFC lose 58 planes in low-level ops (7 German shot down) dropping 40t bombs & firing 242,000rnds.	Lloyd George sends Churchill to Clemenceau via BEF GHQ. King visits W Front (-30). **Occupied Belgium** — French agent Fauquenot escapes Liège prison at 3rd attempt, spies on till Armistice.	**Canada** — Quebec anti-conscription riots (-2 Apr) draw in 4590 troops to quell (*see* 1 Apr).
		Palestine — 13 German planes bomb Shumet Nimrin defile (39 human & 175 camel cas from 2000 supplying British Trans-Jordan ops). **W Front** — Weather curtails ops.	**Lloyd George cables Wilson for immediate commitment of US troops** + 120,000 pm to Europe (Clemenceau also 31, *see* 1 Apr). Czernin urges Emperor Charles to launch Italian Front attack to support Hindenburg.	**Britain** — First Good Friday newspapers due to grave war news. **France** — **Paris Gun causes 165 civilian cas in Church of St Gervais**. Senate votes 1919 class call up.
		Italian Front — Lt Jerrard in Camel of No 66 Sqn RFC (taken PoW) wins VC for destroying 3 of 6 out of 19 Austrian fighters engaging 3 Camels. **W Front** — RFC personnel loss of 199 since 24 highest wkly total of war until 15-21 Sept.	Lloyd George announces Foch's appointment, Clemenceau & Churchill see him at Beauvais.	**Germany** — Adm Müller to Kaiser staff colleague: 'Mars rules the hour'.
Germans have marched 2500 miles through Portuguese territory to date.	**Black Sea** — *Goeben* carries Central Powers Armistice Commission to Odessa. Allied & neutral shipping March losses: 169 ships (79 British with 490 lives) worth 244,814t (British 199,458t incl 3 mined). U-boat fig 190 ships worth	**W Front** — 822 German aircraft supporting Ludendorff Offensive v 645 British, but only 3 Anglo-German combats as Germans claim 19 Allied aircraft for loss of 4. BEF Fifth Army's AA guns claim 17 aircraft since 21. Germans admit Mar loss of	Lloyd George tells Dominions 'the last man may count'. Vienna newspaper *Arbeiter-Zeitung* says greatest land victory cannot defeat Anglo-Saxon seapower.	**Britain** — HMG ends dividends on Russian state loans. 59,316 war widows pensions granted in last yr. **France** — (Mar-Nov) Good medical care returning 60,000w pm to the armies. **USA** — Daylight Saving Time in force. **Austria** — 44,000

MARCH 1918	WESTERN FRONT 1	EASTERN FRONT 2	SOUTHERN FRONTS 3	TURKISH FRONTS 4
Sun 31 contd	after supplies brought up. British capture then lose Hangard; slight French advance between Montdidier & Lassigny. **BEF Mar losses** 173,721, **second worst month of war**, incl 124,462 inf & cav since 21.		offensive which must bring us to the Adige, we shall achieve the military dissolution of Italy.'	
Mon 1 April 1918	**Somme** — Heavy clashes nr Albert, Grivesnes & at Hébuterne. British war poet & painter Pte Isaac Rosenberg k aged 27 E of Arras (4th Div). 1000 British dismtd cav (300 cas) recapture Rifle Wood with 100 PoWs & 13 MGs.	(Apr) 8 German divs transfer to W. Front. Red Army now 114,678, 30 divs planned (88, May). **Finland** — German Baltic Div sails from Danzig escorted by 4 battleships. Whites close ring on 1000 Reds in Battle of Rautu (-5). **Secret War** — (Apr) French Capt E Bordes, officially helping Red Ukraine C-in-C Antonov, moves 3000 rail wagons of munitions to Samara on Volga, out of German reach. Similar convoys (incl strategic minerals) to Tsaritsyn and Baku.	**Salonika** — (Apr) 6000 Serbs from old Russian corps arrive after journey across Siberia to Port Arthur.	**Palestine** — EEF total ration strength a record 316,605 incl 22,400 Anzacs, 865 S Africans, 37,622 Indians, 9272 Egyptians; plus 115,379 followers. 7th Indian Div has relieved 52nd Lowland Div (sails from Alexandria for France 4-11). **Mesopotamia** — (Apr) c200 Turks desert (*see* 26).
Tue 2	**Pershing agrees to brigade troops with British & French** (*see* 23). **Artois** — British 32nd Div recaptures Ayette S of R Scarpe. **Somme** — British Fifth Army renamed Fourth (*see* 23 May).	Sovnarkom decrees barter for grain. Turk Ambassador presents credentials.	**Italian Front** — Cavan & CIGS discuss forming Anglo-Italian Army under British command (-30), but deferred (*see* 9 Oct).	Amman Raid troops (1348 cas) back over Jordan (+ 986 Turk PoWs & 4 guns, *see* 11).
Wed 3	**Beauvais Conference**: Foch further empowered to direct Allied strategy (*see* 14). **Somme** — Local fighting in Scarpe & Hébuterne sectors.	Germans take Ekaterinoslav, NE of Odessa. All-Russian Bureau of Military Commissars formed, works when military regions created from 8,*see* 22. **Finland** — 9445 **Germans**, 18 guns & 165 MGs **land at Hangö** (-5) (*see* SEA WAR). Mannerheim's final assault on Tampere (-6).		**Baluchistan** — Successful British ops v Marris (tribesmen). **Arabia** — Lawrence leaves Abu-el-Lissal with 2000 baggage camels, reaches Atara area, SE of Amman (6), recces town in gypsy clothes.
Thu 4	FINAL GERMAN EFFORT TOWARD AMIENS (-5 Apr): Battle of the Avre begins with 15 German divs v 7 Allied & 1278 guns. After initial panic British & 2250 Australians repulse 9th Bav Res Div before Villers-Bretonneux. 5 French divs counter-attack & gain ground in Castel-Cantigny sector. Since 21 Mar Germans have advanced up to 40 miles			Dr Weizmann's Zionist Commission lands at Jaffa, explains aims at Jerusalem (27).

AFRICAN OPERATIONS 5	SEA WAR 6	AIR WAR 7	INTERNATIONAL EVENTS 8	HOME FRONTS 9
	368,746t, incl 68 ships of 128,620t in Med (4 of 151,273t to Austrians); 5 U-boats sunk (2 to unknown cause).	161 aircraft and claim 447 Allied.		deserters captured since 1 Jan, summary jurisdiction declared v desertion (20).
Tripolitania — (Apr) Ottoman Prince Fuad arrives by U-boat at Misurata to try and unite tribes v Italians. **E Africa** — British ration strength 49,035 (14,366 British, 3720 S Africans, 10,097 Indians, 20,852 Africans) with 18 guns (-11 May) plus 124,447 porters and followers.	**Med** — (Apr) First Sea Lord & RN Intelligence chief Rear-Adm Hall visit Malta to reorganize C-in-C's staff to reduce shipping losses. Fixed Otranto Barrage begun (-Sept) but 121 U-boat passages (-Aug, *see* 3 Aug) despite 58 depth charge attacks. **Atlantic** — (Apr) **Fast US troop convoys begin,** transporting 1,037,000 troops for loss of 3 transports (*see* 2 May); *Aquitania* carries 60,000 men in 9 voyages. **Britain** — (Apr) HMS *Simoom*, first S-class destroyer completed (ordered Apr 1917), 18 more completed by Armistice. (Apr) **Allied shipbuilding for first time exceeds lost tonnage and does so for duration.**	**Britain** — RAF ESTABLISHED by Act of Parlt: world's 1st fully independent air arm amalgamates RFC & RNAS (c2950 aircraft), administered by Air Ministry under Sec of State (Lord Rothermere). CAS: Trenchard (dep CAS Kerr). **Women's Royal Air Force (WRAF) formed.** Retains RFC organization. All ex-RNAS units (add 60 to sqn nos & 200 to wing nos); RNAS officers receive military ranks; 63 RAF sqns & 1 Special Duty Flt in France. (Apr) London Air Defence Area has 282 fighters (14 airfields), 260 guns & 353 searchlights. **France** — 7 Gothas drop 21 bombs on Paris (*see* 11). **Med** — RAF HQ at Malta, 6 aircraft carriers based there or at Alexandria & Mudros. **Salonika** — No 150 Sqn RAF formed with flights from Nos 17 & 47 Sqns, destroys or captures 36 Bulgar aircraft for loss of 1 (-18 Sept). **W Front** — RAF Nos 100 & 216 night bombing Sqns transferred to French zone to raid rail targets in Châlons-sur-Marne sector, 6 nights (-9 May). **Persia** — Martinsyde Scout of No 72 Sqn joins Dunsterville at Hamadan. **Palestine** — (Apr) One British AA section of 2 guns (17 sections with EEF) in action 76 times, firing av of 100 rpd, Germans esp note hampering of recon during 13-19.	Lord Reading cables London from Washington that 480,000 US troops coming to France at 120,000 pm. **Neutrals: Switzerland** — (Apr) 12.4m letters/cards, 3.5m parcels & 133,000 money orders sent to PoWs.	**Britain** — RFP 106% (as Jan), limited tram & rail services, gas & electricity rationing in force (2). **France** — (Apr) Guillaume Apollinaire's war poems (*Calligrammes*) published in small edition. **USA** — (Apr) Newsreel *The German Curse in Russia* showing; *Over the Top* film features veteran Arthur G. Empey. **Canada** — **Troops fire on Quebec anti-conscription rioters**, 4k, 58 arrested curfew (2). **Austria** — Army GHQ forms 'counterpropaganda' dept for PoWs returning from Russia.
		W Front — RAF claims 11 German aircraft shot down (8 S of Somme), but Germans admit no losses and claim 16. McCudden (57 victories) awarded VC.	Gen Dallolio cables Italian support to Churchill. Lloyd George cables India urging redoubled efforts (*see* HOME FRONTS 27). Count Czernin addresses Vienna Municipal Council, blames Western Powers for prolonging war, reveals French 'peace offer' (*see* 9).	**France** — Poincaré visits Renault factories and sees tank trials (*see* 8).
	Baltic — 3 Russian & 7 British submarines blown up outside Helsinki harbour (latter by remaining 26 RN sailors) to avoid capture (-5) together with their mines & torpedoes; crews transferred to Murmansk via Petrograd (*see* E FRONT). Capt Cromie stays behind to continue as Naval Attaché (*see* RUSSIA 31 Aug) & scuttle 3 small British merchantmen (9-10) trapped since 1914.		Allied Blockade Ctee meets. Lloyd George in France for day, meets Foch, Clemenceau & Haig at Beauvais.	**S Africa** — Gen Botha appeals for recruits. Gen Hertzog's secessionist speech (12) denounced by Sir P Fitzpatrick in House of Assembly (18).
	Adriatic — 61 Austrian sailors land N of Ancona (night 4/5) but captured before they can seize a MAS boat & blow up submarines there (*see* 8 May). **Baltic** — Rear-Adm Meurer's Sqn (incl 2 dreadnoughts) supports German landings at Hangö (*see* E FRONT); 2 more Russian battleships, 2 cruisers & 2 submarines escape from Helsinki to Kronstadt (10).	**Palestine** — RAF bomb Amman Stn, hitting train.		**Canada** — Males 16-60 must be usefully employed. **USA** — *Life* Magazine satirizes German professor's claim 'Our culture is largely an imitation of the French'.

APRIL 1918	WESTERN FRONT 1	EASTERN FRONT 2	SOUTHERN FRONTS 3	TURKISH FRONTS 4
Thu 4 contd	& secured 1200sq miles of Allied territory, with 90,000 PoWs & 1300 guns. BEF has received 101,000 inf replacements so far, often teenagers. US 3rd Div lands in France.			
Fri 5	SECOND BATTLE OF THE SOMME (*Michael* Offensive) ENDS; Ancre front stabilized by 4th Australian Div (1233 cas) after 50th Prussian Res Div (c1600 cas) gains 1500yds; counter-attacking British 37th Div take 200 PoWs nr Hébuterne. LUDENDORFF DECIDES 'TO ABANDON THE ATTACK ON AMIENS FOR GOOD... The enemy resistance was beyond our powers' (War Memoirs). 13 German divs are left in awkward Avre salient & W Front 26 miles longer.	**Germans occupy Kharkov. Finland** — Battle of Rautu ends with Whites sealing Karelian frontier. **Siberia** — 500 Japanese marines & 50 Royal Marines land at Vladivostok to protect foreign nationals (-25), Lenin threatens Japan with war (8).		Armenians leave Sarikamish night 5/6 after Turks take village to N (*see* 19). **Turk 5th Div reoccupies Van.**
Sat 6	**Somme** — Severe fighting in Albert & Hébuterne sectors. Arty duels (7) **Meuse** — German attacks nr Beaumont. **Aisne** — Reims heavily shelled. 6 divs of Boehn's Seventh Army drive French Sixth Army from bridgehead N of R Ailette (-9) taking 2300 PoWs.	**Finland** — **Tampere falls** with 11,000 PoWs & 30 guns to Mannerheim who makes his 3 corps cdrs maj-gens.		
Sun 7	**Artois** — British repulse 2 attacks on Bucquoy.	**Finland** — Red Guards evacuating Helsinki; German Col Brandenstein's 2000-strong bde & 8 guns from Reval lands unopposed at Lovisa to E (*see* 19). **Siberia** — French military mission ordered to screen all Czechs.		**Palestine** — 74th (Yeo) Div relieved from Front (-11), embarks Alexandria from 29.
Mon 8	**Flanders** — Germans shell whole BEF front incl 40,000 mustard shells on Armientières. Portuguese bn refuses to march to trenches (relief due evening 9). **Aisne** — Germans reoccupy Coucy le Château, reach Oise-Aisne canal line (9).			
Tue 9	**Flanders** — LUDENDORFF'S SECOND BLOW, BATTLE OF THE LYS (-29) (German *Georgette* offensive against BEF First & Second Armies on R Lys) BEGINS. Ludendorff aims to drive back British & Belgians W of Dunkirk & open road to Calais. After 4½ hr hurricane shelling 14 German Sixth Army divs attack from 0845 on 10-mile front; 4 divs overwhelm Portuguese 2nd Div (6000 PoWs) & drive a 3½ -mile deep wedge, steadily widened, into BEF front although 55th Div holds S wing taking 750 PoWs & 100 MGs (*see* 16). British & Portuguese pushed back to R Lys at Estaires (fighting -11), losing one footbridge. German gas bombardment of Lys (-27) sector: 1m rnds (2000t) mustard gas, phosgene & diphenylchlorarsine; 8424 gassed (30 deaths). **Somme** — French lose & regain Hangard.	**Count Mirbach appointed German Ambassador to Moscow** (arrives 23). Moldavian National Council passes Act of Bessarabian union with Rumania; Ukraine protests (16, Moscow 18), but Germany recognizes. **Kuban** — Kornilov's 6000 Whites repel Red attack on their R Kuban crossing place, and storm ridge W of Ekaterinodar (10), but Avtonomov's 20,000+ Reds in town resist fiercely (-12, *see* 13).		Action of Berukin (-11): British 75th Div (+162 guns) attacks in Judean foothills v Turk 16th & 46th Divs (+85 guns), gains only 2500 yds. Turks capture ops order on 1st day & 2 German bns strike back. (EEF 1498 cas, Turks c700.) **Arabia** — Arabs claim 40,000 Turks neutralised to date.

AFRICAN OPERATIONS 5	SEA WAR 6	AIR WAR 7	INTERNATIONAL EVENTS 8	HOME FRONTS 9
NRFF occupy Mahua (*see* 11).		**Occupied Belgium** — DH4s of No 55 Sqn fly 3 abortive missions this wk v German GHQ at Spa (dense cloud). **W Front** — Despite losing 16 airfields to German advance since 21 Mar, RFC/RAF has made 45 new ones. German bomber & ground attack air gunners awarded badge like pilots & observers.	**Occupied Poland** — Steczkowski new PM.	**USA** — **German immigrant Robert Prager lynched as suspected 'spy'** (Collinsville, Ill), countless other non-lethal incidents. Wilson discusses with cabinet (6) but does not publicly deplore mob spirit till 26 July. Prager buried (10), Germany tries to pay funeral expenses, 12 tried for crime from 13 May but acquitted. War Finance Corp created with $500bn.
Morocco — French attack Abd-el-Malek's entrenched camp (& 8, *see* 16 June).			K George V greets USA on 1st anniversary of entering war. Wilson (Baltimore) says German actions in Russia mean 'force without limit' only answer. Churchill persuades French to continue poison gas use despite Red Cross efforts.	Third US Liberty Loan drive for $3bn begins, passes $4.1bn by 18 May. Memorial to Pte Gresham (first AEF k) laid at Evansville, Indiana.
	N Sea — Keyes addresses Zeebrugge raiders, not one withdraws. Wind & high sea abort attempt on 11 & 12 (*see* 22). **Baltic** — Red Fleet's final 'ice-crossing' evacuation (-11) from Helsinki of 48 destroyers; 2 torpedo boats; 12 mine-sweepers/layers; 10 submarines; 92 other vessels to Kronstadt by 22, only 85 left behind according to 5 Apr agreement with Gemans.	**W Front** — Capt G McElroy RAF (18 victories since 18 Feb) in SE5 collides with tree; he returns to front June, kia 31 July. **Adriatic** — German Navy airship *L59* (Bockholt) catches fire (cause unknown), crashes in Straits of Otranto before planned raid on Grand Harbour, Valletta, Malta (23 k, no survivors).	**Occupied Belgium** — German decree suppresses courts.	**Britain** — **National meat rationing introduced** (-15 Dec 1919, *see* 14 July 1918).
Rosecol recce coy skirmish E of Medo (84 miles from coast). Gambia Coy returns home to Bathurst.			Conference of Nationalities Oppressed by Austria in Rome (-10), votes for national self-determination.	**USA** — National War Labor Board appointed. **Turkey** — Constantinople housing rents fixed at 50% 1 Mar 1916 level for war + 6 months, but law largely dead letter. **France** — First Renault tank bn formed with 72 tanks (*see* 4 May).
Giffard's Kartucol (2 KAR bns) begins march to Medo in pouring rain (*see* 12). Rosecol advances skirmishing on Medo (10).	German torpedo boats shell Belgian coast (*see* W FRONT) & Adinkerke (18).	**W Front** — **Fog delays** Flanders **flying in Ludendorff Lys offensive** till late pm (-11): 492 German aircraft (incl 14 *Jastas*) v 38 RAF sqns, RAF lose 10 planes to German 15 (*see* 12).	**Clemenceau discloses Emperor Charles' 31 Mar 1917 peace letter** to Prince Sixtus. Czernin calls it a lie (*see* 10). Burian diary 'Now we really are tied to the fate of Germany whether we want it or not' (*see* 14).	**Britain** — Lloyd George introduces Manpower Bill (comb-out of munition workers; age up to 50 but over 40s home service only; extension to Ireland, *see* 16). **France** — (c) 10½ oz bread pd for 13-60- yr olds, 2/3 previous. Rail freight charges up 25% (15).

APRIL 1918	WESTERN FRONT 1	EASTERN FRONT 2	SOUTHERN FRONTS 3	TURKISH FRONTS 4
Wed 10	**Flanders — Germans recapture Messines Ridge**: BEF evacuate Armentières after 8 German Fourth Army divs attack on 6-mile front, but British retain Lys line.	**Baltic States** — Estonian Riga assembly refuses union with Germany but Kaiser consents (21, *see* 13). **S Russia** — Germans take Kherson & Belgorod, NE of Kharkov. **Don Cossack Rising** under Esaul Fetisov (*see* 21).		
Thu 11	**Flanders** — Armentières falls to Germans: Germans take Merville. British 25th Div loses Hill 63. Haig's 'Backs to the Wall' Order of the Day: '... there is no other course than to fight it out ... with our backs to the wall...each one of us must fight on to the end.' Germans claim 20,000 PoWs.	Bolsheviks liquidate anarchist clubs.	**Italian Front** — FM Conrad persuades Emperor Charles at Baden to concentrate spring offensive on Trentino sector (*see* 23).	**Palestine** — 4000 Turks (48th Div+) & c40 guns fail to retake Ghoraniyeh Jordan bridge-heads (4500 Anzacs & Camel Bde, 33 guns), lose 472+ cas for 100 defenders. **Hejaz Railway** — Arab regulars storm stns N & S of Maan & hill to SW (-13), take but fail to hold Maan Stn (16), 327 PoWs & 3 MGs taken (*see* 19).
Fri 12	**Flanders — German offensive slackens** 6 miles from Hazebrouck (-16) although Merville falls. British 5th Div arrives from Italy & 1st Australian Div comes up. Battle of Hazebrouck (-15): 4 British divs defend Nieppe Forest (-15), BEF First Army defends Hinges Ridge N of Béthune. Kaiser arrives at Armentières, anticipating victory. **Argonne** — Franco-Americans repulse attacks in Apremont Forest.		Sir H Plumer's British Italian Front dispatch of 9 Mar published; British 5th & 41st Divs now recalled to W Front leaving 3 divs.	
Sat 13	**Flanders — Battle of Bailleul** (-15): Germans gain less than ½ mile v British 34th & 59th Divs. Ludendorff sacks II Bav Corps cdr. British 25th Div reoccupies Neuve Église, but loses it (14).	**Finland — Germans take Helsinki** for 200 cas, White Finn Govt says entirely at their request. White W Army occupies Pori & its railway with Rauma (17). **Baltic States** — United Diets resolve to form separate state within German Empire. **Kuban** — White Volunteer Army repulsed from Ekaterinodar, **Kornilov k** by Soviet shell, **Denikin succeeds** and orders retreat N back to Don.		**Palestine** — Liman vainly asks Enver to let him resign (*see* 22 June).
Sun 14	FOCH APPOINTED ALLIED GENERALISSIMO ON W FRONT. **Flanders** — 1st Australian Div repels massed charges; a German field gun destroys 6 MGs. British First Army repulses 7 attacks nr Merville.	Clemenceau says France does not recognize Bolshevik Govt.	**Salonika** — Anglo-Greek ops across the Struma temporarily occupying 7 villages (night 14/15-20) but, due to poor reconnaissance, Bulgars nearly cut off a British bn (most of 349 cas) & Greeks lose half 33 cas to own premature grenades; Bulgars claim 150 British PoWs & 3 MGs.	
Mon 15	**Flanders** — *Alpenkorps* & 2 other divs capture Bailleul & Wulverghem. Plumer evacuates 5 divs from Passchendaele Ridge. Robillot's French II Cav Corps (3 divs) arrives nr Cassel, 5 inf divs follow (17-18, *see* 19). **Somme** — Fierce arty duel in Luce valley.			**Turk 37th Div takes Batumi** after fighting since 9 (3000 Georgian PoWs, Enver visits '18). **Palestine** — Wavell made Brig-Gen & CoS XX Corps.
Tue 16	**Flanders** — Passchendaele reoccupied by German			

AFRICAN OPERATIONS 5	SEA WAR 6	AIR WAR 7	INTERNATIONAL EVENTS 8	HOME FRONTS 9
	E Atlantic — U-boat shells Monrovia, Liberia destroying radio stn (4k) and armed steamer. **Adriatic** — 8 Franco-Italian destroyers, escorting 3 Italian battleships, move from Brindisi to Taranto, lose 2 of their number in night collisions.		Czernin calls Clemenceau's claims lies and sends Emperor Charles' cable to Kaiser assuring him French claims to Alsace-Lorraine never recognized (*see* 12).	**Britain** — Special Branch Head Thomson reports peace meetings almost ended. **Canada** — £100m war credit bill introduced.
2 coys of 3/1st KAR (40+ cas) engage Capt Müller's 2 coys 25 miles SW of Nanungu (Lettow's HQ).	**Med** — Marseilles-bound British transport *Kingstonian* (9 lost) sunk by U-boat (*see* 12 May). **N Sea** — Dover Patrol shells Ostend & its aircraft bomb Zeebrugge. Dover Barrage claims *UB33* & *UB55* (22). **Baltic** — German dreadnoughts *Westfalen* and *Posen* arrive off Helsinki from Reval (*see* E FRONT 13), but sister ship *Rheinland* crippled by rocks off Lagskär (600t incl all guns removed before refloated for return to Kiel but not repaired).	**W Front** — US I Corps Observation Sqn flies 1st mission over German lines. 94th Aero Pursuit Sqns first successful patrol destroys 2 German aircraft (14, pilots PoWs). **France** — Single Gotha bomber drops 1543lb bomb on Paris (99 cas). **Occupied Belgium** — Only 4 of 7 Handley Pages bomb nr Zeebrugge area (2 FTR).	Report rightly claims British PoWs maltreated and used close to front line (*see* 14 June). **Neutrals: Holland** — Food riots, troops quell (12).	**Britain** — Wastepaper collection 4000t pm. **USA** — National German-American Alliance dissolves itself, gives assets to American Red Cross.
Action at Medo: Kartucol and Rosecol (155+cas) join after former's flanking move ambushed in swamp by Capt Köhl's 800 Germans, 12 MGs and 1 gun; 7hrs fighting before Köhl retreats from Chirimba Hill. Rosecol resumes advance on Mwalia (15), skirmishes (28 cas) with German rearguard (17).	**Adriatic** — Austrian raid on Otranto Barrage (-13). **N Sea** — **Grand Fleet base moved from Scapa to Rosyth for duration.**	**Britain** — **Last Zeppelin raid to cross coast & cause damage or cas.** 5 Navy airships scatter 33,340lb-worth bombs across W Midlands & N England (night 12/13, 27 cas). *L61* (Ehrlich) bombs Wigan (claims attack on Sheffield). 27 defence sorties (5 sightings) cost 3 aircraft. **W Front** — Capt H Woollett RAF in a Camel scores 6 victories. **Flanders** — **Over 170 RAF planes attack at Merville jctn** on R Lys for 13hrs, lose 10 planes for 5 German & 5 German balloons. Little German air support for advance till 25 (*see* 29) but German fighters check RAF from 13.	French news agency publishes all Charles' Sixtus letter.	**Ireland** — Commons 165 maj for conscription. RIC arrest Cp Dowling (ex-PoW in Germany) of 'Irish Bde' in Co Clare, gives misleading account of German landing, 2 more arrests (16) for trying to contact U-boat. **Germany** — Food Dictator says no satisfactory economic solution. **Austria** — Yugoslav-Croat-Slovene Assembly at Agram takes solidarity oath.
				France — 'What do a few kilometres matter, or a few cities in flames?' (*Journal*, André Tudesq). **Austria** — Emperor Charles suffers minor heart attack during Czernin crisis. Union of Czech Deputies renew oath to a Czechoslovak state. **Ireland** — 2k raiding RIC barracks at Gortatlea, Co Kerry (*see* 17 & 18).
	N Sea — *U151* (Nostitz) leaves Kiel for US E Seaboard. She re-enters Kiel 20 July claiming 23 ships sunk of 61,000t (+ 4 mine victims). In all, big U-cruisers carry out 7 transatlantic summer cruises but fail to sink one loaded transport.		**Austrian Foreign Minister Count Czernin resigns**, Baron Burian again in post (16), *see* 22.	**USA** — *A Dog's Life*, Chaplin's latest film, released.
	N Sea — 2 RN minelayers lay deep minefield 10 miles NE of Laeso; escort destroyers *Valentine* & *Vimeira* sink 10 German trawlers off Anholt I deep in Kattegat. **Adriatic** — Adm Horthy orders increased security at Pola (*see* 14 May). Allies begin to lay net barrage from Fano to Otranto (-30 Sept).	**Britain** — CAS **Trenchard resigns**; succeeded by Maj-Gen Sir F Sykes.		
			Holland to send convoy to E Indies; HMG announce right of	**Britain** — Military Services Bill passed (198 maj). **USA** —

APRIL 1918	WESTERN FRONT 1	EASTERN FRONT 2	SOUTHERN FRONTS 3	TURKISH FRONTS 4
Tue 16 contd	**Fourth Army**: Wytschaete & Meteren (with record c1000 NZ PoWs) lost & retaken by Allies. Haig praises 55th Div's gallantry at Givenchy (9-17) in special dispatch. **Artois** — Heavy fighting S of Arras.			
Wed 17	Ludendorff orders Aisne attack preparations by German Crown Prince (*see* 1 May). **Flanders** — German offensive renewed but without decisive effect; Wytschaete & Meteren captured. **First Battle of Kemmel Ridge** (-19). Belgians take 700 PoWs & 42 MGs NW of Dixmude. **Somme** — Heavy German mustard gas attack on Villers-Bretonneux.			
Thu 18	**Flanders** — **Battle of Béthune**: Heavy German attacks from Givenchy to the Lys, 10 miles gained since 9; slight German advance at Givenchy v British 1st Div (-19). **Somme** — Reinforced French 18th Div takes 650 PoWs nr Castel SE of Amiens, 500yd advance with tank support.		**Macedonia** — 4-day British arty harassing in L Doiran sector plus 3 trench raids (20 & 22) cost 136 cas for 100 Bulgars; Italians in Crna bend repel Bulgar attacks (& 24). **Italy** — Italian II Corps (3rd & 8th Divs) begins to entrain (-27) for W Front (*see* W FRONT 13 May); comprises 52,826 men as symbol of Allied unity & affront to Austria.	Anzac Mtd Div demo across Jordan fails (*see* 30).
Fri 19	**Flanders** — Lull in fighting; minor actions (-24). Gen de Mitry assumes command of French N Army Det (-5 July) which relieves British IX Corps, 6 battered British divs withdrawn for rest. **Belgium** — Lt-Gen Gillain replaces Lt-Gen Rucquoy as CoS under K Albert.	**Finland** — Col Brandenstein captures Lahti, cutting off 25,000 Red Guards & joins with Whites (20). Fighting till Reds surrender (-2 May). **S Russia** — **Germans invade Crimea**, occupy capital Simferopol (24).	**Trentino** — Successful British minor action on Asiago (& 25).	**Armenia** — Turk I Caucasian Corps breaks Nazarbekov's 9000-strong Armenian line (350 cas) SW of Kars. **Hejaz Railway** — Lt-Col A Dawnay & Lawrence + 5 armoured cars, 2 aircraft, Egyptian Camel Coy & Bedouin capture Tell-esh-Shakin Stn (54 PoWs, 200 rifles), occupy Ramleh & wreck 80 miles of line; Medina cut off from N.
Sat 20	**Flanders** — German gas bombardment of Kemmel-Ypres: 9m rnds (2000t) mustard gas, phosgene & diphenylchlorarsine fired (-25) at BEF: 8470 gassed (43 deaths). **Somme** — Skirmishes go in favour of British (-22). **Meuse** — Germans gain ground at Seicheprey (Woëvre) v Franco-Americans, who counter-attack successfully (21). **Artois** — Pershing visits Cdn Corps.	**Finland** — Mannerheim attacks towards Viborg with 24,000 men & 40 guns (-29).		
Sun 21	British cas on Somme & in Flanders since 21 Mar total nearly 250,000.	**Petrograd** — Prokoviev's Classical Symphony first performed. **Don** — Prov Govt proclaimed under Janov's Cossack Council.	**Salonika** — CIGS Wilson cables Milne with request for 12 bns (reducing his divs to 9 bns each) for W Front from 15 May (*see* 29 May). **Italian Front** — Austrian corps cdrs ordered to hasten preparations for offensive.	CIGS cable asks Allenby to send 14 more British bns to W Front (sent early June).
Mon 22		Reds decree compulsory military training for men 16-40 (*see* 29 May).		**Tiflis Diet** proclaims independent Trans-Caucasian Federative Republic, which orders ceasefire (23).

AFRICAN OPERATIONS 5	SEA WAR 6	AIR WAR 7	INTERNATIONAL EVENTS 8	HOME FRONTS 9
			search (19).	Schwab made DG Shipbuilding (4 E Coast shipping firms taken over, 11). **Rumania** — League of the People Party formed at Jassy, Gen Averescu leader.
	N Sea — Dover Patrol monitors *Erebus* & *Terror* shell Ostend. **N Atlantic** — 4 RN drifters sink *UB82* in N Channel. **Adriatic** — Italian submarine *H5* sunk in error by HM Submarine *H1*.		Gen Belin succeeds Gen Weygand as Pres, Allied Supreme War Council (announced 21). Croat Dr Trumbic visits Gen Diaz at Italian GHQ.	**Britain** — Irish Nationalists leave Commons (decide to remain in Ireland 20). Churchill cable praises Birmingham tank factory on deliveries. King's message to munition workers (21).
			Lord Derby new British Ambassador to Paris. **Italy** — PM Orlando announces Italian troops sent to W Front. **Central Inter-Allied Propaganda Commission begins work at Padua** (by Oct 70m publications sent to Austrian Army & beyond cause much desertion).	**Britain** — 3RD MILITARY SERVICE ACT becomes law, lowers age to $17\frac{1}{2}$ & raises it to 50, eyesight criteria lessened. **Ireland** — Dublin Mansion House Conference v conscription includes RC bishops (*see* 23).
			German Fatherland Party says Belgium & Flanders must be Germany's 'politically, militarily & economically'.	
Kartucol occupies Mwalia and then captures supply dump on R Mkuti. **Uganda** — c650 KAR and Sudanese resume British ops in Turkana (*see* 15 May).	**N Sea** — British & German destroyers engage in the Heligoland Bight; 1 German destroyer damaged.	**W Front** — Richthofen's 80th (& last) victory, a Camel NE of Villers-Bretonneux.		**Britain** — **Milner replaces Derby as War Minister**. **Canada** — 20-22yr-old men called up. **USA** — Sabotage Act.
	W Med — RN *ML413* depth charges & sinks Cattaro-bound *UB71* off Ceuta.	**W Front** — RICHTHOFEN (the 'Red Baron') KILLED over Somme (aged 25). His blood-red Fokker Dr I Triplane shot down by Capt A Roy Brown of No 209 Sqn RAF in Camel. Australian Lewis gunners (53rd Battery AFA) also claim Richthofen's scalp but probably do not fire the fatal shot (British autopsy report emphasises *flat* trajectory of bullet inflicting entry wound).	German Chancellor vetoes *OHL's* proposal to occupy Dutch Zealand. Japanese Foreign Minister Viscount Motono resigns, Baron Goto succeeds (22). Sir M de Bunsen's British Mission sent to S America (-21 Sept).	
	N Sea — **Zeebrugge Raid**: St George's Day Raid by British Dover Patrol 3 old cruiser blockships; 9 monitors; 5 cruisers; 7 flotilla leaders, 44 destroyers on Zeebruge & Ostend (night 22/23) (2 blockships miss). Zeebrugge Raid lasts 1hr & costs 588 RN cas mainly from 900-strong landing party that tries to storm	**Occupied Belgium** — DH4 bombs Zeebrugge harbour mole (night 22/23) as diversion for RN raid.	German Vienna Ambassador Wedel to Chancellor Hertling 'If we do not win, and do not remain strong and invincible after the struggle, then the first result would be: *"finis Austriae"*. Wedel sees Burian to bind Austria to Berlin (23) & Kühlmann visits Vienna (26). **Neutrals: Holland** — Cabinet Council considers German	**Britain** — Budget raises income tax 1s to 6s in £, doubles duties & stamp duty, letters up to $1\frac{1}{2}$d (in force 3 June). New taxes to yield £67.8m in yr 1918/19. 1st exhibition of British battle photographs in colour. **Germany** — *Das Neue Europa* estimates German losses to 31 July 1917 as 5m. Interior

APRIL 1918	WESTERN FRONT 1	EASTERN FRONT 2	SOUTHERN FRONTS 3	TURKISH FRONTS 4
Mon 22 contd				
Tue 23	Special Haig dispatch reports 102 German divs engaged since 21 Mar. **Somme** — Heavy German attacks at Albert & between Somme & Avre. **US 1st Div enters line** opposite Cantigny (W of Montdidier) between French IX & VI Corps (*see* 3 May).	Lenin tells newly elected Moscow Soviet 'It can be said with certainty that ... the civil war has ended'. Austro-German trade agreement with Ukraine.	**Italian Front** — FM Boroevic proposes Austrian attack across Piave towards Oderzo-Treviso after previously insisting on defensive strategy.	
Wed 24	**Somme** — 2 German divs with 13 tanks (2 lost) capture Villers-Bretonneux (390+ PoWs) & threaten Allied jnctn in Amiens sector. **First tank-v-tank action**: a British Mk IV 'Male' (Mitchell) knocks out German A7V *Elfriede* (after it disables 2 'Females'), which is then captured; 7 British Whippet lt tanks (1 lost) run down 400 German inf.	**Finland** — 8000 Red Guards & 10 guns vainly try to retake Lahti from 800 Germans (-29). **Manchuria** — Col Semenov's White Cossacks defeat 500 armed Hungarian PoWs, drive them towards Chita.		Turks accept armistice for Armenian retreat to Kars forts.
Thu 25	**Flanders** — **Kemmel Hill captured** in 5hrs by 7 German divs (French defeat), British call it Second Battle. Anglo-Australian night attack by 2 bdes (night 24/25) recaptures Villers-Bretonneux with 600 PoWs.			**Armenia** — Turks occupy Kars (first time since 1878), find 212+ field & fortress guns (*see* 15 May). **Persia** — Small British col (aided by 4 RAF aircraft) defeats pro-German Sinjabis NE of Kasr-i-Shirin.
Fri 26	**Flanders** — Germans repulsed at Voormezeele S of Ypres (twice on 27). French lose & retake Locre village W of Mt Kemmel, repulse another attack (28). **Somme** — French Foreign Legion (851 cas) storms Hangard Wood & holds it v 5 counter-attacks.	Bolsheviks protest v German Brest-Litovsk violations. **Finland** — 3000 Germans capture Hämeenlinna & meet Finn Nyland Dragoons (27). Red dictator K Manner flees Viborg with 3 steamers for Petrograd.		**Mesopotamia** — Gen Egerton's 10,500 men (5 cols) wrest Kifri-Tuz Khurmatli from 3000 Turks (-29): 6th Indian Cav Bde charges at Kulawand (27), destroying Turk rearguard (200k, 565 PoWs & 1 gun); 13th Div takes Tuz as 13th Hussars' charge causes 1300 Turks, 12 guns & 20 MGs to surrender (29).

AFRICAN OPERATIONS 5	SEA WAR 6	AIR WAR 7	INTERNATIONAL EVENTS 8	HOME FRONTS 9
	harbour mole. Obsolescent submarine *C3* destroys viaduct linking mole to mainland; 24 CMBs & 60 MLs lay flanking smokescreen; 8 VCs won (King invests them 31 July) & 209 other decorations. Destroyer *North Star* (35 cas) sunk, probably by torpedo from Mole, & German destroyer probably torpedoed on inside. Germans dredge in 24hrs 60-ft wide channel round blockships, canal fully open within 3wks; *UB16* uses it (24), larger boats diverted to Ostend, but raid a great British morale booster at home & in France (*see* 9 May). **Adriatic** — Destroyer action (night 22/23) as 4 Austrian ships chased from W of Valona back to Cattaro by 5 British (*Hornet* suffers 32 cas) & 1 French (*see* 8 May).		demands for unlimited transport of sand & gravel, Foreign Minister Loudan admits relations difficult (25).	Under-Minister writes 'the workers are of the view that now, when the decisive battle is being fought, they should not strike.'
	LAST GERMAN HIGH SEAS FLEET SORTIE (-24): Vain bid from 0500, initially undetected (Scheer eliminates radio traffic), to attack British Norwegian convoys (81 ships off Forth nowhere nr Norwegian waters). Hipper finds nothing, sends back battlecruiser *Moltke* with engine trouble (40 miles SW of Stavanger). Distress signal (24) alerts Room 40 and Grand Fleet's 35 capital ships (incl 4 US) & 111 cruisers & destroyers put to sea from Rosyth in record 1½hrs. Battleship *Oldenburg* takes *Moltke* in tow but she is torpedoed by British submarine *E42* (25) before she & whole fleet (17 battleships) re-enter harbour (*see* 26 May).		GUATEMALA DECLARES WAR ON GERMANY. Hungarian PM Dr Werkerle says Emperor's peace letter had German agreement. Maj-Gen Tom Bridges military adviser to Lord Reading in USA.	**Newfoundland** — Conscription Bill introduced. **Ireland** — National Work Stoppage (exc Ulster) to sign anti-conscription pledge (20,000 at Cork).
Kartucol push checked at Mbalama Hill, but Capt Brodie's recce party storm OP and force German retreat (25). Rosecol advances on Koronje and Nanungu (27-29), Kartucol takes over (30).		**USA** — Bureau of Aircraft Prod & Div of Military Aeronautics founded.	Anglo-Turk PoW exchange agreement ratified. Swiss-German Agreement allows former's cargo free passage.	
	N Sea — World's first dedicated A/S hunter-killer submarines (British *R1* & *R2*) launched at Chatham (class of 12 launched by 5 Oct 1918). **E Atlantic** — U-boat sinks sloop HMS *Cowslip* off Cape Spartel (nr Gibraltar). **Adriatic** — RNAS aircraft bomb Durazzo. **Britain** — First Lord Geddes memo on 'The Future of the Russian Fleets.' **St George's Channel** — RN sloop *Jessamine* depth charges & sinks *U104*. Allied Naval Council, 3rd meeting, in Paris (-27) fails to settle Franco-Italian disagreements (*see* 10 May).	**Britain** — Sir W Weir succeeds Rothermere as Sec of State for Air. **N Sea** — 7 German Zeebrugge seaplanes shoot down 1 of 2 Felixstowe flying boats (down another 6 June). **Flanders** — **96 German planes** fire 60,000 MG rnds & drop 700 bombs on 3 villages **in low-level preparation for assault on Kemmel Hill**; RAF lose 4 planes to only 1 German.		**Britain** — Churchill reviews munitions work for Commons: losses since 21 Mar more than made good; **750,000 women working, doing 90% shell production**; 100,000 released to forces since May 1917. Lord Rothermere resigns from Air Ministry (Sir W Weir succeeds 27). **Exports prohibited to Russia. USA** — Potato eating urged instead of bread. **Australia** — Hughes & Cook made War Conference reps. **France** — 2 meatless days pw become 3 (15 May-16 July). **Portugal** — Decree allows soldiers & sailors on active service to vote, Maj Paes elected Pres (28). **Britain** — Reconstruction Ministry issues Balfour Ctee report on postwar industrial policy.

APRIL 1918	WESTERN FRONT 1	EASTERN FRONT 2	SOUTHERN FRONTS 3	TURKISH FRONTS 4
Sat 27	**First contingent of Italian II Corps arrives** (*see* 13 May).	Soviet CEC abolishes rights of inheritance. At Petrograd White plotters name Grand Duke Alexis Nikolaievich ruler of Russia.		
Sun 28	**Flanders** — Belgians repulse raid at Langemarck.	**Finland** — Reds shoot 26 White PoWs in Viborg prison. Red Guard night attacks throw back Germans, taking 2 guns, but held at Lahti. **S Russia** — Germans reach Taganrog, Sea of Azov, in Donetz coal basin.		
Mon 29	**Flanders — Battle of the Lys ends**: 13 German divs attack at 0540 on 10-mile front but only capture Scherpenberg, a knoll 2 miles NW of Mt Kemmel from French & 2-mile stretch of British-held Salient outpost line, 3 miles S of Ypres. Haig & Plumer contemplate retreat to prepared St Omer line. **Ludendorff suspends the offensive at 2200. Lorraine** — US codebreakers give Doughboys ½ hr warning of attack.	**Finland — Mannerheim captures Viborg. Ukraine** — Gen Gröner establishes military dictatorship (Kiev martial law from 26) under landowner Hetman (ex-Tsarist) Gen Skoropadski, having arrested anti-German League & dissolved Rada.		
Tue 30	**Flanders** — Ludendorff halts Op *Georgette*. OHL decides on major diversionary offensive (*Goerz*) v French designed to draw Allied reserves S from Flanders. Once achieved, a further heavy attack will be mounted to encompass BEF's destruction. (Apr) 118,000 US troops sail for France, BEF losses 143,168, only 48 of 61 divs battleworthy.	Ex-Tsar & family brought to Ekaterinburg in the Urals. **Finland** — Red W Army cut in half by German-White Guard attacks (*see* 2 May). **Russia** — By now 386,000 Austro-German PoWs returned home (*see* 1 May, 30 June). Turkestan Soviet Republic proclaimed.		**Palestine — 2nd Trans-Jordan 'Raid'** (-4 May): Chauvel's 13,000 men & 66 guns v 9000 Turks & Germans & c70 guns. 60th Div & NZ Mtd Bde only take 1st line of Turk Nimrin position E of Jordan, 3rd ALH Bde captures Es Salt (Turk Fourth Army HQ) but 4th ALH Bde checked at Jisr-ed-Damieh bridge. **S Persia** — Sykes' Mission: 3344 British troops & 7898 S Persia Rifles (292 British-Indian officers & NCOs).
Wed 1 May 1918	Supreme War Council endorses AEF autonomy (429,659 men in 9 divs). Ludendorff (now 204 divs in W) orders Aisne attack (*see* 15) to absorb French reserves (47 of 102 divs N of the Oise) so that BEF can be struck again in Flanders. **Flanders** — Small French gains nr Locre, W of Mt Kemmel, repulses German raid to S (6), French raids (23). **Somme** — US units reach Amiens sector.	**Germans occupy Sevastopol & seize part of Black Sea Fleet** (*see* SEA WAR 13). Hoffmann diary on difficulties of repatriating Austro-German PoWs + 3-4m Baltic & Polish refugees. (May) 2 German divs transfer to W Front (-10). Lenin addresses first May Day rally in Red Square & attends flying display. **Finland** — Mannerheim holds victory parade in Viborg.	**Italian Front** — Austrians begin training for offensive on similar terrain, especially river crossing rehearsals on R Livenza; 7 new divs arrive from E Front (May, 21 in all Feb-June).	**Palestine** — 1750 Turks & Germans (Col Böhme's 24th Div) surprise counter-attack across Jordan nearly traps 4th ALH Bde & takes 9 guns; British 60th Div assaults on Shunet Nimrin fail (-3).
Thu 2	French advance in Avre Valley seizing Hill 82, capture wood S of Hailles (15). German arty action in Villers-Bretonneux sector.	**Don** — Cossacks cable Kaiser for help v Bolsheviks (*see* 16). **Finland** — Red W Army collapses, 20,000 PoWs, 50 guns & 200 MGs.	Foch's authority extended to Italian Front.	**Mesopotamia** — Marshall estimates Turk Sixth Army at 18,640 men & 124 guns (*see* 1 June).
Fri 3	**Somme** — Germans fire 10,000rnds (15t) mustard gas at US 1st Div opposite	**Finland** — Whites occupy Kouvola. White ministers meet Mannerheim at Haapamäki.		**Palestine** — Allenby orders retreat from Es Salt (-4); British back over Jordan minus 1649

AFRICAN OPERATIONS 5	SEA WAR 6	AIR WAR 7	INTERNATIONAL EVENTS 8	HOME FRONTS 9
				India — Delhi War Conference (-29). **Britain** — Wheat acreage highest since 1882 but only 500,000 bales of cotton (11 wks supply) left. **Austria** — †Gavrilo Princip, 22, in hospital of tuberculosis, Theresienstadt.
		W Front — First of Rickenbacker's 26 victories: Albatros fighter at Baussant. German aircraft losses since 21 Mar — 059, RAF/RFC 1032 (Mar & Apr).		**France** — *Bonnet Rouge* treason trial opens (*see* 15 May). **Germany** — State Grain Bureau formed in Ukraine. **USA** — 100 US Signal Corps female telephonists now in France, 150 to follow.
	U-boat sinks Canadian Pacific liner SS *Oronsa*. **Irish Sea** — RN convoy sloop *Coreopsis* gunfire sinks *UB85* in N Channel. Allied & neutral shipping losses to U-boats 112 ships (67 British with 488 lives) worth 273,355t (215,543t British from all causes); U-boat fig 134 ships worth 300,069t incl 43 ships worth 80,126t in Med; 6 U-boats sunk.	**W Front** — 180 German triplanes available. Allied Apr losses 232 aircraft & 16 balloons to Germans' 136 aircraft. **Britain** — (Apr) 27 flights of obsolete DH6s on anti-U-boat patrol.	National Ctee of Rumanians of Transylvania & Bukovina formed in Paris. **Neutrals: Holland** — British officer PoW exchange party enter at Venlo. **Norway** — Final trade agreement with Allies.	**Britain** — Maj-Gen Harrington becomes Deputy CIGS. Army billeting provisions extended to women. (Apr) Home Forces fall to record low 1,476,018 troops (727,394 trained) due to reinforcement of BEF. **USA** — German San Francisco Consul & Vice-Consul imprisoned for 2 yrs & fined $10,000 each for conspiracy v British Govt in India.
Kartucol's advance checked nr Koronje Hill (-2), but advances 6 miles (4).	(May) **Brazilian sqn** of 2 cruisers, 4 destroyers & a tender **sails for European waters**, but crew illness delays them at Sierra Leone (*see* 10 Nov). **Adriatic** — Austrians suppress plot in *Tb80* at Pola. **Germany** — (May) Lt cruiser *Stuttgart* converted to carry 3 seaplanes on davits (since Jan). **Britain** — (May) Last of 44 P-Boat type patrol craft launched (since Oct 1915), serve with Dover Patrol, Portsmouth and Nore commands.	**Occupied Belgium** — (May) RAF bombs Zeebrugge with 32t of bombs (& 2, 6, 12 with Ostend & 22) aiming for lock gates. Bruges docks also attacked (25) with 36t of bombs. **Britain** — (May) First flight of super-Handley Page V/1500 'Berlin Bomber' at Belfast, but crashes June, 2nd tested mid-Oct, 3 of 255 ordered ready in Norfolk (No 166 Sqn) on Armistice Day. **N Sea** — Blackburn Kangaroos of No 246 Sqn at RNAS Seaton Carew (Tees) fly 600hrs on A/S patrols 1 May-11 Nov; 12 U-boats sighted, 11 attacked (*see* 31). **Salonika** — RAF bomb Bulgar airfields in Vardar valley. **Palestine** — 2 No 1 Sqn AFC aircraft forced to land & burnt nr Amman. 1 German strafing attack (4). **W Front** — (early May) Fokker DV11s reach German fighter units in quantity, 828 by 31 Aug (*see* 29). Germans have 2551 pilots at front.	Lloyd George, Clemenceau & Orlando attend 5th Supreme War Council at Abbeville (-3), US Army increase & Franco-German PoW exchange sanctioned. Churchill offers US Army 225 6in howitzers & another 50 heavy guns by 1 Nov.	**Britain** — RFP 107% (Mar level). New War Pensions Warrant issued. Anglo-Australian zinc agreement for 250,000t pa war duration + 1 yr. (May) **Record month's gun production** — 1750 pieces with 1275 carriages. **France** — 35,000 armaments workers in May Day strike at Saint Étienne & vicinity (*see* 18). **Turkey** — 1st war loan in Constantinople (-31), (-30 June outside) raises T17.8m. **Germany** — (May) Ludendorff Fund for War Wounded opens. **Hungary** — Gen strike, marches in 4 towns despite ban.
	Atlantic U-boat sinks transport *Tuscania* (211 of 2400 US troops lost) 7 miles N of Rathlin I (*see* 12 & 23). **Channel** — Dover Barrage sinks *UB31* & *UC78* (8).	**Adriatic** — First RAF kite balloon patrol on Otranto Barrage (-5).	**Neutrals: Holland** — Sand & gravel export agreement with Germany. Allied Trade Ctee formed (9).	**Germany** — Prussian *Landtag* votes 235-183 v equal suffrage: pro-equal suffrage meetings banned (25). **USA** — Montana bans German language teaching & textbooks, half states curtail German by summer, much book burning.
		Germany — DH4s of No 55 Sqn seriously damage goods stn rail tracks & rolling stock at	Britain *de facto* recognizes Estonian Diet, France (13), Italy (29). Norwegian-US Agreement	**Britain** — Information Ministry put i/c home propaganda films & photos (*see* 21).

MAY 1918	WESTERN FRONT 1	EASTERN FRONT 2	SOUTHERN FRONTS 3	TURKISH FRONTS 4
Fri 3 contd	Cantigny, 693 gassed (4 deaths, *see* 15). **France** — Maj-Gen James W McAndrew AEF CoS.			cas but plus 981 PoWs & 29 MGs. EEF railway reaches Beersheba. **Georgia** — British military mission leaves Tiflis for Vladikavkas (*see* 27).
Sat 4	**Flanders** — Allied positions in Locre & S Ypres sectors heavily shelled.	Austrians seize German food from Rumania & Ukraine (Russo-Ukrainian armistice signed at Kovenevo). **Siberia** — Novonikolayevsk Soviet arrests Czech Capt Gajda. **Finland** — Whites take Kotka + 3 Red evacuation ships (4000 PoWs, 38 guns & mortars, 50 MGs).	**Serbia** — Serbs capture Bulgar trenches in Mt Dobropolye sector.	
Sun 5	Arty duels & widespread skirmishing. Foch orders army cdrs & higher not to yield ground for defence in depth. **Somme** — British advance at Morlancourt between Ancre & Somme.	Trotsky approves 'in principle' re-routing Czech 2nd Div (still W of Omsk) via Archangel. **Finland** — Last Red Guards surrender in Kymi Valley, 9000 PoWs, 57 guns & 120 MGs; c280 Reds shot (-15) despite orders.	**Salonika** — Greek 13th (Chalcis) Div now available to British Struma line (ordered in from 21).	**Palestine** — Allenby tells Lawrence 'for the moment , we must both just hold on' (*see* 9). **Mesopotamia** — Duncars reach Baghdad by barge (*see* 6 June).
Mon 6	**Flanders** — Germans raid French positions S of Locre. **Aisne** — 3 British divs enter line to 'rest' (-15, *see* 27).	**S Russia** — Hoffmann diary '... *OHL* & Eichhorn are ... driving the Ukraine back into the arms of Great Russia'. Russian ships shell Germans in Mariupol on Sea of Azov, Gen Haller's Poles fight Germans at Kaniow. Denisov's Anti-Soviet Cossacks capture Novocherkassk (reinforced by Drozdovski's 900 Whites, 8), call Krug (Assembly) for the Salvation of the Don, 11, *see* 16).	**Salonika** — British coy trench raid (81 cas) W of L Doiran uses body shields, blows up pillbox (night 6/7).	**NW Persia** — Nuri Pasha arrives at Tabriz.
Tue 7	Heavy rain on Flanders, Artois & Somme fronts. Cdn Corps withdrawn into res (-15 July), 5690 cas since 21 Mar although only Cdn Cav Bde in major battle.	PEACE OF BUCHAREST BETWEEN RUMANIA & CENTRAL POWERS: Bulgaria gets all land lost in 1913, Central Powers to control Danube estuary, 1/3 Army to be demobilized at once; indefinite military occupation (Mackensen C-in-C 11). **Secret War** — Sidney Reilly (MI1c) arrives in Moscow & tries to see Lenin.	**Italian Front** — Foch first requests Italian offensive as soon as posible (*see* 28).	**Mesopotamia** — **Gen Cayley occupies** burning & famine-stricken **Kirkuk** (-8), 600 Turks sick & 3 damaged planes taken but evacuated with 1600 refugees (11-24) due to supply difficulties.
Wed 8		**Germans occupy Rostov**-on-Don. Red Army forms Gen Staff under Lenin's friend Maj-Gen Bonch-Bruevich & 5 fronts.		**S Persia** — 700 British demolish 3 forts at Chah Haq NE of Shiraz (-10); 200 Burma Mtd Rifles defeat c400 tribesmen (10 & 13), storm Kuh-i-Khan (10,700 ft, 16) & race back to Shiraz by 23 (*see* 25).
Thu 9	**Flanders** — German attacks in La Cytte-Voormezeele sector. **Somme** — French success at Grivesnes NW of Montdidier.	CEC decrees Food Dictatorship to control peasants' produce (*see* 20 & 11 June). Ustemovich proclaimed Pres of Ukraine.	**Piave** — Lt Carlo Sabatini & 4 *Arditi* lead Italians onto Mt Corno (Vallarsa valley) & retain it with 100 PoWs v counter-attacks (11, *see* 25).	**Arabia** — Cairo forwards Sherif's message to Feisal at Aqaba 'You and your brother [Zaid] must die at Maan or capture it...'. Feisal wanting to return to Jeddah (*see* INT'L EVENTS 4 June).
Fri 10	**Somme** — British capture front line trench NW of Albert. **Argonne** — 1000 German projectors fire 8t phosgene on French positions; 187 gassed (20 deaths). **Meuse** — German gas attack (500 projectors) on US 26th Div in St Mihiel-Toul sector. **Lorraine** — German gas attack (1000 projectors) on French N of Parroy.	Right SR Moscow conspiracy discovered. **Siberia** — 8000 Czech troops now at Vladivostock.		**Mesopotamia** — 6th Indian Cav Bde, armoured cars & 24 Ford vans drive Turk 2nd Div N of R Little Zab 70 miles from Mosul.

AFRICAN OPERATIONS 5	SEA WAR 6	AIR WAR 7	INTERNATIONAL EVENTS 8	HOME FRONTS 9
		Thionville (*see* 17). **W Front** — RAF claim 36 German aircraft, Germans admit loss of 22 for 33 Allied.	for Allies to furnish supplies not under export restriction to Germany.	
			American magazine *Littell's Living Age* suggests Gustav Krupp as responsible for war as Kaiser.	**Austria** — Emperor closes *Reichsrat* (*see* 16). **France** — 440 Renault tanks delivered, only 216 with units (*see* W FRONT 31).
Rosecol takes over Pamforce advance. **Action of Nanungu** in Kireka Mts (30 miles W of Koronje & 160 miles S of L Nyasa: Lettow's 404 men (107 cas) beat c800 KAR from NRFF (c211 cas inc 106 PoWs), but both sides retire during night (-6).	**N Sea** — U-boat sinks sloop HMS *Rhododendron*.			**Ireland** — **FM Lord French** replaces Lord Wimborne as **Lord Lieutenant** with Edward Short Chief Sec (replaces Duke, *see* 9 &18). **Britain** — 2 meat ration coupons replace 3 pw; boys of 13-18 get extra bacon ration.
				USA — Army Nurse Corps now 9824 strong.
			Arab 'memorial' from 7 leaders in Cairo seeks independence clarification from HMG who reply (9) that independence applies to areas 'liberated by the Arabs themselves'.	**Britain** — Maurice Affair: Ex-DMO letter to *The Times* accuses PM of false statements on Army strength, but Lloyd George wins Commons debate v Asquith 293-106 (9). 2750 Manchester aircraft workers strike (-10) over clerk's victimization.
Rosecol occupies Milinch Hills (160 road miles from Port Amelia).	**Med** — RN convoy sloop *Wallflower* depth charges & sinks veteran *U32* attacking convoy 40 miles NW of Malta. **Adriatic** — 4 Austrian destroyers fail to land raiding party to cut coast railway N of Pescara (night 8/9).	**Salonika** — 6 RAF aircraft drop 4500lb bombs (72 sorties) on Bulgar Drama airfield, 24 aircraft bomb rail stns & dumps (13-14), 27 aircraft bomb Hudova airfield (repeated 21, 23, 29, 30); probable 8 Bulgar aircraft shot down in May. **Britain** — Trenchard accepts command of Independent Air Force for bombing Germany (*see* 5 June).	NICARAGUA DECLARES WAR ON GERMANY & AUSTRIA (*see* 23).	
	Channel — Troop transport *Queen Alexandra* rams & sinks *UB78* N of Cherbourg.	**France** — Allied Supreme War Council first discusses air policy. 3 of 4 'Giant' flying raids on coastal targets destroyed in crash-landings (fog). **W Front** — Fonck in 5min 50sec (in Spad) destroys 6 German aircraft over (again 26 Sept) the Somme firing only 52rnds.		**Britain** — Russian Consul in Glasgow, John McLean, sentenced to 5 yrs penal servitude. **Portugal** — Maj Pais elected Pres (only candidate), calls for support of Allies, forms Cabinet (15). **Ireland** — GOC Mahon resigns, Lt-Gen Sir F Shaw succeeds.
	N Sea — **British blocking attack on Ostend** (49 cas, 3 VCs) night 9/10; war weary cruiser *Vindictive* (laden with concrete) sunk in harbour entrance but only at 25° angle to pier. **E Atlantic** — 6 U-boats attempt to attack convoys (-25), only 2 succeed (*see* 12), 30 convoys pass through group's area. **Britain** — Geddes	**Occupied Belgium** — 7 Handley Pages (1 lost) bomb Ostend in support of RN raid. **N Sea** — Zeppelin *L62* blows up after attack by British flying boat.		**Britain** — Temporary Guards MG Regt formed. **USA** — Congress Act empowers War Sec to sell surplus war material in Europe postwar. **Austria** — Emperor Charles' 4th son Karl Ludwig born at Baden.

MAY 1918	WESTERN FRONT 1	EASTERN FRONT 2	SOUTHERN FRONTS 3	TURKISH FRONTS 4
Fri 10 contd				
Sat 11	**Somme** — German guns in action on the Ancre.	**Ukraine** — Germans v Rada supporters in Kiev (& 21). **Finland** — Peace with Turkey signed.		**Hejaz Railway** — Arab regulars (+ 3 RAF planes) capture Jerdun Stn with 140 PoWs, but another attack cut short by Turk train arriving (17). Nasir destroys 2 stns to N (23-24) without loss. Partial Arab success v bridges 80 miles NW of Medina (23). **Persia** — Dunsterville cables Baghdad that Baku's seizure possible (*see* 1 June), leaves Hamadan for Kazvin & Tehran visits (12-18). **Armenia** — Peace Conference resumes at Batumi, Turk delegates arrive (6) & demand Aleksandropol's evacuation within 24 hrs (14). Ludendorff gets Chancellor's agreement to sending a few bns from Crimea to Caucasus (*see* 27 & 3 June).
Sun 12	All quiet, except for arty duel on Meuse E bank.		**Italian Front** — Austrian Offensive confirmed at Central Powers' Spa meeting (*see* INT'L EVENTS).	
Mon 13	Heavy rain from Flanders to Somme; German arty in action. Italian II Corps enters line W of Verdun.			
Tue 14	**Somme** — German attack on mile front SW of Morlancourt; Australians counter-attack (*see* 18).	Lenin's Report on Foreign Policy to CEC and Moscow Soviet. **Siberia** — **Czech 1st Div first clashes with Bolsheviks** at Chelyabinsk (E of Urals) & seizes town (*see* 18). **Baltic States** — Kaiser proclamation declares Lithuania free & allied to Germany (*see* 4		

AFRICAN OPERATIONS 5	SEA WAR 6	AIR WAR 7	INTERNATIONAL EVENTS 8	HOME FRONTS 9
	proposes to Italian Ambassador Imperiali an Allied Med 'admiralissimo', eg Jellicoe, to settle command differences as on land, Lloyd George cables Clemenceau (13), Anglo-French agreement (17) but scheme founders at Supreme War Council (2 June) due to prolonged Italian objections.			
	E Atlantic — RN submarine *E35* torpedoes & sinks *U154*, 150 miles off Cape St Vincent.	**W Front** — First 'Liberty Plane' (US-built DH4) reaches AEF. **Adriatic** — First of 12 RAF raids on Cattaro (only 4 Austrian Phoenix fighters, Italians bomb 12) & 7 on Durrazo (-31 Aug). U-boat CO at former requests 2 sqns of German fighters (11 June).	Turco-Finnish Agreement signed in Berlin (*see* 29). K George V reviews US troops in London.	**Britain** — No aliens to be given shares or ownership in oilfields, mines or factories inside European neutrals bordering enemy countries.
	St George's Channel — White Star liner/troopship *Olympic* (46,359t) rams & sinks *U103* after she summons 4 others to intercept convoys (*UB72* sunk at RN submarine *D4*). **E Atlantic** — 'Invasion of St Kilda': *U19* (Spiess) shells remote Scottish Western I's only settlement; then lands armed party to shoot sheep. **Adriatic** — Italian destroyers sink transport from Austrian convoy off Durazzo. **Med** — British transport *Omrah* sunk by U-boat off Cape Spartivento (Sardinia); transports *Leasowe Castle* (99 lost) (26) & *Missir* (44 lost) (29) similarly sunk off Alexandria.	**W Front** — Mannock's SE5a flight of No 74 Sqn destroy 6 of 8 German fighters encountered, Mannock scores over 20 May victories incl 3 Pfalzs & a Hannover (21).	**Kaiser & Emperor Charles sign Austro-German *Waffenbund*** at Spa (inc economic cooperation esp in Ukraine; Charles agrees to major offensive in Italy; 1 draft of 'Charles' journey to Canossa' extends political treaty to 1 Jan 1940 (*see* 30).	
Rosecol at Msalu Boma loses 2 KAR sentries to lions (-15).	**Black Sea** — On Moscow's orders 14 Soviet destroyers sail from Sevastopol for Novorossisk, escaping Germans as do 4 more & 2 dreadnoughts (night 14) under fire but Germans seize predreadnoughts & smaller vessels incl ex-Turk cruiser *Medjidieh*. **Adriatic** — Italian naval 'tank' *Grillo* (foiled 6-7) crawls into Pola harbour, is discovered & scuttled to avoid capture, but Austrians raise her & build 2 similar craft (unfinished at Armistice). Early pair of Italian naval 'tanks' scuttled similarly (13 Apr). MAS raid on Trieste also fails (night 14/15). British destroyer *Phoenix* sunk by Austrian *U27* in Otranto Straits.	**Italian Front** — 11 Austrian aircraft destroyed.		**France** — To unions' surprise 40,301 **Paris munition workers strike v war**, 105,131 in 53 factories by 14. Govt impose news blackout, back to normal (21, *see* 18 & 31). **USA** — War Labor Policies Board appointed.
				Canada — PM refuses farmers' sons conscription exemption plea (10,226 drafted — 22 Nov). **Britain** — Compulsory ASW training for Merchant Navy officers.

MAY 1918	WESTERN FRONT 1	EASTERN FRONT 2	SOUTHERN FRONTS 3	TURKISH FRONTS 4
Tue 14 contd		June).		
Wed 15	Arty duels (-16) & skirmishes. **Somme** — US 1st Div ordered to capture Cantigny (*see* 28). **Aisne** — 28 German assault divs begin concentrating opposite Chemin des Dames (1800 trains used).	FINNISH CIVIL WAR ENDS with Whites entering demolished & evacuated Russian Ft Ino. **Volga** — Anarchists & SRs demonstrate in Tsaritsyn (*see* 29).	**Albania** — Franco-Italian troops (5 cols) with air support & pack transport drive back Austrians & their Albanian irregulars W of Koritza & advance up to 12 miles gaining 120 sq miles of mts (-17) for 133 cas to secure Santa Quaranta supply route (*see* 10 June).	**Armenia** — **Vehip Pasha resumes Turk offensive** & occupies Aleksandropol (*see* 18). **Mesopotamia** — British cease recce of Fat-ha, 45 miles N of Tikrit (*see* 18).
Thu 16	**Somme** — British trench raid nr Beaumont Hamel.	Red Army revolt at Saratov on Volga. **S Russia** — Gen Krasnov elected Ataman of Don Cossacks (replaces Popov) seeks arms & recognition from Germans in Ukraine (15m roubles,12,000 rifles, 46 guns & 89 MGs by July). Emperor Charles sacks FM Böhm-Ermolli for rowing with Germans, Gen Krauss from Italy takes over *Ostarmee* (*see* 17 June). **Finland** — Mannerheim leads 16,000 White Army victory parade through Helsinki (Germans only observers).		
Fri 17	Haig directs Rawlinson to plan an attack in Amiens sector with Gen Debeney (French First Army to S) (*see* 4 & 24 July).			
Sat 18	**Somme** — Australians capture Ville-sur-Ancre & take 360 PoWs (night 18/19).	Lenin speaks on financial crisis. **Siberia** — Czech Chelyabinsk Congress (-25) decides v Archangel diversion despite French protests. **Finland** — Parlt votes Svinhufvud provisional head of state, becomes temporary dictator (25) on Ministry's resignation.		**Mesopotamia** — CIGS agrees to postpone Tigris ops till mid-Sept, railway to be extended to Tikrit. **Armenia** — Turk 12th Div attacks S of R Aras v Gen Silikov's 6000-7000 Armenians & 28 guns (-19), occupying Igdir while 5th Div captures 2 passes on Tiflis rd (19).
Sun 19	Fayolle diary: '... still discord between Pétain and Foch. They...ought to be...one single man'. **Flanders** — British raid SW of Meteren, & NW of Merville (20). French attack nr Locre (Kemmel) bags 400 PoWs (20).		**Piave** — Italians storm Austrian trenches at Capo Sile & repulse attack (22,*see* 25).	
Mon 20		**Trotsky orders Czechs' disarming** by arrest or shooting (repeated 25). CEC declares		

AFRICAN OPERATIONS 5	SEA WAR 6	AIR WAR 7	INTERNATIONAL EVENTS 8	HOME FRONTS 9
Uganda — British have killed 141 Turkana raiders & recovered nearly 4000 stock since 6, successful ops end 19 June.	Allies in Rome discuss US plans for Adriatic island capture.	**USA** — New York-Washington air mail service opens, 24c per oz of mail.	Sino-Japanese Military Agreement (published 30) signed in Peking v German-Bolshevik Far East designs; naval convention follows (19 & 23). Supreme Allied War & Naval Councils emergency meeting in London urges US to declare war on Turkey & Bulgaria. Dr Benes in London (10-20) sees Lord R Cecil to press Czech case (*see* 3 June).	**France** — *Bonnet Rouge* trial ends with editor Duval sentenced to death (executed 17 July) for receiving c £40,000 from Germans. **Britain** — Exports to US need British War Mission's approval. **Italy** — G Villa replaces Gen Dallolio (resigned) as Munitions Minister.
		Germany — Air battle over Saarbrücken: 12 DH4s (1 shot down, crew k) shoot down 3 fighters. Direct hits on rail targets (61 cas). **W Front** — French *Aviation Res* designated 1st Air Div under Gen Duval reporting to Pétain (*see* 9 June).	K George V & Queen Mary receive US delegates.	**Britain** — Penalties on excess food profits. **USA** — **Sedition Act** amends 1917 Espionage Act, stiff penalties for insulting US. Overman Act expands Pres' war powers (20). **Austria** — Subject Nationalities Congress in Prague: right-wing Czech Christian Democrats demand independence under federal monarchy (22).
Kartucol resumes Pamforce advance.	**W Med** — French convoy escort *Ailly* sinks *UC35* (destroyed 42 ships worth 65,569t) with gunfire off Sardinia, Germans believe Q-ship the killer.	**Germany** — Metz-Sablon main stn, goods sheds & train hit by 12 DH4s of 55 Sqn (c90 cas). Later, 1 Handley Page & 10 FE2s (2 FTR) attack Thionville (much damage, 35k) & Metz-Sablon (night 17/18).	Emperor Charles visits Sofia & Constantinople (-21).	**Ireland** — c150 Sinn Fein leaders arrested for plotting night 17/18; only Michael Collins & Cathal Brugha escape, but no prosecutions. **Britain** — **All men born 1898 or 1899 called up** (*see* 22). Compulsory meatless day abolished. Pres of Board of Trade estimates half industry on war work, output below pre-war.
Rosecol links with NRFF on R Msalu, bridges it & crosses (19-20).	**W Med** — Heavily damaged (by carrier *Empress* seaplane escorting convoy off Gibraltar 7) *U39* forced into Cartagena (Spain) where interned for duration (*UC56* likewise at Santander 24). French destroyer *Catapulte* sinks in collision with British *SS Warrimoo* off Bône, Algeria.	**Germany** — **First British retaliatory raid on a German city**: 33 bombs from 6 No 55 Sqn DH4s kill 110 at Cologne (some panic on streets), which returning repulse 2 German formations, shoot down 2 fighters. Considerable building damage (est RM340,000). **Adriatic** — Austro-Italian seaplane combats W of Pola.	Allied Munitions Conference in Paris (-19): Churchill first flies (in DH4) from Paris to London (19).	**Ireland** — Lord French proclamation re pro-German conspiracy (Govt blue book (24). **France** — Metal workers strikes until peace (-28) in Loire Dept, 3 inf bns, 9 cav sqns, 560 gendarmes tied down. Mainly peaceful until police officers wounded (23). Clemenceau's deputy PPS Barnier arrives (24); 43 union leaders arrested night 25/26 & 73 workers drafted.
Kartucol occupies Nanungu & its full German hospital.	**Irish Sea** — US destroyers *Patterson* & *Allen* depth charge & sink new *UB119* W of Cardigan Bay.	**Britain** — Largest, LAST & costliest RAID ON LONDON by bomber aircraft: 28 of 38 Gothas sent (6 FTR, 1 crashes), 3 'Giants' with 600 (14.3t) bombs in 1hr cause 226 cas (night 19/20). AA fire destroys 2 Gothas, 88 defence sorties shoot down 3 Gothas in 11 interceptions. **France** — Heavy German raids on railways & munition dumps (12,500t ammo destroyed -22) by *Bogohl 6* (& 20/21); 935 further British wounded & nurses k or injured in 15-Gotha raid (1 shot down) on Étaples hospital complex (key rail bridge missed) (night 19/20), repeated (night 30/3, 47 cas) when 1 span of bridge hit, but alternative soon in use (short breaks 30 June & 24 July).		
		Adriatic — British bomb Cattaro (& 28, *see* 27), Italian seaplanes bomb Durazzo &		**Britain** — Appeal to shipowners to provide extra emergency rafts. 1st min agricultural wage

MAY 1918	WESTERN FRONT 1	EASTERN FRONT 2	SOUTHERN FRONTS 3	TURKISH FRONTS 4
Mon 20 contd		war on kulaks (rich peasants). **Finland** — Svinhufvud & Gen Goltz agree on German-modelled 30,000-strong peacetime army with German troops remaining (*see* 27).		
Tue 21	**Artois** — British trench raids nr Arras (& 23).	**Ukraine** — Peasant revolts v Germans & Haydamak allies. Sovnarkom starts peace talks with Hetman Skoropadski (23).		**Armenia** — Turk 36th & 9th Divs throw back Nazarbekov's c9000 Armenians from Amamli Stn (22); Antranik's 2000 Armenians make rearguard stand nr Jelal-oglu (22-23).
Wed 22		Red rule in Riga ended.		
Thu 23	British Fifth Army reformed under Gen Sir W Birdwood (*see* 1 July).	**British War Cabinet** decides to send 560-man military mission to Archangel to train Whites & 600 troops to Murmansk; they **decide large scale intervention inevitable** (29). Factory delegates in Moscow call for strike v Soviet Govt. **Secret War** — Lockhart sends Foreign Office Savinkov plan 'to murder all Bolshevik leaders on night of Allied landing & form a Govt...in reality a military dictatorship' (*see* 4 June).		**Armenia** — Silikov retakes Sardarabad & drives Turk 11th Div 30 miles N (-24) while other Armenian units drive Turk vanguard back to Amamli.
Fri 24	BEF Tank Corps Lt-Col JFC Fuller writes 'Plan 1919' for Allied tank (4992 req'd) & all-vehicle breakthrough on broad front. Haig receives revised version 21 July. Foch agrees in principle 6 Aug. **Flanders** — Gas shelling of British at Nieppe Forest (Armentières). **Aisne** — 12 tanks from German lines unable to cross French 'Bardonelles Trench'.	**N Russia** — Maj-Gen Poole lands at Murmansk to organize N Russia EF, & cruiser USS *Olympia* joins RN sqn there.		
Sat 25	**Somme** — German arty bombards Villers-Bretonneux, arty duels in Avre sector (26).	1st Congress of Councils of National Economy in Moscow. **Siberia** — c60,000-strong Czech Legion begins revolt v Reds. **W Russia** — Germans arrest 60 conspirators in Dvinsk.	**Piave** — *Bersaglieri* & *Arditi* surprise more Austrian Capo Sile positions & repel 2 counter-attacks (night 25/26). **Trentino** — *Alpini* attack in Tonale-Adamello region (W of L Garda) & capture line of 5 major peaks commanding upper Val Carnonica (*see* 13 June).	**Armenia** — Armenian 2nd Cav Regt charge Turks successfully. Dro's troops hold Bas-Abaran Defile N of Erevan (29) v Turk 3rd Regt (11th Div). **S Persia** — 1600 British (51 cas) & 4 guns defeat Saulat's 4800 tribesmen (est 600-700 cas) at Deh Shaikh 11 miles W of Shiraz & return there (27).
Sun 26	**Aisne** — 2 German PoWs reveal offensive next day, Duchêne's Sixth Army mans overdense first line from 1615.			**Armenia** — Battle of Karakilise (-28): Nazarbekov, outflanked N & S by Turks, escapes via mountain paths & covers Delijan from W with 5000 survivors (-29, *see* 4 June).

AFRICAN OPERATIONS 5	SEA WAR 6	AIR WAR 7	INTERNATIONAL EVENTS 8	HOME FRONTS 9
		Lagosta I (occupied 4 Nov, *see* SEA WAR 3 Nov).		in force. **Hungary** — 2000 troops of 6th Inf Regt mutiny at Pécs v being sent to Front (esp returned Serb PoWs), seize arsenal & aided by armed miners but suppressed by 3 Honved regts.
Kartucol fights 3 actions with Capt Köhl SW of Nanungu. **Ethiopia** — Railway to Addis completed.		**Germany** — 7 Handley Pages (1 FTR) of No 216 Sqn RAF cause 2-day plant closure at Oppau chemical works, Mannheim (direct hit on gas main). Rail workshops & locomotives hit at Karthaus. 2 SVA-5s of Italian 87th *Squadriglia* photograph Zeppelin works at Friedrichshafen (440-mile round trip). 13 FE2s of No 100 Sqn dislocate rail traffic at Saarbrücken (night 21/22). **W Front** — Udet appointed CO *Jasta 4* . **Britain** — Rumpler C VII (Drechsel & Foell) flies daring 375-mile high-altitude undetected photorecon sortie over London, returns safely to Tournai base.	**Occupied Poland** — Germans disband Polish troops for conspiracies (-5 June).	**Britain** — Beaverbrook admits to Balfour Information Ministry in reality subsidiary to Foreign Office.
Action of Korewa (24 miles S of Nanungu): Pamforce & NRFF KAR just fail to trap Capt Köhl in rocky hills, but take most of his baggage (60 cas inc 11 Germans, 67 shells & 70,000 bullets). **Belgian Congo** — Katanga Railway (Bukama-Cape Town) completed.	**N Sea** — British air raid sinks German destroyer in Zeebrugge (lock gates bombed 2 May).	**France** — Single German Gotha of 30 sent bombs Paris: (& 23), 72 bombs cause 23 cas (*see* 27). **Germany** — 11 FE2s & 5 Handley Pages attack Kreuzwald electric power stn. **W Front** — Canadian ace Bishop returns, as CO No 85 Sqn (SE5s, 3 American pilots), scores 27 more victories (-19 June).	Allied Petroleum Conference established.	**Austria** — German Ambassador reports on growing anti-Slav feelings. **Britain** — A Geddes manpower budget says recruits can only come 'at the expense of war industries' ie 3.1m Govt & Allied Govt workers.
Rosecol pursues Köhl's rearguard for 4 miles (-24).	**Channel** — British AMC *Moldavia* escorting convoy HC1 carrying US troops (only 64 lost) sunk by U-boat. **Adriatic** — RN submarine *H4* sinks returning *UB52* 40 miles S of Cattaro.		COSTA RICA DECLARES WAR ON GERMANY.	**USA** — **War Dept issues Work or Fight order**, effective 1 July (*see* 31). **Britain** — Lloyd George Edinburgh speech claims U-boats being out-built & sunk.
Kartucol takes over pursuit S (-30).		**Germany** — Thyssen blast furnaces & iron/steel works Hagendingen attacked by 8 DH9s of No 99 Sqn (which shoot down 1 fighter).		**Hungary** — Opera *Duke Bluebeard's Castle* opens in Budapest with Bartok's music. **Britain** — Empire Day. **USA** — Hotels can hire black waiters due to shortage of white men (draft).
			K Albert of the Belgians thanks USA.	**Britain** — Sir Napier Shaw appointed Meteorology War Scientific Adviser.
	N Sea — US Mine Sqn 1 (Capt Reg Belkap's 19 minelayers with 5530 mines) **arrives** at Invergordon to **help lay Northern Barrage** with 57,000 US-made mines in next 5			**USA** — Food Administrator proposes 2lb meat per person pw.

MAY 1918	WESTERN FRONT 1	EASTERN FRONT 2	SOUTHERN FRONTS 3	TURKISH FRONTS 4
Sun 26 contd				
Mon 27	**Aisne** — THIRD BATTLE OF THE AISNE (-6 June): German *Blücher & Yorck* Offensives v Anglo-French on Chemin des Dames. Bruchmüller 4000-gun bombardment on 24-mile front from 0100. From 0340 25 German divs attack 4 tired French & 4 weak British divs on R Aisne between Soissons & Reims, river first reached in under 6hrs. **Germans** capture Chemins des Dames & Craonne in **record advance up to 12 miles** destroying 4 divs. Kaiser Wilhelm Geschütz bombard Paris (104 shells, -11 June). 1m German rnds phosgene & diphenyl-chlorarsine v French; 4980 gassed (71 deaths) (-5 June).	**Siberia** — Czechs take over Chelyabinsk & refuse to surrender arms at Penza, take town (28, 400 Red cas) but evacuate it 31. **Finland** — **Mannerheim resigns as C-in-C** over future army organization (excessive German influence), leaves for Stockholm 1 June.	**Trentino** — Austrian Eleventh Army report 'Today flour stocks for only another 3¼ days', hence coming attack called 'hunger offensive'.	**Georgia** — **Independent Republic declared** at Tiflis under German protectorate (Col Kress), Trans-Caucasian Federal Govt dissolved. **Azerbaijan** — Tartar National Council proclaims Republic.
Tue 28	**Aisne** — Germans now have 40-mile wide, 15-mile deep bridgehead across Aisne, also cross the Vesle. Ex-BEF GHQ liaison officer Gen des Vallières, French 151st Div Cdr, k by German MG at Juvigny. Allied stand at Vregny plateau & heights of St Thierry as 3 res divs arrive. German officer reports 'regrettable excesses...serious drunken-ness'. **Somme — Battle of Cantigny: First AEF offensive op**, by 28th Inf Regt (3874 men, 823 cas), 1st Div captures village & beats off 3 counter-attacks by German 82nd Res Div (c1000 cas) (-29).	CEC decide 'to direct the maximum number of Party workers to the food front'. **S Russia** — Krasnov & White Volunteer Army fail to agree on united strategy. **E Siberia** — Reds force Col Semenov to E bank of R Onon.	**Italian Front** — **Diaz** informs Foch & CIGS Sir H Wilson that he has **postponed his own offensive** (towards Valsuguna) **to deal with imminent Austrian one.**	ARMENIA DECLARES HER INDEPENDENCE.
Wed 29	**Flanders** — Germans repulsed nr Mt Kemmel. **Marne** — GERMANS CAPTURE SOISSONS, Fère-en-Tardenois, Vregny plateau & heights S of the Vesle, cross R Ourcq French forced off 'Paris Line'. Duchêne tells Clemenceau his army 'simply marching to the rear' (*see* 9 June).	CEC decrees partial conscription for Red Army & forms Supreme Revolutionary Tribunal (*see* 21 June). Martial law in Moscow; Lenin sends Stalin to Tsaritsyn to organize food supplies (*see* 6 June). **Finland** — Govt forms special 5-man courts to try Reds (67,000 convicted, 265 executed); 11,783 Red PoWs die of disease (-Aug).	**Salonika** — Guillaumat and Milne agree to spare 20,000 Allied troops for W Front (*see* 1 June).	
Thu 30	British staff officer notes 'Foch apparently does not think the war can be finished this year. DH [Haig] thinks it can and should.' **Marne** — **Germans reach the Marne in strength**, capturing Château-Thierry & Dormans & advance on Compiègne but 8 divs arriving incl US 3rd. French retire from R Ailette. British form Gater's Force (-19 June) from 21st Div remnants. Foch gives Pétain res Tenth Army (Maistre) from Picardy.	Ataman Dutov leads Orenburg Cossacks v Reds.	**Macedonia — Combat of Skra di Legen**: At 0455 Greek Crete & Archipelago Divs (2659 cas) storm fortified Bulgar 49th Regt salient, rocky outwork of their line 10 miles W of the Vardar, in a morning behind Anglo-French creeping barrage & after diversionary ops since 28; 1812 Bulgar-German PoWs (800k), 50 MGs & 60 mortars taken. Brilliant limited military success of great political value in Greece for Venizelos, makes war fashionable. Bulgar afternoon & night counter-	

AFRICAN OPERATIONS 5	SEA WAR 6	AIR WAR 7	INTERNATIONAL EVENTS 8	HOME FRONTS 9
	months (*see* 8 June), about 5% explode prematurely. Often 1 minelayer laid over 43 miles in 3½ hours (*see* July). **N Sea** — Grand Fleet cruises off Heligoland Bight minefields while Harwich Force goes through, but no German response. Destroyer *Shakespeare* mined but towed home by cruiser *Centaur* (see 10 June). **Channel** — RN patrol yacht *Lorna* depth charges & sinks *UB74* in Lyme Bay.	**Germany** — 12 FE2s (1 FTR) of No 106 Sqn raid Kreuzwald power stn & Metz-Sablon railway. All FE 2 force-lands in enemy lines, crew escape & rejoin sqn (30). 3 Handley Pages attack Mannheim & Kreuzwald (night 27/28). **W Front** — *JG1* & *3*, 5 *Jagdstaffeln* , 14 *Schlachtstraffeln* , 23 *Fliegerabteilungen* & 2 *Bombengeschwader* support Ludendorff's Aisne offensive after lavish air recon, 19 planes lost (-30), mainly to AA fire; 3323 fighter sorties (-18 June). **France** — 15 German aircraft (1 lost) raid Paris (4 bombs, *see* 30). **Adriatic** — British bomb Durazzo, sink Austrian torpedo boat.		
		Germany — 10 DH9s of No 99 Sqn attack rail targets at Bensdorf. **W Front** — Germans capture Magneux airfield on Aisne with all its aircraft. A second French bomber gp joins Aisne air battle.	Anglo-German PoW exchange talks open (*see* 14 July).	**Turkey** — Sultan ratifies banning of all trade in postal & transport permits. **Britain** — Cabinet decide to prohibit racing in 1918/19 winter season.
		Germany — Half 12-strong formation of No 99 Sqn return with engine trouble, rest bomb Metz-Sablon railways. **W Front** — 4 French Spad fighter patrols (1 lost) first encounter new Fokker DVII & shoot 5 down.	Austro-Finnish peace treaty signed at Vienna. US Sec of State Lansing issues communiqué sympathizing with Czechoslovaks & Yugoslavs. Final Allied trade agreement with Sweden.	**Britain** — Food Production Dept reports 4m acres added to tillage, 80% 1918 food will be homegrown. Criminal 'Black Book' libel case about German agents encouraging sexual perversion opens at Old Bailey (-4 June).
Kartucol finds abandoned German field hospital at Kwiri.		**Germany** — 16 DH4s attack Thionville: direct hits on officers' billet (10 cas), rail stn, tracks & rolling stock. **France** — 6 German bombers raid Paris (& 31), 17 bombs cause 6 cas (*see* 1 June). **W Front** — Banks in Camel of No 43 Sqn destroys Friedrichshafen night bomber; RAF bomb towns behind German lines. **Italian Front** — Trentino: 35 RFC Camels bomb (1t) & strafe (9000rnds) Austrian huts N of Val d'Assa. **Secret War** — Italian Voisin lands air observer	Austro-Turk Treaty on Capitulations. **USA** — Masrayk at Pittsburgh promises complete autonomy in the new Czech state.	**Britain** — Churchill protests v War Cabinet announcing no bombing of Cologne on Corpus Christi Day.

MAY 1918	WESTERN FRONT 1	EASTERN FRONT 2	SOUTHERN FRONTS 3	TURKISH FRONTS 4
Thu 30 contd			attacks fail.	
Fri 31	**Battlefield debut of French Renault lt tank: 30 (3 lost) in Retz Forest helps stem German advance** as do 4 more divs. (May) 250,000 US troops sail for France, record 9 divs land.	**Siberia** — Czechs take Petropavlosk & Tomsk.		
Sat 1 June 1918	(June) 1000-2000 flu cases per German div. **Marne** — **Germans** held between the Oise & Marne (US 3rd Div MG bn in action, with 5 more divs arriving incl US 2nd) but reach edge of Villers-Cotterêts Forest **40 miles from Paris**. **Champagne** — French lose then regain Ft de La Pompelle, SE of Reims (*see* 18).	Moscow arrests of 'Union for Fatherland and Freedom' counter-revolutionaries. **S Russia** — Crimean-Tartar Govt formed at Sevastopol (*see* 6 & SEA WAR 18). (June) Germans try to form 1st Ukrainian Cossack Rifle Div.	**Salonika** — (June) 10,000 **French & 10,000 British** (12 British bns transferred from 16) **withdrawn for W Front**; Greek 2nd (Athens) Div becomes operational (in line by 26); 28 Bulgars desert to British in mid month warn of offensive, but cancelled due to mutiny. 80,000t of supplies pw being landed at Salonika (10,109 British cas in hospital). **Italian Front** — Diaz warns his 7 army cdrs not to repeat recent Anglo-French W Front mistakes with their reserves. (June) Czechoslovak Div formed (*see* 1 Sept).	**Mesopotamia** — British assess Turk Sixth Army at 18,800 men, 130 guns & 25 planes (*see* 30 Sept). (June) Khalil Pasha hands it to Ali Ihsan and goes to Caucasus as C-in-C Army Group East (replaces Vehip Pasha). **Georgia** — Tartars massacre Armenians S of Tiflis. **Armenia** — (June) Essad Pasha replaces Vehip Pasha i/c Third Army.
Sun 2	Pershing to ask for 250,000 men pm, June & July. French counter-attacking between the Ourcq & Marne, recapture Faverolles (3).			
Mon 3	Churchill visits BEF GHQ, Paris & Front (-13). Fierce fighting between Soissons & Noyon. French retake Choisy Hill for 5th time. **After 30-mile advance Germans reach the Marne**: US 2nd & 3rd Divs block the advance at Château-Thierry, 'Retreat hell! We just got here' attr to Capt Lloyd S Williams USMC, Belleau Wood. Franco-Americans eliminate German Jaulgonne bridgehead (100 PoWs). Pétain organizes reinforced French cordon round Aisne salient. **Secret War** — 'Le radiogramme de la victoire': French intercept German Eighteenth Army ammo delivery message, hints at Montdidier offensive (9). **Aisne** — Legion stiffens French defence NW of Villers-Cotterêts (night 5/6-c14). 27 Allied divs have arrived since 28 May.	**Japan approves Allied intervention in Siberia. E Siberia** — White Trans-Baikal Cossack Col Semenov retreats on Borsia after defeating Reds, similarly captures Gurks, 93 miles NE (6) but retreats (10).		**Georgia** — 2 German bns from Crimea (217th Div) **land at Poti** (*see* 5, 10,12). **Palestine** — (c) Limited imports allowed through Egypt (*see* 20).
Tue 4	Pétain orders Third Army (Humbert) to thin Matz forward	**N Russia** — 150 Royal Marines land at Pechenga. **Baltic**		Turks sign peace treaty with Armenians, Azerbaijanis &

AFRICAN OPERATIONS 5	SEA WAR 6	AIR WAR 7	INTERNATIONAL EVENTS 8	HOME FRONTS 9
		Lt Camillo de Carlo behind Austrian lines for 3 months, he discovers date of Piave offensive (*see* 14 June). **N Sea** — 5 German seaplanes (from Borkum) destroy Yarmouth-based flying boat (3 PoWs incl US NCF Ensign J J Roe) (*see* 4 June).		
	Empty US transport *President Lincoln* sunk by *U90*. **N Sea** — British destroyer *Fairy* (convoy escort) sinks after ramming & destroying *UC75*. (May) Allied & neutral shipping lost to U-boats 112 ships (59 British with 407 lives lost) worth 294,019t (192,432 British incl ship mined). U-boat figure 139 ships worth 296,558t incl **most successful 1918 month in Med**, 56 ships worth 122,7175t of which 12 (9923t) to Austrians. **Record 14 U-boats sunk** (3 in Med).	**W Front** — Air-to-air combat over R Aisne costs 12 German & 17 French aircraft. Lt Duncan Campbell (94th Aero Sqn) becomes **first American air arm ace** with his 5th victory. Total Allied May losses 362 aircraft & 24 balloons. German non-combat loss 175 aircraft and 201 in action. **Germany** — 10 RAF DH4s (lost) bomb Karlsruhe (78 cas) & stop factory production for 1hr.	**Neutrals: Holland** — Refuses to tolerate British examining convoyed ships. **Switzerland** — British funds are arranged for war exports (*see* 13 June).	**Turkey** — **Great 27-hr fire at Constantinople** causes T£520,000 damage. Maximum prices abolished, trade made free. **Britain** — War Savings certificates reach 2m. (May) Labour Ministry creates Appointments Dept for officers. May's 197,274t new merchant shipping a record. **Belgium** — **Cooreman succeeds Baron de Broqueville as PM**. **USA** — War Sec can conscript conscientious objectors for unpaid farmwork. **France** — Paris munition plants: 'Morale of the workers is excellent'.
Lettow crosses R Lurio to S bank as Kartucol reaches N bank (fords night 3/4). Gold Coast Regt leaves Korewa for Port Amelia and home (*see* 14 Aug).	**Home Waters** (June) British coastal trade increasingly sailing in convoys (*see* July). **Secret War** — (June) British Gyro (gun) Director Training gear has successful trials, equips all capital ships & monitors for rest of war. **N Sea** — (June) RN lays 9049 mines in E Coast Barrage from Flamborough Head NWN to Tyne 15-30 miles from coast.	**France** — 3 German bombers raid Paris (14 bombs, 28 cas), single aircraft raids (3-7, 15, 26) & 3 more (27, 2 lost, 25 cas) (*see* 15 Sept). **Macedonia** — (June) Anglo-French destroy 12 Bulgar aircraft (*see* 15). **W Front** — Germans claim 32 Allied aircraft for loss of 12. Capt P L Weiller made Cmdt of *Groupe des Escs de Grande Reconnaissance* (Breguet recon, arty spotter & bomber units). **Adriatic** — (June) Germans send 6 seaplanes for courier/postal work.	6th Allied Supreme War Council at Versailles (-3) is stormy, Foch v Lloyd George over BEF manpower. Crown Prince Rupprecht of Bavaria writes to Chancellor urges peace talks while still military cards, but Hertling hopes (5) that one Allied power (probably France) may yet collapse (*see* 1 July).	(June) FLU PANDEMIC BEGINS IN INDIA AND BRITAIN. **Britain** — RFP 108% (Feb level). Sugar prod cut to 25% of 1915 for yr. DW Griffith's *Hearts of the World* (starring Lillian Gish) opens in London (June). **France** — Food rationing cards compulsory. (June) André Maurois publishes *Les Silences de Colonel Bramble*. **Germany** — Krupp's Essen Works now has 75,000 men and 23,000 women (*see* 10 Sept). (June) 1920 conscript class called up (*see* 1 Aug). **USA** — Food Administrator warns v boycotting sauerkraut ('liberty cabbage'). War Sec Baker authorizes inquiry into conscientious objectors, 130 Memonites jailed.
	At Allied Supreme War Council Adm Revel says with pride no major Italian warship has left harbour for 6 months & no losses incurred! USN has 150 warships in European waters (*see* 7).	**W Front** — Oblt Göring awarded *Pour le Mérite* (*see* 3 July). Germans claim 38 Allied aircraft for loss of 17.		
	W Atlantic — U-boats sink 9 ships off New Jersey. SS *Pinar del Rio* sunk off Maryland (8).	**Britain** — DFC instituted. **Palestine** — RAF raid Amman (-4, 11 & 18).	**Britain, France and Italy support national aspirations of Poles, Czechs and Yugoslavs** (*see* 28 & 29). Churchill first flies to France, sees Haig and front (-13).	**Ireland** — Lord French calls for 50,000 vols of 18-27 up to 1 Oct. **Britain** — War Office made sole importer of US leather.
		France — Dover Patrol given 82nd Wing (7 sqns) for	Dr Weizmann meets Feisal at Aqaba, latter gives impression	**Clemenceau to Chamber 'I shall fight before Paris... in**

JUNE 1918	WESTERN FRONT 1	EASTERN FRONT 2	SOUTHERN FRONTS 3	TURKISH FRONTS 4
Tue 4 contd	positions for defence in more depth. Americans check Germans at Veuilly Wood.	**States** — Lithuania proclaims royal constitution, Duke of Württemberg accepts throne (elected 31 Aug,*see* 2 Nov). **Secret War** — Lockhart to Foreign Office 'If you do not intervene within...days or weeks....we shall have lost a golden opportunity'.		Georgians. **Persia** — Dunsterville at Kazvin, leaves with Anglo-Russian force (5, *see* 12); 1000 motorized troops & 2 guns (500 vans) forming at Hamadan (2 Duncars arrive 6, *see* 12).
Wed 5	**Aisne** — THIRD BATTLE OF THE AISNE ends with Germans exhausted & overextended in new bulge.			Enver Pasha & Gen Seeck sail from Constantinople for Batumi, Georgia (*see* 10 & 11). **Azerbaijan** — c8500 Armenians attack in 3 cols W of Baku to cover area v Azeri Tartars (-15, *see* 16).
Thu 6	**Marne** — **Battle of Belleau Wood** (-25): US 2nd Div & 4th US Marine Bde counter-attack W of Château-Thierry & capture Vaux, Bouresches & B Wood (1087 cas). Crown Prince orders consolidation of line won. British recapture Fligny village height SW of Reims (-7). Clemenceau sacks d'Esperey from N Army Gp, but sends him to Salonika (11, *see* 9 & 16). Allied Supreme War Council settles Haig-Foch tussle over reserves. Franco-US forces recapture Veuilly-La Poterie & Vinly.	Lenin accepts German ultimatum for Black Sea Fleet's return to Sevastopol (*see* SEA WAR 18). **Volga** — Stalin arrives in Tsaritsyn by train with 2 armoured cars & 400 Red Guards (*see* 23).	Clemenceau recalls Guillaumat to Paris from Salonika & sends Franchet d'Esperey as replacement without consulting Allies (*see* 9 & 17).	Kemal begins regular diary while on sick leave at Carlsbad, Austria for kidney trouble (-27, *see* 7 Aug).
Fri 7	**Champagne** — Italian II Corps joins French Fifth Army (*see* 18).	1st Congress of Red Military Commissars. **N Russia** — 250 Royal Marines land at Kem on White Sea. Lenin orders Murmansk Soviet to oppose Allies. **Siberia** — Czechs occupy Omsk. **Don** — By now Germans have occupied Bataisk S of Rostov (*see* 14).		
Sat 8	Foch warns pessimistic, uncooperative Pétain that 'an important attack in the north [ie in Flanders] is always possible...you must...face having to send back French forces to the British Zone'. **Artois** — Cdn Lewis gunner Cp J Kaeble of 22nd Bn wins posthumous VC repelling c50 German trench raiders nr Neuville-Vitesse.	**Volga** — Czechs take Samara, **White Komuch** ('Ctee of Members of the Constituent Assembly') **Govt established** (*see* 21 July & 4 Oct). **N Russia** — **Soviet Govt orders Allied forces to leave** (*see* 30), 3000 troops ordered N from Petrograd while Moscow/Volga workers & peasants called up (-14).	Italians get final indications of imminent offensive (-14).	**Turkey recognizes independent Armenia & Georgia** with peace treaties; Armenia to let Turk troops through. Ludendorff refuses to recognize treaties (10 & 11). **Palestine** — 7th Indian Div (267 cas) storms 2 low hills 1 mile from sea, taking 110 PoWs & 7 MGs. **Arabia** — Arab raid on Hejaz Railway nr Toweira (105 miles NW of Medina), take Kalaat-el-Almar, 200 miles N of Medina (28).
Sun 9	Clemenceau sacks Gens Duchêne, (Degoutte replaces i/c Sixth Army 10, *see* 28 Sept), Maud'huy & Chrétien (corps cdrs) for Aisne failure. (FOURTH) GERMAN *GNEISENAU* OFFENSIVE V FRENCH ON R MATZ (-14) between Noyon & Montdidier	**Siberia** — 2 Czech forces join in Western advance.	**Albania** — French Annamites (Vietnamese) & Albanian *Tirailleurs* take Austrian-held Mt Kamia (7054ft) & 2 villages (night 8/9) SW of L Ochrid in 5-6-mile advance on 20-mile front (8-14) taking 400 PoWs & 10 guns for 50 cas (*see* 6 July). **Salonika** — Gen Guillaumat	**Armenia/Persia** — Turk Ninth Army (6 divs) formed under Sevki Pasha to invade N Persia (*see* 14).

AFRICAN OPERATIONS 5	SEA WAR 6	AIR WAR 7	INTERNATIONAL EVENTS 8	HOME FRONTS 9
		continued bombing of Belgian coast. **France** — Germans bomb Dunkirk airfields (nights 4/5, 5/6 200 bombs from 24 aircraft disable 52 RAF aircraft (6 & 7) & force Couderkerque airfield's abandonment. **N Sea** — Large 50-min seaplane action off Terschelling I, 2/5 RAF FTR after action with 10 German seaplanes (1 washed ashore). **W Front** — Cmdt Vuillemin's 120 French bombers (*GB6 & 9*) break up German Ninth Army attack E of Retz Forest. Germans claim 18 Allied aircraft for loss of 1.	of not opposing Jewish presence in Palestine. Anglo-American Arbitration Treaty renewed.	**Paris...behind Paris.**', wins vote 337-110. **Britain** — Men of 18 generally lose military service exemption (*see* 14 & 17).
Kartuaal drivos Köhl's rearguards along Malema rd (-7).	**Med** — Armed boarding steamer HMS *Snaefell* sunk by U-boat.	**France** — **Independent Force** (officially **formed** 6) under Trenchard begins ops from Nancy. Organized as 8th Bde RAF, initially with 4 sqns (grew to 9): Nos 216 (Handley Pages), 55 (DHA), 99 (arr 3 May) & 100 (FE2). Only the Handley Pages & DH4s have strategic range & high performance, but 74 attacks made in June. **W Front** — Germans claim 31 Allied aircraft for loss of 7, air fighting diminishes until 9.		**Hungary** — Count Tisza tells Diet Dual Monarchy must be extended (anti-govt riots 22). **USA** — **2nd Registration** adds 750,000 21yr olds to draft list. **Britain** — Madsen (US) MG debate in Commons. Robertson GOC-in-C Home Forces.
	N Sea — Dutch hospital ship *Köningen Regentes* (4 lost) repatriating PoWs between England & The Hague sunk by U-boat (*see* INT'L EVENTS 28).	**Germany** — 6 Handley Pages & 10 FE2s attack Thionville & Metz railways (night 6/7). **W Front** — RAF 9th Bde (200 aircraft, sqn sent 3) reinforces 1000 French aircraft in fierce air fighting over Roye, Montdidier & Noyon (*see* 9).		**Britain** — 535 National Food Kitchens with 500 being negotiated; margarine output up fourfold; dye prod c25,000t (1500t prewar); record corn, wheat & potato cultivation (4), livestock down.
	Med — **Most of first 36 US submarine chasers arrive** with tender *Leonidas* at Corfu, having crossed Atlantic under own power. First hunt (-9) of 37 hunts; CO believes 19 kills achieved, actually none.	**Germany** — 13 DHs attack rail targets at Conz & Thionville: No 55 Sqn unable to reach primary target (Koblenz clouded over), as on (8 & 13).	Allied Supreme War Council decides to move ships for deporting Austro-Germans from China to Australia to Vladivostok for Czechs.	
	N Sea — Areas A & C of Northern Barrage begun. **Britain** — US Ambassador's wife launches 26,000t carrier HMS *Eagle* (ex-Chilean dreadnought *Almirante Cochrane* redesigned by end 1917 as first 'island type' carrier) at Newcastle.	Ludendorff receives Air Force expansion plan for 1 July 1918-1 Apr 1919, he approves 300 more planes pm (to 2300) but actual prod av 1088. **Germany** — No 104 Sqn (arr 20 May) joins RAF strategic bombing campaign with 10-plane attack on Metz-Sablon railways; fighter interceptions (1 shot down) & heavy, accurate flak over objective. 23 DH sorties flown v Hagendingen (8, 9 & 13); cement works badly damaged. **W Front** — RAF 9th Bde with c200 aircraft & French 1st Air Div with 600 aircraft (forerunner of 1939-45 tactical air forces) intervene in Noyon-Montdidier ground battle. Germans claim 38 Allied aircraft for loss of 5. RAF drop 16t of bombs & fire 120,000 MG (-11) rnds	Smuts offers to command US AEF in France, Lloyd George declines to forward request. Anglo-German PoW Conference at the Hague (British delegates' ship sunk by U-boat 6, *see* 14 & 14 July).	**USA** — c5000 Germans interned at 4 camps (7 Irish Americans on conspiracy charges at NY 7). 5000 horse gas masks being made pd. Naval Consulting Board discusses ASW.

JUNE 1918	WESTERN FRONT 1	EASTERN FRONT 2	SOUTHERN FRONTS 3	TURKISH FRONTS 4
Sun 9 contd	(also known as First Battle of Lassigny) begins with midnight barrage which French pre-empt by 10min thanks to deserter intelligence. Germans fire 750,000 rnds (15,000t) mustard gas, phosgene & diphenylchlorarsine: 3918 gassed (32 deaths) (-15 June). Hutier attacks with 11 divs from 0300, advances 6 miles, takes 8000 PoWs, mauls 3 divs & continues at night.		leaves in haste & secrecy for Paris (*see* W FRONT, I4).	
Mon 10	**Noyon/Montdidier** — Germans gain another 2 miles, Humbert withdraws 38th & 15th Divs 6 miles S to N of Laigue Forest (NE of Compiègne). Foch urges Fayolle to launch Mangin's counter-stroke without delay.	Sovnarkom declares war on Siberian Prov Govt.		**Turk 9th Caucasian Div clashes with German-Georgian force** at Vorontsovka, S of Tiflis & drives it back.
Tue 11	**Mangin's** 4 divs & US 2nd & 3rd Divs launch **flank counter-attack** at 1130 without prelim shelling but with 163 tanks (73 lost) & air support, retakes 3 villages, 1000 PoWs & 19 guns before resistance stiffens. **Somme** — Australian 2nd Div 'peaceful penetration' secures 300 PoWs. Monash submits plan for Hamel's recapture (21,*see* 4 July).	Sovnarkom dissolves Czech National Council and decrees Ctees of the Village Poor (*Kombedy*) for food crisis. Britain & France request USA to send 3 bns to N Russia.	**Italian Front** — Heavy rain begins, masks Austrian preparations.	*OHL* telegram threatens to withdraw all German troops & officials from Turkey if Turk advance in Georgia not halted. Enver threatens to resign, but Seeckt patches up quarrel (-July, *see* 22).
Wed 12	**Aisne** — German Seventh Army attacks with 5 divs W of Soissons (-13) but gains minimal v French with 197 tanks, Ludendorff calls off *Gneisenau*. **Noyon/Montdidier** — Mangin again attacks, gains up to 3200yds at heavy cost, but Germans blunted & Clemenceau's critics silenced.	**Finland** — Govt proposes to Diet that monarchy be established.	**Trentino** — Austrian bde attack v Italian ridge of 25 May fails in snowstorms.	**Georgia** — Germans occupy Tiflis. **N Persia** — Anglo-Russian force (1200 Cossacks, 4 guns, c100 Hussars, 2 Duncars & 2 RAF planes) disperses 3000-4000 German-advised Jangali tribesmen at Manjil Bridge, NW of Kazvin; Col Bicherakov soon reaches Enzeli on Caspian (*see* 22).
Thu 13	Foch warns Haig & Pétain to hold back their reserves for rapid mutual support.	Ukraine signs provisional treaty with Moscow. **Siberia** — Fighting at Irkutsk, W of L Baikal.	**Italian Front** — Preliminary Austrian diversionary attack by 2 divs ('Avalanche Action') in Tonale Pass (Trentino, W of L Garda) fails by early afternoon.	
Fri 14	BATTLE OF THE MATZ ENDS: French defensive victory; **First extensive use of mustard gas by Allies** (French) causes 265 cas. Foch instructs Pétain to plan offensive W of Soissons, Mangin makes 8 successful local attacks (-5 July,*see* 28 June). *OHL* reaffirms its cherished 'final' offensive in Flanders (codename *Hagen*). But first Allied reserves must be drawn S by Op *Reims* (*Marneschutz*) (ordered 18). Brüchmuller's 'siege train' to redeploy quickly from Reims to Flanders (Rupprecht to attack 15 days later). French Intelligence predicts 'a continuation of the thrust towards Amiens.. (or) a continuation of the attacks in the direction of Paris by...the Oise and Marne...not before 15 July'. Guillaumat replaces Dubail as Military Governor of	Soviets expel Right Socialist parties. **S Russia** — Don-Kuban Cossack Agreement. 10,000 Russians fight Germans at Taganrog		**NW Persia** — 2000 Turks re-occupy Tabriz.

AFRICAN OPERATIONS 5	SEA WAR 6	AIR WAR 7	INTERNATIONAL EVENTS 8	HOME FRONTS 9
2/3rd KAR at Ndenda (German E Africa) ordered to Lindi to sail for Quelimane (*see* 25).	**Adriatic** — 2 **Italian MAS boats** attack & *MAS 15* (Rizzo) capsizes & **sinks Austrian battleship** *Szent Istvan* (89 dis) off Premuda I despite 7 escort torpedo boats; Austrian Fleet (3 other battleships) abandons sortie to Lower Adriatic for smashing Otranto Barrage. **N Sea** — Harwich Force begins nightly sweeps into Heligoland Bight despite British mine risk (*see* 13 & 19).	**Occupied Belgium** — RAF No 214 Sqn Handley Pages bomb Thourout rail jctn, Bruges docks & steelworks, Zeebrugge lock & canal (night 10/11). **Britain** — 469 AA guns ready for action with 622 searchlights manned by 6136 gunners out of 13,405 personnel in home air defence.	Marshal Joffre 'We ought to have made terms with Austria last year...then Germany would have had to give in'.	**Britain** — Cabinet forms Economic Defence & Development Ctee. Officially claimed that 7 German bombings of hospitals caused 941 cas (15 May-1 June). National Iron & Steel Industry Council formed (11).
S Nigeria — Egba Rising begins N of Lagos: 5 WAFF cols (92 cas) quell by 4 July (500 rebels k); 3400 firearms surrendered (-23 July).	Allied Naval Council 4th meeting, London (11-12) again fails to be unanimous. **Adriatic** — Cattaro U-boat Flotilla CO Lt-Cdr Ackermann reports gloomily on prospects, RAF raids increasing (*see* AIR WAR), fears naval raids.	**W Front** — **Allied close air support for Mangin's counter-stroke** leads to heavy air battles (*see* W FRONT); RAF bombing in error causes 8 French w & 75 horses k. Germans claim 40 Allied aircraft for loss of 19 (-12).	German War Minister Gen Stein claims Central Powers winning.	**Turkey** — **Military & political press censorship abolished** to promote Pan-Turanianism and aid attacks on Allies.
Rosecol broken up. Lettow over R Ligonya.		**W Front** — **First US day bombing mission**: Breguet 14s of 96th Aero Sqn bomb Dommary-Baroncourt rail yds. **Macedonia** — 4 RAF aircraft shoot down at least 3 of 8 hostile aircraft encountered, 2 more collide.	British Imperial War Conference (-26 July) inc 7 PMs. Balfour speech praises Japan (Prince Arthur of Connaught visits 18).	
Kartucol camps just N of Malema (-15) before crossing Inagu Hills.	**Bristol Channel** — U-boat sinks AMC HMS *Patia*. **N Sea** — Cruiser *Conquest* mined off Harwich but towed to Sheerness. Sister ship *Centaur* mined in Heligoland Bight but steams 250 miles stern first to reach Humber (14-15).	**Germany** — Air battle over Trier: 2 fighters shot down by DH4s (1 shot down) by No 55 Sqn; direct hit on iron foundry.	Holland agrees to British conditions (7) for E Indies convoy (*see* 4 July). Burian back in Vienna from 2-day Berlin meeting on Poland and Spa agreement.	
		Occupied Belgium — Germans using Allied PoWs for rail truckloading at Mortagne, later dig training trenches (-15 Oct). **Neutrals: Finland** — Diet fails to vote for monarchy, postpones decision (19) to 1920.		**USA** — Wilson complains at film *My Four Years in Germany* (Warner version of Ambassador Gerrard's memoirs, opened by 30 Mar, PoW atrocity scenes staged in NJ). **Britain** — Men of 50 to report as required (*see* 17).

JUNE 1918	WESTERN FRONT 1	EASTERN FRONT 2	SOUTHERN FRONTS 3	TURKISH FRONTS 4
Fri 14 contd	Paris (potential Pétain replacement, *see* 26). **Flanders —** British night raid along La Bassée Canal succeeds.			
Sat 15	Clemenceau forms ctee for defence of Paris at Bombon (Foch attends); Allied GHQ since 5.		SECOND BATTLE OF THE PIAVE (-24): Austrians (codename 'Radetsky') pre-empted on Asiago sector by Italian barrage for 4hrs before Austrian guns open at 0300 (shell shortage & no phosgene gas given by Germans). Inf attack at 0700. Austrian Eleventh Army penetrates British (3 frontline bns surprised) & French lines but stopped by early pm, repulsed by counter-attack leaving 1500 PoWs & 7 guns. In Mt Grappa sector Austrian XXVI Corps captures 5 features & I Corps takes part of Mt Solaroli salient, max penetration 3300 yds, but Italian Fourth Army counter-attacks make progress. An agitated Emperor Charles (in imperial train at Merano) rings FM Boroevic at noon 'The Army of Tyrol is defeated, the troops have lost all that they had gained and have been driven back to the line of departure'. **Piave —** Code name 'Albrecht', Austrian Isonzo Army crosses Lower Piave under smokeshell & fog cover on a 20-mile front gaining 3 small bridgeheads & laying 1 bridge; Sixth Army crosses onto Montello Ridge, securing bridgehead, takes 4000 PoWs & up to 2 miles but unable to link with Isonzo Army and its bridges & boats hit by RAF (*see* AIR WAR). More troops cross during night.	
Sun 16	Mangin replaces Maistre i/c French Tenth Army, Maistre takes over Centre Army Gp.		**Piave —** British 48th Div (922 cas) after 4 counter-attacks has taken 728 PoWs & buried 576 Austrians. In Mt Grappa sector Italian Fourth Army restores its line except for 2 peaks, releasing 200 Italian PoWs & c12 guns. Austrian Army Gp Conrad losses 35,026. Italian Eighth & Third Army counter-attacks recover some ground incl 4 villages S of the Piave. Heavy rain, Italian & RAF attacks & lack of bridging equipment (due to shortage of horses) hinder river crossings.	**Azerbaijan —** Armenians capture Karamarian (120 miles W of Baku) but fail to advance farther S (*see* 26). **S Persia —** Action of Ahmadabad (W of Shiraz): British spoiling attack inflicts 500 cas on 3200 tribesmen; Shiraz crisis over by 21 (*see* 24).
Mon 17		**Baltic States —** Saxon Minister Seydwitz visits Hoffmann about proposed Saxon-Lithuanian union. **S Russia —** Anti-Red revolt in Tambov. Austrians take 10,000 PoWs in Ukraine (*see* SEA WAR 18).	**Piave —** On Lower Piave Austrian XXIII Corps expands largest bridgehead but still short of Meolo in Italian 2nd line; XXIV Corps makes gains on Montello, but 20 bridges insufficient for supplies, heavy rain makes river rise nearly 3ft (night 17/18) & breaks nearly all of them. **Salonika — Gen Franchet d'Esperey arrives to be Allied C-in-C** (18) tells new subordinates 'I expect from you savage vigour'; Paris directive drawn up (22, *see* 29, 2 July).	
Tue 18	**Marne —** Mudra relieves F Below i/c First Army, latter takes over new Ninth Army at Soissons (-6 Aug). **Champagne —** French repulse German attack from Sillery to Trigny 7 miles W of Reims (&		**Piave —** Slight Austrian Montello gains nr Nervesa rail bridge. Italian 1st Div takes 500 PoWs from Lower Piave San Dona bridgehead, but its reinforced occupiers take 6500 PoWs around Campolunga (-	

AFRICAN OPERATIONS 5	SEA WAR 6	AIR WAR 7	INTERNATIONAL EVENTS 8	HOME FRONTS 9
	Baltic — Last 3 German cruisers leave Finnish waters.	**Italian Front** — Top Italian ace Francesco Baracca scores his last 2 victories (last a 2-seater among 25 escorts, *see* 20). 653 **Allied aircraft** (incl 33 Camels who break 1 pontoon bridge) **attack & help remove Austrian Piave bridgeheads** (-22). **Hejaz Railway** — RAF bomb El Kutrani stn, 30 miles E of Dead Sea S end.	Kaiser's 30th anniversary of accession speech 'a conflict between... the Prussian-Germanic approach ...or the Anglo-Saxon ... enthroning the worship of gold'.	**Germany** — Stressemann writes 'Never had we the occasion like today to believe in German victory'.
Lettow's main body enters Alto Molocque (220 miles W of Mozambique), captures 75,000lb food & valuable maps. **Morocco** — French Oued-Inouen line repulses repeated tribal attacks (*see* 22).				**USA** — Socialist Eugene V Debs speech at Canton, Ohio 'Sooner or later every war of trade becomes a war of 'blood'. (arrested 30 for opposing recruiting, 10yrs jail 14 Sept).
	W Med — RN convoy escorts sloop *Lychnis* & trawler *Partridge II* sink Moraht's *U64* (45 ships or 132,166t sunk since 1916) with gunfire between Sardinia & Sicily. **N Sea** — Sopwith Camel from carrier HMS *Furious* forces German seaplane down for destruction after 2 bombing raids on the ship.			**Britain** — **Men born 1895-7 called up** exc shipbuilders & shale oil miners. Imperial War Conference told soldier's grave will cost £10 (Italy grants land June). **Austria** — **Partial Vienna strike and riots** v reduced bread ration (-21, *see* 21). **Hungary** — Troops cause 24+ cas in Budapest MAV Machine-Factory claiming pay increase (20), capital's workers walk out (-27).
Kartucol coys fire on each other by mistake S of R Ligonha enabling German patrol to escape.	**Black Sea** — Russian dreadnought *Svobodnaya Rossiya* (ex-*Imperatritsa Ekaterina*) destroyed by Reds to avoid capture by Germans. Destroyer *Kerch* torpedoes her at Novorossisk where 7		Emperor Charles predicts Ludendorff Offensive will soon grind to halt, Burian speaks of getting neutral mediation (17).	**Bulgaria** — **PM Radoslavov** (since 1913) **resigns** at Tsar Ferdinand's bidding, Malinov replaces to placate unrest. **Germany** — OHL demands military service for all men 15-60, War Minister opposes (24).

JUNE 1918	WESTERN FRONT 1	EASTERN FRONT 2	SOUTHERN FRONTS 3	TURKISH FRONTS 4
Tue 18 contd	one on Bligny 22 that costs 392 Italian cas).		19).	
Wed 19		Petrograd workers mobilized by Reds. **Baltic States** — Germans remove Polish administrator Michalkiewicz from Vilna. **Volga** — Czechs capture strategic Syzran rail crossing. White demos in Kozlov & Tambov, far SE of Moscow.	**Piave** — Italian Eighth Army counterstroke at 1530 on Montello with 10 divs v 3 Austrian divs & extra arty divs regains Nervesa only to lose it again (20); Gen Vaccari leads his XXII Corps in person. Boroevic sees Emperor Charles at Spilimbergo on the Tagliamento, Arz can offer no reinforcements, munitions or supplies.	**Palestine** — Lawrence at Allenby's HQ, gets latter's letter to Hussein for bringing up Hejaz troops but fails to persuade the Sherif after sailing to Jeddah (*see* 11 July).
Thu 20			**Piave** — Boroevic cables High Command 'As the Monarchy... has loyally fulfilled its duties as an ally...and cannot face the risk of remaining perhaps disarmed, I propose to withdraw...behind the Piave'; Emperor gives permission (*see* AIR WAR). Boroevic plans to retreat at night only. Italians decide shelling bridges better than mass attacks.	**Azerbaijan** — Turk 5th Caucasian Div (6000) arrives at Ganja (Russian Elizavetpol) to be core of Enver's Army of Islam (18,000 under Enver's 28-year-old half-brother Nuri Pasha). A regt marches to support Azeri Tartars (26, *see* 28). **Palestine** — British restore civil law courts in occupied territory (*see* 24 July).
Fri 21		Soviet Supreme Revolutionary Tribunal passes 1st death sentence, Adm Shchastriy of Baltic Fleet shot.	**Piave** — Further Italian inf assaults on Lower Piave bridgehead (-22). Austrian wounded & non-essential troops evacuated (night 21/22). Italians claim 12,000 PoWs to date.	
Sat 22	**Somme** — British Third Army night raid on trenches at Bucquoy incl **first night action by British tanks** (night 22/23), 5 support c150 inf of 62nd Div.	**S Russia** — **Denikin's White Volunteer Army** (9000 men, 21 guns, 3 armoured cars) **begins 2nd Kuban campaign**, captures Torgovaya and Shabilevskaya rail stns, isolating Red Kuban Group and cutting Tsaritsyn railway (25, *see* 10 July). Russian Eastern Railway manager, Gen Horvath, (HQ Harbin, Manchuria) appeals for Allied help.	**Piave** — Austrian Sixth & Isonzo Armies begin recrossing river secretly (night 22/23).	Turk war aims published in *Vorwärts* incl 1914 Empire + Cyrenaica, Dodecanese, Crete, Black Sea Protectorate & influence in Egypt. **Palestine** — Liman submits resignation to Kaiser, but latter prevails on him to stay despite Enver's accusation of hurrying Turks but not Germans to front. Turks repulsed from Hasa Stn on Hejaz Railway. **Persia** — Bicherakov returns to Enzeli after Baku visit & deciding to turn Bolshevik to get there (*see* 28).
Sun 23		**N Russia** — British 'Syren' and 'Elope' forces (600 men under Maj-Gen Maynard) join N Russian EF at Murmansk; Maynard & 30 men head down Murmansk Railway (27), seize it to Soroka (29/30) sending back 3 Red troop trains. **Volga** — Civilian Voroshilov put i/c of 1000-strong Red Tsaritsyn Group (probably by Stalin). **Siberia** — **White Prov Siberian Govt formed at Omsk**, general mobilization soon proclaimed.	**Piave** — Italian Eighth Army reoccupies Nervesa at 1300 & then whole of Montello; Third Army captures 2000 PoWs in Candelu-Zenson sector (Middle Piave).	
Mon 24		Left SRs resolve on terrorism v Germans in Russia(*see* 6 & 30 July). **Siberia** — **Czech newspaper says Legion advance guard of Allied Armies on reformed E Front.**	**Last Austrians recross the Piave**; Third Army clears Austrian bridgehead at its Capo Sile mouth (*see* 2 July). 2,193,659 Allies & 7081 guns in 57 divs (36 in line) hold 188 miles of front (British & French 4 miles each).	War Cabinet Eastern Ctee debates Persian situation, gives India control of S & E Persia, Trans-Caspia & Turkestan ops. **Palestine** — 261,990 Allies (ration strength) & 438 guns v 131,000 Turco-Germans & 523 guns. **Mesopotamia** — 212,131 British & 310 guns v

AFRICAN OPERATIONS 5	SEA WAR 6	AIR WAR 7	INTERNATIONAL EVENTS 8	HOME FRONTS 9
	destroyers & torpedo boats scuttle themselves (*Kerch* scuttles at Tuapse 19). Dreadnought *Volya*, 3 destroyers, 2 torpedo boats & AMC return to Sevastopol as Germans request for internment, but c464 German sailors gradually take them over (*see* 8 July).			*Reichstag* : deputies increased & Act for proportional rep. **Britain** — Commons votes £500m credit (£7342m grand total, £6.8m pd; loans to Allies £1370m).
Fitzcol (2 KAR bns) leave Mbalama, E of Koronje (*see* 30).	**N Sea** — Harwich Force N of Heligoland Bight foiled from launching seaplane attack (3 other abortive attempts in May) but shoots down 1 attacking German seaplane.	**W Front** — Bishop (CO 85 Sqn SE5As) scores his last 5 victories E of Ploegsteert, having already scored 3 on 17 (*see* 3 July).	Franco-US Commissary for war relations formed. **Secret War** — British agent Belgian Lt Baschwitz-Meau arrives by balloon in Luxembourg (night 18/19) from Verdun to run train-watching network via code in newspaper *Landwirt* .	**Germany** — Ludendorff 'We must...think about preparing our people...the war can yet last yet longer.' (*see* 26).
Gen Northey made Gov & C-in-C British E Africa. Brig-Gen Hawthorn takes over NRFF. Kartucol halts for supplies at Vacha farmhouse.		**Italian Front** — Italians shoot down 14 Austrian aircraft over the Piave, but top Italian ace Baracca k strafing in Nieuport. American pilots first fly Italian bombers in action.	Lord Grey's *League of Nations* published. Balfour Commons speech on peace.	**USA** — Women lift operators allowed for duration.
		W Front — RAF No 151 Sqn (Camel night fighters) arrives in France to counter German night raids (*see* 23 July).	Kühlmann says Bulgaria to have N Dobruja (*see* 27).	**Irish Home Rule and conscription abandoned** by HMG. Govt win Clapham (S London) by-election. **Austria** — Emperor Charles refuses PM Seidler's resignation (*see* 22 July).
Morocco — Gen Aubert's 6000 troops storm Abd-el-Malek's citadel N of Taza (-23); his vital base at Kifa taken in Sept (*see* 1 Nov).			Churchill memo to Cabinet urges reforming E Front & organizing 1919 offensive. **Occupied Poland** — New Council of State at Warsaw.	**USA** — Tennessee record US rail collision of 2 trains kills 99, injures 17. Film *To Hell with the Kaiser!* opens, *NY Times* deplores (30).
		Italian Front — First capture of intact Austrian Berg D I fighter (best indigenous Austrian combat type), forced to land at Treviso by Italian fighters. Up to 50 RAF aircraft help harry Austrian retreat.	Lord Reading proposes Anglo-American Union.	**Germany** — 580 LK II light tanks ordered from Daimler, none ever delivered.
	USN & USMC now 450,093 men strong, **larger in manpower than RN.**	**W Front** — 8 sqns of RAF day & night bombers attack German communications in La Bassée-Ypres area, 106t dropped (-6 July).	Lloyd George Commons speech 'We are on the eve of great events'. Italy's recent difficulties greater than Britain's; afterwards meets Kerensky (*see* 27). Kühlmann tells *Reichstag* 'a purely military decision' beyond Germany, enrages Pan-Germans and	**Britain** — Publications on sale or return prohibited.

JUNE 1918	WESTERN FRONT 1	EASTERN FRONT 2	SOUTHERN FRONTS 3	TURKISH FRONTS 4
Mon 24 contd				est 29,500 Turks & 112 guns.
Tue 25	**Marne** — Battle of Belleau Wood ends: US 2nd Div & US 4th Marine Bde (5200 cas) capture objective 5 miles W of Château-Thierry.	CEC decrees a Socialist Academy of Social Sciences. **Ukraine** — Socialist Markiewicz forms Ukrainian Cabinet replacing Lyshub (resigned).		
Wed 26	Clemenceau decrees that Pétain is to 'be placed purely and simply under the orders of General Foch.' But PM refuses Pétain's resignation offer (before 30) over Aisne defeat. **Flanders** — British retake point 10½ miles w of Armentières.	**Baltic States** — Lettish National Council (-29) claims reunion of Latvian territories from Germans.	K of Italy's proclamation from GHQ hails 'a brilliant and certain forecast of future successes which will guide us to the final victory'. Immense psychological impact on Italy, Allies & Central Powers.	
Thu 27		650-member Supreme Soviet enrolled under Zinoviev. Lenin attends 4th Trade Union & Factory Ctees Conference.	**US 332nd Inf Regt lands at Genoa**, enters line end Sept (*see* 8 July & 4 Nov). Badoglio promoted general for his able staff role in the Piave battle. Foch writes to Diaz urging offensive in mts, repeats request 13 July (*see* 6 Aug).	**S Persia** — c800 troops from India land at Bandar Abbas (reach Saidabad 19 July).
Fri 28	**Aisne** — Franco-American local counter-attack gains 3 villages & 1200 PoWs on edge of Villers-Cotterêts forest. **Flanders** — Action of La Becque: substantial raid by 5th & 31st Divs of British First Army NW of Béthune advances nearly 1 mile on 3½-mile front' 440 PoWs. **France** — US Army Chemical Warfare Service created.	Sovnarkom decrees nationalization of major industry (c2000 firms). **N Russia** — Sir E Geddes on visit reports to PM that 5000 troops via Archangel can reach Vologda rail jctn & join Czechs. **S Russia** — Maj-Gen Malleson's Trans-Caspia Mission leaves Simla (India) for Meshed (*see* 6 July).	**Bulgaria** — Last Turk troops (177th Regt) leave for home.	CIGS cables Marshall, urges more vigour by Dunsterforce to control Caspian & destroy Baku oilfields; Dunsterville at Enzeli wires Marshall that Baku situation promising.
Sat 29	**Marne** — French recapture hill nr Treloup.	**E Siberia** — 15,000 Czechs overthrow Vladivostok Soviet.	**Trentino** — Italian Sixth Army recaptures (-30) Mt Valbella, Cols del Rosso & d'Echele with 2087 PoWs, 8 guns & 82 MGs (*see* 2 July). **Serbia** — **Franchet d'Esperey** visits Serb front with Crown Prince & FM Misic & **decides Serbs will have main role in future offensive** (30,*see* 2 July) with 2 French divs under them.	**Azerbaijan** — Azeri Tartars & Turks attack & defeat 8 Armenian bns (800 cas) on heights E of Gök-çay (-30).
Sun 30	Total German cas since 21 Mar: 894,853. (June) 6 US divs land in France.	By now 517,000 Austro-German PoWs repatriated. **N Russia** — Murmansk Soviet, led by non-Red ex-stoker, approves working with Allies (*see* 3 July).		
Mon 1 July 1918	German rifle strength 100,000 below Allied. 1919 class recruits almost used up by 31. 52 British effective divs now in France. 1st Army Co-operation unit (No 8 Sqn RAF) attached to Tank Corps. **Flanders** — Reformed BEF Fifth Army (6 divs) takes over Béthune-Merville sector. **Marne** — US 2nd Div captures Vaux nr Château-Thierry. **Artois** —	Soviet Govt declares strikers enemies of labour. *Pravda* reports 4140 Soviet activists k up to July (6350 Aug-Sept). **Baltic States** — Estonian Diet proclaims independence and rejects German aid.		**Azerbaijan** — 2000 Armenians retreat to Karamarian and Aksu (2).

AFRICAN OPERATIONS 5	SEA WAR 6	AIR WAR 7	INTERNATIONAL EVENTS 8	HOME FRONTS 9
			OHL (*see* 9 July).	
2 coys of 2/3rd KAR land at Quelimane to support Portuguese & advance 26 miles N inland to Nhamacurra (*see* 1 July).		**Germany** — Karlsruhe bombed by DH9s (1 FTR, forced landing) of No 104 Sqn: many houses & workshops damaged. 1 aircraft hit by flak & FTR; 2 fighters shot down; 5 Handley Pages damage permanent way at Metz-Sablon. **W Front** — Fonck destroys 3 German aircraft out of 7 lost today.		**USA** — First of 45 Japan-built ships arrives. Now 5810 US Army dentists, 58 at outset. **Britain** — Gen Smith-Dorrien Gov of Gibraltar.
Kartucol passes through Alto Molocque (burnt).	**N Sea** — British Harwich shore-controlled minefield sinks *UC11* (*see* 19 Aug).	**Germany** — 11 of 20 DHs (1 DH4, 2 DH9s FTR) attack factories & railways at Karlsruhe; a No 104 DH9 loses its way, violates Swiss border & is brought down by AA fire (crew interned). 3 Handley Pages bomb Mannheim, Saarbrücken & Boulay airfields (night 26/27).	Scandinavian Cabinet Ministers' confer at Copenhagen (- 28).	**Germany** — Ludendorff angrily rejects Col Thaer's idea that he be Chancellor or dictator. **Britain** — London Labour Conference (-28) ends political truce. PM appeals to women to help harvest. **USA** — **Sugar rationing**, 3lb per head pm (reduced to 2lb 26 July).
Lettow joins Capt Müller at Mujeba & marches farther S, averaging 19 miles pd spaced over 3 days march, finding much food & clothing but no arms or ammo (*see* 1 July).	**E Atlantic** — *U86* (Patzig) sinks brightly lit homeward-bound British hospital ship *Llandovery Castle* (from Canada) 116 miles off Fastnet Rock (SW Ireland); 283 die, all excl 1 lifeboat with 20. **Last hospital ship sinking** in which Patzig, rare U-boat cdr of both world wars, to fire on survivors (*see* 1 July). **N Sea** — 4 RN destroyers fight 8 German without result.	**Germany** — 27 DHs (1 FTR) attacked by fighters over Thionville (4 shot down). **W Front** — Lt Steinbrecher of *Jasta 46* in Albatros DVa shot down by Camels over Somme is **first fighter pilot to descend successfully by parachute.** (Udet in Fokker DVII shot down by French Breguet 14, parachutes & flies again same day, 29). Germans claim 39 Allied aircraft for loss of 9.	Swedish-German-Finn Agreement for Aaland Is demilitarization. Kerensky addresses London Labour Conference.	**USA** — Smith-Sears Vocational Rehabilitation Act for disabled servicemen. Record 27m cartridges made. **Britain** — 11,000 London & Liverpool aircraft workers win strike (-12 July) over shop steward's dismissal (*see* 3 July). Commons debate recruit stress, too many unfit being admitted.
		W Front — Germans claim 31 Allied aircraft for loss of 2 incl record (so far) 23 victories in single army (Seventh) sector.	Second US communiqué backs Slav freedom from Austro-German rule. Allied Military Supply Board first meets in Paris.	
			France recognizes Czech right to independence & National Council as Allied govt (Italy also 30); Pres Poincaré presents flag to first Czech unit (21st Regt) on W Front at Darney (Vosges 30). German Vienna ambassador urges press campaign to prepare for German intervention v Austria's collapse.	**France** — Customs & other indirect taxes raised (income tax too 30). Money prizes for large families. **Britain** — King addresses 2540 uniformed women at Buckingham Palace, pays tribute to their work.
Kartucol camps at Muneralia having marched 304 miles since early May (*see* 5 July). Fitzcol joins Edforce at Nampula, W of Mozambique.	(June) Allied & neutral shipping losses to U-boats 101 ships (49 British with 453 lives) worth 252,637t (162,990t British incl 2 ships mined), U-boat figure 110 ships worth 268,505t incl 23 ships worth 58,248t in Med; 3 U-boats sunk. **Lowest monthly tonnage loss since Aug 1916.**	**Britain** — (June) RAF Nursing Service formed. **W Front** — (June) Peak French tactical bombing effort in 1918 — 642t (RAF 674t). (June) Germans claim 505 Allied aircraft for loss of 153.		**Britain** — Munitions Ministry claims 114,000 workers shed to armed forces since 1 Jan. Coal miners' war wage raised to 3s pd.
Action at Nhamacurra (-3): at his farthest S, Lettow (25 cas) smashes 630 Portuguese (528 cas) & c300 KAR (223 cas), holding village sugar factory & rail station along R Likungo. Germans take 542 PoWs, 2 Portuguese guns, 10 MGs, c350 rifles, clothing, ammo & 300t food. Allied 209 k inc many drowned or eaten by crocodiles. 155 Gold Coast Mtd Inf sail	**Home Waters** — (July) **Air ASW effort now going to convoy escort** (310 aircraft & airships) rather than air patrols; 167 U-boats sighted (-Nov), 115 attacked & only 6 daylight attacks not frustrated. **N Sea** — Northern Mine Barrage begins to inhibit return voyages (*see* 19). U-boats forced into mined Norwegian waters (*see* 9 Sept). *U86* sinks empty US troop	**Palestine** — (July) Only 7 serviceable German fighters in *Jasta 300* (1 lost to British AA, 19, only 5 in Sept despite reinforcements, 59 aircrew lost cMar-Sept, *see* 25 Aug).	Chancellor Hertling asks Ludendorff 'Can we destroy Britain?' L replies 'We cannot destroy it, but we can seriously weaken it' (*see* 11).	**Britain** — RFP up 2% to record 110%. FLU PANDEMIC RAGES.Household fuel & lighting rationing. Midland (Chilwell, Notts) shell factory explosion (134k, 150w). National Baby Week (-7). (July) Sassoon's 2nd poetry volume *Counter-Attack* published. **Germany** — (July) Ruhr metal workers demand 56 not 60hr wk but no serious strikes (*see* 2

JULY 1918	WESTERN FRONT 1	EASTERN FRONT 2	SOUTHERN FRONTS 3	TURKISH FRONTS 4
Mon 1 contd	Almost 50,000 Cdn troops celebrate Dominion Day at Tincques, 14 miles W of Arras; Cdn PM inspects 2 divs (2).			
Tue 2	1,019,115 US troops now sent to France, only 291 lost at sea (*see* 31). **Aisne** — French gains nr Moulin-sous-Touvent, continue (3) taking 1000 PoWs.		**Piave** — (Mt Grappa sector) 3 Italian bdes recapture Col del Migio & Mt Solaroli but lose latter to counter-attack (*see* 15). Italian 4th & 54th Divs clear Austrians from between old & new river delta channels, taking 3000 PoWs, 20 guns & 80 MGs (-6). **Salonika** — Franchet d'Esperey receives Paris directive for local attacks before autumn offensive. Clemenceau soothes British at Supreme War Council over his unilateral action. British ration strength 162,332 lowest since 1 Nov 1916.	
Wed 3	**Flanders** — *OHL* informs Rupprecht *'Hagen* offensive will be carried out...the *Kurfurst* ['Elector'] offensive [towards Paris] will only be got ready.'	**Allied Supreme War Council approve N Russia intervention** with 1200 more British troops & French colonial bn (Allied-Murmansk Soviet defence agreement 7,*see* 31).		†**Sultan Mohammed V** aged 73 at Yildiz, **brother Mohammed VI succeeds.**
Thu 4	**Somme** — Actions of Hamel & Vaire Woods: US troops, brigaded with British, in action for first time. Tank-aided (62 Mk V tanks, 3 lost) Australian Corps (Monash, 775 cas) & 1000 men of 33rd US Div (134 cas) capture Hamel S of Somme in model 93-min all-arms op (600-gun creeping barrage) on 3$\frac{1}{2}$ mile front to 1$\frac{1}{2}$-mile depth; 1472 PoWs, 2 guns, 171 MGs & 26 mortars taken (*see* AIR WAR). Australians advance 2000yds NE of Villers-Bretroneux (5). **Champagne** — Foch & Pétain bring in reserves to meet impending German offensive (confirmed by PoWs & deserters 5,*see* 11). *GQG* 2eme Bureau (Intelligence) correctly says German main effort will be on Marne. **Marne** — US I Corps (Liggett) relieves French III Corps W of Château-Thierry.	Siberia declared independent republic by new Prov Govt at Vladivostok, but latter resigns (*see* 23). (Czechs defeat Reds nr Nikolaievsk & occupy 50 miles N.)		
Fri 5	Buat replaces Anthoine as Pétain's CoS (Foch's change). Berthelot takes over Fifth Army from Micheler, belatedly orders defence in depth (7).	Lenin's speech to 5th Congress of Soviets interrupted by Left SRs (expelled 9).		**Azerbaijan** — Bicherakov's 1200 Cossacks, 6 guns & 4 Duncars land at Alyat (sailed from Enzeli 3), 40 miles S of Baku, arrive at Kurdamir (8, Duncars in action 9-19).
Sat 6	**Flanders** — Kuhl, Rupprecht's CoS, told by Ludendorff all *Hagen* preparations approved but a diversionary attack to preface this major blow. **Artois** — BEF Highland regts' Gathering at Tincques, 14 miles W of Arras.	**German Ambassador Count Mirabach murdered at Moscow** by Left SR bomb (*see* 23). Left SRs rebel v Reds there, besiege Lenin in Kremlin ('Comrade, can we hold out until morning?', *see* 8) & in Petrograd. Savinkov rebels v Reds at Yaroslav N of Moscow	**Albania** — **Italian offensive** (-14): Ferrero's XVI Corps (53 bns) & 300 guns (+ 2 RN monitors) attacks N of its Valona entrenched camp & to E, crosses R Vojusa & Gen Nigra's cav capture Fieri (8), 20 miles NE, and Austrian Bde HQ of Berat (10). 10-mile advance	

AFRICAN OPERATIONS 5	SEA WAR 6	AIR WAR 7	INTERNATIONAL EVENTS 8	HOME FRONTS 9
from Port Amelia for Mussuril Bay off Mozambique Is (*see* 11).	transport *Covington* (6 lives lost). **Adriatic** — 5 British aircraft bomb Cattaro with success. **Med** — (July) 27 German U-boats but 5 in dock & 2 on Tripolitania supply runs, so av 8 at sea for duration. **Kaiser refuses to extend unrestricted U-boat war to US waters,** but 3 U-cruisers operate according to prize rules, sink c 100,000t of shipping (7 June-Oct), 42 steamers & small craft (*see* 10 Aug).		**Wilson declares that over 1m Americans have sailed for France** (only 8165 cas *see* 31). Allied 7th Allied Supreme War Council. Allied Parliamentary Commercial Conference in London on postwar anti-German trade steps. Kaiser & Chancellor at Spa war aims conference veto proposed U-boat blockade of US E Coast (& 16), but Soviet Black Sea Fleet remnants to be German-crewed (*see* RUSSIA 27 Aug). Ludendorff wants colonies, citizenship and conscription for German-speaking Russians. **France** — Pershing attends Cdn Corps' Dominion Day celebration (*see* W FRONT).	&11).**USA** — Naval Appropriation Act grants $1.57bn. **S Africa** — PM Gen Botha speaks at Pretoria on security measures (Smuts' London speech on SA's future 24). **Germany** — Ludendorff says German workers 'too reasonable and too patriotic' to ruin war effort (*see* 11 & 12).
		Britain — First Sopwith 'Cuckoo' torpedo plane delivered to Torpedo Aeroplane School, Scotland for operational training (*see* 19 Oct). **W Front** — Hermann Göring takes command of *JG1* (at ex-French airfield of Beugneaux, SE of Soissons, since 1) with Udet as his aide after CO Reinhard dies in crash. Mannock takes over No 85 Sqn despite flu attack during leave (*see* 26).		**Britain** — †Food Controller Lord Rhondda, JR Clynes MP succeeds (9), allocates fish supplies (c23). Aircraft unions accept Churchill's arbitration, but unofficial leaders extend strike (*see* 11).
		N Sea — 7 German Zeebrugge seaplanes damage 4 Felixstowe flying boats (1 shot down), down another British seaplane (18). **W Front** — RAF drop 100,000rnds ammo to Australian machine-gunners, capturing Hamel on Somme, **first air supply in mobile battle**; 5 RAF aircraft lost to 5 German fighters & a balloon.	At Mt Vernon Independence Day celebration Wilson proclaims Allies' 4 great aims: 1) 'Destruction of arbitrary power'; 2) national self-determination; 3) national morality to be like individual's; 4) peace organization to prevent war. **Britain** — Churchill main speaker at Anglo-Saxon Fellowship, Central Hall, Westminster. **Neutrals: Holland** — HMG waive right of search on E Indies convoy.	**USA** — 95 ships & 14 destroyers launched (*see* SEA WAR 9). **Ireland** — W Coast declared military area.
Kartucol fords R Likungo in rain (*see* 14), Lettow also re-fords to march NE while British dash past to protect Quelimane.			*Reichstag* passes Treaty of Bucharest. Rumanian Social League formed in Washington to explain Rumanian problem (*see* 19).	**Austria** — Over 250,000 military deserters, many in armed bands with MGs & even artillery (*see* 11).
	N Adriatic — Italian submarine *F12* torpedoes & sinks Austrian *U20* off Tagliamento estuary.	**Albania** — RAF drop 3t bombs & fire 3000 MG rnds in support of Italian offensive (1 DH9 lost), but fail to hit Kuchi bridge (hit twice 8). **USA** — First flight of first Americanized HP O/400.	**Occupied Belgium** — Germans suppress provincial councils.	**India** — Montagu-Chelmsford Report on constitutional reforms. **Britain** — King's & Queen's Silver Wedding. **Germany** — *Reichstag* SDP Deputy 'The black market has become the one really successful organization in our food supply system'.

JULY 1918	WESTERN FRONT 1	EASTERN FRONT 2	SOUTHERN FRONTS 3	TURKISH FRONTS 4
Sat 6 contd		(-21) but Red Army retakes town using artillery and poison gas (apparently). **Siberia** — **Vladivostok declared under Allied protectorate.** Pres Wilson unilaterally suggests 12,000 Japanese troops for E Siberia to rescue Czechs. **Trans-Caspia** — Anti-Red 'Turkestan Union' obtain 2m roubles from British Col Redel at Meshed which Gen Malleson reaches (16), sends 250 troops to border (19-24).	on 60-mile front also gains 2000 PoWs, 26 guns & 6 aircraft for 850 cas, but malaria subsequently creates havoc; French 57th Div conform in Devoli valley taking 700 PoWs (*see* 20 Aug).	
Sun 7	1st & 35th **Austrian Divs arrive on W Front. Somme** — Australians advancing in hills N & S of the river (59th Bn refuses to advance, 8).	**Volga** — Stalin cables Lenin, demands full military powers (*see* 19). **Siberia** — **Czechs defeat Reds nr Chita & occupy Irkutsk** (8).		**Mesopotamia** — Marshall leaves Baghdad for leave in India (-1 Sept), having cabled that Dunsterforce supply problem not realized; GOC 18th Div Fanshawe i/c. **S Persia** — Action at Ft Chenar-Rahdar (-8): British end any tribal threat to Shiraz, leader Saulat flees to Firuzbad 70 miles S (*see* 17).
Mon 8	**Aisne** — French advance E of Villers-Cotterêts, taking 346 PoWs. **Flanders** — British X Corps relieves last French corps.	Left SRs in Moscow disarmed by Col Vatsetis' loyal Red Latvian riflemen whom Lenin visits after Red Guards mistakenly fire at his car.	**Piave** — First American wounded in Italy: 18-yr-old American Red Cross canteen driver Ernest Hemingway severely w at Fossalta di Piave with *Arditi* by Austrian heavy mortar; he receives *Croce de Guerra* & is hospitalized at Milan.	
Tue 9	Foch & Pétain agree (at Provins) on Mangin counterstroke & Fifth Army blow to follow Ludendorff onslaught.	**Volga** — Red E Front C-in-C Col Muraviev (militant Left SR) rebels at Kazan, sails down Volga to Simbirsk with 1000 men (10,*see* 11). **E Siberia** — Gen Horvath declares himself Prov Ruler at Grodekovo NW of Vladivostok.		
Wed 10	**Marne** — French reoccupy Courcy, N of R Ourcq.	5th Congress of Soviets adopts RSFSR Constitution. **Volga** — Vatsetis named new E Front Commander (*see* 4 Sept). **N Caucasus** — Denikin's Volunteer Army defeats Red Army (-14, *see* 15). **Siberia** — HMG announce 25th Middlesex Regt sailing from Hong Kong to Vladivostok.		Kress wires Berlin from Tiflis that Armenians threatened with extermination; Hindenburg cables Enver 'as a Christian' to let 500,000 starving go home (29, *see* 3 Aug). **Persia** — RAF plane flies to Urmia, arranges ammo convoy supply (22) for Christian Assyrian Jelus beset by Turks (*see* 2 Aug).
Thu 11	**Flanders** — Rupprecht seriously considers postponing *Hagen* because of influenza epidemic. Australian Lys sector trench raid nr Merris (captured 29). **Marne** — French deserter informs Germans that Allied tank-led offensive imminent. **Lorraine** — First of 4 US radio stns (at Toul) starts to monitor German traffic. First AEF field code in service (15), 9 more by Armistice.	Red Simbirsk Province Chm ambushes & kills Muraviev (*see* 24), but Whites rise at Arzamas, Murom, Rostov (Yaroslav Prov) & Rybinsk. **Baltic States** — Prince William of Urach (Württemberg) accepts title of Mindove II, King of Lithuania, from Council of State (*Taryba*) (*see* 2 Nov).	At Supreme War Council **Gen Guillaumat says Balkans autumn offensive will succeed,** Greeks had entered war to regain E Macedonia, Clemenceau (18) instructs d'Esperey to continue preparations (see 22).	**Lawrence** at Allenby's HQ **told outline of Palestine Sept offensive.** Allenby informs CIGS that it will be mid-Sept (12), he replies no winter reinforcements from France (20), *see* 1 Aug.
Fri 12	**Somme** — French capture Castel-Auchin Farm, NW of Montdidier. Foch asks Haig to be ready to attack in Flanders from La Bassée canal N to liberate Bethune mining district. Haig demurs citing 'waterlogged' terrain, counterproposes early advance 'east and SE of Amiens, so as to	Red Foreign Affairs Commisar Chicherin protests v Allied intervention.		**Mesopotamia** — I Indian Corps det occupies Tikrit to cover rail extension from Samarra.

AFRICAN OPERATIONS 5	SEA WAR 6	AIR WAR 7	INTERNATIONAL EVENTS 8	HOME FRONTS 9
				France — Flu now an epidemic.
		Flanders — German night bombing of ambulance park at La Panne (Yser) kills 43 female drivers.	**Neutrals: Spain** — Stringent espionage law passed.	
	Adriatic — British monitors give gunfire support to Franco-Italian advances in S Albania (*see* S FRONTS). **Black Sea** — German naval staff meeting has acute problems trying to crew ex-Russian Fleet. Ludendorff opposes any gifts to Ukraine or Bulgaria (10); gets Kaiser approval (12) to put 1 dreadnought, 5 destroyers and submarines into German service (*see* 15).	**Occupied Luxembourg** — 12 DH4s of No 55 Sqn bomb rail targets.		**Britain** — Commons prolongs session to 30 Jan 1919. **USA** — Army Appropriation Act grants $12bn.
	HMG announce that homeward-bound shiping loss rate since 1 Jan over 1%. **N Adriatic** — Austrian *U19* mined off Caorle, beaches & later plundered by Austrian troops. **USA** — Henry Ford launches first 'Eagle Boat' patrol vessel, 60 of 100 ordered built, *PEI* commissions 28 Oct 1918.	**W Front** — Maj James **McCudden** VC CO No 60 Sqn RAF (57 victories since 6 Sept 1916) **k** in landing accident (*see* 26), aged 23.	Rear-Adm **Hintze German Foreign Minister** on Kühlmann's resignation (8, Hintze formally appointed 20). Central Powers' Salzburg economic conference.	**Britain** — Churchill memo warns PM v drafting munition workers, needed to equip 1m Americans as well (*see* 19).
	U-boat sinks Cunard liner *Carpathia* (5 lives lost) W of Ireland.		Asquith speech on Wilson & League of Nations. Clemenceau receives Kerensky, but refuses him Bastille Day participation.	**Britain** — Imperial War Conference votes for postwar statistical bureau, news service, dye industry, & parcels delivery; forms Military Demobilization Ctee (22) & several other socio-economic bodies (-27).
Gold Coast Mtd Inf reach Edforce HQ at Nampula (80 miles W of Mozambique).	US supply ship *Westover* (10 lost) sunk in European waters.		Count Hertling tells *Reichstag* foreign policy unchanged, Belgium, 'A pawn ...' (Balfour retorts 20). Churchill to Sinclair '... England and US may act permanently together'.	**Austria** — German Ambassador reports 'People have only one more hope - the German Front. Even a hope in a separate peace does not exist anymore'. **Germany** — (c) Silesian mines strike for reduced hrs, but are militarized (-Aug). **Britain** — Revised Aliens policy announced. Churchill takes over Alliance aeroplane works, blames management. Clyde-Forth oil pipeline begun.
	Pacific — Japan's first dreadnought 21,900t *Kawachi* blown up by magazine explosion in Tokuyama Bay, 700k.		HAITI DECLARES WAR ON GERMANY. Australian PM Hughes says no return of German Pacific Is.	**Germany** — **Col Bauer note to Ludendorff 'We will win if the Homeland no longer stabs the Army in the back.'**; repeats view to Düsseldorf Industry Club (20). **Britain** — 'Propaganda is advertising ...', Northcliffe.

JULY 1918	WESTERN FRONT 1	EASTERN FRONT 2	SOUTHERN FRONTS 3	TURKISH FRONTS 4
Fri 12 contd	disengage that town and the railway'. Foch agrees & reveals that Debeney (French First Army) is 'studying an offensive with the same objective'. Pétain letter to Haig: 'I have the honour to request a more complete participation of the British Army in the burdens ... weighing on my armies for 3½ months: either by ... at least 3 divisions or by an attack launched before 18 July on a suitable part of the front.' Ludendorff's 5th offensive postponed to 15.			
Sat 13	Pétain fixes Mangin's D-day as 18 (*see* 15). Gen Haller made C-in-C Polish Army (1 regt). **Aisne** — British XXII Corps transferred S to Ardre Sector.	**Turkestan** — **White** railwaymen massacre Tashkent's Cheka chief & bodyguard in Ashkabad, but Red Guards repulse drive on Tashkent (24,*see* 1 Aug).	French Gen Gramat made CoS Greek Army.	
Sun 14	**Marne** — 27 German PoWs (chiefly Alsatian) reveal to French Fourth Army timings of impending Champagne-Marne offensive. **Champagne/Marne** — Germans gas shell US 3rd Div: 7500 rnds (15t) mustard gas & phosgene; 600 gassed (9 deaths); US 26th Div at Château-Thierry endures 10,000rnds (20t) mustard gas & phosgene (-17); 518 gassed (no deaths).	**Volga** — White Govt formed at Astrakhan.	**Trentino** — **FM Conrad resigns from active service** (especially due to Hungarian protests at Piave failure), is made Count & Col of all the Guards; Gen Krobatin (Tenth Army) takes over his Tyrol army gp.	**Palestine** — Action of Abu Tulul: 5800 Turks & Germans (1000 cas inc 475 Germans & 540 PoWs, 6 MGs lost) attack 2500 Anzacs & Indian cav (c200 lancers cause 192 Turk cav cas E of Jordan), unsupported Germans repelled for 70 ALH cas (189 total).
Mon 15	**Champagne/Marne** — FOURTH BATTLE OF CHAMPAGNE (-18)/SECOND BATTLE OF THE MARNE (-4 Aug): Ludendorff launches his 5th offensive since 21 Mar (codenamed *Friedensturm* 'Peace Storm') v French & 9 US divs from E of Reims to the Marne. Seventh, First (watched by Kaiser) & Third Armies (0435-0530) attack with 43 divs on 50-mile front after 4-hr barrage (0010, pre-empted by French 2330, 14), Germans advance rapidly to the Marne at Fossoy. German fire 500,000rnds (9000t) mustard gas, phosgene & diphenylchlororsine; 2600 gassed (47 deaths) (-18). Pétain's 'recoiling buffer method of defence' (Liddell Hart) absorbs initial attack's 2-mile impetus in lightly-held forward zone & awaits wearying, entangled attackers on a strong rear position. E of Reims German 21-div offensive fails on a 25-mile front N of Roman Road; 20 German tanks in sector all knocked out by French guns. More success achieved W of Reims v Italians (8th Div annihilated) & 2 French divs. Foch countermands Pétain's 1000 order to Fayolle postponing 18 July attack. German 10th & 36th Divs' try to force Marne crossing v reinforced US 38th Inf Regt. Outnumbered 3:1, pounded by 336 German guns & with both flanks dangling, 3600 Americans stand firm in savage hand-to-hand fighting. 8 German divs achieve 9-mile, 13-mile deep bridgehead astride Dormans to E. Paris	**Kuban** — Denikin's Volunteer Army (now 20,000) captures Tikoretskaya Stn, and Red C-in-C's HQ train, 50 guns, rifles, ammo and 1 plane (*see* 21).		**Azerbaijan** — Bicherakov orders general Armenian retreat; Turk 36th Div to join Nuri Pasha's 12,000 troops (*see* 26). **Palestine** — First through train for Cairo leaves Jerusalem.

AFRICAN OPERATIONS 5	SEA WAR 6	AIR WAR 7	INTERNATIONAL EVENTS 8	HOME FRONTS 9
				Britain — *The Times* reports biggest Trafalgar Sq crowd since outbreak in protest v aliens supposedly at large.
Kartucol returns to Munevalia (left 3) after 187-mile march (*see* 20). Lettow occupies Ociva.	**Med** — *UB105* sinks French transport *Djemnah* (442 lost) off Cyrenaica. British Australia-bound SS *Barunga* (ex-German SS *Sumatra*) sunk by U-boat.	**W Front** — 9 RAF sqns fly to reinforce French in Champagne despite rainstorms, lose 15 aircraft in action (-17).	Prov Anglo-German PoW agreement at the Hague, better treatment and equal exchange.	**Britain** — **National rationing for sugar** (-29 Nov 1920), **butter** (-30 May 1920), **margarine** (-16 Feb 1919) **and lard** (-16 Dec 1918), national bacon/ham rationing discontinued 29. Local jam, cheese & tea rationing for 500,000-17.5m people since early 1918.
	Black Sea — (c) Germans have in service only 1 ex-Russian destroyer (Turco-German crew), submarine *UJ4* (ex-*Gagora*), 5 shallow draft craft in Sea of Azov, 1 repair ship & 4 tugs (*see* 1 Oct & INT'L EVENTS 27 Aug).	**W Front** — 225 French bombers (25 lost) in 20-30 formations drop 44t bombs on makeshift German Marne bridges. Constant air attacks (-20) till Germans evacuate bridgehead. Germans shoot down 37 Allied aircraft for loss of 9.	US Treasury estimates Allies have 303m people & $495bn wealth v Central Powers' 147m people & $134bn. British War Cabinet to inform Berlin that British Army will continue to use paper-cored bullets (instead of aluminium) as fully legal & not like dum-dums. **Austria** — Count Burian peace memo published. **Britain** — Ex-Empress Eugenie to Col Vernier 'This "League of Nations", what folly!'"	**Belgium** — Bank formed in London, Paris & The Hague for economic recovery. **Turkey** — Anti-war Interior Minister appointed. **Britain** — (c) 1st British welded steel ship launched. Coal gas-powered bus experiment announced.

JULY 1918	WESTERN FRONT 1	EASTERN FRONT 2	SOUTHERN FRONTS 3	TURKISH FRONTS 4
Mon 15 contd	Gun, in new emplacement nr Fère-en-Tardenois, fires 14 shells at French capital (-19).			
Tue 16	**Champagne/Marne** — French hold Germans E of Reims, but fall back slightly at Prunay; W of Reims German advance up Marne to Renil threatens Épernay (7 miles E), US 42nd Div counter-attacks N of St Agnan La Chapelle.	EX-TSAR & IMPERIAL FAMILY MURDERED at Ekaterinburg by Red Ural Regional Council's order or by Moscow's (*see* 25). Tsarina's sister and 5 Romanov princes murdered in nearby Alapaevsk (17).		**Persia** — 1100 Dunsterforce lorried inf (39th Bde, 13th Div) at Hamadan, halfway to Kazvin by 26. Dunsterville allowed to send them to Baku (19).
Wed 17	**W Front at its longest, 532 miles. Champagne/Marne** — Germans advancing on Épernay, reach Montasin-Chêre la Rare (French later recapture Chêre) between Marne & Reims. Germans reach Nanteuil-Pourcy but Italians counter-attack successfully. E of Reims Germans defeated S of Prunay (retaken 18) as Gouraud advances N. German losses 50,000; Boehn stops Seventh Army attacks. Violent thunderstorms (night 17/18).	Definitive **US memo on Siberian intervention proclaims principle of political non-interference** (Japan approves 18,*see* 2 Aug).		**S Persia** — 150 British besieged at Abadeh relieved by c800 from Shiraz 170 miles away. Persians occupy Firuzbad (24) but Saulat escapes.
Thu 18	**Champagne/Marne** — SECOND BATTLE OF THE MARNE: ALLIED COUNTER-STROKE. Franco-Americans, backed by 2000 guns, attack at 0435 on 27-mile front, Fonteroy-Belleau. French Tenth Army (Mangin) incl US 1st & 2nd Divs (among 9) supported by 223 tanks (62 hit), **achieve complete surprise** advances up to 4^1/$_3$ miles to within a mile of 'Mt Paris', Soissons & Crive Valley. Allies take 12,000 PoWs & 250 guns from 11 German divs. Farther S, Franco-Americans (Degoutte) advance 3-5 miles N of Marne. Germans reach St Agnan S of Marne. **Flanders** — Ludendorff morning Mons conference (with Rupprecht, army cdrs & staffs for projected 'final offensive' *'Hagen'* scheduled early Aug), thrown into confusion by news of Marne debacle. Ludendorff immediately sends 2 divs to threatened front, but news of fresh defeats abruptly ends conference. Army Gp Crown Prince William orders 14 German divs S of the Marne to retire, Ludendorff cancels planned thrusts around Reims & halts transfer of Brüchmuller`s arty to Flanders. At 1535 Rupprecht is ordered to dispatch 2 more divs to Reims, his diary comments 'no doubt that we have passed the zenith of our successes'. **Ludendorff rows with Hindenburg twice** as latter insists on counter-attack from N of Soissons.			War Office approves Basra-Baghdad Euphrates through railway (156-mile Nasiriya Hills gap).
Fri 19	**Flanders** — British 9th Div recaptures Meteren (300 PoWs). **Champagne/Marne** — Franco-Americans with 195 tanks (50 hit) take 3000 PoWs & 150 guns, advance 2 miles	**Volga** — Stalin made Chm of N Caucasus Military Council, signs Tsaritsyn Order No.I for city's defence (22).	**Salonika** — 'hottest day in the Struma 101°F', Milne diary records visit to Greek Corps HQ with d'Esperey.	

AFRICAN OPERATIONS 5	SEA WAR 6	AIR WAR 7	INTERNATIONAL EVENTS 8	HOME FRONTS 9
	N Atlantic — *U54* sinks sloop HMS *Anchusa* off N Ireland. **W Med** — Destroyer night collision between HMS *Cygnet* & Italian *Garibaldino* sinks latter off Villefranche (S France).	**Germany** — 12 DH9s of No 99 Sqn & 6 DH4s of No 55 attack Thionville (93+ cas): 15-wagon munition train explodes; another train hit; serious fires started, & goods stn badly damaged. Handley Pages drop 5 bombs in Saarbrücken centre (heavy damage). 10 FE2s bomb Hagendingen; bomb destroys tunnel shelter (23 cas) and burns large stocks of fodder & coal. **W Front** — Germans claim 37 Allied aircraft for loss of 14.		**France** — Treason trial of ex-Interior Minister Malvy begins (*see* 6 Aug). **USA** — Congress authorizes Govt telecommunications control. **Austria** — Emperor & Empress visit Slovak Pressburg by Danube steamer for harvest festival.
		Germany — 17 DHs attack Thionville (alternate target for Stuttgart). **W Front** — German fighter units airborne 7 times trying to stem Allied air attacks on Marne bridges, claim overall 23 aircraft for loss of 6.		**Britain** — HG Wells resigns as German propaganda chief after row with Northcliffe whom US adviser E House informs (18) that Germans saying 'The English are doing more to defeat us in this way than the armies in the field.'
		W Front — **French 1st Air Div gives close support to Allied ground attack** (for heavy losses) at Château-Thierry & Soissons. Comprises 590 aircraft in 2 *Groupements* each with 12 *escs* of Spad S13 fighters; *1st Groupement* has 9 *escs* Breguet 14 day bomber/recon aircraft; *2nd Groupement* 6 Breguet *escs*. RAF (aircraft attached to French XI Corps) also gives support. Allies lose 34 aircraft (14 to *JG1*) to 8 German. Sgt Willi Gabriel of *Jasta 11* scores 4 victories. Germans regain air supremacy over parts of Marne battlefield (22, when 41 Allied aircraft lost for 2 German, -6 Aug).		**Austria** — *Reichsrat* debate on German course of policy, Count Czernin says Austria destined to mediate in Anglo-German duel. **Hungary** — Diet rejects female suffrage.
Gold Coast Mtd Inf reach Metil on R Ligonha having ridden 102 miles in 57hrs (*see* 26).	**N Sea** — **The Tondern Raid**: 7 Sopwith Camels (each 2 50lb or 65lb bombs) fly 80 miles from carrier *Furious*, escorted by 6th Lt Cruiser Sqn, destroy double Zeppelin shed at Tondern nr	**N Sea** — **Tondern Raid**: German airships *L54* & *L60* bombed & burned in Tondern sheds by 6 Camels (4 FTR) from British carrier *Furious*; 3 pilots fail to locate carrier, land	HONDURAS DECLARES WAR ON GERMANY. Franco-Swiss Economic Agreement. New British Asst Foreign Secretary Lord Cecil's statement of Allied trade policy. Rumanians' Action	**India** — Rowlett Sedition Ctee report. **Britain** — War Cabinet refuses Churchill's plea to halt 'combing out' which has halved tank production, Milner wants men now not

JULY 1918	WESTERN FRONT 1	EASTERN FRONT 2	SOUTHERN FRONTS 3	TURKISH FRONTS 4
Fri 19 contd	towards Soissons-Château-Thierry road, but German 20th Div regains this artery; S of Marne Allies recapture Montoisin. British 51st & 62nd Divs replace Italians. US 2nd Div relieved after 5000 cas.			
Sat 20	**Champagne/Marne** — GERMANS RECROSS THE MARNE. Total Allied captures since 15: 20,000 PoWs, 400 guns. Mangin has only 32 tanks but makes 8 attacks. British 51st & 62nd Divs attack but gain only a mile & 500 PoWs v hidden MGs (Battle of Tardenois -31). **Flanders** — Ludendorff cables Rupprecht: 'In view of the situation of the Army Group Crown Prince Wilhelm which...will absorb a still great amount of troops, and...the possibility of a British offensive action the *Hagen* operation will probably never come into execution.'			Turk deserter amnesty to get returns to front, followed by sterner measures (29). **NW Persia** — Action at Resht (-22): 450 British & Gurkhas (51 cas), 2 guns & 2 Duncars repel 2500 Austro-German led Jangali tribesmen (150+cas) from consulate (*see* 12 Aug).
Sun 21	**Champagne/Marne** — CHÂTEAU-THIERRY RECAPTURED BY FRENCH after Germans retreat 5 miles (night 20/21). French reach Lassery-Château-Thierry road on broad front. Between Marne & Reims, Anglo-French recapture Bois de Courton, advance down Ardre valley, capture (then lose) Marfaux & Coutrim. US 1st Div relieved (7200 cas) by British 15th (Scottish) Div.	**Kuban** — White guerilla Col Shkuto captures Stavropol by threatening artillery bombardment (no guns but Reds evacuate). Denikin has to help to keep town and barely repels Sorokin's Red counter-stroke (*see* 7 Aug).		**Hejaz Railway** — 1800 Arabs (80+k), guns, armoured car & RAF planes repulsed by Jerdun Stn's 400 Turks & Maan garrison resupplied. **Palestine** — Yeomanry Div renamed 4th Cav Div, 5th Cav Div joins DMC (2).
Mon 22	**Champagne/Marne** — ALLIES CROSS THE MARNE nr Dormans, Germans retreat 5-6 miles beyond Château-Thierry between the Ourcq & the Marne. Franco-Americans reach Bézu-Epieds. Ludendorff finally orders S half of salient to be abandoned (*see* INT'L EVENTS). **France** — Gen Rogers AEF QMG at Tours.		**Salonika** — Milne cables CIGS '... The time may be approaching when this Army should be able to take action in this theatre with possibly far reaching results'. Franchet d'Esperey instructs Milne (25) to prepare for offensive in late Sept.	
Tue 23	**Champagne/Marne** — German defence tenacious by 27 divs in line: French advance on 2-mile front N of R Ourcq, across Lassons-Château-Thierry road to reach Faux; S of the Ourcq they advance on Fère-en-Tardenois, British recapture Marfaux. Foch letter to Pétain urges one main thrust on Fère-en-Tardenois. **Somme** — Battle of Moreuil or Sauvillers: French 3rd Div (1891 cas) with 36 British tanks (11 disabled) advance 2 miles on 4-mile front towards Avre valley, capture 3 villages, 1858 PoWs, 5 guns & 275 MGs.	**Helfferich** (ex-Interior Minister) **new German Ambassador to Moscow** (arrives 28). **Siberia** — Govt Council at Omsk proclaims independence, restores Duma & landowners, annuls Red decrees and appeals for Allied recognition (25).		
Wed 24	**Champagne/Marne** — Army Gp Crown Prince reports 18 divs unbattleworthy. Allies advance N of Château-Thierry towards Fère-en-Tardenois, reach line Oulchy-le-Château-Gaulgonne, & push along the Marne in Fère Forest. British advance N of the Ardre. Bombon Conference of C-in-Cs	**Volga** — 1500 Czechs & Whites take Simbirsk (railbridge, granary, Lenin's birthplace).		Allenby and 6000 people attend Dr Weizmann's corner-stone laying of Hebrew Univ of Jerusalem where law courts reopen.

AFRICAN OPERATIONS 5	SEA WAR 6	AIR WAR 7	INTERNATIONAL EVENTS 8	HOME FRONTS 9
	Sylt (Schleswig). Destroyer HMS *Garry* (ramming) & *ML23* convoy escorts sink *UB110* off Yorkshire coast. **Med** — U-boat sinks French liner *Australien* (20 lost). **W Atlantic** — Cruiser USS *San Diego* (6 lost) sunk by mine off Fire I (New York). The culprit — *U156* herself mined off Bergen 25 Sept.	in Denmark, another drowned at sea (future MRAF Dickson one of the 2 who returned) (*see* SEA WAR).	Ctee formed in Italy to organize Rumanian-Austrian PoWs into legions (*see* 6 Sept).	**machines later** (*see* 23). National Service Ministry finally convince Army of civil doctor priority need. **USA** — Baseball 'non-essential' under 'Work or Fight' law.
Kartucol engages Köhl's rearguard at Tipe on R Molocque & beyond (-22).	**E Atlantic** — Troopship White Star liner *Justicia* (32,234t, 10 lost) sinks off W Scotland after persistent attacks (19) by *UB64* (Schrader) & *a coup de grace* from *UB124* despite up to 40 escorts. (*UB124* sunk by destroyer HMS *Marne* 's depth charges in N Channel).			**France** — Foch asks Clemenceau to call up 1920 conscript class at end of 1918 (*see* 1 Aug).
			Austria — Gen Arz to Count Burian '... we are the victors on the Balkan Peninsula, no one will argue with us about that'.	**Turkey** — Food Ministry created, Kemal Bey Minister; uneatable bread still sold at exorbitant prices.
Action at Ft Namirrue (-23): Lettow night attack destroys 3/ 3rd KAR Bn of Fitzcol after its river crossing. Germans take fort & 1st mortar, some ex-German askaris rejoin.			**At Avesnes Hindenburg tells Kaiser 1918 offensive a failure**, Wilhelm tells diners at Spa 'I am a defeated War Lord to whom you must show consideration.'	**Britain** — Munitions Ministry declares threatened Coventry strike 'an attempt to overthrow the policy of the state'. **France** — Civilian exodus back to Paris begins. **Austria** — **PM Dr Seidler finally resigns.** Ex-Education Minister Baron Hussarek succeeds (24).
	E Atlantic — U-boat sinks AMC HMS *Marmora* (100 lives lost) off S Ireland. **N Sea** — K George again visits Grand Fleet.	**W Front** — Marne Allied losses (since 16) 150 aircraft & 6 balloons to 27 German (since 15). RAF Camel night fighter (Capt A Yuille) forces down a Gotha over Étaples (3 PoWs, *see* 10 Aug), first of No 151 Sqn's 26 bomber victims without loss (-11 Nov).	US Food Controller Hoover says at Mansion House, London 'We are eating at a common table' (Lloyd George addresses Allied food controllers 25). Burian suggests to Emperor Charles Allied-Central Powers meeting on neutral soil (*see* 29; 14 Aug).	**Britain** — 35,000 Midlands engineers on unofficial strike affecting tank production (-2 Aug, *see* 26). Advisory Ctee on ex-officers/soldiers training appointed 24.
		Occupied Belgium — Handley Page (Dell) of No 215 Sqn drops 1st **1650lb SN 'block-buster' bomb** at Middelkerke.		**Austria** — *Reichsrat* secret session attacks military leadership & Piave failure. **Germany** — **29 British officer PoWs tunnel out of Holzminden camp**, 10 get home. **USA** — Fuel Administra-tor orders 4 lightless nights pw. No German in letters sent from US allowed from 15 Aug.

JULY 1918	WESTERN FRONT 1	EASTERN FRONT 2	SOUTHERN FRONTS 3	TURKISH FRONTS 4
Wed 24 contd	at Foch's HQ decides to expedite general counter-offensive. Foch aims first to free 3 great rail routes: (1) Paris-Verdun, (2) Paris-Amiens & (3) Verdun-Arricourt. (1) to be achieved by the on-going French counter-offensive; (2) by Haig's proposed Amiens offensive (Foch directive 26, *see* 28); (3) by reducing St Mihiel salient (proposed by Pershing, Lt -Col Marshall begins study today). Other follow-up ops to liberate N France coalmining districts & clear Calais-Dunkirk region. French Ninth Army (de Mitry) abolished due to narrowing front.			
Thu 25	**Champagne/Marne** — Allies advance 2 miles, occupying Fère Forest & capturing La Croise Range, Oulchy-le-Château & Villemontoire (6 miles S of Soissons), last stormed by French 67th Regt (12th Div) from Prussian 79th Regt. Ludendorff sanctions night pullback to Fère-en-Tardenois line for night 27, orders Aisne-Vesle line defences (26).	Allied Diplomatic Corps from Vologda reaches Archangel. **Urals** — Czechs take Ekaterinburg & form Regional Govt.	**Salonika** — CIGS Wilson writes to War Cabinet that '... we economise British troops to the utmost [for W Front] by the gradual substitution of Indian units as they can be made available' (*see* 3 Aug).	
Fri 26	**Champagne/Marne** — GENERAL GERMAN RETREAT begins towards Eperrau, then extends to Marne & Ourcq valleys.	Lenin addresses Moscow Soviet & unions. HMG tells Red envoy Petrov it has no intention of infringing Russia's territorial integrity. **N Russia** — French troops join British at Murmansk.		**Azerbaijan** — Central Caspian Dictatorship of five topple Reds in Baku and invite Dunsterforce (*see* 4 Aug). Turks capture 1 Duncar & 2 lorries to W.
Sat 27	**Champagne/Marne** — Allied tanks & cav units pursue retreating Germans, but they have rail alternative to Soissons & still hold city.			**Mesopotamia** — RN parties from gunboats *Moth* and *Mantis* leave Baghdad with 3 guns for Caspian (Cmdre Norris follows 28). **Palestine** — c150 Sikhs trench raid 3 miles from sea.
Sun 28	**Champagne/Marne** — Since 26, Allies (most of 5 US divs engaged -31) have advanced 4 miles on 20-mile front. They cross the Ourcq & capture Fère-en-Tardenois. British retake Bligny in Ardre valley. Foch puts French First Army under Haig for Amiens op & asks that Rawlinson's planned 20 Aug attack be advanced to 8 Aug due to critical Marne situation.			
Mon 29	Kaiser allows retreat to *Blücher* position N of Vesle, Ludendorff orders on 30. **Champagne/Marne** — French pincers close NE of Oulcq-le-Château, capture Grand Rozoy & surround Buzancy: German Gen Cappard resists fiercely between Fère-en-Tardenois & St Euphrasie. Pétain concedes Germans have escaped trap. **Somme** — Australians advance on 2-mile front at Morlancourt, take 138 PoWs & 36 MGs (*see* 6 Aug). British Amiens concentration begins at night, with camouflage & strict security.	**Lenin proclaims *de facto* state of war v Allies. Sovnarkom allows Trotsky to mobilize ex-officers** (22,315 by 30 Nov), those refusing to face concentration camps. Trotsky calls Czechoslovak Corps 'Almost the most important factor.'		
Tue 30	**Champagne/Marne** — Allies capture Romigny-St Gemme.	**Ukraine** — FM Eichhorn & Capt Dressler murdered at Kiev		Maj Buxton's 300 British camelry met by Lawrence at

AFRICAN OPERATIONS 5	SEA WAR 6	AIR WAR 7	INTERNATIONAL EVENTS 8	HOME FRONTS 9
		W Front — RAF drops 288t+ bombs on German Amiens sector rear areas (-7 Aug). Germans claim 31 aircraft for loss of 4. **Aegean** — Turks bomb RAF Imbros stn (night 25/26), 60 bombs, one fires hangar destroying 7 Camels. RAF retaliate v Galata (25/26, 27).	Balfour at Yugloslav National War Aims Ctee's inauguration.	
28 Gold Coast Mtd Inf surprise German baggage train on R Ligonha, take 21 porters & 2 Germans, but most captors & PoWs taken (27) leaving only 65 out of 165 troopers.		**W Front** — Maj E 'Mick' **Mannock** DSO, CO No 85 Sqn RAF (73 victories since 7 June 1917) k aged 31, **shot down** by rifle shot in petrol tank turning for home after final victory (an LVG). Top-scoring British ace & war's outstanding fighter patrol leader, awarded posthumous VC 18 July 1919.		**Britain** — PM threatens to conscript workers after 29 (as Churchill urged) but ctee settles strike.
Kartucol finds Namirrue empty, joins Fitzcol remnants, marches 143 miles (-31) ;	**N Sea** — Armed yacht *Vanessa* depth charges & sinks *UB107* off Scarborough.			
				Brazil — German banks ordered to cease ops (finally closed 16 Oct).
	E Med — British transport *Hyperia* (52 lives lost) sunk by U-boat 84 miles from Port Said. **St George's Channel** — Asst USN Sec Franklin Roosevelt & First Sea Lord Sir E Geddes visit Queenstown base, S Ireland.		Emperor Charles tells Finance Minister that peace talks will begin in autumn and finish in spring 1919.	**France** — Socialist Party National Council votes for revised war aims & Bolshevik peace.
	Channel — Collier Q-ship *Stock Force* (Lt H Auten wins		Onondaga Indians (NY State, USA) declare war on Germany.	**Britain** — First Lord states shipping position maintained.

JULY 1918	WESTERN FRONT 1	EASTERN FRONT 2	SOUTHERN FRONTS 3	TURKISH FRONTS 4
Tue 30 contd	Fierce German resistance continues. American poet & journalist Sgt Joyce Kilmer k on Ourcq (165th Inf, 42nd Div).	by Left SR bomb. Gen Kirchbach succeeds as German C-in-C Army Gp Kiev (8 Aug); Kathen replaces him i/c Eighth Army in Baltic area (31).		Aqaba after 162-mile ride from Suez Canal (see 2 Aug)
Wed 31	**Meuse** — German gas shell French Neuilly sector with 340,000rnds (850t) mustard gas, 3400 gassed (68 deaths). **Marne/Champagne** — French now control main E rail line between Château-Thierry & Épernay. Severe fighting round Seringes. (July) **Record 313,410 US troops land in Europe** incl 6 divs & 34 aircraft (total now 1,210,703). The 4 British divs return to BEF zone (-7 Aug).	**N Russia** — **Allies seize Archangel** (-1 Aug) with little shooting (2 cas) thanks to Russian Navy officers' help. Some of the 1500 British Elope Force also take Onega on White Sea.		
Thu 1 August 1918	**Marne/Aisne** — Franco-British advance N of the Ourcq; 2-mile advance along Fère-en-Tardenois road; 600 PoWs. 100 PoWs taken at Cierges. German retreat to Vesle begins in rain (night 1/2). **Somme** — British Fourth Army in Amiens sector secretly doubled by 8 Aug; 290 special trains bring up 6 inf & 2 cav divs incl Cdn Corps from Arras, 8 tank bns & huge ammo stock piles. Small Canadian force sent N to Flanders (Mt Kemmel), part of deception plan incl **first land use of radio traffic deception.** (Aug) *OHL* reduces 400-strong bns from 4 coys to 3.	New German Ambassador Helfferich's memo urges Reds' overthrow, Kaiser agrees. Lenin via Chicherin asks for German help v counter-revolutionaries (see 6 & 27). **Trans-Caspia** — Ashkabad Whites appeal to Maj-Gen Malleson; he sends Punjabi MG detachment which covers 1800 Whites' defeat by 3000 Reds at Bairam Ali (13); Reds take Merv Oasis (c18, see 28).	**Italian Front** — (Aug) Numerous Anglo-French trench raids (8-27) on Asiago take 586 PoWs. **Piave** — (Aug) 33,000 Austrian malaria cases leave them 198,000 understrength.	**Palestine** — Allenby issues personal & secret instructions to his 3 corps cdrs for Sept offensive (greatly extended 22). **Armenia** — Parlt opens at Erivan.
Fri 2	FRENCH (11th Div *chasseurs*) REOCCUPY SOISSONS (300 of 15,000 pop left) & advance up to 6 miles; 50 villages retaken. Germans regroup behind Rs Vesle & Aisne. Hindenburg & Ludendorff Press Conference at *OHL*, latter claims 'limited tactical success' on Marne. Both slight AEF — comparing it with France's Black African 'auxiliaries'. Hindenburg insists his goal is 'a peace of honour'.	Lenin tells 5 meetings 'The Soviet Republic is in Danger'. **N Russia** — 870 French colonial inf & Maj-Gen Poole land at Archangel. **Siberia** — Japan declares she will land troops at Vladivostok but not to create new E Front. **Secret War** — US War Sec Baker tells Maj-Gen Graves, Cdr designate for Siberia 'Watch your step, you will be walking on eggs loaded with dynamite' (see 16). US Vice-Consul at Petrograd notifies state of war between US & Russia.		**Persia** — Turks occupy Urmia; all 80,000 Jelus flee, only 59,000 reach Bijar. **Azerbaijan** — Petrov's 1200 Reds & 2 guns (from Astrakhan) land in Baku & secure Bolshevik leaders' release.
Sat 3	**Marne/Aisne** — Allied advance on 30-mile front to Fismes, US III Corps marching towards the Vesle takes Fismes (4). **Somme** — Germans withdraw behind the Ancre.	**E Siberia** — **British** (25th Middx Regt, 521 men) & **Japanese** 12th Div troops (12,000 by 21) **land at Vladivostok. Volga** — White Samara Govt invites Allied intervention.	Allied Supreme War Council debates Balkans offensive & agrees to preparations continuing without detriment to W Front (US Gen Bliss' insistence) (see 4 Sept).	Enver replies to Hindenburg's 29 July appeal that 500,000 Armenian refugees in league with British (see 20).

AFRICAN OPERATIONS 5	SEA WAR 6	AIR WAR 7	INTERNATIONAL EVENTS 8	HOME FRONTS 9
	VC) sunk after engaging *UB80* 25 miles SW of Start Point, nr Plymouth (severely damaged).			Export prohibitions extended to Spain. Small Holdings (Colonies) Act: 60,000 acres to be acquired for ex-servicemen. **USA** — Film *America's Answer* opens NY, 2nd highest box office after *Allied (Official) War Review.*
	N Sea — Flt Sub-Lt Culley successfully takes off in Sopwith Camel from a lighter towed by destroyer *Truculent* (*see* 11 Aug). (July) Allied & neutral shipping losses 95 ships (37 British with 202 lives) worth 259,901t (British 165,449t); U-boat figure 113 ships worth 280,820t incl 39 ships of 76,864 in Med (10 of 235t to Austrians); 6 U-boats sunk.	**Italian Front** — Austrian ace Oblt F Linke-Crawford (c30 victories) k, his Phoenix fighter shot down at Montello by Cuttle of No 43 Sqn RAF in Camel. **Germany** — 12 DH9s (7 FTR) of No 99 Sqn (Taylor) dispatched to Mainz (alternate Saarbrücken); 5 aircraft bomb Saarbrücken, attacks by 3 fighter waves (total 40) decimate formation; 2 fighters damaged, No 99 non-operational until 20 Aug. IAF's July losses 15 bombers. **W Front** — German night bombing of Allied troops S of Aisne. Allies have lost 200 aircraft & balloons over German Seventh Army alone since 15. French July loss of 67 aircraft worst month in 1918. (July) Germans claim 505 Allied aircraft for loss of 129. Record 1478 German aircraft delivered in July.	(July) Record 313,410 US troops shipped to Europe. Lord Cecil accepts Royal Commission's recommended union of Foreign Office & Diplomatic Service.	**Britain** — Month's coal output record lowest at 15,760,000t due to flu epidemic. Sir Charles Fielding new DG Food Prod (Lord Lee resigned 22).
		German Army Air Service has 318 front-line units with estab of 2569 aircraft (excl depot res) incl 1053 fighters & c253 bombers. **W Front** — (Aug) *Jastas* equipped with Fokker DVII fighters claim 565 victories but serious fuel shortages beginning to affect all German flying units (150 or 250 litres pd per aircraft from mid-Aug). French have 2970 aircraft.	(Aug) Siam sends Military Mission to Europe, lands Marseilles (incl motor ambulance & air corps). Balfour speech on League of Nations. Lloyd George learns from Canadian PM of Haig's impending Amiens offensive (CIGS not informed).	**Britain** — RFP up 8% to record 118%. **Commons passes record £700m credit**. Postwar rationing of raw materials & scheme of pay compensation for torpedoed seamen announced. **France** — Chamber votes for 1920 class call up. **Turkey** — (Aug) Political exiles allowed to return. **Germany** — (Aug) 1920 conscript class reaches field depots but not used in front line for political reasons. Ludendorff raises soldiers' pay 1RM pd. **USA** — 1m women now working in factories.
	N Sea — British minelayer destroyers *Vehement* & *Ariel* mined & sunk (97 lives lost) by German mines close to Dutch neutral zone. (Aug) RN lays 9000 mines off Yorkshire & Durham coasts (-Sept).	**W Front** — US 'Liberty Planes' (DH4s) first in action. **Britain** — RAF Capt Prince Albert joins St Leonards-on-Sea Air Cadet School (K George V inspects 30).		
	Adriatic — *UB53* scuttles after fouling Otranto Barrage & exploding 2 mines. **Channel** — U-boat sinks British ambulance transport *Warilda* (125 lost) on Havre-Southampton route.			**Cuba** — Conscription for men aged 21-28 plus compulsory military training for 19-25 (*see* INT'L EVENTS 11 Sept). **Britain** — Churchill message to constituents v war weariness 'The Appearance of power is with the enemy & the Reality of power is with us'. **France** — Pétain & Clemenceau (7) thank Renault for their tanks. Louis Renault awarded *Légion d'Honneur* 6 Sept.

AUGUST 1918	WESTERN FRONT 1	EASTERN FRONT 2	SOUTHERN FRONTS 3	TURKISH FRONTS 4
Sun 4	**Marne/Aisne** — SECOND BATTLE OF THE MARNE ENDS: Allies have taken 35,000 PoWs & 700 guns. German rearguards withdraw to N bank of Vesle. **Somme** — Germans withdraw on 10-mile front (Montdidier-Moreuil) on E bank of the Avre. Cp Hitler awarded Iron Cross 1st Class for 'personal bravery and general merit'. Ludendorff order of the day tries to raise morale, says Second Army ready for an 18 July-style tank offensive.	**Volga** — Stalin letter to Lenin reports Cossacks have cut Tsaritsyn-Moscow railway (*see* 13).		**Azerbaijan** — **First British** (Col Stokes & 44 men) **reach Baku**. **N Persia** — Dunsterville arrests Bolsheviks at Enzeli.
Mon 5	4th and final Paris Gun bombardment (66 shells -9).	Anglo-French nationals arrested in Moscow. **E Siberia** — 1150 French colonial troops land at Vladivostok (arrive at front under shellfire 11-12), Marines land (9). **Volga** — 2500 Czechs & Whites land at Kazan but are driven back (*see* 7).		**Azerbaijan** — 1st Turk attack on Baku repulsed by 8000 defenders (620 cas); 2 Duncars & 200 British reach city & help (2 more Duncars & 150 British land 7). **Georgia** — Kress radios Berlin 'I have hampered every shipment of munitions [for Turks] from Batumi via Tiflis up to the present'. US intercept stn, picks up & solves in 1hr (another signal decoded 8).
Tue 6	**Foch created Marshal of France** (receives baton 24). **Marne/Aisne** — Franco-Americans reach R Vesle & straighten out Salient (Soissons-Reims). Carlowitz takes over German Ninth Army from F Below. Army Gp Boehn formed (*see* 12). Vienna newspaper *Arbeiter Zeitung* praises Foch: '... the Allies now possess a leader whose name arouses confidence and ...they believe that, unlike his predecessors, he will not fall far short of the mature skill...possessed by Hindenburg and Ludendorff'. **Somme** — German div counter-attack at Morlancourt regains much ground & 250 PoWs (British 18th & 58th Div replacing Australians).	Sovnarkom authorizes unions to send armed men to get bread from villages. Recalled German Ambassador leaves Moscow (arrives Pskov 11). **Britain issues non-interference declaration to Russian people** (published 9).	Foch writes to Diaz urging offensive, grants 40,000 gas shells & 75 Renault light tanks as requested (6 July). Diaz replies (13) that Asiago attack preparations ready by 10 Sept.	
Wed 7		**Volga** — **Czechs & Whites capture Kazan** from Red First Army whose Col Vatsetis just escapes. Red gold reserve moves to Samara. Largest workers rebellion v Red rule at Izhevsk (arms factory town 150 miles NE of Kazan, -7 Nov). **Trotsky leaves Moscow** in armoured train **for Volga**. **Kuban** — Denikin breaks Reds before Ekaterinodar after week's fighting (*see* 14).		**Palestine** — Kemal re-appointed C-in-C Seventh Army (sees Sultan & Enver for last time 9, *see* 20).
Thu 8	FOCH BEGINS HIS 'FREEING ATTACKS' (-18 Sept). **Somme** — BATTLE OF AMIENS (French Battle of Montdidier) (-11): BEF Fourth Army, with French First Army (Moreuil captured with 3150 PoWs & 161 guns), & 430 tanks (96 Whippets) attacks at 0420 on 15-mile front E of city. 5 German divs routed (27,700 cas incl 15,565 PoWs from 11 divs & 400 guns). Newly arrived Cdn Corps (3868 cas) advances 6 miles taking 12 villages, 5033 PoWs & 161 guns; Australians (3000 cas) take 7 villages, 7920 PoWs and 173 guns. The 'BLACK DAY OF	Balfour tells Lockhart to maintain existing relations with Bolsheviks. **Finland** — Britain says she is not hostile to Finn aspirations in Karelia & Murmansk Coast.		Enver becomes CGS instead of Deputy C-in-C. **Hejaz Railway** — Maj Buxton's 300 British camelry (17 cas) storm Mudauwara Stn taking 150 PoWs & 2 guns, 4 aircraft support.

AFRICAN OPERATIONS 5	SEA WAR 6	AIR WAR 7	INTERNATIONAL EVENTS 8	HOME FRONTS 9
				Japan — Toyama fishing families riot v high rice prices, unrest spreads to Kyoto, Kobe & other cities. Govt requisitions all stocks for sale at fair prices (17). **Britain** — **PM's 4th anniversary war message** in 4000-5000 theatres & cinemas etc. Bishop of London consecrates war shrine in Hyde Park.
Lettow short of supplies in Chalaua district.	**USA** — Hog's I, Philadelphia, launches first fabricated ship SS *Quistconck* & 7 completed by 8 Jan 1919, yard having been built from scratch since 20 Sept 1917 (16 ships launched, *see* 28 Sept).	**Britain** — **Final attempted Zeppelin raid** by *L70, L65* (hit) & *L53 & L56* (all bombs into sea). *L70* (Lossnitzer, Leader of Airships Strasser) shot down from 18,000ft off Norfolk coast by 2 DH4s (Cadbury/Leckie, Keys/Harman). 35 defence sorties (2 lost) incl USN Air Service F2A (Lt E Lawrence, Ensign A Hawkins) from Killingholme S of Humber (*see* 11).	Lloyd George's 'Hold Fast' message to British Empire.	**USA** — Manpower Bill introduced into Congress, passed 24. War Industries Board orders 15% page reduction in daily newspapers, weeklies 20%. **Britain** — Only Commons debate on propaganda. Admiralty £4m concrete ship programme announced (1st concrete barge launched at Poole 24).
Morocco — Lyautey Fez proclamation urges tribes to submit to a stronger France.	**Med** — U-boat sinks destroyer HMS *Comet*. Allied mining conference at Malta (-9), USN to lay 2nd Otranto mine barrage & a S Aegean one.			**Austria** — Czechs, Yugoslavs & some Poles vote v budget (*see* 17). **France** — Malvy sentenced to 5yrs exile.
Lettow marches 3hrs NE of Chalaua, receives British flag of truce for medical/ PoW exchange, suspects trap.	**N Atlantic** — French cruiser *Dupetit Thouars* (13 lost) sunk by *U62* (Hashagen).	**W Front** — RAF night flying helps drown noise of 589 tanks moving up for Battle of Amiens.	**Lloyd George Commons speech says German high water mark reached, their economic position desperate.**	**Turkey** — *Daily Vakit* complains v Turks in Germany smuggling sugar & paper (*see* 13).
Tripolitania — Gen Garioni replaces Gen Ameglio i/c 30,000 troops (*see* 23 Sept). **E Africa** — Kartucol leaves Calipo for Nametil (18 miles E), Fitzcol moves on Chalaua, Durcol formed to march on Alto Ligonha.	**Channel** — Destroyer HMS *Opossum* & MLs depth charge & sink *UC49* off Start Point nr Plymouth. 6 **RN** destroyers **lay first** 234 **magnetic mines** off Dunkirk. Officially designated Sinker Mk1(M) they are prone to explode prematurely, but Germans never discover.	**Somme** — **Record losses of aircraft in 1914-18 air combat** — 83 Allied + another 52 RAF written off (90 cas), 49 German during Battle of Amiens which 800 RAF (376 fighters) & 1104 French aircraft (612 fighters) support v 365 German planes (140 fighters). Some German pilots (incl Göring) 10hrs in air successfully defending Somme bridges (14 permanent) from 205 RAF sorties (12t bombs dropped). 9 RAF fighter sqns drop 1563 bombs & fire 122,150 MG rnds at ground targets (-9). RAF shoot down 9 German balloons, ace Beauchamp-Proctor shares in	Balfour Commons speech says Pacifist peace means set-back to civilization (*see* 20). Kaiser at Spa entertains Archduke William, Austrian Pretender to Ukraine; Crown Prince Boris of Bulgaria at Spa (11, *see* 29).	**Britain** — Fisher Education Act raises school-leaving age to 14. Trading With the Enemy Act extended 5yrs after war. Maternity and Child Welfare Act benefits mothers & under 5s.

AUGUST 1918	WESTERN FRONT 1	EASTERN FRONT 2	SOUTHERN FRONTS 3	TURKISH FRONTS 4
Thu 8 contd	THE GERMAN ARMY IN THIS WAR' (Ludendorff *War Memoirs*). From a German HQ BEF obtain map of all 'Hindenburg Line' dug-outs, emplacements, HQs, OPs, dumps, railheads, billets, balloon sheds & landing grounds between R Oise & Bellicourt. BEF loss under 9000 & 109 tanks (8 to 1 anti-tank gun).			
Fri 9	**Flanders** — British advance W of Merville to Locon. **Somme** — Germans momentarily reoccupy Chipilly N of the river Somme, British with 145 tanks (39 knocked out) (US 167th Regt joins), capture Morlancourt & Rosières-Lihons; advance up to 3 miles despite facing 6 extra German divs, 3884 Canadian (capture 8 villages & Australian cas. French take 2 villages & encircle Montdidier with 6 divs.	Lenin writes to Nizhni Novgorod (renamed Gorki) Soviet demanding searches, executions & deportations v planned White uprising and prostitutes.		
Sat 10	Total Allied PoW haul since 8 Aug: 24,000, plus 400+ guns. **US First Army operational** under Pershing; Col Hugh A Drum CoS. AEF combat strength 822,358 (*see* 12 Sept). Churchill (flew to France 8) at BEF GHQ Shell conference. **Amiens** — Montdidier garrison surrounded & captured by French First Army in 7-mile advance. 7 new German divs arrive, drunken Bavarians shout at 38th Div 'What do you war-prolongers want ?' Rawlinson asks Haig 'Are you commanding the British Army or is Marshal Foch?' & gets Amiens thrust ended (*see* 15); he has 85 tanks (30 knocked out) in action (38 on 11, 6 on 12). **Oise** —French Third Army (7 divs) drives 3-4 miles NE into German Eighteenth Army flank below Montdidier in Second Battle of Lassigny (-22).	**Lenin orders anti-German screen troops to Volga** (*see* 18) despite Trotsky's doubts (still 37 German divs in E). Anglo-French Moscow consuls arrested in reprisal for Archangel landings. **E Siberia** — Czechs & 400 Cossacks repulse 5000 Reds in Stepanovka-Kraevsk area.		
Sun 11	Although counter-attack now stabilizing Amiens-Montdidier line, **Ludendorff offers resignation** to Kaiser who refuses but replies '... we must strike a balance. We have nearly reached the limit of our powers of resistance. The war must be ended' (*see* INT'L EVENTS 13). **Somme** — 9074 Canadian cas since 8.	Semenov defeats Reds N of Manchuria Stn, joined by Japanese force (22), again beats Reds & drives them to R Onon (28).		**Azerbaijan** — 600 Allies & 2 Duncars repulsed from Mastagi village (first 2 British cas, *see* 17).
Mon 12	Kaiser relieves Crown Princes William & Rupprecht of Ninth, Eighteenth & Second Armies, all heavily engaged at Amiens & formed into Boehn's new Group (-31 Oct) whose Seventh Army goes to Eberhardt. **Somme** — Lull in ops (-20), Australians take Proyart. K George decorates US 33rd Div Doughboys.			**Palestine** — British 10th & 60th Divs' raids on Gharabe Ridge (164 cas) & E of Nablus road cause 570 cas & take 14 MGs (239+ Turk PoWs). Lawrence & Lt-Col Joyce meet Buxton's force at El Jefir E of Hejaz Railway, reach Azrak in armoured car (14). **N Caucasus** — Bicherakov (c2200) captures Derbent; Red warship foils Dunsterville's bid to recall him (20).
Tue 13	**Somme** — Cdn Corps has defeated elts of 15 German divs, routing 4 since 8 Aug.	**Volga** — Stalin declares state of siege at Tsaritsyn, bourgeoisie to dig trenches.		

AFRICAN OPERATIONS 5	SEA WAR 6	AIR WAR 7	INTERNATIONAL EVENTS 8	HOME FRONTS 9
		all these kills. **Italian Front** — 4 No 139 Sqn Bristol Fighters destroy 2 of 3 Austrian Albatroses over Pergine airfield (E of Trent) during Emperor Charles' visit.		
		Austria — **The Vienna Raid**: Gabriele D'Annunzio organizes daylight leaflet drop: 7 SVA 5s & 1 2-seater SVA9 (Palli & D'Annunzio) fly 625 miles San Pelagio-Vienna & back, loitering 30mins over city, drop 200,000 manifestos calling on the Viennese to throw off 'Prussian servitude'. **W Front** — Allies again lose heavily attacking Somme bridges, RAF loses c35 of 45 aircraft lost for 3 German.	Ludendorff to Col Mertz 'We cannot win the war any more, but we must not lose it either'.	**USA** — War Industries Board orders all car makers to convert fully to war work by 1 Jan 1919. Meat restrictions abolished. **Britain** — Miners Federation appeal for greater output (yr to 17 down 8% on 1917).
	W Atlantic — U-boat gas attack on USCG stn & lighthouse, Smith I, NC. **N Sea** — Harwich Force (4 cruisers & 13 destroyers) off W Frisian Is launches 6 CMBs to attack German minesweepers across minefields, but all lost to German seaplane attacks (1 lost), other aim of trapping Zeppelin achieved (*see* AIR WAR 11 & SEA WAR 15).	**W Front** — RAF Amiens offensive bombing switches to railways as well, 90 extra fighters bring strength to 480, but Péronne stn raid costs 6 of 52 aircraft involved (Péronne attacked 3 times, 11). Capt FMF West in FK 8 of No 8 Sqn RAF wins VC on tank contact patrol. Oblt Erich **Lowenhardt** (53 victories) **k** in mid-air collision (**Germany's 3rd-ranking ace**), one of 15 aircraft lost (38 Allied planes claimed). Capt A Yuille (Camel, No 151 Sqn) shoots down first Giant bomber behind British lines nr Talmas (night 10/11, *see* 24).		**Britain** — Churchill writes to PM that Tank Corps requires 100,000 men by June 1919 (*see* 9 Sept). **USA** — 100 IWW leaders fined & jailed in Chicago for conspiracy v war. **Austria** — CoS Arz offers to resign if staying might hinder new policy re Berlin.
Lettow leaves Chalaua SW in night march while Kartucol marches in rain NE 4 miles away in bush (-12), occupies deserted German camp (13) & returns to Tipe with food poisoning.	**Scheer replaces Holtzendorff as CNS. Hipper to command High Seas Fleet.** Hindenburg & Ludendorff tell Scheer (12) that only U-boats can win the war.	**N Sea** — German airship *L53* (Prolss) shot down off Terschelling by Culley in Camel launched to 19,000ft from a lighter towed by British destroyer *Redoubt*. **All Zeppelin ops suspended.** **France** — 9 German bombers raid Calais, cause 47 military & 13 civ cas, 100 vehicles destroyed & fire spreads to spare parts worth £1¼m for 19,566 BEF motor vehicles. **W Front** — Germans claim 38 Allied planes for loss of 15.		
	E Med — U-boat sinks British transport *Anhui* (4 die) off Cyprus.			**Italy** — Ex-PM Giolitti speaks on postwar reconstruction. **USA** — **Liquor sale ban on railways**. Britain — 30,000 see British Scientific Products Exhibition (250 firms) in London (-7 Sept).
	Behnke replaces Capelle as German Minister of Marine (-7 Oct). **N Sea** — Convoy escort	**Occupied Belgium** — 50 Camels (incl No 17 US Aero Sqn, *see* 26) surprise	**Britain recognizes Czechs as Allied nation**, latter declare war on Germany (*see* 3 Sept).	**USA** — 1st woman marine recruited. **Germany** — German-Turkish Society says

AUGUST 1918	WESTERN FRONT 1	EASTERN FRONT 2	SOUTHERN FRONTS 3	TURKISH FRONTS 4
Tue 13 contd		**E Siberia** — Czech Gen Dieterichs appeals for Allied help from Vladivostok (*see* 15).		
Wed 14	German Crown Council decides victory in the field now most improbable. LUDENDORFF RECOMMENDS IMMEDIATE PEACE NEGOTIATIONS. **Somme** — Germans evacuating Ancre sector.	Latvian agents provocateur tell Lockhart unrest among their Red Kremlin Guard (*see* 22). **Kuban** — Denikin column takes Timashevskaya trapping 30,000 Reds in Taman Peninsula (they escape Sept by 300-mile march).		
Thu 15	**Somme** — BEF recrosses the Ancre (for last time). Cdn Corps actions around Damery (-17, repulse counter-attack 16). Haig refuses to obey Foch's order (11) for attack on Roye-Chaulnes, but will attack N of Somme (21 qv). French Third Army captures Lassigny Massif & town (21) halts on R Divette (22). **Flanders** — Rupprecht warns Prince Max of Baden 'Our military situation has deteriorated so rapidly that I no longer believe we can hold out over the winter; it is even possible that a catastrophe will come earlier.'	**US severs relations with Soviet Govt. E Siberia** — Heavy Red shelling (-17) answered (16) by HMS *Suffolk* 12pdr in armoured train. Siberian Regional Duma meets in Tomsk. **Kuban** — **Volunteer Army captures capital Ekaterinodar** (Denikin enters 16, *see* 26).		**Arabia** — Lawrence's 30th birthday.
Fri 16	Pershing requests return of 3 out of 5 US divs training with BEF. **Somme** — Anglo-French advance in Roye sector.	Lenin tells Moscow Party that young people must be won over. **N Russia** — Whites occupy Shenkursk, 175 miles SSE of Archangel. **E Siberia** — 27th US Inf (from Philippines) lands at Vladivostok (*see* 2 Sept) as does Japanese C-in-C Gen Otani. Czechs foil Red landing attempt on L Khanka. Sir Charles Eliot British High Commissioner in Siberia; Regnault (ex-French Tokyo Ambassador) made Allied rep at Vladivostok (21).	**Salonika** — War Office promises Milne additional gas shell for Sept offensive, but only 3000 rnds of 6in arrive in time. Milne submits plans to d'Esperey (17).	
Sat 17	Mangin's Tenth Army (1138 guns) gains c2000yds between Rs Oise & Aisne with 2000+ PoWs (-18, *see* 20).	**N Russia** — 2/10th Royal Scots march through Archangel behind US Marine band, reach Bereznik on R Dvina by barge (31).		**Azerbaijan** — Dunsterville arrives at Baku in SS *President Kruger*, 2 bns follow, inspects defences (18) while defenders lose Fatmai village on N flank.
Sun 18	**Flanders** — British Second Army (671 cas) advance between Vieux Berquin & Bailleul takes 697 PoWs incl Fifth Army 5-mile advance (-6 Sept). **Lorraine** — AEF gas attack at Mervillor nr Baccarat: 800 projectors fire 12t phosgene (250 gassed, 30k). 2 British Second Army divs capture Outtersteene & Hoegenacker Ridges E of Hazebrouck, Merville retaken (19).	**Volga** — 30,000+ Red troops transferred from W since 25 July. **E Siberia** — Cossack MGs repulse Red R Ussuri crossing S of Runovka. 2 more *Suffolk* 12pdrs back defence though Japanese refuse gun battery (17), but c3000 Allies retreat 6 miles to Syvagino by train after Cossack lines stormed (20,*see* 24).		
Mon 19	**Aisne** — French capture Le Hamel. **Somme** — French First	People's Commisariat for Military Affairs decreed.		Turk commercial treaty with Azerbaijan.

AFRICAN OPERATIONS 5	SEA WAR 6	AIR WAR 7	INTERNATIONAL EVENTS 8	HOME FRONTS 9
	armed trawlers depth charge & sink *UB30* off Whitby. **Med** — 17 destroyer-escorted fast storeships from USA have docked at French ports, via Spanish waters, since 1 July, 4000t pd discharged by autumn.	Varssenaere airfield W of Bruges, destroy 28-38 aircraft.	At Spa Hindenburg & Ludendorff, Chancellor & Foreign Minister, agree war cannot be ended militarily.	that over 2000 students in Germany.
Gold Coast Regt (917) sails home for Accra from Port Amelia (*see* 7 Sept).		**Somme** — RAF has flown 700 sorties & dropped 57t bombs on bridges (mainly 112lb) since 8 without inflicting serious damage. Fonck destroys 3 German aircraft (8 admitted losses for 29 Allied). **Palestine** — Nos 144 & 45 Sqns reinforce RAF.	**Emperor Charles & Kaiser meet for last time at Spa**, Arz warns 'Austria-Hungary could only continue the war until December'; Austrians plead for peace. Kaiser instructs Hintze to seek Queen of Holland's mediation but only to aid German recovery. Allied Propaganda Conference at Crewe House, London (-17) opened by Northcliffe.	Ludendorff meets Kaiser & Chancellor, demands 'Severer internal discipline', War Minister so instructed.
	N Sea — Harwich Force destroyers *Ullswater* & *Scott* sunk (torpedo & mine respectively) escorting Dutch convoy.	**W Front** — German fighters break up Allied formations, claim 25 Allied aircraft for 4 lost.	**Neutrals** — Spain tells Germany she will replace her future sunken ships with interned German tonnage (Germany accepts 25, *see* 14 Oct).	**France** — Churchill at Allied Munitions Council in Paris (-16), sees Clemenceau. US agrees (16) to Anglo-French steel, tank engine & gun supply for US Third Army (forming). **Britain** — National war bonds reach £1bn.
		W Front — 65 Allied fighters attack La Bassée fighter base. New German Fokker EV parasol monoplane fighter (*Jasta 6*) scores first victory out of 18 claimed (*see* 21). **Germany** — First RAF raid on Darmstadt, by No 55 Sqn, 3 DH4s lost to fighters.		
				Austria — Emperor Charles' 31st birthday, receives FM's baton as Army salute and decorates 12 all ranks with Maria Theresa Order at Villa Wartholz, Reichenau. National Slovene Council meets at Laibach (*see* 24 Sept). **Britain** — 11,000 bus & tram workers strike & secure 5s pw rise for women (-23). Tube strike secures equal pay (25-28).
		W Front — Current leading US ace (94th Sqn) David Putnam (12 victories) shot down & k.	HMG announce Dominion rights in Imperial War Cabinet. Churchill in Paris urges closer Anglo-French cooperation in long-range bomber production.	Kaiser leaves Spa for Homburg where Kaiserin had heart attack, stays with her at Wilhelmshoe nr Kassel (20 Aug—9 Sept).
	Channel — British Folkestone shore-controlled minefield sinks			

AUGUST 1918	WESTERN FRONT 1	EASTERN FRONT 2	SOUTHERN FRONTS 3	TURKISH FRONTS 4
Mon 19 contd	Army takes over Cdn Corps line; latter transferred to British First Army (night 19/20, *see* 26).			
Tue 20	**Battle of Noyon** (-29) & the **Ailette**: Mangin's 12 divs and 220 tanks advance 3 miles between Rs Oise & Aisne, taking 8000 PoWs, ('another black day', Ludendorff), reaches Oise (21), but repulsed N of Soissons (22). Foch letter to Clemenceau says victory in 1919. **Somme** — Since 8, Cdn Corps (11,822 cas) has advanced up to 14 miles on a 6-mile front, liberating 65 sq miles & 27 villages, capturing 9000+ PoWs, nearly 200 guns & 1000+ MGs & mortars.	**CEC abolishes right to own land.** Lenin's letter to Armenian workers.	**Albania — Austrian counter-offensive** (-26): Col Gen Pflanzer-Baltin flown in to command XIX Corps incl fresh 45th Div & Bulgar 12th Div (43 bns) v Ferrero's 23 Italian bns (13,000 Aug sick).	**Palestine** — Kemal reports to Liman at Nazareth GHQ. **Trans-Jordan** — Lawrence & Buxton's force spotted by Turk plane 15 miles SE of Amman, decide to withdraw after spreading rumours of larger numbers. **Persia** — Turk 11th Caucasus Div advancing SE from Tabriz (-23). **Georgia** — Kress' final cable appeal to Berlin for Armenians, but Hintze replies diplomatic means exhausted (24).
Wed 21	ALLIED OFFENSIVE RENEWED (-3 Sept). Haig tells Churchill chances of 1918 victory good. **Somme** — SECOND BATTLE OF ALBERT (-29) opened on 10-mile front at 0455 by BEF Third Army's 9 divs , 1294 guns (486 heavy), 500 tanks, c120 aircraft in intensely hot weather. Prelim fog & smoke-aided advance of 2-3 miles, gains 2000 PoWs and reaches Arras-Albert railway as planned. German Seventeenth Army counter-attack held (22).			**Persia** — 250 British & 6 guns & 2 armoured cars sent from Kazvin (-22) to reinforce Mianeti post & irregulars (SE of Tabriz). (300 Indian troops reinforce Shiraz 20).
Thu 22	Haig diary 'Foch's strategy is a simple straight forward advance by all troops...to keep the enemy on the move'. **Somme** — **British Fourth Army** (incl 66 tanks) **recaptures Albert** with 18th Div. 1st Australian Div shatters 2 German counter-attacking divs. Haig tells army cdrs 'It is no longer necessary to advance...step by step'. 32 Allied divs have beaten 42 German on 47-mile front since 8.	Hoffmann diary 'If the Entente set up a Tsar in Russia, then Russia will be closed to us.' Wilson says US troops at Vladivostok purely to rescue Czechs. **Secret War** -(c) Col Berzin tries to get British agent Sidney Reilly to plot Lenin & Trotsky's murder; Reilly prefers public de-bagging.	**Albania — Last Central Powers' military success** in full swing, regaining Devoli & Semeni river lines.	
Fri 23	**Somme — Main attack by BEF Third & Fourth Armies now on 33-mile front** supported by 100 tanks, former advances 2 miles, across Arras-Bapaume road (5000 PoWs taken); Australians capture 2000 PoWs and 23 guns, Bray & Chuignes (incl 15in gun, disabled 9, used from July to shell Amiens 15 miles to W); 4 Fourth Army divs continue advance by moonlight.	Lenin tells Moscow Polytechnic Museum meeting that world revolution will come, time not predictable. **Volga** — Red First Army defeats Czechs, retakes 3 villages S of Kazan. **Siberia** — **Battle of Dukhovskaya** (-24), **Allies win 1st real action v Reds**, regain Krevsk position, take 2 MGs & destroy 2 armoured trains but little Japanese co-operation.		
Sat 24	**Somme** — British 38th Div recaptures Thiepval Ridge & reaches Bapaume outskirts. British 99th Bde (2nd Div) captures Mory Copse. **Flanders** — British 55th Div captures Givenchy Craters.	**Siberia** — Gen Horvath topples Col Tolstov from White command in Vladivostok (Allies disarm 400 Horvath men 26). **Clemenceau appoints Gen Janin** (still in France) **C-in-C Allied Forces**, Maj-Gen Knox to head British Military Mission.	**Albania** — Austrians recapture Fieri & Berat as Italians withdraw to Malakastra heights N of R Voyusa (-26). French conform. **Salonika** — Tank Corps Capt D Mackay arrives to investigate possible use of tanks, rules it out (14 Sept).	**Persia** — Dunsterville settles peace with Kuchik Khan, returns to Baku (27) where now c1200 British troops.
Sun 25	**Somme** — British now again hold Albert-Bapaume road, Mametz Wood, 2nd Div recaptures Behagnies & Sapignies, N of Bapaume.			

AFRICAN OPERATIONS 5	SEA WAR 6	AIR WAR 7	INTERNATIONAL EVENTS 8	HOME FRONTS 9
	UB109 (*see* 28 Oct).		German Colonial Minister Dr Solf replies to Balfour's speech, Pan-Germans only minority; colonial questions should be settled according to care of coloured people and economic state (*see* 23).	
		W Front — All 80 parasol-wing Fokker D VIII (EV) withdrawn due to structural failures (reinstated after modifications 24 Oct). Fog hampers RAF support of tank-led BEF Albert Offensive, but No 73 Sqn does attack German anti-tank guns (& 23). Germans claim 37 Allied aircraft for loss of 7. Night bombing incl 12t bombs on Cambrai rail jctn (repeated 22/23). First flight of French Nieuport-Delage NiD 29 fighter.	Lord Reading speech to American London Club urges redoubled effort.	**Germany** — Hintze informs *Reichstag* party leaders of peace efforts.
Kartucol leaves Tipe N for Alto Molocque, 64 miles N (*see* 28).	**Britain** — Battlecruiser *Hood* launched by John Brown yard on Clyde, completed May 1920.	**Germany** — No 104 Sqn loses 7 DH9s over Karlsruhe & Mannheim.	U-boat sinks Belgian Relief Commission ship *Gasconier* off Haugusemb in Norwegan waters, kills 6 & wounds others firing on lifeboats.	**USA** — Senate report attacks airship production delays.
		W Front — 2 **German** *Jasta 34b* **fighters disable 2 British tanks** with armour-piercing ammo, 1 is Bavarian Oblt Ritter von Greim's 23rd (of 26) victories (last *Luftwaffe* C-in-C in 1945). Wireless Central Info Bureau co-ordinates RAF ground attacks.	Lord Cecil replies to Solf's speech (20) Pan-Germans still influential, colonial policy brutal & militarism incompatible with League of Nations.	
Lettow crosses R Likungo & storms Numarroe from 2 KAR coys & 6 MGs (44k & 43 PoWs + 2 MGs lost).		**W Front** — Both sides' night bombers active, RAF v 4 rail jctns, Boulogne hit by 37 bombs; but 2 German aircraft downed by No 151 Sqn Camel. No 48 Sqn loses 10 Bristol Fighters on ground to 5 German raiders (night 24/25).	US-Italian Reciprocal Military Service Convention (with Greece 30). US NY District Court declares *Lusitania* sinking an act of piracy.	**USA** — 158,000 21yr-olds registered for draft since 5 June. **Germany** — Gen Wrisberg meets 'disdainful mocking laughter' telling *Reichstag* Budget Ctee that High Command confident of future. **Britain** — 1,250,000-signature petition & Hyde Park mass rally demands internment of all aliens.
Fitzcol reaches Ille after 13-day pursuit at 18-20 miles pd.		**Germany** — 2 Handley Pages (Lawson & Purvis) devastatingly dive-bomb Mannheim Badische Anilin Works from 200ft & 500ft (night 25/26). **W Front** — RAF attack 2 German airfields, loses 2 DH9s but shoots down 3		**USA** — War Industries Board exempts movie industry employees from draft. **Germany** — Berlin rioters smash pictures of the Kaiser. **Hungary** — Govt expels Jews & confiscates their assets.

AUGUST 1918	WESTERN FRONT 1	EASTERN FRONT 2	SOUTHERN FRONTS 3	TURKISH FRONTS 4
Sun 25 contd				
Mon 26	**Somme** — GERMAN 10-MILE RETIREMENT on 55-mile line S to N Noyon-E of Péronne-Bapaume-Lens (night 26/27). Ludendorff overrules army gp cdrs urging major retirement (up to 70 miles) to Antwerp-Meuse position (Verdun-Sedan-Charleroi-W of Brussels-Antwerp). **Artois** — Second Battle of the Scarpe (-30): 3rd Cdn Div & 2 tanks capture Monchy-le-Preux in First Army's 4-mile advance (45 tanks & 600 guns) for 1500 cas.	**Kuban** — **Volunteer Army captures Black Sea port of Novorossiisk** (ex-Imperial officers from Crimea able to join, *see* 1 Sept). Denikin forms civil admin (28). **Finland** — Govt repudiate alleged help for German Murmansk expedition. Duke of Mecklenburg-Schwerin no longer candidate for throne (*see* 9 Sept).	**Albania** — Italian retreat over, causes concern for Otranto Barrage's E end to Cmdre British Adriatic Force who cables Valona endangered. *Comando Supremo* sends *Puglia* Bde & later 13th Div, plus shifting div to Brindisi as reserve.	**Trans-Jordan** — Buxton's force back at Bair (*see* 6 Sept); Lawrence leaves for Abu-el-Nissal by armoured car to patch up Feisal-Hussein row (-30). **Azerbaijan** — Baku: 1000 Turks overrun British position (82 cas) on Mud Volcano at 5th attempt; another coy repels 2 attacks on Binagadi Hill, but later (31) Turks force unsupported British (36 cas) off it back 2-3 miles to inner line.
Tue 27	**Somme** — British III Corps recaptures Delville & Trônes Woods & Greenland Hill. French recapture Roye & Chauny (Oise).	GERMANY AND RUSSIA SIGN SUPPLEMENTARY PEACE TREATY: **Russia promises to fight Allies in N Russia** & can free troops to move E; Germany to prevent Finland attacking; **Russia to pay £300m in more reparations** & allow **Germans secret use of Black Sea Fleet** remnants (*see* 7 Sept). Russia to export to Germany $\frac{1}{3}$ of her oil once Turks return Baku. Red negotiator Joffe regards terms as '... worse than Brest-Litovsk'.		
Wed 28	GENERAL GERMAN RETREAT FROM THE SCARPE TO ABOVE R AISNE. **Somme** — Chaulnes reoccupied by French. Crown Prince William Special Order claims 'There is no reason for depression. Even 24 enemy states [actually 23] will not overcome the German nation.' **Artois** — Cdn 2nd & 3rd Divs (5801 cas) have fought 5+ miles forward astride Arras-Cambrai road since 26, capturing 3300+ PoWs, 53 guns & 519 MGs, but II Bav Corps clings to part of Fresnes-Rouvroy line.	Miliukov leaves Cadets & forms Constitutional Monarchist Party. **Volga** — Col Kappel's 2000 Whites just fail to seize Romanov railbridge (Moscow-Kazan line) & Trotsky's HQ train in Red Fifth Army rear. Trotsky shoots 20 men from Red regt that fled (29). **Trans-Caspia** — 500 Punjabis (32 cas) & Whites repel Reds from Merv nr Kaakhka (*see* 4 Sept).		
Thu 29	GERMANS BEGIN EVACUATION OF FLANDERS: Sniper kills British war poet Lt H L Simpson at Hazebrouck (*see* 31). CIGS telegram warns Haig 'the War Cabinet would become anxious if we received heavy punishment in attacking the Hindenburg Line without success'. **Somme** — NZ Div recaptures Bapaume. **Aisne** — French re-occupy Noyon & cross R Ailette. **Artois** — Canadians advance nearly 1000yds, taking 2 villages on R Sensée.	Lenin proposes that all Sovnarkom write reports on work since Revolution. Petrograd Cheka Chief Uritsky murdered by military cadet. Soviet decree orders arrest of all Anglo-French nationals aged 18-40.		
Fri 30	AEF now holds 90 miles of front (68 on 30 July), BEF holds 87. **Flanders** — British 25th Div reoccupy Bailleul. **Somme** — British take & lose Bullecourt-Hendendcourt. Australian Corps crosses Somme S & W of Péronne. **Meuse** — US First Army now has 16 divs. Pershing concentrates 3 AEF (I, IV & V) Corps & 1 French (II Colonial) with 3020 (1329	LENIN WOUNDED (pistol bullet through hip, another in shoulder) by SR Dora Kaplan (executed 4 Sept).		**Trans-Jordan** — First 600 supply camels begin 300-mile march to Azrak.

AFRICAN OPERATIONS 5	SEA WAR 6	AIR WAR 7	INTERNATIONAL EVENTS 8	HOME FRONTS 9
		German fighters. Germans claim 19 Allied aircraft for loss of 10. **Palestine** — Germans unable to fly any recon over British lines (-14 Sept) after loss of 2 *Jasta 301* aircraft (25-31).		
Lettow declines to attack Regone supply dump (3/4th KAR reinforced 24) & moves NW on Lioma followed by Shortcol over ravine-cut terrain.		**Somme** — A No 59 Sqn RE8 calls down arty fire on 3 bodies totalling 1500 German infantry. Fokkers (1 lost) destroy 6 of 9 US No 17 Sqn Camels over Bapaume-Cambrai road. **Artois** — 5 RAF fighter sqns support BEF First Army with 553 bombs & 26,000 MG rnds for loss of 5 aircraft (646 bombs & 47,570 MG rnds, 6 aircraft lost, 27).	Oxford University MP Lord H Cecil's letter v Lord Lansdowne's peace policy says war is for civilization & Allies already prototype League of Nations. Ukrainian National Council in Paris appeals for moral support v Germany.	**Germany** — Col Bauer to Col Haeften 'The black market is destroying our entire moral and economic life....eg 30 marks for a pound of butter in the industrial district'.
	Adriatic — Germans at Cattaro forecast 5 bomb-proof U-boat shelters by 15 Apr 1919. Cmdre Grasshoff replaces Pullen i/c U-boats until typhus restores latter (-15 Oct).			**First 2 cases of American 'Spanish 'flu'**: 2 sailors at Boston, USN Receiving Ship has 106 by 31. All over E Coast by mid-Sept (*see* 26 Sept). Fuel Administrator bans Sunday driving E of Mississippi.
Kartucol reaches Inagu E of Lioma.	**N Sea** — Destroyer HMS *Ouse* (with Blackburn Kangaroo seaplane) depth charges & sinks *UC70* off Yorkshire coast.	**W Front** — Low clouds & ground mist hamper flying. **N Sea** — Blackburn Kangaroo (Waring & Smith) helps destroy *UC70* off Whitby (*see* SEA WAR).	US London Ambassador Page to retire (*see* 19 Sept).	
	Spanish SS *Casara* sunk by U-boat (*see* 2 Oct).	**W Front** — 16 RAF DH9s cause fires at Cambrai & Valenciennes stns, but 20 German fighters (4 lost) thwart 12 DH9s (2 lost) from bombing Somain stn & their 15 escorting Camels lose 5. Germans claim 40 aircraft for loss of 4.	Kaiser visits Tsar Ferdinand at Nauheim. Dutch Berlin Minister ready by now to invoke his Govt's mediation.	**France** — German Eighteenth Army order warns of British 'Ministry for the Destruction of the German confidence' (MI7 has already sent 26m leaflets). **USA** — Labor Dept show 17% cost of living rise in yr to July.
Action at Lioma (-31): Lettow attacks camp from 3 sides but is repulsed as Kartucol arrives, losing 95 cas (inc 29 Europeans), 200 carriers, ammo, baggage & medical stores. Kartucol just fails to trap Lettow, having pursued 435 miles in month.			**Count Burian notifies Berlin of Austrian intention to take independent peace action.** HMG welcome Gompers, Pres of American Labor Federation, in London.	**Britain** — 10,000 of 19,000 London Metropolitan Police strike for higher war bonus and reinstatement of dismissed colleague (PM meets leaders at No 10 and concedes pay 31).

AUGUST 1918	WESTERN FRONT 1	EASTERN FRONT 2	SOUTHERN FRONTS 3	TURKISH FRONTS 4
Fri 30 contd	French) guns, 267 tanks, 1500 aircraft (609 US-piloted) round St Mihiel Salient (-11 Sept). **Aisne** — US 32nd Div (2600+ cas) storms Juvigny in 2½ mile penetration (-1 Sept) as Mangin crosses the Ailette and turns E behind Chemin des Dames with 300 tanks in support. **Artois** — British 52nd Div capture Hendecourt behind Fresnes-Rouvroy line.			
Sat 31	**Flanders — Germans evacuate Mt Kemmel.** **Cambrai** — 3 German tanks attack British lines nr Bapaume but repulsed by arty fire; 2 captured. **Somme** — Second Battle of Bapaume (-3 Sept): British Third Army with tanks & armoured cars. **Australians capture Péronne**: After crossing river 5 miles S of Péronne 1320 men of 2nd Australian Div drive German 2nd Guard Div (700+ PoWs) off Mont St Quentin, 1 mile N of Péronne (-2 Sept). Rawlinson calls it 'The finest single feat of the whole war' (8 VCs won). Pershing letter to Foch insists on integral US First Army. (Aug) Germans disband 10 divs to stiffen remainder. BEF (108,712 cas incl some to 3 Sept) has taken 63,579 PoWs & 870 guns among total German Aug loss of 228,000, only 130,000 replacements. French (c100,000 cas) take 31,000 PoWs & 890 guns. US Tank Corps receives 144 Renault light tanks.	Petrograd Cheka murder Capt Cromie, RN Attaché in British Embassy; Lockhart arrested in Moscow (*see* 4 Sept). **Volga** — Stalin letter to Lenin says Cossacks breaking up, asks for Caspian naval force inc 2 submarines. **Siberia** — **The 3 Czech Legion groups link up to control whole Trans-Siberian railway.**	**Macedonia** — By now, after 2 wk operation, French have hoisted 24 heavy 6.2in guns by tractors & tackle onto Mt Floka (6700ft) & neighbouring peak to support Serbs (*see* 14 Sept). d'Esperey briefs his generals.	
Sun 1 September 1918	BEF peak 1918 est strength of 1,916,464 (record 163,635 Canadians). **Somme** — British 52nd and 57th Divs finally secure Bullecourt & Hendecourt after fighting since 28 Aug; BEF Third Army clears 8 more villages E & SE of Bapaume (-2), has gained 8-13 miles, & 11,000 PoWs from 23 German divs since 21 Aug. 5th Australian Div reoccupies Péronne (-2) after 2nd Australian Div captures Mt St Quentin. 3 British divs capture 4 villages & farm to N. AMIENS SALIENT ELIMINATED. **Flanders** — British 30th Div (Second Army) recaptures Neuve Église & Wulverghem (2,*see* 4). **Aisne** — French recapture 5 villages N of Soissons (-2).	(Sept) 3 German divs & Austrian 106th Div leave for W Front. **Siberia** — By now White Siberian Army 38,000 men & 70 guns. **Urals** — (Sept) Future Soviet marshal V K Bliukher first Order of the Red Banner winner (instituted 16). **S Russia** — By now White Volunteer Army 35,000-40,000 (Lt-Gen Wrangel joins from Crimea 7).	**Salonika** — British 27th Div (298 cas) using 700 inf & 89 guns/mortars captures Bulgar Roche Noire Salient W of R Vardar with 67 PoWs & 1 MG after 10 days' rehearsal on replica, repulses counter-attack (2). British affected by flu. **Italian Front** — Czechoslovak Div enters line.	**Mesopotamia** — Marshall returns from leave. **Azerbaijan** — Dunsterville threatens to evacuate Baku after 600 Turks take Digya to N (71 British missing in retreat); 500 Bicherakov troops & 10 MGs arrive from Derbent (8). **Palestine** — EEF total ration strength 306,274 incl 23,113 Anzacs, 1161 S Africans, 90,327 Indians, 8437 Egyptians; plus 147,355 followers, with 154,637 animals (31 Aug) incl 43,938 mules & 36,057 camels.
Mon 2	**Artois** — CANADIANS STORM DROCOURT-QUÉANT 'SWITCH LINE' (*Wotan* sector of Hindenburg Line) in 4 hrs from 0500: 1st & 4th Divs (7 VCs won) break through & reach open country except on extreme left, 57 tanks in support. Advance defeats 11 German divs & claims 10,000 PoWs. LUDENDORFF ISSUES ORDER FOR 2ND PHASED RETIREMENT to 4 armies shortly after 1400 — in S to main 10-mile deep Hindenburg position, in N behind & along Canal du Nord (av fall back of 13 miles). BEF has advanced	**Red Terror declared** (Petrograd Cheka announce 512 executed). Red Revolutionary Military Council formed with Trotsky Chm. Sovnarkom accuse Anglo-French reps of plotting. **N Russia** — Italian bn lands at Murmansk. **E Siberia** — Czechs from L Baikal join Semenov at Manchuria Stn. US Maj-Gen Graves lands at Vladivostok. **N Caucasus** — Bicherakov occupies Petrovsk. Muslim Checen overthrow Shura Soviet (3).		**Trans-Jordan** — 800 camels, 450 regular camelry, 2 British armoured cars & French mtn bty march for Azrak, Lawrence & Nasir follow in Rolls Royce (4).

AFRICAN OPERATIONS 5	SEA WAR 6	AIR WAR 7	INTERNATIONAL EVENTS 8	HOME FRONTS 9
	(Aug) Allied & neutral shipping lost to U-boats 104 ships (41 British with 217 lives), 278,876t (British 145,721t); U-boat figure 154 ships worth 310,180t incl 38 ships of 71,490t in Med (1 of 2209t to Austrians); 7 U-boats sunk (2 to unknown causes).	**W Front** — No 110 (Hyderabad) Sqn RAF reaches France, equipped with Liberty-engined DH4s. **RAF Aug aircraft losses a record** so far, 215 (French 55) but record 948t bombs dropped (French drop 550t). (Aug) **Germans claim record 655 Allied aircraft for record loss of 174**. **Britain** — All London Air Defence Area sqns fitted with radio telephone linked to central ops room (12 Sept). **Aegean** — RAF Aegean Gp has 116 aircraft (38 seaplanes). **Italian Front** — 3 No 45 Sqn Camels destroy all 6 Austrian fighters encountered over Allied lines.	Allied Intelligence Co-ordination Meeting in London.	**France** — Loire police inspector: 'Agricultural workers seem to ignore the war.... cupidity having apparently supplanted everything else.' **Britain** — 708,000 working days lost in month. **Hungary** — Ministerial council agrees to increase gendarmerie by 50%.
Lettow's 1663 men, 1 gun & 40 MGs pursued 18 miles along Muanhupa road by Kartucol. **Tripolitania** — (Sept) Senussi leader Sayyid Ahmed leaves Gulf of Sirte in U-boat (Misurata-Pola) for Turkey.	US Shipping Board has 331 Allied & neutral ships on charter worth 1,084,986t. **Med** — Only **8 of 979 ships sailed in convoy lost** (Sept). Allied Otranto Barrage Force: 280 ships incl 31 destroyers; 8 submarines; 10 sloops & torpedo boats; 36 US subchasers; 153 trawlers. **E Atlantic** — 3 US battleships stationed at Berehaven (SW Ireland) to cover Atlantic convoys from surface attack, sail for that purpose (Oct).	**Britain** — 16,224 American mechanics have arrived to work & train with RAF (3931 by 1 Mar). **Germany** — (Sept) **Peak month of RAF raids**, 62. **W Front** — Germans claim 27 Allied aircraft for loss of 8. RAF FE2b night bombers attack 3 defended villages before BEF First Army with 300 bombs (night 1/3, tactic repeated 18). **Russia** — (Sept) **Aviadarm** formed with 315 planes (mainly Anglo-French made) to support Red Army.		**Britain** — RFP down 2% to 116%. (Sept) Tank appears at Birmingham Win-the-War Day. Allied Tin Executive formed. **Germany** — (Sept) 774 torpedoes produced (4x 1913 total). **Turkey** — All fuel & several food items up in price 11-120% since Jan. **India** — Indian National Congress at Bombay condemns Montagu-Chelmsford reforms, want autonomous govt in 15 yrs. **Austria** — (Sept) Est 400,000 deserters.
	Atlantic/N Sea — Kurt Beitzen 'the man who killed Lord Kitchener' k when his *U102* is sunk by mines off Northern Barrage (*see* 9). **Secret War: Britain** — Weymss indicates to Beatty that new German naval cipher broken.	**Germany** — 5 Handley Pages inflict RM400,000 damage on Saarbrücken's Burbach works (night 2/3). **W Front** — *JG3* destroys 26 Allied aircraft without loss, but up to 90 RAF single-seaters strafe ahead of Canadian Corps. British lose 36 aircraft (incl 4 Camels of US No 148 Sqn) fighters & 13 balloons, claim 8 German. Germans claim 50 Allied aircraft for loss of 6.		**Germany** — Hindenburg on Sedan 1870 anniversary warns Army & people v Allied propaganda 'His airmen throw... leaflets intended to kill the soul'. Kaiser refuses to leave his bed (*see* 5). **Britain** — TUC Golden Jubilee at Bristol represent s 4.5m members (-7, *see* 5), US Labor leader Sam Gompers addresses it.

SEPTEMBER 1918	WESTERN FRONT 1	EASTERN FRONT 2	SOUTHERN FRONTS 3	TURKISH FRONTS 4
Mon 2 contd	av of 14 miles on 28-mile front since 21 Aug, taken 46,241 PoWs for c89,000 cas, defeated 66 German divs (c115,600 cas in total). Foch, Pétain and Pershing meet.			
Tue 3	FOCH GENERAL ORDER SPECIFIES UNREMITTING ATTACKS ALL ALONG THE LINE. Ludendorff secret order deplores defeatist talk by men on leave. **Artois** — British re-enter Lens; rapid German retreat. Cdn Corps suffers 5622 cas (1-3) and takes 6000 unwounded PoWs (1-4). **Somme** — French cross river to E at Epenancourt S of Péronne.	Soviet unemployed forbidden to refuse work.	**Italian Front** — Austrians retake 2 Italian OPs between Mts Mantello & S Matteo. **Salonika** — Milne cables CIGS '... it is impossible to say what the Serbs may or may not do'.	
Wed 4	**Flanders** — British 29th Div captures Ploegsteert & Hill 63. **Somme** — NZ Div captures Ruyaulcourt, 7 miles E of Bapaume.	Lockhart again arrested. British War Cabinet cable threatens reprisals if British lives not guaranteed. **N Russia** — 4500 **US troops** (Col Stewart's 339th Regt, embarked Newcastle 26 Aug) **land at Archangel** (ann 11). Allies occupy Obezerskaya 73 miles S.	**Lloyd George approves Macedonia offensive** after Guillaumat visits London, latter then visits Rome who approve (10).	
Thu 5	**Somme** — French Third Army (Humbert) advances on St Quentin from Noyon, retakes Ham (6), fights across Crozat Canal at 2 points, retaking 5 villages (8), another 3 & Ft Liez (9). **Aisne** — French & AEF reach the river in Condé sector. Legion's 3rd Bn, storms MG-studded Terny-Sorny, then held at Allemant (6,*see* 14). **Meuse** — AEF St Mihiel attack set for 12.	**Ukraine** — Hetman Skoropadski in Berlin (1918-19 Economic Ageement signed at Kiev 11). **E Siberia** — Japanese take Khabarovsk & 120 guns, and Blagoveschensk (18) with 2000 Austro-German PoWs, 326 rail cars & 55 steamers.		**NW Persia** — Up to 2000 Turks & 2 guns (11th Caucasian Div) advance along Tabriz road v 660 British & irregulars, occupy Turkmanchai (7) & Mianeh (9), patrols reach Zenjan after British Kuflan Kuh mountain position outflanked (12), but by 21 recalled to Constantinople.
Fri 6	**Flanders** — GERMAN EVACUATION OF LYS SALIENT COMPLETE. At *OHL* Conference Hindenburg stresses gravity of situation; Boehn recommends 45-mile retirement to Antwerp-Meuse position, instead decision taken to halt (if necessary) on *Hermann-Hunding-Brunhild* position, 20 miles back. BEF field guns & 6in howitzers have fired 8,382,200 rnds since 8 Aug.	**Col Vatsetis made first Main C-in-C of Red Army**, Col S S Kamenev takes over E Front. **Volga** — Stalin reports Cossack retreat over Don from Tsaritsyn (*see* 18).		**Palestine** — Buxton's British camelry rejoin EEF at Beersheba having covered 900 miles in 44 days.
Sat 7	**Flanders** — Skirmishing in Armentières-Lens sector. **Somme** — BEF Fourth Army retakes Roisel rail jctn (Cambrai-St Quentin line).	Lenin cables Trotsky 'Recovery proceeding excellently'. First £12.5m of war indemnity sent from Moscow. Germans receive at Orsha (10).	**Italian Front** — 9 British bns withdrawn (-14) to reform 25th Div in France. Diaz returns from Paris, Cavan urges offensive (9) but Italians waiting for Hindenburg Line breakthrough (*see* 17 & 24).	
Sun 8	Foch visits K Albert & Haig (who tells Churchill 'the Allies should aim at getting a decision as soon as possible'), decides to add Flanders offensive (*see* 28). OHL orders signals concerning tanks be given priority. **Occupied France** — †German writer & poet Lt Bernhard von der Marwitz (relative of army cdr,*see* 22) dies of wounds aged 28 at Valenciennes Lazarett. **Aisne** — US III Corps transferred from the Vesle (crossed 4) to Souilly. **Meuse** — Ludendorff orders St Mihiel salient evacuation (*see* 12). Allied PoW haul since 8 Aug 150,000, 2000 guns and	White state conference of 170 delegates at Ufa in W Urals (-23), welcomes Allied Vladivostok landings (12). Neutral diplomats protest v Red Terror. Soviet-Allied agreement on diplomat exchange.		**Palestine** — Turk ration strength 103,500.

AFRICAN OPERATIONS 5	SEA WAR 6	AIR WAR 7	INTERNATIONAL EVENTS 8	HOME FRONTS 9
	N Sea — 6 RN monitors fire 550 shells (incl 52 18-in shells from *General Wolfe* at 36,000yds) at Snaeskerke rail jctn & bridge 4 miles S of Ostend despite German aircraft bombing (repeated 29, 2 & 3 Oct, *see* 14 Oct). **Neutrals: Chile** — 7 of 32 interned German steamers partially sabotaged by crews, but Chilean troops board (*see* INT'L EVENTS 7).	**W Front** — Allies claim 55 German aircraft (Germans admit loss of 8 for 30 Allied). **Salonika** — 6 RAF SE5as & Camels destroy 4 of 6 German aircraft encountered after lone Bristol photo recon monoplane shot down into L Doiran.	USA recognizes Czechs as having *de facto* govt. Franco-American reciprocal Military Service Convention. Hintze sees Burian in Vienna in vain effort to prevent separate peace attempt (-6, *see* 11 & 14). **Occupied France** — Germans evacuate Cambrai and Douai civil populations to Belgium.	**Germany** — Hoffmann diary 'Public feeling in Berlin is not good'. Hertling tells Prussian Ministerial Council of peace-feelers via neutrals. **Turkey** — Telegraph operator writes that his family starving.
Kartucol crosses R Lurio (-5).		**W Front** — RAF day bombers raid Valenciennes, Douai & Cambrai, air combat costs 15 RAF & 11 German aircraft.		**Italy** — Munition factories close due to general coal shortage. **USA** — War Dept appeals for more women workers in munition factories.
Lettow halts for day to complete food supplies.		Royal Canadian Naval Air Service founded. **W Front** — **RAF reduces low-flying fighter ops to recuperate**, losses fall dramatically until 15.	Bolshevik envoy Litvinov & others arrested in London as bargaining counters (*see* RUSSIA 8).	**Britain** — Food Controller tells TUC no fears of shortage if war prolonged. Churchill memo to War Cabinet asks if war to be won in 1919 or 1920. **Germany** — Anglophile shipping magnate Ballin vainly meets Kaiser at Ludendorff's request, Kaiser confident that Hindenburg will stabilize front (*see* 10). State of siege declared in Berlin and Brandenburg.
Action at Pere Hills: Lettow's main force (90 cas plus 30 porters) bumps into Kartucol's transport, but is held by dusk for 132 KAR cas (53 PoWs); Germans disengage 3 miles NW. Shortcol continues pursuit (7).			Provisional Rumanian Council formed in Paris (see 3 Oct). Sultan Mohammed VI receives 2 Armenian envoys & welcomes independent Armenia. Talaat Pasha in Berlin on Caucasian matters. 2nd Sino-Japanese Military Convention (*see* 24).	**Britain** — Manchester aircraft workers' strike for shop stewards (-11) wins inquiry. Mrs Gwynne-Vaughan Cmndt WRAAF.
W Africa — Gold Coast Regt lands at Sekondr to return to base at Kumasi.	British Admiralty publishes names of 151 U-boat commanders sunk or captured by RN, this very accurate list affects morale of surviving crews.	**Germany** — No 104 Sqn loses 5 DH9s in Ludwigshafen raid.	**Neutrals: Chile** — Churchill negotiates British contract for 1918 delivery of 1.5m tons nitrate to Allies.	**Britain** — Household Coal Requisitioning. Munition workers get pay rise.
Capt Köhl's rearguard skirmishes with Shortcol at Milweberg.			US War Sec Baker arrives in France at Brest. King of Bavaria visits Sofia (K of Saxony also 14, see HOME FRONTS 25).	

SEPTEMBER 1918	WESTERN FRONT 1	EASTERN FRONT 2	SOUTHERN FRONTS 3	TURKISH FRONTS 4
Sun 8 contd	13,000 MGs.			
Mon 9	Lt-Col Wetzell, strategic adviser at *OHL*, superseded owing to rows with Ludendorff. **Somme** — British gain high ground commanding Hindenburg Line N of Havrincourt Wood (*see* 12). **Aisne** — 2 German counter-attacks at Laffaux fail (& 11).			**Palestine** — Allenby issues orders for offensive.
Tue 10	Haig (in London to impress need for 1918 victory -12) issues Special Order of the Day claiming 75,000 PoWs & 750 guns taken by BEF in 4wks, his diary notes 'It seems to me to be the beginning of the end.' US Army Radio Corps formed for signals intelligence.	**Volga** — **Red Fifth Army** (aided by 4 Baltic Fleet destroyers) **retakes Kazan**; Czechs and *Komuch* People's Army retreat to avoid trap.		
Wed 11	K Albert meets Foch at Bombon and agrees to lead Allied Flanders offensive (*see* 28). **Cambrai** — German counter-attacks at Gouzeaucourt & Moeuvres. British retake 3 villages to S. **Meuse** — Lt-Col Patton instructs 34th Bde (US) Tank Corps in St Mihiel Sector: 'American tanks do not surrender ...as long as one tank is able to go forward. Its presence will save the lives of hundreds of infantry and kill many Germans...'.	**N Russia** — Allies from Murmansk capture Ft Ukhtinskaya. 200 R Scots & 2 guns from Archangel repel 500-Red night attack & occupy Priluki on R Dvina (-12), occupy 5 more villages astride river up to 25 miles SE (14-17). **Trans-Caspia** — 136 British & 2 guns (arr 4) aid repulse of Reds from Kaakha (& 18).		
Thu 12	**Meuse** — BATTLE OF ST MIHIEL (-16): After 4-hr barrage from 0100 by 3010 guns, 216,000 men of (10 divs) US First Army (Pershing), supported by 48,000 French (4 divs) advance in heavy rain 5 miles on 12-mile front v Fuchs' 75,000-strong Det C (already withdrawing its 13 divs) & take 8000 PoWs. AEF fires 100,000rnds (200t) phosgene; 9000 gassed (50 deaths). Patton & MacArthur meet under fire, former outwalks his tanks (70 of 174 reach startline). **Cambrai** — BATTLES OF THE HINDENBURG LINE BEGIN: Battle of Havrincourt won on 5-mile front by 6 divs of Byng's Third Army who take village SW of Cambrai, 1000 PoWs & beat 4 div counter-attacks.	Tukachevksi's Red First Army retakes Simbirsk, Lenin cables Trotsky with thanks.		
Fri 13	**Meuse** — St Mihiel: Pershing takes 13,000 PoWs & 200 guns as salient closed at Vigneulles by 0600 as US 26th and 1st Divs meet (200,000 Americans in res). BAR first used in action by US 79th Div. **Somme** — Anglo-French close on St Quentin.			
Sat 14	**Aisne** — French Tenth Army storms Allemant (Legion's last major action)-Laffaux Mill (Marine bn) in 5-miles of Hindenburg Line and captures 2500 PoWs + guns; recaptures Vailly on river (16); advances NE of Soissons (17), & repulses 5 counter-attacks nr Allemant (20).	**Finland** — German Helsinki Minister offers no German attack in E Karelia if Allies evacuate N Russia (*see* 18).	**Macedonia** — ALLIED FINAL OFFENSIVE: Battle of the Vardar (-25) (French Battle of the Dobropolje (-17), Serb Battle of the Moglenitsa) begins with record Balkans 650-gun bombardment from 0800 along 80-mile Vardar-Monastir line esp on 6-mile Mts Sokol-Vetrenik sector. Scholtz wrongly moves Bulgar regt &	**Azerbaijan** — Turks capture **Baku**: 8-10 bns capture Wolf's Gate. Dunsterforce evacuation ordered at 2000 after 180 cas & 5 RAF sorties. 3 RN-manned ships take 1300 British & 8000 Armenians to Enzeli (-15). Tartars massacre 8988 Armenians (-16). Turks install Khan Khoiski's Tartar Govt (16).

AFRICAN OPERATIONS 5	SEA WAR 6	AIR WAR 7	INTERNATIONAL EVENTS 8	HOME FRONTS 9
	N Sea — *U92* sunk on Northern Barrage; *UB104* (19); *U156* (25).		Prince Frederick Charles of Hesse (Kaiser's brother-in-law) accepts Finnish throne offer (*see* 9 Oct).	**Turkey** — Constantinople papers state 98 firms worth T£16.6m formed during war. **Britain** — (c) Register formed for British subjects' claims in Russia (some not compensated till 1987). Churchill writes to PM on 1919 manpower problems, urges 100,000 Tank Corps (55,000 agreed). **France** — 2 deputies mortally wounded visiting front.
	N Sea — *UB83* sunk in Pentland Firth by destroyer HMS *Ophelia*'s depth charges.		Hindenburg urges peace moves to Emperor Charles.	**Kaiser addresses** 1500 **Krupp workers** on only visit to Essen Gusstahlfabrik and gets no response (*see* 25).
324 KAR defeat 2000 Masai (revolt v recruiting) 20 miles W of Narok; talks restore quiet till Feb 1919.			**Lloyd George cable thanks Czech Legions for service to Allies. Hintze instructs appeal to Holland for mediation.** US declines Cuban troop offer due to shipping shortage.	**Britain** — Lloyd George finally clarifies Information Ministry powers, but Beaverbrook ill, Arnold Bennett & Roderick Jones supervise for duration (*see* 21 Oct). Lt-Gen Macdonogh Adjt-Gen Home Forces (*see* 17). **Turkey** — Daily *Vakit* 'our social bonds have become dangerously loose'. Record syphilis cases in Constantinople.
	E Atlantic — U-boat sinks Union liner *Galway Castle* (154 lives lost). **Med** — Armed boarding steamer *Sarnia* sunk by U-boat.	**W Front** — St Mihiel Op: **Greatest Allied air concentration of war**: US units; 25 French *escs* ; *le Div Aerienne* (600 aircraft) & 9 sqns of Indep Force (c100 bombers); single Italian, Brazilian, Portuguese, Belgian sqns. Total 1483 planes under US Brig-Gen Mitchell, bombers & recon planes spearhead Pershing's advance while fighters maintain local air supremacy ('barrier' technique, as pioneered at Verdun). US 3rd Pursuit Gp specializes in lorry-busting. Rickenbacker shoots down *JG2* Fokker (6th kill), but *JG2* claims 81 victories for 2 losses (12-18).	British Blue Book issued describing cruel German rule in SW Africa.	**Canada** — Dept of Public Instruction for propaganda. **USA** — 3rd Draft Registration 13,228,000 (18-21yrs, 32-35 yrs).
Kartucol resumes pursuit.	Allied Naval Council, 5th meeting, Paris (-14) incl Wemyss, Sims & Revel.	**France** — Marshal Foch memo to Premier Clemenceau on 'The bombardment of the Interior of Germany' by an 'inter-allied bombing force'. **W Front** — Handley Pages of No 207 Sqn attack Le Cateau stn with 79 bombs (night 13/14). RAF night raids on 3 German Paris bombing bases (night 15/16).		
		Germany — Largest Handley Page effort (night 14/15), 40 v various targets (1 FTR). **Macedonia** — First of 3 RAF pre-final offensive bombing raids (-16) on Hudova airfield.	**Austria sends note to US, all belligerents & neutrals** suggesting 'non-commital discussion' on neutral soil. Allies spurn (*see* 16) & Germans irritated.	**France** — Pres Poincaré visits newly-liberated St Mihiel and returns to his ruined house at Sampigny across the Meuse.

SEPTEMBER 1918	WESTERN FRONT 1	EASTERN FRONT 2	SOUTHERN FRONTS 3	TURKISH FRONTS 4
Sat 14 contd			12th Saxon *Jäger* Bn to N of Monastir, only at 2230 discovers the point of attack.	
Sun 15	French losses since 1 July 279,000. Construction of *Hermann* Line behind Army Gps Rupprecht & Boehn begun. German gas response to BEF autumn offensive: 2m rnds (4000t) mustard gas expended; 24,363 gassed (540 deaths) (-11 Nov). **Flanders** — †Belgian composer & soldier for duration Georges Antoine from influenza.	**Volga** — Red E Front (5 armies) 70,000 men, 225 guns, 1059 MGs (*see* 7 Oct).	**Macedonia** — At 0530 36,000 Serb, French & Italian inf attack 12,000 Bulgars & Germans, capture Mt Vetrenik (4725ft), Mt Dobropolje (6125ft, French first use flamethrowers) & Mt Sokol with nearly 3000 PoWs & 33 guns for 2520 cas. Advance continues at night up to 6 miles.	
Mon 16	**St Mihiel salient fully straightened out** for 7511 US & 597 French cas (15,000 beds available), 15,000 PoWs & 450 (or 443) guns taken. Germans commit 4 res divs. Metz fortress guns fire (15), but c400,000 Americans now switched 60 miles NW (*see* 22).	**Lenin recovers**, attends meetings (-17), but moves to Gorki (24 or 25) to convalesce (-mid Oct).	**Macedonia** — Serb Yugoslav Div attacks Mt Kozyak all day (Bulgar 3rd line) & finally takes it, but German 13th Saxon *Jäger* Bn covers breach. Scholtz cables Hindenburg, asking for German div from W Front; request forwarded to Austrians, who hedge. Bulgar 2nd Div withdraws to 3rd line without warning. **Bulgaria** — Tsar Ferdinand replies to Gen Lukov peacefeeler suggestion 'Go out and get killed in your present lines'. **Italian Front** — Italian raid N & NW of Mt Grappa takes 300 PoWs & some MGs, counter-attacks beaten (17).	Cox becomes HM Ambassador in Tehran, Col A Wilson replaces him as Chief Political Officer Mesopotamia. **Trans-Jordan** — Lawrence blows up Deraa-Amman railbridge (1200 Arabs left Azrak,14).
Tue 17	**Flanders** — Localized fighting incl British 55th Div capture of Canteleux Trench. **Cambrai** — More German counter-attacks at Moeuvres beaten (-19), village falls (20).		**Macedonia — Franco-Serb breakthrough now 6 miles deep & 20 miles wide.** Gen Ruser orders his Bulgar 2nd Div to retreat from 3rd line behind R Crna leaving 5-mile gap for Serbs to reach river. Two Bulgar 3rd Div regts mutiny. **Scholtz orders general retreat behind R Belasnica. Italian Front** — After visit to Paris Diaz tells PM Orlando no premature autumn offensive until clear Allied success on W Front (*see* 20 & 25).	**NW Persia** — Dunsterville recalled, GOC 14th Div Thomson replaces i/c 'Norper Force', Enzeli to be held. Cmdre Norris says Caspian Flotilla possible, plans 12 ships (27), 1st ready 6 Oct. **Palestine** — DMC secretly concentrated in Plain of Sharon, betrayed by Indian Muslim sgt deserter, but Liman believes him to be a plant. **Trans-Jordan** — Arab Army captures Tell Arar bridge N of Deraa. Lawrence gets slight bomb splinter arm wound; 350 Arab regulars then capture stn 5 miles W of Deraa, drawing in reserve German troops from Afuleh.
Wed 18	Ludendorff warns Adm Scheer of plans for abandoning Flanders coast (*see* 11 Oct). **Somme** — Battle of Epéhy: British Third & Fourth Armies (1488 guns & 300 MGs) attack from 0700 in heavy rain with 21 tanks on 16-mile front NW of St Quentin, 6800 Australians (1260 cas) advance 5000yds, capture 4243 PoWs, 76 guns & 330 MGs & mortars in total of 9000 & 100 guns. British 12th & 58th Divs capture Epéhy.	**N Russia** — Karelians beat German-led force at Ukhtinskaya and drive it back into Finland. **S Russia** — Red S Front created with Stalin as Military Council Chm (first meets 28 and forms Eighth-Twelfth Armies,*see* 20).	**Salonika — Anglo-Greek attack astride L Doiran** with 231 guns: Battle of Doiran (-19) at 0508 v Bulgar 9th Div & 122 guns, British enter Doiran town & take Petit Couronné with 777 PoWs but British 65th Bde (22nd Div) has only 200 survivors (30 poisoned by British gas) from attempt to storm Grand Couronné, (thrice-w CO 7th S Wales Borderers Lt -Col Burges awarded VC). Greek losses 1232, British failure E of lake (900 Anglo-Greek cas) due to grass wildfire started by Bulgar arty. Bulgar Deputy C-in-C Todorov cables Hindenburg pleading for at least 6 German divs. Serb cav reach Polosko.	**Trans-Jordan** — Lawrence blows his 79th rail bridge N of Nisib Stn S of Deraa as Arab Army turns E. **Palestine** — On Allenby's E flank 53rd Div storms across Wadi-es-Samieh and advances 7 miles (night 18/19).
Thu 19	**Cambrai** — British take Lempire (SE of Epéhy) & French, Essigny Le Grand. Haig tells Foch BEF ready to assault Hindenburg Line on 26.	**Trans-Caspia** — Krasnovodsk Whites murder 26 Red Commissars from Baku despite Maj-Gen Malleson's request. British bn sails there from Enzeli (29).	**Salonika** — Renewed Anglo-Greek attack fails in 6 bloody hrs as some British caught in own shellfire. Milne tells d'Esperey British can do no more. Bulgar First Army Cdr	**Palestine** — BATTLES OF MEGIDDO (-25): Bulfin's XXI Corps (35,000) advances from 0430 behind 385-gun barrage. DMC follows by 0700, takes 7000 PoWs & 100 guns in 22-

AFRICAN OPERATIONS 5	SEA WAR 6	AIR WAR 7	INTERNATIONAL EVENTS 8	HOME FRONTS 9
		Germany — Stuttgart (Bosch & Daimler works) attacked by 9 DH4s of No 55 Sqn; 2 fighters shot down. **France** — **Last bombing of Paris**: 50 Gothas (2 lost) drop 85 bombs (37 cas). **W Front** — German pilots destroy 6 & damage 4 balloons on BEF First & Third Army fronts (RAF manage 3 & 3). Germans claim 58 Allied aircraft for loss of 12 in air fighting above all but one of the 14 German armies.	**German peace offer to Belgium** on basis of no indemnity or reparations (*see* 19). New York Congress of Austrian subject peoples demands Empire's dismember-ment.	Churchill's offer of 2000+ guns to USA for 1919 accepted. **Britain** — Mr CHE Stubb gives Stonehenge to nation. (c) Labour Minister GH Roberts visits BEF in France (-30) to explain postwar betterment and demobilization.
	Channel — Monitor HMS *Glatton* scuttled at Dover following magazine explosion & fire. *UB103* , sighted by British blimp SS *21* (Pilot US Ensign NJ Learned), sunk by several RN drifters' depth charges off Cap Gris Nez.	**Trans-Jordan** — 6 RAF DH9s raid Deraa for first time; 8 German planes from there cause Arab Army only 2 cas thanks to BE12 (destroyed). **W Front** — RAF destroy 8 German aircraft for loss of 4 over BEF Third Army but, overall, Germans claim 59 Allied planes for loss of 10. **Germany** — 7 RAF Handley Pages FTR from Cologne, Saarbrücken & Trier etc, 6 lost to flak (16,063rnds & 173 searchlights, night 16/17).	**Wilson rejects Burian 'Peace Note'** (Vienna receives l9). Balfour calls Austro-German offers unacceptable. Count Hertling tells Conservative leader that Austrian peace move has prejudiced Dutch mediation. Japan recognizes Czechs as belligerent Allies. K George V cables Pres Wilson with congratulations on St Mihiel salient removal.	**USA** — *Joanna Enlists* film premiere includes stars in uniform.
Lettow reaches Mwembe area, flu causes 19 deaths from 207 sick since mid-Aug.			Clemenceau in Senate spurns Austrian peace offer. Allied Labour & Socialist Conference in London (-20) accepts 14 Points & calls on Allies to formulate war aims. **Secret War** — †Allied agent 'Alice Dubois' (alias Louise de Bettignies) in Cologne Prison.	'Worry whitens Hair of Kaiser' *Detroit Free Press* headline. **USA** — Smith & Wesson arms Co machinists return to work after strike vote (6), Presdential warning & War Dept takeover (13). **Britain** — Maj-Gen Thwaites to be DMI.
2/4th KAR Bn embarks at Fort Johnston for Mbamba Bay (E shore of L Nyasa) & Songea.	**N Sea** — **Scheer told to prepare for evacuation of Flanders coast** (*see* 28).	**Salonika** — RAF sends 372 calls for arty fire (-19), only 1 aircraft lost & shoots down 2 aircraft. **W Front** — Rain & clouds restrict flying over Somme (-19), both sides' aircraft losses much lower (17-20).	Final Allied neutral trade agreement, USA & Denmark.	
	E Med — RN destroyers *Druid* & *Forester* give gunfire support to Allenby's Megiddo offensive in Palestine.	**Palestine** — RAF strike Tulkarm-Nablus road, 2 army HQs, telephone exchanges & 3 airfields. No 113 Sqn twice smokescreens XXI Corps' advance. Jenin airfield captured	**Belgium rejects German peace offer**. J Davis new US London Ambassador.	**Germany** — Industrialists meet to discuss Scheer U-boat progamme. **Canada** — 'Khaki University' established. **Britain** — Railway workers win half pay demand.

SEPTEMBER 1918	WESTERN FRONT 1	EASTERN FRONT 2	SOUTHERN FRONTS 3	TURKISH FRONTS 4
Thu 19 contd			Gen Nerezov proposes counter-offensive to take Salonika but German-Bulgar (Steuben & Todorov) Prilep conference decides on gradual withdrawal prior to cutting off Allied salient. Franco-Greek attack storms Mt Dzena (7000ft).	mile ride. Turk Eighth Army HQ at Tulkarm falls to 60th Div after 18-mile march. **Trans-Jordan** — Lawrence destroys Turk plane on ground & engages train in his armoured car. **Egypt/Palestine** — Egyptian Labour Corps 100,000 strong in 99 coys and 30 camps (Palestine).
Fri 20		**Sovnarkom repudiates 3 Mar Russo-Turk Treaty. Don** — Krasnov's 20 Cossack regts attack again, breaking Red S Front (*see* 27).	**Salonika** — Bulgar First Army receives order to retreat in 'a stunned silence'. **Austria** — Vienna *Neue Freie Presse* mentions rumours of coming Italian offensive (*see* 25).	**Palestine** — 2nd Indian Lancers seize Musmus Pass & their charge wipes out 516 Turks. **Liman** (in pyjamas) **just escapes** 13th Cav Bde's swoop on **Nazareth** (1250 PoWs). **4th Cav Div seizes Jordan crossings** after 70-mile ride in 34hrs. 3rd ALH Bde captures Jenin & 1869 PoWs. Allenby sees Lawrence at GHQ after latter's RAF Bristol Fighter flight from Azrak.
Sat 21	War Minister warns Haig v heavy cas due to poor recruiting at home, but FM resolves to continue planned offensive. **Cambrai** — British 12th & 18th Divs (with 9 tanks) capture Le Petit Priel farm, E of Epéhy (21). 119 Australians of 1st Bn refuse to attack & go to rear.	Adm Kolchak & Czech Legion C-in-C Gajda leave Vladivostok on Trans-Siberian line (*see* 13 Oct).	**Salonika** — 2 RAF DH9 observers report 500 Bulgar wagons & lorries in retreat at 1040 (*see* AIR WAR). Bulgar morale plummets as they burn stores. Italians seize Hill 1050 after 1530, advance 6 miles (-22). Only 5000 Bulgar PoWs so far.	**Palestine** — **Last serious infantry action**: 10th Div captures Nablus, where Allenby meets Chetwode. RAF massacre Turk Seventh Army col in Wadi Fara descent to Jordan. Mopping up (-24) yields 87 guns, 55 lorries & 842 wagons (*see* AIR WAR).
Sun 22	Carlowitz replaces Marwitz i/c German Second Army (St Quentin), who takes over Fifth Army from Gallwitz his army gp cdr (*see* 26). **Argonne** — US First Army relieves French Second Army.		**Serbia** — **Serb Second Army** reaches Negotino on R Vardar, **20 miles N of 14 Sept line**. Prilep-Gradsko rail line cut, d'Esperey orders cav pursuit.	NZ Mtd Bde seizes Jisr-ed-Damieh Jordan bridge with 786 PoWs. Djemal Kuchuk belatedly orders Fourth Army retreat E of Jordan while Col Oppen's 2000 Asia Corps (700 Germans) survivors ford Jordan (night 22-23).
Mon 23	French reach R Oise, 3 miles N of La Fère.	Helfferich resigns as German Ambassador. **W Urals** — Ufa State Conference elects 5-man compromise Directorate inc ex-Tsarist corps cmdr Gen VG Boldyrev as White Siberian C-in-C.	**Serbia** — French Cav Bde Jouinot-Gambetta begins 57-mile 6-day advance from Novak, C-in-C gives Uskub (Skopje) as their objective, reaches evacuated Prilep at 1300 (*see* HOME FRONTS). Serb Second Army forces the Vardar despite stiff resistance.	**Palestine** — 500 **British cav capture Acre and Haifa** with 889 PoWs & 18 guns. Liman arrives in Damascus (-29), sends staff to Aleppo (25). **Trans-Jordan** — NZ Mtd Bde occupies Es Salt and the Arabs Maan.
Tue 24	*OHL* informs Berlin Govt that armistice talks inevitable (*see* 28). **Somme** — Anglo-French attack on 4-mile front E of Vermand to within 2 miles of St Quentin. British 1st & 6th Divs with 20 tanks attack Quadrilateral & Fresnoy (NW of St Quentin); French capture 2 villages to W. **BEF's best week of war for taking PoWs**, 30,441 (-30).		**Macedonia** — Milne diary 'the Bulgar has stopped us a bit...by rearguards'. British 27th Div bridges Vardar with 500ft bridge. **Italian Front** — Diaz orders Gen Caviglia to make preparations for autumn Middle Piave attack as well as Trentino (*see* 4 & 10 Oct) at DMO Col Cavallero's urging.	**Palestine** — 4th Cav Div takes 8000 PoWs at Jordan fords (23-24), Kemal only just escapes.
Wed 25	**Cambrai** — German counter-attacks fail nr Moeuvres & Epéhy. **Aisne** — Arty exchanges.		**Serbia** — French & Serbs capture vital Bulgar supply centre of Gradsko on the Vardar with 19 guns & 40 locomotives; Gen Pruneau of 17th Colonial Div 'My *poilus* have their clothes in rags and most...are barefooted' (26). Cav Bde Jouinot-Gambetta reaches	**Trans-Jordan** — 2750 **Anzacs capture Amman** with 2563 PoWs & 10 guns. 400 ALH (78 cas) storm Semakh rail stn S of L Galilee with 364 PoWs (c150 Germans) & 1 gun. Tiberias surrenders. EEF haul (since 19) 45,000 PoWs & 260 guns.

AFRICAN OPERATIONS 5	SEA WAR 6	AIR WAR 7	INTERNATIONAL EVENTS 8	HOME FRONTS 9
		(28) with 11 burnt German aircraft.		
	Adriatic — *U47* sinks French submarine *Circe* (1 survivor) off Albania.	RAF bomb & leaflet Constantinople (*see* 18 Oct). **Palestine** — RAF drop 10t bombs & fire 40,000 MG rnds, use captured El Afuleh airfield.		
		RAF'S MOST DEVASTATING 1914-18 BATTLEFIELD INTERVENTIONS: **Palestine** — Bristol Fighters & SE5s (105 planes in theatre) in 4hrs block, massacre or disperse Turk corps column descending to Jordan, 9¼t bombs & 56,000 MG rnds delivered in 84+ sorties (2 aircraft lost) (*see* TURK FRONTS). **Macedonia** — RAF (45 serviceable planes) bomb Bulgars fleeing through Kosturino defile to Lyumnitsa, at least 700k, 300 wagons destroyed; then attack Kryesna Pass & block Kresni defile (28-29). Total of 782 bombs dropped (-29).	Report to Lloyd George on Zahroff's 3rd visit to Switzerland for talks with Abdal Kerim.	
		Trans-Jordan — 2 Bristol Fighters & 1 DH9 reinforce Arab Army E of Deraa, destroy 2 German 2-seaters & a Pfalz scout. Handley Page joins (23) with fuel & spares & bombs Deraa rail stn. W of Jordan RAF drop 41t bombs & fire 30,000 MG rnds at Turk fugitives.		**Britain** — Meat retail price up c2d per lb.
Tripolitania — Italian col from Zuara defeats rebels at Gasr Tellil (*see* 5 Oct).		**W Front** — 13 German bombers raid RAF Marquise depot, destroy or damage 99 aircraft (172 cas) (night 23/24). **Palestine** — RAF (at least 22 attack) drop 6¼t bombs & fires 33,000+ MG rnds E of Jordan (resumed 25 with 39 sorties).		**Austria** — Count Tisza's arrogant Sarajevo speech during tour (13-26) kills last S Slav Habsburg sympathies. Yugoslav charter signed at Agram (24). **Bulgaria** — Socialist students organize Soviets in 3 towns (-24, *see* 25).
			OHL inform Berlin that **armistice talks inevitable** (*see* 29). Turkey backs Austrian note. US CPI publishes suspect Sisson documents to show Bolsheviks German stooges (Britain does not copy till after 23 Oct). Secret Sino-Japanese Agreement over Shantung (*see* 30 Apr 1919).	**Germany** — Kaiser visits Kiel U-boat School, speaks to 400 U-boat officers and minelayer crews. **France** — 4th War Loan authorized. **Britain** — Army educational scheme issued. (c) Churchill first meets S Sassoon.
Patrol from Mitimoni discovers Lettow's columns but barely escapes.		**W Front** — Rickenbacker awarded CMH; posthumous award to Texas 'balloon-buster' Lt Frank Luke, 29 (k 19 after 14 victories in 8 days, incl 3 aircraft & 2 balloons, 18). Germans claim 41 Allied aircraft for loss of 13 (inc 24). **Germany** — 4 DH9s of No 110 Sqn lost in raid	**Italy recognizes Yugoslav State.**	**Bulgaria** — **Tsar Ferdinand orders Stamboliski freed to calm mutineers in Sofia**, 1500 cas as loyal cadets & German 217th Div from Odessa & Varna disperse them (*see* 27). **Britain** — 'Italy's Day' in London.

SEPTEMBER 1918	WESTERN FRONT 1	EASTERN FRONT 2	SOUTHERN FRONTS 3	TURKISH FRONTS 4
Wed 25 contd			Babuna Pass and strikes N through mts for Uskub covering 11 miles (26). **British** XVI Corps **cross Bulgar frontier** & enter Kosturino. Bulgar deserters try to seize GHQ at Kustendil (*see* HOME FRONTS) & commandeer trains to go home, GHQ moves to Sofia (27).	
Thu 26	FOCH LAUNCHES GENERAL OFFENSIVE: 1st Phase (-15 Oct). BATTLE OF MEUSE-ARGONNE (-11 Nov): After 3hr barrage **37 Franco-American divs attack** at 0530 **on 40-mile front from Champagne to Meuse** with 705 tanks available, av advance 3 miles. AEF gas effort: 800rnds (1600t) mustard gas & phosgene; 10,600 gassed (278 deaths) (-11 Nov).		**Bulgaria** — N of Kosturino at 0800 (95°F in shade) Derbyshire Yeomanry meets Bulgar car with white flag & Todorov letter to Milne. Bulgar capital Sofia still 130 miles & 5 mtn ranges to N. **Serbia** — Serb cav capture Kocharia, Drina & Morava Divs liberate Veles after hard fighting v 4 German bns. Allies now have 10,000 PoWs & 200 guns.	**Palestine** — **Allenby** meets corps cdrs at Jenin, **orders advance on Damascus**. **Trans-Jordan** — 10th Cav Bde at Irbid fails v Turk Fourth Army flank guard. Arab Army (3000) crosses Hejaz Railway N of Deraa (Col Oppen's 700 Germans reach, railed to Riyak 27), takes 2 stns & 600+ PoWs.
Fri 27	Franco-American advance slows. Montfaucon behind *Michel* Stellung & Varennes (Crown Prince's 1916 Verdun OP) captured, 23,000 PoWs. Battle of Flanders Ridges begins (-10 Oct). **Cambrai** — BEF ATTACKS HINDENBURG LINE with Third (15 divs) incl 16 tanks (5 lost) & First Armies (12 divs) on 14-mile front from 0530. Battle of Canal du Nord (-1 Oct): British within 3 miles of Cambrai as 4th Cdn Div & 2 tanks capture Bourlon & Wood. 2 other villages fall in 3-mile advance, incl Graincourt to Gds Bde, 10,000 PoWs & 200 guns taken. Rupprecht writes that peace must be made in winter. US 106th Regt (27th Div) loses 1540 of 2000 men attacking 3 Hindenburg Line outposts.	**N Russia** — **Allied Archangel advance blocked** by far larger Red force at Nizhne-Toimski after 60-mile push, retreat to Borok and dig in (-28). **S Russia** — Stalin signals Trotsky for 30,000 rifles, 150 MGs and 50 guns or else retirement E of Volga.	**Macedonia** — British officer's diary 'The men have marched well in spite of heat and dust'. US diplomat from Sofia Mr Walker arrives at Salonika to mediate but not admitted.	Australian Mtd Div begins ride for Damascus by crossing Jordan. **Trans-Jordan** — Arab Army cuts in at Sheikh Saad, makes 2000 PoWs & wipes out 2000 Turks in revenge for Tafas village massacre.
Sat 28	HINDENBURG & LUDENDORFF AGREE AFTER 1800 GERMANY MUST REQUEST AN IMMEDIATE ARMISTICE (KAISER APPROVES 29). FINAL BATTLE OF FLANDERS (-11 Nov): Allied Flanders Army Gp (K Albert, CoS Gen Degoutte) of 28 divs with 2550 guns (12 Belgian or 170,000 men, 10 BEF, 6 French) after 3hr barrage advances on 23-mile front. Houthulst Forest (4-mile advance) & Wytschaete captured: 4000 PoWs. Belgian 4th Carabineers storm Passchendaele. British Second Army fights **Fourth Battle of Ypres** (-2 Oct), in 4½-6 mile advance (9 miles by end 29) recaptures Gheluvelt & Messines. **Aisne** — Italians cross E of Condé in surprise night attack.		**Armistice talks begin in Salonika** at 1600 incl Gen Lukov & Bulgar Finance Minister who hope for neutral status but d'Esperey unyielding. **Serbia** — French 57th Div occupies Ochrid. **Dolomites** — Austrian attack in Val Guidicaria repulsed.	**Palestine** — British 54th Div begins advance on Haifa (-4 Oct). **Trans-Jordan** — Arabs occupy Deraa where Lawrence meets Barrow, GOC 4th Cav Div. **Syria** — DMC reaches Kuneitra, 40 miles SW of Damascus. **S Persia** — British break Bushire tribal blockade.
Sun 29	Ludendorff severely depressed (*see* INT'L EVENTS). BEF RIGHT WING (Fourth Army, 17 divs) & FRENCH LEFT (First Army, 14 divs) ATTACK HINDENBURG LINE in dense fog. BEF fires all-time record of 943,947 shells (since noon 28). Canadians suffer 2089 cas. **Somme** — British Fourth Army offensive (now 39 BEF & 2 US divs v 41 German) on 12-mile	**N Russia** — Allied N Dvina Force formed, Canadians land at Archangel (30). **S Russia** — S Front C-in-C ex-Tsarist Gen Sytin clashes over HQ site with Stalin who removes him (*see* 4 Oct).	**French Cav Bde** Jouinot-Gambetta (3000) **captures Serbia's 2nd city Uskub** (Skopje) in heavy rain at 0900 by advances from N & S with 339 PoWs & 5 guns; German armoured train escapes fighting. 3 French aircraft take news to Salonika. Main Serb Army still 30 miles to S, but close to Bulgar frontier S of Kustendil &, storming Bulgar	**Syria** — Turco-German rearguard (1500 with trucks) delays 3rd ALH Bde at Sasa (-30), but eventually loses 350 PoWs. Liman sends Kemal to Riyak (NW of Damascus). **Trans-Jordan** — Turk II Corps (4602 & 14 guns) marches into Amman to **surrender to Chaytor's Force** (terms agreed 28).

AFRICAN OPERATIONS 5	SEA WAR 6	AIR WAR 7	INTERNATIONAL EVENTS 8	HOME FRONTS 9
		on Frankfurt (bombed from 17,000ft) to 50 fighters.		
	French request Italian naval action v Durazzo (*see* 2 Oct).	**Germany** — 4 Handley Pages of No 216 Sqn damage railways & bridge at Metz-Sablon causing delays & dislocation for 24hrs. **W Front** — Mitchell's 842 US aircraft v 302 German for Meuse-Argonne Offensive (- 11 Nov), but weather restricts close support. **Germans claim 63 Allied aircraft for loss of 3.**	BULGARIA REQUESTS ARMISTICE.	**France** — Dreyfus promoted Lt Col. **USA** — 6139 Army flu cases (170 deaths) in last 24hrs, total ill 35,146 **Britain** — Revised certified occupations' list (age 18-51).
	Med — All available U-boats ordered to N Aegean to cover Thrace & Dardanelles.	**W Front** — **57 RAF sqns with 1058 aircraft support BEF assault on Hindenburg Line;** 6 fighter sqns make low-lying attacks using 700t bombs & 26,000 MG rnds; 3 German airfields attacked. Germans claim 44 Allied aircraft for loss of 10. Handley Pages drop 6t bombs on Busigny rail jctn (night 27/28).	Austrian Crown Council: Burian says 'In jumping clear from us, Bulgaria has knocked the bottom out of the barrel', urges peace & solution to S Slav danger. **USA** — Wilson New York speech calls League of Nations 'indispensable instrument', adds 5 Particulars to 14 Points.	**Austria** — Emergency Crown Council: Charles urges peace and internal reform, but ministers want it in Dual framework (*see* 2 Oct). **Britain** — Army Council put i/c of waste. **Bulgaria** — Republic proclaimed at Radomir (factory town between Sofia & Küstendil), 6000 men march on Sofia.
Lettow recrosses R Rovuma into German E Africa, opposite Nagwamira (8 hippos shot for meat to celebrate return). Kartucol reaches R Lugenda.	**N Sea** — British ships & aircraft attack Zeebrugge. 11 German destroyers evacuate port (30) & reach Germany thanks to moonless nights, shoals & rough weather which thwart Harwich Force. **Britain** — Swan Hunter yard launches first fabricated 'straight line' ship SS *War Climax*, 31 weeks from laying keel.	**W Front** — Udet destroys 2 US-crewed DH & receives bullet graze. Lt F Rumey (45 victories) of *Jasta 4* kia. *Bogohl 3* & other German units drop 167,154lb bombs. Most crews carry out 3 sorties (night 28/29). **RAF loss of 424 men since 15 severest of war,** av 15.5 per 100 planes flown (1404 serviceable). **Palestine/Syria** — RAF bomb Damascus airfield from new Kuneitra landing ground, supplied with fuel by air. Aircraft land at Damascus 1 Oct. **Flanders** — **24 RAF sqns support final Allied advance,** helped by radio telephone. 6-main rail targets attacked, 27 aircraft lost in low-flying attacks (*see* 20 Oct).	**Ludendorff persuades Hindenburg to call for immediate armistice.** Germany refuses British PoW proposal (*see* 4 Oct). Japanese Foreign Minister Baron Goto resigns, Count Uchiba succeeds (29). **Neutrals: Switzerland** — Stravinsky's ballet *A Soldier's Tale* first staged.	**Germany** — Kaiser leaves Wilhelmshoe for Spa by train. **USA** — 4th Liberty Loan (-19 Oct) for $6.96bn, redeemable after 15 Oct 1933. Films *Kultur* & *Why America Will Win* showing. **Britain** — National War Bonds 2nd series ends after £1120m raised.
Fitzcol disbands at Dar-es-Salaam, most units transferred to Cenforce.	**N Sea** — *UB115* (oil patch sighted by rigid airship *R29*) sunk off Sunderland by depth charges from several RN destroyers (incl HMS *Ouse*) & trawlers.	**W Front** — 337 RAF aircraft (17 sqns) support BEF Fourth Army's rupture of the Hindenburg Line although smoke & mist hampers them; 5 German balloons shot down, 6 fighters for loss of 3 incl fight between 20 German & 29 RAF fighters, although Germans concede only 2 losses for 8 Allied.	**Occupied Luxemburg** — At Spa Crown Council **Hindenburg & Ludendorff insist on armistice & new govt,** Kaiser agrees (*see* 30). **Japan** — 1st commoner Takashi Hara succeeds Count Terauchi as PM.	**Japan** — War Minister Lt-Gen Oshima resigns, Tanaka succeeds (30).

SEPTEMBER 1918	WESTERN FRONT 1	EASTERN FRONT 2	SOUTHERN FRONTS 3	TURKISH FRONTS 4
Sun 29 contd	front begins with 1600 guns. **Battle of St Quentin Canal** (-2 Oct): British 46th Div (800 cas) fights across it in epic style at Bellenglise using boats, ladders & 3000 lifebelts from Channel ferries, advances 3½ miles taking 4200 PoWs (of 5300 total) & 70 guns (of 100 total) in 2½ hrs. 5th Australian & US 30th Divs storm Bellicourt Tunnel defences to N (141 tanks support, incl US 301st Bn in British Mk Vs, but 75 hit). **Flanders** — Belgian 4th Div recaptures Dixmude but 9th Div repulsed 6 times from Westroosebeke (evacuated 30).		position 11 miles NE of Veles, Greek 14th Div occupies Yenikoi after 382 cas. BULGARIA SIGNS 7-clause ARMISTICE at 2210. Austrian 9th Div from Italian Front still 50 miles N of Uskub.	
Mon 30	**Flanders** — British 2 miles from Menin. **Cambrai** — British in Cambrai outskirts; 6 villages captured. German incendiarists at work. **BEF first uses mustard gas**, v Hindenburg Line. Foch, back from Flanders sees Haig at Arras. **Champagne** — French capture Marfaux-Aure & St Marie-a-Py as Fifth Army attacks. **Argonne** — AEF heavily engaged as its ill-organized motor/horse transport becomes increasingly traffic-jammed. Allied max advance now 8 miles with 18,000 PoWs & 200 guns. German Sept losses 236,200. Total 160 Allied divs (+57 in res) v 113 German front-line divs (+84 in res), but only 59 German divs classed as 'fit'. British Army adopts 24-hr clock (French Army throughout) from midnight 30 Sept/1 Oct. (Sept) 10 more German divs disbanded (3 more early Oct) to strengthen depleted remainder. Lack of horses reducing medium btys from 4 guns to 3.	Trotsky orders arrest of families of officers who desert to Whites.	BULGARIA HOSTILITIES CEASE AT NOON, conceding Allied occupation of key points & use of railways v remaining Central Powers; Bulgar Army to be reduced to 3 divs & 2 cav regts. British Sept sick admissions 9855 (mainly flu & malaria), 3137w. **Albania** — Italian cav patrols reach R Skumbi (see 7 Oct). **Serbia** — German *Alpenkorps* (from W Front) reaches Nis with 219th (Saxon) Div (from E Front) behind.	**Syria** — Arab flags flown in Damascus as Turks retreat N on 2 roads and Germans blow ammo dumps. Australian Mtd Div blocks Barada Gorge (Beirut road) and takes 4000 PoWs; 5th Cav Div makes 1294 for 10 cas; Arabs take 600 from Turk Deraa col after Lawrence fetches 4th Cav Div arty. **Mesopotamia** — Turk Sixth Army estimated at 13,725 (4 divs+), 154 guns & 237 MGs.
Tue 1 October 1918	LUDENDORFF CABLES GOVT TO TRANSMIT PEACE OFFER WITHOUT FURTHER DELAY (see HOME FRONTS). BEF about to break through Hindenburg Line last defences after 7-mile advance since 27 Sept. This *Wotan* position runs W of Lille, Douai & St Quentin to Reims. Behind, Germans have begun 2 other positions: *Hermann* (Ghent-Valenciennes-Le Cateau-Aisne) & Antwerp-Meuse Line (W of Antwerp & Brussels to Mézières & Sedan). Ludendorff sends staff officer Maj Bussche to Berlin to explain to new Chancellor military situation makes peace moves essential. German cas since 21 Mar 1,222,299, and German Ninth Army disbanded due to shortened front. **Artois** — Germans evacuate Lens & Armentières (night 1/2). British 2nd Div captures Mont sur l'Oeuvre. Canadians (1000+ cas) fight another mile forward N of Cambrai, have captured 7000+ PoWs & 205 guns since 27 Sept, from up to 12 German divs. **Champagne** — French Fourth Army (Gouraud) advances on 14-mile front.	(Oct) 4 German divs transfer to W Front. Lenin writes to Sverdlov & Trotsky that international revolution imminent (urges preparations & 3 million man army, 3). (Oct) Red Army c430,000-strong. **N Russia** — Maj-Gen Ironside lands at Archangel as new Allied C-in- C. **W Russia** — (Oct) White Northern Corps formed from Petrograd officers under German protection at Pskov, Russian PoWs released to it.	**Albania** — Italians reoccupy Berat in advance N, then Elbasan (7) & Karaje (12, see 14).	FALL OF DAMASCUS (pop c250,000): 3rd ALH Bde enters before 0630, Lawrence & Arabs 0730; but both claim to be first; 13,746 Turks surrender to 6000 DMC and 28 guns. Lawrence makes Shukri Pasha military gov. **Palestine** — 7th Indian Div enters Haifa, Tyre (4), Sidon (6), (see 8).
Wed 2	Bussche briefs *Reichstag* party leaders: sustained Allied	**Baltic States** — German *Armeeabteilung* D disbanded	Franchet d'Esperey writes 'I can with 200,000 men cross	**Syria** — Last Australian action: 9th ALH takes 1481

AFRICAN OPERATIONS 5	SEA WAR 6	AIR WAR 7	INTERNATIONAL EVENTS 8	HOME FRONTS 9
	U-boats sink US SS *Ticonderoga* (121 of 243 soldiers lost). **Adriatic — Otranto Barrage completed**. **N Sea** — British seaplane sqn over Heligoland Bight. (Sept) Allied & neutral shipping lost to U-boats 79 ships (48 British with 521 lives) worth 186,600t (British 136,859). U-boat figure 91 ships worth 171,972 incl 38 ships of 42,693t in Med (incl last Austrian score, 16 ships worth 5004t); 9 U-boats sunk.	**W Front** — (Sept) **German airmen make 130 parachute descents** as new Heinecke equipment comes into general use. **RAF Sept loss** (excl IAF) **a record 235 aircraft** (French 59). German loss 115 aircraft (excl 21-23 & 30). *Jasta Boelcke* scores its monthly record of 46 kills for loss of 2 pilots. **Bulgaria** — RAF photo-recon flight to Sofia.	ALLIED-BULGARIAN ARMISTICE AT NOON. **German Chancellor** Count Hertling **& all Ministers resign** (*see* 4 Oct).	**USA — Wilson tells Senate woman suffrage 'a vitally necessary war measure'.** **Britain** — Bonar Law opens 'Feed the Guns Campaign' to raise 2nd £1bn war loan (*see* 17 Oct).
	(Oct) 179 operational U-boats. Largely propaganda 'Scheer Programme' (1) envisages increasing monthly U-boat prod from 13 to 37 boats (Dec 1919) building 376-450 U-boats using 69,000 workers & 11 yards. Only 257 (5.1%) of 5018 RN warships on convoy escort duty. US Shipping Board has 3115 ships of 17,276,318t building. **Arctic** — British flag raised at Ebeltoff Harbour, Spitzbergen. **Black Sea** — c200 Germans take over Russian battleship *Volya*; 4 destroyers; 2 torpedo boats; & 1 auxiliary cruiser, *Volya* enters service (15). By 26 Berlin urging return to Russians. **N Sea/Channel** — Flanders U-boat Flotilla recalls all 8 boats at sea for return to Germany (*see* 4), 4 others scuttled (-5, *see* 17).	**W Front** — Fine weather all day. Only 11 of 49 DH9s reach & bomb Aulnoye rail jctn am, mainly due to engine trouble, but 18 of 21 bomb it pm, exploding ammo train. (Oct) Maj-Gen Salmond, GOC RAF in France complains DH9 day bomber so inadequate it has 'to accept battle when, & where, the defending forces choose ...'. **Flanders** — RAF drop c24t bombs & destroy 16 German aircraft.	Austrian PM Hussarek in Vienna Parlt says open to peace offers. *Tageblatt* publishes German Majority Party's programme, includes Belgium's restoration & joining League of Nations.	Ludendorff tells staff 'Our own Army is...heavily infected with the poison of Spartacist-Socialist ideas'. U-boat Programme feasibility study in Cologne. **Britain** — RFP 129% (up 13% due to meat, butter, milk & egg rises). Max horse ration 7-13lb pd. (Oct) Film *Mrs John Bull Prepared* . **Austria** — Row in *Reichsrath* as PM Hussarek proclaims reconstruc- tion. **USA** — Senate rejects women's suffrage 3rd time; (Oct) **Flu pandemic at height** (2-3) suspends draft in several cities, shuts war plants; 14,636 army cases (300 deaths) in last 24hrs, total 88,461 (1877 deaths *see* 12). Student Army Training Corps opens in 500+ colleges.
	Adriatic — Allied Fleet (3 Italian battleships; 3 Italian & 5	**Flanders** — 80 **Allied aircraft drop 15,000 rations** (13t) from		Kaiser & Hindenburg arrive in Berlin to appoint new

OCTOBER 1918	WESTERN FRONT 1	EASTERN FRONT 2	SOUTHERN FRONTS 3	TURKISH FRONTS 4
Wed 2 contd	attacks on whole W Front make formation of reserves impossible; *OHL* can no longer make good losses suffered; Germany can continue for some time inflicting heavy losses & implementing a 'scorched earth' policy, but she cannot win the war. Every day reduces likelihood of acceptable peace terms (*see* INT'L EVENTS 4). 3017 BEF officer weekly cas since 25 Sept, second highest of war. **Argonne** — Surrounded **US 'Lost Battalion'** (308th Inf, 77th Div) holds till relief (-7), 194 survivors from 600+. **Flanders** — Fourth Battle of Ypres ends: Allies stopped short (*see* AIR WAR) of key objectives (Roulers jctn & Menin), but gain 11,000 PoWs, 300 guns & 600 MGs for 4500 Belgian & 4695 British cas (*see* 14). **Somme** — French First Army's L wing (XV Corps) liberates a ruined St Quentin.	(formed 8 Oct 1915). **Volga** — Stalin signals Trotsky & Lenin 'Situation on South Front unsteady due to lack of armament and the failure to send submarines.' In fact 40,000 Red troops & 240 guns at Tsaritsyn.	Hungary and Austria, mass in Bohemia covered by the Czechs and march immediately on Dresden' (*see* 7).	PoWs, 3 guns & 26 MGs; only 17,000 of 100,000 Turks have escaped. N. Lawrence's Arabs disperse Algerian/Druze riot in Damascus. **Mesopotamia** — Marshall told to begin Tigris advance without delay (*see* 18). Trading with enemy limits raised in Baghdad & Basra districts.
Thu 3	**Somme/Cambrai** — BATTLE OF BEAUREVOIR LINE (-5): British Fourth & Third Armies attack on 8-mile front incl tanks & 2nd Cav Div, capture Le Catelet & 350 guns. **Meuse/ Argonne** — Gallwitz stalls US advance, after 7-mile gain, on Apremont-Brieulles line. **Champagne** — French take Challerange. US 2nd Div storms key Blanc Mont Ridge (15 miles NE of Reims) -4 to aid Gouraud's hitherto stalled advance for 5 miles (-10) taking c2000 PoWs for 6300 cas.	**N Russia** — Action near L Pyavozera (Murmansk sector). **Volga** — Red Army retakes Syzran & Krasnoufimsk. **S Russia** — Red Army C-in-C Vatsetis signals that Stalin's 'disregard of orders... intolerable' appeals to Trotsky (*see* 6). **Urals** — Prov All-Russian Govt declares all Soviet treaties void, fixes capital at Omsk (9). **E Siberia** — Japanese reportedly join Semenov at Ruchlevo, 1500 Hungarian PoWs taken.	Hindenburg writes to Chancellor 'As a result of the collapse of the Macedonian Front...there is no longer a prospect of forcing peace on the enemy'. **Serbia** — 19,000 Bulgars surrender to Italian 35th Div & French 11th Colonial Div at Sop, 7000 Bulgars surrender to Serbs who drive back Austrian 9th Div. **Italian Front** — British raid on N Asiago sector, heavy fighting & 500 Austrian PoWs (11).	**Allenby visits Damascus & meets Feisal for first time,** tells him France will be protecting power in Syria, but he can set up military admin Aqaba-Damascus E of Jordan. An exhausted & disillusioned Lawrence asks for leave & departs for Cairo (4).
Fri 4	Allies announce capture of 254,012 PoWs, 3669 guns, 23,000 MGs (15 July-30 Sept). **Meuse/Argonne** — US advance resumed W of river, takes Hill 240 & 4 villages in mile or so advance. '...Bullard's Corps forces the enemy back to the *Kriemhilde* positions south of the Bois de Forest' (US communiqué). A US 1st Div bn has 242 men left out of 820, 3rd Div takes 1366 cas v Curel Heights. Lull follows (5) after 8-mile advance.	CEC pledges support for German proletariat. **N Russia** — RN monitor *M25* sails for Archangel to avoid freeze; 30 Red gunboats dominate R Dvina (-14). **Galicia** — German-aided Ukrainians attack Poles.	**Italian Front** — PM Orlando to Diaz 'Of inaction and defeat, I would prefer defeat. Act at once !' (*see* 12). **Serbia** — French Tranie Det from Uskub (Skopje) captures Kacanik with 30 guns & Lipljan with 22 guns (7), 40 miles NNW. **Macedonia** — Greeks occupy Seres & Demi Hissar, Aegean port of Kavalla (9), Drama (10). **Italian Front** — Sharp fighting in Mt Grappa area. Austrian High Command appoints Armistice Commission.	**HMG learns Turkey has cabled Berlin that she is about to seek peace** (*see* INT'L EVENTS 14). **E Persia** — Insp-Gen of Communications Dickson reaches Juzzah border railhead, cables need for 14,600 camels or 1450 vans.
Sat 5	**Somme/Cambrai** — British 25th Div (Fourth Army) with 6 tanks captures Beaurevoir; Germans retire from Scheldt Canal. Kaiser Order of the Day mentions peace offer, but urges continued stern resistance. *The Times*, London 'Our Armies in the West hold the front from the east of Ypres to the north of St Quentin. Since August 8 we have advanced practically at every point.' **BEF has captured 35,000 PoWs & 380 guns since 27 Sept & broken through Hindenburg Line in 9 days** on 30-mile front. Victorious Australian Corps withdrawn to rest after capturing Montbrehain, having captured 29,144 PoWs & 388 guns since 27 Mar (21,243 cas incl only 79 missing), liberated 116 towns & villages since 8	**N Russia** — Royal Scots repulse Red attack. **Siberia** — British High Commissioner Eliot arrives at Omsk.	**Serbia** — Serb First Army liberates Vranje 50 miles S of Nis & liberates Leskovac (7) S of Nis having taken 3000 Austrian PoWs. Serb Second Army begins transfer from Bulgar frontier W to Montenegro/Albania (-20).	

AFRICAN OPERATIONS 5	SEA WAR 6	AIR WAR 7	INTERNATIONAL EVENTS 8	HOME FRONTS 9
	British cruisers; 16 British & 7 Italian destroyers; 8 Italian torpedo boats; 4-6 MAS boats) shells Durazzo, 3 Austrian destroyers & torpedo boats slightly damaged in harbour (Austrian evacuation ordered 28 Sept). Hospital ship allowed out. Austrian *U31* torpedoes cruiser *Weymouth*'s stern off (*see* 22). **W Med** — U-boat shells & sinks Spanish SS *Francoli* (292 lost) off Cartagena.	300ft in 4hrs **to leading Franco-Belgian troops** in swamp terrain. German communications bombed (3-4). **Albania** — RAF from Andrano in heel of Italy make 4 raids on Durazzo (total 29 aircraft), drop 6280lb bombs (*see* SEA WAR).		Chancellor (*see* INT'L EVENTS 3). **Turkey** — Interior Minister resigns. **Austria** — Common Ministers Council reaches no agreement on peace or internal reform; PM Hussarek warns of Austrian German irredentism. **France** — Liberation saves St Quentin Cathedral from German demolition.
	N Sea — RN submarine *L11* torpedoes & sinks German destroyer *S33*.		**Prince Max of Baden** (Kaiser's 2nd cousin) **becomes last Imperial Chancellor**, also replaces Hintze as Foreign Minister; Hindenburg urges peace at his first council. **Bulgaria** — TSAR FERDINAND ABDICATES in favour of son Boris, who signs decree demobilizing Army (*see* 1 Nov) and issues peaceful manifesto (6). Ferdinand's train told to leave Austrian territory (5), leaves for Coburg (6). **Rumania** — Prov Nat Council forms Nat Council of Unity (France recognizes 12).	**France** — 1st speculation as to when Germans will be expelled. New Gov of Paris Gen Moiner.
Lettow passes Songea to W; Spangenberg's advance guard fights N Rhodesia Police 15 miles to W as Capt Müller's rear guard clashes with 2 KAR coys 16 miles to S.	**E Atlantic** — U-boat sinks Japanese liner *Hiramo Maru* (292 lost) off Ireland. **Med** — British convoy escorts & SS *Greenland*'s gunfire sink *UB68* SE of Malta, her cdr Dönitz a PoW, having sunk 7 ships or 16,993t incl 1 in this convoy. **N Sea** — Harwich Force hoping to find returning U-boats only finds 2 armed trawlers to sink (*see* 23).	**Italy** — 48 Camels (no cas) bomb Austrian flying schools at Campoformido, SW of Udine & Egna, S of Bolzano (5), destroying 13+ aircraft.	**Germany & Austria send armistice pleas to Wilson** (via Berne) on basis of 14 Points (*see* 8).	**Germany** — Socialist Deputies Grober & Scheidemann become ministers without portfolio. **Britain** — Churchill requests 1000 dummy tanks for Feb 1919. **USA** — 90k in shell loading plant explosion, Morgan, NJ. 26-year-old Mae West sings 'Any Kind of Man' in *Sometime* Broadway premiere.
Tripolitania — Italian Zuara garrison heavily defeats Senussi attack and with Tripoli force counter-attacks successfully (6).	**N Channel** — AMC *Otranto* (Orient Co) carrying US troops (431 lost) sinks in collision, destroyer HMS *Mounsey* rescues 596. **E Med** — French Syrian Sqn occupies Beirut, then Tripoli & Alexandretta (both 14).		Prince Max outlines peace plan in *Reichstag*, makes Dr Solf Foreign Minister. Allies announce 1,766,160 US troops in Europe (*see* 15).	**Germany** — Prince Max tells *Reichstag* that it will approve all future chancellors. **Austria** — Nat Council at Laibach extended to all Yugoslav parties, moves to Agram (10), adopts constitution (21, *see* INT'L EVENTS 29). **Turkey** — Peace rumours cause 35% price fall, but soon rise again. **USA** — 1761 American prisoners in Germany & Turkey (281).

OCTOBER 1918	WESTERN FRONT 1	EASTERN FRONT 2	SOUTHERN FRONTS 3	TURKISH FRONTS 4
Sat 5 *contd*	Aug, engaged 39 German divs (30 twice or more, 6 disbanded). **Artois** — Germans burn Douai (*see* 12). **Champagne** — German First & Third Armies fall back on entire front, French finally occupy Moronvilliers Massif. Guillaumat replaces Berthelot (to Bulgaria) i/c French Fifth Army.			
Sun 6	Haig meets Foch, announces new offensive for 8. Italians 9 miles S of Laon (burning) then withdrawn after 2159 cas since 28 Sept.	British Petrograd officials reach Swedish border. **S Russia** — **Trotsky recalls Stalin from Tsaritsyn** to Moscow (-11), returns till 19 (*see* 8).	**Bulgaria** — Prince Regent Boris promoted General (*see* 11). **Salonika** — Milne cables CIGS urging his troops be used v Turkey (*see* TURK FRONTS 7).	**Syria** — DMC occupies Rayak & Zahle (177 PoWs), 30 burnt planes at former.
Mon 7	Supreme War Council learns new German Chancellor has approached Pres Wilson with request for armistice (*see* INT'L EVENTS 8 & 12). **Aisne** — French capture Berry-au-Bac.	General Berthelot proposes Salonika army use in S Russia to Clemenceau to protect Denikin's White build up; Franchet d'Esperey opposes (27). **Volga** — **Red Fourth Army retakes Samara.** (Red E Front now 103,000, 298 guns, 1627 MGs.) **N Russia** — US 339th Inf coy wins skirmish at Borok, but Reds force Allied outposts back (9-10). Allies retreat 20 miles to Kurgomin-Tulgas (13-17) and repel Red attack (23).	Clemenceau telegram orders d'Esperey to liberate Serbia, regain touch with Rumania & isolate Turkey (*see* INT'L EVENTS).	**Supreme Allied War Council decides Salonika Army will march E through Thrace to Constantinople**, Milne to command (10), ready with 4 divs (29), *see* S FRONTS.
Tue 8	**Somme/Cambrai** — SECOND BATTLE OF CAMBRAI (-9): British Third, Fourth & First (takes Fresnoy-Rouvroy line NE of Arras) Armies attack with 82 tanks (22 lost) on 20-mile front between St Quentin & Cambrai, advance 3 miles, take 10,000 PoWs & 150 guns (incl 1500 PoWs & 30 guns by US 30th Div). Third Army captures Villers-Outreaux, Forenville & Niergnies SE of Cambrai despite 15 German tanks (6 lost) heading 3 local counter-attacks & hitting 4 British tanks (4A7Vs deliver another, 11). Army Gps Rupprecht & Boehn ordered back to *Hermann* position. Boehn's gp then to be broken up; its Second Army to Rupprecht, Eighteenth to Crown Prince, Boehn sent on leave. **Argonne** — Marksman Cp York (328th Inf, 82nd Div) captures 132 Prussian Guardsmen having shot dead 15.	Lenin appoints Stalin to Revolutionary Military Council. **S Russia** — †Gen Alexeiev at Ekaterinodar (60), **Denikin becomes White supreme commander & civil dictator.** **Occupied Poland** — Regency Council dissolves Council of State & takes over German admin (12, *see* 22).		7th Indian Div occupies Beirut after 2 French destroyers' arrival, 600 Turks handed over. Col Piépape, French military gov, whose troops arrive 20.
Wed 9	**Cambrai** — HINDENBURG LINE COMPLETELY BROKEN: **Canadians enter Cambrai**, link with Third Army, begin BEF pursuit to the Selle (-12,*see* 17), 3rd Cav Div (329 cas) takes 500 PoWs, 10 guns & 60 MGs in 8-mile advance, finishes only 2 miles from Le Cateau (2 armoured cars briefly enter). **Meuse/Argonne** — 20,000 AEF deaths to date from flu & pneumonia.		**Italian Front** — Diaz forms Tenth and Twelfth Armies under British and French command.	Allenby orders occupation of Homs & Tripoli.
Thu 10	FOCH'S ORDERS FOR FINAL ALLIED ADVANCES: Belgians advance on Bruges, BEF upon Maubeuge & Mons, & Franco-Americans upon Mézières & Sedan, to cut German forces' main lateral line of communication — Brussels-Maubeuge-Mézières-Sedan railway & to drive Germans into forested		**Serbia** — After 170-mile advance in 25 days **Serbs recapture Nis** from Germans who begin retreat to Krusevac & Knjazevac (night 9/10). FM Kövess made Austro-German C-in-C Balkans (HQ Belgrade), decides on retreat behind Danube & Sava. **Bulgaria** — British 26th Div reaches	**Syria** — British 5th Cav Div armoured cars occupy Baalbek.

AFRICAN OPERATIONS 5	SEA WAR 6	AIR WAR 7	INTERNATIONAL EVENTS 8	HOME FRONTS 9
		W Front — US airmen Bleckley & Foettler posthumously awarded CMH for suicidal supply-dropping mission to 'Lost Bn' at Binarville (*see* W FRONT 2).	Prince Max's 12 Jan anti-peace letter published. France warns Germany re crimes on her territory.	**India** — Record 768 flu deaths in Bombay.
	Germany — Vice-Adm E Mann replaces Vice-Adm Behncke as Navy Sec (-Feb 1919).	**W Front** — French pioneer aviator Roland Garros k aged 30 (having escaped to Holland from Magdeburg PoW camp Feb).	Poles in Warsaw proclaim independence, as do deputies in German *Reichstag*. Sir E Geddes & Naval Mission arrive in New York.	**Germany** — Spartacist Gotha Conference urges Soviets in Germany (*see* 22). **Britain** — Churchill addresses Glasgow munition workers, deprecates a negotiated peace (in Sheffield 11, Manchester 15). Merchant Navy war risks bonus granted. Lady Cynthia Asquith diary 'I am beginning to rub my eyes at the prospects of peace' .
	N Sea — Rear-Adm Trotha CoS German High Seas Fleet recommends a 'final sortie' v Grand Fleet if U-boat campaign abandoned completely or Fleet threatened by a 'humiliating end'. Hipper sanctions (10) detailed planning for this *Flottenvorstoss* ('Fleet Attack'); Scheer's CoS Cmdre Levetzow supports (16, *see* 22). Scheer does not inform Army, Kaiser or politicians (*see* 18). **Med** — Adm Calthorpe leaves Malta in cruiser *Foresight*, arrives Mudros (11, *see* 15).	**W Front** — **RAF support Second Battle of Cambrai** incl **laying smokescreens** with 40lb phosphorous bombs, few air combats. Night bombers strike rail jctns (night 8/9).	Pres Wilson replies to German peace note, occupied territories evacuation first condition. Foch note gives his armistice terms to Allied PMs.	Hoffmann diary (Berlin) 'But they have all lost their nerve' .**Britain** — Food Controller takes over milk distribution.
		Germany — 8 Handley Pages of Nos 215 & 216 Sqns attack Metz, bomb detonates magazine on island in R Moselle, fire burns for 4 days (RM1m damage done, night 9/10). **Syria** — RAF bombs Homs stn (10 & 12) from new Haifa base, refuelling at Damascus. **W Front** — Mainly low-flying RAF ops, wet weather hampers flying (-13).	Prince Frederick Charles of Hesse elected King of Finland by *Lantag* (renounces crown 31 Dec).	Bank of England gold reserves war record £73.1m. **Germany** — Maj-Gen Scheuch succeeds Lt-Gen Stein as War Minister (*see* 17 Dec). Leading iron industrialists meet in Düsseldorf & decide to cultivate unions.
	Aegean — *UB48* (Steinbauer) torpedoes French battleship *Voltaire* (night 10/11) nr Cerigotto. **Irish Sea** — Irish packet *Leinster* sunk between Kingstown & Holyhead by U-boat in heavy seas (176 dead); SS *Dundalk* torpedoed (20). Kaiser & new liberal German Govt demand that Navy halt U-	**W Front** — German *JG4* (Schleich) fighter formation formed with *Jastas 23b, 32b, 34b* and *35b*.	Count Burian 'We must strive for the Germans concluding an armistice only under the condition that we also receive one'. Lord Grey speaks on League of Nations, peace in sight but not yet at hand.	**S Africa** — Flu epidemic.

OCTOBER 1918	WESTERN FRONT 1	EASTERN FRONT 2	SOUTHERN FRONTS 3	TURKISH FRONTS 4
Thu 10 contd	hilly Ardennes. **Flanders** — Battle of Flanders Ridges ends. **Somme/Cambrai** — British advance continues to last line of Hindenburg line (*Hermann* position) along R Selle; Horne's First Army fights its way along Sensée Canal to N (-16). British 66th Div retakes Le Cateau. **Meuse/Argonne** — **Over 1m Americans** (record 29 divs) **in action**, US Second Army (Bullard) formed (HQ Toul) for Meuse-Moselle sector. AEF holds record 101 miles.		Livunovo (Struma valley) in advance on Radomir (*see* 21). **Italian Front** — 21 divs, 1600 guns, 500 mortars & 2.4m shells moved up for offensive since 25 Sept (*see* 14).	
Fri 11	GERMANS forced by pressure on flanks into GENERAL WITHDRAWAL between Rs Oise & Meuse to *Hunding-Brunhild* line. **Flanders** — German Army & Marine units hasten evacuation of coastal bases & defences (ships & aircraft leave, guns moving since 7). **Artois** — 2nd Cdn Div (First Army) capture Iwuy, NE of Cambrai, before handing over to British XXII Corps; since 26 Aug Cdn Corps has gained 23 miles v 31 German divs in 47 days. For 30,806 cas since 22 Aug Canadians have captured 18,585 PoWs, 371 guns & almost 2000 MGs, liberating 116 sq miles with 54 towns & villages. **Champagne** — French advance up to 6 miles on 37-mile front, have taken 21,500 PoWs & 600 guns since 26 Sept, incl Italian reoccupation of Chemin des Dames.		**Bulgaria** — C-in-C Gen Gekov dismissed (had been on sick leave in Vienna). **Albania** — Austrians evacuate Durazzo (*see* 14).	
Sat 12	Hindenburg warns troops that favourable armistice terms depend on successful resistance. *OHL* sanctions Sixth Army retirement (begins early 15). Mudra replaces O Below (recalled to Germany to organize home defence) i/c Seventeenth Army. Eberhardt takes over Mudra's First Army. **Meuse/Argonne** — Pershing transfers First Army to Liggett. **Artois** — British First Army reaches Douai suburbs but is checked by German flooding (*see* 17).		**Serbia** — French Tranie Det occupies Pristina, French cav enter Pirot (13). **Italian Front** — More orders modify Italian offensive plans (*see* 18, 21). Diaz confers with his 9 army cdrs.	
Sun 13	**Aisne** — **French Tenth Army enters Laon** (pop 10,000) after 11-mile advance in 36hrs, presses N to R Serre (*see* 18), has taken 26,000 PoWs & 400 guns since 17 Aug. **Oise** — French First Army liberates La Fère.	**Siberia** — Adm Kolchak reaches Omsk (*see* 4 Nov). **Finland** — **Govt ask German troops to leave** (*see* 16 Nov).		**Syria** — Yeomanry Regt & armoured cars occupy Tripoli (19th Inf Bde arrive 18, whole 7th Indian Div by 28 having covered 270 miles since 19 Sept).
Mon 14	**Flanders** — BATTLE OF COURTRAI (-19): BEF Second Army (16 divs) & Franco-Belgians renew offensive at 0530 v German Fourth Army (16 divs) between Dixmude & R Lys; 12,000 PoWs & 550 guns taken in 18-mile advance (-19). French with tanks take Roulers rail jctn. **Selle** — German counter-attacks repulsed (& 16,*see* 17). **Meuse/Argonne** — US First Army attacks *Kriemhilde* Line, 32nd Div	**Siberia** — 25th Middlesex Regt reach Irkutsk. **Trans-Caspia** — Action of Dushak Stn (90 miles W of Merv): 550 British (204 cas), 9 guns & 1600 Whites (c30 cas) inflict 1000 Red cas & force their retreat (18), Whites reoccupy Tegend (20,*see* 1 Nov).	**Albania** — Italian *Tanaro* Bde occupies Durazzo from land side after defeating Austrian rearguard. *Palermo* Bde enters Tirana (15), finds Serb det which withdraws (*see* 31). **Piave** — Italians begin to bring up material for 24+ bridges & camouflage them (*see* 18 & 24).	

AFRICAN OPERATIONS 5	SEA WAR 6	AIR WAR 7	INTERNATIONAL EVENTS 8	HOME FRONTS 9
	boat attacks on passenger ships 'since any incident that might disrupt the peace negotiations is to be avoided at all costs'. Scheer replies that Navy will demonstrate its 'fullest loyalty' by recalling all commerce-raiding U-boats (*see* 15).			
		Persia — 3 RAF RE8s attack Turk cols (2 lost, but 3 aircrew walk 120 miles to safety).	New German Minister Erzberger announces German militarism is dead.	**Austria** — Hungarian & Austrian Govts resign on German acceptance of Wilsonian terms, but Emperor Charles keeps PM in de facto office & receives *Reichsrat* nationality deputations. **Canada** — Strikes & lockouts forbidden.
			Germany accepts Wilson conditions (message of 11 received 12, *see* 14). Luxembourg begs Wilson to protect her rights. Britain recognizes Polish National Army (in France) as an ally.	**USA** — 11,724 Army flu cases in past 24hrs, total since 13 Sept 234,868 (338,257 cases & c17,000 deaths by 1 Dec, *see* 1 Nov). Wilson attends Metropolitan Opera for Queen Margherita's Fund for the Blinded Soldiers of Italy. **Britain** — Lloyd George given list of rebels & revolutionaries, includes Sylvia Pankhurst, GDH Cole & unions. **Germany** — Ex-Interior Minister Delbrück replaces Berg as Kaiser's civil cabinet chief. **Austria** — In Transylvania Rumanian National Party demands recognition as admin (*see* INT'L EVENTS 16).
			Young Turks resign; Gen Izzet Pasha (War Minister 1913/14) replaces Talaat & Enver (*see* 2 Nov). Venizelos arrives in London.	**Portugal** — Govt crushes Democrat military rising in Lisbon, Oporto & Coimbra (-14) with 1000+ arrests, but violent crime already rampant.
Lettow reaches Pangire (Jacobi) Mission Stn after many Wangoni carriers go home; restocks supplies.	**N Sea** — British destroyers torpedo SS *Brussels* at Zeebrugge. 5 RN monitors (incl 2 with all-time heaviest 18in naval guns) shell Snaeskerke German btys for last time. **E Atlantic** — Portuguese auxiliary gunboat *Augusto de Castilho*, hopelessly outgunned & escorting passenger ship (saved), sunk in gallant duel with *U139* (Arnauld) between Madeira & Azores.	**Occupied Belgium** — **US Northern Bombing Gp flies first raid** (8 by 27), 100t bombs dropped (-11 Nov). RAF drop 2000+ bombs (40t) in Flanders offensive.	US Sec of State Lansing answers Germany's note (12) imposing further military conditions & will only deal with democratic govt (Berlin receives 15, *see* 17 & 20). **Turk armistice proposal note delivered at Washington** by Spanish Ambassador. HMG threatens reprisals if Germany does not redress PoW grievances within 4 weeks. (Germany threatens reprisals 23.) Mr Justice Youngers' 1918	**Britain** — King presents £10,000 to Red Cross (Prince of Wales £3000, 18). Colonial Sec W Long urges united 'Civil Secret Service', Thomson agrees, urges Director of Home Intelligence (15). **Austria** — Gen strike in Bohemia.

OCTOBER 1918	WESTERN FRONT 1	EASTERN FRONT 2	SOUTHERN FRONTS 3	TURKISH FRONTS 4
Mon 14 contd	storms Côte Dame Marie ridge (*see* 16).			
Tue 15	Since 26 Sept, 43 German div res divs committed. **Flanders** — British 34th Div return to Menin as to S Second Army reaches & crosses R Lys (-16), Belgian 3rd Div also reaches (-16).	**Volga** — **Krasnov's Don Cossack offensive threatens Tsaritsyn**; Vatsetis orders it not to be given up. **Occupied Poland** — Austrian Lublin Govt agrees to give Poles E districts (*see* 19).	**Serbia** — Serb First Army again in action with enemy incl Austrian 30th Div (from Ukraine), pursues (-18). First Allied train reaches Veles. **Salonika** — Milne & RN C-in-C Mediterranean Adm Calthorpe discuss combined ops v Turkey.	
Wed 16	**Flanders** — **Last German shelling of Dunkirk.** L/Cp Hitler (16th Bav Res Regt) w by BEF gas shell (evacuated half-blinded to Pasewalk hospital, Pomerania). **Aisne** — FRENCH (Gouraud) CROSS RIVER, storming Vouziers heights & capturing Grandpré. **Meuse** — AEF BREAKS THROUGH *KRIEMHILDE* LINES in fierce attacks (16, 17 & 18). German coy cdr writes home '... a quick end is to be hoped for, there is nothing more to be saved'. **Artois** — *OHL* orders Sixth and Seventeenth Armies to retreat into *Hermann* line.	CEC forms Unified Labour School. **Volga** — Red Fifth Army retakes Buyulma. Zhloba's Steel Div (arrived from N Caucasus) surprise attack causes 1500 Cossack cas 12 miles from Tsaritsyn and temporarily saves city.	**Greece** — Proclamation announces clearance of Bulgars. **Bulgaria** — French 54th Colonial Inf Regt (17th Div) enters Sofia; 227th Inf Regt reinforce (18).	(c) 2 British officer PoWs exchanged from Smyrna to Alexandria having feigned madness (famous 1919 book *Road to Endor*). **Syria** — British 5th Cav Div col reaches Homs. **Armenia** — Gen Andranik harrassing Turk communications around Erivan (*see* 24). **Arabia** — British given Fakhri Pasha (Medina) cable to Ibn Saud offering help.
Thu 17	**Flanders** — **Belgians reoccupy Ostend.** British Second Army reach Tourcoing outskirts. Allied advance since 14 has turned Lille defences, BEF FIFTH ARMY (57th Div) OCCUPIES LILLE without firing a shot (Clemenceau visits 20,*see* 24). **Selle** — BATTLE OF THE SELLE (-25): BEF Fourth, Third & First Armies (8th Div occupies Douai and Canadians cross Sensée Canal) & US II Corps assault *Hermann* position at 0530 (*see* 20) on 10-mile front S from Le Cateau (captured) & line 3 miles to E (18) with 5000 PoWs & 60 guns. Full German Cabinet: LUDENDORFF DEMANDS A FIGHT TO THE FINISH denounces Wilson's 2nd Note & declares '... on my conscience a breakthrough [by Allies] is unlikely'; in 4wks campaigning season will be over; that, provided with promised reinforcements he can retire to Antwerp-Meuse Line, to resume in spring 1919. If necessary, Belgium must again become a battleground 'so that 1914 will be child's play compared to it'. Ludendorff, interrogated by Imperial Chancellor, calls situation grave but not hopeless ('perhaps Germany's luck may return'). War Minister Scheuch says c600,000 reinforcements raisable but warns that if Rumanian oil ... is cut off Army (& Air Force) can only continue ops for another 6wks (*see* INT'L EVENTS 20 & S FRONTS 19). **Britain** — K George V becomes Col-in-Chief, Tank Corps.	British War Cabinet E Ctee decide to stop Bicharakov subsidy.	**Serbia** — Franco-Serbs liberate Krusevac & Knjazevac. **Montenegro** — Rising v Austrians as French liberate Ipek with 600 PoWs.	

AFRICAN OPERATIONS 5	SEA WAR 6	AIR WAR 7	INTERNATIONAL EVENTS 8	HOME FRONTS 9
			PoW Report published, reveals ill-treatment close to front line under British fire. **France** — Czech Prov Govt formed (*see* 17). **Neutrals: Spain** — 7 German ships taken over in agreed compensation.	
	Lloyd George letter to Clemenceau insists a British admiral shall command in Aegean; French PM refuses (21), LG insists (25).		US says she will continue to ship 250,000 troops pm to Europe.	**Germany** — **Imperial Order subjects military to civil authority**. 1500 Berliners die of flu. **Austria** — Hungarian PM Wekerle arrives in Vienna & gets manifesto exemption for Hungarian crown lands.
	N Sea — RN submarine *L12* sinks *U90* in Skagerrak, *G2* likewise dispatches *U78* (28). **Germany** — Fast lt cruiser *Frauenlob II* launched at Kiel.		**Austria** — **Emperor Charles' 'Peoples' Manifesto'** proclaims federations with 6 self-governing nationalities, but Transylvania to remain Hungary's, & Austrian PM denounces.	Berlin peace demos; Federal Council accepts amended constitution limiting Kaiser's rights (*see* 28).
Lettow leaves Ubena (Maj-Gen Wahle left with other sick & w, KAR coy captures 18) & reaches Kidugala. KAR coy surprises Müller's rearguard nr Njombe.	**N Sea** — **German Navy evacuates Ostend, Zeebrugge & Bruges**, abandoning 9 coastal torpedo boats. **Med** — Austrian U-boats ordered home.	**W Front** — (c) **Rain & mist restricts flying** (-27) **& aids retreating Germans.** RAF pilots land at Ghistelles, Ghent & in Ostend market sq, just as Germans leave.	Kaiser, Ludendorff & Prince Max confer on reply to US note (*see* W FRONT). **Austria** — **Czechs proclaim Republic at Prague** (Council in Paris declares formal independence 18 *see* 27 & 28); Hungarian Parlt declares independence except for Crown as figurehead.	**Britain** — Londoners raise £31m in National War Bonds in 9 days at Trafalgar Square ruined French village replica. **Italy** — Upper Adige Germans Ctee present local autonomy plan (*see* 18 Nov).

OCTOBER 1918	WESTERN FRONT 1	EASTERN FRONT 2	SOUTHERN FRONTS 3	TURKISH FRONTS 4
Fri 18	Mangin's French Tenth Army wins final victory breaking *Hunding* line astride R Serre (Czechs in action 22), N of Laon. Mangin & HQ withdrawn for planned Lorraine offensive (27, *see* 20). Rupprecht letter to Chancellor describes exhausted troops short of arty, horses, ammo, fuel & officers, ends '... we must obtain peace before the enemy breaks into Germany'. Foch moves his HQ N to Senlis.	Lenin tells Berlin envoy to increase publications hundredfold and writes to Spartacus Group (*see* 23). **N Russia** — Murmansk Allies advance to Sovoka.	**Bulgaria — Last Germans leave. Italian Front** — Heavy rain postpones Allied offensive to 24 (*see* 21).	Allenby orders advance to Aleppo for 20. **Mesopotamia** — Gen Cobbe completes preparations for final Mosul op v Turks 35 miles to N (*see* 23).
Sat 19	FOCH'S LAST GENERAL DIRECTIVE to his 14 armies. Haig visits CIGS & War Cabinet in London, considers 'enemy was not ready for unconditional surrender' but urges terms for 1918 armistice to prevent winter recovery by Germany. **Lys** — Ludendorff directs Rupprecht to hold *Hermann* Lys position for at least 8 days as Plumer's Second Army forces river in 6-mile advance taking Courtrai (20). **Flanders — Belgians occupy Zeebrugge & Bruges** (K Albert flies in 23). **Artois** — 4th Cdn Div liberates Denain in record day's advance of nearly 7 miles; Prince of Wales attends thanksgiving ceremony.	**Galicia** — Ukrainian National Council at Lemberg assumes control of E. Austrian Ukraine independence declared (23).	**French** (227th Inf Regt by rail from Sofia) **reach Danube** at Lom-Palanka (Bulgaria), capture convoy of lighters (21); d'Esperey reports first French guns heard on Danube since 1809. Jouinot-Gambetta's cav reach Danube at Vidin (21) after 437-mile march in 36 days.	**Mesopotamia — Germans withdraw** all 1200 advisers, planes, guns & transport (-21). **S Persia** — Despite flu (1453 sick 23) British occupy Ahram, but Zair Khidar & Wassmuss have fled; c1000 British leave Shiraz (20) to relieve Firuzabad from 2000 tribesmen (25) before flu strikes (*see* 20 Dec).
Sun 20	ALL BELGIAN COAST IN ALLIED HANDS, Belgian N wing on Dutch frontier. **Selle** — 2nd phase (-22): British storm *Hermann* line & extend advance to N (-25); Third Army (7 divs) crosses Selle (4 tanks support) & captures Solesmes. US 27th & 30th Divs withdrawn to rest (11,500 cas since 27 Sept). **Lorraine** — Foch directs Pétain to prepare to launch offensive as latter requested (14). **Meuse/Argonne** — US losses now 54,158.	**Urals — Heavily-mauled Czech 4th Regt mutinies**, 1st Regt soon follows.	**Serbia** — Battle of Paracin (-23): Serb First Army attacks strong counter-attacking German rearguards in Upper Morava valley. Serb Second Army relieves French at Pristina before advance to W Morava valley via Kossovo.	Gen Townshend (freed 18) & Turk ADC sails into Mytilene then Mudros for separate peace talks as Izzet Pasha's envoy. **Syria** — British 5th Cav Div (2500) repairs R Orontes bridge (-21) 10 miles N of Homs, is 5 miles N of Hama 40 miles on (21).
Mon 21	**Meuse/Argonne** — Clemenceau, furious at AEF lack of progress, asks Foch to appeal for Pershing's removal; the Generalissimo declines.	**Lithuania** — Police fire on Polish demo in Vilna. **Siberia** — Maj-Gen Knox arrives in Omsk, gets White C-in-C Gen Boldyrev to resign in Gen Janin's favour.	**Bulgaria** — British 26th Div arrives by rail (-23) at Mustapha Pasha on Bulgar-Turk frontier W of Adrianople (*see* 28) where garrison of only I bn & 2 guns. **Italian Front** — Diaz's final orders stress aim 'to separate the Austrian forces on the Trentino from those on the Piave'.	
Tue 22	**Scheldt** — British First Army closes in on Valenciennes, 3rd Cdn Div clears Fôret de Raismes in 4-mile advance.	Lenin addresses CEC, Moscow Soviet, factory ctees & unions 'Three months ago people used to laugh when we said there might be a revolution in Germany.' **Occupied Poland** — Swierzynski forms National Democratic anti-German cabinet (*see* 8).	**Italian Front** — 2 Croat regts refuse to relieve 2 other Austrian regts in trenches, but soon made obedient (*see* 23, 26, 27).	**Syria** — British armoured cars capture Turk armoured car & 2 lorries after 15-mile running fight halfway to Aleppo. **Aden** — 75th Carnatic Inf lose 50 cas at Imad until rescued from Turks & Arabs by 26th Cav (*see* 8 Dec).

AFRICAN OPERATIONS 5	SEA WAR 6	AIR WAR 7	INTERNATIONAL EVENTS 8	HOME FRONTS 9
Lettow learns of Bulgaria's surrender from captured newspapers.	**N Sea** — Scheer deceives the Kaiser: 'The Fleet shall again become available for other tasks' (ie the final sortie) if ending U-boat warfare not followed by an immediate ceasefire. *UB123* sunk on Northern Barrage. **Adriatic** — 16 RN destroyers leave Otranto Barrage (mine net barrage completed to Fano I) for Aegean, 24 trawlers follow.	**W Front** — RAF Handley Pages drop 4t bombs on Namur rail stn & Charleroi. **Aegean — Last RAF raid** (10th since July) **on Constantinople**, 12 DHs report hits on War Office & rail stn.	Wilson rejects Austrian peace note; recognizes Czechs at war with Empire. **Hungary** — Rumanian Transylvanian Deputy reads independence declaration in Parlt.	**Britain** — Bonar Law drops luxury duties in Budget. **France** — War Minister empowered to suspend court martial sentences. **USA** — War Dept says soldier overseas costs $423.47pa, 1 at home $327.78.
		Syria — 2 Australian No 1 Sqn Bristol Fighters destroy German 2-seater 25 miles SW of Aleppo (bombed 23), & Babannet airfield to N attacked. **Britain** — Canadian W Front ace Quigley (34 victories) dies of 'flu. **First torpedo plane sqn** (20 Sopwith Cuckoos) **embarked in British carrier *Argus*. W Front** — K Albert letter to Curzon praises RAF support in Allied victory of 28-30 Sept.	**Rumania** — At Jassy Nat Ctee of Rumanian Emigrants demands Transylvania's union with Rumania.	Kaiser tells Prince Max envoy 'A successor of Frederick the Great does not abdicate' **Britain** — Govt decides to sell some of its ships after the war to depleted private companies. **USA** — 4th Liberty Loan ends after estimated 20m people contribute. **France** — Clemenceau visits devastated Lens.
1/4th KAR take over pursuit from Tandala with 200-mile to-in school atlas.	ALL U-BOATS ORDERED HOME by Scheer (17 recalled), *UB86* last outwardbound boat to cross Northern Barrage for Irish Sea. **Channel** — RN monitor *M21* strikes 2 mines off Ostend, towed back to Dover but sinks.		**3rd German note accepts US conditions** (of 14) including renunciation of U-boat war (Washington receives 22). **Neutrals** — Denmark proposes Schleswig-Holstein plebiscite.	**Turkey** — **General amnesty to exiles & refugees** (part of Izzet Pasha Govt programme read to Assembly (19). Press meet & agree to act together (21).
	Irish Sea: Last merchant ship (coaster *Saint Barcham*, 8 lost) **sunk by U-boat in British home waters.** Beatty insists to War Cabinet meeting on German Fleet's surrender as well as all U-boats and Heligoland.	**Germany** — 7 DH9As (No 100 Sqn) FTR (4 lost to fighters) from daylight Frankfurt raid.	K George receives Allied Parliamentary delegates in London. **Occupied Belgium** — German Gov Gen 'pardons' Belgians & neutrals convicted by court martial (Belgian reparations bill already nearly £400m).	Ludendorff approves Scheer U-boat plan, inc release of skilled workers from front. Kaiser meets *Reichstag* at Berlin Bellevue Palace, ISP leader says 'Crowns are rolling about the floor'. **Austria** — **German Austrians declare independence at Vienna** & form National Provincial Assembly (2nd mtg passes fundamental laws 30). **France** — *Le Matin*'s 'Panorama of the Battle of Liberation' map posted up in Paris. **Britain** — Beaverbrook resigns as Information Minister (ill health). Labour Minister reports that Special Branch & GHQ Home Forces preparing supply of auxilliary labour. Thomson (Special Branch) writes that working-class morale 'Probably at its highest point', but warns of union strike plans.
	N Sea — Levetzow delivers verbal operational order (Operations Plan No 19) to Hipper at Wilhelmshaven: **'High Seas Fleet shall attack and engage in battle the English Fleet.'** Nothing is to be allowed to delay the op because the country 'is rushing toward an	**Adriatic** — 142 Italian flying boats & 56 Caproni bombers raid Pola (*see* 24).	Prince Max says Germany will not submit to a 'peace of violence', Alsatian Gov for Alsace-Lorraine, bill for *Reichstag's* greater share in govt. K Albert thanks Belgian Relief Commission on its 4th anniversary for saving nation from starvation.	**Germany** — **Liebknecht released in general amnesty.** Chancellor presents *Reichstag* with constitutional reform, equal suffrage voted (26). **Austria** — Czech Socialist Klofac tells Emperor Czech lands slipping away from Crown. **Britain** — New l0s note design issued.

OCTOBER 1918	WESTERN FRONT 1	EASTERN FRONT 2	SOUTHERN FRONTS 3	TURKISH FRONTS 4
Thu 22 contd				
Wed 23	**Selle** — 3rd phase: Byng's Third Army (incl 6 tanks) attacks Forest & Ovillers, captures Grand Champ Ridge, Rawlinson's 18th Div (with 6 tanks) captures Bousies. BEF drives 6-mile deep, 35-mile wide breach into German line (-24).	Lenin telephones Berlin envoy to congratulate Karl Liebknecht on his release. Stalin rejoins Lenin in Moscow, asks for S Front reinstatement (*see* 17 Nov).	**Serbia** — Serbs liberate Paracin, Kraljevo & Zajecar. **Montenegro** — German rearguard of LXII Corps reaches Adriatic at Teodo Bay after epic march from S Serbia, shipped to Fiume. Austrians evacuate San Giovanni di Medua. **Italian Front** — Mutinous Croat troops seize Fiume but are suppressed. Emperor Charles cables Pope to prevent offensive & issues last appeal to troops 'The people of the Monarchy have always found their country in her army'.	**Syria** — GOC 5th Cav Div MacAndrew summons Aleppo to surrender but Ismet Pasha refuses. 54th (E Anglian) Div marches from Haifa for Beirut (31). **Mesopotamia** — Cobbe's 18,400 troops & 136 guns ready for attack astride Tigris, but Hakki Bey's 2600 Turks & 26 guns retreat (-24) to Humur, 20 miles NW (*see* 25).
Thu 24	Ludendorff telegram to troops for continued resistance v Allied unconditional surrender demands never sent. **Artois** — Portuguese bns attached to BEF Fifth Army bdes for first action since Apr, take part in official Allied entry into Lille (28).		**Italian Front** — BATTLE OF VITTORIO VENETO (THIRD PIAVE) (-4 Nov) begins in rain on Caporetto 1st anniversary at 0500 with 1402-gun shelling on Mt Grappa sector & at 0700 Fourth Army inf assault on 13-mile front gains little ground & 1800 PoWs v fierce, skilled defence. 2 **British** bns **seize** N half of **Papadopoli I in Piave** & 6 Italian bns Caserta I (night 23/24) & take 350 PoWs, but Austrian arty destroys most bridges. On Asiago Anglo-French diversion takes 1000 PoWs.	**By now new Turk Govt withdrawing 4 divs from Armenia/Azerbaijan** (Germany informed) & Enzeli advance abandoned, only 3 divs left in Caucasus after early Oct advance N to Derbent.
Fri 25	Foch, Haig, Pétain & Pershing meet at Senlis, formulate stiff proposals incl surrender of arty, railway stock & U-boats, agree to preventing fresh fighting after any armistice. **Selle** — 4th phase ends: 24 British divs have forced 31 German divs well back from river & stand in outskirts of Valenciennes & Le Quesnoy & S edge of Mormal Forest. Total captures: 20,000 PoWs & 475 guns. LAST EFFECTIVE GERMAN LINE OF DEFENCE ON W FRONT BROKEN. **Flanders** — British Second Army success at Ooteghem (*see* 31). **Oise** — French 79th Regt (XX Corps, First Army) with 4 tanks storms Villers-le-Sec in *Hunding* Line, taking 150 PoWs, 1 gun, 58 MGs & 1 mortar for 40 cas despite counter-attack.		**Austro-German retreat over Sava & Danube** (-1 Nov) by bridges & streamers between Smederovo & Sabac covered by river monitors. Serbs reach Kragujevac 60 miles to S of Danube (*see* 28). **Salonika** — First 5 Indian bns from Mesopotamia land. **Piave** — British overrun rest of Papadopoli I (night 25/26) but flooding river delays main crossing. Italian Grappa attacks continue at heavy cost capturing & losing Mt Asolone again with 600 PoWs, *Pesaro* Bde & *Arditi* take Mt Pertica; Austrian *Edelweiss* Alpine Div thrown into battle.	**Syria** — Col Nuri Bey's 1500 Arabs enter Aleppo at 2nd attempt but again driven out by Kemal as 500 British cav join armoured cars 13 miles SW. **Mesopotamia** — British armoured cars approach Sharqat from desert as 40th Bde (13th Div) again takes Kirkuk.
Sat 26	LUDENDORFF RESIGNS as First QMG & *de facto* C-in-C W Front (*see* INT'L EVENTS). **Succeeded by Gröner** whose railway expertise proves invaluable during the retreat. Kaiser refuses Hindenburg's tendered resignation. BEF GHQ: Churchill chairs senior gas officer conference (flies home 30).	Sovnarkom authorizes issue of 35.5bn roubles in bank notes, levies 10bn rouble tax on bourgeoisie (30), and decrees universal labour duty (31). **N Caucasus** — Soviet C-in-C Sorokin shoots 5 members of Republic's CEC during breakout attempt N, is outlawed and shoots himself (c2 Nov, *see* 18 Nov).	**Piave** — Italian Grappa attacks mainly fail, gaining only Peak 1186 & Col del Cuc (Aosta *Alpini* Bn 568 cas to date). FM Boroevic thanks defenders, confident 'that they would convince the enemy that their blood had been shed in vain', but 3 Hungarian divs ask to be withdrawn home (-27). Italians begin 4 bridges (Middle Piave).	**3 Turk envoys begin armistice talks at Mudros** (-30). **Syria** — **British enter Aleppo** at 1000 after c1000 Turks leave; 500 Jodhpur & Mysore Lancers (80 cas) charge Kemal's 3000 Turks & 8 guns N of city at Haritan but beaten off after lancing 50 & taking 20. **Mesopotamia** — Cassels' 1000 cav & 6 guns (11th Cav Bde) ford mile-wide Tigris 13 miles N of Sharqat after 83-mile ride in 2 days as 17th Indian Div (-27) repulsed from Turk Humur line with 618 cas.

AFRICAN OPERATIONS 5	SEA WAR 6	AIR WAR 7	INTERNATIONAL EVENTS 8	HOME FRONTS 9
	armistice at full speed' (*see* 29). Plan envisages coordinated raids into Thames Estuary and down Flanders coast with 22 U-boats off Scotland. **Adriatic** — Italian warships shell S Giovanni di Medua, Albania as Austrians evacuate.			
	N Sea — Harwich Force last in action. Though weather prevents its seaplanes taking off & 3 of 4 Camels broken on lighters, German aircraft driven off (*see* 7 Nov). **Adriatic** — **Austrian Fleet discipline breaking down with demands to go home. Secret War** — Admiralty warns Beatty of German Fleet sortie preparation.	**W Front** — More activity than for several weeks, RAF No 20 Sqn's Bristol Fighters destroy 5 Fokkers for no loss, Hirson rail jctn bombed. Handley Page destroys Kaiserslautern Greist munitions factory with 1650lb bomb (night 21/22). Similar devastation in Wiesbaden city centre (nights 23/24, 49 cas). Prince Albert flies in Handley Page to join IAF HQ nr Nancy (*see* 26).	**Wilson refers German note** (of 20) **to Allies suggesting armistice terms be drafted** (*see* W FRONT 24). Balfour speech at Anzac lunch says Germany's colonies can never be returned.	**Britain** — **Commons votes 274-24 for women MPs**. **Hungary** — PM Wekerle resigns (*see* 31). Emperor Charles & Zita open Debrecen University. **USA** — Chaplin secretly marries actress Mildred Harris at Los Angeles (announced 9 Nov).
		Italian Front — **600 Allied aircraft** (93 Anglo-French) **support final offensive**; wreak havoc among fleeing Austrian columns (esp 29-30). RAF drop 20,000lb bombs & fire 51,000rnds, losing 7 aircraft (-4 Nov).	Austrian Foreign Minister Count Burian resigns, Count Andrassy succeeds.	**Germany** — Mark drops to 33 to £. **Britain** — Cheap housing scheme announced. Red Cross 'Our Day' appeal.
	Med — **Scheer orders all seaworthy Med U-boats to sail home,** 12 do so (29-31, *see* 9 Nov).	**Mesopotamia** — c1500 Turks attacked by RAF (1 SE5 damaged).		**Germany** — Papers publish Ludendorff appeal to fight on. Chancellor goes to Kaiser, either Govt or Ludendorff resign. **Hungary** — Independence Party forms National Council under Karolyi. **Britain** — Lord d'Abernon outlines partial postwar retention of liquor control measures. **USA** — 4339 AEF wounded landed since 1. Wilson open letter calls for Democrat Congress majority, Republicans say using war to party advantage (26, *see* 5 Nov).
		France — **Trenchard appointed C-in-C Inter-Allied Indep Air Force** under Foch.	LUDENDORFF RESIGNS in Berlin: Kaiser says 'The operation is done. I have split the Siamese twins'. K of Montenegro's manifesto backs confederated Yugoslavia with autonomous states. **USA** — Mid-European Union meets in Independence Hall, Philadelphia, under Masaryk, resolves on united action. **France** — US special rep arrives in Paris where Clemenceau & Poincaré receive Foch's armistice text.	Emperor Charles leaves Budapest with Karolyi for Vienna in court train (his children return by car 31). **Britain** — 2225 London flu deaths since 20.

OCTOBER 1918	WESTERN FRONT 1	EASTERN FRONT 2	SOUTHERN FRONTS 3	TURKISH FRONTS 4
Sun 27	German attack NW of Le Quesnoy repulsed. **Aisne** — French Fifth Army attacks on 7½-mile front NW of Château Porcien (W of Rethel), major bombing of Seraincourt to NW (28). **Meuse/Argonne** — US 78th Div (c5000 cas) captures Grandpré after fighting since 25.	**N Russia** — R Scots surprise attack on Topsa fails.	**Piave** — Austrian counter-attacks recapture Mt Pertica (briefly), Istrice & Valderoa (600 PoWs). After wading across from 0645 **Italians & British form 3 bridgeheads over Piave** up to 2½ miles deep, taking 7800 PoWs & 74 guns. Austrian guns destroy 3 bridges by 0800 but parts of 2 Austrian divs refuse to counter-attack. Eighth & Twelfth Armies rely on swimmers (82 *Caimani di Piave*) & air supply as 5 new bridges shortlived, only allowing 17 bns to cross (night 27/28).	Count Bernstorff leaves German Constantinople Embassy. **Syria** — Australian Mtd Div leaves Damascus for Alexandretta (nr Homs 31). Kemal retreats 3 miles W of Haritan & 5 miles farther (28-30); covers Alexandretta with 4 very weak divs (c8000). **Mesopotamia** — Cassels blocks Turk attacks on both sides, but 17th Div still 25 miles S.
Mon 28	**Scheldt** — British 51st Div captures Mont Houy S of Valenciennes but driven back to S slopes, 3 German divs counter-attack (-29).		**Serbia** — Serbs reach line Uzice-Arandelovac-Pozarevac. **Albania** — Italians enter Alessio (*see* 31). **Bulgaria** — **British 22nd Div lands at Dedeagach** (sailed from Stavros) from 17 destroyers (after 2 bad weather postponements) **for invasion of European Turkey** 10 miles away, transport & cav arrive (30) after gruelling overland march (*see* 31). French Army of the Danube formed under Berthelot (-25 Jan 1920). **Piave** — Italian XVIII Corps reinforces Anglo-Italian Papadopoli bridgehead, taking 3000 PoWs, 7 guns & 150 MGs with aid of British barrage. **Austrian Sixth Army orders retreat** at 2030 after Italians join up the 3 bridgeheads & are up to 4 miles from river. King watches ops from Montello. Austrian Armistice Commission meets. Boroevic tells Emperor Charles situation 'untenable' (night 28/29).	**Mesopotamia** — **Battle of Sharqat** (-30): 1/7th Gurkhas ferried over to Cassels after 33-mile march in 21hrs as he fights 6000 Turks & 24 guns from Mosul.
Tue 29	**Oise** — French First Army (Debeney) retakes Guise.	**Volga** — Tukachevski's Red First Army retakes Buguruslan and Buzuluk.	AT 0830 AUSTRIANS SEEK ARMISTICE: Capt Ruggera takes white flag to Italian lines at Serravak in Adige valley. **Piave** — *Calabria* Bde storms Mt Asolone (Grappa), but loses it to Austrians; Italians suspend ops in sleet & fog after 24,500 cas. All 21 Italian Eighth Army bridges rebuilt as Austrian guns fall silent (night 28/29) & British cross R Monticano by intact bridge after beating 2-div counter-attack. Italians play for time as Austrian collapse worsens. French capture Segusina with 3000 PoWs & 18 guns. Austrian GHQ announces decision 'to evacuate the Veneto...to show its goodwill towards peace' (*see* INT'L EVENTS 29). Italian general 5-mile advance captures Conegliano & Susegana. **Salonika** — Lt-Gen T M Bridges arrives to be British Military Mission Chief to Franchet d'Esperey.	**Mesopotamia** — British 7th Cav Bde (c 3100) storms Cemetery Hill on foot taking 990 PoWs & 12 MGs as 3000 men of 17th Div (509 cas) make slow progress v 4000 Turks. **Syria/Palestine** — EEF has 4345 motor vehicles & 1523 motor cycles.
Wed 30	**Lorraine** — German 18th *Landwehr* Div refuses to enter line. Pershing exhorts Supreme War Council to continue Allied offensive until Germany is compelled to surrender unconditionally: 'An armistice would revivify the low spirits of the German Army and enable it to reorganize and resist later on ...' **Flanders** — US 37th & 91st		**Piave** — **Italian *Firenze* lancers & *Bersaglieri* cyclists enter Vittorio Veneto** (old Austrian Sixth Army HQ). Third Army storms Lower Piave at 4 points as Italian cav & armoured cars begin pursuit; Austrian Sixth Army split in two. PoWs total 33,000. Austrian Belluno Gp begins general retreat (night 30/31). Austrian	ARMISTICE SIGNED AT 2140 aboard battleship HMS *Agamemnon* in Mudros harbour; 25 clauses begin with Dardanelles opening and occupation (published 2 Nov). **Mesopotamia** — **Turk Tigris Group** (Col Ismail Hakki Bey) **surrenders at Sharqat**: 11,321 PoWs, 51 guns, 130 MGs, 2000 animals for 1886 British cas

AFRICAN OPERATIONS 5	SEA WAR 6	AIR WAR 7	INTERNATIONAL EVENTS 8	HOME FRONTS 9
		W Front — Cdn Maj W Barker in Snipe of No 201 Sqn single-handedly battles 5 formations totalling c60 aircraft over Mormal Forest. He shoots down 4 (50 victories total), receives 3 wounds, & crashlands behind British lines (VC awarded 30 Nov). **Italian Front** — 6 RE8s drop 5000rnds by parachute to forward British troops. 9 Camels destroy 3 Austrian balloons. Austrians bomb Allied Piave bridges without success.	Emperor Charles cables Kaiser 'My people are neither capable nor willing to continue the war…. I have made the unalterable decision to ask for a separate peace and an immediate armistice'. AUSTRIA ASKS FOR ARMISTICE (via Stockholm) AS DOES GERMANY. **Austria** — Lammasch succeeds Hussarek (resigned) as PM (-31), receives Czech Ambassador (30).	
	N Sea — Final U-boat sortie: Flanders Flotilla *UB116* (Emsmann) with volunteer crew undertakes 'suicide' mission v Grand Fleet flagship *Queen Elizabeth* (erroneously believed lying at Scapa). Raider destroyed in electrically-controlled minefield. **Adriatic** — German personnel evacuate Pola, Cattaro ones sail (30), scuttle 10 U-boats there & at Fiume (-1 Nov).	**W Front** — 3 Fokkers (2 lost) intercept DH9s (1 lost) over Mons & RAF No 205 Sqn bombs Namur (-30).	Allied armistice Conference in Paris (-30). **Austria** — Galicia severed from Empire. Czech Nat Council at Prague takes over internal administration. CZECHOSLOVAKIA INDE-PENDENT.	**Germany** — **Kaiser signs amended constitution**, says '…(his) office is one of service to German people', but at Hindenburg's request returns to Spa by train (29) refusing to meet Prince Max. **Austria** — Agram military command surrender to Yugoslav Council (*see* INT'L EVENTS 29). **France** — BEF march past in liberated Lille (Churchill present). **Canada** — 5th War Loan.
	Allied Naval Council prepares naval armistice terms (-4 Nov). **N Sea** — High Seas Fleet prepares for 'death or glory sortie', but already passive resistance hampering it in all battleships & 3 small cruisers. Red Flags hoisted in dreadnoughts *Thüringen* & *Helgoland*.	**Germany** — 14 Indep Air Force aircraft bomb 9 different targets (night 29/30, 40+ cas). **W Front** — German fighters (2 lost) turn back No 107 Sqn's DH9s (1 escort lost) from Mariembourg, but bombed (30). **Italian Front** — Seaplane sqn CO Lt Casagrande Eugenio completes last of 15 agent landing/recovery ops behind Austrian Piave lines since 30 July.	YUGOSLAV INDEPENDENCE DECLARED by Nat Council at Agram. Slovak Nat Council votes for union. EMPEROR CHARLES ASKS DIAZ FOR ARMISTICE. Arz cables Hindenburg that Austrian Army in Italy finished, over half divs refuse to fight (*see* S FRONTS).	**Hungary** — Emperor Charles makes Hadik PM (-31) & Archduke Joseph Regent. **Britain** — Doctors to be increased for civil work. 13,000 Liverpool wood workers win strike (-2 Nov) v national aircraft factory bonus system.
	N Sea — Room 40 intercepts **High Seas Fleet** 0800 signal. 'All officers on board the Flagship' as first hint of mutiny. **Order to leave port defied five times** & crews too denuded by 1000 arrests to do so (-31, *see* 2 Nov). Hipper disperses Fleet to the Elbe, Kiel & Wilhemshaven.	**W Front** — Dolphin fighters of No 19 Sqn & DH9s (No 98) attacked by many German fighters (10 lost) covering vital rail targets; 10 Dolphins & 4 DH9s FTR; 2 DH9s crashland, but 12 Bristol Fighters (88 Sqn) destroy 9 of c17 Fokkers over Tournai for no loss. 62 RAF aircraft (3 FTR) attack Rebaix airfield N of Ath, hit 4 hangars &	German note to US says armistice terms awaited. **Austria** — Fiume declares independence & desires union check with Italy (*see* 5 Nov). **Emperor Charles gives Fleet to Yugloslav Nat Council (***see* SEA WAR 31), **Danube Flotilla to Hungarians; allows officers to serve in new national armies** (*see* 2 Nov).	Kaiser 'I would not dream of abandoning the throne because of a few hundred Jews and a 1000 workers'. Socialist S German newspaper says 'We have lost the war'. **Austria** — Vienna workers & students demo v Habsburgs. **Japan** — Kawasaki launches 9000 dwt SS *Raifuku Maru* at Kobe, laid down 7 Oct. One of 233

OCTOBER 1918	WESTERN FRONT 1	EASTERN FRONT 2	SOUTHERN FRONTS 3	TURKISH FRONTS 4
Wed 30 contd	Divs suffer 2593 cas in final Allied advance (-11 Nov).		Armistice Delegates reach Villa Giusti nr Padua at 2000. **Adriatic** — Hungarians surrender Fiume to Croats. **Balkans** — 122,000 Austrian troops (5½ inf +1 cav divs) & 540 guns in Albania and Serbia v 144,000 Italians & 373 guns among 730,850 Allies & 1883 guns.	since 23 incl 7th Cav Bde 16-mile N pursuit taking 1200.
Thu 31	(Oct) ALLIES have CAPTURED 108,343 POWS & 2064 GUNS. Since 1 Aug BEF has taken 172,659 PoWs, 2378 guns, 17,000 MGs, 2750 mortars and suffered 358,149 cas (121,046 in Oct). Kaiser leaves Berlin (for last time) by train for *OHL* at Spa. Foch tells Supreme War Council: '... since July 18 we have forced the enemy to retreat. We have attacked him along 400 kilometres and we are continuing to do so...we can continue it if the foe desires it right up to their complete defeat ...'. **Flanders** — British Second Army success at Tieghem takes 1000 PoWs as it reaches R Scheldt. Allies have taken 19,000 PoWs & advanced 31 miles since 14.		**Piave** — Italian Fourth & Sixth Armies occupy empty Austrian Grappa & Asiago lines, by 1700 2 *Alpini* bns clear Feltre. British & Italians reach R Livenza. British recapture Sacile. **Albania** — Italians & Serbs capture Scutari (*see* 1 Nov). **Bulgaria** — 2 British & 1 French div on R Maritsa close to Turk frontier (*see* TURK FRONTS).	HOSTILITIES CEASE NOON LOCAL TIME. Liman hands over to Kemal at Adana, repatriation of 10,000 Germans begins. **Mesopotamia** — Only 3280 Turks & 44 guns est in Mosul or en route. Gen Lewin occupies Altun Kopri on Little Zab. **S Persia** — 600 British (35 cas), 4 guns & 2 MGs take Lardeh village & 30 PoWs (-1 Nov).
Fri 1 November 1918	FOCH'S PLAN FOR FINAL PHASE OF GENERAL OFFENSIVE (-11): major thrusts by BEF in N & AEF in S, both supported by French armies on their flanks. BEF is to force the Scheldt, advance to Maubeuge & press on to seize Meuse crossings from Namur to Dinant. If taken before Germans evacuate Flanders they are to be pressed back against border of neutral Holland & captured. In S, US First & French Fourth Armies to advance by forced marches to seize Mézières & Sedan, so isolating Germans facing French Centre Army Gp & sever the great lateral railway Bruges-Ghent-Maubeuge-Mézières-Metz, key artery to half of W Front. **Scheldt** — BATTLE OF VALENCIENNES (-3): Haig turns Scheldt defences (*Hermann* position) & pushes E & N to Maubeuge, Mons & R Dendre. BEF Third & First Armies attack on 6-mile front & reach Valenciennes outskirts (4th Cdn Div captures Mont Houy) despite German 28th Res Div counter-attack with 4 (captured BEF) tanks (2 lost), last such effort. BEF Fourth Army's 32nd Div & 3 tanks attacks Happegarbes Spur SW of Landrecies. Constant rain (-11). **Aisne/ Meuse** — FRANCO-US OFFENSIVE begins: US First Army (7 divs) with 19 tanks & r wing of French Fourth Army; US V Corps in centre, drives a 5-mile deep wedge into German lines astride Bourgogne Wood incl **first AEF use of mustard gas** (41t of gas, 36,000rnds), as 4 German divs overrun. US 5th Div crosses Meuse isolating Dun-sur-Meuse (*see* 4).	(Nov) 2 German divs transfer to W Front (1-11). **N Russia** — (Nov) A A Samoilo made C-in-C Sixth Detached Red Army (HQ Vologda). Red W Front formed and Ukrainian Soviet Army (late Nov). **Don** — Red Army takes offensive v Denisov's Great Don Host (50,000). **Trans-Caspia** — (c) British & Whites reoccupy Merv (*see* 17). **Siberia** — British War Cabinet decide to recognize Prov Govt (*see* 18). **Russia** — (early Nov) Communist Youth League *Kom somol* founded, 100,000 members by end 1919.	SERBS LIBERATE BEL-GRADE & SERBIA: Bojovic's First Army enters as last Austrian boats reach Hungarian shore & engages Austrian monitors from Topcider btys; Second Army reaches R Drina in W. **Italian Front** — *Comando Supremo* receives Allied armistice terms by telephone from Paris by 0615, Badoglio tells Austrians' actual text available only on 2nd. Allies progress on Asiago plateau, Italians reoccupy Belluno & Longarone. Last Austrian GHQ communiqué 'In the Veneto the evacuation operations proceed'.	**Mesopotamia** — MEF ration strength 222,399 comprising 102,034 British, 305 Anzacs, 120,060 Indians with 366 guns & 183 mortars (1 Oct); plus 185,739 followers. British occupy Ana on Euphrates and reach 12 miles S of Mosul. **Azerbaijan** — At Baku Nuri Pasha retitles himself C-in-C Azerbaijan Army; Marshall refuses to recognize change (6). **Palestine** — Land transfer forbidden in Jerusalem *sanjak* (province).

AFRICAN OPERATIONS 5	SEA WAR 6	AIR WAR 7	INTERNATIONAL EVENTS 8	HOME FRONTS 9
		destroy 9 aircraft in air. c30 German fighters scatter 2 DH9 sqns (2 bombers & 4 fighter escorts shot down). Lt Degelow downs RAF DH4, wins last of 75 air *Pour le Mérite* awards. **RAF claims record 67 German aircraft for loss of 41.**		steamers built 1914-18.
Lettow sends patrol v Fife (N Rhodesia) as his pursuers reported on Neu Langenburg-Rwiba road.	**Austrian Fleet at Pola transferred to S Slav National Council** in Agram. Non S-Slavs free to go home, ships fully illuminated for first time, Adm Horthy makes farewell signal, relinquishes command at c1645. Allied and neutral shipping Oct losses to U-boats, 52 ships (23 British with 318 lives) worth 112,427t (British total all causes 25 ships worth 59,229); U-boat figure 73 ships worth 116,237t. **Lowest monthly tonnage score since July 1916**; 5 U-boats sunk.	**Germany** — 9 bombs from No 55 Sqn DHs cause 86 cas at Bonn. **W Front** — (Oct) **Record 5,360,000 leaflets dropped by Allied balloons**; AEF reports 80% German PoWs with one by 15, BEF say 12% of theirs. RAF losses 161 aircraft, French 40.	REVOLUTIONS IN VIENNA & BUDAPEST; Red Guards murder Count Tisza in latter. Polish troops occupy Cracow. Slovenes in Laibach Nat Assembly proclaim independence.	**Britain** — (Oct) Over 10,000 ships reported as repaired since June 1917. Shipbuilding up nearly 50% over 1917, little change in jobs or days lost. **Hungary** — **Emperor Charles appoints Count Karolyi new PM. Austria** — Egon Schiele, Expressionist painter and soldier, aged 28 from flu at Vienna. 700,000 PoWs have returned from Russia since 3 Mar.
Lettow recces Fife. KAR strength record 35,424 (22 bns). British ration strength 26,234 (10,697 British & S Africans, 1262 Indians, 14,275 Africans), 5 guns, 16 mortars & 222 MGs with 37,690 followers. **W Africa** — 2nd WA Bde (4 bns & 4 guns) formed for Palestine under Brig-Gen Rose. **Morocco** — Abd-el-Malek flees into Spanish zone, his 11 German advisers desert to Mellila after 11.	**Adriatic** — **Italian frogmen** Paolucci & Rossetti mine, capsize & **sink former Austrian flagship *Viribis Unitis*** (Capt Vukovic, Yugoslav Fleet cdr) in Pola harbour & liner *Wien*.	**W Front** — DH9s bomb Brussels rail stn & Maubeuge. **N Russia** — (Nov) 2 air sqns (White & RAF + 6 Camels late Nov) go into action above Dvina Force. **W Front** — Fonck's 75th & final victory, a German leaflet-dropping 2-seater. **Germany/Black Sea/Med** — German Naval Air Service 1478 aircraft & seaplanes with 16,122 men (2116 aircrew) at 32 seaplane & 17 land air bases.	**K Boris of Bulgaria abdicates**; Peasant Party leader Stamboliski becomes PM at Tirnova. **Serbia** — Great Serb National Council proclaimed at Sarajevo. **Diplomacy** — Versailles Conference opens. Baron Flotow provisionally succeeds Count Andrassy as Austrian Foreign Minister. (c) Supreme Allied Council for Supply & Relief formed.	**Turkey** — **Talaat Pasha** addresses last Congress of Party of Union & Progress, **admits massacre of innocent Armenians by many officials** (*see* TURK FRONTS 2). **USA** — 306,719 Army flu cases since 12 Sept, 19,429 deaths. **Britain** — RFP up 4% to 133%. Shipbuilding control transferred from Admiralty to Shipping Ministry.

NOVEMBER 1918	WESTERN FRONT 1	EASTERN FRONT 2	SOUTHERN FRONTS 3	TURKISH FRONTS 4
Sat 2	**Aisne/Meuse** — Germans retreat before US I Corps which captures Buzancy & links with French Fourth Army. **Sambre — Mutiny of E Front reinforcements** for German Seventeenth Army: they have to be disarmed by a storm bn. **Scheldt** — Cdn Corps (c380 cas) captures Valenciennes with 1800 PoWs & 7 guns, 800+ German k.	**Poland** — Regency Council orders forming of regular standing army. Republic's Directorate formed at Cracow (*see* 8). **Lithuania** — State Council retracts Duke of Württemberg's election as King vests power in 3-man Ctee (5) who invite Prof Voldemar to form govt (*see* 11). **Russia** — Sovnarkom appropriates 1bn roubles for collective farming & abolishes private trade (21).	Allied Supreme War Council (-4) approves plan for up to 40 Italian divs (incl 5 British & French) to invade Bavaria from Innsbruck & Salzburg areas in early 1919 under Foch's direction. **Italian Front** — Italian First Army begins advance, occupies Rovereto & Calliano in Adige valley (night 1/2) & Col Santo. Italian Seventh Army begins advance W of L Garda, captures Mt Pari nr it. First armistice meeting 2100-0300 (night 2/3), Austrians reluctantly accept 24hr delay for end of hostilities.	**Enver, Talaat & Djemal leave Constantinople in German naval ship for Ukraine.** **Mesopotamia** — Marshall gets full armistice terms; Gen Cassels sees Ali Ihsan, arranges advance to within 2 miles of Mosul.
Sun 3	**Flanders — Belgians reach outskirts of Ghent. Aisne/ Argonne** — Franco-American offensive ends: Lille-Metz rail line severed. French IX Corps takes Basancourt Farm.	Lenin addresses rally to honour Austrian revolution: 'The time is near when the first day of the world revolution will be celebrated everywhere.' **Bukovina** — Ukrainians seize Czernowitz.	AUSTRIAN ARMISTICE SIGNED AT 1800 by Gens Weber & Badoglio at Diaz's Villa Giusti HQ nr Padua. Austrian Army Gp cdrs suspend hostilities from 0330. Italians (from Venice) land at Trieste, occupy Trento. British 48th Div completes haul of 23,000 PoWs with 14 bns. Italian cav cross Tagliamento & regain Udine.	**Egypt** — Saad Zaghlul Pasha demands independence from British High Commissioner (refuses to see Egyptian nationalist delegation 27).
Mon 4	**Sambre** — BATTLE OF THE SAMBRE: British Fourth (3 divs with 26 tanks & 6 armd cars, 1200 cas), Third (8 divs with 11 tanks) & First Armies (6 divs) attack on 30-mile front from E of Valenciennes to Guise; Landrecies falls to 600 men of 25th Div. NZ Div storms Le Quesnoy taking 2500 PoWs & 100 guns. **Lt W Owen** (Manchester Regt), **war poet, k** aged 25 by MG fire at Sambre Canal assault. BEF 5-mile advance captures 10,000 PoWs & 200 guns. Haig orders Plumer to be ready to cross R Scheldt c11. German Second Army begins retreat to Antwerp-Meuse position (night 4/5). **Meuse/Argonne — Franco-Americ**ans clear Argonne; AEF take Stenay & Dun-sur-Meuse.	British Admiralty asked to send ships to Baltic (*see* 13, 20, 22). **Siberia** — Kolchak joins Prov Govt as War & Navy Minister (*see* 18).	AUSTRO-ALLIED HOSTILI-TIES END AT 1500. Diaz cables Paris that Italy will intervene to enforce Germany's armistice terms if necessary. **Italian Front** — US 332nd Inf Regt gets into action a few hours before ceasefire, capturing Austrian MGs on E bank of R Tagliamento (*see* 13). Italian 1st & 4th Cav Divs reach frontier in Carnia & Caporetto beyond. Italian 54th Div captures 10,000 Austrians at Muzzanella bridge W of coastal frontier after Cdr Borghese cuts road with Bafile Bn & *Arditi* (3-4) who are forced to surrender at 0800. **Montenegro** — Serb Second Army liberates Cetinje (capital, *see* 8).	Liman reaches Constantinople, put i/c evacuation; most Germans have or are sailing to Odessa (-19). **Mesopotamia** — **British** under Gen Fanshawe **enter Mosul** (Marshall arrives 7).
Tue 5	**Sambre — Pursuit after Battle of the Sambre begins**: BEF Fourth, Third & First Armies engaged; Mormal Forest cleared. Cdn Corps & 3 British divs with tanks force R Grand Honnelle (mainly just inside Belgium) (-7). French take Château-Porcien (Aisne). *OHL* ORDERS GENERAL RETIREMENT INTO ANT-WERP-MEUSE POSITION (issued 0400). Foch given 'supreme strategical direction of all forces operating against Germany on all fronts'.		**Bulgaria** — British bn occupies Black Sea port of Varna, sails on to Constanza (13).	**Syria** — Whole British 54th Div now at Beirut.

AFRICAN OPERATIONS 5	SEA WAR 6	AIR WAR 7	INTERNATIONAL EVENTS 8	HOME FRONTS 9
Lettow bombards Fife in N Rhodesia but declines to assault (premature shell explodes mortar) while 1/4th KAR 23 miles to E. **Lettow advances into N Rhodesia** with 400 cattle; at Mwenzo Mission increases quinine supply to over 30lb (enough to last to June 1919).	**Baltic** — Mass meeting of 3rd Sqn sailors in Waldweisse meadow, Kiel. Stoker Karl Artelt urges men to persist for their imprisoned shipmates' release & gain support from shipyard workers; 5 other speakers demand continuing resistance & refusal to obey orders (reactionary officers deserve to be 'clubbed to death'), and an immediate end to war. Kiel Governor Adm Souchon (of *Goeben* fame) attempts to disperse crowd with 2 naval inf coys, but both units refuse to open fire. **Constantinople** — Germans hand over *Goeben* & U-boats to Turks.	**W Front** — **First attempted 'cloud' (blind) bombing** (using dead reckoning): lone DH9a of No 99 Sqn RAF drops 3 x 112lb bombs in area of Avricourt rail jctn & nearby dump.	Emperor Charles at Schönbrunn receives Allied abdication demand & 5 Austrian State Council leaders who refuse to share armistice responsibility. **Neutrals: Switzerland** — Prince Windischgrätz talks to Allied envoys at Berne (-7) until latter reply that Empire's peoples have decided.	**Austria** — 69th Hungarian Inf Regt deserts Schönbrunn Palace (Hungarian troops later officially allowed to go home) but Wiener Neustadt military cadets (military academies close) replace them. Emperor Charles refuses Archduke Joseph's call to abdicate as King of Hungary. Slovenes take over Carniola Province. **Germany** — Hindenburg appeals for unity. Unions & industrialists demand demobilization office instead of Imperial Economic Office (*see* 7). **USA** — New York's worst subway accident (97k, 100 injured).
	Baltic — GERMAN NAVY MUTINY AT KIEL: 3000 sailors & workers converge on Waldweisse in Kiel; a USPD rep & shipyard workers proclaim solidarity. The elated crowd then marches towards Feldstrasse naval gaol, but is fired on in Karlstrasse by 48 officer cadets & shipmates (Lt Steinhauser), 8k, 39 wounded. Crowd retaliates with stones & a few rifle shots (Steinhauser k), then disperses. **Adriatic** — **Italian Navy** from Venice, Ancona, Brindisi & Albania **begins occupying 32 Dalmatian Islands & Adriatic ports** (-5 Dec) beginning with Trieste & Pelagosa I (4 small craft) & Lissa I.		AUSTRIAN ARMISTICE WITH ALLIES signed at noon (effective 4, published 6) after **Emperor Charles relinquishes supreme command to Arz** (Kövess nominated 4). **Allies agree to Germans request for armistice.** Republic declared at Warsaw. Serb Govt re-enters Belgrade. Yugoslav Republic declared at Agram (*see* 7). **Occupied Rumania** — Mackensen proposes immediate evacuation (US decrypt message, Mackensen receives Rumanian ultimatum 9 & begins pullout 10, *see* 16 Dec).	**Britain** — National jam rationing to 15 Apr 1919 (4oz per adult pw). Lloyd George tells Northcliffe 'to go to Hades' when he requests peace terms propaganda campaign (*see* 4 & 12).
	Baltic — Enraged by 'Karlstrasse Bloodbath' thousands of sailors, 20,000 garrison troops & workers join Kiel mutiny. Crew of battleship *Grosser Kurfurst* overpower their officers & march to Karlstrasse to swear an oath of vengeance. At mass meeting in 1st Torpedo Div, Artelt demands immediate establishment of a 'sailors' council'. Officers attempting to silence him are savagely disarmed. Council elected with Artelt as chairman drafts programme of '14 demands'. Troops of 1st Dock Div arrive but refuse to fire, hand over their weapons. Even the staunchly loyal U-boat Div now turns against officer corps. At 1345 Kiel town Cmndt informs Souchon 'The mutiny ... continues to spread ... we no longer possess any reliable troops...'. Souchon dismissed & replaced by Socialist Gustav Noske.	**W Front** — Air activity revives after mist & rain (2-3).	ALLIED-AUSTRIAN HOSTILI-TIES END. US recognizes Polish Army as co-belligerent. Chile seizes 84 German interned merchant ships.	**Germany** — KIEL MUTINY: Revolution spreads to Lübeck & Travemünde (5), Hamburg, Bremen, Cuxhaven, Wilhelmshaven (6), *Landwehr* & workers. Gen Gröner goes to Berlin & learns no armistice if Kaiser does not abdicate; meets Chancellor Ebert (6). Stuttgart founds 1st Workers Council. **Austria** — High mass at St Stephen's Cathedral for Emperor's name day. **Britain** — Northcliffe's 'From Peace to War' tirade v PM in *Daily Mail* & *The Times*.
	Adriatic — **Italians enter Pola**. **Baltic** — Capt Weniger and 2 other officers of battleship *König*, shot dead while attempting to prevent hoisting of red flag on their ship (Kiel town cadet also k by sailors 6 Nov). Kaiser's brother Grand Adm Prince Heinrich flees in a truck flying the red flag. **N Sea** — British carrier *Campania* sunk in collision with battleship HMS *Revenge*, Firth of Forth.		Lloyd George announces Armistice conditions in Commons. **Wilson tells Germany she must apply to Foch for terms.** USA recognizes Rumanian Unity National Council (Britain 11, Italy 22). Soviet Ambassador Yoffe expelled from Germany for subversion, but gives Independent Socialists 4m roubles for propaganda (6).	**USA** — Congress elections oust Democrat majority in both Houses. **Germany** — General strike in Berlin. Chancellor dissuades Kaiser from 'suicidal' scheme of ordering 'Lion of Flanders' Adm Schröder to retake Kiel with few hundred combat troops.

NOVEMBER 1918	WESTERN FRONT 1	EASTERN FRONT 2	SOUTHERN FRONTS 3	TURKISH FRONTS 4
Tue 5 contd	GENERAL RETREAT OF GERMANS from the Meuse to Condé on the Scheldt begins, French Centre Army Gp joins in pursuit. Gröner in Berlin informs German Cabinet '… one thing must not be allowed to happen. The American Army…must be prevented from advancing north of Verdun`. **Meuse/Argonne** — MacArthur i/c 42nd 'Rainbow' Div (-22) on advancing US I flank after AEF link with Gouraud.			
Wed 6	**Meuse** — US 1st DIV REACHES SEDAN: traffic halted on key Mézières-Montmédy railway; only line to W Front still available S of Ardennes; 4 German armies are virtually cut off. Army Group Gallwitz ordered to retire to Antwerp-Meuse position. Gröner warns Chancellor: '… even Monday will be too late [for an armistice], it must be Saturday at the latest'. **Scheldt** — **Canadians enter Belgium**, forcing Rivers Aunelle & Honelle N of Valenciennes-Mons road; they take 1750 PoWs from 7 German divs (1-8). **Sambre** — British Third Army makes v limited advances owing to Seventeenth Army rearguards & repeated shelling of river crossings; added to heavy rain, bad roads & limited room for manoeuvre. **Oise-Aisne** — French recapture Vervins & Rethel. **Lorraine** — Foch decides to attack as soon as possible & assigns troops from US Second Army (see 14).	Lenin tells 6th Soviet Congress 'Germany has caught fire, and Austria is burning out of control.' **Caspian** — 5 RN ships reach Petrovsk (N Caucasus) to fetch Bicherakov (see TURK FRONTS 12).		**French High Commissioner in Syria & Armenia, Picot, lands at Beirut** (see 14). **Georgia** — 15th Bavarian *Jägers* begin 4-month march home via Ukraine.
Thu 7	Germans radio Foch with names of armistice envoys, (leave Spa at noon) he stipulates they must come to Forest of Compiègne. Haig orders that on 8th 'The Fourth, Third and First Armies should continue their present operations…reaching the line Avesnes-Maubeuge-Mons (Avesnes road): advanced guards and mounted troops should then be pushed forward beyond …to keep touch with the enemy…the Fifth and Second Armies… with the Flanders Group of Armies should on the 11th November…force a passage of the Scheldt and then drive the enemy back over the river Dendre.' **Sambre** — British advance 5 miles through Avesnes & Bavai to Haumont, 3 miles W of Maubeuge. **Scheldt** — German arty 'hate shoot' on Oudenarde, heavy civilian cas. At 1915 Pétain cables '..Res Army Gp is to support the British right wing, making its principal effort by the Chimay gap [before Givet on Meuse]; Centre Army Gp is to secure Mézières, Charleville & Sedan & establish bridgehead on the Meuse'. **Meuse/Argonne** — US 29th Div & French 10th Colonial Div meet on Borne de Cornoiuller (15,000 US cas since 26 Sept) above Meuse after fighting since 3. US Third Army formed. **France etc** —	Lenin unveils Marx & Engel's statue before Bolshoi Theatre, singing in Red Sq to mark 1st anniversary of revolution. **Siberia** — Pres Asksentiev appeals to US for recognition.	Franchet d'Esperey & Serb Crown Prince enter Belgrade under triumphal arches & meet Karolyi's Hungarian delegation (see 10) which left Budapest (5), hand them the armistice terms (see 13). **Austria** — Austrians inform Italians that elements of II Bavarian Corps approaching Brenner Pass (see 10).	**Allenby makes Anglo-French declaration of Eastern Peoples' liberation** from Turk oppression. **Syria** — *Yilderim* & Seventh Army HQs closed, Kemal recalled to Constantinople, Nihad Pasha i/c Second Army takes over.

AFRICAN OPERATIONS 5	SEA WAR 6	AIR WAR 7	INTERNATIONAL EVENTS 8	HOME FRONTS 9
Lettow's main body at Kajambi Catholic Mission (missionaries had fled); Capt Köhl's rearguard has patrol skirmish.			**K Peter re-enters Belgrade. Rumania** — Marghiloman Govt resigns at Jassy, Gen Coanda succeeds.	**Austria — Emperor formally demobilizes armed forces. Britain — Lloyd George** lunches & dines **ministers**; they **agree to call General Election. Germany** — A dozen sailors persuade all 12,000 workers at Hamburg's Blohm & Voss shipyard to down tools.
	N Sea — Harwich Force sorties (-8) but cannot prevent some German steamers interning themselves in Holland by sailing in Dutch territorial waters. **First Sea Lord** Adm Sir R **Wemyss made British Naval Representative for Armistice talks.** Beatty writes 'The Fleet, my Fleet, is broken-hearted [at being denied battle], but are still wonderful, the most wonderful thing in creation.'		BAVARIA DECLARED REPUBLIC by Prussian Jew Kurt Eisner at Munich as K Ludwig III flees into Austria (formally deposed 8, 'abdicates' 16). Yugloslav Conference at Geneva decides on joint govt (*see* 23).	**Germany** — Majority Socialists demand Kaiser & Prime Minister's abdication by noon 8, resign from *Reichstag* & call General Strike (8). **Demobiliza- tion Office set up**. Gen Linsingen i/c Brandenburg forbids Soviets. **Sailors seize Cologne despite 45,000- strong garrison. USA** — False armistice celebrated in New York due to erroneous UP dispatch. **Britain** — Labour Ministry forms Civil Demobiliza- tion & Resettlement Dept. Churchill announces munitions 'carry on at reduced speed' (not less than halftime 9, in force 11, *see* 21). **Alsace** — Pro-French demo at Stras- bourg.

NOVEMBER 1918	WESTERN FRONT 1	EASTERN FRONT 2	SOUTHERN FRONTS 3	TURKISH FRONTS 4
Thu 7 contd	Record 190,564 US soldiers in 23 hospitals & 21 hospital trains. French Army has 185 hospital trains (8 in 1914).			
Fri 8	GERMAN ARMISTICE DELEGATION led by Erzberger SEES FOCH at 0900, refer terms to Berlin 1300. GERMAN SENIOR CDRS UNANI-MOUSLY IMPLY TO IMPERIAL CHANCELLOR THAT ARMY CANNOT BE RELIED ON, IF ORDERED, TO SUPPRESS UPRISINGS AT HOME. **Germans retire from** *Hermann* **position**. (Oudenarde-Tournai-Condé). **BEF begins advance to Armistice Line** (18,000 PoWs taken since 1). **US Second & First Armies & 4 French Armies begin final advance**. **Sambre** — British 32nd Div (Fourth Army) captures Avesnes. **Scheldt** — Germans begin withdrawing opposite BEF Fifth Army at 0200. British patrols soon discover abandoned German bridgehead W of Antoing-Tournai, British quickly reach W bank from Bruyelle to Froyennes & cross river.	**Poland tells Austria she has assumed sovereignty over Galicia.**	*The Times* publishes Bishop of London's letter vindicating British Salonika Army's ordeal, but message lost in subsequent Armistice euphoria. **Bulgaria** — British 79th Bde reaches Ruschuk on Danube (-12), rest of 26th Div arrives by 26 (*see* 27). **Herzegovina** — Serbs occupy Cattaro (*see* 19).	Izzet Pasha resigns having refused to dismiss remaining Young Turk ministers. **Azerbaijan** — Marshall ordered to reoccupy Baku as soon as possible. Turk evacuation to Batumi begins. British warn Nuri Pasha (9) to evacuate Baku by 17.
Sat 9	KAISER 'ABDICATES' following a final showdown with Hindenburg & Gröner at *OHL* Spa (after 39 div/bde & regt COs give Army's opinion). Hindenburg offers to resign rather than say that situation both at the front & at home is hopeless. Gröner boldly states 'The Army will march back home under its own generals in good order but not under the leadership of Your Majesty'. Kaiser retorts 'I require that statement in writing, I want all the commanding generals to state...that the Army no longer stands behind its Supreme Commander. Has it not taken an oath on the colours?' Gröner replies that in this situation oaths lose their meaning (see INT'L EVENTS). **Scheldt** — Germans in general retreat on British Second Army front; British take Tournai. **Sambre** — Gds Div bn (Third Army) occupies Maubeuge. BEF Fourth Army organizes Maj-Gen Bethell's mobile force (incl 5th Cav Bde & 5 armd cars) to pursue Germans across Belgian frontier E of Avesnes (-11). **Aisne** — French capture Hirson rail jctn.	**Poland** — Govt formed at Lublin. **Urals** — Czechs at Ekaterinburg proclaim national independence. Kolchak visits & presents new colours to 4 Czech regts (10).		Anglo-French declaration on future of Syria & Mesopotamia. **Syria** — Small Anglo-French force occupies Alexandretta (*see* 14).
Sun 10	German Chancellor radios Armistice delegation after 1800 to sign. **Flanders** — BELGIANS REOCCUPY GHENT. **Sambre** — CANADIAN 3rd DIV (264 Cdn cas) ENTERS MONS overcoming diehard MG squads; town cleared of German 62nd Regt (12th Div) by dawn 11. **Meuse** — **Gouraud's right wing** (French Fourth Army) **reaches Mézières**; Germans abandon gun parks, huge store dumps & rolling stock. **US First Army assault crosses Meuse.**	Lenin cables to 'All Soviets of Deputies, to Everyone' hails German Revolution. **Poland** — Pilsudski arrives in Warsaw.	**Allies cross Danube**: 2 French bns at Ruschuk into Rumania (also at Sistova & Nikopol 11), Serb First Army crosses unopposed around Belgrade into Hungary. Some German troops cross Austrian frontier into N Tyrol but soon dissolve into desertion & Italians occupy Brenner Pass where CO 4th Bavarian Div says he will retire to Germany on 11.	**Sultan appoints Tewfik Pasha** (ex-London Ambassador) **to form pro-Allied govt** (Assembly approves 18). **Mesopotamia** — **Turks evacuate Mosul** for Nisibis.

AFRICAN OPERATIONS 5	SEA WAR 6	AIR WAR 7	INTERNATIONAL EVENTS 8	HOME FRONTS 9
			German Armistice delegates reach Foch's HQ. Prince Max's proclamation to Germans abroad. K of Württemberg & Duke of Brunswick abdicate. Pilsudski released from Magdeburg fortress to Berlin, arrives Warsaw 10 (*see* 12). Wilson cables congratulations to new govts at Vienna, Budapest & Prague. British Blockade Minister warns enemy ships' transfer will not be recognized.	**Germany** — **Revolutionaries seize 11 major cities.** Munich crowd demand Kaiser's abdication. Troops occupy Berlin essential services. Bavarian bns reach Brenner Pass to guard it v Allies but go home (10). Belgian Brussels Burgomaster Adolphe Max escapes from Goslar (*see* 21). **Austria** — War Minister & Emperor order that new loyalty oath replaces imperial one. **Britain** — Final wartime import restrictions (first relaxation 14).
Capt Spangenberg's 3 coys take Kasama (100 miles SW of Abercorn), a little ammo & 20 Boer wagons. 1/4th KAR (Maj Hawkins & 750 all ranks) fords R Chambezi guided by Rhodesian settler.	Kaiser tells Scheer (at Spa) 'I no longer have a Navy'. Hipper's flagship hoists red flag and he goes ashore. **E Atlantic — Last U-boat sunk:** *U34* (sinker of 121 ships of 262,886t since 1915) sunk off Gibraltar by British ex-Q-ship *Privet* & MLs. British battleship *Britannia* sunk (40men lost to toxic smoke) by *UB50* (Kukat) off Cape Trafalgar, but stays afloat 3½ hrs. **N Sea** — Grand Fleet heavily afflicted by flu, 2 captains die. U-boat Cmdre Michelsen orders last c20 loyal U-boats + small craft to home ports.	**W Front** — RAF 80th Wing bombs troops & transport on crowded Ath-Enghien road, Enghien rail stn & 2 airfields nearby.	KAISER 'ABDICATES', REVOLUTION IN BERLIN as **Scheidemann proclaims German Republic** from *Reichstag* , Prince Max becomes Regent (having announced Kaiser's 'abdication') & Ebert becomes Chancellor. Gen Gröner tells Kaiser at Spa Army will not follow him ('Treason, gentlemen, barefaced treason!'). **Saxony declared a Republic** (*see* 13). Eisner PM & Foreign Minister in Bavaria. Lloyd George in Guildhall speech says Germany's choice immediate surrender or worse fate. Wilson directs Hoover to Europe (in London 23) for food relief.	**Germany** — BERLIN REVOLUTION. **Prince Max hands Chancellorship to Ebert.** Liebknecht Sparticists seize Old Palace & hang red flag. Republic of Hesse declared. Krupp Works at Essen close; Gustav Krupp decides to keep pre-war workers (10) & sends 70,000 (inc 30,000+ Poles) home with 2 weeks pay & rail tickets (-18). **France** — †War poet Guillaume Apollinaire from flu after March 1916 headwound (38). **Austria** — Emperor to his advisers 'I will not abdicate and I will not flee the country' (*see* 11). **Britain** — Lloyd George on Kaiser's 'abdication' 'Was there ever a more dramatic judgment?' **Italy** — PM Orlando Rome speech claims 'it is a Roman victory'.
	N Sea — Paddle minesweeper HMS *Ascot* (53 lost) sunk by *UB67* off NE England. **Britain** — Naval staff discuss desirability of abolishing the submarine. **W Med** — Newly arrived Brazilian Sqn fires in error on US submarine chasers during ASW op.	**Germany** — 11 DH4s (1 FTR) of No 55 Sqn bomb railways at Ehrang. Low cloud, mist & heavy flak prevent them reaching Cologne; 5k, 7inj in central Metz by Handley Page bomber (night 10/11).	**Kaiser crosses into Holland** at Eysdin at about 0700 with 70 staff in 11 cars, waits for & reboards imperial train for journey through Liège (Crown Prince follows him 12 with 4 staff). **K of Rumania announces nation has resumed war on Allied side** (Gen Berthelot crosses Danube in Wallachia). **Czechoslovakia** — Masaryk elected Pres in Geneva (*see* 14). 2 Hungarian divs drive 1100 Czechoslovaks from Slovakia. **Occupied Belgium** — German troops	Belgian Govt sequestrates all enemy property. **Italy** — Mussolini one of several Milan victory speakers.

NOVEMBER 1918	WESTERN FRONT 1	EASTERN FRONT 2	SOUTHERN FRONTS 3	TURKISH FRONTS 4
Sun 10 contd	**Moselle** — US Second Army (Bullard), incl 92nd (Negro) Div (1000 cas), attacks towards Briey Basin (blast furnaces & iron ore workings). **Lorraine** — Mangin gives Legion *RMLE* its 9th, final & record citation in Army Orders, unit in sight of Metz (11).			
Mon 11	ARMISTICE SIGNED in Foch's *wagon lit* at Rethondes, Compiègne Forest at 0505, COMES INTO FORCE 1100 & fighting ceases all along front. Allied line from Selzaete & Ghent to Thann & Swiss border: BEF stands on 55-mile line; Franco-Belgian frontier E of Avesnes-Jeumont-Givry, 4 miles E of Mons (captured by 3rd Cdn Div & 5th Lancers) - Chièvres 4 miles E of Ath-Lessines (captured at 1055 with 150 PoWs) - Grammont. Since 18 July Allied Armies have taken 385,500 PoWs & 6615 guns (BEF share totals 188,700 PoWs & 2840 guns). Pétain weeps in frustration that Armistice has denied 'decisive' victory, but at 2000 writes GHQ order **'Closed due to victory'**. **Meuse** — Vanguards of US Second Army & 3 French corps are within 6 miles of Montmédy. AEF strength 1,981,701 (1,078,222 combat troops).	Germans have 26 divs from Finland to Georgia, Austrians have 7 divs in Ukraine. **Britain recognizes Latvia. Poland** — Directorate formed at Warsaw, deposes Regency Council. **Lithuania** — Hoffmann diary (Kovno) 'A Soldiers' Council has been formed here also.' **N Russia** — Archangel Allies (53 cas) at Kurgomin-Tulgas (R Dvina) repulse 1000 Reds (600+ cas) & gunboats.	**Balkans** — 80,000 Germans (53 bns or 6 divs) & 338 guns on SE (Danube) front. British effective other ranks strength 103,996 (1 Nov ration strength 158,707).	Adm Calthorpe to be British High Commissioner, Constantinople.
Tue 12	Foch's Message to Allied Armies: 'You have won the greatest battle in history and saved the most sacred cause: World Freedom.' Lt-Gen Sir R Haking British delegation chief to Permanent International Armistice Commission.	**Poland** — Pogroms reported.		**Allied Fleet** (60 ships) **passes the Dardanelles. Caspian** — Bicherakov's 8500 troops & 3000 refugees & 3 gunboats arrive at Enzeli. **S Persia** — Bushire reinforcements from India arrive (-23) & occupy Mallu Pass (18).
Wed 13	Germans begin retreating passing through Dutch Limburg (*see* 19 Dec).	**Soviet CEC repudiates Brest-Litovsk Treaty. Baltic States** — Britain decides to supply arms (*see* 20). **Finland** — Dictator Svinhufvud resigns (*see* 11 Dec).	**Hungary signs final Central Powers' armistice** at Belgrade, FM Mišić & Gen Henrys sign for Allies. French Army of Hungary formed (-10 Sept 1919). **Italians & Serbs occupy Fiume**, Serbs withdraw (19); US 2nd Bn, 332nd Infantry and British bn arrive from Venice to keep peace (26). **Bulgaria** — Italian 35th Div reaches Kustendil to be main Allied occupation force (-July 1919) & rescues Italian PoWs from old Austrian Empire.	**Allied Fleet arrives at Constantinople** (landing parties 14) as does Kemal, who says 'They will go as they have come'. Liman meets Gen Curry in Pera suburb.
Thu 14	Retiring Germans blow up munition dump at Jamioulx, S of Namur (*see* 18). Foch warns	**Ukraine** — Hetman Skoropadski tries to change sides, but Denikin & Whites		**Syria** — French Armenian bn lands at Alexandretta. Picot cables Paris '... send 20,000

AFRICAN OPERATIONS 5	SEA WAR 6	AIR WAR 7	INTERNATIONAL EVENTS 8	HOME FRONTS 9
			hoist red flag in Brussels. **Britain** — Mannerheim arrives at Aberdeen.	
Lettow cycles into Kasama. Armistice news reaches Deventer. **Morocco** — †Spanish zone High Commissioner Gen Jordana at his desk.	ARMISTICE TERMS stipulate delivery of 11 German battleships, 5 battlecruisers, 8 cruisers, 50 destroyers (all modern warships) & all U-boats to internment (see 20 & 21). Germany to retain only 6 battleships, 6 cruisers & 24 destroyers (all oldest classes). Record 20 Q-ships under SNO Scotland. Germany has 171 U-boats plus 149 building. **Britain** — Lt cruiser *Carlisle* completed by Fairfield Yd, joins Harwich Force (see 26). **N Sea** — Naval Council of 21 i/c at Wilhemshaven.	**W Front** — **French Breguet 14** (Minier) **carries German plenipotentiary** Maj Geyer from Tergnier to German GHQ at Spa **with Armistice terms.** They include IMMEDIATE DEMOBILIZATION OF GERMAN ARMY AIR SERVICE & SURRENDER OF 2000 FIGHTERS & BOMBERS (eventually reduced to 1700). Special importance is attached to confiscation of all Fokker DVIIs & Zeppelins — **2713 planes handed over by 16 Jan 1919**. RAF now has 22,647 aircraft (incl trainers), (1576 serviceable out of 1789 on W Front) with 291,170 personel (54,075 in France). French first-line strength 4511 aircraft & 61,000 men in 80 fighter, 32 bomber & 146 recon sqns; German 2390 (2709 estab) incl 1134-1296 fighters & 168 bombers in 284 flying units with c4500 airmen. Since 16 May French 1st Air Div (600 aircraft) alone has claimed 637 German aircraft & 125 balloons, dropping 1360t of bombs.	ARMISTICE SIGNED AT 0505, HOSTILITIES END 1100. Germans to evacuate France & Low Countries in 14 days. New German Foreign Minister Dr Solf appeals for lighter terms & immediate talks (12). EMPEROR CHARLES RENOUNCES RULE (& as K of Hungary 13). PM Lammasch & last Imperial Cabinet resign. Wilson Washington speech says Allies will feed Central Europe. **Neutrals** — Bolshevik Swiss Mission expelled. Kaiser given refuge at Count Bentinck's Amerongen moated house nr Utrecht. **Occupied Belgium** — First German Army Soviet at Malines.	**USA** — AP flash brings armistice news at 0300. Wilson reads terms to joint session of Congress. Greatest nationwide celebration ever known. **Britain** — King's message to Empire. Joyous pandemonium in London & elsewhere from 1100. CIGS Wilson records No 10 dinner 'Lloyd George wants to shoot the Kaiser. Winston does not ....'. War Risks Insurance reduced 50% since 1 Nov. **Austria** — Emperor accepts his last PM's resignation. **Imperial family leave Schönbrunn for Eckartsau, 37½ miles NE of Vienna** (see 13). **Germany** — Berlin workers delegates appoint council of Six Peoples Commissars (non-Bolshevik). **France** — From 1100 church bells salute the Armistice, Paris AA guns fire 1200 shots.
LAST AFRICAN ACTION OF THE WAR: Hawkins' KAR force R Milina v Capt Köhl's rearguard as German main body reaches Kasama.	**Dardanelles** — Battleship HMS *Superb* leads Allied Fleet of 7 battleships, 7 cruisers & 18 destroyers to Constantinople (13) after 600 mines cleared from Dardanelles.		**German Austrian Republic proclaimed in Vienna.** K George V decorates Emir Feisal (see 28).	**Germany** — Council of Peoples Commissars abolish Auxiliary Service Law & censorship; declare amnesty, 8hr day (from 1 Jan 1919) & universal suffrage. **France** — Paris celebrates even more enthusiastically (-13). **Britain** — Lloyd George addresses selected Liberals 'Revolution I am not afraid of. Bolshevism I am not afraid of. Reaction I am afraid of.' Northcliffe resigns as Director of Propaganda in Enemy Countries. Reconstruction Minister Dr Addison says a year's unemployment benefit for demobilized soldiers (those with jobs waiting to be demobilized first); 6 months unemployment pay for civilians. Commons votes £700m credit (total £2.5bn 1918), £8743m since war began.
Lettow advances from Kasama for Chambezi ferry & depot, cycles ahead to select camp site when told by Müller of Armistice after British motorcyclist captured in Kasama. **KAR meet German white flag** at 1442, 4 miles N of Kasama. Lettow receives Deventer unconditional surrender cable about midnight, orders march N to Abercorn.	**N Sea** — German cruiser *Königsberg* sails with Rear-Adm Meurer & 4 other plenipotentiary officers, representing Workmen's and Soldiers' Council of the Fleet, to meet British Admiralty.		Wilson conditionally promises food to Germany. K of Saxony renounces throne. **Hungary signs separate armistice at Belgrade.** Hungary — Rumanian talks in Arad over Transylvania (-15, see 18). **Neutrals: Holland** — Amsterdam disturbances, German troops retreat through Limburg.	**Germany** — New Cabinet published. Grand Duke of Saxe-Weimar & Prince Leopold of Lippe abdicate. Republics declared in Württemberg & Prussia. **Britain** — Lloyd George addresses Govt-Employers TU Conference on prewar restrictions restoration. John Buchan made Information Ministry liquidator (it & Crewe House formally closed 31 Dec). **Austria** — Hungarian delegation fail to get Emperor Charles to abdicate as K of Hungary.
HOSTILITIES CEASE. Lettow meets British Prov Commissioner on R Chambezi, hands	**Irish Sea** — Cruiser *Cochrane* runs aground in Mersey, becomes total loss.		INDEPENDENT CZECHOSLOVAK REPUBLIC declared at Prague with Masaryk elected	**Germany** — Grand Dukes of Baden, Anhalt (12), Saxe-Coburg & Mecklenburg

NOVEMBER 1918	WESTERN FRONT 1	EASTERN FRONT 2	SOUTHERN FRONTS 3	TURKISH FRONTS 4
Thu 14 contd	*OHL* such acts must cease. Day of projected but now unnecessary 26-div Franco-American Lorraine (Castelnau) offensive with 2456 guns & c600 tanks v 6 German divs.	reject offer. Gen Petlyura rebels v Ukrainian Govt (*see* 20).		soldiers to Syria and ask England to hand it over to us'.
Fri 15	Inter-Allied Armistice Commission (IAAC) assembles at Spa. Gen Plumer makes formal entry into Mons. First 2 trainloads of Allied PoWs (1000 men) reach Calais from Germany.	**Don** — Cossacks withdraw S. **Estonia** — Diet declares independence (*see* 16 & 18).		
Sat 16	ALLIED ARMIES OF OCCUPATION BEGIN MARCH INTO GERMANY.	POLAND DECLARES INDEPENDENCE: Pres Gen Pilsudski, Poles demand Posen's surrender. **Ukraine** — **German evacuation begins**. **Finland** — **German troops** (4 divs) **leave** (-16 Dec). **Rumania** — White Russian politicians at Jassy approve Allied landings in S Russia (*see* 26) & claim pre-1914 frontiers (excl Poland). **Baltic States** — New Latvian Nat Govt under PM Poska, Estonia orders general mobilization.		
Sun 17	ALLIED ARMIES OF OCCUPATION (40 divs) BEGINS MARCH EASTWARD FROM ARMISTICE LINE TO RHINE in N-S order: Belgian Army, BEF Second Army (Plumer), British Fourth Army (Rawlinson), US Third Army (Dickman), French Tenth Army (Mangin), French Eighth Army (Gérard), French Fourth Army (Gouraud), French Second Army (Hirschauer). Latter reoccupies Mulhouse. Foch tribute calls BEF 'decisive factor in final German defeat'.	**S Russia** — Crimean Tartar Govt yields to Prov Govt at Sevastopol. Stalin appointed to Ukraine Front in Kursk area. **Trans-Caspia** — White Govt asks British for £1m + £130,000pm, given 5m roubles (9 Dec).		German Asia Corps interned at Haida Pasha, Hadikoi & Prinkipo. **Azerbaijan** — 2000 **British** (39th Bde from Enzeli) & Bicherakov **reoccupy Baku** from 30 ships.
Mon 18	BRUSSELS REOCCUPIED BY BELGIANS. **Last German troops leave French territory**. Retiring Germans blow up munition dump at Beez, E of Namur. **Lorraine** — AEF enters Longwy & Briey.	**Siberia** — Directorate of Five overthrown at Omsk (night 17/18), **Adm Kolchak proclaimed White Supreme Ruler**; 3000 Czechs only protest while White C-in-C Boldyrev resigns in protest. British 25th Middx Regt guard roads to Kolchak's HQ. **Estonia** — Treaty with Germany confirms authority surrendered (11), evacuation agreement signed (19). **Poland** — German Gov Gen Beseler resigns. **N Caucasus** — White Gen Wrangel retakes Stavropol after leading cav charge, pursues Reds to E (*see* 20).		Adm Amet to be French High Commissioner Constantinople (French troops land 21). Gen Franchet d'Esperey saluted by Allied & Turk troops as he crosses Ottoman European frontier from Bulgaria (22), soon cruises along the Bosphorus.
Tue 19	METZ REOCCUPIED BY FRENCH under Pétain and Fayolle (*see* 26). ANTWERP REOCCUPIED BY BELGIANS, King returns. Gérard reoccupies Saverne.	Lenin speaks to 1st Working Women Congress. Hoffmann diary 'Our troops ... belong to the oldest classes...we have got most of the Alsace — Lorrainers....the older men , naturally, want to get home.' Admiralty orders Vice-Adm Calthorpe to enter Black Sea as soon as possible (*see* 26).	**Herzegovina** — Col Gen Pflanzer-Baltin, former Austrian C-in-C Albania, evacuated from Cattaro in French warship.	
Wed 20	AEF crosses Luxembourg frontier (Germans leave Grand Duchy 22). Pétain given title Marshal of France (*see* 8 Dec). Gen Rawlinson makes a formal	**N Russia** — Marushevski made White Russian Gov-Gen & C-in-C at Archangel. **W Russia** — Red Army takes Pskov. **Ukraine** — Soviet Govt		

AFRICAN OPERATIONS 5	SEA WAR 6	AIR WAR 7	INTERNATIONAL EVENTS 8	HOME FRONTS 9
acceptance telegram for Kaiser; British PoWs released.			Pres, Dr Kramarzh PM. **Neutrals: Holland** — Interned RND members sail home.	abdicate. *Bundesrat* ordered to continue functions. **USA** — Wheat substitute bread regulations suspended. **Britain** — **Labour** Conference **decides to leave war coalition** & issues Labour programme.
	N Sea — Beatty receives Meurer aboard his flagship *Queen Elizabeth* at Rosyth in Firth of Forth for first of 4 meetings. **E Med** — **Last French warship loss**: destroyer *Carabinier* scuttled under Turk fire after being stranded off Latakieh, Syria.		German Foreign Minister appeals to Wilson for new Hague Conference, US replies (16) all Armistice messages to be sent to all Allies. **Belgium** — Brussels Burgomaster returns from German captivity (*see* 21).	**Germany** — Prussian Upper House abolished. **Britain** — **Sir E Geddes to coordinate demobilization on Smuts' resignation from War Cabinet.** Meat rations to be doubled for Christmas. War Savings Certificates to be permanent. **USA** — War Sec Baker issues 1st demobilisation order. Censorship Board abolished.
Lettow's column marches through KAR camp; Lettow declines lunch invitation for him & all his officers. (1/4th KAR follows for Abercorn 17).			POLAND & HUNGARY DECLARE INDEPENDENCE, Karolyi elected Pres of Hungarian People's Republic. Hungarian Bolshevik Bela Kun arrives from Moscow on forged passport & founds Communist Party (24).	**Lloyd George London speech opens election campaign. Rumania** — 1 man 1 vote decreed.
			Yugoslav National Council at Agram protests v Italy occupying Fiume (but Gen Grazuli persuades Serb troops to evacuate 19). Serb Govt formed at Paris, Pasic PM (*see* 12 Dec).	**USA** — Flu deaths exceed 53,000 war kia.
			Wilson announces he will attend Peace Conference personally. Rumanian Nat Council manifesto 'to the Peoples of the World' for Transylvania's union (*see* 22).	**Italy** — Proclamation pledges Germans can stay in Upper Adige. **Britain** — Asquith tells Liberals 'Election, a blunder and a calamity'. Churchill tells constituents 'The victory ... belongs to all', warns v excessive harshness to Germany. Special Branch chief Thomson reports pacifists 'reappearing in their proper garb as revolutionaries'. **USA** — Film *Under Four Flags* celebrates Allied victory, CPI's 4th biggest earner.
				Italy — Orlando's speech opens Parlt. **Britain** — Naval censorship abolished. NUR announce withdrawal from War Truce. Govt announce over 3m war cas incl nearly 1m dead.
	N Sea — Harwich Force meets **first 20 U-boats** (of 170) to **surrender** 20 miles off Lowestoft & puts prize crews aboard; German crews sent		Bonar Law says feeding Germany dependent on safe PoW return (first British sail in Danish liner 21). Australian Parlt votes v German colonies	

249

NOVEMBER 1918	WESTERN FRONT 1	EASTERN FRONT 2	SOUTHERN FRONTS 3	TURKISH FRONTS 4
Wed 20 contd	entry into Charleroi. **France — First US-made tank lands.**	formed. **Baltic States** — British War Cabinet agree on RN show of force (*see* 22). **N Caucasus** — Volunteer Army breaks up Red Taman army.		
Thu 21	BELGIAN GOVT REINSTATED AT BRUSSELS. BEF occupies Namur. Hindenburg cables govt any renewal of war impossible even v French Army alone.			
Fri 22	Procession of King of the Belgians into Brussels where Parliament receives him. BEF composite bn of English (29th Div), Highland (9th Div), Irish (9th Div) coys under NZ Brig-Gen Freyberg, VC, DSO & headed by massed pipe bands of 26th Bde & 9/Seaforth Highlanders (Pioneers), march 8-abreast with fixed bayonets. **Alsace — French Fourth Army enters Strasbourg**, Gouraud proclaims 'France comes to you!' and becomes military governor. Castelnau enters Colmar.	Rear-Adm Alexander-Sinclair's 23 warships sail from Forth for Baltic, also covering 2 minelayers taking 10,000 rifles to **Estonia** where **Red Seventh Army crosses frontier** nr Narva (*see* 28). **Latvia — Republic proclaimed at Riga** with Farmers' Political League leader K Ulmanis as Pres.		
Sat 23	BEF GHQ lays down guidelines for Cologne bridgehead '... Tactical features will be prepared for defence , trenches dug, wire entanglements erected....No more damage should be done to houses, trees, etc, than is absolutely necessary for military reasons'. **Germany** — †Gen F Below, army cdr since 1915, at Weimar aged 65.	**Galicia** — Poles capture Lemberg. **Estonia** — Prov Govt at Reval. **Don** — Cossacks briefly take Liski rail jctn (50 miles S of Voronezh) from Red Eighth Army. **Siberia** — Kolchak proclaims 'only the armed forces...offer salvation'.	**Austria** — Italians occupy Innsbruck & Landeck (Tyrol).	
Sun 24	BEF & AEF REACH GERMAN FRONTIER. Foch's instructions to Allied Cs-in-C in Rhine Bridgeheads & Neutral Zone.			
Mon 25	Marshal Pétain enters Strasbourg. Canadians reach the Meuse at Namur.	**E Siberia** — 1/9th Hampshire Regt (1023) lands at Vladivostok after 27-day voyage from Bombay (*see* 15 Dec).		

AFRICAN OPERATIONS 5	SEA WAR 6	AIR WAR 7	INTERNATIONAL EVENTS 8	HOME FRONTS 9
	home in own transport after boats berth at Harwich. 39 U-boats surrender (21, *see* 24). K George inspects Grand Fleet (388 ships incl 15 US & 3 French with total crews of 90,000). German destroyer *V30* mined & sunk en route to Scapa internment.		return.	
	SURRENDER OF GERMAN FLEET TO GRAND FLEET off Firth of Forth; 9 battleships, 5 battlecruisers, 7 cruisers, & 49 destroyers escorted in (taken to Scapa 24).		Belgian Govt reinstated with Delacroix PM. British Asst Foreign Sec Lord Cecil resigns.	**USA** — **Wilson signs Wartime Prohibition Act**, forbids liquor manufacture from 1 May & sale from 30 June 1919. McAdoo resigns as Treasury Sec & Railway DG. **Britain** — Food Controller Klynes resigns due to Labour Party policy. Termination of War Act empowers King-in-Council to fix official dates. Munitions Act 1919 empowers Minister to divert production to peace purposes (11 Nov wages to be paid for 6 months). **Belgium** — War Minister Gen de Ceuninck resigns, Masson succeeds. King appoints Adolphe Max a minister of state.
	RN sqn sent to Baltic (*see* E FRONT hereon), reaches Copenhagen (28). **N Sea** — Battleship *Malaya* collides with destroyer *Penn*.		Rumanian Nat Council of Transylvania asks Hungary for recognition (*see* 28). (c) Allied Banking Corpn formed with £1bn capital.	**Austria** — National Assembly's fundamental law assumes sovereignty over German-speaking parts of former Empire. **Germany** — Spartacists' attack on Berlin police HQ defeated. **USA** — Fuel Administrator lifts lightless nights ban. **Britain** — Lloyd George & Bonar Law's election manifestos issued. London Metropolitan Police starts official force of 100 police-women. **France** — Act guarantees mobilized workers' ordinary contract resumption.
			Yugloslav Nat Council votes for union with Serbia & Montenegro (*see* 25). T Roosevelt to Kipling on League of Nations 'A product of men who want everyone to float to heaven on a sloppy sea of universal mush.'	**Britain** — **Lloyd George says Govt's task to make 'a country fit for heroes to live in'.** League football resumes. **Hungary** — Electoral law adopted.
1/4th KAR enters Abercorn having marched 1830 miles since May.	**N Sea** — 28 more U-boats surrender at Harwich (27 more on 27, *see* 1 Dec). **Canada** — 2 Canadian-built 640t French Navy trawlers lost in L Superior bound for Boston, remaining 10 disarmed there. **Uruguay** — 8 interned German steamers seized.		Bavarian Minister Count Lerchenfeld's 1914 dispatches published to prove Germany's war guilt. Soldiers & Workers Councils in NW Germany decide to form Republic with Hamburg as capital. **Neutrals: Spain** — *UC74* interned.	**Italy** — D'Annunzio in *Corriere delle Sera* first refers to 'mutilated victory'.
LETTOW enters Abercorn & **SURRENDERS** in hollow square to Brig-Gen Edwards. German force comprises Gov Schnee; 20 officers; 6 doctors; 1 vet; 1 chemist; 1 field telegraph officer; 125 German NCOs (inc at least 15 *Königsberg* crew); 1156 askaris; 1598 carriers plus women & children. Lettow hands over 1 Portuguese gun (40 shells); 37 MGs (7 German); 1071 rifles (mainly British & Portuguese with 208,000rnds).	**N Sea** — 5 German battleships leave Firth of Forth for Scapa Flow internment, rest of fleet follows (-27).		Montenegrin *Skupshtina* votes for union with Serbia, deposes K Nicholas (26, Prince Regent accepts 16 Dec). German States Chancellor Ebert opens German States Conference at Berlin, agrees Soldiers & Workers Councils have authority till Constituent Assembly meets.	**Britain** — **Parlt dissolves**. Bulk of lighting restrictions lifted. Out-of-Work Donation Scheme begins (24s pw, disabled servicemen to get more). 2 months paper allowed for yr ending 28 Feb.

NOVEMBER 1918	WESTERN FRONT 1	EASTERN FRONT 2	SOUTHERN FRONTS 3	TURKISH FRONTS 4
Tue 26	**Last German troops recross Belgian frontier; French cross German frontier**. Lt-Gen Fergusson appointed British Military Governor of Cologne (*see* 11 Dec). Foch reviews his old 39th Div on Place de l'Hotel de Ville at Metz where Gen Maud'huy, a native, named first French military governor since 1870.	Sovnarkom decrees science & arts' nationalization. Allied declaration defines their Russian relations. **S Russia — Allied troops land at Odessa**. Allied Fleet takes Russian Black Sea Fleet remnants at Sevastopol + 4 U-boats (500 Royal Marines land). **N Russia** — 3 British bns land at Murmansk.	**Bulgaria** — Gen Milne sails from Dedeagach for Constantinople (arrives 27).	Court martial of Enver & Djemal in absentia begins (*see* 1 Jan 1919).
Wed 27	In note to French Govt Foch asserts that Rhine must be future W frontier of Germany; advocates Rhineland as buffer state, separated from Germany & unarmed, while under French military control: 'Whoever holds its [the Rhine's] bridges is master of the situation; he can easily repulse invasion, and, if attacked can carry the war into the enemy's country.' France will thus be safe-guarded v an ever-more populous, resurgent-militaristic Germany: 'Any other frontier is bad for us, and may give us illusory security, but not genuine security.' Marshal Foch is hailed by Strasbourg.	Lenin addresses Moscow Party workers.	**Italy** — K of Italy reviews British 23rd Div.	
Thu 28		**Baltic States — Red Seventh Army** (16,000 by Dec) **captures Narva, Estonia** & sets up Soviet Govt (-June 1919) & advances 130 miles by mid-Dec (*see* 8 & 13 Dec).	**Austria** — British HAC bn sent to Trentino for occupation duties.	
Fri 29	K George V confers OM on Foch. BEF cav reach German frontier.	**N Russia** — New Allied White Provincial Govt fixes currency rate at 40 roubles to £.		**Arabia** — Philby warns London that Ibn Saud's patience running out with Hussein.
Sat 30	K George V visits Front (-10 Dec). Belgians occupy Aix-la-Chapelle, and fix HQ there.	**Soviet CEC establishes Council of Defence** (Lenin chm, Trotsky, Stalin & Sverdlov) & War Production Ctee. **N Russia** — White-US force captures Korpayaskoi, 200 miles SE of Archangel.		
Sun 1 December 1918	**BEF & AEF cross pre-1870 German frontier**: British Second Army (11 divs + 1st Cav Div) cross between Oudler & Eupen. **US Third Army** (243,707 men) **enters Trier** at 0530. Foch in London urges a grand Confederation of the Rhine: 'All the French, Belgian , Luxembourg and Rhenish provinces. With a population of 54m it will counter-balance the 65 to 76 million over the Boches' Rhine.' Both Lloyd George & Bonar Law oppose as it will create 'another Alsace and Lorraine'. Foch obtains permission to extend Armistice & to exact further pledges if necessary. He urges British to keep 10 divs in Occupied Territory even after peace signed & another 10 in Belgium & France.	Lenin attends Defence Council first meeting. (Dec) 143,000 Red combat troops in E & S Fronts.	**Rumania** — British 10th Devonshire Regt present at King's return to Bucharest, having crossed Danube 27 Nov.	

AFRICAN OPERATIONS 5	SEA WAR 6	AIR WAR 7	INTERNATIONAL EVENTS 8	HOME FRONTS 9
	Black Sea — Allied Fleet arrives at Odessa & Sevastopol to take surrender of 4 U-boats (former Constantinople Flotilla) & German-owned Russian warships incl 6 submarines. All Turk & Russian warships accounted for by 5 Dec (announcement). **Britain** — 5 laid down light cruisers cancelled.			**Germany** — Bavarian councils demand German war criminals' trials. Spartacist manifesto calls for revolution. **Britain** — Churchill speaks in Dundee; much of world 'in various states of anarchy and starvation'. **Poland** — 8hr day compulsory. Electoral law for over 21s (28).
		K George V visits Paris.		**Britain** — Asquith E Fife speech (Huddersfield 28). General demobilization not yet possible, 'pivotal men' to be released in advance, then by trades or work offers. Germany — 1.5m+ Allied PoWs released to date (see 29).
Lettow and KAR camp nr Bismarckburg.	**Baltic** — Polish Navy created, initially with 6 vessels on Vistula.		**Bavaria severs relations with Berlin** (threatened 26). **Kaiser signs formal abdication** (document brought by Govt delegation) as Emperor & K of Prussia, releases all officials from oath (Kaiserin joins him from Potsdam). **Bukovina** — General Congress decides for Union with Rumania (see 7 Dec). **France** — Lawrence & Feisal meet Col Brémond at Lyons (see 9 Dec).	**Bulgaria** — PM Malinov resigns, Todorov forms coalition govt. **Britain** — PM and Bonar Law pledge no forced separation of Ulster and Ireland. Belgium first requoted on Stock Exchange. **Austria** — Govt says it will try those starting war.
				Germany — K of Württemberg abdicates. **Ebert Govt decides to convene National Assembly** 16 Feb 1919. **Britain** — Lloyd George Newcastle speeches. PoW ship docks at Hull.
	(Nov) Allied & neutral shipping losses 15 ships worth 26,857 (1 life lost) to Med U-boats. Other Allied & neutral tonnage lost 2159 (-4 Dec). U-boat fig 3 ships worth 10,233t.		**Rumanian Govt returns to Bucharest.** British censorship of neutrals' parcel post ceases.	**Germany** — Commissars of the People's electoral law (universal secret ballot with proportional rep). **USA** — War casualties given.
	N Sea — 8 U-boats surrender at Harwich (total now 122); 62 seaworthy boats left. Total of 176 surrender; Britain gets 105, France 46, Italy 10, Japan 7, US 6, Belgium 2.	(Dec) RAF suffers 51 flying cas & 231 non-flying (see 31). (Dec) 3 German flying units formed to support E border ops incl many W Front veterans.	Clemenceau, Foch, Italian PM Orlando & Baron Sollino arrive in London for Allied Conference (-3). **Rumania — K Ferdinand re-enters Bucharest in triumph.** 100,000-strong National Assembly of Rumanians in Hungary proclaim union with Rumania at Alba Julia (Transylvania), form Prov Govt (2). **Italy** — Rome Conference votes to annex Fiume, Sibenik, Spoleto etc. **Neutrals: Holland — Crown Prince renounces all rights to Prussian & Imperial crowns**, but connives at officers' rescue plot which Dutch foil (5).	**Britain** — RFP down 4% to 29%. Car drivers allowed to travel freely within 30 miles of home (unlimited distance 16). **USA — First troops return to New York** in British liner *Mauretania* (3798 return 23).

DECEMBER 1918	WESTERN FRONT 1	EASTERN FRONT 2	SOUTHERN FRONTS 3	TURKISH FRONTS 4
Mon 2	Belgians occupy Julich, München-Gladbach (5), Crefeld on the Rhine (6), cav enter Neuss (4), Urdingen (8).	**Trans-Caspia** — Red attack on armoured trains repelled. White raid captures Ravnina (8), but CoS India disapproves Anglo-White advance to Oxus (11).		
Tue 3	K George V visits British 5th Div nr Le Quesnoy, France.	**S Russia** — Red Army takes Valuiki.		
Wed 4	**Advance of British Second Army into Germany resumes after halt enforced by rail supply problems** (see HOME FRONTS). Canadians cross German frontier just N of Luxembourg.			
Thu 5		CEC forms Soviet Propaganda Dept and decrees literates' mobilization for it (10).	**Balkans** — War Office informs Gen Milne that British forces remain under Franchet d'Esperey's general control excl troops sent to E end of Black Sea. **Adriatic** — Italians complete occupation of Dalmatian coast.	
Fri 6	**Cologne entered by British** 2nd Cav Bde & armoured cars. (City designated HQ Allied Occupation Zone 3): local authorities had requested British cav help to keep order. British 28th Bde, 9th Div, reaches Cologne by train (7).	**W Russia** — Red Army retakes Dvinsk.		
Sat 7				**Armenia** — Turk evacuation complete to 1877 frontier.
Sun 8	British 1st Cav Div reaches Rhine on broad front & secures crossings (see INT'L EVENTS). AEF enters Koblenz. Pétain ceremonially created Marshal of France at Metz before Joffre, Allied C-in-Cs & reps. Poincaré presents baton. Pétain French C-in-C till Feb 1920. K George V visits Ypres.	**Caspian** — 2 RN ships drive off 3 Red ships attacking in fog off Cherchen. Red destroyer flees (9). RN has 8 ships by 30. **Baltic States** — Red Seventh Army 40 miles inside Estonia (see 13). Latvian Govt allows Baltic *Landeswehr* (7), see 17 & 29.		**Allied Military Administration set up in Constantinople.** **Aden** — British reoccupy Lahej & 2500+ Turks surrender (-15); 4100 more by 1 Mar 1919, but 800 take most arms & ammo to Imam of Yemen at Sana & enter his service (incl Gov Gen Mahmoud Nadim Bey).
Mon 9	German delegates for renewal of Armistice (Erzberger, Oberndorff & Vanselow) leave Berlin for Trier. K George V at Zeebrugge; Pres Poincaré at Strasbourg. AEF REACH RHINE (from Brohl to Rolandseck Koblenz-Bonn).	**Poland severs relations with Moscow.**		
Tue 10	Pres Poincaré & PM Clemenceau enter Mulhouse, Alsace. AEF occupy W bank of Rhine from Andernach to Rolandseck & from Trechtingshausen (N of Bingen) to Boppard.	**Red Army reoccupies Minsk.**		Emir Feisal in London as Arab delegate to Peace Conference (met by Lawrence at Boulogne 9, see INT'L EVENTS 28).
Wed 11	British Military Governor (Lt-Gen Fergusson) hoists Union Flag over his HQ Hotel Monopol, Cologne. AEF take formal possession of Koblenz. French (Mangin) enter Mainz: civil admin had broken down,	**Mannerheim elected Regent of Finland** (returns to Helsinki in triumph 22, white 'Mannerheim' bread comes from Allies). **S Russia** — Gen Petlyura's Ukrainians surround Odessa (see 20).		

AFRICAN OPERATIONS 5	SEA WAR 6	AIR WAR 7	INTERNATIONAL EVENTS 8	HOME FRONTS 9
	Baltic — RN destroyers arrive at Libau (*see* 5 & 12).		British War Cabinet decides to press for Kaiser's extradition (*see* 5).	Wilson tells Congress he is going to Europe (*see* 4). **Britain** — Iron and steel subsidies' removal for 1919 announced. Final war factory worker pay rise 5s pw (total 28s 6d).
Lettow receives Deventer's telegram saying despite former's protest German troops will be treated as PoWs; they embark in 4 ships on L Tanganyika.	**N Sea** — Harwich Force detaches cruisers *Centaur* & *Coventry* for Baltic service.		**Rumania** — Last Bulgar troops evacuate Dobruja.	**Germany** — Sailors rebel for Liebknecht (*see* 6). **USA** — Fuel Administrator resigns.
	Admiralty publishes estimate of world's war shipping losses to 31 Oct: 15,053,786t lost, net loss of 1,811,584 after new construction & 2,392,675t of Central Powers' shipping captured. British loss 9,031,828t with net loss of 3,443,012t.		Pres Wilson sails for France. **Yugoslav National Council proclaims union of all Serbs, Croats & Slovenes** (*see* 20 & 29). Polish ultimatum for German evacuation (*see* 15). Switzerland sends 19 trucks of food to starving Austrians.	**Britain** — **Army Demobilization begins** (*see* 9 & 31). Queen calls on women to help reconstruction. Candidates nominated for general election. **USA** — Wilson sails from New York in ex-German liner *George Washington*. **Germany** — Cologne Centre Party votes for Rhine-Westphalia Republic.
Lettow's troops arrive at Kigoma to generous Belgian reception before boarding train (flu caught en route); askaris held at Tabora Camp until repatriation.	**Baltic** — Cruiser HMS *Cassandra* mined & sunk. **Home Waters** — Adm Bayly makes last Queenstown (Irish Command) report. Q-ships *Suffolk Coast* & *Hyderabad* open to the public in R Thames.		**Lloyd George says Kaiser must be prosecuted** by an international court (& 10, 11). K Albert visits Paris. Germany hands back 300m gold francs extracted under Brest-Litovsk Treaty. British reps at Versailles call for Europe to abolish conscription.	**France** — Alsace-Lorraine Diet convened as National Assembly to **announce formal return of French rule**. **USA** — Congress asked for Allied credit extension for one yr. **Britain** — Potato crop (4,209,000t) 25% up on 1917.
			Koreans appeal to USA for help to end Japanese domination. Pres Masaryk leaves London (arr from NY 29 Nov) for Paris (-14), met by Foreign Minister Dr Benes & Prague (*see* HOME FRONTS 21).	**Germany** — Govt troops v Spartacist parade in Berlin (180 cas). Krupp advertising drive 'We make Everything'. **Britain** — War pensions increased as from 1 Nov (granted to parents of unmarried soldiers 18). Rail strike ends with 8hr day conceded from 1 Feb 1919.
Lettow & officers arrive at Dar-es-Salaam by train, Lettow finds everyone 'extraordinarily kind'. Deventer invites him, Schnee & Maj Kraut to lunch.			Bukovina deputation arrives at Jassy to pursue union with Rumania. **Sweden & Switzerland sever relations with Russia.**	**Britain** — Forces instructed to fill in civilian employment forms. **USA** — 'British Day'. New York Narrows anti-U-boat steel net raised.
				Britain — War Risks Insurance policies discontinued. Shop lighting limits removed for Christmas. 'Pivotal' men's release from forces begins (*see* 31). 100,000 cotton workers win strike (-18) for 40% pay rise.
	N Sea — Cruiser HMS *Galatea*, ordered to Black Sea, collides with SS *Moto* off Northumberland but continues.		Bessarabia votes for unconditional union with Rumania (see 9 April 1919). Only Nobel Prizes go to Germans Max Planck (Physics) & Fritz Haber (Chemistry), poison gas developer.	**Czechoslovakia** — Law passed to aid unemployed ex-soldiers (*see* 19). **Canada** — $5m war savings stamps authorized. **Britain** — Lloyd George's 6 points election speech (in Bristol 11). Special bonuses for 2-4yr enlistments in Regular Army (produces 75,000 men by Sept 1919).
			Dr Solf resigns as German Foreign Minister, Brockdorf-Rantzau succeeds.	**Portugal** — Lisbon Revolt (-16): Pres Paes murdered (14), Adm Antunes elected Prov Pres (16). **Britain** — Food rationing discontinued on all edible offals (meat).

DECEMBER 1918	WESTERN FRONT 1	EASTERN FRONT 2	SOUTHERN FRONTS 3	TURKISH FRONTS 4
Wed 11 contd	order rapidly restored.			
Thu 12	BRITISH 1st CAV DIV CROSSES RHINE (Hohenzollern Bridge) AT COLOGNE & BONN, to begin occupation of 38-mile Cologne bridgehead. Allied & German Armistice delegates meet at Trier.	Lenin writes to Astrakhan urging speculators' execution and cables Trotsky that Perm needs reinforcing. Norwegian Legation leaves Moscow.		
Fri 13	PROLONGATION OF THE ARMISTICE (-17 Jan 1919). British inf complete occupation of Cologne bridgehead: British 29th & 9th Divs & Cdn Corps follow cav across Rhine at Cologne-Bonn. AEF cross Rhine at Koblenz, occupy bridgehead with 3 divs & incl 2nd Div crossing at Remagen.	**Estonia** — RN cruisers *Cardiff* & *Caradoc* & 5 destroyers shell Red Seventh Army rear at Wesenberg, destroying river frontier bridge; **with Estonian guerrillas halt Red march.**		**Yemen** — LAST ANGLO-TURK FIGHTING: 2/101st Bombay Grenadiers (sent from Egypt) land & storm Hodeida (-14) covered by HM cruisers *Juno*, *Proserpine* & *Suva* (AMC). Turk GOC 40th Div escapes to Sana.
Sat 14	ARMISTICE RENEWED TILL 17 JAN 1919. Allies reserve right to occupy neutral zone on E bank of Rhine.	Ukrainian Directory leftist-nationalists topple Skoropadski and proclaim People's Republic at Kiev. Soviet Belorussia united with RSFSR (-17).	**Salonika** — British GHQ leaves for Constantinople by sea, reopens at Turk Military School in Pera (17). Milne, ex-C-in-C Salonika Army, arrives in England for first leave since Sept 1915 prior to commanding at Constantinople, receives no awards & little recognition.	
Sun 15		**Estonia proclaimed Soviet Republic**. Lenin urges Trotsky's deputy to strengthen S Front. **E Siberia** — 1/9th Hampshire Regt leaves Vladivostok for Omsk (-18).	**Italy** — All quiet at Taranto after 2 British West Indies bns disarmed following mutiny over having to do dock duties instead of fighting.	**S Persia** — Brig-Gen Sykes leaves Shiraz for India.
Mon 16	Allies complete occupation of Rhine bridgeheads.	**Finland** — **Last German troops leave. Baltic States** — Hoffmann diary 'The evacuation [4 divs on 11 Nov] is becoming very disorderly'. (*see* 26). **Urals** — Red reverse N of Ekaterinburg. **Siberia** — Gen Janin reaches Omsk but rows with Kolchak and leaves for front (20).		
Tue 17	British occupation of Cologne bridgehead & US occupation of Koblenz bridgehead completed, 40 Allied divs deployed.	**Latvia declared a Soviet Republic**. German *Oberost* HQ to move to Königsberg.		
Wed 18		Germans evacuate Dorpat, Estonia. Announced that Reds have entered Walk, Livonia. **S Russia** — French warships arrive at Odessa (*see* 20).		
Thu 19	The 'Limburg Passage': Dutch Foreign Minister Van Karnebeek reports to Parlt that 70,300 German soldiers have passed through S Holland since Armistice; disarming proce-dures strictly observed;	Lord Milner defends British intervention in Russia.		Liman ordered to Prinkipo, Germans to be quartered there or on other Princes' Is.

AFRICAN OPERATIONS 5	SEA WAR 6	AIR WAR 7	INTERNATIONAL EVENTS 8	HOME FRONTS 9
	Baltic — RN Sqn arrives at Reval, Estonia (*see* E FRONT 13 & 26).		New Zealand PM leaves for Peace Conference in Paris.	**Germany** — Republican Guard formed. **Britain** — Men over 41 called up in 1918 to be demobilized. Horseflesh prices fixed due to rise in consumption. Churchill's final election speech at Dundee stresses need for unity at Peace Conference.
	Red Sea — *see* TURK FRONTS.		**Pres Wilson lands at Brest, arrives Paris 14** (receives freedom of city 16). Lloyd George election press statement backs universal abolition of conscription. Indian Peace Conference delegates arrive in London.	**Britain** — King holds Buckingham Palace investiture (incl VCs).
			Armistice renewed at Trier to 17 Jan 1919. New US Ambassador arrives in England. **Rumania** — Bratianu new PM & Foreign Minister (*see* 24).	**Britain** — GENERAL (THE 'KHAKI' OR 'COUPON') ELECTION, first since 1910 (RESULTS 28 to allow forces' votes to be counted). Munitionette volunteers released (*see* 17). Soldiers released for civil work to return to units. Scheme for forces higher education & training announced.
			Poland severs relations with Germany (*see* 27 & 28).	**Austria** — Emperor Charles ill at with flu at Eckartsau (all his 5 children too). **Germany** — People's Party programme.
			FM Mackensen's forces surrender to Hungarians nr Budapest, FM interned by French (-Dec 1919). Botha arrives in London for Peace Conference.	**Germany** — Conference of Workers & Soldiers Councils at Berlin (-20), 450 deputies. **Britain** — Demobilization scheme for Army & RAF men with jobs to go to. Lard rationing discontinued.
				Germany — War Minister Maj-Gen Scheuch resigns. **Britain** — Scheme announced for household training of soldiers' wives & fiancées formerly on war work. Churchill writes to PM that Munitions Ministry (3m work people & 17,000 staff) 80% of demobilization & should handle it.
†Capt Spangenberg from flu at Dar-es-Salaam + 9 other Germans before 114 embark with Lettow & 194 women & children (17 Jan 1919) for home via Cape Town & Rotterdam.				**Britain** — **Information Ministry abolished**. Govt to grant up to £10m for road & bridge repairs. RND ex-PoWs land at Leith. Restrictions on new newspapers & poster sizes lifted. **Germany** — **Berlin Conference decides on Ebert Prov Govt pending National Assembly elections** (fixed for 19 Jan 1919). **Austria** — Electoral law passed. **USA** — 5 Philadelphia *Tageblatt* staff jailed for Espionage Act violations.
			King of Italy visits Paris.	**Czechoslovakia** — 8hr day, 48hr week. **Britain** — Haig & his 5 army cdrs return to London. Sir E Geddes made Coordinator for Army demobilization. Military gratuities scale issued (Navy's 24).

DECEMBER 1918	WESTERN FRONT 1	EASTERN FRONT 2	SOUTHERN FRONTS 3	TURKISH FRONTS 4
Thu 19 contd	baggage searched for war material; no consultation with German authorities, only unit cdrs in transit. Haig, CoS Lt-Gen Lawrence & five Army cdrs receive official welcome home in London.			
Fri 20		Gen Borius' 1800 **French African troops** (156th Col Div) **land at Odessa**. Petlura's Ukrainians capture Kiev and end Skovopadski's rule.		Gen Hamelin's French troops (incl 2 bns Armenians) occupy Cilicia and Taurus rail tunnels (29) from landing at Mersin. **S Persia** — c2000 men of Bushire Field Force clear Kamarij Pass; **German agent Wassmuss still refuses to yield** (23).
Sat 21		**Siberia** — Bolshevik plot crushed in Omsk, but White reprisals indiscriminate.		Sultan dissolves National Assembly after it censures Govt.
Sun 22		**Georgia** — British bde (from Salonika Army) lands at Batumi to link with Baku garrison as Armenian/Georgian fighting in progress (peace signed with British mediation 17 Jan 1919).		
Mon 23	Erzberger, head of German Armistice delegation, praises Foch's 'benevolent attitude': 'At first the Allies regarded the German Armistice commission with great and genuine distrust, but during the four weeks (sic) of the Armistice Marshal Foch, as he frankly admitted, convinced himself that we were honourably exerting ourselves to fulfill the conditions imposed, although he emphasised that not all conditions had been fulfilled...', Foch declared 'I understand that you have three things in particular at least, first, the provision of food supplies; second, bringing about the speediest possible peace; third, the German prisoners.' [Foch cannot yet discuss the PoW question.] With reference to the two other matters, however, he assumed a benevolent attitude ' (Interview in *National Zeitung*).	CEC resolves to recognise Baltic States as independent Soviet Republics; and closes Teachers' Union.	**Italy** — First British demobilization train leaves, others (29 & 30).	
Tue 24	**Occupied Germany** — snow.			**N Syria** — 28th Indian Bde (7th Div) occupies Killis & Aintab, N of Aleppo, & Baghdad Railway.
Wed 25	Pres Poincaré tours Ardennes, visiting Sedan, Mézières, Charleville, Rethel & Vouziers. At Sedan, he replies to a welcome address, 'The name of Sedan is inseparable from the mournful memory of a painful past, but today she is liberated and the ray of glory which illuminates her will not be extinguished.' **Pres Wilson spends Christmas Day with AEF** at its Chaumont HQ .	**Urals** — Gen Pepelyayev's **White Siberian Corps** of Gen Gadja's Northern Army (Kolchak) **captures** and loots **Perm** (prov capital & industrial city) in surprise thrust, takes 30,000 PoWs; 50 guns; 10 armoured cars; 248 MGs; 260 engines and 4000 rail cars from drunken Lashevich's Red Third Army (unaided by Second Army). Whites lose 5000k or frozen to death inc 444 officers. **N Russia** — British subaltern found murdered nr Murmansk (murderer shot 5 Feb 1919). **S Russia** — French troops land at Sevastopol.		

AFRICAN OPERATIONS 5	SEA WAR 6	AIR WAR 7	INTERNATIONAL EVENTS 8	HOME FRONTS 9
			Serb PM Pasic (since 1912) resigns.	Hindenburg protests v Berlin Conference military resolutions. Spartacists raid *Vorwärts* Berlin office.
				Britain — Children's sugar rations increased (manufacturers allowance doubled 30). **Germany** — Prussia National Assembly elections fixed for 16 Jan 1919. **Czechoslovakia** — Pres Masaryk arrives in Prague (inaugurated 22).
			1st US food mission sent to Warsaw.	US Food Administrator suspends all food regulations; *Too Fat to Fight* film comedy showing.
				Germany — Spartacists & Marines seize Berlin Chancery but Govt troops eject with 29k (-24).
			K Ferdinand's decree on Transylvania's union with Rumania, to have minister in central govt (*see* HOME FRONTS 26)	**Austria** — Toasts to Emperor drunk all over Vienna (prov Pres Renner tells State Council 22 that dynasty still in its midst).
51 KAR establish post at Dolo in Jubaland, NE corner of British E Africa adjoining Abyssinia & Italian Somaliland.			Polish leader Paderewski lands at Danzig en route for Posen (*see* 28, arrives Warsaw 1 Jan 1919).	**Albania** — National Assembly at Durazzo elects Turkhan Pasha Pres & Head of Peace Conference delegation. **Germany** — Hindenburg's Kassel manifesto to officers. **Britain** — Christmas holidays extended to 28.

DECEMBER 1918	WESTERN FRONT 1	EASTERN FRONT 2	SOUTHERN FRONTS 3	TURKISH FRONTS 4
Thu 26		**Baltic States** — 2 RN cruisers & 3 destroyers capture Red destroyers *Spartak* and *Avrotil* (-27) after chase off Reval, 247 PoWs; ships later given to Estonian Navy. W Ukraine Republic declared. Lithuanian Voldemar Govt resigns, new PM Slezevicius forms coalition with Voldemar as foreign minister. Hoffmann diary records Polish offer to hold Vilna v Reds.		**N Syria** — Allenby has Turk Second Army withdrawn W of Bozanti (Cilician Gates), it is then demobilized.
Fri 27		Lenin writes to Chicherin urging Berlin or Holland conference to found Third Communist International by 1 Feb 1919 (platform basis to be that of Bolsheviks and Spartacus League 31). Red Army Central Commission for tackling desertion formed.		
Sat 28				
Sun 29		RN shore patrols (withdrawn 2 Jan l9l9) evacuate 350 Allied subjects & Latvian Govt from Riga (20,000 Reds 25 miles away defeating Baltic *Landeswehr* at Hintzenberg). Cruiser HMS *Ceres* fires on mutinous Latvian regt's barracks & subdues it (-30).		
Mon 30		**N Russia** — Allies take Kadish. **Siberia** — Kolchak takes Birsk.		
Tue 31	Demobilization of German *Landssturm*. Foch told AEF will be reduced by 5 divs pm in occupied area from 1 March 1919.	Red Second Army retakes Ufa (gateway to the Urals) & Sterilitamak.		
		Baltic States — 2 RN cruisers & 3 destroyers capture Red destroyers *Spartak* and *Avrotil*		**N Syria** — Allenby has Turk Second Army withdrawn W of Bozanti (Cilician Gates), it is

AFRICAN OPERATIONS 5	SEA WAR 6	AIR WAR 7	INTERNATIONAL EVENTS 8	HOME FRONTS 9
			Wilson arrives in London, met by King at Charing Cross Stn.	**Rumania** — Workers' Bucharest demonstration dispersed (100+ k).
			Polish Gen Dowbor-Musnicki seizes Prussian Pomerania (-28). Wilson meets Lloyd George and Balfour, attends King's state banquet.	
			Wilson Guildhall speech on Peace Treaty features. Polish-German fighting at Posen (Poznan).	BRITISH GENERAL ELECTION RESULTS: Govt Coalition 478 seats (Tory 384; LG Liberal 138, Coalition Labour 14) v 219 Opposition (58 Labour, Asquith Liberals 27; Irish Nationalists 7; Sinn Fein 73). Liberal vote falls 50% to 25% of total (Asquith loses seat after 32 years as MP). Tories dominant for 1st time since 1906. Countess Markiewicz only successful woman candidate (of 17) for Dublin but will not take oath of allegiance to King. National War Bonds record £1388.5m in last year. **Germany** — 3 Commissars resign but replaced by SDs. **Italy** — Socialist Minister Bissolati (Civil Aid & War Pensions) resigns v Govt anti-Yugoslav policy.
			Clemenceau and Pichon speak on balance of power, peace terms and Russian intervention. Stoyan Protich first PM of Yugoslavia. Wilson visits Carlisle (his mother's home).	Majority Socialist demo in Berlin v Spartacists, but 3 Independent Socialists leave Govt. **France** — Liberated Districts Ministry formed. **Britain** — Meat ration coupon value raised from 4d to 5d (pork, poultry, game & pre-served meats unrestricted). Churchill vainly asks for Admiralty rather than War Office.
			Wilson receives freedom of Manchester.	**Germany** — **German Communist Party founded.**
	N Sea — Fisher visits aircraft carrier *Furious* at Rosyth and predicts the next war will be in 20 yrs' time.	**Britain** — †Capt W Leefe Robinson VC aged 23 of flu, PoW returned home (14).	Wilson and Balfour leave London for Paris. **Neutrals** — Holland allows normal river passage.	**USA** — War Industries & Railroad Board dissolved. **Germany** — *Vorwärts* publishes draft German constitution. *Landsturm* demobilized & dissolved. **Britain** — 288,438 troops demobilized so far; 124,680 British ex-PoWs reach dispersal camps. National munition workers reduced from 306,000 to 136,000. 12,276/21,698 war contracts terminated. Last coalition War Cabinet meeting. During 1918 unemployment rose to 1.1%; TU membership up 19%; only 5000 working days lost to strikes before Armistice; imports up 19%, exports down 5%; shipping tonnage almost 20% down on end 1914; annual births lowest of war (848,519).

FOCUS ON THE FRONTS

1917

During this 'Year of Agony', that in so many ways began the modern world as we know it, Russia discarded absolute monarchy, underwent two revolutions and submitted meekly to an Austro-German 'peace' Diktat. Britain's Army was bled white in Flanders and U-boats slaughtered her merchant sailors; the French Army was rent by mutiny and defeatism; Germany suffered increasingly severe shortages, sparking off food riots and acts of disobedience in the blockaded fleet; Austria experienced near-famine and serious unrest among her subject nationalities; worst of all, Italy sustained a near-fatal blow in the field. In East Africa, Germany's last colony was lost but the indefatigable Lettow-Vorbeck took his surviving troops into Portuguese Mozambique, prolonging this side-show by a year.

The war had become 'an ever-widening all-consuming siege of peoples in which fighting fronts and home fronts were merged in a single, indivisible ordeal'. The Allies made contradictory promises of independence to Arabs and Jews as Turkey lost Baghdad and Jerusalem to ably-commanded British armies.'Its only independent event, so to speak still prompted by free will and not by necessity, and ultimately its outstanding and decisive event, was America's declaration of war on Germany.' [*This Age of Conflict* by Frank P Chambers *et al* (New York 1943), p 70]

The severe attrition experienced during the Battle of the Somme, had induced the German High Command to abandon their advanced positions in France and withdraw to a strong fortified line which they could hold with limited forces while giving Russia a knock-out blow. This 'Hindenburg' (or 'Siegfried') Line was constructed during the winter of 1916-17. More accurately, the 'Line' was a complex zone of trenches, concrete shelters, gun emplacements, and barbed (or 'razor') wire. It was extended even farther to the rear by the 'Hunding' and 'Brunhilde' lines completed in 1918. Germany's propagandists and apologists trumpeted the 'impregnable' character of the Line during 1917-18 to counteract the growing war-weariness of their undernourished people. Ludendorff ventured the opinion that the Line could be held until the unrestricted U-boat campaign had brought the English to their senses (and their knees!).

Early in 1917 German forces withdrew to the Hindenburg Line, carrying out ruthless deportations and demolitions as they did so. Army Group Commander Prince Rupprecht protested against this unnecessary and self-defeating savagery and threatened to resign. Allied offensives in April freed Vimy Ridge, but appalling French losses during the excessively promoted and inept Nivelle Offensive on the Aisne sector sparked off large-scale mutinies. Thanks to the masterly intervention of Pétain, these outbreaks were quickly and secretly suppressed.

In June, the British, under Plumer seized the Messines Ridge and other key points in the Ypres Salient. But prolonged attempts from 31 July to advance eastward from Ypres towards the U-boat bases on the Flanders coast (Third Battle of Ypres/Battle of Passchendaele) achieved very little at appalling cost. Many hundreds (if not thousands) of British and Empire soldiers simply disappeared, drowned in the bottomless mud. Perhaps the British offensive did (as Haig and Robertson claimed) hold German attention at a critical period while the battered French Army staged a slow recovery. But surely similar results could have been achieved with superior strategy (for example, detailed plans existed for an amphibious assault on the German-occupied Belgian coast, utilizing special landing craft and tanks) at far less cost in human life. During August-October, the French made significant gains before Verdun and took the Chemins des Dames Ridge in well-planned and executed limited attacks.

The Italians had continued their repeated offensives against the Austrian line along the Isonzo River north-east of Venice. Small gains had resulted and the Italian line became overextended. Repeated appeals for the despatch of Anglo-French heavy guns had elicited a meagre response. Italian C-in-C Cadorna had suspected an impending Austro-German offensive but his precautionary measures had not been implemented by dilatory corps commanders. The Italian gas masks offered only limited protection, and Italian airmen were, in general, outclassed by German veterans from the Western Front. Unbeknown to the defenders, a crack German expeditionary force of seven divisions had been railed secretly from the moribund Eastern Front. Its junior leaders — all converts to the novel 'storm troop' infiltration tactics associated with General Hutier — included a certain Württemburger, Erwin Rommel.

On 24 October 1917 the blow fell at Caporetto. The Italian line collapsed and was pushed back 70 miles to the Piave river with the loss of 320,000 men and 3000 guns. Eleven divisions of British and French reinforcements were rushed to the Piave and a 'Supreme War Council' was established to secure a unified strategy. At this dark hour, a ray of hope was provided by the surprise attack of massed British tanks at Cambrai (20 November). True, the breakthrough was shortlived and soon eliminated by German reinforcements railed from the Eastern Front and from Italy, but the potential of massed armour had been proved beyond a doubt. It was, according to the *Daily Mail* correspondent, H W Wilson, 'the vindication of mechanical war'.

1918

With the end of fighting on the Eastern Front in December 1917 and the Italians still psychologically reeling from the Caporetto 'Catastrophe', Germany's *de facto* supreme commander, General Erich Ludendorff (his official title was

'First Quartermaster General'), had a breathing space to devote all his organizational and tactical skills to the problem of of the stalemated Western Front. He calculated that the American Army would be unable to intervene decisively in France before the early summer of 1918: 'It seemed to Ludendorff, therefore, that Germany could take no other course but to transfer divisions from Russia to the West and, by exploiting her temporary superiority in the field, achieve a decisive victory over Britain and France before the Americans began to arrive *en masse*...Germany's last hope of winning the greatest conflict in history.' ['Offensive 1918' by Correlli Barnett in *Decisive Battles of the Twentieth Century* (London 1976)].

After prolonged discussion and disagreement, Ludendorff rather belatedly reached a decision to direct the main weight of his grand offensive on the British-held St Quentin (Somme) sector (code name 'Operation *Michael*'). The aim was to drive west between Péronne and Arras towards the Channel coast. 'If this blow succeeded, the strategic result might indeed be enormous, as we should separate the bulk of the English army from the French and crowd it up with its back to the sea...' [*My War Memories 1914-1918* by Erich Ludendorff (London 1919)].

The ambitious plan depended for success on the maximum exploitation of the novel 'storm troop' tactics evolved in Russia (notably by General Hutier and artillery Colonel Brüchmuller) and first employed at Riga. These specially trained formations — armed with light machine-guns, rifles, flamethrowers, mortars and a sprinkling of field guns — had orders to infiltrate as fast as their legs could carry them, bypassing Allied strongpoints. In a reversal of accepted tactical doctrine, reserves would be put in where the attack was progressing, not where it was held up.

Special artillery tactics involved a crushing short bombardment of a fews hours' duration using a 4:1 preponderance of gas projectiles, to dislocate and paralyse the defenders. But, despite the vital need to maintain the momentum of advance, no attempt was made to create a German tank corps on the British or French model, and both cavalry and supply units were seriously embarrassed by a lack of horses.

Nevertheless, the German *Kaiserschlacht* ('Emperor's Battle') offensive began in spectacular fashion on 21 March 1918. Between 23 and 25 March Ludendorff was within reach of victory as the outnumbered British Third and Fifth Army began 'the Great Retreat'. However, Ludendorff's Teutonic inflexibility and his basic flaws of character and intellect now revealed themselves: '...the nearness of the Allied front and Allied solidarity to final collapse was not apparent from the reports of his own armies. *Above all, the pattern of success on the ground had failed to correspond with the strategic character of the Michael plan*... [of the three attacking generals] only Hutier [Eighteenth Army] had achieved the kind of swift, deep advance which Ludendorff had been counting on... . Yet under the original Michael strategy, Hutier's role was the subsidiary one of the flank guard. The German success was all on the wrong wing.' (*Ibid.*, p73)

If on 23 March 1918, Ludendorff had chosen to throw all his 'attack' divisions behind a single thrust by Hutier and the left-wing of Marwitz's Second Army towards Amiens ('hinge' of the Anglo-French front), there is every possibil-ity that an ineradicable wedge could have been driven between the British and French with devastating psychological effects on the defeatist Pétain (no longer the indomitable 'Victor of Verdun'). Instead Ludendorff waffled and ordered no fewer than three separate thrusts by his three armies. 'It was all a fatal dispersion of effort,' maintains Correlli Barnett (*Ibid.*, p74), 'a plan beyond the powers of his rapidly tiring troops'. Although Hutier crossed the Somme on a broad front, even he fell 6-10 miles short of his objectives. On 25 March Ludendorff drastically revised his directive of the 23rd, but only succeeded in dissipating his chances of a decisive breakthrough. Only on 28 March (four days too late), did he order an all-out attack on Amiens. By then, the crisis in the Allied command set-up had been overcome, Foch being appointed Supreme Commander.

Throughout April, late May, early June and half of July, Ludendorff continued to ring the changes with another four massive blows, and bellow down the field telephone at his increasingly resentful and frustrated generals. Even so, by June the Allies had lost all they had gained since 1915 and the Germans had reached the River Marne for the second time in the war. But they had nowhere succeeded in permanently breaking the Allied line, while American troops were now in action in ever-increasing numbers. Fifteen US divisions landed in France between April and June 1918.

On 15 July the Germans attacked simultaneously on both sides of Reims (Aisne Salient). East of that constantly bombarded city, they made slight gains. To the west, they crossed the Marne. Foch replied with a massive artillery bombardment followed by a decisive counter-attack (18 July-6 August) spearheaded by swarms of fighters, light bombers and 'fast' light Renault tanks. Nine American divisions supported powerful French units. In this Second Battle of the Marne, the Germans were forced back to the River Vesle.

On 15 September 1918, Salonika-based British, French, Serb and Greek units attacked the Bulgarian line in Macedonia. Bulgarian resistance soon collapsed. The following month Serbia was cleared of Austrian occupation forces and Germany's Balkan flank lay exposed. The final Austrian offensive against Italy had soon petered out on the Piave (15-25 June 1918). An eleventh hour Allied offensive (Battle of Vittorio Veneto) from 24 October broke initial stubborn resistance and quickly developed into an Austrian rout, accelerated by the ever-increasing disaffection, desertion and mutiny by Serb, Croat, Czech and Polish troops and sailors of the finally disintegrating Imperial armed forces. Austria signed an armistice on 3 November 1918, her non-German subject peoples had already seized independence.

The British General Allenby captured a Turkish army at Megiddo in September and overran Syria. The surrender of the Turkish army on the Tigris followed. The Ottoman Empire signed an armistice on 30 October.

Foch launched a general counter-offensive in September. The tank-led British drove the Germans back 8 miles at Amiens on 8 August and attacked the Hindenburg Line in September. That same month, the Americans stormed the four-year-old Saint Mihiel Salient and Allied armies broke through the Hindenburg Line after 18 days' continuous battle (26 September-13 October). During October, an Anglo-French-Belgian army group freed the Flanders coast, the British reached the River Scheldt, the French drove east over the Aisne and the Americans down the Meuse to Sedan.

Mutiny gripped the German Fleet in the last days of October, and revolution quickly followed in all the main cities. Armistice negotiations, on the basis of US President Wilson's famous 'Fourteen Points' programme, began on 6 November; the Kaiser 'abdicated' on 9 November and, on 11 November, the Armistice was signed in Foch's converted *wagon-lit* at Compiègne. The Great War had ended after 1567 days.

ARMISTICE TERMS 11 NOV 1918

Summary of significant conditions affecting W Front:

1   Cessation of hostilities 6hrs after signature.

2   Immediate German evacuation of Belgium, N France, Luxembourg & Alsace-Lorraine in 3 stages within 15 days. 'Joint occupation by the Allied and United States Forces shall keep pace with evacuation in these areas.'

3   Repatriation of all hostages.

4   Surrender of 5000 guns; 45,000 MGs; 3000 trench mortars & 1700 aircraft .

5   German Armies to evacuate left (W) bank of the Rhine (in 4 stages). Allied & US garrisons to hold principal crossings of the Rhine (Mainz, Coblenz, Cologne), together with adjacent bridgeheads (radius 18 miles) on right (E) bank. 6 miles wide demilitarized Neutral Zone on right (E) bank.

6   German High Command to disclose all mines & delay-action bombs on former occupied territory.

7   Immediate repatriation (without reciprocity) of all Allied and United States prisoners of war.

8   Duration of Armistice: 36 days (option to extend).

JANUARY 1919

Wed 1
Britain — RFP 130% ie 11. 6% l9l8 rise. Gas & electricity ration increased 25% in England & Wales. *The Times* Red Cross Appeal closes at £14m. 200 sailors on leave drown in the yacht *Stornoway* off Scotland. **Germany** — Ruhr strikes. **France** — National debt 147 4bn fr. **Turkey** — Enver & Djemal cashiered. **Russia** — (Jan) According to its C-in-C Red Army has 600,000 rifles (for 788,000 men), 8000 MGs & 1700 field guns. White Russian Gen Eugene K Miller (1914-17 corps & army cdr) arrives in Archangel (from Rome exile) to be Gov-Gen.

Thu 2
Russia — Reds advance on Reval & Riga; Ukraine fighting; White offensive in Caucasus. **Danube** — Czechs fight Hungarians at Pressburg. **Britain** — Trenchard Independent Air Force dispatch & Brig-Gen Cockerill's Special Intelligence report published. Union leader Clynes deplores 'industrial action' for political purposes. **France** — Railways back in private ownership.

Fri 3
Diplomacy — Pres Wilson arrives in Rome (sees Pope 4, at Milan 5). Food Council under Hoover formed in Paris to feed Central Powers (asks for £20m 4, Congress votes 13). Feisal-Weizmann Agreement in London (T E Lawrence present) welcomes Jewish settlement in Palestine. **Baltic States** — RN sqn sails from Riga for Copenhagen & sails thence to Rosyth (10). **Red Latvian Army occupies Riga** & sets up Latvian SSR. **S Russia** — Denikin's Volunteer Army (25,000 men & 75 guns) splits typhus-ridden Red Eleventh Army (70,000) in three (-10, *see* 20), takes 50,000 PoWs. **Britain** — **19,000 soldiers protest at Folkestone over slow demobilization**, refuse to return to France from leave (*see* 7). Rutherford splits the atom at Manchester Univ.

Sat 4
Baltic States — 2 RN cruisers & 1 destroyer help Estonian Army smash Red Seventh Army (*see* 8). Estonia appeals for arms from Britain (6). **Germany** — †Ex-Chancellor Count Hertling aged 76.

Sun 5
Poland — Prince Sapieha's Warsaw coup column. **W Russia** — Red W Army occupies Vilna and advances farther W (11, *see* 18 Apr).

Germany — **Spartacist revolutionary workers rise v Govt** which they declare deposed at Berlin, 700,000 said to be in protest demo over Govt's dismissal of left-wing Berlin police chief (2), but garrison and sailors not won round and under 1000 Spartactists are armed (-13); Munich, Stuttgart, Dresden & Essen *Army & Freikorps* kill est 1000 (*see* 8). Munich locksmith Anton Drexler founds German Workers' (future Nazi) Party (*see* 19 Sept).

Mon 6
Yugoslavia — PM Protich notifies Allies of union. **Britain** — Engineering & shipbuilding strike (40,000) v I break system (-1 Mar). Raw materials rationing no longer necessary. **USA** — †Ex-Pres Theodore Roosevelt aged 60. **Russia: Urals** — Kolchak orders halt at Perm & shift S to centre of his front, ie to reach Volga. **Germany** — SPD politician Gustav Noske made C-in-C Berlin garrison, he encourages formation of 28 *Freikorps* nationwide by end Jan.

Tue 7
Diplomacy — Wilson arrives in Paris. **Russia** — British force sent to Caucasus. Siberia: 1/9th Hampshire Regt (1023) relieves 25th Middlesex at Omsk (-May). **Britain** — War Cabinet's Eastern Ctee dissolved. Revised de-mobilization rules issued after 2 soldiers' demos in Whitehall. Lloyd George appeals for patience (8, *see* 29).

Wed 8
Germany-Berlin: Pro-Govt demos as garrison, Socialist People's Militia & *Freikorps* reoccupy seized public buildings. **Armenia** — Turk **evacuation complete**. **Turkey** — Milne replaces Sir HFM Wilson as C-in-C at Constantinople (35,000 Allied troops) and GOC Army of the Black Sea (*see* 10 & 15). **Baltic States** — Estonians retake Narva & 3 other towns (-18). **Britain** — Haig's penultimate (21 Dec 1918) dispatch published. **S Russia** — White Don & Volunteer leaders meet at Torgovaia and arrange operational unity under Denikin as AFSR.

Thu 9
Diplomacy — Italian PM Orlando & Foreign Minister Sonnino arrive in Paris. **Peace Process** — French Conference reps designated; the 5 Allied Great Powers to have 2 reps each on Peace Conference Supreme Council. Hoover's Allied Supreme Council of

Supply & Relief formed (1st meets 19). **Germany** — Martial law in Berlin. Riots in Westphalia & Saxony. **S Persia** — First RAF planes join Bushire Field Force (*see* 27). **Britain** — 150,000 Yorkshire miners strike & secure 20-min mealbreak per shift (-23).

Fri 10
Diplomacy — Gen Smuts' League of Nations pamphlet. Foch's memo on French Rhine frontier sent to Allies. **Germany** — Radicals seize Bremen declaring Soviet Republic (-4 Feb). **N Russia** — Allies occupy Rugozerski (*see* 19). **Baltic States** — Red Army takes Mitau, SW of Riga. **S Russia** — Ukrainians take Poltava. **Galicia** — Poles relieve Lemberg from Ukrainians. **Turkey** — British formally take over Baghdad's administration, French i/c European Turk railways (*see* 15) **Britain** — New Coalition Govt announced. Car use restrictions withdrawn, petrol allowance increased.

Sat 11
Peace Process — British Ministers arrive in Paris for Peace Conference. **Germany** — Cuxhaven 'Republic' proclaimed. 3000 *Freikorps* troops enter Berlin after *Vorwärts* newspaper offices recaptured (night 10, *see* 13 & 15). **Italy** — Mussolini among band ending ex-Minister Bissolati's speech on League of Nations at Scala Opera House, Milan (*see* 23 Feb).

Sun 12
Diplomacy — Supreme War Council considers Armistice renewal (*see* 16). **Peace Process** — Chief reps discuss Peace Conference procedure, all countries who severed relations with Germany entitled to attend plenary (1st session 18). **Hungary** — National Council names Count Karolyi Prov Pres, he asks Berenkey to form Govt (20). **Britain** — Butter ration increased to 1oz & margarine to 5oz pw.

Mon 13
Arabia — Fakhri Pasha's starving 16,645 **Turk garrison** (12 bns) **of Medina finally surrenders** holy city to K Hussein of Hejaz (Turk evacuation -31 Mar). **Germany** — Govt troops crush Spartacists in Berlin (*see* 15). **Britain** — Air raid casualty tables published.

Tue 14
Italy — Nitti's resignation causes ministerial crisis, PM Orlando leaves Paris. **Germany** — Dortmund rioting.

Wed 15
Germany — Hiding Spartacist leaders **Liebknecht & Rosa Luxemburg** (body found in canal 1 June) arrested and **shot dead** in Berlin en route to prison by officers of the Gd Cav Rifle Div (2 sentenced to death 14 May). **Britain** — Disabled soldiers given priority in Govt factories; employers asked to replace civilian war workers with them. **Trans-Caspia** — Gen Milne put i/c, sees Gen Malleson at Askabad (27); cables London for policy decision 1 Feb. **Turkey** — Allies take military control of Constantinople (British, French and Italian zones).

Thu 16
Diplomacy — **Germany signs new Armistice terms** at Trier (-17 Feb); she is to give up many farm implements & her merchant fleet; Allies reserve right to occupy Strasbourg defences on Rhine's E bank. **Poland** — Paderewski PM, forms National Govt with Pilsudski as C-in-C (27). **Trans-Caspia** — 900 British & Whites (c116 cas) defeat c5000 Reds & 8 guns (est 600 cas & 7 MGs lost) at Annenkovo, NE of Merv. **Italy** — National Institute of Ex-Soldiers formed, 900,000 now demobilized.

Fri 17
Baltic States — Rear-Adm Cowan's cruiser *Caledon* & 3 destroyers arrive at Libau, Latvia. **Britain** — 538,912 troops demobilized so far (*see* 31).

Sat 18
PEACE CONFERENCE OPENS at 1530 in Quai d'Orsay, Paris, 48 years to day since German Empire's proclamation at Versailles: Clemenceau unanimously elected Chairman with 27 countries represented by up to 5 delegates each; secretariat appointed. **Britain** — National War Bonds issue closed at £1645.3m (£148m in last week).

Sun 19
N Russia — Red Sixth Army attacks 2000 Allies in 37° of frost at Shenkursk (on R Vaga, 180 miles S of Archangel), forcing Allied retreat (24-25, *see* 26). **Germany** — National Assembly elections (30m of 35m over 20 vote) for 421 deputies (*see* 23).

Mon 20
Allied Council of Supply & Relief approves Commissions at Trieste, Bucharest, Constantinople & in Poland. **Britain** — 161,953 British PoWs (4624 civilians) re-

patriated since Armistice, camps in Germany practically empty; 3330 German interned civilians repatriated. Peak PoW total in British hands 507,215 (incl 43,308 civilians). **France** - 514/654 export restrictions lifted (19 left 14 May). **S Russia** — Denikin's Whites take Piatigorsk (capital N Caucasus SSR), Kislovodsk & Georgievsk (22). Gen Milne visits Tiflis (HQ British 27th Div) and Baku (22) seeing Caucasus govts (*see* 6 Feb).

Tue 21
Britain — Gen Milne's 1 Dec 1918 final Salonika dispatch published. **Ireland** — Sinn Fein Dublin Congress of MPs (except 36 in prison) convenes first Dail (Parlt) & declares Ireland independent; 2 policemen killed in Co Tipperary by 9 Irish Vols, 'troubles' resume. IRA lose 600 killed (more than British) by July 1921 truce (*see* 2 Feb).

Wed 22
Peace Conference approves Wilson's fruitless 'Prinkipo proposal' (by radio) to get Russian parties to meet on Sea of Marmara Island (off Constantinople) beginning 15 Feb (*see* 24, 26, 29 & 5 Feb). **Siberia** — Reds take Orenburg & hold through long siege.

Thu 23
Germany — Election results give Social Democrats majority (163 deputies). **Britain** — 150,000 miners begin strike for shorter working week (*see* 25).

Fri 24
Peace Conference appoints Arms Control Commission for Germany; Supreme War Council fixes occupation army strengths. Ukraine & Estonian reps refuse 'Prinkipo proposal', likewise Archangel (27). **Russia** — Red Central Ctee calls for 'the most merciless mass terror in relation to all Cossacks involved, directly or indirectly, in the struggle with Soviet power'. **Galicia** — Czechs beat Poles (-28). **Britain** — Govt refuses to recognize Police & Prison Officers National Union.

Sat 25
Peace Process — League of Nations recognized as part of Peace Treaty & 8 Int'l Ctees formed in 2nd Plenary Session. **Britain** — Sugar ration increased to 12oz pw. 67,000 workers begin unsuccessful Clydeside strike (-mid Feb) for 40hr wk (*see* 31); 40,000 Belfast engineers strike for 44 (instead of 54) hr wk, gain 47 (-9 Feb).

Sun 26

Petrograd *Red Gazette* calls 'Prinkipo proposal' 'Universal surrender of bourgeoisie' (*see* 29; 5 Feb). **N Russia** — Red Sixth Army attacks Allied defences at Tulgas till it is evacuated & burned (30). **Bavaria** — Eisner wins only 3 of 160 seats in elections as law & order breaks down.

Mon 27
Peace Process — Japan presents Pacific claims (China 28). **Russia** — †Gen Ivanov (ex-Tsarist SW Front cdr 1914-16) of typhus, aged 67. 2nd Czech Div's evacuation ordered. **S Persia** — British occupy Kazerun; Bushire & Shiraz cols unite (28). RAF attack Nasir Diwan.

Tue 28
Peace Process — France presents Togo & Cameroons claims.

Wed 29
Peace Process — Commission of Polish Affairs formed & sent (permanent Ctee from 12 Feb). **Britain** — Churchill announces Army pay bonus of 10s 6d pw (cost £36.5m pa) and only 900,000-strong Occupation Army (3,676,473, 1 Jan) to be retained of men under 36 enlisted after 1 Jan 1916 or 1-yr volunteers. Release of Admiralty's 3000 trawlers urged. **Urals** — Red First Army takes Uralsk, disorganizing Orenburg & Ural Cossacks. **Siberia** — Gen Knox cables re 'Prinkipo Proposal', 'suddenly the whole of Russia is informed by wireless that her Allies regard the brave men who are here fighting for part of civilization as on a par with the bloodstained, Jew-led Bolsheviks'.

Thu 30
Peace Process — Supreme Council adopts mandate system, provisional arrangements for German colonies & occupied Anatolia. Weizmann tells Col Meinertzhagen 'Zionism is constructive Bolshevism'. S African war losses published. **Russia** — 3 ex-Grand Dukes shot in Petrograd.

Fri 31
Peace Process — Teschen Commission appointed & sent (*see* 1 Feb). Serb claims heard. **France** — 3 RN gunboats arrive at Strasbourg via Rhine. **Britain** — Army demobilization 977,525 so far (*see* 3 Feb). Govt announces railway control until 2 yrs after Peace Treaty signed. 678,702 (incl 53,000 ex-servicemen & 425,000 women) receiving out-of-work donations during Jan. **'Red Friday'**, Clydeside dock strike riot clashes with police & army (incl tanks) in Glasgow. Strike ends 11 Feb. **Baltic Provinces** — Red Army occupies Windau (-1 Feb), 40 miles miles N of Libau (*see* 9 Feb). **S Russia** — Gen Wrangel of 1st Cav Div made C-in-C Caucasus Volunteer Army v Gen Gittis

(ex-Tsarist Col aged 38) put i/c Red S Front (both late Jan). Red Eighth Army suffers 150 Cheka executions (2000 sentenced) in Jan. **Japan** — (Jan) French mission begins teaching the Army to fly (144 aircraft by 1920).

FEBRUARY 1919

Sat 1
Britain — New 5% National War Bonds issue. Supply Ministry replaces Munitions Ministry in organizing for peace & reconstruction. British air casualties announced. **Peace Process** — Czech-Polish Teschen Agreement signed. Rumanian claims presented. **Baltic States** — Estonians retake Verro & Walk in Livonia (*see* 7). Latvians retake Shavli. German Gen Goltz arrives at Libau (*see* 3 Mar). **Russia** — (Feb) Reds form combined Lithuanian Belorussian SSR '*Litbel*' (-Aug), wound up when Poles take Minsk. 152,000 Reds face Denikin in S (*see* May). Bashkir Corps deserts to Reds from Kolchak, S of Urals.

Sun 2
Britain — Michael Collins helps Sinn Fein leader de Valera escape from Lincoln prison (*see* 1 Apr). The other Sinn Fein prisoners released 6-10 Mar.

Mon 3
Peace Process — Venizelos presents Greece's Smyrna claims (-4). League of Nations Ctee first meets (*see* 14). **France** — Sugar ration increased 50%. **Britain** — Army demobilization 1,112,339 so far (*see* 14). Tube strike (-8) wins meal breaks. **Switzerland** — International Socialist Conference at Berne admits 2 Irish (non-British) delegates (7).

Tue 4
Britain — London waiters strike (-10) for 8-hr day and tipping reform fails. Canadian PM Sir R Borden opens London Exhibition of nearly 400 war memorial paintings.

Wed 5
Peace Process — Soviet Govt accepts 'Prinkipo Proposal' invitation (*see* 8). **Britain** — Guards Memorial Service at St Paul's Cathedral (*see* 25). **Ukraine** — Red Army retakes Kiev. **S Russia** — Denikin's Whites capture Grozny & Kizliar (6) linking with Terek Cossacks, only 10% Reds reach Astrakhan. **France** — Pétain letter thanks departing Italian Corps. **Aviation** — First sustained daily air passenger service begun by *Deutsche Luft-Reederei* using converted military biplanes between Berlin and Weimar (120 miles in 2hrs 18min).

Thu 6
Allied-German Agreement on food supplies. Emir Feisal heard at Peace Conference. British trade allowed with W bank of Rhine, Alsace-Lorraine, Czechoslovakia & Occupied

Austria. **Germany - National Assembly opens at Weimar** (*see* 11). **S Russia** — Milne at Constantinople cables CIGS that the 3 Caucasus republics unlikely ever to 'be wholly independent'.

Fri 7
Peace Process — Special Commission on German Materials of War & Disarmament formed. Italy's claims heard. **Baltic States** — Reds cleared from Estonia (*see* 9, 20, 24). **N Russia** — Allied success nr Kadesh (Archangel) & defence of Shredmekrenga (8-11).

Sat 8
Peace Process — Supreme Allied Economic Council announced. Prince Lvov's Paris 'Russian Political Conference' denies Soviet claim to represent Russia. Lloyd George returns to London (-6 Mar). **Germany** — Fighting in Berlin. **Ireland** — Lord-Lt FM French catches influenza, absent from work until 7 Apr. **Turkey** — Franchet d'Esperey fixes HQ at Constantinople as C-in-C *Armées Alliées en Orient*, clashes with British (17).

Sun 9
Baltic States — Cruiser HMS *Caledon* shells Reds out of Windau , Latvia (2 cruisers & 5 destroyers sail for Baltic 13). Estonians take Marienburg (10). **Aviation** — First London-Paris passenger flight, by Farman F60 Goliath, 3½ hrs at 97mph from Kenley to nr Versailles (*see* 22 Mar).

Mon 10
Peace Process — Armistice Ctee appointed, Marshal Foch President. French Finance Minister Klotz heard on German devastations in France. Italy refuses to submit Adriatic dispute with Yugoslavia to Wilson. **Britain** — Labour Ministry's Industrial Training Dept formed for the demobilized. Cabinet deluded by forged document that Germans aiming to subdue Allies by Bolshevism in their armies. **S Russia** — Denikin's right wing reaches Caspian.

Tue 11
Ebert elected first President of German Republic; provisional Weimar constitution published. Allied Maritime Transport Council announces use of surrendered tonnage for repatriation & food transport to Central Europe. **Peace Process** — Belgian claims heard. **Britain** — New naval prize money regulations. Parliament reassembles. Anglo-US Reading-Hines Agreement settles 3 payment classes for British transport of AEF soldiers in Europe.

Wed 12
Peace Process — Allies settle Armistice conditions renewal and form Military & Naval Ctee with Foch as President.

Germany — New Chancellor Scheidemann forms Cabinet, Count Brockdorff-Rantzau Foreign Minister. **Poland** — Allied Mission arrives at Warsaw. **S Russia** — Ukrainians defeat Reds nr Kiev. **USA** — 3-yr naval programme passed. **Britain** — Coalminers reject Govt's 6s pw wage offer & inquiry in reply to 30% claim, 6-hr day & nationalization, decide to hold strike ballot (13, *see* 20). War Cabinet agrees on Russia 'that intervention on a large scale was not possible'; Lloyd George tells Churchill 'if we were going to do any good we should need a million men at least' (*see* 16).

Thu 13
Peace Process — Syrian claims presented (Druses' 15). **S Russia** — French Gen Berthelot arrives at Odessa & enrages Whites by saying he will give it to Ukrainians. **Britain** — Labour amendment to Commons loyal address regretting measures to meet industrial unrest defeated 311-59.

Fri 14
Peace Process — **League of Nations Covenant** (published 15) **approved** by 27 nations at 3rd Plenary Session. **Germany** — Ruhr general strike (-19), Spartacists seize several towns. **Russia** — (c) Red E Front 84,000 combat troops, 372 guns, 1471 MGs v Kolchak's 256 guns & 1235 MGs. Red S Front 117,000 men, 460 guns, 2040 MGs v 38,000 Don Cossacks, 165 guns & 491 MGs (*see* 15 & 20). Red W Front 81,000 men, Red Ukrainian Front 47,000. **Britain** - Demobilization to date 1,411,936.

Sat 15
Peace Process — **Allied Supreme Economic Council raises Dardanelles blockade** (British trade may resume with Turkey, Bulgaria & Russian Black Sea ports). Pres Wilson leaves France from Brest in liner *George Washington* for US. **Diplomacy** — British Military representative in Vienna cabled to send officer to Emperor Charles (*see* 21). **S Russia** — Gen Krasnov resigns as Don Cossack Ataman, pro-Volunteer Gen Bogaevski replaces. **Trans-Caspia** — British withdrawal ordered by end Mar, Gen Malleson informs Whites 1 Mar (*see* 6 Mar). **E Persia** — 1640 British-Indian troops plus 10,000 men on supply lines with 23,300 animals. **Britain** — Requisitioned passenger liner release begins. Treasury bills outstanding below £1bn for first time since May 1918.

Sun 16
Peace Process — **Armistice extension terms signed** at Trier, to last till peace signed (presented by Foch 14). Foch demands 'cessation of the German attacks against Poles in Poznan, E Prussia and

Upper Silesia'. †British Middle East expert Mark Sykes in Paris of double pneumonia. **Austria** — National Assembly election makes Social Democrats largest party. **Russia** — Lloyd George in Paris tells Churchill in 2 telegrams that British policy pro-Whites but they not foreigners must oust Reds . This remains HMG policy despite Churchill's continued efforts for greater intervention.

Tue 18
Peace Process — Yugoslav claims heard. **Britain** — PM instructs Food Ministry to lower prices.

Wed 19
Clemenceau wounded by anarchist Cottin (sentenced to death 15 Mar), absent from Conference (-27, *see* 25). **Bavaria** — 600 Bavarian sailors' coup bid crushed by Left and Right.

Thu 20
Amir Habibullah Khan of Afghanistan murdered by pro-war party while on hunting expedition; 3rd son Amanulla succeeds (*see* 8 May). **Baltic States** — Estonians occupy Oesel Island. **S Russia** — Red S Front defeats Don Cossacks N of R Donetz, latter reduced to 15,000. **Britain** — Food Controller announces mild controls' retention & increased beer (price reduced 24) & spirits supply. Miners postpone strike for wage report by 20 Mar. Zeebrugge Raid 9 May 1918 dispatch published. **Britain** — Gen Marshall's 1 Oct 1918 Mesopotamia dispatch published. **Hungary** — 4-8 policemen killed in Communist demo, Béla Kun and other Communist leaders imprisoned (*see* 21 Mar).

Fri 21
Peace Process — Danish claims on Schleswig-Holstein heard. **Germany** — Bavarian PM Eisner murdered by royalist ex-Lt Count Arco auf Valley, 3 others killed & 3 wounded in Munich Diet; city riots for 2 days. Central Ctee declares martial law. **Diplomacy** — Emperor Charles writes to King George V, thanking him for sending British officer for his protection (*see* 27).

Sat 22
Galicia — Polish-Ukrainian truce at Lemberg (-3 Mar).

Sun 23
Pres Wilson lands at Boston and speaks for League of Nations (arrives NY 24, *see* 26 & 27).

Mon 24
Peace Process — Albanian claims heard. Sinn Fein 'envoy' O`Kelly in Paris. **Russia** — Trotsky tells Red Army cadets in Moscow 'situation is completely favourable'. Red Caspian Flotilla surrenders to Allies (*see* 1 Mar). **Baltic States** — C-in-C Gen Laidoner announces Estonia clear of

foreign troops. **Britain** — 1919 British Industries Fair opens in London (-7 Mar).

Tue 25
Peace Process — Neutral zone created between Hungary & Rumania. GER Antwerp service restored. Britain and USA oppose Clemenceau's proposed independent W bank of Rhine (see 14 Mar). **Britain** — Guards Div returns (see 22 Mar).

Wed 26
Peace Process — Armenian claims heard (Zionist claims to national home in Palestine, 27). **USA** — Wilson fails to win round 34 hostile Congressmen at White House dinner.

Thu 27
Siberia — Reds take Orsk. **Austria** — Over 100 at Imperial Court, Eckartsau. Lt-Col Strutt arranges British lorryload of rations (28) incl first white bread since early 1916. **Britain** — Govt summons National Industrial Conference to solve unrest. **USA** — Wilson discusses League of Nations Covenant with Congress Foreign Affairs Ctee.

Fri 28
Peace Process — Russian 'Prinkipo' conference not to be held. **Blockade of Bulgaria ends. Italy** — War losses published. **USA** — Lord Reading arrives in New York. Senators Lodge & Knox oppose League of Nations. **Britain** — 948,620 people on out-of-work donations. **Bavaria** — Motion for declaring a Soviet republic defeated (see 7 Apr).

MARCH 1919

Sat 1
(Mar) Spanish influenza pandemic severe. British, French, US, German & Austrian war losses published. (Mar) Allies decide on Victory Medal (inscribed 'The Great War for Civilization'), over 5m issued. **Peace Process** — Feisal's famous welcoming letter to Jewish 'cousins'. **Russia** — Reds call up 1899 conscript class (1900 soon after Kolchak's offensive, 4). **Baltic States** — (Mar) Gen Yudenich arrives in Reval, Estonia as Kolchak's area C-in-C. **Siberia** — (Mar) Kolchak's front line strength 110,000 plus 118,000 foreign troops between Omsk (bulk of British supplies incl 600,000 rifles, 192 guns, 6831 MGs arrive there from Vladivostok -June). **S Russia** — (Mar) No 47 Sqn RAF arrives at Ekaterinodar. **Caspian** — 2 Russian gunboats (first ever diesel-engined warships) surrender to British at Baku. **N Russia** — Allies retreat 1 mile at Vistavka, 140 miles SE of Archangel (-9). **Britain** — RFP falls 10% to 120%. British Army Estimates reduce 2. 5m men to 952,000 at £287m pa. Paper allowances trebled. **France** — (Mar) 1000 AEF veterans form American

Legion at Paris caucus (see May). **Occupied Germany** — (Mar) British Rhine Army daily newspaper *Cologne Post* launched -Nov 1929). **Bavaria** — Prov Govt formed under Johannes Hoffmann (see 7 Apr). **Spain** — Martial law declared after food shortage riots.

Sun 2
Britain — Margarine unrationed. **Germany** — Lettow-Vorbeck and his 100-odd *Ostafrikaners* march in triumph through the Brandenburg Gate.

Mon 3
Germany — More Berlin fighting kills c1500 (-14), Communist-called general strike (3-6). **Galicia** — Ukrainians bombard Lemberg. **Austria** — Emperor Charles tells Lt-Col Strutt 'I first tried to rule autocratically, and then democratically; both were errors, but of the two the latter was the greater'. **Turkey** — Damid Ferid Pasha Grand Vizier (Sultan's brother-in-law), Tewfik Pasha resigns. **Britain** — Coal Industry Commission opens. Meat prices down 2d/lb. **Italy** — Last US troops sail from Genoa. **Russia** — 3rd Communist International (*Komintern*) founded at Moscow; 8th Communist Party Conference (350,000 party members) changes emphasis to win 'middle peasants' v Kolchak; party organs defined (see 19). **Baltic States** — Gen Goltz's 25,000 Latvian-Germans (incl *Freikorps* Iron Div) begin advance from Libau on Riga, retake Murayeva (5) from Reds (see 10).

Tue 4
Siberia — Kolchak's White **'Ufa' Offensive** begins on 700-mile front, advances up to 250 miles in 8 weeks taking 115,000 sq miles & 5m people. **USA** — Wilson New York speech on League but 37 senators back Lodge's Anti-League resolution. US Army CoS gives total loss estimate. **Austria** — New Parliament assembles. **Britain** — **War Cabinet decide to evacuate N Russia** as soon as possible, ie June. PM addresses National Industrial Conference. (c) Cloth commandeered for demobilization suits. Canadian riot (over demobilization) at Rhyl, N Wales.

Wed 5
Peace Process — Montenegrin claims heard. **France** — Meat control ended (milk also, 22). **Britain** — Labour Party demands conscription's abolition.

Thu 6
Allied German Spa food relief talks end due to Germany's refusal to surrender ships (talks resume at Brussels 13). Rumanian war losses published. **Trans-Caspia** — By now 900 White Russians from Caucasus in Askabad, British

withdrawal publicly announced (11, achieved by 2 April). **France** — Lloyd George returns to Paris (-14 Apr). **USA** — Wilson sails for France in *George Washington* having failed to win support for his League policy. **Britain** — Board of Trade announces 1.2m women added to work force by the war.

Fri 7
Britain — Record 790,521 civilians receive out-of-work donations.

Sat 8
Peace Process — Belgian report demands 1839 Treaty neutrality revision. **Germany** — Gen Plumer cables Lloyd George urging Rhineland food relief (see 18). **Egypt** — Zaghlul Pasha & 3 other nationalist leaders deported to Malta (-14); Cairo riots (-11) & countrywide (11-20). **Britain** — PM appeals to employers to engage disabled ex-service-men.

Mon 10
German Army to be limited to 100,000 volunteers, Navy 15,000 (see 19). **Baltic States** — Latvians & Germans retake Tukkum (see 18). **S Russia** — Cossack Maj Grigorev's 15,000 Reds take Kherson on R Dnieper despite stern resistance by 1000 (mainly) Greeks, Reds shoot PoWs after 500 hostages found massacred; then storm Nikolayev (12). **USA** — Prewar shipping tonnage trebled to 3,834,760t, 45% US cargo in US-owned ships v 9. 7% prewar.

Wed 12
Peace Process — Air Commission appointed. **Egypt** — Allenby leaves Cairo for Paris. **Russia** — Final Soviet concessions to US diplomat William Bullitt. **Germany** — Interned ships in Chile to be given up for food.

Thu 13
At Brussels Allies agree to supply Germany 370,000t food pm for her merchant marine & £7m gold in Bank of Belgium (+ £11m within 10 days). **Britain** — **Army demobilization reaches 2m** incl 52,000 officers (see 31). Robertson C-in-C Rhine (see 19 Apr), Haig GOC-in-C Home Forces (i/c from 15 Apr). **Germany** — Some cities restricted to 2lb potatoes pw, only 45% of food home grown.

Fri 14
Britain & USA offer France defence treaties in lieu of Rhineland Republic on W bank. Clemenceau asks for guarantees, demilitarized W bank & 31-mile strip on E bank (17, see 20). Pres Wilson back in Paris. **France** — Franc falls against £ (-18) due to ending of HMG London market support.

Sat 15
Russia — Whites take Ufa, Ossa & Birsk. (c) Cheka chief

Dzerzhinsky also made Interior Commissar. **Austria** — Coalition Govt under Chancellor Renner who decides to force issue with Emperor, internment or exile if no abdication (see 17, 19, 22). **Britain** — c22,500 Army animals still being treated (60,000 at Armistice).

Mon 17
Peace Process — Baltic States & Ukraine demand recognition. **Baltic States** — Germans take Bausk, Latvia. **N Russia** — Archangel sector: Reds overwhelm French garrison nr Bolshe Ozerki (-18) & repel British counter-attack (23). **Britain** — **Liquor control relaxation**, 9.30pm uniform closing hour. **Diplomacy** — Emperor Charles writes to Alfonso XIII of Spain via special courier urging Allied military support v radicalism in Danube area. Alfonso forwards to King George V (29), letter sent to Lloyd George in Paris for Peace Conference. Lt-Col Strutt cabled to get Habsburg royal family into Switzerland at once, tells Emperor, who refuses to leave (see 19).

Tue 18
Egypt — 8 British soldiers murdered in train in Deirut. **Britain** — Over 1m (incl 305,256 ex-servicemen & 519,047 women) on out-of-work donation scheme. **Baltic States** — Goltz's Latvians & Germans retake Mitau, find many hostages massacred by Reds in citadel, but offensive halts (31).

Wed 19
Peace Process — German Navy to be limited to 36 ships. Supreme War Council orders Poles & Ruthenians to stop fighting. Indian delegation asks for Turkey to control Islam's holy places, Constantinople & Thrace. **Russia** — 8th Communist Party Congress heralds 'the era of the worldwide proletarian Communist revolution'. **Austria** — Lt-Col Strutt persuades Empress Zita that Switzerland best choice 'A dead Habsburg is no good to anyone, whereas a live one, with a family, may yet be'; Strutt sees Chancellor Renner (20, see 22).

Thu 20
The Big Five discuss Near East with Allenby, who is made Egypt Special High Commissioner (21) and returns there (25, see 7 Apr). **Britain** — Coal industry Sankey Royal Commission interim report (see 24). **Hungary** — Allied ultimatum (by French Military Mission Chief) demands extensive crown lands within 10 days incl Debrecen and Oradea, second and third cities.

Fri 21
Danube navigation resumes. **Hungary** — Count Karolyi's **Govt in Budapest (resigned) replaced by Communist-Socialist coalition in which**

Communist Béla Kun foreign minister among 16 people's commissars whom Soviets support. Allied Missions leave (26). **Hungarian Soviet Republic declared.**

Sat 22
Peace Process — League of Nations first meeting since 14 Feb. **Egypt** — Gen Bulfin C-in-C. **Austria** — Lt-Col Strutt gets Chancellor Renner to drop final abdication demand by drafting telegram (without authority) ordering stop to food trains. **Britain** — Guards Div victory march through London. **Aviation** — Farman brothers open Paris-Brussels weekly air passenger service.

Sun 23
Italy — Mussolini founds Fascists (200) at hall in Piazza San Sepulchro, Milan, during year of constant strikes, inflation & Bolshevik demos. **Austria** — Imperial family (25 persons) **leave for Swiss exile** in imperial train with 7 British military police as escort, watched by 2000 people, many weeping.

Mon 24
Peace Process — Council of Ten reduced to Council of Four at Lloyd George's suggestion (Wilson, Lloyd George, Clemenceau, Orlando) to speed treaty, first meets 25. **Switzerland** — British-protected Emperor Charles arrives via Innsbruck (Italian Third Army). **Britain** — Tea prices and distribution de-controlled. 100,000 miners strike (-29) but await national ballot on Royal Commission.

Tue 25
Germany — **First food ship docks at Hamburg,** c400,000t of food delivered by 13 May. **Switzerland** — Austrian imperial family stay at Bourbon-Parma Chateau of Wartegg on Lake Constance; (c) Charles signs the Feldkirch Manifesto of 24 March disowning the Republic, but only privately distributed for the record (see 3 Apr). **USA** — US 27th Div triumphal march through New York.

Wed 26
German Armistice Commission refuses Allied request to let Gen Haller's Polish troops from France through Danzig (Paris talks since 21) but suggest 4 other Baltic ports (28). League of Nations Revision Ctee appointed (Lord R Cecil, M Larnaude, Venizelos, Col House). **Italy** — Ex-Austrian Fleet, taken prize to Venice, surrenders to Italian Navy.

Thu 27
Britain — National Industrial Conference backs 48-hr week. Railway Agreement confirmed.

Fri 28
Peace Process — French Saar memo discussed. Morocco Commission appointed. **Balkans** — Hungary declares

war v Czechoslovakia and her Red troops invade Slovakia (*see* 16 & 26 Apr). **Britain** — Rouble note import prohibited except Archangel Prov Govt's.

Sat 29
Peace Process — War Responsibilities Commission's final report. **Diplomacy** — **France announces no more troops going to Russia** (*see* 18 Apr). **Turkey** — 2 companies of Italian sailors occupy Adalia (S Anatolia). **Britain** — 326,741 motor vehicle licences issued, about same as 1916. **Holland** — Ex-Kaiser says he prefers suicide to trial by Allies (*see* 9 Apr).

Sun 30
Peace Process — Wilson refuses Clemenceau Rhineland annexation but concedes Saar mines. **Diplomacy** — Lenin offers German alliance with Hungary v Allies & Poland. **India** — Delhi riots during 'Passive Resistance' to Rowlatt Acts.

Mon 31
Peace Process — Foch vainly reads the Big Four his memo on Rhine frontier necessity. **N Russia** — Red attack on Archangel front repulsed. Anglo-French platoon & White Siberian patrol meet at Ust Ujva on R Pechora, 400 miles SE of Archangel. Gen Maynard crushes Red revolt at Murmansk. **Britain** — Demobilization to date 2,414,000; 192,678 widows' & 10,605 orphans' pensions granted so far affecting 355,211 children.

APRIL 1919

Tue 1
Gen Haller's 35,000 troops (incl 7 French aircraft sqns) return to Poland from France via Danzig (-8). **Peace Process** — Council of Four decide on Rhineland's demilitarization, appoint Saar Valley Commission, decide to lift blockade, & send Smuts to Hungary, but his mission fails (2-6). King Albert flies into Paris, meets Lloyd George (2) & Wilson (4), flies out (5). German Financial Delegation meets Economic Council. **Ukraine** — (Apr) Red plane (ex-German) makes first flight Vinnitsa-Budapest; Hungarian Communist leader Szamuley flown out to Moscow (late May). **N Russia** — Second British attack on Bolshie Ozerki fails. **S Russia** — (Apr) 12 British tanks with 70 instructors delivered to Denikin at Ekaterinodar (*see* 22). **Trans-Caspia** — Last British troops (c130) leave (*see* 23 May). **S Persia** — (Apr) Most British troops withdrawn to India. **Britain** — RFP falls 7% to 113%. Free trade with Poland & Estonia. Regular Army recruiting re-opened. **Ireland** — Eamon de Valera elected President of Sinn Fein Dail (*see* 5 July). Limerick general strike (14-25).

Wed 2
Baltic States — 2 RN cruisers & 10 destroyers bring 20,000 rifles, 18 guns & 20 lorries for Latvian Army. **S Russia** — **Reds enter Crimea.** Gen d'Anselme announces **Odessa evacuation** causing panic as 30,000 civilians & 10,000 White troops embark (-5), many suicides (-5). **Britain** — Jellicoe & Beatty made Admirals of the Fleet. 10% rent increases permitted. Household Cavalry memorial service.

Thu 3
Peace Process — Council of Four consider Adriatic (Fiume) question. Wilson sick with 'flu. Spain first neutral to apply to join League of Nations. **Austria** — So-called 'Habsburg Law' passed unopposed, Habsburgs banished for good & private property forfeit. **Britain** — Meat rationing to cease end June. Commons debate German war indemnities (200 MPs cable Lloyd George for firmness 8).

Fri 4
Peace Process — Versailles agreement to make Danzig a Free City (*see* 15 Nov 1920).

Sat 5
N Russia — British again repulse Reds (180 cas incl 80 PoWs) on Archangel front. British 5000-volunteer relief force sails for Archangel (9, *see* 27 May).

Sun 6
Polish PM Paderewski arrives in Paris. Clemenceau tells Foch independent Rhineland W bank not feasible (*see* 18). **S Russia** — French & Greek troops evacuate typhus-infected Odessa (announced 8).

Mon 7
Peace Process — Saar talks deadlock, Wilson considers US withdrawal. **Egypt** — Allenby announces Zaghlul Pasha & associates' relief from Malta. Rushdi Pasha PM (9-23). **Siberia** — Whites take 3 towns incl Sterlitamak. **Britain** — **Grand Fleet dissolved** (Beatty farewell speech 5). **Bavaria** — Soviet Republic formed (-1 May). Hoffmann Govt flees to Bamberg (*see* 16).

Tue 8
Britain — Free passage to Dominions for ex-servicemen & women (later).

Wed 9
Peace Process — **Saar to be under League of Nations control for 15 years** until plebiscite, but France to own coal mines. Council of Four sign Kaiser's indictment for trial. 200 MPs cable Lloyd George urging no recognition of Soviet Govt. **Germany** — Brunswick revolt (-17).

Thu 10
Peace Process — League of Nations accepts Monroe Doctrine, Geneva to be its HQ (8, *see* 28). **India** — Amritsar

rioting begins. Rioting at Kansur (12) & in Punjab (14-18, *see* 13). **Siberia** — Reds retire on Ural front (-15), but Trotsky & Red Army commanders at Simbirsk plan counter-attack v Kolchak. **N Russia** — Canadian Malmoot Coy & armoured train take Urosozero on Murmansk Railway, causing 90+ Red cas; White battalion takes Voyomosalmi 50 miles to E (*see* 1 May). **Britain** — Haig's 1918 post-Armistice dispatch published. **Portugal** — Riots (-14).

Fri 11
Peace Process — 4th Plenary Session approves International Labour Organization. **Balkans** — Rumanians temporarily withdraw from Hungary but resume advance (15, *see* 16 & 21). **Switzerland** — Emperor Charles writes to King George V thanking him for help; moves to Villa Prangins, Lake Geneva in May. **Britain** — Marshall's final Mesopotamia 1 Feb 1919 dispatch published.

Sat 12
Peace Process — Syrian & Arab affairs. **S Russia** — Reds occupy Yalta & Zhitomir. Churchill enlarging British Military Mission to Denikin to 1500 (340 already sailed, *see* 22) **Siberia** — Whites take Buguruslan & Belebei; Ural Cossacks retake Orsk.

Sun 13
India — Amritsar Massacre; martial law declared (15-9 June).

Mon 14
Rumania adopts Gregorian calendar. **Britain** — Trade allowed with Yugoslavia, Montenegro, Albania, Latvia & Lithuania.

Tue 15
Siberia — (c) White military control extended to railways & towns, but official i/c Urals industry resigns v lack of support from Omsk. **S Russia** — (c) Red S Front offensives v Donbas & from Tsaritsyn. Trotsky claims 'the collapse of the Kolchakites will lead at once inexorably to the complete collapse of Denikin's volunteers (volunteers under the lash)'.

Wed 16
Rumania invades Red Hungary with 4 divs (+ 3 in res) to forestall any attempt to reconquer Transylvania (*see* 21). **Baltic States** — Gen Goltz's Germans overthrow Latvian Govt at Libau (*see* 3 May). **S Russia** — Last White Volunteers leave Crimea covered by French troops (*see* 19, 22, 25). **Britain** — Lloyd George triumphantly defends his decisions in Commons. Coalminers ballot accepts Sankey proposals. Naval, Military & Air Force Act extends conscription where needed to June 1920. **Bavaria** — 'Red Victory of Dachau': bn of new Bav Red Army (c20,000 strong) captures Dachau, NW of

Munich, routing or capturing c2000 *Freikorps* of previous govt which now accepts Berlin's help (*see* 18).

Thu 17
Allies refuse Dr Nansen's food offer to Russia unless fighting ceases. **N Russia** — Gen Maynard's Whites rout Reds at Lake Vigo, Murmansk sector; 2nd action nr Bolshe Ozerki, Archangel sector.

Fri 18
Peace Process — German Armistice Commission invited to Paris by French War Minister for 25, Foch refusing (*see* 25) to receive Treaty; his views deliberately leaked to *Le Matin* & *Daily Telegraph*. Clemenceau has already sounded Pétain on replacing him (*see* 25). Berlin announces sending 6 delegates (19, *see* 25). **W Russia** — **Poles invade**, take Lida, then Vilna & Baronivichi (19). **Black Sea** — French Navy mutinies (-28). **India** — Gandhi advises Passive Resistance's suspension; Delhi rioting. **Bavaria** — Munich: 14 die in Red Army faction fighting. Weimar Govt aircraft leaflet city (19 & 20) to say help coming (*see* 27).

Sat 19
Peace Process — Wilson refuses to participate in Dalmatian coast talks. **Germany** — Gen Robertson arrives at Cologne, relieves Plumer (22) as C-in-C, Rhine. **Russia** — Red attack on Sevastopol begins. c400 picked British troops land at Murmansk (reach Maselskaya 6 May, 438 miles S). †Adm Eberhardt, ex-Black Sea Fleet C-in-C at Petrograd aged 63. **Britain** — Last of 4126 conscentious objectors released from work.

Sun 20
Peace Process — Zaghlul Pasha, Egyptian nationalist, arrives in Paris. **Montenegro** — *Skupshtina* assembly pronounces King Nicholas dethroned. **Ukraine** — Red First Army surrenders to Ukrainians.

Mon 21
Austria — Vienna rioting. **Hungary** — Rumanians resume advance in Hungary, reach R Theiss (26). **Russia** — Lenin tells Red Army C-in-C Vatsetis help for Donbas comes before secure rail link with Red Hungary (*see* 23 & 27). Kolchak's troops 100 miles E of Kazan.

Tue 22
Peace Process — Italian PM Orlando & Foreign Minister Sonnino refuse to continue work. Former leaves for Italy (24). Alsace-Lorraine Commission appointed. **Diplomacy** — US recognizes British protectorate over Egypt. **Crimea** — French Armistice with Reds (*see* 25). **S Russia** — Gen Milne arrives at Novorossisk, sees Denikin at Ekaterinodar (23, *see* 28).

Wed 23
Soviets invade Bessarabia. **Peace Process** — Wilson appeals to Italian people to renounce Fiume & Dalmatia. Supreme War Council calls for end to German meddling in Baltic States, Gen Goltz must be recalled (*see* 4 May).

Thu 24
Germany — Plundering in Hamburg. **Britain** — Army demobilization totals 2,536,866.

Fri 25
Peace Process — First German delegates arrive at Versailles (80 by 28). Foch addresses Clemenceau & Cabinet on Rhine frontier not having been shown draft Treaty (*see* 28). Chinese Shantung Province proposals presented re Japan (*see* 30). **Baltic States** — Adm Cowan sails with cruiser *Caledon* & 2 destroyers from Libau after Red Fleet reported at sea. **N Russia** — 3rd N Russian Rifle Regt (White) mutinies v officers, murders 7 & fights British; 300 desert to Reds. **S Russia** — Red Army enters Sevastopol, but Whites hold Kerch Isthmus (E Crimea) with RN help (scuttle 14 Russian submarines off Sevastopol 26). **Britain** — Anzac Day march through London. 379,799 ex-servicemen & 474,613 women on out-of-work donation.

Sat 26
Britain — Gen Deventer's last E Africa dispatch (-20 Jan 1919) published. Blacklist of neutral firms withdrawn. Football 'Victory Cup' Chelsea beats Fulham 3-0. **Hungary** — Yugoslav Sava Div and 2 French divs invade from S, latter install anti-Soviet govt at Arad. Czech 6th Div invades from N (*see* 3 May). Yugoslav Drina and Dunaj Divs attack (28 & 29).

Sun 27
Britain — Removal of Govt control of nearly all home commodities by 31 May announced. **Bavaria** — Weimar Govt troops surround Munich, reach outskirts (30) after Lenin telegram hails doomed Red republic (28).

Mon 28
S Russia — Lt-Gen C J Briggs Liaison Officer & Head British Military Mission 'Denmiss' to Denikin (-June, Holman succeeds). **Peace Process** — 5th Plenary Session approves revised League of Nations Covenant, appoints Sir J Drummond first Sec-Gen; also approves International Labour Organization's convention. Foch threatens resignation but withdraws it (Lloyd George & Pres Wilson agree to Pétain as replacement Generalissimo) *see* 6 May. **Siberia** — Khanzhin's W Army (Kolchak's Whites) takes Chistopol & Sergievsk but Red Fifth Army counter-attacks, drives Whites 200 miles E by end-May.

NW Russia — Finn partisans attack unofficially NE of Lake Ladoga, but, forced to abandon 2 places, taken by Reds landed from lake behind them (-3 May).

Tue 29
Peace Process — German Foreign Minister Count Brockdorff-Rantzau arrives. **Italy** — Chamber vindicates Govt 382-40. **Britain** — Labour Minister says 3m of 4m demobilized from forces & munitions already in work. Unlimited exports allowed to Switzerland & northern neutrals. **Turkey** — 12 former officials incl ex-minister face war crimes trials.

Wed 30
Peace Process — Japan granted Shantung subject to verbal promise of eventual restoration to China, Chinese delegation protest (6 May). **Britain** — Budget: no income tax change; excess profits duty halved; death duties increased on estates over £15,000; beer & spirit duties increased. All iron & steel industry subsidies now gone. Over 3m workers have reduced hours since 1 Jan. Press Bureau closed. **Turkey** — Kemal appointed Insp-Gen Ninth Army, Anatolia (*see* 17 May).

MAY 1919

Thu 1
Peace Process — Commission for protection of minorities in new & other states appointed. **Austria** — Yugoslavs take Klagenfurt. **Germany** — **Govt troops retake Munich** from Spartacists after they murder 10 hostages. Reprisals & death sentences (-14 June) raise deaths to 719 since 7 Jan (incl 58 Russian ex-PoWs who joined Bav Red Army). **Russia** — (May) In South 228,000 Reds & 400-550 guns v Denikin's 50,000 (Gen Mai-Maevsky new C-in-C Volunteer Army). Trotsky visits Ukraine for first time, 'The prevailing state of chaos, irresponsibility, laxity and separatism exceeds the most pessimistic expectations.' Cheka gets 100,000 internal security troops. Communist International May Day Appeal 'Before a year has passed, the whole of Europe will be Soviet.' Murmansk sector: 3000 Allies advance & take Maselskaya (-3). Archangel sector: Reds repulsed (2 & 10). **W Russia** — Poles take Svensiani. **S Russia** — Reds take Mariupol on Sea of Azov. RAF No 47 Sqn destroys 15 Red planes (-31). **Britain** — RFP falls 6% to 107%. **Civil flying allowed.** FM Lord French's *1914* published (*see* 16). HMG appoints Special Commission to help Belgium industrial reconstruction & in principle accept 48-hr week & minimum wage proposals. **France** — 2 die & over 800 injured in Paris Socialist Anarchist riots. **USA** — (May) American Legion 2nd Caucus at St Louis, Mo, completes constitution (*see* Nov).

Fri 2
Allies agree to occupy Budapest. **Germany** — **Hindenburg announces his resignation as Army C-in-C as from peace** (*see* 3 July). **Britain** — Admiralty publishes March 1915 Dardanelles dispatches.

Sat 3
Baltic States — German Latvian coup. Supreme Allied Council demands Gen Goltz's recall (4, 10 *see* 22). **Central Europe** — Hungarians invade Czechoslovakia & beat Czechs (24). **Britain** — **Ration book issue ended**; butter ration increased to 2oz per head pw. Overseas troops march through London. **Ireland** — 3 Irish-American 'Friends of Irish Freedom', having lobbied Wilson in Paris, arrive to report (3 June).

Sun 4
Peace Process — Supreme Allied Council invites Italians' return, they do (5). Senior US official, probably E House, sees Kerensky who feels Reds can last 'only a few months now' but fears Kolchack regime will be scarcely better. **China** — **15,000 Peking students 'May the 4th' protest over Shantung going to Japan.**

Mon 5
Rumanian terms presented to Hungary (*see* 8). **Switzerland** — Emperor Charles & Empress Zita's 5th son born. **Russia** — C-in-C Red Army Vatsetis sacks Col Kamenev for insubordination on E Front but Lenin re-instates him i/c E Front 3 weeks later. Vatsetis warns Defence Council that SAA supply heading for 'catastrophe'.

Tue 6
Peace Process — 6th Plenary session approves draft peace treaty; Foch, unhappy with French security guarantees, speaks against. Council of Three dispose of German colonies (SW Africa to S Africa, E Africa to Britain) & decides to allow Greeks to occupy Smyrna (*see* 13). **Diplomacy** — Britain recognizes Finland, & USA does (7). **Britain** — Food Controller envisages closing Food Ministry by Dec. **Aviation** — British Admiralty announces helium as non-inflammable hydrogen substitute for airship gas.

Wed 7
Peace Process — 7th Plenary Session: **draft treaty read by Clemenceau to German delegation** at Trianon Palace (Versailles) with 15 days for consideration in writing (deadline extended 20 to 29). Count Brockdorff-Rantzau in speech, remaining seated, refuses to admit whole war guilt. All German colonies mandated except Togo & Cameroons which await Anglo-French recommendations. **Ukraine** — Maj Grigorev rebels v Red Ukraine Front & disrupts

its rear areas till killed late July.

Thu 8
Peace Process — German delegation protests v specific peace terms (also 10, 11, 13, Saar 16, 19 PoWs, each on 1 topic). Complaints transferred to 13 ctees for specific clauses. Zionist delegation leader writes to Wilson and gets unequivocal statement of support. **E Europe** — Allies stop Rumanian advance in Hungary. Paderewski leaves Paris for Warsaw. **Siberia** — Reds retake Bugaruslan, Bugulma (12) & Belebei (18). Ural Cossacks take Aktiubinsk. **S Russia** — Denikin counter-offensive (-15) takes 25,000 PoWs from Red Tenth Army. **N Russia** — Archangel sector: 2 White bns repel surprise Red attack on Korelka. **India** — **Third Anglo-Afghan War begins** as Afghans invade across NW Frontier but repulsed by Maj-Gen Fowler at Bagh Springs with loss of 400 cas & 5 guns (11, *see* 13).

Fri 9
Britain — 408,491 ex-servicemen on out-of-work donations.

Sat 10
Baltic States — Pro-German Balt Govt established in Latvia. **Britain** — Labour Corps recruiting opens for military cemetery work in France (15,445 men by Apr 1920). Govt awards RN pay scheme with back pay from 1 Feb. **Aviation** — AV Roe & Co begin first regular air service in England with 3-seat Avros (Manchester to Southport & Blackpool -30 Sept for 4 guineas).

Mon 12
Peace Process — Economic Council decides on further blockade measures if Germany refuses to sign Treaty. **Germany** — National Assembly meets in Berlin, Chancellor Schiedemann asks 'What hand would not wither' if treaty signed. **Britain** — Covent Garden Opera House reopens.

Tue 13
Peace Process — Count Brockdorff-Rantzau note to Clemenceau refuses Germany's unique responsibility clause (& 24). **Baltic States** — Estonian Army (20,000) moves nearer Petrograd, lands at Kaporia Bight with RN support (*see* 17 & 18). **Turkey** — **Greek troops land at Smyrna** (-16) initially to protect Christian population and keep order, but about 20 Turks soon shot in streets; Greeks courtmartial 74 Greeks, Turks and Armenians for rioting (3 Greeks executed). Greeks occupy Magnesia (24), Aidin (27) & Aivali (28, *see* 28) inland. **Britain** — War shipping losses announced as 2197 ships (7,638,020grt). **Afghanistan** — British Khyber Pass force occupies Ft Dakka. Afghans counter-attack (16)

after falsely suing for peace (14), daily NW Frontier fighting till 3 June.

Wed 14
Peace Process — Dr Renner's Austrian delegation arrives at St Germain-en-Laye, terms for Austria discussed (15). Allies nominate Baltic Commission. Smuts to friend on peace terms '. . . the dimensions of the problem are beyond me, perhaps beyond human power'. **Britain** — Nurse Cavell's body brought home & buried at Norwich (15) after London services. Wartime Govt rail traffic valued at £112m plus £95m compensation excluding 'extra wear and tear'.

Thu 15
France — Zionist leader & master spy Dr Aaronsohn drowned in RAF DH4 mail plane crash, Boulogne Harbour, returning to Peace Conference. News not published till 20. **Siberia** — (c) Red E Front 361,000 men plus 195,000 in 3 rear MDs as Kolchak's armies retreat. **N Russia** — Murmansk Railway: 400 British storm 60th Village (named in honour of the 60th Rifles), Whites occupy Povyenets (18) & Allies take Medyezhya (21).

Fri 16
Britain — Asquith answers Lord French re Kitchener's supercession. Limited price coal exports to Allies ended.

Sat 17
Peace Process — Count Brockdorff-Rantzau leaves Versailles for Spa, returns (19) with long reply. **Baltic** — RN cruiser & 3 destroyers pursue 5 Soviet warships back into Kronstadt. **Belgium** — War damage official estimates $7.6bn. **S Russia** — Gen Ulagai's White cav charge & rout 6 Red cav regts on steppe N of R Manych which Wrangel bridges with causeway of village wooden fences (-18, *see* 20). **Britain** — Free petrol purchase restored. **Turkey** — Kemal leaves Constantinople, arrives at Black Sea port of Samsun (19, *see* 22; 11 July).

Sun 18
Baltic States — Gen Alexander P Rodzianko's White N Corps (6000) begins drive towards Petrograd from Estonia, Narva & Gdov taken (21, *see* 24). **Poland** — Paderewski resigns as PM.

Mon 19
Peace Process — Poles refuse to accept Allied decisions on Ukraine (*see* 27). **USA** — Army CoS & Sec of State Polk approve permanent 'Black Chamber' code & cypher organization. **Baltic States** — **Estonia declares herself independent republic.**

Tue 20
British Rhine Army ready to march farther into Germany to enforce peace terms. **S Russia** — Wrangel smashes

Red Tenth Army Manych front, taking 15,000 PoWs, 55 guns & 150 MGs; way to Volga & Tsaritsyn open (*see* 13 June). **France** — Chamber votes women vote.

Thu 22
Peace Process — German delegates leave for Spa to consult. **Baltic States** — Baltic Baron Manteuffel's German-Latvian *Landeswehr*, with air support, liberate Riga from Reds, but many hostages slaughtered and Manteuffel killed, German Maj Fletcher succeeds (*see* 2 June). **Turkey** — Kemal issues the Amasya Decisions, new national body needed (*see* 23 July).

Fri 23
Baltic — RN cruiser *Galatea*, destroyers, 3 minesweepers, fleet oiler & submarines reinforce Adm Cowan (-24, *see* 29). **Trans-Caspia** — Reds capture Merv.

Sat 24
Afghanistan — RAF Handley-Page bombs Kabul (4 hits on royal palace). Afghan ground counter-attack (26). **Britain** — Food exports to Germany allowed via Allies & neutrals (*see* 28). **W Russia** — Whites take Pskov, securing base area outside Estonia. **S Russia** — Denikin retakes Mariupol on Sea of Azov. CIGS cables Milne that British troops to to evacuate Caucasus, Italians to replace. **Siberia** — Reds re-occupy Sterlitamak.

Sun 25
France — 1,259,098 US troops now repatriated, all home by end Aug (*see* June). **Mesopotamia** — Kurd rising captures British officers (rescued 18 June).

Mon 26
Allied Supreme Council offers conditional recognition plus military & food support to Adm Kolchak (terms accepted 7 June). **Allied Mediterranean blockade raised** (*see* 12 July). Sweden requests Aaland Is plebiscite. **Britain** — Ex-servicemen demonstrate in London (Commons debate 28). Consumers' Council proposes permanent Food Ministry. (c) Passports only needed for Paris, Russia, enemy territory & military zones.

Tue 27
Peace Process — Draft treaty presented to Poland. German counter-proposals published in Berlin. **N Russia** — British 238th Relief Bde lands at Archangel, reaches front 6 June. **Afghanistan** — British Baluchistan Force (57 cas) captures Spin Baldak fortress (356 Afghan cas, 250 escape), posing threat to Kandahar

Wed 28
Central Europe — Yugoslavs attack Austrians in Carinthia (-6 June armistice). **Britain** — Limited food & clothing gifts to Germany, Austria & Hungary

allowed via recognized agencies. Govt inquiry into London traffic begins (London Traffic Board urged 21). **Afghanistan** — Amir Amanullah of Afghanistan writes to Viceroy of India requesting armistice (*see 2 June*). **Turkey — First Greco-Turk armed clash** at Odemis. **Syria** — Emir Feisal writes to Allenby with hopes for international commission, but Feisal already negotiating with the French. **S Russia** — French repulse Red attack on Benderi.

Thu 29
Peace Process — 7th Plenary Session receives incomplete draft Austrian Treaty (*see 2 June*). Allies offer Italy, Brenner Pass frontier better than in 1915 Treaty. German counter-proposals to Allies include RM100bn reparations; Alsace-Lorraine plebiscite; fixed coal supply to France for Saar's retention; colonies to go to arbitration; occupation armies to leave 6 months after Peace Treaty signed. **Germany** — Naval war losses published. **Russia** — Lenin tells E Front commissars 'If before winter we do not take the Urals I consider that the defeat of the Revolution will be inevitable'. **Baltic** — RN submarine *L16* misses Soviet destroyer *Azard*, but Estonian plane damages minesweeper forcing Reds back into Kronstadt (*see 31*). **Hungary** — Anti-Soviet rising in SW suppressed (-2 June). Gen Szombathelyi joins anti-Soviet govt (C-in-C Adm Horthy) at Arad.

Fri 30
Peace Process — Yugoslavia rejects 'Tardieu Compromise' Fiume buffer state proposals (League of Nations mandate). Britain agrees to transfer part of German SW Africa to Belgium. **Britain** — Metropolitan Police pay increase of 15s pw, no union recognition.

Sat 31
Allied note to Germany re troops in Baltic States. **Baltic** — 3 RN cruisers & 6 destroyers drive several Soviet warships back into Kronstadt. Reds withdraw from Gulf of Riga (*see 2 June*). **Aviation** — First Transatlantic air crossing completed at Plymouth by USN Curtiss NC4 flying-boat from Rockaway, NY (left 8, covered 3150nm in under 44hrs Newfoundland-Lisbon 25-27, *see 14 June*).

JUNE 1919

Sun 1
Russia — (June) Red Army High Command estimates 657,000 foes incl Poles & Finns (latter 100,000 of which 25,000 N of Petrograd, *see 6*) whereas 356,000 Red combat troops at fronts in total of 899,000 men plus 538,000 in interior MDs & 111,000 paramilitary. Trotsky realizes Allied intervention powerless. **Siberia** — (June)

Kolchack's paper strength 450,000 (Reds estimate 129,000 combat troops), but whole White units desert & shoot officers; Anglo-Russian Regt withdrawn to Omsk, never sees action. **S Russia** — 259,000 Reds v Denikin's AFSR (early June); Gen Sidorin's White Don Host links up with Veshenskaia Cossack rebels. **France — Bread cards abolished. Germany** — Rhineland Republic proclaimed at Gen Mangin's prompting (*see 2, 3 & 8*). **Britain** — RFP falls 3% to 104%; average family spending 4s 9d pw less on food since 1 Nov 1918. **USA** — (June) Record 434,786 troops return home across Atlantic, making 1,610,074 by 30 (*see 13*).

Mon 2
Peace Process — Draft treaty handed to Austrian delegation (Dr Renner leaves for Vienna 3, returns 7). **Balkans** — Rumania & Yugoslavia divide the Banat region. HMG recognize Yugoslavia as Kingdom of Serbs, Croats & Slovenes. **Baltic States** — RN occupy Bjorko Sound on Finnish coast (with permission), 30 miles NW of Kronstadt. Red destroyer *Gavriil* sinks British submarine *L55* with gunfire & with another destroyer shells Bjorko (9). Allies back Estonians in fighting at Venden NE of Riga to check German Maj Fletcher's Baltic *Landeswehr*, nominally Latvian but German dominated. Armistice (11) broken. More fighting nr Rup (13) finishes with Estonian push on Riga (*see 3 July*). **Britain** — Enemy firms creditworthy. **India** — Viceroy replies to Afghan armistice request (*see 14*). **France** — Clemenceau laments 'I have to struggle every day against generals who leave their own domain and commit faults that I regret'.

Tue 3
Peace Process — Germany protests v French support for newly-independent Rhineland Republic. **Britain** — Asquith answers Lord French on 1915 shell shortage controversy.

Wed 4
S Russia — Trotsky assures Kharkov, in no more danger than any other city incl Moscow (*see 27*). **Siberia** — Red Fifth Army drives Kolchack's left wing back on Ufa (*see 9*). **Britain** — Out-of-work donation extended 13 more weeks for ex-servicemen & women (*see 24 Nov*). Lord Glanely's horse Grand Parade wins the Victory Derby.

Thu 5
Peace Process — Paderewski heard on Polish frontiers. Austro-Yugoslav armistice. **N Russia** — 1st Lake Onega flotilla action. **Siberia** — Gen Gadja's Whites retake Galazov (but lose it 16). Reds take Sarapol. **S Russia** — Denikin takes Berdiansk (on Sea of

Azov) & Lugansk. **Britain** — Army demobilization 2,830,146 incl 107,743 officers.

Fri 6
Finland declares war on Soviet Russia, but of little practical effect (*see 23*).

Sun 8
Peace Process — Count Brockdorff-Rantzau returns to Versailles. Allies request Béla Kun to stop attacking Czechoslovakia & invite him to Paris; he complies (9, *see 11 & 16*). **Germany** — Govt troops suppress Rhineland Republic. **Rumania** — German population forms single political party.

Mon 9
Siberia — Red 25th Rifle Div captures Ufa with many supplies & much grain after surprise R Belaia crossing (7). By c15 Whites driven back 50 miles E into Urals. **Turkey** — Fire destroys Sultan's Constantinople palace.

Tue 10
Peace Process — Austria protests at Allied terms. **Baltic States** — Estonians take Jakobstadt & Kreutzburg on R Dvina. **N Russia** — British storm Murmansk Railway Siding 10 (-11) after 500 Whites refuse to attack, but British repulsed 4 miles to S (23) in scorching heat & temporarily relieved by Italians (26 June-3 July). **USA** — Senator Knox's resolution asks for League Covenant's separation from Peace Treaty.

Wed 11
Czechoslovakia — Hungarian Red Army advancing victori-ously in Slovakia (*see 16*). **USA** — Sinn Fein leader de Valera arrives in New York on visit.

Thu 12
Peace Process — Turk delegation arrives. **S Russia — Denikin recognizes Kolchak as White Supreme Ruler**, in speech at farewell dinner for British Military Mission chief Lt-Gen Briggs. **S Persia** — Capture of Kadarjan. **Britain** — Haig & Beatty receives the OM from the King (*see 6 Aug*).

Fri 13
Baltic — Forts Krasnya Gorka & Seraya Loshad covering Kronstadt naval base rebel v Reds & shell port (-17). Stalin orders 2 battleships to counter-bombard & Reds retake forts while garrison survivors & Estonians retreat (*see 18*). **Siberia** — Czech troops mutiny at Irkutsk but soon put down; French Gen Janin blames US for incident. **S Russia — Wrangel's Caucasus Volunteer Army** (mainly cav) **attacks Tsaritsyn** (-15) but Red defences too tough, Whites lose nearly 25% incl 8 generals & 11 regimental COs. Wrangel withdraws a day's march to S (*see 28*). Civilian river & rail exodus from city. **Britain** — New Victory Loan

issued, 4% bonds. **France** — AEF *Stars and Stripes* weekly newspaper closes (peak circ 522,000).

Sat 14
FIRST NON-STOP ATLANTIC FLIGHT (Alcock & Brown -15). **S Russia** — 5 Camels of No 47 Sqn RAF kill 800 of Budenny's Red cav bde, 15 miles N of Tsaritsyn. **India** — Afghan reply to armistice terms received at Peshawar.

Sun 15
NW Russia -(c) Red deserters swell White N Corps to 25,000, becomes NW Army.

Mon 16
Peace Process — Final Allied reply to German objections requires acceptance in 5 days; early League of Nations membership, Upper Silesia plebiscite & slight Polish frontier changes conceded. German plenipotentiaries return to Berlin. Clemenceau and Lloyd George oppose Foch's plan of Main valley S Germany advance instead of march on Berlin; Foch's aide Weygand rows with Clemenceau. **Central Europe** — Hungarians evacuate Czechoslovakia (-4 July, *see 24*) after Allied Supreme Council demand (15) and having declared Slovak Soviet Republic. 8k in Vienna Communist riot. **Britain** — Disabled ex-servicemen estimated at 720,000 pensionable, 350,000 eligible for re-training. Free export to Denmark allowed, food to unoccupied Germany, Poland & Balkans.

Tue 17
Peace Process — Austrian counter-proposal. Wilson leaves Paris for Brussels. German Versailles delegates stoned by Berliners. **N Russia** — 7 RAF & White planes destroy Red airfield & 4+ planes at Puchega.

Wed 18
Baltic — RN *CMB4* torpedoes & sinks Red cruiser *Oleg* off Fort Krasnya Gorka, Lt Agar wins VC. Stalin executes 67 actually loyal officers of Kronstadt garrison. **Siberia** — Reds take Ossa & Okhansk. **S Russia** — White Volunteer Army clears Crimea (-29); Reds join Whites or are shot. **Turkey** — Turks retake Nazli from Greeks & advance on Aidin (21).

Fri 20
Peace Process — Count Brockdorff-Rantzau refuses to sign Peace Treaty, as does Scheidemann Govt which resigns (Bauer-Erzberger Ministry formed 21). **Allied Supreme Council orders Marshal Foch to advance into Germany if Treaty not accepted by 1900 hrs 23 June**. **N Russia** — Archangel sector: Allies take Topsa but not Troitsa on R Dvina N bank. **Italy** — PM Orlando resigns, Nitti succeeds (22). **Britain** —

Govt war risks insurance scheme for trade with Russia.

Sat 21
GERMAN HIGH SEAS FLEET INTERNED AT SCAPA FLOW SCUTTLES from 1215: 9 of 1800 German sailors k as 10 dreadnoughts, 5 battlecruisers, 8 cruisers, 32 destroyers sunk by crews at Rear Adm Reuter's order in under 6hrs. 14 destroyers beached along with flagship battleship *Baden*. **Turkey** — Kemal issues 'Declaration of Independence' from Ankara.

Sun 22
Peace Process — German Assembly at Weimar votes 237-138 for Peace Treaty. Supreme Council refuses to accept German war guilt/criminals reservations. **S Russia** — Denikin's Volunteer Army 24 miles from Kharkov, takes Belgorod & Valuiki (23, *see 27*).

Mon 23
Peace Process — Herr Haniel indicates (25 min before ultimatum expires) **Germany will sign under protest after delay refused. Germany** — Soldiers burn captured French 1870-1 flags in Berlin. **Britain** — Revised Household Fuel & Lighting 1918 Order increases coal allowance. 450,000 cotton spinners strike (-12 July) wins 30% pay rise & 48-hr wk. **Siberia** — Kolchak cables Regent Mannerheim in Finland begging attack on Petrograd, but not willing to recognize independent Finland.

Tue 24
Peace Process — Belgium to have priority in German reparations up to $500m. **Central Europe** — Hungarian-Czech Army truce. Anti-Communist Budapest rising suppressed as are 3 others (22-25).

Wed 25
Peace Process — Allied note protests at Scapa scuttle & at retention of captured French flags. **Siberia** — Reds 20 miles from Perm & advancing E of Ufa.

Thu 26
Germany — Berlin & Hamburg fighting. **Britain** — Haig appeals to workmen & unions to help unemployed ex-servicemen find work (*see 1 July*).

Fri 27
Peace Process — China says she will not sign Treaty due to Shantung clauses. **Germany accepts final protocol. S Russia** — White Gen Kutepov's Corps of Volunteer Army takes Kharkov. **Britain** — Labour Party Southport Conference votes for Allied ceasefire in Russia & press censorship removal.

Sat 28
TREATY OF VERSAILLES (75,000 words, 200 pages, 440 clauses) signed at 1550 during

9th Plenary Session in Hall of Mirrors, Versailles. Foreign Minister H Muller & Empire Minister Dr Bell sign for Germany. League of Nations Covenant Part I signed. Anglo-French-US Defensive Treaty signed, also Allied Poland Minorities Treaty & Rhineland Military Occupation Agreement. Marshal Foch comments at his Kreuznach HQ 'This is not peace, it is an armistice for 20 years'. **Mediterranean** — British rail ferry *Duchess of Richmond* mined & sunk. **S Russia** — Panic intensifies in Tsaritsyn as White inf & guns reinforce Wrangel. **Britain** — Demobilization scheme to release all 1914 recruits by 28 July; 1915 recruits & those aged over 37 at end 1917 by 28 Aug; other classes by 28 Sept.

Sun 29
Pres Wilson & Lloyd George leave Paris for home. **S Russia — Wrangel storms Tsaritsyn** aided by 6 tanks (incl 1 British-crewed) of which 4 break through followed by cav incl 4th Kuban Cossack Div.

Mon 30
S Russia — Tsaritsyn Volga docks burn as Whites take city after some street fighting; 4 looters shot. Whites' booty incl over 40,000 PoWs, 10,000 lorries, 131 rail engines & 2 armoured cars. (c) New Red Ninth Army C-in-C ex-Tsarist Gen Vsevlodov deserts to Whites with family. **USA** — CPI abolished. **Britain** — War pensioners total 2,340,081. Meat rationing abolition delayed by drought & cattle fattening. Bonar Law says Govt not committed to coal nationaliza-tion.

JULY 1919

Tue 1
Russia — (July) Veteran Communist Rykov made Defence Council's Extraordi-nary Plenopotentiary for the Supply of the Red Army (excl food). Reds return 1,426,000 deserters to Red Army (July-Dec, v 334,000 in Feb-June). **Siberia** — Red Second & Third Armies capture Perm, Kungur (8) & Krasnoufimsk (14). (July) Kolchak replaces Gen Khanzhin i/c Third Army with Gen Sakharov (8). **Britain** — RFP up 5% to 109%. **Haig declares war pensions totally inadequate** (see 31).

Wed 2
S Russia — Wrangel formally enters Tsaritsyn to enthusiastic welcome, orders cathedral's cleaning (used by Reds as food store) for victory *Te Deum*; Denikin arrives by train. **Britain** — Peace proclaimed at St James's Palace & in City of London (see 6).

Thu 3
Baltic States — Gen Gough secures Latvian-Estonian armistice; German volunteers to evacuate Riga, 6000 Baltic-German *Landeswehr* (with 12

guns & 8 planes) to have British CO, Col (later FM) Alexander, Irish Guards (see 18, see 20). **Russia** — Col Sergei S Kamenev, aged 38 (ex-Tsarist officer) **replaces Vatsetis as Red Army Main C-in-C** after Central Ctee backs advance to Urals, Frunze i/c E Front. Trotsky offers own resignation but refused (see 23). **N Russia** — 2nd Lake Onega Flotilla action. **S Russia — Denikin issues** secret order 08878 or **'Moscow directive'** from Tsaritsyn for 3-pronged White advance on Russian capital. **Germany — Hindenburg** retires from active service. **Italy** — Riots in 5 cities during Fiume disturbances (2-6).

Fri 4
Turkey — Turks occupy Aidin & Pergamum. **Britain** — Record 2271 ex-servicewomen receiving out-of-work donation. **Ireland** — Sinn Fein, Irish Volunteers & other bodies proclaimed illegal associations in Co.Tipperary.

Sat 5
N Russia — Murmansk Railway: British & Whites storm Kapaselga on Lake Onega (see 17 Aug). Archangel sector: Slavo-British Legion mutiny kills several British officers (see 22). **Turkey** — Young Turks sentenced to death *in absentia*. **Britain** — King reviews London troops. Food Ministry to continue after 1919. Postal censorship ended: DMI thanks Jules Silber (undetected German spy). **Ireland** — Sinn Fein declared illegal.

Sun 6
Baltic States — RN carrier *Vindictive* (12 planes) runs aground off Reval (-13), Estonia. **S Russia** — Denikin's AFSR take Dubovka, Ekaterinoslav (Gen Shkuro 8), Balashov (10) & Liski (12, see 15). **Britain** — **National Peace Thanksgiving Day**: King & Queen at St Paul's (see 19).

Mon 7
Britain — Army demobilization 2,993,454 (see 14). Labour Ministry issues training grants for unemployed women (2000+ by mid-Oct).

Tue 8
USA — Wilson home for Treaty campaign. **Britain** — Capt Fryatt buried at Dover after London memorial service.

Wed 9
Germany ratifies Versailles Treaty, 208-115 (99 abstain). Pres Ebert signs (10) & courier takes document to Versailles. **Russia** — Lenin's circular speech 'All out for the Fight against Denikin'; Soviet Republic 'must be a single armed camp'. **France** — Army demobilization resumes (-23 Oct).

Thu 10
Austria presents counter peace proposals (see 20).

Fri 11
Turkey — Govt outlaws Kemal (see 23).

Sat 12
ALLIED BLOCKADE OF GERMANY RAISED. **Britain** — Victory loan closes at £574,704,000. Coastal shipping tonnage fall reported of 71,381,720t (1914) to 35,470,337t (1918). **Siberia** — Kolchak sacks Czech Gen Gajda from his Siberian Army command (who leaves for Vladivostok); Gen M K Dieterichs made C-in-C.

Sun 13
Urals — Tukhachevski's Red Fifth Army breaks through & takes Zlatoust, then Chelyabinsk (24) after battle costing 15,000 cas for 5000+ Whites (Sakharov's Third Army). **France** — Joffre, Foch and Pétain receive their marshals' batons from Pres Poincaré before the Hôtel de Ville, Paris. **Aviation** — British airship R-34 completes first two-way Atlantic crossing, landing in Norfolk, England (left Edinburgh 2).

Mon 14
Britain — Army demobilization 3,018,644 (121,615 officers) see 27 Aug. **France** — Bastille Day Victory Parade by Allied troops. **USA** — Foreign trade practically de-controlled. **Afghanistan** — Final fighting (-22) apart from tribal raiding.

Tue 15
Siberia — Col Shorin's Red Second Army re-enters Ekaterinburg after 200-mile advance in 4 weeks. **Britain** — (c) Liquor Control Board's early abolition announced.

Wed 16
W Russia — Reds drive White NW Army back to Yamburg (see 4 Aug). Poles take Luninetz from Ukrainians then drive them back to R Zbrucz thus gaining Galicia (25). **S Russia** — Denikin takes Kherson. **Trans-Caspia** — Reds take Kaakha, enter Askhabad (22).

Thu 17
Britain — Improved Navy officers' pay, RAF too (21).

Sat 19
British Empire Official Peace Day. London Victory Parade lasts 2½ hrs, led by US Gen Pershing. War Medal issued. Other Peace Celebration parades across country.

Sun 20
Peace Process — 2nd draft Treaty handed to Austrian Chancellor Dr Renner. **Central Europe** — Hungarians (5 divs) attack Rumanians (7 divs) on R Theiss who defeat them (-26). **Baltic States** — Latvian-Estonian mutual help treaty.

Mon 21
Rumania — Pro-Soviet strikes (-Aug).

Tue 22
N Russia — Murmansk sector: 4000 Whites mutiny, British 2nd Hampshire Regt sent. **W Russia** — Estonians repulse Red attack on Pskov. **Britain** — Wartime wooden huts to be used for temporary housing. Commons approve bill to ratify Versailles Treaty.

Wed 23
S Russia — New Red C-in-C Kamenev issues general directive No 1116 for counter-offensive along Volga (see 15 Aug). **Turkey** — National Congress meets at Erzerum (-6 Aug), Kemal elected President (joined by Raouf Bey), he affirms loyalty to Sultan (see 5 Aug). **Britain** — Triple Union Alliance decide to ballot members on political strike but postponed (12 Aug). 24,278 ex-servicemen have applied for 424,000 acres of land so far.

Thu 24
Italy — Caporetto Enquiry Commission Report leads to 4 generals' retirement incl Cadorna. **Britain** — CIGS Wilson promoted FM.

Sat 26
Peace Process — Allied warning to Hungarian Soviet. PM Theodorov's Bulgar Peace Delegation arrives in Paris (see 19 Sept). **India** — Anglo-Afghan Peace Conference at Rawalpindi (see 8 Aug). **Britain** — (c) Average daily Govt spending £4. 44m pd.

Sun 27
Baltic — Two RN destroyers damage Red submarine *Vyepr* in Kaporia Bight (see 30).

Mon 28
S Russia — Wrangel's Cossacks storm Kamyshin on the Volga, taking 13,000 Red PoWs. By early Aug within 60 miles of Saratov on Volga but then Red counter-offensive. Caucasus Army patrols E of Volga meet Kolchak's Ural Cossacks nr Lake Elton. **USA** — Chicago race riots (90 cas) cause arrival of 4000 troops.

Tue 29
Secret Greco-Italian Treaty for mutual claims in Turkey. **S Russia** — Denikin in Poltava.

Wed 30
Baltic — 11 RNAS planes bomb Kronstadt, causing 100 cas & hitting Red submarine depot ships (10 raids during Aug, see 18). **Britain** — K George presents Foch with his British field-marshal's baton.

Thu 31
Germany — National Assembly approves Weimar Constitution (federal one for 17 states). **Central Europe** — Yugoslavs evacuate Klagenfurt on Allied Supreme Council's order. **Britain** — Allenby & Plumer promoted FMs; Rawlinson to direct N Russia evacuation. T E Lawrence demobilized as Lt-Col. War pensions increase to minimum £2 pw for single man,

£2 10s for married men. 1919 imports 20m tons so far v 30.7m tons in same 1913 period. (July) Hours reduced 5hrs pw for 1.55m workers.

AUGUST 1919

Fri 1
Baltic States (Aug) — Russo-German 'Army of W Russia' (10,000 men under adventurer Col Prince Bermondt-Avalov) persuaded by Gen Goltz (see 16) to attack Latvian Riga despite White pleas to aid advance on Petrograd. **Hungary** — **Béla Kun's Soviet Govt overthrown** after 133 days; he escapes to Vienna & is interned as Rumanians advance nr Budapest (see 4). **Britain** — RFP up 8% to 117%. Bread restrictions removed. Police union recognition strike strike flops. Civil servants total record 409,561.

Sat 2
N Russia — 3rd Lake Onega flotilla action (& 4th, 28).

Sun 3
Britain — Liverpool riots ended by Army's arrest of 300 (4).

Mon 4
Hungary — **Rumanians occupy Budapest** (-16 Nov). **NW Russia** — Reds retake Yamburg.

Tue 5
Russia — Trotsky memo urges CEC to begin long-term preparations for 'a military thrust against India. . . the road to Paris and London lies via the towns of Afghanistan, the Punjab and Bengal'. **Turkey** — Kemal at Nationalist Congress declares himself independent (see 8).

Wed 6
Peace Process — Austria submits counter-proposals. **Hungary** — Prov Govt falls, Habsburg Archduke Joseph 'State Governor', accepts Versailles Treaty (9) (see 22). **Britain** — Lloyd George given OM for wartime leadership, Haig & Beatty made Earls; Allenby Viscount; Haig's 4 Army cdrs Barons; 4 admirals Baronets; as are CIGS Wilson, Gens Robertson, Birdwood & Trenchard. **Turkey** — Gen Milne visits Gen Paraskevopoulos at Smyrna (-8) and fixes 3000yd neutral zone between Greeks and Turks.

Thu 7
Britain — Chancellor Austen Chamberlain warns existing expenditure 'would head straight to national bankruptcy', economies proposed (12). Gen re-registration of food rationing retailers for Sept to secure stricter distribution.

Fri 8
Third Anglo-Afghan War ends. Turkey — Young Turk & 1916 captor of Kut Khalil Pasha escapes his Constantinople prison to join Nationalists in

Anatolia. **W Russia — Poles take Minsk**, take Dubno & Rovno (10 *see* 24). **Siberia** — Reds take Tyumen & Kurgan (18) on R Tobol after 350-mile march across the Urals; (c) Whites down to 50,000 combat troops. **S Persia** — British capture of Teraghah.

Sat 9
Diplomacy — Anglo-Persian Agreement signed at Tehran, 'a triumph of Curzon's policy of barring the way to India' (repudiated Feb 1921). **Russia** — Politburo orders Trotsky to hold Odessa & Kiev 'to the last drop of blood'.

Sun 10
Hungary — Banat Swabians adhere to union with Rumania. **N Russia** — Archangel sector: **Battle of Troitsa** on N Dvina, Allies (55+ cas, mainly British) with 23 guns, 5 RN gunboats & monitors (shelling 9-11), 3 seaplanes (1 lost) & with use of use of 600 mustard gas shells defeat 6000 Reds (3964 cas) incl 2164 PoWs, 9 guns, 5 mortars & 16 MGs. Allied aim of covering imminent evacuation achieved. **Britain** — Labour MP J Thomas condemns strike threats in Yarmouth speech.

Mon 11
Britain — Butter ration reduced from 2oz to 1^1/2oz pw. (c) British fishermen allowed to fish in all non-dangerous waters. **Germany** — Weimar Constitution formally adopted.

Tue 12
Belgian troops occupy Malmédy under Versailles Treaty (formal possession 25).

Thu 14
White Russian NW Govt formed at Helsinki (Yudenich War Minister & C-in-C), grudgingly recognizes Estonia to whom US loans $50m. **S Russia** — Red Thirteenth & Fourteenth Armies begin 95-mile advance taking Kupiansk (25), but *see* 15 Sept.

Fri 15
Volga — Red Ninth & Tenth Armies drive Whites 140 miles downriver (*see* 22). **Britain** — Transport Ministry created. Prewar union practices restored. Police Federation created. Prince of Wales visits North America (-Nov). **France** — Air Force losses reported as 60%.

Sat 16
Baltic States — Gen Goltz recalled from Latvia, but stays incognito under Gen Eberhardt from 12 Oct (*see* 26). **Azerbaijan — British evacuate Baku.**

Sun 17
N Russia — Murmansk Railway: Allies advance S for 6 miles after repelling Red attacks on Kapaselga (6 & 17) then retire.

Mon 18

Baltic — Kronstadt Raid: 7 RN CMBs (3 lost with 17 cas) sink 2 Soviet battleships & depot ship under air raid (8 planes) cover at night; 2 VCs, 4 DSOs & 8 DSCs won. **S Russia** — Denikin's III Corps enters Nikolayev & Elisavetgrad (19). Gen Mamontov's IV Don Cav Corps (9000) raids Tambov, provincial town 125 miles behind Red lines, drafts or sends home 20,000 Red recruits, moves W to S Front HQ & rail junction at Kozlov (raid lasts 10 Aug — 18 Sept). **Britain** — Lloyd George Commons speech calls for increased production to pay nation's way (*see* 25).

Tue 19
Britain — Trade with Arabia licensed. 6-month Profiteering Act passed (extended to May 1921).

Thu 21
Peace Process — Supreme Council accepts Anglo-French Togo/Cameroons partition & Anglo-Belgian Ruanda/Urandi mandate agreement (30).

Fri 22
Allied Supreme Council refuse Archduke Joseph recognition, he resigns (23). **S Russia** — Intense fighting just N of Tsaritsyn, Wrangel stops Red advance with aid of British-supplied tanks (*see* 5 Sept).

Sat 23
S Russia — White landing, aided by battleship *General Alexeiev* (former Tsarist dreadnought *Imperator Alexander III*) & Allied warships, **retakes Odessa. Denikin takes Kiev** & ousts Petlyura's Ukrainians. **USA** — Senate Ctee rejects Shantung clause of Versailles Treaty.

Sun 24
W Russia — Poles reach R Beresina.

Mon 25
Austria — 1st Lt Wittgenstein home in Vienna from Cassino PoW camp in Italy. **Britain** — Warship & airship programmes curtailed. Cabinet Finance Ctee formed.

Tue 26
Baltic States — Germans refuse to evacuate Latvia.

Wed 27
Britain — Army demobilization 3,166,834 (133,272 officers). **S Africa** — †PM Gen Botha (aged 56), Smuts succeeds (31) . **N Russia** — Vologda front (Archangel sector): Actions of Svyatnavolotski & Yemtsa (29) as 3000 British & 1000 Whites advance.

Thu 28
Siberia — Reds enter Tobolsk. **S Russia** — Reds retake Kumishin. **Trans-Caspia** — Reds beaten at Keliata.

Fri 29
Peace Process — Germany signs coal delivery protocol at

Versailles. **Britain** — Paper imports unrestricted. Revised food rationing scheme for 13 October issued.

Sat 30
Siberia — Whites begin counter-offensive. **W Russia** — Ukrainians take Zhitomir from Red Twelfth Army having taken Berdichev (*see* 11 Sept). **Britain** — RN demobilization complete.

Sun 31
Baltic States — Estonia accepts Soviet peace overtures, but 17 Sept talks abortive (*see* 5 Dec). Red submarine *Pantera* sinks RN destroyer *Vittoria* E of Seskar Island, Gulf of Finland (largest warship sunk by a Soviet submarine). **Britain** — Out-of-work donations down to 478,084 (141,132 civilians). **Ireland** — Press censorship abolished.

SEPTEMBER 1919

Mon 1
Russia — (Sept) Anarchist bomb at Moscow Ctee HQ kills Moscow Party chief & 11 others, 55 wounded incl Bukharin. Cheka execute 67 pro-White Moscow National Centre supporters. Trotsky *Pravda* article threatens Finland with 'merciless extermination' if she attacks; his Sept slogan is 'Proletarians, to horse!' to increase Red cavalry. **N Russia** — (Sept) 16,000 British, 1400 French & Serb & 26,000 White troops. **Baltic** — 10 RNAS Sept air raids on Kronstadt area, 70 bombs dropped, 1 plane lost. **Siberia** — (Sept) Gen Belov's White (Kolchak) S Army surrenders to Reds rather than face starvation in Turkestan desert. Reds take Orsk then Aktiubinsk (3). **S Russia** — Denikin takes Konotop, only 375 miles from Moscow, but overstretched & he writes to Gen Mai-Maevski of 'this gloomy picture of grandiose looting and plunder'. **W Russia** — Polish-Ukrainian armistice. **Britain** — RFP down 1% to 116%. Bread price raised to 9^1/2d, 1st change since Sept 1917. Import restrictions generally removed. First regular London-Paris civil air service by Handley Page (London-Brussels 22). **Repatriation of Central Powers' PoWs begins**, 135,821 by 1 Oct (*see* 1 Nov)

Tue 2
Peace Process — Germany **accepts Allied ultimatum** to drop Article 61 from Weimar Constitution admitting Austrian deputies to Imperial Council. Supreme Council reply to Austrian 6 Aug Treaty note, Radkersburg rail junction returned to Austria. **New Zealand ratifies Versailles Treaty.**

Wed 3
USA — Wilson begins countrywide tour to promote League of Nations (*see* 22),

---

says choice is 'peace partnership or armed isolation' (5). Pershing (sailed home 1) given unique rank of General of the Armies.

Thu 4
N Russia — 2nd Action of Ust Pocha, Limja captured (14). **Turkey** — *De facto* Nationalist Govt declared at Sivas Congress.

Fri 5
France — Paris court martial sentences Georges Quien to death for Nurse Cavell's betrayal. **S Russia** — Wrangel saves Tsaritsyn with cavalry flank attack that takes 18,000 PoWs & 31 guns from the almost successful Red Tenth Army (-8, *see* 9 & 15). **Britain** — Govt refuse British toymakers' demand for 3 years protected trade with Germany.

Sat 6
Peace Process — Austrian National Assembly votes 97-23 to accept Treaty terms (*see* 10). **NW Russia** — Yudenich defeats Reds E of Gdov & strikes E (27, *see* 12 Oct).

Sun 7
Belgium — 45 Flemish wartime separatists imprisoned. **Ireland** — Irish Vols' 2nd Cork Bde fire at British troops in Fermoy (latter loot shops 8-9, *see* 12).

Mon 8
Baltic — Aircraft carrier HMS *Furious* at Copenhagen with 20 mainly useless replacement planes. **Britain** — TUC at Glasgow (-13) now represents 5m workers. Govt Export Credits Dept opens to give up to 80% guarantee on exports to war-devastated European countries.

Tue 9
N Russia — Archangel sector: British retreat begins, rearguard actions (11, 12, 14-16). **S Russia** — Wing-Cdr Collishaw in Sopwith Camel destroys Red Albatros DV, 20 miles N of Tsaritsyn; 2 RAF DH9s help repulse Red Volga Flotilla (10, *see* 15). **Georgia** — British HQ leaves Tiflis (*see* 15).

Wed 10
AUSTRIA SIGNS TREATY OF ST GERMAIN: Rumania & Yugoslavia refuse to sign. Austria cedes S Tyrol, Istria, part Dalmatia & Adriatic Islands to Italy; Bukovina to Rumania; recognizes Hungary, Czecho-slovakia, Poland & Yugo-slavia (who share prewar debt); minorities protection; Austrian Army to be reduced to 30,000 volunteers; no aircraft or warships except 3 Danube patrol boats; reasonable reparations (Art 77) to be paid by 1 May l921; Austria not to join German Republic (Art 88); Adriatic rail access guarantee. Allied-Czechoslovak Minorities Treaty. Allied Arms Convention to prevent exports to non-signatories; most of Africa, Central & W Asia prohibited zones.

Thu 11
Ukraine — Reds retake Zhitomir from Ukrainians.

Fri 12
Canada & S Africa ratify Versailles Treaty. D'Annunzio & his 1000 volunteers seize Fiume & proclaim city Italy's though Rome disowns him. **Ireland** — British declare Sinn Fein illegal after rioting since 16 Aug.

Sat 13
Russia — Frunze's Red First Army, 300 miles from Orenburg, meets Reds from Tashkent (900 miles distant).

Sun 14
Polish PM Paderewski vainly offers Lloyd George 500,000 Poles for march on Moscow if £600,000 given for weapons (*see* 12 Dec).

Mon 15
ALLIES DECIDE TO EVACU-ATE RUSSIA. **S Russia** — Gen Selivachev's Red Armies back on 14 Aug start-line; †Selivachev (17) supposedly of typhus. c4 RAF DH9 bombers repulse 40-strong Red flotilla shelling Tsaritsyn; a DH9 sinks Red Volga barge carrying 8 seaplanes (17). **Caucasus** — British evacuated save at Batumi. **Diplomacy** — Anglo-French Syria-Palestine-Mosul Agreement. **China ends state of war with Germany. Britain** — King's Roll Scheme begun to employ ex-servicemen (est 700,000 of 800,000 employable already employed).

Tue 16
Britain — Allenby returns from Egypt.

Wed 17
Britain — 100,000 fewer farm workers reported since Aug 1914.

Thu 18
S Russia — Churchill via British Military Mission urges Denikin to issue proclamation v anti-Semitism. **Britain** — National Volunteer Force disbanded.

Fri 19
Peace Process — Draft treaty presented to Bulgar delegation. **Germany** — Hitler joins German Worker's Party (7th member) in Munich (*see* 24 Feb 1920).

Sat 20
S Russia — White Volunteer Army armoured trains seize Kursk; Red 9th & 55th Rifle Divs destroyed. Whites also occupy Lgov & Rilsk (24), Bakhmach & Fastov (30). **Austria** — Govt reveals that Kaiser backed ultimatum to Serbia.

Sun 21
Paris-Constantinople Orient Express service resumes for first time since 1914.

Mon 22
Britain — Iron founders strike

for wage increases involves 65,000 workers directly (-26 Jan 1920). Lloyd George writes fierce rebuke to Churchill telling him to concentrate on public spending cuts and 'throw off this obsession' with Russia, points out it has cost £100m-150m in 1919 to date: 'We cannot afford it. The French have talked a great deal about Anti-Bolshevism, but they have left it to us to carry out the Allied policy'. **USA** — Wilson suffers nervous breakdown in Pueblo, Colorado (see 2 Oct).

Tue 23
Britain — Railway Executive Ctee abolished as NUR warns of strike (24, see 26).

Wed 24
Britain — White Star liner *Vedic*, with troops & refugees from Archangel, runs aground off Orkneys; US minesweepers tow her into Invergordon.

Thu 25
Peace Conference gives Norway sovereignty over Spitzbergen. **Holland** — Allies return last requisitioned ships. **Britain** — Highest silver price since 1859 (-30). Scafell Pike Mt, Cumbria, presented to nation in memory of war dead.

Fri 26
Russia — Red CEC orders best Petrograd district units to S Front. **Britain** — Rail strike (NUR want 100% above prewar pay rates) from midnight (-5 Oct). PM calls it 'an anarchist conspiracy' (27).

Sat 27
N Russia — **Last of 11,000 British troops sail from Archangel. Siberia** — Gen Knox to Kolchak's CoS on 'worse chaos than anything I have seen in the past twelve months'. **Peace Process** — Supreme Council decides for Teschen plebiscite, later abandoned; also demands immediate German troop withdrawal from Baltic States. **Britain** — **State of National Emergency declared;** demobilization & Army leave suspended (-6 Oct); food rations reduced (-13 Oct) to 6oz sugar per head pw, 1oz butter, 1s 8d worth meat; Emergency Fuel Orders (-9 Oct, see 3).

Mon 29
W Russia — Poles take Dvinsk's South forts. **Siberia** — Czech Legion's evacuation ordered. **Britain** — (c) Free export of aircraft, balloons etc allowed except to Russia & ex-enemy countries.

Tue 30
Siberia — Gen Dieterichs' White counter-offensive re-takes Tobolsk, regains R Tobol (4 Oct). **Britain** — Air-mail service to 5 major cities.

OCTOBER 1919

Wed 1
Germany — Berlin Exchange RM100 to £ (20.8,1914), 127-

130 by 31. **Russia** — (Oct) 40,000 Party members added to c120,000 in Red Army during 'Party Weeks'. By now Red Army has 59 armoured trains. **N Russia** — Allied Murmansk Evacuation (-12). **Poland** — (Oct) 17 US airmen join Polish 7th Sqn nr Lemberg (Lvov). **Syria** — (Oct) Gertrude Bell writes report on Syria 'Syria in October 1919' after 2-week visit, backs Sherifian rule for Iraq. **Britain** — RFP up 6% to 122%. Govt rail talks resume (see 5).

Thu 2
Australia ratifies Versailles Treaty. USA — **Pres Wilson suffers massive stroke** in Washington after breaking off countrywide tour. Able to work a little from 1 Nov but on one side physically **paralyzed for rest of his term.**

Fri 3
Baltic States — Gen Goltz ordered back to Germany; Alexander's Baltic *Landeswehr* capture Lievenhof, advance 10 miles & repel 3-day Red counter-attack (-6). Germans not to recruit White Russian volunteers. **Russia** — Stalin agrees to be S Front Commissar, Col A I Egorov made C-in-C S Front (11) aged 36; Red S & SE Fronts 677,000-strong + 575,000 in Volga, Moscow & Orel MDs. **Britain** — Home Sec appeals to mayors to raise a Citizen Guard.

Sat 4
N Russia — Murmansk sector: British evacuate Kem on White Sea (see 10).

Sun 5
Turkey — Grand Vizier Damad Ferid resigns & elections ordered (see 11 Jan 1920). **Britain** — Rail strike ends with new pay rates by end 1919 agreed. Estimated cost to Govt £10m plus 375,000 put out of work.

Tue 7
Italy ratifies Versailles & St Germain Treaties. Britain — Cabinet ctee to consider Irish self-govt.

Fri 10
Britain ratifies Versailles Treaty. N Russia — 5000 **British & 1400 French & Serb troops leave Murmansk** (-12); battleship HMS *Glory* last to leave. **Britain** — Sir A Geddes says trade prospects excellent, no immediate fear of German competition. Teachers ask for 100% increase over prewar pay.

Sun 12
Baltic States — Col Bermondt's 15,000 Russo-Germans attack Latvians in the rear, bombard Riga (16). **NW Russia** — Yudenich's **White NW Army** (14,400 men & 44 guns) **begins final & surprise offensive on Petrograd**, taking Yamburg & Pskov. **S Russia** — Denikin's farthest NW advance takes Chernigov, squeezing

Reds v Polish positions.

Mon 13
France & Belgium ratify Versailles Treaty. S Russia — Denikin estimates he has control of 350,000 sq miles & 42m people. **Trans-Caspia** — Muslims of Ferghana region rise v Reds who are beaten W of Askabad (16). **Britain** — Sugar & meat rations raised to 8oz & 2s per head pw respectively. **France** — Clemenceau announces retirement after Nov elections (see 30 Nov).

Tue 14
S Russia — Denikin's elite Kornilov Div captures Orel (-20) with 8000 PoWs, **culminating point of White offensive 250 miles S of Moscow**. Reds throw in 200 planes incl Moscow Flying School to aid ground forces. RAF RE8 unit prepares to bomb Moscow (not done). **Baltic States** — RAF drop 300 bombs (-19) on 2 fortresses resisting Estonian advance, 2 planes lost. **Turkey** - Ali Riza Pasha made Grand Vizier. **France** — General demobilization decree.

Wed 15
Russia — Politburo decides to give Moscow Tula sector priority v Denikin. **Baltic States** — 5 Anglo-French warships bombard Germans in Riga when they refuse to evacuate, cruiser HMS *Dragon* hit 4 times (14 cas) by shore guns (17, see 19). **Britain** — Wrens demobilized. Naval Welfare Advisory Ctee first meets.

Thu 16
Baltic States — Latvians retake Dunamunde from Russo- Germans. **NW Russia** — Yudenich takes Gatchina. **Britain** — Housing Minister says 500,000 houses needed.

Fri 17
Austria ratifies St Germain Treaty (in force from 16 July 1920), changes country's name from German-Austrian Republic to Austrian Republic. **NW Russia** — White NW Army only 20 miles from Petrograd where Trotsky arrives by special train (on line not cut as ordered by Yudenich). He doubles food ration & is once on horseback to rally panicking troops (see 21). **Britain** — Lloyd George Sheffield speech on economy without endangering interests.

Sun 19
Baltic States — Russo-Germans besiege Libau (see 3 Nov). Estonians take Marienhausen (31). **Japan** — Govt to spend £c30m on aviation.

Mon 20
S Russia — Red Estonian & 13th Rifle Divs re-occupy Orel. **France** — Amnesty Act for all wartime crimes excluding some cases of mutiny & desertion.

Tue 21
NW Russia — Whites (incl 6

British-manned tanks, but held back) on Pulkovo heights 8 miles from Petrograd, but exhausted & short of supplies as Red Seventh Army (reinforced from Tula) begins counter-attack supported by 11,000 sailors & 87 planes. Whites retreat towards Gatchina (23). **Britain** — 3 Red destroyers sink on RN mines off C Dolgy Nos, no survivors.

Thu 23
General French Army demobilization ceases.

Fri 24
Germany — Gen Degoutte succeeds Fayolle ic Allied Army of Occupation. **Peace Process** — Bulgar Treaty protests to Supreme Council incl land settlement & conscription abolition (see 3 Nov). **N Russia** — Reds clear Lower Onega Valley. **Don** — Budenny's Red Cav Corps retakes Voronezh from Gen Shkura (see 15 Nov). **Siberia** — Red Fifth Army retakes Tobolsk (see 31). **Britain** — Balfour resigns as Foreign Secretary, Curzon succeeds (27).

Sat 25
Britain — Scheme to ease wartime domestic servant shortage.

Sun 26
NW Russia — Yudenich back at Gatchina, Reds retake Krasnoe Selo (27, see 3 Nov).

Mon 27
Britain — Revised capital debt figure £8075m. Anglo-French imports normalized.

Wed 29
1st International Labour Conference in Washington (-29 Nov). **Britain** — Army demobilization 3,598,215 (153,875 officers).

Fri 31
Siberia — Reds take Petropavlovsk. **Baltic** — Monitor HMS *Erebus* (2 x 15in guns) bombards Fort Krasnaya Gorka, but no Estonian ground assault. **Britain** — Aliens Repatriation Ctee recommends 16% repatriation of enemy aliens interned at time of Armistice. Russian operations since Armistice estimated cost £79,830,000. Trade with Germany since, British exports £16m; German imports £216,000.

NOVEMBER 1919

Sat 1
Siberia — (early Nov) Red Third & Fifth Armies have nearly 100,000 men, 504 guns & 1211 MGs v Kolchak's c55,000 under Sakharov. **S Russia** — Denikin claims only 97,000-99,000 combat troops v 148,000 Reds, 864 guns & 3974 MGs. **Syria** — **French begin replacing British** (-19 Jan 1920), take over Cilicia (18). **Britain** — RFP up 9% to 131%. Beatty becomes First Sea Lord. (Nov)

Women's Emergency Corps disbanded. Cambridge economist J M Keynes publishes anti-Versailles Treaty & anti-Lloyd George best-selling book *The Economic Consequences of the Peace*. **Ireland** — (Nov) 37,259 British troops. **France** — Repatriation of BEF's German PoWs completed, likewise from Britain by 20 (77,279 24 Sept — 20 Nov) via 7 ports. **USA** — (Nov) Congress charters American Legion, Franklin d'Olier elected first national cdr (12). **Germany** — Railways to shut for 10 days to save coal.

Sun 2
Siberia — Reds 40 miles W of Omsk where evacuation of tripled population & Allied missions already long under way (see 14).

Mon 3
Peace Process — Supreme Council reply to Bulgar 24 Oct note only promises early League membership (see 13). **Baltic States** — Gen Balodis' Latvians counter-attack Russo-Germans at Riga with Allied naval gunfire support routing Bermondt (-10). **NW Russia** — Red Seventh Army retakes Gatchina & Luga from Yudenich who loses Gdov (7) & is smashed at Yamburg & Narva (14, see 20). **Britain** — All docks' war controls removed.

Tue 4
Baltic States — RN cruiser *Phaeton* & 5 destroyers (+ monitor *Erebus* from 8) smash German attacks on Libau (-12). **Siberia** — Kolchak speech admits reliable manpower problem insuperable. **Bulgaria** — All ex-Radoslavov (excluding Radoslavov in Germany) cabinet ministers arrested for signing war declaration without National Assembly consent.

Fri 7
Russia — Lenin & Trotsky in 2nd anniversary of Revolution celebrations, Red Square, Moscow. **Britain** — First Olympia Motor Show since 1913.

Sat 8
Britain — WRAF demobilization complete. Lloyd George Guildhall speech hints at end to support of Whites.

Mon 10
Baltic States — Latvians drive Germans back (see 18), recapture Mitau (21), relieve Libau (24, see 28). **Britain** — Pres Poincaré arrives in London. Meat ration can be exceeded due to ample supply. **Occupied Germany** — GOC Rhine Army (65,260 strong 1) issues trade regulations.

Tue 11
Britain — FIRST ARMISTICE REMEMBRANCE DAY: 2-minute silence & standstill before 11am. 2509 ex-servicemen now in Civil Service

(12,000 target). **Ireland** — Dublin Armistice ceremony street clash between University & Trinity Colleges' students. Sinn Fein *Irish Bulletin* launched.

Thu 13
Peace Process — New Bulgar Govt accepts peace terms (*see* 27). **USA** — Senate resolution (46-43) v League of Nations Covenant. **Siberia** — Czech National Council condemns Kolchak in letter to Allies; Kolchak tries to sever relations (25) with Czechs. Kolchak leaves Omsk in 7-train convoy with Russian Imperial gold reserve (£100m, *see* 19).

Fri 14
Siberia — After 60-mile advance in 1 day **Red 27th Div takes Omsk** across frozen R Irtysh, 30,000 PoWs, 40 locomotives, 1000+ trucks.

Sat 15
S Russia — Budenny's capture of Kastornoe rail junction (Voronezh-Kursk railway) forces White Volunteer Army retreat from potential encirclement. (c) Budenny's First Red Cavalry Army (4th, 6th, 11th Divs) formed.

Sun 16
Hungary — After Supreme Council ultimatum (7) **Rumanians evacuate Budapest** taking food, cattle, 1151 locomotives, 40,950 rail carriages, all city's post office motor cars & 4000 telephone installations, plus many other items (*see* 20). **Egypt** — 60 cas in Cairo nationalist rioting (Britain grants new constitution 19). **France** — Clemenceau coalition wins general election (women first have vote, *see* 17 Jan 1920).

Mon 17
Britain — Gas & electricity household limitations suspended. (c) Unsold enemy property valued at £111,499,000; British property in enemy countries £64,814,000 (£42,693,000 in Germany).

Tue 18
Baltic States — Latvian C-in-C Balodis refuses German armistice request (*see* 28). **Hungary** — Adm Horthy enters Budapest with national army. **S Russia** — Red S Front retakes Kursk, Lgov, Rilsk, then Bakhmut (20), but again repulsed from Tsaritsyn (24).

Wed 19
US SENATE DEFEATS VERSAILLES TREATY RATIFICATION (51-41). Separate US peace treaties with Austria & Germany 24-25 Aug 1921. **Siberia** — Omsk White cabinet arrive in Irkutsk.

Thu 20
Italy — Mussolini & 37 Fascists arrested after rioting v socialist election victory. **Baltic States** — Estonians take over White NW Army's Front & block Reds

at Narva (22, *see* 3 Dec). **N Russia** — Reds raid Pechora valley, attack in Onega & Valogda sectors (28). **Peace Process** — Allies tell Rumania to sign peace treaty or be dropped as an Allied power (*see* 27).

Fri 21
Allied Supreme Council gives Poland Galicia mandate for 25 years.

Sat 22
Britain — Petrol Control Dept closed.

Mon 24
Britain — Civilian out-of-work donation scheme ended but ex-servicemen & women receive till end July 1921 at 20s & 15s respectively. City of London meeting to employ ex-officers.

Tue 25
Baltic — RN evacuate airfield & seaplane mooring nr Björkö (Finland); seaplane patrols flown until 11 Dec when Kronstadt reported frozen-in (*see* 18 Dec); RAF have flown 837hrs since July with 55 planes (33 lost, 6 aircrew cas).

Thu 27
BULGARIA SIGNS PEACE TREATY OF NEUILLY (signed at Neuilly-sur-Seine): Rumania (*see* 7 Dec) & Yugoslavia (*see* 5 Dec) refuse to sign; Thrace ceded to Allies (assigned to Greece later); S Dobruja to Rumania; Strumitza & Tsaribod to Yugoslavia; Bulgaria assured Aegean trade outlets; reparations of 2. 25m gold francs every 6 months for 37 years; Army of 20,000 volunteers; Navy, 4 torpedo & 6 gunboats; no aircraft or submarines; reparations in kind include 50,000t coal pa for 5 years to Yugoslavia.

Fri 28
Germany — Berlin Exchange RM197 to £ (172. 6 on 29) **Baltic States — Germans evacuate Courland, Latvia** (- Jan 1920, *see* 13 Dec). **Trans-Caspia** — Whites retake Kizil Arvat. **Britain** — Virginian-born Nancy Astor elected (in Plymouth by-election) first woman MP to sit in Commons (1 Dec). **Egypt** — Mohammed Said Pasha replaced by Yusef Wahba Pasha as PM.

Sun 30
Russia — (late Nov) Trotsky tells Red Army 'Your task is not to conquer the Ukraine but to liberate it'.

DECEMBER 1919

Mon 1
Russia — (Dec) Lenin defends Cheka's record at 7th Soviet Congress. Denikin moves typhus-wracked Wrangel to Volunteer Army (Mai-Maevski sacked); AFSR have 42,700 sick & wounded (late Dec), Gen Ulagai reports 'in general, we have no cavalry'. Denikin cracks down on Kuban

Cossack separatists, several hanged, others exiled. **Britain** — RFP up 3% to 134% (passed I Nov 1918 level). Coal prices reduced. 1919-20 Naval Estimates £157.5m, down from £334m (1918-19).

Tue 2
£ worth below $4 (New York Exchange). **N Russia** — Reds attack on Pinega sector.

Wed 3
Estonian-Soviet Armistice signed at Dorpat, hostages exchanged (4, *see* 2 Feb 1920). **Italy** — General strike in several cities.

Fri 5
Peace Process — Yugoslavia signs Austrian & Bulgar peace treaties & Minorities Treaty. **Siberia** — Reds take Slavgorod, Semipalatinsk (7), Barnaul (14, *see* 20). **S Russia** — Reds re-enter Konotop, retake Kalach & Valuiki (10) & Kharkov (13). **Trans-Caspia** — Red advance on Krasnovodsk begins (*see* 6 Feb 1920).

Sat 6
S Russia — British Mission & RAF evacuate Taganrog under Red attack, then Rostov.

Sun 7
Siberia — Kolchak rows with PM & arrests Army C-in-C Sakharov who is released by successor Kappel.

Mon 8
Allied ultimatum to Germany demands Scapa scuttle reparation. **France** — 24 Alsace-Lorraine deputies take their seats in Chamber.

Tue 9
Peace Process — Rumania signs Austria & Bulgaria peace treaties & Minorities Treaty. Supreme Council Fiume proposal. US delegates leave. **Germany** — RM200 to £ (temporarily).

Wed 10
Still 15,000-18,000 British railway trucks in France (49,687 at Armistice). **Aviation** — First Britain-Australia flight. **Diplomacy** — Pres Wilson awarded Nobel Peace Prize.

Fri 12
Clemenceau & Lloyd George decide to transfer Allied aid to Poland (really starts mid-Jan 1920, mostly incl Austrian war surplus stockpiled in Rumania, now that Whites seem doomed. **Britain** — (c) Reported that 2,297,000 ex-servicemen absorbed into industry, 107,000 on leave, 356,000 unemployed. War paintings exhibition at Royal Academy, Piccadilly (-7 Feb 1920).

Sat 13
Baltic States — Germans finally evacuate Mitau-Shavli-Tauroggen area.

Sun 14
Siberia — Red Fifth Army takes Novonikolaevsk (*see* 7

Jan 1920).

Mon 15
Siberia — Czech Legion C-in-C Gen Syrovy orders all White Russian train movements under his control (*see* 18). **Britain** — **Meat rationing ended**, but butter ration reduced to 1oz pw due to shortage.

Tue 16
Ukraine — Reds retake Kiev.

Thu 18
Baltic — Adm Cowan evacuates Björkö Sound for Reval as Gulf of Finland freezing up, sails for England (28) with 2 cruisers & 1st Destroyer Flotilla. **Siberia** — Kolchak's trains leave Krasnoyask (*see* 24); garrison mutinies & yields to Red partisans (19).

Fri 19
S Russia — Reds retake Kremenchug & Cherkassy, and Lugansk (24). **Ireland** — Ashtown Ambush: 11 members of IRA (1k, IRA new name of Irish Vols) nearly murder Lord-Lt FM French in Dublin, his personal detective wounded. IRA wreck *Irish Independent* production plant (21) after newspaper calls dead IRA man 'would-be assassin'.

Sat 20
Diplomacy — Lord Kilmarnock British Chargé d'Affaires at Berlin. **Siberia** — Reds retake Tomsk.

Tue 23
A brig-gen now i/c British troops in France (38,440 1 Feb 1920). **Siberia** — Kolchak reaches Czech-held Nizhne Udinsk (stays till 8 Jan 1920) 300 miles W of Irkutsk having made Semenov C-in-C (23). French Gen Janin averts White Army v SR Menshevik bloodbath at Irkutsk (Gen Sychev flees 4 Jan 1920). Semenov intervention with 3 armoured trains from E ends (-29). **Britain** — Sex Disqualification Act comes into force.

Sat 27
Siberia — Reds take Karkavalinsk. **Turkey** — Kemal fixes HQ at Ankara and Nationalist Council of Representatives at Ankara (visits Damascus & Aleppo by 20 Jan 1920 for talks with Emir Feisal's reps, attacks N Mesopotamian towns).

Mon 29
Rumania — Parliament ratifies Union of Bessarabia, Bukovina & Transylvania.

Tue 30
Britain — Women's Land Army disbanded. **Austria** — Acute food shortage, Vienna bread ration 4oz pw.

Wed 31
Anglo-US-Japanese agreement over E Siberia. **Britain** — War Savings Organization to continue. Army demobilization 3,475,026 (incl 144,444

officers) plus 230,976 discharged medically unfit. (c) Coal nearly treble 1913 price. Over £13m spent in 1919 for European relief & reconstruction.

JANUARY 1920

Thu 1
Italy — (Jan) Bulk of British troops gone by 31 Jan. **Britain** — (Jan) One demobilization centre left. **S Russia** — (Jan) Denikin's belated slogan 'Land to the peasants and the labouring Cossacks', promises Constituent Assembly, forms separate Kuban Army but it dissolves. **USA** — FBI arrest 4000 suspected Russian Communists in 33 cities; 'Do not let the country *see* Red' pleads Pres Wilson.

Fri 2
W Russia — Latvian-Polish offensive takes Dvinsk (3). **Ireland** — RIC recruits first of c4000 'Black and Tans' (British ex-servicemen) to combat IRA. **Baltic** — Last RN submarines sail for home (*see* 31 Mar).

Sat 3
Siberia — Irkutsk anti-Kolchak rising (-4). **S Russia** — Denikin replaces Wrangel as C-in-C Volunteer Army (reduced to Corps) with Gen Sidorin. Reds regain Tsaritsyn. **France** — Last US troops leave.

Sun 4
Russia — Kolchak resigns in Denikin's favour. Red E Front HQ broken up (Jan).

Mon 5
Holland — 2 American officers on own initiative try to escort Kaiser from Amerongen exile to Paris, but are foiled (*see* 16).

Tue 6
S Russia — Reds retake Mariupol & Taganrog cutting Denikin's AFSR in two.

Wed 7
Peace Process — Count Apponyi's Hungarian delegation arrives in Paris, receives draft Treaty (15). **Siberia** — Red Fifth Army & partisans take Krasnoiask, 60,000 White PoWs & 200 guns; only Gen Kappel & few Whites escape by sledge (*see* 26). **S Russia** — Reds retake Rostov & Novocherkassk.

Sat 10
PEACE WITH GERMANY FORMALLY RATIFIED IN PARIS; Clemenceau, Lloyd George, Italian PM Nitti, Matsui (Japan) & Baron Lersner sign from 1600 in the Quai d'Orsay Clock Room. **League of Nations** (31 founder members) **& Mandate system come into effect**. League Council first meets (16). Germany signs protocol agreeing to reparations for Scapa ships. **S Russia** — British High Commissioner assures Denikin that all available Allied ships will evacuate White officers' wives and families with British Mission

as rearguard (see 26).

Sun 11
Germany — Allied Commission takes over Rhineland (HQ Koblenz). **Baltic States** — Latvian Army (c30,000) recaptures E province of Lettgallen from Reds (800 PoWs), capital Rjeshiza falls (21), reaches frontier (31) for only 29 cas, 28° below zero (see 18 Feb).

Mon 12
Versailles Treaty in force in Brazil.

Tue 13
Germany — Police open fire to defend *Reichstag* v workers' demo.

Thu 15
Siberia — Czech Legion hand Kolchak over to hostile Political Centre who hand him over to Reds for interrogation (21, see 7 Feb). **Ireland** — Sinn Fein win 172 of 206 borough & urban district councils in elections.

Fri 16
Allied Supreme Council note to Holland demands Kaiser's release for trial. Holland refuses (23). US Senate votes v joining League. PROHIBITION BEGINS.

Sat 17
S Russia — Red attempt to cross Don bloodily repulsed. **France** — Clemenceau defeated in Presidential election by Deschanel, Millerand becomes PM (19).

Tue 20
Siberia — Retreating Whites wipe out Nizhne Udinsk Red garrison & try to rescue Kolchak (23). **S Russia** — Reds retake Perekop & Genichesk. Typhus in Crimea.

Wed 21
Allied Supreme Council & Peace Conference closed, Conference of Ambassadors to supervise treaties.

Thu 22
Baltic States — Yudenich formally disbands Russian NW Army. **Syria** — French besieged in Marash by Arabs & Turks (-7 Feb) see 9 Feb.

Sat 24
Allied Reparation Commission organized (Poincaré Pres 20 Feb).

Sun 25
Siberia — Revolution at Nikolsk & at Vladivostok (31) where Zemstvos Govt seizes power.

Mon 26
Siberia — †White Gen Kappel of frostbite & pneumonia during ice march of 5 weeks to Lake Baikal. **S Russia** — Gen Milne visits Odessa, White Gen Schillings pleads for evacuation.

Tue 27

Hungary — First universal suffrage election (see 29 Feb).

Wed 28
S Russia — Reds take Sv Kresta & Kherson. **Turkey** — New Ottoman Parliament's National Pact declaration moves towards Nationalists.

Thu 29
Siberia — Reds declare martial law in Irkutsk. **Britain** — 1784 German Scapa Flow scuttle sailors repatriated.

FEBRUARY 1920

Sun 1
Germany/Poland — Allied troops occupy plebiscite area (pop 2,124,433) of Upper Silesia (see 19 Aug).

Mon 2
SOVIET-ESTONIAN PEACE; **first Moscow settlement with border state**. **S Russia** — Reds retake Nikolayev. (Feb) Azerbaijan Communist Party set up. Khiva's feudal ruler toppled by Red Army & Muslim reformers.

Tue 3
Siberia — Whites demand Irkutsk's surrender, Kolchak's release & rations for 50,000 men, skirmishing in outskirts (see 7). **Germany** — Allies ask for 890 military & political leaders to face trial on war crimes, Berlin refuses (5), but ex-Crown Prince offers himself as solo defendant (10, see 13).

Fri 6
Germany — League of Nations take over Saar region, mines under French control. **N Russia** — Reds attack in Dvina sector. **Trans-Caspia** — Reds occupy Krasnovodsk (E shore of Caspian Sea).

Sat 7
Siberia — **Kolchak shot at Irkutsk**. Czechs sign evacuation agreement with Reds.

Mon 9
Turkey — French evacuate Marash, Cilicia.

Tue 10
Germany — By now 1,824,828t of shipping surrendered to Allies.

Fri 13
Allied Supreme Council agrees to 25 Jan German request that war criminals be tried at home & not internationally (list handed over 3 Feb, see 10 Jan 1921).

Sat 14
S Russia — Tukachevski's new Red Caucasus Front, 215,000-strong (71,000 combat troops but typhus-afflicted), attacks v 60,000 Whites. **Britain** — K George V inspects W Front veteran 'Ole Bill' Motor Bus, back with London Gen Omnibus Co since 1919.

Sun 15
Baltic States — Allies take over Memel.

Mon 16
S Russia — Denikin retakes Perekop.

Wed 18
N Russia — Archangel: White Gen Miller & several hundred followers escape aboard icebreaker (see 21). **Baltic States** — Red peace overtures to Latvia.

Thu 19
Foreign Secretary Curzon disbands British Arab Bureau, absorbed into Cairo residency.

Fri 20
S Russia — Denikin's Volunteer & III Don Corps recapture Rostov in last success.

Sat 21
N Russia — Red 18th & 54th Divs occupy Archangel. Murmansk revolution (see 26). **S Russia** — Denikin dismisses Wrangel completely along with Gen Lukomsky & other Crimean White leaders. British Military Mission to Denikin numbers 1725 Army & RAF personnel under Maj-Gen H C Holman.

Sun 22
Germany — 21 Berlin arrests for violent anti-semitism.

Mon 23
Ireland — Midnight -0500 curfew in Dublin police district. **Britain** — Churchill says Army will be 220,000 volunteers (see 30 Apr).

Tue 24
Hitler addresses first public meeting of German Workers' Party in Munich beer hall. Renamed National Socialist German Workers' (Nazi) Party (Apr) when about 50 members.

Wed 25
Ireland — Govt of Ireland Bill introduced in Commons. **Britain** — Asquith re-elected MP, for Paisley nr Glasgow.

Thu 26
Lenin offers democratic parlt & payment of 60% of Russia's debt, US says propaganda ploy. **N Russia** — Reds occupy Povyenets & Segeja en route for Murmansk (see 13 Mar).

MARCH 1920

Mon 1
Hungary — Adm Horthy appointed Regent & Head of State, dissolves parlt (28), but does not answer Emperor Charles' 4 June message from Switzerland to prepare his return as king. **Russia** — (Mar) 9th Party Congress (600,000 members). State Commission for the Electrification of Russia set up. South Reds take Bataisk rail junction from Denikin, then Tikhoryetskaya (9). British Army cas in Russia since Armistice Day 986. USA — Railways returned to their 280 private owners.

Tue 2

W Russia — Red Army attacks Poles between Pripet & Dniester reaching latter between Mogilev & sea (7). **S Russia** — Reds take Stavropol. **Siberia** — Reds take Verkhne Udinsk.

Wed 3
S Russia — Gen Milne ordered to evacuate British 'Denmiss', sends 2nd Scots Fusiliers' coy in 2 sloops (8) to cover withdrawal (see 23).

Thu 4
N Russia — Reds take Kem on White Sea.

Fri 5
Siberia — Red Fifth Army reaches Irkutsk. **W Russia** — Poles take Mozyr (see 25 Apr).

Tue 9
Syria — At Damascus Syrian & Mesopotamian Arab Ctees elect Abdulla King of Mesopotamia & his brother Feisal King of Syria (see 25 Apr).

Wed 10
Latvia — *Landeswehr* reorganized as Latvian 30th Tukkum Regt, British CO Col Alexander leaves (20) with Baltic Cross of Honour. **Britain** — Home Rule Act partitions Ireland.

Thu 11
Near East Relief Campaign requests aid for 1.25m Armenians still alive (14,000 reported massacred 1).

Sat 13
N Russia — Red 1st Div reaches Murmansk, takes Pechenga (27). **Germany** — Kapp Putsch by Gen Luttwitz with former Erhardt Bde of 8000 Baltic *Freikorps* veterans seizes Berlin installing American-born journalist Wolfgang Kapp as Chancellor (with Ludendorff support), but Army & Police do not join, workers strike & regime soon flees (-17). Nationwide Spartacist risings. Weimar Govt returns (21).

Tue 16
Turkey — Allies occupy Constantinople more strictly as protest v Armenian massacre, 6 Indian cas taking GOC Turk 10th Div's home, (9k); 24 Turk leaders incl Rauf Bey deported to Malta as hostages.

Wed 17
S Russia — Reds take Ekaterinodar. **Britain** — Queen Alexandra unveils Nurse Cavell statue nr National Gallery, London.

Thu 18
Turkey — Last meeting of Imperial Ottoman Parliament.

Fri 19
Pilsudski made Marshal of Poland. **US Senate finally rejects Versailles Treaty**. **Turkey** — British 1/25th Punjabis retreat from Eskishehr on Anatolian Railway to Izmid (-22, see 22).

Sat 20
Ireland — Lord Mayor of Cork (alias Cmdt IRA 1st Cork Bde) shot dead (RIC blamed). Ulster Unionist Council accepts Govt of Ireland Bill. Dublin magistrate searching for Sinn Fein finances, shot and murdered by IRA (26).

Mon 22
Turkey — British repair rail bridge at Akhissar and heavily repulse Nationalists (-27, see 10 June).

Tue 23
S Russia — Milne arrives at Novorossisk aboard destroyer HMS *Venetia*, sees Denikin, arranges evacuation (-27).

Wed 24
Churchill warns Lloyd George he cannot militarily enforce a peace on Turkey 'on this world so torn with strife I dread to see you let loose the Greek armies — for all our sakes and certainly their sakes'.

Sat 27
S Russia — **Whites evacuate Novorossisk**: 10 Anglo-French and US warships help lift 35,000 White troops & 22,000 PoWs to Crimea, 200,000 fugitives never reach port.

Tue 30
Portugal ratifies Versailles Treaty.

Wed 31
Baltic — RN ordered not to attack Reds; battlecruisers *Hood* & *Tiger* recalled from Copenhagen. **Germany** — All *Freikorps* disbanded at Allied request. Last Spartacists put down (1-10 Apr).

APRIL 1920

Thu 1
S Russia — Denikin resigns, Wrangel succeeds (see 4). Red CEC sets up Caucasus Bureau. **Siberia** — US forces evacuate Vladivostok, Czechs begin to leave (-Dec). (Apr) Japanese Army takes over Primorskaia Region driving Reds underground. Brig-Gen J M Blair's British Military Mission withdrawn. **Diplomacy** — (Apr) Britain asks Moscow to spare Whites in Crimea. **Ireland** — (Apr) Londonderry disturbances (& May and from 19 June) cause 18 deaths.

Sun 4
S Russia — Denikin's farewell order 'To all those who honourably accompanied me in the heavy struggle — a low bow. God grant victory to the Army and save Russia.' He sails for Constantinople (CoS Gen Romanovski murdered there 5) in British destroyer, then on to Malta (6). **Siberia** — **Japanese occupy Vladivostok** & disarm Whites. **Caspian** — Red Flotilla beats White sqn (latter interned at Enzeli, N Persia, 8).

Mon 5
Ireland — 1916 Easter Rising

anniversary marked by Sinn Fein burning 22 tax offices & 13 police stns, 300,000 workers strike (13, see 14).

Tue 6
French occupy Frankfurt, Darmstadt & Hanau (-17 May) to force 40,000 German troops from Ruhr.

Thu 8
Reds enter Tuapse in N Caucasus & take Alexandrovsk in Siberia (Ural Cossack remnants).

Sun 11
Turkey — Sheikh-ul-Islam denounces Nationalists as rebels; Sultan dissolves Parliament (12).

Mon 12
Siberia — Siberians besiege Japanese in Khabarovsk till defeated (-22), latter repulse attack on Spasskoe (16) & land at Nikolayevsk on Sea of Okhotsk. **Syria** — French Urfa garrison wiped out, but French relieve Aintab (16) from Nationalists.

Tue 13
S Russia — Reds retake but then lose Perekop, take Derbent in Caucasus.

Wed 14
Ireland — Govt decide to release 89 Sinn Fein hunger strikers on parole, but 100 remain in jail (40 released 10 May from Wormwood Scrubs Prison, London).

Fri 16
S Russia — Whites take Sivash, Chongav & Genichensk but Reds retake latter (18).

Sun 18
Latvia — Constituent Assembly elections.

Mon 19
Russo-German PoW Repatriation Agreement signed at Berlin.

Fri 23
Turkey — Grand National Assembly meets at Ankara after elections and forms new govt (2 May).

Sat 24
Ukraine — **Polish offensive** (4 armies c150 planes) between Pripet & Dniester advances 150 miles in 2 weeks taking Mogilev (27), Berdichev, Zhitomir & Vinnitsa (30); Pilsudski signed alliance with Ukrainian leader Petlyura (21) but Red Twelfth & Fourteenth Armies escape.

Sun 25
British Palestine and Mesopotamia Mandates announced by League of Nations at San Remo, military rule ends in Palestine (29). Arabs attack British troops (26).

Wed 28
S Russia — First Red armoured trains reach Baku; Azerbaijan SSR declared.

Thu 29
Tukachevski made C-in-C Red W Front v Poles.

Fri 30
Britain abolishes conscription. France — 456,125 disablement pensions granted so far.

MAY 1920

Sat 1
Britain — QMAAC ceases to exist.

Mon 3
Ukraine — Poles take Fastov & Vapnyarka (6).

Tue 4
Britain — Commons debate unanimously confirms uniformity for war graves.

Wed 5
Russia — Lenin addresses troops bound for Polish Front in Moscow's Sverdlov Square (famous photograph, Trotsky often cropped out). *De facto* Red-White ceasefire in Crimea. **Palestine** — Arabs attack Jews in Plain of Sharon (-6).

Thu 6
Peace Process — Turk delegation arrives in Paris, handed draft Treaty (11).

Fri 7
Ukraine — **Poles take Kiev** but their offensive ends (10). **S Russia** — Reds land at Lenkoran. Soviet-Georgian Non-Intervention Treaty, still British troops in Batumi. Georgian Communist Party set up (May).

Sat 8
Germany — Army Air Service officially ceases to exist.

Tue 11
Turkey — Kemal condemned to death in absentia by Ottoman Govt. **Georgia** — Gen Milne visits Batumi for last time (-13). Intended Allied evacuation announced 8 June (see 9 July); 634-strong French bn arrives (20).

Wed 12
Britain — Dockers embargo munitions to Russia (-24).

Fri 14
W Russia — Tukachevski's Red offensive S of Dvina, takes Disna & Polotsk (16), Lepel (18), but fails overall (see 4 July). **Siberia** — Japanese repel Reds at Chita.

Sat 15
Holland — Ex-Kaiser moves into final place of exile, his purchased moated country house at Doorn, 12 miles E of Utrecht. **Lithuania** — 112-member Constituent Assembly meets & adopts provisional democratic republican constitution (2 June). **Crimea** — Gen Milne visits Whites for last time.

Sun 16
Ireland — Knockalong Dairy,

Co Limerick, forms a Soviet. Rail munitions strike in Co Dublin (23) soon becomes countrywide and extend to not carrying armed troops (-21 Dec).

Tue 18
Caspian — Reds force British to leave Enzeli, N Persia.

Wed 19
Britain has repatriated 370,855 Central Powers' PoWs and 9309 friendly nationals since 1 Sept 1919; 33,739 (all but 771 are Turks in Egypt, Mesopotamia and India) remain.

Thu 20
Syria — French order Feisal to leave Damascus.

Tue 25
W Russia/Ukraine — General Red offensive v Poles (see 10 June). **Siberia** — Red partisans massacre 700+ Japanese at Nikolaievsk (mouth of R Amur); Japan seizes oil-rich N Sakhalin as compensation (see 4 July).

Thu 27
USA — Senate rejects League of Nations offer of US mandate over Armenia (Britain also rejects 9 June).

Mon 31
Britain — **Butter rationing ends.**

JUNE 1920

Tue 1
Diplomacy — Khalil Pasha delivers Kemal letter to Soviet Commissar for Foreign Affairs in Moscow, so gains arms, ammunition & T£100,000 in gold.

Thu 3
Mesopotamia — Explosion at Tel Afar nr Mosul sparks off **insurrection v British** (81,907 troops on 27 Mar, 416k July-Sept); Army convoy wiped out nr Mosul (13). Mesopotamian League & Feisal's Syrian Ctee issue proclamation to free Mesopotamians (17). **S Russia** — Rear-Adm G Hope of RN Black Sea Fleet cables Wrangel warning him of no further British help if he attacks Bolsheviks (see 7).

Fri 4
ALLIED PEACE TREATY OF TRIANON WITH HUNGARY: Transylvania to Rumania which partitions Banat with Yugoslavia which gets Croatia; Slovak & Ruthene provinces to Czechoslovakia; Hungarian Army not to exceed 35,000; reparations to be fixed. Hungary reduced from 125,000 sq miles (1914) to 36,000 sq miles, population from 22m (1914) to 8m.

Mon 7
S Russia — Wrangel starts **White offensive from Crimea** into Ukraine, reaches Lower Dnieper in week, doubles territory, takes 8000 PoWs, 30 guns & 2 armoured trains. Red I Cav Corps wiped out in its

counter-raid, 3000 horses taken. White Gen Slashev lands on Sea of Azov coast. British Military Mission withdrawn (11) but French resume support for a time.

Tue 8
Italy — Riots follow bread price increase.

Wed 9
Britain — K George V opens Imperial War Museum at Crystal Palace.

Thu 10
Poles evacuate Kiev, Cabinet resigns. **Turkey** — Allies disarm Turk Constantinople garrison. British estimate Nationalist strength at 63,000 with 42,000 being recruited (14, see 15).

Sat 12
Red Army reoccupies Kiev, 16th & final change of ownership since 1917.

Tue 15
Turkey — Across Bosphorus from Constantinople, British Ismid Peninsula garrison (5bns with RN help incl 2 battleships firing) repulses up to 8000 Nationalists (c400 cas, -19) for c50 cas (see 12 July).

Wed 16
Holland — League of Nations Permanent Court of Justice opens in The Hague.

Sat 19
Allied Hythe Conference (Kent, England) agrees on Greek help for Allies in Anatolia (-20, see 22).

Sun 20
Latvian-Soviet war refugee evacuation agreement (100,000 Latvians supposed to be in Russia, see 11 Aug).

Mon 21
Peace Process — Allied Supreme Council agrees Germany to make 42 annual reparation payments, mainly to France, Britain, Italy & Belgium (see 5 July.

Tue 22
Turkey — **Greek offensive in Anatolia** v Turk Nationalists, reaches Usak 125 miles E of Smyrna (29, see 2 July).

Sat 26
Ireland — 2 British colonels and a general kidnapped while fishing on R Blackwater.

Mon 28
India — Irish Connaught Rangers Regt mutinies at Jullundur, Punjab.

Wed 30
Lithuania-USSR Peace Treaty.

JULY 1920

Thu 1
Aviation — Largest Zeppelin *L71* surrendered to Britain. **Palestine** — British Mandate takes effect, Sir H Samuel High

Commissioner.

Fri 2
Turkey — Greeks capture Panderma and Brusa (9) S of Sea of Marmora (see 20 & 25).

Sun 4
Siberia — Maritime Province Prov Govt agree to hand Japan parts of the coal & oil-rich Sakhalin Islands. **W Russia** — Tukachevski's Red W Front (4 armies = 108,000 men & 595 guns) attacks Poles, retakes Minsk (11), Vilna (14) & Grodno (19, 500 Polish PoWs).

Mon 5
Peace Process — Allied PMs Spa Conference Protocol (-16) apportions German reparations: France 52%; Britain 22%; Italy 10%; Belgium 8%; Japan & Portugal 3/4%; 6 1/2% to Greece, Rumania & Yugoslavia. Lloyd George says German Army still 150,000+. Germany signs Disarmament Protocol (9). **Schleswig is transferred to Denmark from Germany.**

Thu 8
Britain renames her East African colony Kenya.

Fri 9
c1000 British troops sail from Batumi, Georgians enter (7).

Sat 10
Britain — †Admiral of the Fleet Lord Fisher, aged 79.

Sun 11
Germany — East & West Prussia plebiscite votes to be part of Germany, but Polish corridor left through latter to connect with Danzig. **Spain** — †French Empress Eugenie, aged 94 at Madrid.

Mon 12
Diplomacy — British Foreign Secretary Curzon draws up Curzon Line to define Poland's Eastern frontier & so informs Moscow (see 17). **Turkey** — British form Ironside's Force to clear Ismid Peninsula of Nationalist irregulars, skirmishes to at least 30.

Thu 15
Latvian Peace Protocol with Germany.

Fri 16
Treaty of St Germain with Austria ratified in Paris (comes into force 24).

Sat 17
Politburo reject Allied note. **Red Army invades Poland in drive for Warsaw.**

Sun 18
Germany — Ex-Kaiser's youngest son Joachim takes his own life at Potsdam.

Mon 19
Peace Process — Allied ultimatum to Turkey demands treaty signing within 10 days (see 10 Aug).

Tue 20
Turkey — Greeks land a div at

Tekirdag and Eregli on N coast of Sea of Marmora.

Wed 21
Ireland — Street fighting between Sinn Fein & Unionists in Belfast. (12+ deaths - 24) **Syria** — King Feisal recognizes French mandate. French occupy Damascus (25).

Fri 23
Ukraine — Kamenev orders Red SW Front to march on Lemberg (Lvov). **Poland** — Tukhachevski reaches R Bug.

Sun 25
Turkey in Europe — **Greeks under King Constantine occupy Adrianople. Poland** — Anglo-French Missions arrive in Warsaw.

Tue 27
Pripet — Red Army takes Pinsk & crosses into Poland.

Wed 28
Czech-Polish Teschen Agreement signed in Paris.

Fri 30
Poland — Reds form Provisional Polish Revolutionary Ctee at Bialystok, 100 miles E of Warsaw.

Sat 31
Britain — Communist Party of Great Britain founded.

AUGUST 1920

Sun 1
Poland — Tukhachevski's Red Sixteenth Army takes Brest-Litovsk, but Polish Army 740,000 + 5000-strong French training mission incl Major de Gaulle. **S Russia** — (Aug) France gives Wrangel de facto recognition but sends very little help.

Sun 8
Moscow again rejects proposed armistice with Poland. **S Russia** — Wrangel lands 4500 Whites back in the Kuban, but forced to re-embark by 30.

Mon 9
Britain — Trade unions form Council of Action to arrange general strike if Britain declares war on USSR. Restoration of Order in Ireland Act.

Tue 10
TURKEY SIGNS PEACE TREATY OF SÈVRES: Greece to acquire Thrace & Aegean-Turk Islands with 5-year control of Smyrna + hinterland, pending plebiscite; Syria, Mesopotamia, Arabia & Armenia recognized as independent; **Dardanelles & Bosphorus to be demilitarized** & League of Nations-administered; Italy to retain Dodecanese & Rhodes; all Turk claims to lands inhabited by non-Turk peoples renounced. Ottoman Army limited to 50,000. Terms cause fury in Turkey and are replaced by the TREATY OF LAUSANNE (24 July 1923) after Kemal's nationalists (who

refuse to accept Sèvres) win the Greco-Turkish War & regain Smyrna; Turkey also regains Imbros, Tenedos & Eastern Thrace, thus giving virtually her present boundaries. Allies evacuate Constantinople 23 Aug 1923. **Diplomacy** — New States treaty between Allies, Rumania, Czechoslovakia & Poland; also Frontier Treaty with Rumania, Czechoslovakia & Yugoslavia.

Wed 11
Latvian-Soviet Peace Treaty of Riga.

Fri 13
Poland — Red Sixteenth Army storms Radzymin 15 miles E but Poles using Renault tanks recapture (15). Foreign diplomats except Papal Nuncio leave Warsaw for Lodz. **France** — Visiting Greek PM Venizelos wounded by 2 Greek soldiers.

Sat 14
Yugoslav-Czechoslovak alliance, joined by Rumania (17) to form **'Little Entente'**. **Poland** — Tukhachevski belatedly given control of Red Twelfth and First Cavalry Armies.

Mon 16
BATTLE OF WARSAW or 'MIRACLE OF THE VISTULA' (-25): Pilsudski's Poles defeat Red Army at the gates of their capital in a series of actions that the British Ambassador calls 'The 18th Decisive Battle in World History'. Poles claim 66,000 PoWs, 44,000 Reds interned in E Prussia, 231 guns, 1023 MGs, 10,000 vehicles. Up to 19 Polish aircraft (200 sorties) delay Budenny in south (16-19, see 31). US warships sent to Danzig.

Tue 17
Polish-Soviet talks begin at Minsk (see 12 Oct).

Thu 19
Silesia — Poles raid Germans in attempt to seize area (see 20 Mar 1921). **Russia** — Politburo gives Crimea priority over Poland.

Mon 23
Ireland — Belfast incidents cause c30 deaths and a curfew (-31).

Tue 24
Kemal draws up draft treaty with Communists in Moscow.

Thu 26
USA — The 19th Amendment gives women the vote.

Tue 31
S Poland — Poles maul Budenny's Red First Cavalry Army in Battle of Zamosc-Komarow ('Zamosc Ring'), 6 years to the day since many participants fought each other in the Habsburg & Tsarist Imperial Armies across the same ground (see 23 Sept).

SEPTEMBER 1920

Wed 1
S Russia — (Sept) 'Congress of Peoples of the East' at Baku. Red Army topples Emir of Bukhara. **Syria** — France creates state of Lebanon.

Tue 7
Franco-Belgian Military Convention.

Fri 10
Britain — Soviet attempt to fund *Daily Herald* suspends Anglo-Soviet negotiations.

Sun 12
Pripet — Gen Sikorski's Poles begin offensive, capture Kovel, Lutsk, Rovno & Tarnopol (18), & Pinsk (20), crushing Red Twelfth & Fourteenth Armies (see 20).

Thu 16
USA — Wall St bomb explosion causes 330 cas, Russian A Brailovsky arrested (18).

Mon 20
Poland/W Russia — Battle of the Niemen (-29): Pilsudski destroys Red Third Army, re-occupies Grodno (26) & drives Tukhachevski's remnants back to Minsk in Battle of the Shchara. Takes 50,000 PoWs & 160 guns in these 2 victories (see 15 Oct). **Armenia** — Turks invade South Armenia: Dashnak Govt surrenders power to Reds (see 21 Oct). **Peace Process** — League of Nations approves Belgium's annexation of Eupen & Malmédy from Germany.

Thu 23
Ukraine — Kamenev orders Budenny's First Cavalry Army away from Poles to Wrangel front (300 mile ride).

Sat 25
Ireland — †CO IRA 1st Cork Bde & City's Lord Major T MacSwiney on 74th day of hunger strike, Brixton prison, London.

OCTOBER 1920

Fri 1
Ukraine — (Oct) New C-in-C Red S Front Frunze to Lenin from Kharkov 'I feel that I and the front HQ are surrounded by hostile elements'.

Wed 6
S Russia — Wrangel 'Trans-Dneiper' spoiling attack by Gen Kutepov's First Army forced back across river after a week (see 28).

Sat 9
Polish 'rebel' Gen Zeligowski drives Lithuanians from Vilna (Polish-Lithuanian armistice 30 Nov).

Tue 12
Red Army C-in-C Kamenev comments 'simultaneous battle with Poland and Wrangel has not given us success ... it should be against Wrangel'. **Soviet-Polish Armistice signed** at Riga.

Fri 15
W Russia — **Poles re-occupy Minsk.**

Sun 17
Trotsky suggests in *Izvestia* that Wrangel may last winter.

Thu 21
Turkey — Turk Nationalists recapture Kars from Armenians.

Wed 27
Poland signs treaty with Danzig (declared a free city 15 Nov).

Thu 28
S Russia — Final Red offensive: Frunze's 5 armies (133,000) v 37,000 Whites in N Tauride, Whites lose 20,000 PoWs, 100 guns & 7 armoured trains but veterans win race back to Crimea.

NOVEMBER 1920

Sun 1
(Nov) Red Army takes over Armenia and declares SSR (29). **Ireland** — First execution since May 1916: Kevin Barry for soldier's murder (20 Sept).

Mon 2
USA — Warren G Harding elected Pres in place of Wilson.

Sat 6
Lenin tells meeting in Bolshoi Theatre 'Today we can celebrate our victory'.

Sun 7
S Russia — Red Sixth Army infantry outflank Crimean Turk wall (Perekop Isthmus) by surprise night attack across Sivash salt sea.

Thu 11
Crimea — Latvian Div & Bliukher's 51st Div (from Siberia) storm White Iushun Line. Frunze radios surrender terms incl pardon for war crimes & right to emigrate (Lenin annoyed). British Adm de Robeck told to remain neutral. **Britain** — CENOTAPH UNVEILED in Whitehall to 'The Glorious Dead of 1914-18'; THE UNKNOWN WARRIOR (brought from France 10) BURIED IN WESTMINSTER ABBEY. **France** — UNKNOWN FRENCH SOLDIER BURIED UNDER THE ARC DE TRIOMPHE. **Ireland** — Sinn Feiners chant through 2-minute silence.

Fri 12
Black Sea — RN destroyer *Tobago* mined, towed to Constantinople & Malta, but not repaired. **Crimea** — Red Sixth Army pauses crucially. **Diplomacy** — Italy & Yugoslavia temporarily resolve Adriatic disputes by Treaty of Rapallo: Italy has Istria and Yugoslavia Dalmatia.

Sat 13
League of Nations first full session has 5000 delegates from 41 countries.

Sun 14
Crimea — Wrangel embarks at

Sevastopol in battleship *Gen Kornilov*.

Mon 15
Crimea — **Red Sixth Army enters Sevastopol. Europe** — First League of Nations Assembly, **Danzig declared a free city.**

Tue 16
Crimea — White evacuation of 146,000 people completed at 5 ports for voyage to Constantinople (350 miles), helped by French Navy and US destroyers. **Greece** — Venizelos resigns after election defeat.

Sun 21
Ireland — 'Bloody Sunday': IRA murder 12 British officers in Dublin, paralyzing Special Branch (7 IRA gunmen later hang). Black and Tans slaughter 12 from Gaelic football match crowd. IRA arson attacks in Liverpool (27).

Thu 25
Japan — World's first 16in gun and largest battleship completed, 38,500t *Nagato* at Kure (see 11 July 1921).

Mon 29
Britain — Sugar rationing ends.

DECEMBER 1920

Wed 15
China & Austria joins League of Nations.

Sat 18
France & Britain agree on Syria-Palestine frontiers.

Sun 19
Greece — Ex-K Constantine returns despite Anglo-French objections after referendum in his favour (5).

JANUARY 1921

Mon 3
SW Africa — Martial law lifted.

Thu 6
Germany — 25% of Berlin's 485,000 children malnourished or diseased.

Mon 10
Germany — German supreme court war trials begin at Leipzig (Ludendorff acquitted 24 Apr). First sentence, 26 Oct, 9 months for cruelty to PoWs.

Fri 28
Allies fix German reparations at £10bn over 42 yrs = RM 200bn plus 12.5% tax on German exports (see 8 Mar).

FEBRUARY 1921

Wed 9
Soviet-Polish Peace Treaty of Riga (to 18 Mar). **Georgia** — (Feb) Rev Ctee declares SSR (25) and calls in Red Eleventh Army which secures Tiflis after wk-long battle.

Wed 16
Britain — Unemployment 1,039,000 incl 368,000 ex-

servicemen.

Sat 18
US representative recalled from Reparation Commission.

Sat 26
Soviet Russia recognizes Persia-Afghanistan frontiers.

MARCH 1921

Tue 1
Russian Baltic Fleet mutiny at Kronstadt eventually crushed (-18). **Britain** — (Mar) By now 1,187,450 men (37,450 officers) receiving war disability pensions, of which 243,250 (11,250 officers) 50% disabled or worse (ie at least partial amputees); 531,666 pensioner disabilities due to disease, 324,722 due to wounds.

Thu 3
Japan — Crown Prince Hirohito begins visit to Europe in battleship *Katori* (-3 Sept); reaches Britain (8 May); tours W Front battlefields after 29 May.

Tue 8
French troops occupy Düsseldorf & other Ruhr towns v Germany's failure to make preliminary reparations payment (*see* 23).

Wed 16
Anglo-Soviet trade agreement.

Fri 18
Soviet-Polish Treaty of Riga; Poland abandons her claim to the Ukraine.

Sun 20
Silesia — 63% vote for Upper Silesian union with Germany but, after continued Polish-German fighting, League of Nations partitions province with Poland (25-26 Oct).

Wed 23
Germany says she cannot pay £600m reparations due on 1 May (*see* 27 Apr).

Thu 24
British Reparation Recovery Act imposes 50% duties on German goods (reduced to 26%, 20 May). **Germany** — Communist riots in Hamburg (20+k).

Thu 31
Britain — Last Volunteer Force Units disbanded.

APRIL 1921

Tue 5
International Red Cross proposes new limits on warfare.

Tue 19
Germany — Monarchist demo at ex-Kaiserin Victoria's funeral (she died 11, aged 62).

Sun 24
Tyrol plebiscite favours union with Germany but Allies give region to Italy.

Wed 27
Allied Reparations Commission fixes Germany's bill at £6650m.

MAY 1921

Mon 2
French troops mobilized for Ruhr occupation.

Thu 5
Allied Supreme Council warns Germany that non-payment of reparations by 12 will cause Ruhr occupation.

Wed 11
Germany accepts Allied ultimatum on reparations (French troops evacuate Ruhr 30 Sept).

Sat 14

Italy — Fascists win 29 seats in parliament.

Tue 24
British Legion for Great War veterans founded.

Tue 31
USA — First Austrians & Germans become US citizens since 1917.

JUNE 1921

Mon 20
Russia — First food ship for 3 yrs docks at Petrograd. Lenin appeals for international famine relief (9 Aug), 18m starving esp in Volga region due to drought & civil war.

JULY 1921

Sat 2
USA — Pres Harding signs Peace Decree with Germany & Austria (*see* 24 Aug).

Mon 11
Ireland — British Army-IRA truce (leads to Anglo-Irish Treaty 6 Dec). **USA** — Pres Harding issues Washington Naval Conference invitations (talks begin 21 Nov, warship limitation treaty signed 6 Feb 1922).

Fri 29
Germany — Hitler becomes Nazi Party leader (3000 members Nov).

AUGUST 1921

Sat 6
Germany — Tax increases to pay reparations.

Tue 23
Emir Feisal crowned King of Iraq.

Wed 24
US signs Peace Treaty with Austria (resumes diplomatic relations 7 Dec), with **Germany** (25) & **Hungary** (29). US troops evacuate Koblenz and leave Germany Jan 1923. Unknown soldier buried in Arlington National Cemetery 11 Nov.

Fri 26
Germany — Armistice signatory & Catholic Party leader Erzberger murdered by ex-*Freikorps* men.

Wed 31
BRITISH TERMINATION OF WAR IN ALL ASPECTS.

THE PEACE PROCESS 1918-1923

The Great War took longer to end by treaty than the fighting itself. Not until 23 August 1923 did the Allied occupation forces evacuate Constantinople in conformity with the definitive Turkish peace treaty, signed at Lausanne a month earlier. Their military occupation of the former Ottoman imperial capital and its strategic straits had lasted $4^3/4$ years. It had almost led to a new war in the autumn of 1922 (Chanak Crisis) when Mustapha Kemal's triumphant Turkish Nationalists, after their decisive eviction of the Greeks from Asia Minor, confronted British troops. The war scare was enough to clinch the fall of Lloyd George's wartime coalition government.

Such events remind us that the Great War settlement was more than just a matter of Germany, however much that country had dominated the former Central Powers and bulked foremost in the minds of peacemakers. The Treaty of Versailles with Germany (28 June 1919) was the first of six settlements with the defeated powers and the model for them all. No international agreement has undergone more analysis or remained so controversial. Not for the Allies the clearcut unconditional surrenders that concluded the Second World War whose own causes owed so much to the Peace Treaty of 1919.

The Treaty was divided into 15 parts containing almost 450 articles and numerous annexes. Germany lost 13% of her prewar territory and 6 million people or 10% of her population. By Articles 51-79 France regained Alsace-Lorraine (120,000 Germans departed by 1921) 47 years since their annexation. Belgium received the mainly German-speaking enclaves of Moresnet, Eupen and Malmédy (population about 70,000; Articles 32-34) that Prussia had gained in 1815. The Baltic port of Memel went to the new independent state of Lithuania (Article 99). Czechoslovakia received the Hultschin district (40,000 Germans emigrated). Poland gained West Prussia and the Posen area (Article 87); parts of Upper Silesia (by referendum in 1921) under Article 88; and a corridor to the Baltic Sea where the new Free City of Danzig (Articles 100-108) was to be administered by the League of Nations (its Covenant formed Part 1 of the Treaty). East Prussia was, therefore, cut off from the remainder of Germany. Northern Schleswig went to Denmark by plebiscite (Articles 109-114).

The 1000-square mile Saar Basin was put under League of Nations administration subject to plebiscite after 15 years. In the meantime, France was to control its valuable coalfields as direct reparation in kind for the damage done to hers (Articles 45-50). The Rhineland, containing Germany's Ruhr industrial heart, was to be demilitarized and occupied for 15 years (Articles 42-43). Reparations were to be paid (Article 232) with an immediate payment of RM20bn in gold by 1 May 1921. Reparations including handing over every merchant ship of 1600grt and over (half the ships of 1000-1600grt and a quarter of fishing vessels) to compensate the Allies for wartime losses.

All Germany's colonies became League of Nations' mandates for disposal to the victors (Article 22) and 20,000 German colonial settlers returned home. Economically Germany lost 45% of her coal (10 years of massive supplies to Belgium, France and Italy); 65% of her iron ore; 57% of lead; 72% of her zinc. The Kiel Canal (Article 380) and five major rivers became international waterways. A ban was placed on the union of Germany and Austria. Provision was made for the trial of the Kaiser and about 100 other war leaders (Articles 227-230) including Hindenburg; this was an unfulfilled but natural extension of the war guilt clause (Article 231). The German Army was reduced to a 100,000-strong volunteer force including a maximum of 4000 officers (Article 160). Conscription was abolished (Article 173). No tanks, armoured cars, heavy artillery, flamethrowers, poison gas, Zeppelins, military aircraft, air force or general staff were permitted. No arms were to be imported or exported. The Navy was limited to 15,000 men manning 6 battleships, 6 light cruisers, 12 destroyers and 12 torpedo boats (Article 181). No new warship over 10,000 tons was to be built and no U-boats were allowed (Article 181).

Little wonder that Germany signed under duress and protest. The High Seas Fleet was scuttled a week before the hated Diktat came into force. Much opinion in Britain and the USA turned against the harsh provisions to the extent that the US Senate never ratified the Treaty, itself a major weakness of the postwar settlement. Yet there were those who argued and still do that Versailles was too lenient, a compromise between the Big Four. The European Allies were keenly aware of their financial indebtedness to the USA ($10bn owed, only $2.7bn repaid 1920-32) and even the French felt obliged to refrain from claiming the Rhine frontier that Foch wanted. Versailles humiliated and hurt Germany, but, as events soon proved, did not permanently remove her capacity to wage aggressive war. Probably only the most ruthless partition of Germany into scores of 18th century-style small states and military occupation of a post-1945 scale and length could have achieved that.

The Reparations issue was to sour Allied-German relations into the 1930s. Fixed at £6.6bn plus interest in April 1921, the Weimar Republic promptly paid £50m but halted payments during the 1922 inflation crisis thus triggering a Franco-Belgian occupation of the Ruhr. The American-compiled Dawes Plan (Apr 1924) gave a loan to secure future payments and stabilized matters until the June 1929 Young plan cut the original figure by 75%, proposing annual instalments until 1988. Germany made a first payment in May 1930 but the world economic depression and Hitler prevented any more. All told Germany had paid RM21.6bn, or an eighth of the original demand, but received more in loans (mainly from the USA) to aid her economic recovery.

The Austrian Republic signed next at St Germain (10 September), admitting responsibility for the war (Article

77). Austria now consisted of only two thirds of the former Habsburg German-speaking territories, losing 3.5 million Germans to Czechoslovakia and 250,000 South Tyroleans to Italy. Bulgaria's fate was similar (Neuilly 27 Nov) but her reparations were the only ones wholly specified from the start — £90 million; 278,000 Bulgarians left the ceded territories.

Peace with Hungary was delayed by Béla Kunn's Communist takeover until 4 June 1920 (Trianon). It proved the harshest of all the settlements. Privileged Dual Monarchy Hungary was reduced to one third in area and population. She lost Transylvania to Rumania, the most enlarged Allied Power, and her ancient capital of Pressburg (Bratislava) to the entirely new state of Czechoslovakia. No fewer than 280,000 Hungarians fled the ceded lands by 1924.

Turkey, alone of the defeated Central Powers, had the opportunity to mitigate her treatment by force of arms against a former Allied power — Greece. So crucial were these events to the modern republic that they are known as the Turkish War of Independence. Nevertheless the main territorial difference between Sèvres (10 Aug 1920) and Lausanne (24 July 1923) lay in the restoration of Turkey-in-Europe and the inviolability of Anatolia. The Great War had swept away the old Ottoman Middle East hegemony and Sultanate for good.

Conspicuous of course by her absence from the peace process was Russia. Yet the fear of a Bolshevized Europe was a great influence throughout. By the end of 1920 the Red Army had won the Civil War but had failed to export the Revolution on its bayonets. The Polish Army was the first foreign foe to defeat it conclusively until the Afghan mujahideen in 1989. The internally victorious but fragile Soviet Union began to recognize its new western neighbours and borders culminating in the March 1921 Treaty of Riga with Poland. Not so fortunate were the USSR's southern neighbours in the Caucasus who had enjoyed a fractious independence since the upheavals of 1917. Between April 1920 and February 1921 Azerbaijan, Armenia and Georgia in turn became Socialist and Soviet Republics.

By 1924-25 non-Communist Europe could be said to be recovering prewar levels of prosperity and to have removed the most obvious scars of war. The political and emotional legacies of the Great War, and on the Western Front even its physical imprint, are with us still.

TABLES

Arras Forces 9 Apr 1917

British Third Army (Allenby) 350,000 men, 48 tanks, 2817 guns (961 heavy) in 21
divs + 3 cav divs, 450 aircraft
German Sixth Army (Falkenhausen) 230,000 men, 1014 guns (237 heavy) in 13 divs,
195 aircraft

Arras Losses 9 Apr - 26 May 1917

British 158,660 (87,226 in Third Army); c30+ tanks
German 180,000+ (20,834+ PoWs); 252 guns; 227+ mortars; 470+ MGs

Nivelle Offensive Forces 16 Apr 1917

French Res Army Gp (Micheler) 1,200,000 men, 128 tanks, 5544 guns (1466 heavy)
in 56 divs (26 in res)
Sixth Army (Mangin) 17 inf + 1 cav div, 1659 guns, 594 mortars
Fifth Army (Mazel) 16 inf + 1 cav div + 2 Russian bdes, 128 tanks, 1967 guns, 1056
mortars
Tenth Army (Duchêne) c12 inf + 3 cav divs
French Centre Army Gp (Pétain)
Fourth Army (Anthoine) c11 inf divs
German Army Gp Crown Prince 2531 guns (790 heavy) in 38 divs (17 in res)
Seventh Army (Boehn) 8 inf divs
First Army (F Below)
Third Army (Rothmaler)

Nivelle Offensive Losses 16 Apr - 9 May 1917

French 187,000 (incl 5183 Russians & 4000+ PoWs); 38 tanks
German 163,000 (28,815 PoWs); 194 guns; 530 MGs; 149 mortars

Messines Ridge Forces 7 June 1917

British Second Army (Plumer) 12 divs, 2266 guns (738 heavy), 428 mortars, 72 tanks
& 300 aircraft
German Fourth Army (Arnim) 5 divs + 4 later, 640 guns (296 heavy)

Messines Ridge Losses 1 - 12 June 1917

British 24,562 (10,521 Anzacs); 11 tanks disabled
German c23,000 (7264 PoWs); 154 guns (48 captured); 218 MGs; 60 mortars

Third Ypres Forces 31 July 1917

BEF (Haig) 3091 guns,406 aircraft in sector
British Fifth Army (Gough) 9 divs, 136 tanks
British Second Army (Plumer) 5 divs
French First Army (Anthoine) 6 divs, 500 guns, 200 aircraft
German Army Group Crown Prince Rupprecht
German Fifth Army (Gallwitz)
German Fourth Army (Arnim) 13 divs, c600 aircraft
German Sixth Army (O Below) 6 divs

Third Ypres Losses 31 July - 10 Nov 1917

British (-12 Nov) 244,897 (14,000 PoWs, nearly 40,000 gassed since 12 July); 50+
tanks
French (8 July-31 Oct) 8525
German (73 divs engaged) c230,000 (37,000 PoWs); 86 guns? lost/captured

Cambrai Forces 20 Nov 1917

British Third Army (Byng) 19 inf divs + 5 cav divs, 476 tanks (98 supply & support),
1003 guns, 289 aircraft
German Second Army (Marwitz) 5 divs, 440 guns, 78 aircraft

Cambrai Losses 20 Nov - 8 Dec 1917

British 44,207 (9000 PoWs); 166 guns; c300 tanks; 53+ aircraft
American 18
German 41,000+(11,000 PoWs); 142 guns; 456 MGs; 79 mortars; 14+ aircraft

W Front Losses 1917

British 817,790 (27,200 PoWs); 172 guns; c400 tanks (988 engaged)
French 569,000 (excl officers); 38 tanks
Belgian
Portuguese
American 108+ (cas singled out, total certainly only a few hundred)
German 883,979 (73,131 PoWs to BEF, 50,000+ PoWs to French); 955+ guns (531
to BEF); 605+ mortars; 2407+ MGs
Austrian (to 31 July, mainly arty) 965 (92 missing & PoWs); 29,510 sick

1917 French dead by arm

Infantry	134,710
Cavalry	3180
Artillery	15,500
Engineers	5475
Air arm	820

Kerensky Offensive Forces 1 July 1917

Russian SW Front (Gutor) 224,701+ , 1114 guns, c120 aircraft
  Eleventh Army (Erdeli) 12 inf + 1 cav div + Czech Bde, 575 guns, c50 aircraft
  Seventh Army (Heroys) 20 + inf + 4 cav divs + 2 cyclist bns, c70 aircraft
  Eighth Army (Kornilov) 8 inf + 3 cav divs
Austro-German Army Group Böhm-Ermolli
  Austrian Second Army (Böhm-Ermolli) 5 German + 5 Austrian divs =83 bns, 1
  Austrian cav div + 1 cav bde, 460 guns (60 heavy)
  Südarmee (Bothmer) 528 guns in 6 German, 3 Austrian & 1 Turk div
  Austrian Third Army (Tersztyanszky) 1 German + 5 Austrian divs + 1   Austrian
  cav bde

Riga Offensive Forces 1 Sept 1917

German Eighth Army (Hutier) 760 guns & 544 mortars in 8 inf + 2 cav divs
Russian Twelfth Army (Klembovski) 9 inf + 2 cav divs, c500 guns

Riga Offensive Losses 1 - 10 Sept 1917

Russian 25,000 (9000 PoWs and c1000 gas cas); 262 guns
German 4200

Rumanian Front Forces July 1917

Rumanian First Army (Cristecu) 170,000, 584 guns, 52 aircraft in 6½ inf 2½ cav divs
Rumanian Second Army (Averescu) 228 guns, 448 MGs, 21 aircraft in 4 inf +1/2 cav
divs
Russian Fourth (Ragoza), Sixth & Ninth Armies with 37 inf + 7 cav divs
Central Powers Forces 27 inf + 10 cav divs, 1440 guns
Archduke Joseph Ferdinand Army Group with Austrian Army Rohr; Austro-German
Army Gerok; German Ninth Army (Eben) with 10 Austrian + 12 German divs
Mackensen Army Group with Turk VI Corps (Cevad Pasha) of 2 divs & Bulgar Third
Army (Mezerov) 3 inf + 1 cav div

1917 Russian Front Losses

German & Austrian 56,061+ (49,861 PoWs); 124 guns
Turk (-Aug) unavailable but incl 191 PoWs
Bulgar unavailable but incl 338 PoWs
Russian 693,000 (281,000 PoWs); 584+ guns; 200+ MGs
Rumanian (May-Nov) 383,000 (213,000 PoWs); 22+ guns

1917 SOUTHERN FRONTS TABLES

Macedonia Forces May 1917

Allied Armies in the Orient (Sarrail) 274 bns
    French Army of the Orient (Grossetti) c195,000 in 6 divs + 3 cav regts
    British Salonika Army (Milne) 180,000 in 6+ divs & 2 mtd bdes
    Serb Army (Crown Prince Alexander, Gen Boyovic) 152,000 in 6 divs + 1cav div
    Italians (Petitti/Pennella) 55,000 in 1 div (18 bns)
    Russians (Dietrichs) 17,367 in 2 bdes (12 bns)
Bulgar-German-Turk forces 255 bns
    Bulgar First Army (Gesov) in 2 divs + German 9th *Jäger* Regt
    German Eleventh Army (Scholtz) in 5 divs (1 German) 1 Turk regt & other bns
    Bulgar Second Army (Todorov) in 4 divs (1 Turk)

Macedonia Losses Mar - May 1917

British 5024; 11+ aircraft
French c3000
Italians 3000
Serb c3000
German/Bulgar 2924+ (2111+ PoWs); 3+ bombers

Caporetto Forces 24 Oct 1917

German Fourteenth Army (O Below) 15 divs (168 bns), 1845 guns (incl 239 heavy &
    492 German 9.45in mortars), 1000 gas projectors
    Krauss Gp 3 Austrian + German *Jäger* div, 430 guns
    Stein Gp 3 German (incl Bavarian *Alpenkorps*) + 1 Austrian div
    Berrer Gp 2 German divs
    Scotti Gp 2 Austrian + 1 German div
    Army Res 3 Austrian divs
Italian Second Army (Capello, Montuori) 21 divs (224 bns), c2200 guns, 800 mortars
    IV Corps (Cavaciocchi) 4 divs
    XXVII Corps (Badoglio) 4 divs
    XXIV Corps (Caviglia) 3 divs
    II Corps (Albricci) 2 divs
    VI Corps (Lombardi) 2 divs
    VIII Corps (Grazioli) 3 divs
    Army Res VII Corps (Buongiovanni) 2 divs

Caporetto Losses 24 Oct - 9 Nov 1917

Italian 320,000 (265,000 PoWs); 3152 guns; 1732 mortars, 3000 MGs; 2000 SMGs;
    300,000+ rifles
Austro-German c20,000

Piave Losses 10 Nov - 25 Dec 1917

Italian c140,000 (70,000 PoWs)
British 371 (3 PoWs & missing)
French 259
German *Jäger* Div (17-27 Nov) 1206

1917 Macedonia Losses

French 14,947; 8+ aircraft
British 12,460 (1069 died of disease); 11+ aircraft
Serb 8494 (exc 2917 died in hospital Aug 1916-28 Feb 1918)
Russian 1477 (to 15 Nov)
Greek 1544 (incl Dec 1916, exc 15 Jan-15 May)
Italian 4775; 5+ MGs
Bulgar 1095 PoWs to British
German 6+ aircraft

1917 Italian Front Losses

Italian 807,736+ (380,000+ PoWs); 3152+ guns; 1732 mortars; 3000 MGs
French 259+
British 371 (3 PoWs & missing)
Austro-German 193,603+ (58,795 PoWs+); 135+ guns (before Caporetto, perhaps
    recaptured)

1917 TURKISH FRONTS TABLES

Gaza-Beersheba Offensive Forces 31 Oct 1917

British EEF (Allenby) 75,000 inf, 17,000 cav, 8 tanks, 475 guns, 74 aircraft in 3 cav
    divs + 7 inf divs + 1 camel bde + 3 inf bdes
Turk *Yildirim* Army Group (Falkenhayn) 38,500+ inf, 1500 cav, c300 guns, 390+ MGs
    Eighth Army (Kress) 7 divs
    Seventh Army (Fevzi) 2 divs + 1 cav div

1917 Palestine Losses

British 37,351 (1760 died of disease, 843 PoWs); 5 tanks; 1 armoured car; 12+ MGs;
    138,821 sick admissions; 3033 camels; 245 donkeys
Turk 35,118+ (17,646 PoWs) + many more sick; 108 guns; 15+ mortars; 172+ MGs;
    24+ aircraft

1917 Mesopotamia Losses

British 31,540 (2425 died of disease, 383 PoWs); 1 gun; 7 mortars; 3 MGs; 8 aircraft;
    110,613 sick admissions exc Indians
Turk 25,347+ (15,944 PoWs) many more sick; 124 guns; 22 mortars; 37+ MGs; 7+
    aircraft

1917 Arabia Losses

Turk 1785+ (935 PoWs); 4 guns
Arabs 34+

1917 Aden Losses

British 190 (7 died of disease)

Senussi Revolt/W Desert Losses 1915 - 17

British 667+ (80 PoWs)
French 853 among 2560 men lost in Tunisia
Italian incl 700 PoWs released 1917-18
Senussi 1883+ (161+ PoWs); 5 guns; 9+ MGs

1917 AFRICAN OPERATIONS TABLES

1917 E Africa Losses

British 8878 (3310 died of disease, 441+ PoWs & missing); 18+ MGs
Portuguese 700+ ; 6 MGs
Belgian not available
German 7249+ (6728 PoWs); 18 guns; 47 MGs

1917 SEA WAR TABLES

1917 Royal Navy Losses

63 warships including 2 battleships; 1 cruiser; 1 monitor; 10 sloops; 23 destroyers; 7
    submarines; 6 AMCs. Total 103,785t
313 auxiliaries incl 136 colliers & oilers and 133 trawlers & drifters.Total 538,322t
Total naval cas 7899 or 2.13% of av 370,100 strength

1917 British A/S Air Effort

RNAS aircraft sight 135 U-boats (85 attacked, 1 sunk)
RNAS airships sight 26 U-boats (15 attacked)
RFC aircraft sight 8 U-boats (6 attacked)
Total hours flown 1,526,746

1917 Allied & Neutral Shipping Losses

2673 ships (1197 British) worth 6,184,000t (4,011,000t British with 6408 lives)
U-boat figure 6,256,399t (532,272t to U-boat-laid mines) of which 1,514,501t in Med
New British ships built only 1,163,000t or just over 25% of losses; 6,401,845t
    available for imports but includes 925,000t damaged

1917 U-boat Losses & Gains

63 (only 3 in Med) but 87 commissioned making total strength 169
Most successful 1917 U-boat *U35* (in Med) 62 ships worth 170,672t

Baltic Losses to Nov 1917

German   6 cruisers; 12 destroyers; 3 torpedo boats; 1 minelayer; 3 U-boats; 23
    minesweepers; 14 small craft; c50 merchant ships

Russian   1 predreadnought; 1 cruiser; 5 destroyers; 2 minelayers; 5 torpedo boats;
    3 gunboats; 5 submarines; 18 minesweepers; 15 merchant ships

1917 AIR WAR TABLES

1917 Air Raids

Paris	1 : No cas
Britain	37 : (8 Zeppelins lost, 23 Gothas); 580 Zeppelin bombs; 2341 cas; 1507 defence sorties (32+ aircraft damaged, 12 aircrew deaths)
London	13 : 719 bombs; 1302 cas; 365 buildings hit; 87 fires caused
Germany	175 : 5234 bombs
Constantinople	1
Venice	1

1917 RFC Expansion

70 service sqns become 115
50 training sqns become 109 (15 in Canada by Aug)
1491 aircraft (691 in France) become 3238 (934 in France & Italy)
53 balloon units become 89
5796 vehicles become 8173
57,897 personnel become 114,260
41 boys for labour become 9601 women & boys
3379 cadets in training become 14,097
1679 graduated pilots become 3974
24,895 personnel sent overseas (22,289 to France)
4227 aircraft sent to France
941 aircraft sent to Middle East
5770 aircraft issued to home units
127,000 aerial photographs taken (3.9m prints developed)

1917 RFC W Front Air Victory Claims

1073 German aircraft shot down
885 German aircraft driven down out of control
76 German aircraft to BEF AA guns
45 German balloons destroyed or captured

1917 INTERNATIONAL EVENTS TABLE

US Forces Apr 1917

127,588 regular troops, 504 field guns + coast arty (21,000), 1110 MGs, 80,436 National Guard; 55 aircraft (c75 trained pilots); 14 dreadnoughts

1917 HOME FRONTS TABLE

Austrian War Losses -1 Feb 1917

579,258 k; 1,361,462 PoWs or missing; c1.5m w; 1.8m sick (1m of latter 2 categories died or disabled)

1918 WESTERN FRONT TABLES

Second Somme Forces 21 Mar 1918

German Army (Hindenburg & Ludendorff) 74 divs, 6473 guns, 3532 mortars, 9 tanks, 730 aircraft (82 sqns)
Army Gp Rupprecht (CoS Kuhl)
  Seventeenth Army (O Below) 18 divs, 2234 guns (824 heavy), 1197 mortars, 241 aircraft
  Second Army (Marwitz) 20 divs, 1751 guns (714 heavy), 1080 mortars, 232 aircraft
Army Gp Crown Prince (CoS Schulenburg)
  Eighteenth Army (Hutier) 27 divs, 2623 guns (970 heavy), 9 tanks, 1257 mortars, 257 aircraft
Reserves 9 or 11 divs
BEF (Haig) 34 inf + 3 cav divs, 2804 guns, 1400 mortars, 217 tanks; 579 aircraft (31 sqns)
  Third Army (Byng) 14 divs, 1120 guns (461 heavy), 98 tanks; 261 aircraft
  Fifth Army (Gough) 12 divs + 3 cav divs, 1684 guns (532 heavy), 119 tanks; 357 aircraft
  GHQ Reserve 8 divs
French Third Army (Humbert) 4 divs (2 cav)

Second Somme Losses 21 Mar - 5 Apr 1918

British (46 inf + 3 cav divs engaged) 177,739 (72,000 PoWs); 1100+ guns, c200 tanks; 2000 MGs; c400 aircraft
French (16 inf + 4 cav divs engaged) c77,000 (c15,000 PoWs)
American (2 coys engaged) 77
German (90 divs engaged) 239,000; 76 aircraft

Lys Forces 9 Apr 1918

Portuguese Corps (Tamagnini d'Abreu) 19,000, 64 guns
British First Army (Horne) 5 divs, 504 guns (200 heavy)
British Second Army (Plumer) 6 divs, 245 guns (105 heavy)
German Army Gp Rupprecht 39 divs, 2208 guns (1009 heavy), 492 aircraft
  German Sixth Army (Quast) 18 divs, 1686 guns (794 heavy), 10+ tanks
  Fourth Army (Arnim) 8 divs, 522 guns (214 heavy)

Lys Losses 9 - 29 Apr 1918

Portuguese 6000 PoWs
French (8 divs engaged) 35,000; 12+ guns
British (25 divs engaged) 76,300; 108+ guns; 63 aircraft
German (42 divs engaged) 109,300; 38 aircraft
Germans took 29,100 Allied PoWs; 453 guns & 233 MGs

Third Aisne Forces 27 May 1918

German Army Gp Crown Prince 41 divs, 5263 guns (1631 heavy), 1233 mortars, 30 tanks, 500 aircraft,
  Seventh Army (Boehn) 30 divs
  First Army (F Below) 7 divs
French North Army Gp (Franchet d'Esperey)
  French Sixth Army (Duchêne) 16 divs (5 British), 1400 guns (600 heavy)
  French Fourth Army (Gouraud) 6 divs (2 cav)

Third Aisne Losses 27 May - 6 June 1918

French 98,160; 642+ guns; 3+ tanks ⎤
British (-19 June) 28,703; 158 guns ⎦ 130 aircraft, 23 balloons (-18 June); 2500+ MGs
American (-6 June) 474 but 9777 (Belleau Wood - 1 July)
German (-13 June) 130,370 (1687 PoWs to AEF); 56 aircraft (in June)

Noyon/Montdidier Forces 9 & 10 June 1918

German Eighteenth Army (Hutier) 23 divs, 2276 guns (784 heavy)
French Res Army Gp (Fayolle) 1200 aircraft (600 bombers)
French Third Army (Humbert) 15 divs, 1058 guns (474 heavy)
French Tenth Army (Mangin) 5 divs, 165 tanks, 4 British armoured cars

Noyon/Montdider Losses 9-14 June 1918

French 35,000 (15,000 PoWs); 70 tanks (144 engaged); 208 guns; 62 aircraft (incl RAF)
German 30,000 ; 19+ guns; 11 aircraft

Second Marne Forces 15 July 1918

German Army Gp Crown Prince 2,352,000 men in 50 divs (21 res, only 7 first class in Allied rating), 6353 guns (2091 heavy), 25 tanks, 2200 mortars; 900 aircraft
  Seventh Army (Boehn) 22 divs, 5 tanks
  First Army (Mudra) 16 divs
  Third Army (Einem) 12 divs, 20 tanks
French Centre Army Gp (Maistre) 46 inf + 3 cav divs, 2991 guns (1551 heavy); aircraft incl 70 US (1st Pursuit Gp)
  Sixth Army (Degoutte) 9 divs (incl 2 US)
  Fifth Army (Berthelot) 11 divs (2 Italian)
  Fourth Army (Gouraud) 16 divs (incl US 42nd Div)
  2 British divs res
  Polish *Chasseur* regt
  Ninth Army (Mitry) 8 divs.

Second Marne Forces 18 July 1918

French Reserve Army Gp (Fayolle) 24 divs (4 US), 493 tanks, 2133 guns, 1143 aircraft
  Tenth Army (Mangin) 16 divs (2 US), 3 cav divs, 346 tanks, 1545 guns, 581 aircraft
  Sixth Army (Degoutte) 8 divs (2 US), 147 tanks, 588 guns, 562 aircraft
Army Gp Crown Prince 26 divs (10 res), 918 guns (232 heavy), c800 aircraft
  Ninth Army (Eben) 7 divs
  Seventh Army (Boehn) 4 divs

Second Marne Losses 15 July - 5 Aug 1918

German (-2 Aug) 168,000 (29,367+ PoWs); 600 guns (145 to AEF); 3723 MGs; 300 mortars; 36 aircraft
French 95,165; 175 tanks ⎤
British 16,000; 15 aircraft (-17 July) ⎥ 150 aircraft; 6 balloons (-23 July)
Italian 9334; 29 guns ⎥
American (excl non-div units) 40,353 ⎦

W Front Losses Mar - July 1918

British 447,921 (114,895 missing & PoWs); 1366+ guns; c200 tanks; 601 aircraft
French 490,000; 862+ guns; 248+ tanks; 230 aircraft
American 51,207+
Portuguese (6000 PoWs)
Belgian 1800+
German 1,062,853+ (13,067 PoWs to BEF); 22 tanks; 217+ aircraft

Amiens Forces 8 Aug 1918

Allied Army Gp (Haig)
    British Fourth Army (Rawlinson) 14 inf + 3 cav divs, 2 US regts (33rd Div), 2070 guns (684 heavy), 430 tanks (96 Whippets), 12 armoured cars; 800 aircraft
    French First Army (Debeney) 7 divs, 1606 guns (826 heavy), 90 tanks, 1104 aircraft
German Second Army (Marwitz) 14 divs (4 in res), 749 guns (289 heavy); 365 aircraft

Amiens Losses 8 - 11 Aug 1918

British 22,000; 480 tanks; 148+ aircraft; 1800 cav horses (-15)
French 24,232 (6-15 Aug incl Third Army); 38+ aircraft
American 983
German c75,000 (29,873 PoWs); 500 guns; 49+ aircraft

St Mihiel Forces 12 Sept 1918

US First Army (Pershing) 550,000 men in 18 divs (4 French), 3010 guns (1329 French-crewed), 267 tanks (113 French-manned)
French II Colonial Corps (Blondlat) 110,000 men in 3 divs, 439 guns
German Army Det C (Fuchs) 75,000 men, 450+ guns in 7 divs

Hindenburg Line Forces 26 - 29 Sept 1918

BEF 60 divs, 345 tanks; 1058 aircraft
French 102 divs (2 Italian), 385 tanks
Belgian 12 divs, 170,000 men
US 39 divs, 1 million + men, 320 tanks
Portuguese 2 divs
TOTAL 217 (57 in res)
German 193 divs (84 in res)
Austrian 4 divs

Meuse-Argonne Forces 26 Sept 1918

US First Army (Pershing) 300,000 men, 2700 guns, 189 tanks, 842 aircraft in 16 inf divs
French Fourth Army (Gouraud) 250,000 men, 75,000 horses, 385 tanks in 27 inf divs
German Army Gp Gallwitz 24 inf divs, 302 aircraft
    Fifth Army (Marwitz) 10 divs (3 in res)
German Army Gp Crown Prince
    Third Army (Einem) 14 divs (4 in res).

Meuse-Argonne Losses 26 Sept - 11 Nov 1918

American (22 divs engaged) 117,000 men; 20+ aircraft (Sept)
German (47 divs engaged) 100,000 men (26,000 PoWs); 846 guns; 5+ aircraft (Sept)

Allied Captures 18 July - 11 Nov 1918

British 188,700 PoWs; 2840 guns; 29,000 MGs
French (incl Italian) 139,000 PoWs; 1880 guns
American 43,300 PoWs; 1421 guns
Belgian 14,500 PoWs; 474 guns

Allied Somme/Montdidier Gains 8 - 22 Aug 1918

	Strength	Opposition	Advance	PoWs	Guns taken
BEF Fourth Army	13 divs	27 divs	12 miles	27,000	400+
French First Army	12 divs	20 divs	10-15 miles	12,000	100+
French Third Army	7 divs	8 divs	6 miles	5000	100

1918 Western Front Losses

British 952,981 (189,010 PoWs & missing); 981 guns lost captured (21 Mar-7 July); 819+ tanks (2245 engaged); 1215 aircraft (Mar-Oct, exc IAF)
French 1,015,000 (excl officers); 440 Renault lt tanks; 390 aircraft (Mar-Oct)
Belgium 30,000
Portuguese 6000 PoWs
Italian 14,658; 29 guns
American c278,875 (c4283 PoWs); 357 aircraft; 35 balloons
German 1,498,138 (excl Oct/Nov 1918); 6615+ guns; c27 tanks; 1244+ aircraft (Mar-Sept)
Austrian 7548 (3915 missing & PoWs); 59,068 sick (31 July 1917-30 Sept 1918)

1918 French dead by arm

Infantry	182,120	
Cavalry	7690	
Artillery	27,725	— worst year of war
Engineers	7155	
Air arm	1965	

W Front Losses 1914-18

Belgian 58,401 k & w (incl Africa); 10,203 PoWs (incl Africa); c170+ guns
French c4,888,474 (1,300,000k, 507,800 PoWs); 7100+guns; 478+ tanks
British 2,706,154 (564,715k incl 32,098 dd or injury, 175,624 PoWs); 1237 guns (captured); c1235 tanks
Russian 5183+
Portuguese (1917-18) 14,411 (1935k or dd, 6895 PoWs)
American (1917-18) 278,983 (48,909k, 9294 PoWs)
Italian 20,870 (incl 6000 Italian Legion 1914-15); 29 guns
German c4,846,340 (1,493,000k, 774,000 PoWs of which 319,138 to BEF); 9850+ guns; 32,639+ MGs; 4567+ mortars; c27 tanks; 2000+ aircraft
Austrian (-30 Sept 1918) 8583 (3201k, 4077 PoWs & missing but BEF counted 10,429 PoWs); 88,578 sick.
Germans claimed 7067 Allied aircraft

Allied Western Front Strength 11 Nov 1918

	France	Britain	USA	Belgium	Italy	Portugal
Total strength	2,600,000	1,966,727	1,981,701	145,000	50,000	35,000
Combat strength	1,554,000	1,202,000	1,078,222	115,000	23,000	
Inf divs	102 (1)	58	31	12	2	2
Cav divs	6	3	-	1	-	-
Horses	630,000	388,000	151,000	38,000	7000	
Field guns	6000	4202	2400	416	80	
Heavy guns	5600	2204	406	333	20	
Trench mortars	1600	2500	750	293	94	
Light MGs	50,000	20,000	18,000	1000	168	
MGs	30,000	5000	6000	3000	276	
Tanks	2300	610	90	-	-	
Aircraft	3600	1576/1799 serviceable	740	134	12	
Motor vehicles	98,000	57,051				768
Length of front	214 miles	70 miles	83 miles	25 miles		

Note: (1) includes 1 Czechoslovak & 2 Polish divs

BEF Advance to Victory 8 Aug - 11 Nov 1918

	Cas	Advance	Battles	PoWs taken	Guns taken	MGs
First Army (Horne)	26,405	55 miles	7	23,000	405+	950+
Second Army (Plumer) (27 Sept-)	c17,534	53 miles	2	17,200	c300	
Third Army (Byng)	115,429	60 miles	7	67,000	800	
Fourth Army (Rawlinson)	122,427	72 miles	9	79,743	1108	5473
Fifth Army (Birdwood)	554	54 miles	skirmishes	c1000		
Tank Corps (Elles)	2416	(565 tanks lost to 24 Oct in c2000 actions; 2523 tanks repaired & reissued)				
MG Corps	13,665					

Central Powers W Front Strength 11 Nov 1918

	German	Austrian
Ration strength	3,403,000	124,000
Combat strength	2,911,700	100,000
Inf divs	183½	5
Cav divs (dismtd)	4	-
Field guns	9074	348
Heavy guns	5624	235
Motor vehicles	40,000	

1918 EASTERN FRONT TABLES

Finnish Civil War Forces 28 Jan - 15 May 1918

White Guards 80,000 (incl 84 Swedish officers) in 18 regts
Germans 12,000, 26 guns
Red Guards 140,000 incl former Russian XLII Corps + fortress coast & frontier troops (c30,000 in Jan 1918)

Finnish Civil War Losses 28 Jan - 15 May 1918

White Guards 3537 (467 PoWs); 1+ MG
German 950
Red Guards/Russians 90,000 (69,400+ PoWs, 8380+ murdered by Whites); 493+ guns; 633 MGs, 2 armoured trains; 3 ships

1918 SOUTHERN FRONTS TABLES

Piave Forces June 1918

Austrian SW Front (Archduke Eugene)
55 divs (642 bns incl 5 divs in res), 6833 guns (362AA), c8700 MGs, 280 aircraft
  Army Group Conrad 4 divs in res + 1 cav
  Tenth Army (Krobatin) 7 divs, 1360 guns
  Eleventh Army (Scheuchenstuel) 21 inf + 3 cav divs, 2935 guns
  Army Group Boroevic 2 divs in res
  Sixth Army (Archduke Joseph) 3 inf + 2 cav divs, 768 guns
  Isonzo Army (Wurm) 12 inf + 2 cav divs, 1770 guns
Italian Army (Diaz) 2,193,659 incl 74,659 British, 44,000 French & 19,100 cav in 61 divs (12 in res), 7542 guns (524AA), 2049 mortars (180 British), 676 aircraft (86 British); 37 balloons; 4 airships
  Seventh Army (Tassoni) 6 divs ⎤
  First Army (Pecori-Giraldi) 9 divs ⎦ — 2339 guns
  Sixth Army (Montuori) 10 divs (3 British & 2 French with 437 guns), 1214 guns
  Fourth Army (Giardino) 8 divs, 881 guns
  Eighth Army (Caviglia) 4 divs, 744 guns
  Third Army (Duke of Aosta) 7 divs, 1273 guns
  Ninth Army 10 res divs (1 Czech with 15,000 men), 567 guns

Piave Losses 13-24 June 1918

Austrian l35,000-150,000 (24,475 PoWs); 70 guns; 75 mortars; 1234 MGs; 151 flamethrowers; 37,000 rifles; 107 aircraft; 9 balloons
Italian 84,830 (30,000 PoWs)
British (June) 1959 (319 PoWs & missing)
French (15-20 June) 564

Macedonia Forces 1 July 1918

Allied

French 225,373; 65,501 horses & mules; 12,200 wagons; 3982 cars
British 136,531
Greek 129,465
Serb 117,344
Italian 44,697
Total 653,710

Central Powers

Bulgar 400,000

Macedonia Forces 14 Sept 1918

Allied Armies of the Orient (Franchet d'Esperey)
c550,000, 1522 guns, 2682 MGs, c200 aircraft in 28 divs (8 French, 6 Serb, 4 British, Italian & 9 Greek) with 291 bns
  British Salonika Army (Milne) 152,301 British (1 Sept), 337 guns & 136 mortars in 9 divs (5 Greek), 43 RAF aircraft
  French Army of the Orient (Henrys) 202,061, 596 guns in 7 divs (1 Italian & 1 Greek)
  1st Group of Divisions (d'Anselme) 3 divs (2 Greek)
  2nd Group of Divisions (Patey) 4 divs
  3rd Group of Divisions (de Lobit) 1⅓ divs + 5 bns (2 Serbs & 2 Albanian with c2039 (1 Sept) Albanians)
  Serb Army (Crown Prince Regent Alexander, CoS Mišić) 117,344 Serbs, 278 guns in 8 divs and 1 cav div
  Serb First Army (Bojovic) 3 divs
  Serb Second Army (Stepanovic) 5 divs (2 French)
  Greek Army (Danglis) 183,229 (incl 18,692 in Epirus), 252 guns split up as above
  Allied reserves 2 divs
Bulgar Army (Crown Prince Boris, Deputy C-in-C Todorov) 450,000, 1597 guns (c200 German), 3062 MGs (16 German coys with 8 guns each), 1652 mortars, 180 aircraft in 15 divs with 302 bns & 61½ sqns
  Macedonian Army Gp (Scholtz) 158 bns, 18 sqns, 560 guns, 1575 MGs, 781 mortars in 7 divs (3 with total of 4 German bns)
  Bulgar First Army (Nerezov) 67 bns, 4½ sqns, 454 guns, 694 MGs, 599 mortars in 3 divs
  Bulgar Second Army (Lukov) 44 bns, 17 sqns, 271 guns, 461 MGs, 124 mortars in 3 divs
  Bulgar Fourth Army (Toshev) 33 bns, 22 sqns, 312 guns, 332 MGs, 148 mortars in 1 div + 2 cav divs + 3 Landwehr regts

Battle of Lake Doiran Losses 18 - 19 Sept 1918

Greek 3528
British 3511; 1 aircraft
French c155
Bulgar 2726; 2 aircraft

Macedonia Offensive Losses 14 - 30 Sept 1918

Bulgar 77,000 PoWs; 400 guns; 10,000 horses, 20,000 oxen & sheep
Germans & Austrians c1000 PoWs by Serbs alone up to 15 Oct
British 3703
French 3268 (Sept)
Greek 5168
Serb 4019 (1 Sept to end of hostilities)
Italian

PoWs taken by Allies 15 Sept - 15 Oct 1918

French 71,111
British 776
Greek 1595
Italian 8239
Serb c8016

Balkans Losses Oct - Nov 1918

Austrian & German c3216 PoWs by Serbs alone

1918 Balkans Losses

French 6997
Serb 6120 (excl Aug, incl 71 deaths in hospital 1 Mar-15 Apr)
Italian (Macedonia) 722 (Jan-Aug)
Italian (Albania) 850+; 13,000 sick (Aug)
British 8718 (2164 deaths from disease)
Austrian (1 June-4 Nov) est 55,000 (5000 PoWs); 36 guns; 6 aircraft
Bulgar 79,807+ (78,907 PoWs); 400 guns; 60+ mortars; 50+ MGs; 43+ aircraft (incl German)

Vittorio Veneto Forces 24 Oct 1918

Italian Army (Diaz) 2,075,000 Italians (24 June), 78,661 British (1 Oct), 44,000
    French (24 June), 5000 Americans in 57 inf + 4 cav divs with 725 bns (47
    Anglo-French) & 149 sqns, 7720 guns (3136 heavy), 1745 mortars' 600 aircraft
    (93 Anglo-French)
    Seventh Army (Tassoni) 4 divs
    First Army (Pecori-Giraldi) 5 divs
    Sixth Army (Montuori) 6 divs (1 British & 1 French)
    Fourth Army (Giardino) 9 divs
    Twelfth Army (Graziani, Fr) 4 divs (1 French) ⎱ 1402 guns
    Eighth Army (Caviglia) 14 divs
    Ninth Army (Morrone) 7 divs (1 Czech + US regt)
    Tenth Army (Cavan, Br) 4 divs (2 British)
    Third Army (Aosta) 4 divs
    Cav Corps (Count of Turin) 4 divs
Austrian SW Front (Arz) c1,809,700 men in 54½ inf + 6 dismtd cav divs with 757
    bns, 26 sqns, 6145 guns (1800 heavy), 564 aircraft
    Army Group Krobatin 21 divs
    Tenth Army (Krobatin) 10 divs (1 dismtd cav)
    Eleventh Army (Scheuchenstuel) 11 divs (2 dismtd cav)
    Army Group Boroevic 37 divs
    Belluno Group (Goglia) 12 divs, 1385 guns, 3130 MGs
    Sixth Army (Schönburg) 7½ divs
    Isonzo Army (Wurm) 14½ divs
Reserve 3 dismtd cav divs (3900)

Vittorio Veneto Losses 24 Oct - 4 Nov 1918

Austrian 30,000 k & w; 427,000 PoWs (34,046 to British), 5000 guns (240 to British)
Italian 37,819
British 2135
French (21 Oct-5 Nov) 778 (81 missing)

1918 Italian Front Losses

Austrian 508,573+ (453,048 PoWs), 5104 guns, 1616+ MGs; 367 aircraft to RFC/
    RAF
Italian 122,819+ (30,000+ PoWs)
French 1342+
British 6709 (754 missing & PoWs); 32 Camel fighters
Czech 291
American 7

1918 TURKISH FRONTS TABLES

Baku Forces 4 Aug - 15 Sept 1918

Turk Army of Islam (Nuri Pasha) 13,000-15,000 (7000-8000 regular inf in 5th & 36th
    Divs), 32 guns
British 1300, 3 armoured cars, 6 guns, 2 aircraft
Russo-Armenian c6500, 3 armoured cars, 24 guns; 2 seaplanes

Baku Losses 4 Aug - 15 Sept 1918

Turk 2000+, 16 MGs
British 156, 3 armoured cars, 2 aircraft
Russo-Armenian 8988 & incl all heavy weapons

Megiddo Forces 19 Sept 1918

British EEF (Allenby) 11,000 cav (25,618 horses), 56,000 inf, 552 guns, 105 aircraft
Arab Northern Army (Feisal) 3000, 2 armoured cars, 4 mtn guns
Turk Yilderim Army Group (Liman) 3000 cav, 32,000 inf, 402 guns, 850+ MGs; 106
    aircraft
Eighth Army (Djevad Pasha) 10,000 inf, 157 guns (30 German) in 5 divs + 3 German
    bns
Seventh Army (Kemal) 7000 inf, 111 guns in 4 divs
Fourth Army (Djemal the Lesser) 2000 cav, 6000 inf, 74 guns in 3+ inf 1 cav div + 3
    German bns
Gen Reserve 3000 inf, 30 guns
Hejaz Railway to Maan 6000 inf, 30 guns

Megiddo Losses 19 Sept - 26 Oct 1918)

British 5566; 82 camels; 3+ aircraft (16 Sept on)
Arab unknown
Turk 75,000+ PoWs (3700 Austro-German); 360+ guns; 784-800 MGs; 210 lorries;
    89 rail engines & 468 rail carriages; 45+ aircraft

1918 Palestine Losses

British 25,705 (472 PoWs); 9 guns; 33 aircraft; 274+ camels; 23 donkeys
Arab 432+
Turk 90,179+ (79,880 PoWs); 366 guns; 815-831 MGs; 106 aircraft

1918 Mesopotamia Losses

British 11,536 (15 PoWs); 13 aircraft
Turk 23,317+ (20,777 PoWs), 76 guns, 223 MGs; 6 aircraft; 7 vessels

1918 AFRICAN OPERATIONS

1918 E Africa Losses

British 3811 (2271 died of disease, c361 PoWs & missing), 2 MGs
Portuguese 529+; 2 guns; 10 MGs
German 3230+ (2910 PoWs); 1 gun; 37 MGs

1918 SEA WAR TABLES

1918 Royal Navy Losses

79 warships including 1 battleship; 6 cruisers (used as block ships); 1 coast defence
    ship; 3 monitors; 4 sloops; 19 destroyers; 1 aircraft carrier; 5 AMCs; 10 CMBs.
    Total 113,682t
186 auxiliaries incl 65 colliers & oilers and 80 trawlers & drifters. Total 232,590t
Total naval cas 6867 or 1.75% of av 391,700 strength

1918 Allied & Neutral Shipping Losses

1077 ships (544 British) worth 2,649,748t (1,694,749t British with 4122 lives) of which
    3 to surface ships; 1035 (530 British) to U-boats; 27 (10 British) to mines
U-boat official figure 1305 ships worth 2,754,152t (820,950t in Med)
Most successful 1918 U-boat U151 (U-cruiser, Atlantic) 39 ships worth 109,236t

1918 U-boat Losses & Gains

69 U-boats lost, but 88 commissioned making total strength 171
Another 18 boats completed after Armistice

1918 British A/S Air Effort

Hours flown: 4,801,152
U-boats sighted: 192
U-boats attacked: 131
U-boats sunk: 1

Convoy Statistics 1916 - 18

	Ships sailed	Sunk	Loss rate
Ocean	16,070	96	0.6%
Home Waters	67,888	161	1.24%
Med	11,509	136	0.84%
Total	95,000	393	0.41%

Only 84 successful U-boat attacks on convoys June 1917-Nov 1918 (1 ship only sunk
in 69 of them)

Sea Mine Warfare 1914 - 18

British minesweepers cleared 23,873 mines (11,487 moored, 12,386 drifting)
214 British minesweepers lost
595 British ships sunk (673,417t) or damaged (incl 44 warships sunk)
British & US minelayers laid 156,417 mines in home waters
48 U-boats sunk by mines
German mines claimed 8 battleships; 5 cruisers; 44 destroyers; 207 auxiliaries

Declared Sea Mines Laid 1914 - 18

Austria	5650
Britain	128,652
Bulgaria	748
France	223
Germany	43,636
Italy	12,293 (only 599 declared)
Russia	19
Turkey	423
USA	56,033

Most Successful Minelaying U-boats 1915 - 18

UC17 94 ships worth 143,870t
UC21 95 ships worth 129,502t
UC65 103 ships worth 112,859t

Most Successful German U-boat Commanders 1914-18

	Merchant Ships	Tons	Warships	Tons	Cruises
Kapitanleutnant Lothar von Arnauld de la Périère (*U35* , *U139*)	194	453,716	2	2500	10
Kapitanleutnant Dr Walther Forstmann (*U12* , *U39*)	146	384,304	1	820	16
Kapitanleutnant Max Valentiner (*U38* , *U3* , *U157*)	141	299,326	1	627	17
Kapitanleutnant Otto Steinbrinck (*U6* , *UB10* , *UB18* , *UC65* , *UB57*)	202	231,614	2	11,810	24
Kapitanleutnant Hans Rose (*U53*)	79	213,987	1	1265	12

Most Successful Ocean U-boats 1914-18

U35	224 ships worth 539,741t
U39	154 ships worth 404,478t
U38	137 ships worth 299,985t
U34	121 ships worth 262,886t
U33	84 ships worth 229,598t
U53	90 ships worth 215,769t

Most Successful Coastal U-boats 1915-18

UB57	63 ships worth 100,100t
UB40	103 ships worth 133,358t
UB18	126 ships worth 128,555t
UB48	36 ships worth 109,273t

1918 AIR WAR TABLES

1918 Air Raids

Paris 31 : 787 cas
Britain 10 : (1 Zeppelin lost, 5 Gothas); 188 Zeppelin bombs; 687 cas; 528 defence sorties (8+ aircraft damaged, 5+ aircrew deaths)
London 5 : 121 bombs; 513 cas; 220 buildings hit; 10 fires caused
Germany 353 : 7117 bombs
Constantinople 10
Venice 5

German Night Bombing in BEF Zone, France May-Oct 1918

Bombing nights	127
Av bombers per night	29
Bombs dropped	16,075
Casualties	4156
Bombers lost to night fighters	20
Bombers lost to AA fire	82
Bombers damaged by AA fire	62
Bombers lost to small arms	15

Allied Air Strength June 1918

	British	French	Italian	US	Belgian	Total
W Front	1736	3149	-	180	127	5192
Italian Front	104	-	477	-	-	581
Macedonia	41	363	24	-	-	428
Middle East	269	-	28	-	-	297
Mediterranean	144	-	-	-	-	144
Home defence	336	345	-	-	-	681
Total	2630	3857	529	180	127	7323

1918 HOME FRONT TABLES

Rationing pw per head (ordinary adult)

	Bread	Meat	Fats	Sugar	Potatoes
Germany(Hamburg)	4³/₈lb	9oz	2¹/₂oz	¹/₃lb	7¹/₈lb
Austria (Vienna)	2¹/₂lb	4¹/₂oz	1¹/₂oz	None	1¹/₈lb
Britain (by 14 July)	6¹/₂lb (1)	1lb	6oz butter	8oz	
Holland (Neutral)	3lb 1oz	7oz	6oz	8oz	
USA	70% of 1917 flour used	-	-	4-8oz (1 Jul-Nov)	-

Note (1) Britain: Bread not rationed, av consumption figure computed with 6lb 2oz pw prewar.

1914-1918 GENERAL TABLES

1914-18 MILITARY STATISTICS

<table>
<tr><td colspan="2">Allied Guns in Line at Armistice</td></tr>
<tr><td>British</td><td>6690</td></tr>
<tr><td>French</td><td>11,608</td></tr>
<tr><td>Italian</td><td>7709</td></tr>
<tr><td>American</td><td>3308</td></tr>
</table>

<table>
<tr><td colspan="2">Generals Killed 1914-18</td></tr>
<tr><td>Britain</td><td>70</td></tr>
<tr><td>France</td><td>98 (43k in accidents or died of illness)</td></tr>
<tr><td>Germany</td><td>150 (to mid-Sept 1918)</td></tr>
<tr><td>Italy</td><td>7+</td></tr>
</table>

Note: Readers are invited to provide totals for Italy and the omitted countries.

Allied Military Effort and Losses 1914 - 18

	Mobilized	Total Cas	Deaths All Causes	Wounded	Prisoners/Missing
Belgium	380,000	200,130	45,500	78,624	73,976
British Empire	8,904,467	3,428,535	947,023	2,289,860	191,652
Australia	416,809	215,514	59,330	152,100	4084
Britain	5,704,416	2,555,799	722,785	1,662,625	170,389
Canada	628,964	236,233	59,544	172,950	3729/6
Colonies	134,837	51,781	45,967	4826	988
India	1,679,998	140,015	62,056	66,889	11,070
Newfoundland	11,922	3661	1082	2314	152/18
New Zealand	128,525	58,492	16,645	41,317	530
South Africa	136,070	18,913	7121 or 9050	11,444	1538
French Empire	8,660,000	6,220,800	1,397,800	4,266,000	557,000
France	8,091,000		1,322,100		531,300
French N Africa & Colonial	569,000 (1)		75,700		
Greece	230,000	38,310	23,098	14,145	1067
Italy	5,903,140	2,197,000	680,000	947,000	600,000
Japan	800,000	13,245	1344	11,901	n/a
Montenegro	50,000	20,000	3000	10,000	7000
Portugal	200,000+	35,247	8145	14,784	12,318
Rumania	1,234,000	535,706	335,706	120,000	80,000
Russia	12,000,000	9,300,000	1,600,000-1,850,000	4,950,000	2,500,000
Serbia	707,343	413,641	127,535	133,148	70,423/82,535
USA	4,743,826	325,236	116,708	204,002	4480/46

Note: (1) On 11 Nov 1918 the French Army included 176,000 Algerians; 50,000 Tunisians; 34,000 Moroccans; 136,000 Senegalese; 34,000 Madagascans; 42,000 Indochinese, and 3000 Somalis. A total of 475,000 troops from her overseas territories. Colonial troops also included white settlers and officers.

Central Powers Military Effort and Losses 1914 - 18

	Mobilized	Total Cas	Deaths all causes	Wounded	Prisoners/Missing
Austria	8,000,000	4,650,200	1,496,200(1)	1,943,000	1,211,000
Bulgaria	1,200,000	346,869	101,224	155,026	90,619+
Germany	13,250,000	7,209,413	1,808,555(2)	4,248,158	1,152,800
Turkey	2,998,321	1,965,000-2,415,000	550,000-600,000	1,565,000	c250,000

(1) Austria: includes 480,000 PoW deaths in captivity
(2) Germany: includes 55,006 PoW deaths in captivity; some sources give deaths at 1,950,000 or 2 million and over.

Poison Gas Casualties & Production 1915 - 18

	Total cas	Deaths	Production (t)	Used (t)
British Empire	188,706	8109	25,735	14,000
France	190,000	8000	36,955	26,000
Italy	60,000	4627	6300	6300
Russia	419,340	56,000	4700	4700
USA	72,807	1462	6215	1000
Austria	100,000	3000	7900	7900
Germany	200,000	9000	68,100	52,000
Others	10,000	1000	-	-

<table>
<tr><td colspan="2">French Army Courts-Martial/Desertions</td></tr>
<tr><td>1914</td><td>3000/409</td></tr>
<tr><td>1915</td><td>14,000/2433</td></tr>
<tr><td>1916</td><td>25,000/8924</td></tr>
<tr><td>1917</td><td>21,871</td></tr>
<tr><td>1918</td><td>n/a</td></tr>
</table>

<table>
<tr><td colspan="2">Animal Losses on Military Service 1914 - 18</td></tr>
<tr><td colspan="2">Britain 484,143 horses, mules, bullocks and camels</td></tr>
<tr><td colspan="2">France 541,714 horses to 1 Oct 1917</td></tr>
</table>

1914 - 18 EASTERN FRONT TABLE

Eastern Front Losses 1914 - 18

German   c900,000+ (159,390+ PoWs); 28+ guns; c200 MGs; 189 aircraft
Austrian   2,770,428+ (1,736,764+ PoWs); c2324 guns; 1678+ MGs
Turk   (1916-17) 24,521 (incl 1089 deaths from disease)
Bulgar   (1916-17 v Rumania) 670 PoWs taken by Russians (-1 Sept 1917)
Russian   c7,412,000 (2,216,200 PoWs); 6827+ guns; 6411+ MGs; 500 aircraft
       captured (1918 only); 358 aircraft shot down (incl Rumanian)
Rumania   533,000 (363,000 PoWs); 359 guns; 346 MGs

1914-18 SOUTHERN FRONTS TABLES

Italian Front Losses 1915 - 18

Austrian 1,420,451 (653,444 PoWs & missing); 1,482,220 sick; 5239+ guns; 367+ aircraft
German (1917-18) 12,006+
Italian c2,150,000 (530,000+ PoWs); 3512+ guns
French (1917-18) 2872 from, 120,000 troops deployed
British (from June 1917) 7080 (757 missing & PoWs), 50,552 sick, 11,514 flu cases (481 died from 145,764 troops deployed); 32 Camel fighters.
Czech (1918) 291 from 15,000 troops deployed
American (1918) 7 from 5000 troops deployed

Macedonian Campaign Losses 1915 - 18

Serb 42,165 (Aug 1916 to end incl 3106 deaths in hospital but exc Aug 1918)
French 38,489
British 23,762 battle cas (1194 PoWs); 481,262 sick (3744 died) from 404,207 troops deployed; 8 guns; 3 mortars; 24 MGs
Italian 8401 k & w; 80,000 sick (Sept 1916 on) from 143,000 troops deployed
Greek 26,000 (Dec 1916 on)
Russian 3180 (Sept 1916-Nov 1917)
Bulgar 239,742 (c13,619 PoWs before Sept 1918 collapse)
Austrian 174 PoWs
Turk 743 (180 PoWs), 4804 sick (671 died) (Sept 1916-June 1918)
German 84,303 (incl Serbia 1915 & Dobruja 1916-17 & 2334+ PoWs before Sept 1918 collapse)

1914-18 TURKISH FRONTS TABLES

Armenia & Persia Losses 1914 - 18

Turk c250,000+ (64,509 PoWs inc E Front), 482 guns
Russian c200,000 (incl 3000 in Persia and 100,000 evacuated sick winter 1916-17); 10+ guns; 2 MGs

Egypt & Palestine Losses 1914 - 18

British 54,261 (10,145k, 6012 died of disease, 34,106w, 3998 PoWs), total incl 5302 Anzacs and 11,026 Indians; 9 guns; 5 tanks; 12+ MGs; 33+ aircraft; c12,600 horsesetc & c9300 camels (July 1917-Oct 1918)
British sick admissions (8 Jan 1916 - 14 Feb 1920) 556,048 (717,853 British combatants & 474,658 non-combatants employed to 1 Oct 1918 with 17,736 animals sent from India); 63,000 horses & 31,000 camels (July 1917-Oct 1918)
Turk 134,157+ (103,491 PoWs), 482 guns, 1015+ MGs, 15+ mortars; 106+ aircraft

Mesopotamia Losses 1914 - 18

British 92,501 (14,814k, 12,807 died of disease, 51,386w, 13,194 PoWs); 52 guns; 48+ MGs; 25+ aircraft
British sick admissions (12 Aug 1916 - 17 Jan 1920) 261,169 (400,905 British combatants & 488,596 non-combatants employed of which 675,391 Indian with 102,840 animals sent from India)
Turk 90,179+ (45,500 PoWs); 250 guns; 275+ MGs; 17 aircraft

Persia & Gulf Losses 1914 - 18

British (incl S Persia Rifles and died of disease) 4030
(51,248 British and Indian combatants and non-combatants sent with 6995 animals to end 1919)
Tribesmen 2568+ (97+ PoWs)

Aden Losses 1914 - 18

British 1279 (1179 Indian incl 6 PoWs; 34,424 British and Indian combatants and non-combatants sent with 3500 animals to end 1919)

India Frontier Losses 1914 - 18

British 6677 (incl 103 British regulars, 743 missing and PoWs)

1914-18 AFRICAN OPERATIONS TABLE

E Africa Losses 1914 - 18

British 18,626 (3445k or died of wounds, 6100 died of disease, 7777w, 1304 PoWs); 5 guns; 36 MGs
British sick admissions (20 Aug 1916 - 8 Feb 1919) 267,645 (12,000 S Africans invalided)
African & Indian follower cas (-28 Feb 1919) 47,071 (44,956k or died of disease)
112,052 British combatants & 260,898 non-combatants incl 52,339 troops, 43,477 S Africans, with 1501 animals sent from India & 1500 mules from S America)
Belgian 1276+ ; 2 guns; 4 MGs (c15,000 troops used)
Portuguese 4723 (30,701 troops employed); 4 guns; 16 MGs
German 15,200 (10,638+ PoWs); 43 guns; 104 MGs (30 Allied retaken); 3 gunboats

1914-18 SEA WAR TABLES

Allied Warship Losses 1914 - 18						
	Britain	France	Italy	Japan	Russia	USA
Tonnage	651,907	172,261	92,104	48,453	126,528	41,365
Personnel	41,058	11,400	3065	1039+k	5000k	8106
Dreadnoughts	2	-	1	-	2	-
Battlecruisers	3	-	-	-	-	-
Predreadnoughts	10	4	2	1	1	-
Cruisers	13	5	2	1	2	-
Light cruisers	12	-	1	3	-	-
Monitors	4	-	2	-	-	-
Coast defence ship	1				-	-
Aircraft carriers	3	-	-	-	-	-
Destroyers	66	11	8	2	22	2
Torpedo boats	11	8	5	1	1	-
Gunboats	5	2	-	-	2	1
Sloops	18	1	-	-	-	-
Patrol boats	2	-	-	-	-	-
Minelayers	2	2	1	-	3	-
Minesweepers	18	-	2	-	25	-
Armed merchant cruisers	17	13	14	-	1	-
Armed boarding steamers	13	-	-	-	-	-
Coastal motor boats	13	-	17 MAS boats	-	-	-
River gunboats	2	-	-	-	-	-
Submarines	54	12	8	-	20	2

Note: Portugal lost 1 auxiliary gunboat and 1 river gunboat with 142 men. Greece lost 1 destroyer (in French hands). Rumania lost 1 torpedo boat and 1 river torpedo boat.

Central Powers Warship Losses 1914 - 18

	Austria	Germany	Turkey
Tonnage	58,416	362,371	30,640
Personnel	-	24,955	n/a
Dreadnoughts	2	-	-
Battlecruisers	-	1	-
Predreadnought	-	1	1
Coast defence ship	1	-	1 obsolete
Cruisers	-	6	-
Light cruisers	2	20	-
Destroyers	4	53	3
Torpedo boats	2	63	5
Gunboats	-	5	6
River gunboats	-	3	1
River monitors	3	-	-
Minelayers	-	1	3
Minesweepers	-	28	3
Motor torpedo boats	-	2	-
Armed merchant raiders	-	11	-
U-boats	7	192	-

Note: Bulgaria lost 2 torpedo boats totalling 195t.

Allied & Neutral Merchant Shipping Losses 1914 - 18

Belgium	105,000t	
Brazil	31,000t	
Britain	7,759,090t	(2479 ships)
Denmark	245,000t	
France	891,000t	(500 ships to U-boats)
Greece	415,000t	
Holland	c230,000t	
Italy	872,341t	(633 ships)
Japan	128,000t	
Norway	1,177,001t	
Portugal	28,637t	
Rumania	n/a	
Russia	183,000t	
Spain	260,000t	
Sweden	264,000t	
USA	531,000t	

Note: Reputable sources publish a wide range of different figures. They can be due to differing tonnage measures, ownership rules and chronological periods. In general the Chronicle opts for the higher figures.

Central Powers Shipping Losses 1914 - 18

Austria	15,116t
Bulgaria	
Germany	4,900,000t (643 ships)
Turkey	61,470t

Merchant Ships Registered 1913 - 19 (Nos, thousands of tons)

	Austria	Belgium	Britain	France	Germany	Greece	Italy	Russia	Turkey	USA
1913 sail nos	16,781	12	8336	15,824	2765	788	4696	5998	-	1508
tonnage	51	13	847	602	488	137	356	625	47	-
steam nos	528	112	12,602	1895	2170(a)	389	931	1998	-	5333
tonnage	570	222	11,273	980	2832(b)	434	877	608	110	-
1914 sail nos	-	-	8203	15,682	-	-	4773	-	-	1433
tonnage	-	-	794	586	-	-	349	-	-	-
steam nos	-	-	12,862	1935	2090	450	949	-	-	5428
tonnage	-	-	11,622	1043	-	493	933	-	-	4287
1915 sail nos	-	-	8019	15,161	-	784	4737	-	-	1384
tonnage	-	-	779	561	-	107	322	-	-	-
steam nos	-	-	12,771	1939	-	474	644(d)	-	-	5944
tonnage	-	-	11,650(c)	1066	-	550	934	-	-	-
1916 sail nos	-	-	7669	14,470	-	-	4464	-	-	1311
tonnage	-	-	715	520	-	-	262	-	-	-
steam nos	-	-	12,405	1942	-	-	659	-	-	6070
tonnage	-	-	11,037	1027	-	-	1036	-	-	-
1917 sail nos	-	-	7186	13,777	-	-	4084	-	-	1278
tonnage	-	-	625	417	-	-	218	-	-	-
steam nos	-	-	11,534	1880	-	-	559	-	-	6433
tonnage	-	-	9608	886	-	-	896	-	-	-
1918 sail nos	-	-	6856	13,378	-	700	-	-	-	1210
tonnage	-	-	604	409	-	120	-	-	-	-
steam nos	-	-	11,334	1842	-	205	448	-	-	7471
tonnage	-	-	9497	850	-	291	679	-	-	-
1919 sail nos	-	-	6555	13,137	-	1056	-	-	-	1200
tonnage	-	-	593	427	-	133	-	-	-	-
steam nos	-	-	11,791	1969	-	282	408	-	-	10,416
tonnage	-	-	10,335	879	-	430	632	-	-	-

(a) Germany: Not surpassed till 1959
(b) Germany: Not surpassed till 1957
(c) Britain: Not surpassed till 1928
(d) Italy: Steamships under 250 tons not included 1915-18

1914-18 AIR WAR TABLES

Personnel Losses 1914 - 18

Britain	16,623
France	5333 k & missing
Germany	15,906 (389 in Zeppelins)

Aircraft Combat Losses 1914 - 18

Britain	c4000 (+15,000 in training)
France	c3000
Russia	358 (German claim on E Front)
Italy	267 (Navy only)
USA	357
Germany	3128 (incl 460 to Turkey)
Austria	423+(+231 Navy aircraft in accidents or worn out)

Aircraft Production 1914 - 18

	Austria	Britain	France (a)	Germany	Italy
1914	-	-	429	-	-
1915	400	2542 (incl 1914)	4500	4400	382
1916	1000	6642	7500	8100	1255
1917	1740	14,832	14,900	19,400	3871
1918	2378	30,782	23,000 (?)	6528+(b)	6523

(a) France: 2676 to AEF
(b) Germany: Jan-Jun 1918
(c) Russia: 5600, 1914-17

Airship Production 1914 - 18

Britain	213 (23 to Allies)
Germany	62

Airship Losses 1914 - 18

Britain	99 deleted
France	4
Germany	67 (17 on raids over Britain, 17 by Allies elsewhere)
Italy	7

Air Raid Casualties & Damage 1914 - 18

Britain	4830 cas; £2,962,111 from 8575 bombs (270t)
(London)	2630 cas; £2,043,199 from 1824 bombs
France	(Paris only) 914 cas (+880 to Paris Gun)
Germany	2589 cas; RM24m = £1.2m, from 14,208 bombs

British Air Raid Losses & Damage by Cause 1914 - 18

	Zeppelins	Gothas/Giants	Other Aircraft
Numbers bombing	202 of 277	330 of 446	61
Raids	54	27	37
Bomb tonnage	196.4t	73.55t (1)	
Bombs dropped	5751	2471	301
Killed	557	835	22
Wounded	1358	1973	85
Property damage	£1,527,585	£1,418,274	£16,252
Raiders lost	17	28	6+ damaged
Defence sorties	788	1637	315

(1) German figure 113t

Total Fighter Aces by Country (5 victories or more)

Austria	25-30 (1 with 40 victories)
Belgium	At least 45
British Empire	784 (14 with 40 or more victories)
France	158 (4 with 40 or more victories)
Germany	363 (12 with 40 or more victories)
Italy	43
Russia	18 or 19
USA+	6+

Top-scoring Fighter Aces

Name	Nationality	Victories	Period	Months
Manfred Baron von Richthofen	German	80	Sept 1916-Apr 1918	19
René Paul Fonck	French	75	Aug 1916-Nov 1918	27
Edward Mannock	British	73	June 1917-July 1918	14
Godwin Brumowski	Austrian	c40	-	Nov 1918
Willy Coppens de Houthulst	Belgian	37*	July 1917-Nov 1918	16
Francesco Baracca	Italian	34	Apr 1916-June 1918	27
Edward Vernon Rickenbacker	American	26	April-Nov 1918	6
Alexander Alexandrovich Kazakov	Russian	c17	Mar 1915-? Dec 1917	30

*Includes 26 balloons (ringed with AA guns)

1914-18 INTERNATIONAL EVENTS TABLES

British Supplies to Allies 1914 - 18

	Belgium	France	Italy	Rumania	Russia	USA
Aircraft	34	11	-	19	308	452
Tanks	-	101	-	-	-	18
Motorcycles & bicycles	25,000	27,600	2500	1098	10,000	2219
Lorries & ambulances	878	1171	-	177	4533	4553
Motor cars	-	37	-	-	1323	811
Explosives (t)	17,000	416,000	140,000	-	217,000	-
Iron & Steel (t)	4,332,000	950,00	-	-	64,000	-
Non-ferrous metals (t)	4,536,000	-	-	-	-	-
Grenades	151,000	4,811,000	-	-	8,400,000	300,000
Mortar shells	998,000	-	-	-	-	-
Mortars	1430	213	-	-	264	1800
MGs (a)	296	12,849	8358	520	1602	268
Bullets	50m	140m	100m	18m	2500m	11m
Rifles	189,000	-	50,000	-	1m	15,000
Shells (b)	75,520	119,324	821,035	54,000	2,985,528	427,71
Guns (c)	53	17	174	8	756	164

(a) Japan 21
(b) Serbia 2000; Portugal 41,863; Greece 83,908
(c) Greece 40; Portugal 17

British Loans to Europe 1914 - 25 (£m)

	War	Relief & Reconstruction
Austria	-	11
Belgium	110	9
France	626	-
Greece	21	-
Italy	590	-
Poland	-	5
Portugal	23	-
Rumania	26	-
Russia	757	
Serbia	30	

Britain's Balance of Payments 1913 - 19 (£m)

	Visible balance	Invisible balance	Overall Current Balance
1913	-82	+317	+235
1914	-120	+254	+134
1915	-340	+285	-55
1916	-350	+440	+90
1917	-420	+470(a)	+50
1918	-630(b)	+355	-275(c)
1919	-470	+425	-45

(a) Record till 1920   (b) Record till 1941   (c) Record till 1940

US Loans to Europe 1914-25 ($m)

	War	Relief & Reconstruction
Armenia	-	12
Austria	-	24
Belgium	349	-
Britain	4277	-
Czechoslovakia	62	-
Cuba	8	-
Estonia	-	14
Finland (a)	-	8
France (b)	2997	-
Greece	15	-
Hungary	-	1
Italy (c)	1640	-
Latvia	-	5
Liberia	4	-
Lithuania	-	5
Poland	-	160
Rumania	25	-
Russia	187	-
Serbia	24	-
Yugoslavia	-	25

(a) Finland: only country to repay in full by 1969
(b) France: 60% cancelled 1926
(c) Italy: 80% cancelled 1925

German Aid to Bulgaria & Austria 1914-18

	Bulgaria	Austria
Aircraft		447
Rifles	230,000	112,747 (12,000 Russian)
MGs	1950	632 Bergmann
Pistols	22,000	10,000 + 2000 flare pistols
SAA	235m	136m
Helmets		100,000
Guns	403	4135 guns (22 Russian & 13 Belgian)
Shells	8,225,000	1,827,700
Gas masks	400,000	966,475
Gas shells	80,000	
Motor vehicles	450	548
Locomotives	140	
Wagons	1200	
Longe-range radio stns	6	
Army & field telephones	5000	
Telegraphs	450	
Uniforms & trousers (each)	560,000	94,500 blankets
Coats	600,000	
Pairs of boots	1,420,000	

German Raw Material Aid to Austria 1914-18

	Pig Iron	Rubber
1914	6823t	
1915	20,515t	19.6t
1916	100,000t	1.7t
1917	167,540t	3.9t
1918 (Jan-July)	97,700t	25.0t

+ RM 690m worth of metals

German Aid to Turkey 1914-18

386,000t coal (14 coal trains pw to Constantinople 1916-18)
10,814 wagons of war material incl 460 aircraft
4707 wagons of rail, field & tram material
28,841 wagons of coal
2615 wagons of prviate goods

Austrian Aid to Germany 1914-18

1,827,700 SAA
Guns worth RM 21.5m
39,302 horses
Chemical warfare material worth RM 27m
Aviation & motor fuel worth RM 173m
10,742t of coal & graphite
Metals worth RM 487m

Bulgarian Aid to Germany 1916 - 1 July 1918

1.69m, tons of metal, oil, etc, worth RM 167m
103,087t farm produce (1916)
825lt farm produce (1917)
597t farm produce (1918)

Gold Reserve Gains & Losses 1913-19 (£m)

Allies	Central Powers	Neutrals
Australia +1	Austria -55	Argentina +49
Belgium -4	Bulgaria -1	Denmark +9
Britain -42	(Finland) -0.5	Holland +41
Canada +9	Turkey n/a	Sweden +10
France -25		Spain +84
Greece +5		Switzerland +12.5
Italy -19		Uruguay +10
Japan +183		
New Zealand 0		
Portugal -1.5		
Rumania -7		
South Africa -0.5		
USA +278.5		

1914-18 HOME FRONTS TABLES

Civilian Dead 1914-18

Belgium	30,000
Britain	30,633 (15,313 merchant sailors & fishermen)
France	40,000 (3000 merchant sailors)
Greece	132,000
Italy	
Japan	
Montenegro	
Portugal	
Rumania	275,000
Russia	2,000,000 (incl c500,000 Poles & Lithuanians)
Serbia	650,000
USA	
Austria	300,000 (2/3rds+ Polish)
Bulgaria	275,000
Germany	760,000 (controversially attributed to Allied blockade)
Turkey	2,150,000 (at least half massacred or starved Armenians)

Note: Some figures include 1918-19 'Spanish' flu pandemic which killed 21.64m people worldwide (incl 5m in India), others do not. Only c100,000 deaths due to land, air or naval action, remainder to wartime privations.

Financial and Economic Costs 1914-18 (in £/$)

ALLIED		
Belgium	£2039m	($10,195m)
Britain	£7852m	($39,260m)
British Empire	£10,395m	($51,975m)
France	£9975.4m	($49,877m)
Greece	£111.2m	($556m)
Italy	£3628.6m	($18,143m)
Japan		
Portugal	£60-80m	($300-400m)
Rumania	£520.2m	($2601m)
Russia	£5121m	($21,600m)
Serbia	£480m	($2400m)
USA	£6464m	($32,320m)
CENTRAL POWERS		
Austria	£4921m	($23,706m)
Bulgaria	£203m	($1015m)
Germany	£11,614.4m	($58,072m)
Turkey	£689m	($3445m)
NEUTRALS		
Denmark	£18m	($90m)
Holland	£134.4m	($672m)
Norway	£26m	($130m)
Sweden	£859.6m	($4298m)
Switzerland	£50m	($250m)

Note: These figures include government spending, loans and material damage valuation. They can only be taken as an approximate relative guide. £=$5 (1914 exchange rate).

Births, Deaths & Marriages 1914 - 19 (b, d & m) (thousands)

	Austria (a)	Belgium	Britain	Bulgaria	France	Germany (c)	Italy	Rumania
1914 b	801	156	1002	191	753	1819	1114	327
d	558	109	662	88	1130	1291	643	183
m	183	41	353	53	205	461	252	65
1915 b	664	124	1025	172	480	1383	1109	320
d	612	101	720	85	1065	1450	810	194
m	90	25	421	27	86(b)	278	186	56
1916 b	408	99	987	99	382	1029	882	n/a
d	525	101	650	97	695	1298	855	n/a
m	92	30	333	10	125	279	106	n/a
1917 b	384	87	851	81	410	912	714	n/a
d	529	125	636	99	855	1345	949	n/a
m	105	33	310	21	180	308	99(d)	n/a
1918 b	74	85(e)	849	100	470	927	655	n/a
d	646	157	769(f)	152	1115	1606	1268(g)	n/a
m	100	44	040	45	202	333	107	n/a
1919 b	119	128	887	157	504	1261	771	366
d	131	113	668	97	737	978	676	328
m	80	97	440	75	553	844	333	107

(a) Austria: Area of subsequent Republic plus Hungary till 1918
(b) France: Lowest on record
(c) Germany: Includes deaths attributed to Allied blockade (controversial figures) 1915 - 88,235; 1916 - 121,114; 1917 - 259,627; 1918 - 293,760
(d) Italy: Lowest on record
(e) Belgium: Lowest on record
(f) Britain: Highest on record partly due to world flu pandemic
(g) Italy: Highest on record partly due to world flu pandemic

Central Government Expenditure/Revenue (millions) 1913 - 19

	1913	1914	1915	1916	1917	1918	1919
Austria (kronen)	3692	2193(a)	17,357/10,039	n/a	n/a	n/a	-
Britain (pounds)	192/198	559/227	1559/337	2198/573	2696/707(c)	2579/889	1666/1340
Bulgaria (leva)	350/169	291/224	314/195	476/193	973/338	1294/567	1316/844(d)
France (francs)	5067/5092	10,065/4549	20,925/4131	28,113/5529	35,320/6943	41,897/762	39,970/13,282
Germany (RM)	3521/2095	9651/2399	26,689/1769	28,780/2045	53,261/7682	45,514/6830	54,867/9712
Greece (drachma)	261/194	482/218	376/222	215/226	317/234	n/a	1446/516(e)
Hungary (kronen)	2319/1839	1444/889(b)	6659/1829	12,248/2283	10,911/2772	12,251/5015	11,200(f)
Italy (lire)	3137/2529	3009/2524	5795/2560	12,543/3734	21,622/5345	26,502/7533	33,335/9676
Portugal (escudos)	n/a	n/a	n/a	163	204/86	242/100	128
Rumania (lei)	522/639	543/755	747	/379	1027/187	787/419	/1115
Russia (roubles)	383/3417	4865/2818	n/a	n/a	n/a	n/a	n/a
Serbia (dinars)	131/131	214/214	n/a	n/a	n/a	n/a	n/a
USA (dollars)	724/724	735/734	760/697	734/782	1977/1124	12,696/3664	18,514/5152

(a) Austria: 1914 & 1915 half-year figures only
(b) Hungary: Half-year figures only
(c) Britain: Expenditure not surpassed till 1940
(d) Hungary: Revenue for year ended 31 Mar 1920
(e) Greece: Expenditure for 15 months ended 31 Mar 1920
(f) Hungary: Period 1 Nov 1918-6 Aug 1919

Cost of Living Indices 1914 - 19

	Austria	Britain	Bulgaria	France	Germany	Greece	Italy
1914	90	61	3	17	67	5	22
1915	142	75	4	20	84	6	24
1916	303	89	n/a	23	110	8	30
1917	605	107	n/a	27	164	8	43
1918	1047	124	n/a	35	196	19	59
1919	2243	131	41	44	269	17	60

Personal Taxation Rates

	Prewar	Postwar
Australia	8%	9.5%
Britain	9%	27%
Canada	11%	13%
France	13%	18%
Germany	8%	12%
Italy	11%	11%
Japan	20%	13%
USA	2%	8%

Food Production Decline 1914 - 18

	Meat	Milk	Butter	Sugar	Fish
Britain	17%	20%	-	35%	40%
France	-	45%	-	-	-
Germany	42%	50%	40%	-	-

Livestock 1913 - 18 (thousands)

		Horses	Cattle	Pigs	Sheep	Goats
Austria	1914		17,300	7700		
	1918			3500	200	
Belgium	1913	267	1849	1412		
	1919(a)	162	1286	770		
Britain	1914	1609	7093	2634	24,286	
	1915	1487(b)	7288	2579	24,598	
	1916	1567	7422	2314	25,007	
	1917	1583	7437	2051	24,043	
	1918(c)	1586	7410	1825	23,353	
France	1913(d)	3222	14,788	7036	16,131	1435
	1914	2205	12,668	5926	14,038	1308
	1915	2209	12,520	4910	12,262	1231
	1916	2246	12,342	4362	10,845	1177
	1917	2303	12,242	4165	9881	1161
	1918	2233	12,251	4377	9061	1197
Germany	1913	4558	20,994	25,659	5521	3548
	1914	3435	21,829	25,341	5471	3538
	1915	3342	20,317	17,287	5073	3438
	1916	3304(e)	20,874	17,002	4979	3940
	1917	3324	20,095	11,052	4954	4315
	1918	3425	17,650	10,271	5347	4321
Turkey	1913	339	2397	1373 mules & donkeys 314 camels		

(a) Belgium: Horses fewest recorded since figures began (1816).
Cattle & pig figures lowest since 1880
(b) Britain: Fewest horses since 1890
(c) Britain: Fewest pigs & sheep since figures began (1867)
(d) France: Cattle figure surpassed 1927, pigs 1934, sheep never again, and goats 929
(e) Germany: Fewer horses than in 1883

Coal Output 1913 - 19 (thousands of metric tons)

	Aust	Belg	Brit	Bulg	Fr	Ger	Gr	Ital	Port	Rum	Russ (b)	Turk	USA
1913	43,838	24,371	292,042(a)	369	40,844	277,342	0.2	701	25	250	36,050	826	478,435
1914	39,027	16,714	269,927	421	27,528	245,331	20	781	29	230	31,900	651	422,704
1915	38,354	14,178	257,269	533	19,533 (c)	234,816	40	953	60	254	31,440	420	442,624
1916	n/a	16,863	260,489	640	21,310	253,350	117	1306	143	300	34,470	408	502,520
1917	n/a	14,931	252,487	761	28,915	263,200	158	1722	189	n/a	33,310	146	551,791
1918	n/a	13,891	231,404	673	26,259	258,854	213	2171	185	n/a	13,100	186	579,386
1919	n/a	18,483	233,467	583	22,441	210,355	183	1158	130	1353	9450	n/a	465,860

(a) Britain: All-time record
(b) Russia: Soviet figures applied to 1923 borders
(c) France: Received 22mt of coal from Britain
(d) Rumania: New expanded borders

Pig Iron Output 1913 - 19 (thousands of metric tons)

	Austria	Belgium	Britain	France	Germany	Italy	Lux	Russia	USA
1913	2381	2485 (a)	10,425 (b)	5207	16,761	427	2548 (c)	4641	34,036
1914	1847	1454	9067	2736	12,481	385	1827	4137	24,935
1915	1817	68	8864	584	10,190	378	1591	3764	34,031
1916	1930	128	9062	1311	11,327	467	1951	3804	43,821
1917	2380	8	9488	1408	11,601	471	1529	2964	43,246
1918	n/a	n/a	9253	1293	10,680	314	1267	597	42,618
1919	n/a	251	7536	1333	6284	240	617	117	33,858

(a) Belgium: Not surpassed till 1924
(b) Britain: Not surpassed till 1952
(c) Luxembourg: Not surpassed till 1926

Iron Ore Output 1913 - 19 (thousands of metric tons)

	Austria	Britain	France	Germany	Italy	Lux	Russia	USA
1913	3039	16,254 (a)	21,918 (b)	28,608 (c)	603	7333	9537 (d)	61,980
1914	2281	15,107	11,252	25,505	706	4900	7660	41,440
1915	2547	14,463	620	17,710	680	6140	5940	55,526
1916	n/a	13,712	1681	21,334	942	6958	7250	75,168
1917	n/a	15,084	2035	22,465	994 (e)	4502	5330	75,289
1918	n/a	14,847	1672	18,392	694	3131	590	69,658
1919	n/a	12,451	9413	6154	613	3112	90	60,965

(a) Britain: Best since 1884, passed again 1940
(b) France: Record till 1923
(c) Germany: All time record

(d) Russia: Not surpassed till 1930
(e) Italy: Not surpassed till 1937

Crude Steel Output 1913 - 19 (thousands of metric tons)

	Austria	Belgium	Britain	France	Germany	Italy	Lux	Russia	USA
1913	2611	2467	7787	4687	17,609 (a)	934	1326	4918 (b)	n/a
1914	2190	1396	7971	2802	13,810	911	1136	4466	23,513
1915	2686	99	8687	1111	12,278	1009	980	4120	32,151
1916	3460	99	9136	1784	14,871	1269	1312	4276	42,773
1917	1650 (c)	10	9873 (d)	1991	15,501	1332 (e)	1087	3080	45,060
1918	n/a	11	9692	1800	14,092	933	888	402	44,462
1919	n/a	334	8021	1293	8710	732	369	199	n/a

(a) Germany: Not surpassed till 1936
(b) Russia: Not surpassed till 1930
(c) Austria: Half year only

(d) Britain: Not surpassed till 1935
(e) Italy: Not surpassed till 1924

Electric Energy Output 1913 - 19 (in giga Watt hrs)

	Britain	France	Germany	Italy	Russia	USA
1913	2.5	1.8	8.0	2.0	2.04	n/a
1914	3.0	2.15	8.8	2.2	n/a	n/a
1915	3.5	1.90	9.8	2.58	n/a	n/a
1916	4.1	2.18	11.0	2.93	2.58(a)	n/a
1917	4.7	2.4	12.0	3.43	n/a	4.34
1918	4.9	2.7	13.0	4.0	n/a	n/a
1919	4.9	2.9	13.5	4.3	n/a	n/a

(a) Russia: Not surpassed till 1925

Railways (miles) & Rolling Stock 1914 (standard gauge only)

	Miles	Locomotives	Carriages	Wagons
Austria	28,400	10,000	21,000	245,000
Belgium	5370	4300	10,000	90,000
Britain	23,718	22,998(a)	72,888	1,380,520
Bulgaria	1320	-	-	-
France	31,200	14,500(b)	33,500	364,000
Germany(c)	38,950	28,000	60,000	600,000
Greece (1915)	1431	-	-	-
Italy	11,884	6000	12,000	112,000
Rumania	2229	-	-	-
Russia	45,350	17,200	20,000	370,000
Serbia (1913)	993	-	-	-
Turkey	3882	280	720	4500
USA (d)	387,208	67,012		

(a) Britain: 600 locomotives sent overseas including 208 to Russia, 43+ to Salonika, & 22 to Mesopotamia; 1217 locomotives supplied to BEF in France
(b) France : Only 83 locomotives lost to Germans in 1914 but 45,000 wagons were

(c) Germany: In occupied territory on 11 Nov 1918 Army alone running 6627 locomotives and 178,046 wagons on 12,038 track miles
(d) USA: 1303 locomotives sent to France during hostilities

Railway Freight Traffic 1913 - 19 (thousands of metric tons)

	1913	1914	1915	1916	1917	1918	1919
Belgium	88,427	-	-	-	-	-	-
Britain	570,544 (a)	-	-	-	-	-	309,753
Bulgaria	1947	2536 (b)	2002	2834	3455	2926	1782
France	136,000	88,200	71,500	79,700	83,700	64,700	77,000
Germany	676,627 (c)	528,882	367,600	415,600	-	387,000	287,200
Greece	743	771	747	789	616	756	766
Italy	41,422	37,660	38,283	40,535	38,653	38,994	39,727
Rumania	9043	9872	9286	4322	2368	1656	3548
Russia (d)	132,000	123,000	126,000	147,000	115,000	37,000	31,000

(a) Britain : All time record
(b) Bulgaria: Level surpassed 1921

(c) Germany : Not surpassed till 1961
(d) Russia : Not surpassed till 1927. Figures for 1914-19 apply to Soviet 1923 borders

Railway Passenger Traffic 1913 - 19 (millions)

	1913	1914	1915	1916	1917	1918	1919
Belgium	224.3	-	-	-	-	-	-
Britain	1423.5	-	-	-	-	-	1522.6
Bulgaria	1.9	4.2	3.5	1.5	1.6	2.7	5.4
France	529.0	355.0	209.0	325.0	352.0	377.0	463.0
Germany	1798.0	-	-	-	-		
Greece	12.6	12.3	13.4	17.1	14.1	14.7	15.0
Italy	106.0	98.7	93.2	90.6	82.1	92.4	118.3
Rumania	11.1	11.6	-	-	-	4.9	14.2
Russia	185.0	235.0	264.0	348.0	354.0	386.0	202.0
USA	1043.6	1063.2	985.6	1048.9	1109.9	1122.9	1211.0

Women in War Production 1914 - 18

	Britain	France	Italy	Germany	USA
1914	175,000	18,815 (metals)			
1915	246,000	35,000/44,162 (Jan-June/July)	few thousand		
1916	-	109,910 (1Jan)	89,000		
1917	-	300,000	175,000		
1918	c759,000 (July)	426,000 (1 Nov)	200,000		2,250,000

Strikes 1914 - 19 (incl total workers & days lost)

	Austria	Britain	France	Germany	Italy
1914	260	972	672	1223	905
	33,000w	447,000w	162,000w	238,000w	217,000w
	n/a	9,878,000dl	2,187,000dl	2,844,000dl	n/a
1915	n/a	672	98(a)	141(b)	608
		448,000w	9000w	48,000w	180,000w
		2,953,000dl	55,000dl	46,000dl	
1916	n/a	532	314	240	577
		276,000w	41,000w	423,000w	138,000w
		2,581,000dl	236,000dl	245,000dl	838,000dl
1917	n/a	730	696	562	470
		872,000w	294,000w	1,468,000w	175,000w
		5,647,000dl	1,482,000dl	1,862,000dl	849,000dl
1918	n/a	1165	499	532	313(c)
		1,116,000w	176,000w	716,000w	159,000w
		5,875,000dl	980,000dl	1,453,000dl	912,000dl
1919	n/a	1352	2026(d)	3719(e)	1871(f)
		2,591,000w	1,151,000w	2,761,000w	1,551,000w
		34,969,000dl	15,478,000dl	33,083,000dl	22,325,000dl

(a) France : Lowest number of strikes since 1879 with fewest workers since 1874
(b) Germany: Lowest since 1894
(c) Italy : Lowest since 1896
(d) France : Highest until 1936
(e) Germany: Highest yet
(f) Italy : Highest ever

Unemployment 1914 - 19 (%)

	Britain (unions only)	France	Germany
1914	3.3	4.7 (1913)	7.2(a)
1915	1.1	n/a	3.3
1916	0.4(b)	n/a	2.2
1917	0.7	n/a	1.0(c)
1918	0.8	n/a	1.2
1919	2.4	n/a	3.7

(a) Highest since 1887 when records begin
(b) Lowest ever recorded
(c) Lowest since 1898

Artillery Production 1914 - 18

	Britain	France (a)	Germany	Italy	Russia	USA
1914	91	5pd	100pm +20 heavy (Sept)		355	
1915	3226		120pm (June) 270pm (Aug) c60pm (Sept)		2065	
1916	4551	30pd	480pm +300pm (Sept)		8289	
1917	6483	36pd	400pm (Sept)		4302	3160 (b)
1918	10,680	60pd				
Totals	25,031			11,789	15,031	

(a) France: 7000 for Allies incl 4000 for AEF   (b) USA: 1102 for Allies; 464 US-made 75mm guns delivered to Army (Oct 1918)

Tank Production 1916 - 18

	Britain	France	Germany	Italy	USA
1916	150				
1917	1277	800			
1918	1391	4000 (a)	20	6	64 (b)

(a) Renault light tanks: 514 supplied to AEF, 100 to Italy (cAug 1918), 100 to Russia
(b) Renault light tank redesign built under licence as 6-ton Model 1917, 10 in France by Armistice

---

Armoured Car Production 1914 - 18

Belgium	20+
Britain	300+
France	333+
Germany	37
Italy	19 types
Russia	n/a
USA	84

Italian War Production 1915 & 1918

	1915	1918
MGs (pm)	25	1200
Shells (pd)	10,400	88,400
Aircraft (pa)	382	6523
Aircraft engines (pa)	606	14,820
Motor vehicles (pa)	9200 (1914)	20,000

British Mortar and Small Arms Production 1914 - 18

	Rifles (a)	MGs	SAA (thousands)	Mortars	Mortar Bombs	Grenades
1914	120,093	274	121,995	12	545	2152
1915	616,111	6064	1,261,546	976	352,882	12,282,182
1916	1,168,899	33,200	2,955,425	5554	6,493,555	34,867,966
1917	2,123,287	79,438	1,573,864	6194	5,669,619	29,226,753
1918	1,062,052	120,864	2,724,282	6360	4,477,714	23,723,666
Totals	5,090,442	239,840 (b)	8,637,112 (c)	19,096	16,994,315	100,102,719 (d)

(a) Rifles: 118,486 in Canada 1915-17; 1,117,850 in USA 1916-17. USA made 2,819,185 for own use 1917-18
(b) MGs: Italy 31,030 1915-18
(c) SAA: 876,587 in USA 1914-17
(d) Grenades: Germany 300m; Italy 7.3m

German Small Arms Production

	Rifles	MGs	Carbines
4-31 July 1915	110,329	611	24,350
2 July-5 Aug 1916	230,791	1608	30,000
7 July-3 Aug 1917	180,395	8676	38,400
2-30 Aug 1918	97,145	11,354	47,350

German Mortar Strength

Aug 1914	160
July 1916	1684
Sept 1916	2484
Aug 1917	15,933
Jan 1918	17,027

German Heavy Guns in the Field

1914	2000
1 March 1917	6819 (1112 captured guns)
Dec 1917	6353
Mar 1918	6172
Nov 1918	5624 (W Front)

German Monthly Sandbag Consumption

1915	15m
1916	20m
to mid-1918	600m

German Weekly Trench Obstacle Production (tons)

July 1915	2000
Aug 1915	3000
Dec 1915	7000
1916	5000-7000
1917	7000
1918	4000-5000
Apr-Nov 1918	2000
Total to mid-1918	635,000

German PoWs Working in France

End 1915	64,171 (20,000 on land)
End 1916	122,773 (35,000 on land)
End 1917	208,082
Armistice Day	306,044 (a)

(a) A record 64,250 were working in Britain (7 Nov)

ABRUZZI, Duke of the, Prince Luigi Amedeo Giuseppe Maria Ferdinando Francesco   C-in-C Italian Fleet

b Madrid 29 Jan 1873 3rd son of Amedeo, King of Spain & Duke of Aosta, cousin of Victor Emmanuel II, King of Italy; d Mogadishu, Italian Somaliland 18 Mar 1933 aged 60

Distinguished naval cdr, mountaineer, explorer, man of science, writer.

First to climb 18,008ft Mt St Elias, Alaska 31 July 1897. Organized Arctic expedition 1899-1900. A sledging party from his ship *Stella Pollare* reached lat 86°33'N. Climbed 16,763ft Mt Ruwenzori, central Africa, 1906 & reached 24,600ft on Mt Godwin-Austen, Himalayas 1909. Commanded naval sqn during 1911-12 Italo-Turk War.

C-in-C Italian Fleet 1913-17, but basic defensive strategy inhibited his desire for action. Enjoyed good relations with Allied navies. Published *Farther North Than Nansen* (London 1901); *On the Polar Star in the Arctic Sea* (London 1903). After the war became a colonist in the Horn of Africa.

ALBERT I, King and C-in-C of the Belgians 'Albert the Brave'

b Brussels 8 Apr 1875 2nd son of K Leopold II's brother, Prince Philip of Saxe-Coburg; d nr Namur 17 Feb 1934 in Ardennes rock-climbing accident aged 58

Heir apparent on elder brother's death 1891; entered Army as Lt 1892; married Duchess Elizabeth of Bavaria 1900; Col 1901; Lt-Gen 1907; succeeded to throne Dec 1909 aged 34; visited bellicose Kaiser, his cousin 1913.

Personal and unsuccessful appeal to Kaiser 3 Aug 1914. Dramatic 4 Aug speech to Parlt ensured whole of Belgium would be defended. Named C-in-C by constitution. Stopped generals counter-attacking after 5 Aug German repulse at Liège. Withdrew Army to Antwerp entrenched camp. Inspired heroic stand on Yser (13-30 Oct) retaining last corner of country. Elder son Leopold enlisted as private aged 13 (in 12th Regt, 5 Apr 1915).

Opposed Anglo-French attempts to treat him as ally, saw himself as leader of injured neutral state, so cautioning govt Apr 1915. Welcomed German peace feelers winter 1915/16 thus split from Cabinet in seeking compromise peace. Refused to come under Haig's command for Third Ypres. Lost pro-compromise Foreign Minister & PM Broqueville (Jan-May 1918) to pro-Allied Paul Hymans. With Allied turn of tide accepted Foch's offer of Flanders Army Group (Sept 1918) to advance on Nieuport and liberate homeland.

First peacetime speech called for equal voting and language rights as well as end to Belgian neutrality. Visited USA to thank for support 1919. More complex in 1915-18 than Allied propaganda lauding a young warrior king and his devoted nursing wife. Nevertheless, one of only three pre-1914 monarchs to regain a lost throne and the only one to strengthen it.

ALEXANDER KARADJORDJEVIC Prince Regent of Serbia

b Cetinje, Montenegro 16 Dec 1888 2nd son of Peter & Princess Zovka; d Marseilles 9 Oct 1934 aged 45 murdered by Croat & Macedonian revolutionaries.

Educated Geneva & School for Pages, St Petersburg; Russia may have given taste for autocracy; Crown Prince from 1909 when elder brother renounced rights to throne; briefly linked to Black Hand nationalist group; diplomat & army commander in Balkan Wars 1912-13; took over from father weeks before Sarajevo.

Both men became symbols of Serb resistance & aspirations. Alexander's proclamation of 4 Aug 1914, as nominal C-in-C to Army, called Slavs in Austria-Hungary 'our brethren'. Peter rose from sickbed to hold a rifle in the trenches & led Army back into Belgrade (2-15 Dec 1914). Father & son shared the Great Retreat. Alexander, despite appendicitis, insisted the Army would recover & fight on. Alexander met Croat exile leader Ante Trumbic in Paris (April 1916) while on tour of Allies with PM Pasic Alexander may have instigated execution of anti-royalist officers early 1917, certainly benefited from Yugoslav plans of Corfu Conference (20 July 1917).

Breakout from Salonika gave Alexander his chance to return home victorious & become regent of the new kingdom, unfettered by PM Pasic sent off to Versailles. Alexander formally gained the crown on his father's death.

ALEXEIEV, Gen Mikhail V (1857-1918) (*see* RUSSIAN GENERALS)

ALLENBY, Edmund Henry Hynman   British General 'The Bull'

b Brackenhurst, Southwell, Notts 23 Apr 1861, 2nd child of country gentleman; d London of brain haemorrhage 14 May 1936 aged 75

Educated Haileybury & Sandhurst 1875-81, 2/Lt 6th Inniskilling Dragoons and first action in S Africa 1882-8; Maj and Staff College 1896-7; sqn & regt CO, then Flying Column cdr in Boer War 1899-1901; Col & CO 5th Royal Irish Lancers; GOC 4th Cav Bde 1905; Maj-Gen & Insp-Gen of Cav 1909-10.

Stalwart regular career cavalryman with violent temper. Took BEF mounted troops to war in 1914. Ably covered retreat from Mons and as Lt-Gen i/c Cav Corps (9 Oct) made sacrificial stand at First Ypres. Took over V Corps 6 May 1915 and Third Army as General 23 Oct 1915. Loyally carried out costly attacks but disliked Haig.

Achieved shortlived success at Arras 9 Apr-3 May 1917, chosen by Lloyd George to take over EEF 28 June. Lost only son killed on W Front 29 July.

Like Maude restored morale of baffled army, securing reinforcements and supplies. Nurtured Lawrence and the Arab flank diversion. Third Battle of Gaza, begun by bold and cleverly disguised cavalry pounce on Beersheba, fractured Turk armies and gained Jerusalem in sustained advance. Twice thwarted in trying to break out E across the Jordan (19 Feb-4 May 1918). Integrated Indian replacement troops into depleted EEF and masterminded cavalry exploitation at Megiddo that brought Turkey to armistice in 38 days.

Supervised Near East occupation before becoming High Commissioner for Egypt (25 March 1919-14 June 1925). Field-Marshal 31 July 1919. In biographer and subordinate Wavell's opinion 'the best British General of the Great War'.

ARAB LEADERS

The Hashemite leaders of the Arab Revolt came from the Sherifite House of Hashim, Mecca, in authority since 1827, descended ultimately from the Prophet's tribe and his daughter.

Hussein, ibn Ali ibn Mohammed   Sherif of Mecca, King of Hejaz
b Constantinople 1856 grandson of 1st Abdillah clan Sherif (d1858); d Amman 4 June 1931 aged 75

From age of 8 studied at Mecca; lived from 1893 in Constantinople having links with Pan-Islamic and Pan-Arab movements as well as British in Egypt; 4 sons born 1880-97; nominated Sherif of Mecca by Ottoman Grand Vizier 1908 to succeed uncle Abdulla who died en route 1908; anti-Turk policy from c1913; in touch with British Resident Kitchener in Cairo 1914.

White-bearded conspirator but cautiously edged way towards open revolt of 5 June 1916 once assured of British money and arms. Left military leadership to 4 sons but proclaimed himself 'King of the Arabs' 4 Nov. Fearful of Ibn Saud even before Turks expelled from Hejaz. Gave victory banquet to Allied reps Feb 1919 but refused to sign Versailles Treaty in protest at Allied Middle East mandates.

Declared himself Caliph of Islam Mar 1924. Abdicated Oct in favour of son Ali when Ibn Saud had conquered almost all Hejaz. Cyprus exile till 1930.

Eldest son Ali (1880-1935), old for his years and suffering from consumption that caused outbursts. Hesitantly commanded blockade of Medina for his father. As Hussein's successor held Jeddah for over a year v Ibn Saud 1924-5. Second son Abdulla (b Mecca 1882, d Jerusalem 29 July 1951) best known as Emir then King of Trans-Jordan 1921-51 who held secret talks with new state of Israel. As Deputy for Mecca in Ottoman Parlt often quarrelled with Enver. Foreign Minister and captor of Taif in 1916 revolt. Short, stocky and convivial unlike his stiffer brothers.

Fourth son Zaid b c1897 to Circassian Turk mother. Humorous and unpolitical. Brought British news of revolt at Jeddah 6 June 1916.

Feisal, ibn Hussein   C-in-C Arab Northern Army

b Taif, Hejaz 20 May 1885; d Berne 8 Sept 1933 aged 48

Educated Constantinople 1893-1909, Deputy for Jeddah in Ottoman Parlt 1913. Prewar clever but rash intriguer with Arab Nationalist Committees and Young Turks.

Dignified and complex third son. Twice in Damascus with Djemal Pasha and Germans 1915-16 and there until May 1916. Led Arab Army outside Medina and in Hejaz with little success until Capt T E Lawrence saw his tall regal figure as the best leader for the revolt. Fortunes rose with switch north to Wejh and Aqaba. By summer 1918 led 8000 increasingly regular and well-equipped troops. Reached Damascus but lost it to French imperialism. Gained throne of Iraq thanks to Gertrude Bell and 96% plebiscite. Crowned 23 Aug 1921. Died having begun dynasty that lasted to 1958.

ARZ von Straussenburg (1857-1935) (see AUSTRIAN GENERALS)

ASQUITH, Herbert Henry   British Prime Minister 'Wait and See'

b Croft House, Morley, Lincolnshire 12 Sept 1852 son of non-conformist woolspinner; d The Wharf, Sutton Courteney, Berks 15 Feb 1928 aged 75

Scholar to Balliol College, Oxford 1870; barrister 1876; Liberal MP for E Fife 1886; Home Sec 1892-5; opposed leader's Boer War criticisms; Chancellor of Exchequer 1906-8; Prime Minister 1908-16.

Great peacetime Prime Minister and seeker of consensus. Longest occupant of No10 this century until Margaret Thatcher. Picked Churchill and Lloyd George for his Cabinet. War saved him from Irish Home Rule deadlock. Brilliantly chose Kitchener for War Ministry. Carried on extraordinarily indiscreet correspondence with Venetia Stanley until her May 1915 marriage. This may have weakened his opposition to coalition that month. Bears heavy share of responsibility for Gallipoli. The French compelled him to back Salonika. Not a single-minded war leader, played bridge 2 hrs every evening with forceful diarist wife Margot. Son Raymond's W Front death (15 Sept 1916) probably undermined his will to resist Lloyd George's machinations. In opposition made only mild criticism of war in which he embodied ordinary English reasonableness. Published *Memories and Reflections* (2 vols 1928).

AUFFENBERG, Baron von (1852-1928) (see AUSTRIAN GENERALS)

AUSTRIAN GENERALS

Habsburg generals lacked recent modern battle experience, even colonial (Bosnia 1878), and soon faced humiliating dependence on the Germans. Viktor **Dankl** (1854-1941) won the first battle v the Russians (Krasnik) and defended the Tyrol ably until 17 June 1916. Moritz, Baron von **Auffenberg** (1852-1928) lost his Fourth Army command in the Lemberg fiasco. Cavalryman Eduard, Baron von **Böhm-Ermolli** (1856-1941), longest serving Eastern Front army and army group commander had little impact until quarrels with the Germans cost his job. Transylvanian **Arz** von Straussenburg (1857-1935) proved a loyal but uninspired successor to Conrad after competent field commands. Harsh Croat infantryman **Boroevic** von Bojna (1856-1920) performed best leading Fifth Army in defence against the hated Italians. Hungarian Baron **Pflanzer-Baltin**, (1855-1925), recalled from retirement, proved adept in the Carpathian (1914-15) and Albanian mountains (1918) although Brusilov cost him his command (while ill) in between.

The Archdukes did not win laurels. Francis Joseph's godson, **Joseph Ferdinand** (1872-1942), led Fourth Army to successive disasters till June 1916. FM **Frederick** (1856-1936), fine prewar trainer and nominal C-in-C, played a largely diplomatic role in patching up Austro-German rows. Hungarian Archduke **Joseph** (1872-1962) handled VII Corps bravely in defence (Carpathians; Isonzo; Transylvanian Alps) but was the only commander to vote for a split Army. FM **Eugene** of Austria (1863-1954) merely presided over Balkan and Italian Fronts till January 1918.

Hungarian FM Baron von **Kövess** von Kövessháza (1854-1924) uniquely led successful attacking armies on all 3 fronts (1915-17).

AVERESCU, Alexandru   Rumanian General & PM

b Ismail, Bessarabia 9 Mar 1859 of peasant stock; d Bucharest 2 Oct 1938 aged 79

Rumania's most famous soldier. A strategist of note, but extremely ruthless & with increasingly political ambitions &

fascist tendencies.

Enlisted 1876; fought in Rumano-Turk War of Independence 1877-8; Italian Gen Staff College, Turin; military attaché, Berlin 1895-8; Brig-Gen 1906; War Minister 1907-12, bloodily suppressed 1907 peasant rebellion. Army CoS during Balkan War 1912-13. Directed invasion of Bulgaria July 1913.

CO Second Army Aug 1916. Led initially successful invasion of Transylvania. Given Third Army for bold, but unsuccessful counter-stroke v Mackensen in the Dobruja. Returned to Second Army & directed Carpathian rearguard actions. After supporting Lt-Gen Prezan's final counter-offensive at gates of Bucharest, conducted fighting withdrawal to R Prut. Won Battle of Marasti 23 July 1917-1 Aug, occupying salient & defending it v furious Austro-German attacks, in Battle of Marasesti 6 Aug-3 Sept 1917. As Premier 9 Feb-12 Mar 1918 failed to ameliorate draconian German peace terms after collapse of Russian resistance in winter 1917-18 (Treaty of Bucharest). Founded People's Party 1918.

Twice more PM (1920-1 & 1926-7); FM 1930. Laid to rest on battlefield of Marasesti.

BALFOUR, Arthur James   British First Lord of Admiralty & Foreign Secretary 'AJB'

b Whittinghame, E Lothian 25 July 1848 son of country gentleman; d Fisher's Hill nr Woking, Surrey 19 Mar 1930 aged 81. Veteran Tory statesman

Eton & Trinity Coll, Cambridge; Tory MP 1874; Congress of Berlin with uncle Lord Salisbury 1878; Irish Chief Sec 1887; Tory Commons leader 1891; PM 1902-6, established CID and Entente Cordiale; resigned Tory leadership over Irish Home Rule 1911.

Tall, suave, complex bachelor-intellectual of great charm and experience but also dilatory. Attended War Council on occasion even before May 1915 coalition gained him the Admiralty in place of Churchill. Lacked energy and resource in job. Congratulated Jellicoe on Jutland but told Beatty that it was 'a missed opportunity'. Called U-boat threat 'an evil which unfortunately we cannot wholly cure'. Moved by Lloyd George to more suitable Foreign Office, AJB's greatest triumph was winning US support after her entry into war. Underestimated Austrian peace offers and Bolshevik threat. Famous 'Declaration' laid Middle East powder keg. Told friend before Versailles '... not so much the war as the peace that I have always dreaded'. Rescued negotiations and main architect of Treaty of St Germain.

BEATTY, David   British Battlecruiser and Grand Fleet C-in-C 'David'

b Howbeck Lodge, Stapeley, Co Meath, Ireland 17 Jan 1871 son of Anglo-Irish capt in 4th Hussars; d London 11 Mar 1936 aged 65

Handsome, vain & well-connected, his dashing leadership had Nelsonian echoes.

Entered RN Academy, Gosport 1884; served in Sudan 1896-8, esp i/c Nile river gunboats at Khartoum (DSO, promoted Cdr); Boxer Rebellion 1900 (twice w), promoted Capt. Married US heiress Ethel Field 1901; commanded 3 cruisers & battleship *Queen* in turn. Rear-Adm 1910 at age 39 (same as Nelson). Naval adviser to First Lord but serious row led to being put on half-pay. Naval Sec to First Lord Churchill 1912-13.

Led Battle Cruiser Sqn (later BCR Force) 1913-16. Won Battles of Heligoland Bight and Dogger Bank. At Jutland drew German Fleet towards Jellicoe but at controversial cost of 3 of his 6 battlecruisers. C-in-C Grand Fleet 29 Nov 1916. Remedied Jutland design & shell deficiencies. Kept morale high for duration, ably

fostering American naval friendship & shipboard aviation. Received off Rosyth surrender of High Seas Fleet 21 Nov 1918. At 1104 made historic signal: 'The German flag will be hauled down at sunset today, and will not be hoisted again without permission.'

Received earldom (of Brooksby & the North Sea) & made Admiral of the Fleet 2 Apr 1919. First Sea Lord 1919-27. Represented Britain at Washington (Disarmament) Conference 1921. Laid to rest in St Paul's Cathedral. See *The Beatty Papers* Vol 1 1902-1918 (Scolar Press for Navy Records Society, 1989).

BEF ARMY COMMANDERS PROFILES

Byng, Julian Hedworth George, 1st Viscount Byng of Vimy, British General

b Wrotham Park, Barnet, N of London 11 Sept 1862 son of 2nd Earl of Strafford; d Thorpe-le-Soken, Essex 6 June 1935 aged 72

Charm & affability made him generally popular, the Canadian Corps successfully stormed Vimy Ridge under his cmnd.

Joined 10th Hussars India 1883; first active service Red Sea 1884; Capt 1889; Staff College 1894; Major raising SA Light Horse 1899; Relief of Ladysmith & flying col cdr 1900-2; CO 10th Hussars 1902; i/c 1st and 2nd Cav Bdes 1905-7; Maj-Gen 1909.

Left Egypt garrison to be GOC 3rd Cav Div, Flanders Oct 1914; i/c Cav Corps June-Aug 1915. GOC IX Corps at Gallipoli, GOC XVII Corps, BEF, Feb 1916, to Cdn Corps 28 May 1916 — 9 June 1917. Took over Third Army from Allenby. Executed Cambrai tank attack but largely negated by German counter-stoke; staunchly held Arras sector in spring 1918 & played a leading role in the BEF's 'Hundred Days' of victory.

Left Army 1919. Gov-Gen of Canada June 1921-26. Commissioner of London's Met Police 1928-31; FM 1932. See *Byng of Vimy* by Jeffery Williams (London 1983).

Gough, Sir Hubert de la Poer   British General, 'Goughie'

b London 12 Aug 1879 son of Gen Sir Charles Gough VC; d London 18 Mar 1963 aged 92

Unlucky Fifth Army cdr at Passchendaele & Second Battle of the Somme.

Educated Eton & RMA Sandhurst; joined 16th Lancers 1889; Tirah Expedition (Indian NW Frontier) 1897-8. Wounded in S African War & able CO of mtd inf regt; Staff College Instructor 1903-6; Col 1906; Brig-Gen i/c 3rd Cav Bde at Curragh Camp, Ireland 1911-14, leading officers' 'mutiny' there during Irish Home Rule crisis.

Took bde to France, soon GOC 2nd Cav Div (9 Oct), Maj-Gen (27 Oct); transferred to command 7th Inf Div 18 Apr 1915 & led I Corps 18 July 1915-16. Controversial & at 45 youngest British army cdr (23 May 1916) whose 'cavalry spirit' may not have been a requirement for step-by-step trench warfare. Pre-Third Yres staffwork much criticized & Haig soon gave Plumer control of ops. Recalled by Lloyd George after German Somme breakthrough 21 Mar-5 Apr 1918 which he had done all he could to meet & which his army's sacrifice blunted.

Chief Allied Baltic Mission 1919; retired as General 1922. Briefly held high cmnd 1940-5 in Home Guard; chmn & director in electrical industry. Died almost totally forgotten. See his self-justifying *The Fifth Army* (Hodder, London 1931) & autobiographical *Soldiering On* (London, 1954). A Farrar-Hockley's *Goughie* (Macgibbon & Kee, London 1975) is a modern general's assessment.

Horne, Henry Sinclair, 1st Baron   British General & artillery expert

b Stirkoke, Caithness, Scotland 1 Feb 1861; d Stirkoke 14 Aug 1929 aged 68

Quiet professional Scottish gunner, least well-known of Haig's army cdrs, whose Artois sector First Army took brunt of Ludendorff's Apr 1918 Lys offensive & had a full share in the advance to victory.

Educated Harrow & RMA Woolwich; joined RA 1880. Extensive staff service in S African War; Inspecting Gunner 1905-12; Col 1906.

CRA BEF I Corps 1914; Maj-Gen Oct 1914; GOC 2nd Div Jan-Nov 1915 sending it into the Loos gas cloud ; with Kitchener to Gallipoli & Egypt 1915; GOC XV Corps (to France Apr 1916), using arty ably on the Somme & First Army, BEF Sept 1916; KCB Oct 1916; Lt-Gen 1917.

Gen 1919 & Baronetcy with £30,000; GOC- in-C E Cmnd 1919-23; Col Cmdt RHA 1918-29; retired 1926.

Plumer, Herbert Charles Onslow, 1st Baron Plumer of Messines 'Daddy' or 'Plum', British General

b Torquay 18 Mar 1857; d London 16 July 1932 aged 75

Won victory of Messines Ridge June 1917 by skilful use of surprise, arty & mines.

Educated Eton; joined 65th Foot 1876, first fought in Red Sea campaign 1884; Staff College 1885; Matabeleland 1896 (raised own mtd inf regt, Rhodesian Horse, at Bulawayo); S African War (led Rhodesian Field Force at Relief of Mafeking & flying col cdr); Maj-Gen 1902; GOC 5th Div 1905; Lt-Gen 1908; GOC N Cmd 1911-15.

Led V Corps at Ypres Jan-May 1915; Second Army 27 Apr 1915-9 Nov 1917. BEF in Italy, 10 Nov 1917-10 Mar 1918; Second Army 17 Mar-Dec 1918. Methodical & cautious cdr who used an able CoS Harington & liaison officers to keep the pulse of his army. Visually, but not in fact, the prototype walrus moustache for David Low's cartoon Col Blimp yet v popular with Dominion troops.

FM & GOC Rhine Army 1919; Gov of Malta June 1919-24; High Commissioner for Palestine 1925-8. Viscount 1929. See *Plumer, The Soldier's General* by Geoffrey Powell (Leo Cooper, London 1990).

Rawlinson, Henry Seymour, 2nd Baronet & 1st Baron Rawlinson of Trent, Dorset, British General 'Rawly'

b Trent Manor 20 Feb 1864 son of a maj-gen; d India 28 Mar 1925 aged 61

'... broke the Hindenburg Line, winning fame, a peerage in 1919 & a grant of £30,000' (Thorne & Collocott)

Educated Eton & RMA Sandhurst; commissioned into 60th King's Royal Rifles, India/Burma 1884-9 (ADC to Ld Roberts); transferred to Coldstream Gds 1892; Staff College 1892-3; on Kitchener's Sudan staff 1897-8. At Siege of Ladysmith Bvt Lt-Col 1899; led 2400-strong anti-Boer mobile col 1901-2; Brig-Gen & Cmndt Camberley Staff College 1903-6; GOC 2nd Bde 1907-9; Maj-Gen 1909; GOC 3rd Div 1910-14.

At War Office till selected to lead IV Corps for Antwerp's relief being diverted to Ypres, Neuve Chapelle & Loos; KCB 1915. Lt-Gen i/c Fourth Army 5 Feb 1916 & learnt the hard way on the Somme in Britain's first major attrition offensive. Not in the 1917 limelight but recalled (27 Mar 1918) from the Allied Supreme War Council to lead Fourth Army before Amiens, the outstanding British formation in 1918 victory.

Published *The Officer's Note-book* . Postwar, military worth recognized by dispatch to N Russia for the Allied evacuation and as C-in-C India from 1920. See *Life* from his journals & letters by Maj-Gen Sir F Maurice (London, 1928).

BETHMANN HOLLWEG, Theobald von   Imperial German Chancellor 'Lanky Theobald'

b Hohenfinow 29 Nov 1856 son of estate owner/district magistrate; d Hohenfinow 1 Jan 1921 aged 64

Read law at Strassburg, Leipzig & Berlin; entered civil service 1879; district magistrate (*Landrat*) 1886-96; rose in Prussian bureaucracy to Brandenburg Lord Lt 1899 and Interior Minister 1905; Reich Interior Minister & Deputy Chancellor 1907; Chancellor 1909; liberalized Alsace-Lorraine constitution 1911, but financial reforms failed, 1912 resignation rejected.

A tall stoic patrician who lacked debating and diplomatic skills, but studied Kant and played piano. Convinced Russo-German War inevitable but hoped Britain would stay out. Unable to assert political primacy over military before and during war or woo powerful interest groups. Lost a cavalryman Rhodes scholar son on Russian Front Jan 1915. Bungled Dec 1916 peace initiative and forced to allow unrestricted U-boat warfare. Fell over longstanding issue of Prussian voting reform that he wanted as basis of constitutional monarchy. Published 2 vols of memoirs (1921).

BÖHM-ERMOLLI, Baron von (1856-1941) (*see* AUSTRIAN GENERALS)

BOROEVIC, von Bojna (1856-1920) (*see* AUSTRIAN GENERALS)

BOTHA, Louis   S African General & PM

b Honigfontein, nr Greytown, Natal 27 Sept 1862 son of Boer farmer; d Pretoria 27 Aug 1919 aged 56

Orange Free State farmer; fought in 1884 Zululand succession war; Field-Cornet c1886; voted v Boer War but led commando, soon promoted Asst-Gen; Boer hero of Colenso & Spion Kop 1899-1900; Cmndt-Gen of Transvaal fighting at Doornkop & Diamond Hill 1900; Guerrilla campaign till 1902 Peace of Vereeniging which he signed with Kitchener; PM Transvaal 1906; first PM of Union of S Africa 1910 (*see* SMUTS for 1914-18).

BRUSILOV, Alexei Alexeievich   Russian General

b Tiflis 31 Aug 1853 son of noble-born general; d Moscow 17 Mar 1926 aged 72 from pneumonia

The one really talented Eastern Front senior Russian commander whose 1916 offensive crucially aided Italy and Verdun by mauling the Austrian Army, but unable to match this success in 1917.

From noble Corps of Pages into cavalry 1872; won gallantry medal in 1877-8 Russo-Turkish War; Cavalry School service ended as Commandant 1902-6; Divisional (2nd Gds Cav Div) and XII Corps Commander 1906-14; returned to Poland from German holiday 29 July 1914.

Led Eighth Army Aug 1914 - 4 Apr 1916 for Galicia's conquest and Carpathians campaign. Performed well in 1915 retreat, striking lethally at Austrian pursuers. Replaced the gaga Ivanov as C-in-C SW Front (4 armies). Planned offensive that achieved surprise (4 June) by hiding reserves and attacking along whole

200-mile front. Advanced 60 miles before stalled by Austro-German reserves and having to help a Rumania his success had brought in. Accepted March 1917 Revolution and made C-in-C by Kerensky (22 May). Replaced by Kornilov (1 Aug) after Germans counter-attacked his demoralized Army's short-lived July offensive. Retired until May 1920 Polish invasion when became Red cavalry adviser. Inspector of Cavalry 1923-4. Wrote *A Soldier's Note-Book 1914-1918* (1930).

BYNG, Julian Hedworth George, 1st Viscount Byng of Vimy, British General (*see* BEF ARMY CDRS)

CADORNA, Count Luigi   Italian Chief of Staff

b Pallanza on L Maggiore 4 Sept 1850 son of Gen Count Raffaele Cadorna; d Bordighera 21 Dec 1928 aged 78

A good organizer & strategist, but his Piedmontese aloofness & draconian discipline made him extremely unpopular.

Educated at Turin military school; entered Infantry 1866, on father's staff in 1870 capture of Rome and Papal States; Capt 1875; CO 10th Bersaglieri; General Staff Academy; Col 1892; Maj-Gen 1898; Lt-Gen 1905; offered post of CoS but his demand of right to overrule war minister rejected 1908; i/c VIII (Genoa) Corps 1910; Army-cdr designate 1911 but lost that year's manoeuvres. Accepted post of CoS July 1914.

Reorganized & expanded Italian Army Aug 1914-May 1915. Selected the French-made 75mm Deport field gun instead of a Krupp. Launched 11 (mostly futile) offensives on Italo-Austrian (Isonzo) front 23 June 1915 - 18 Sept 1917 that locked both sides into unrelenting attrition. Repulsed dangerous Austrian offensive in the Trentino (spring 1916). Captured Gorizia E of the Isonzo (8 Aug 1916). Ruthless in purging senior officers but slow to improve front-line conditions. Received most blame (perhaps unjustly) for 'Caporetto Catastrophe' (Twelfth Battle of the Isonzo) 24 Oct-9 Nov 1917. Replaced by Diaz, having selected Piave line of defence, & transferred to Supreme War Council at Versailles until Feb 1918. Recalled when Caporetto Parliamentary Commission of Inquiry set up, put on half pay (29 Aug), retired 2 Sept 1918.

Commission's indictment (belatedly published 1919) provoked his outraged reaction. Mussolini elevated a still-aggrieved general to Marshal of Italy 1924. See his *La Guerra alla Fronte Italiana* (Rome, Mar 1921).

CHARLES I, Francis Joseph   Emperor of Austria, King of Hungary 'The Peace Emperor'

b Persenbeug, Lower Austria 17 Aug 1887 son of Archduke Otto; d Madeira 1 Apr 1922 of lung infection aged 34

Educated Scottish High School, Vienna and Prague Univ; Lt-Capt 4th Dragoons 1905-12; married Princess Zita of Bourbon-Parma 1911; Maj 39th Inf Regt (Vienna) 1912; Heir-apparent after Sarajevo; served Galicia Aug/Sept 1914; promoted Maj-Gen summer 1915; CO new XX (Edelweiss) Corps in S Tyrol Mar-July 1916; Army Gp Cdr Russian/Rumanian Front 20 July-11 Nov 1916.

Francis Joseph's inexperienced 29-yr-old great nephew ascended tottering throne. Humanitarian and religious reforms but undermined Habsburg loyalists and encouraged separatists. Met Zita's Bourbon Belgian brothers but unwilling to press 1917 peace initiative to separate one without Germany so increased dependence on Berlin. Called off Battle of Piave 20 June 1918. Tried to keep throne as federal union and stepped down rather than abdicated. Failed in two 1921 attempts to regain Crown of St Stephen (Hungary). Died in exile on Portuguese Atlantic island.

CHURCHILL, Winston Leonard Spencer   First Lord of the Admiralty, Munitions Minister

b Blenheim Palace 30 Nov 1874 son of Lord Randolph Churchill; d London 24 Jan 1965 aged 90

Educated Harrow and Sandhurst; 2/Lt 4th Hussars 1895; Cuba, India and Sudan 1896-8; Boer War correspondent and PoW 1899-1900; Tory MP for Oldham 1900; Joined Liberals 1904; MP for Manchester 1906; Pres, Board of Trade 1908 (introduced 8hr coalmining day & labour exchanges); Home Sec 1910-11 prison reforms; First Lord of the Admiralty 1911, created War Staff, RN Staff College and RNAS; encouraged oil-fired warships.

Had Fleet ready for war and not a soldier lost at sea in 1914. Blamed for *Goeben-Breslau* Escape and Antwerp fiasco. Brought Fisher back to mastermind Falklands victory, but conceived Dardanelles-Gallipoli venture without adequate military or political backing. A tank pioneer and Room 40 enthusiast. Forced to resign and spent 1915/16 winter in trenches as CO 6th Royal Scots Fusiliers. Lloyd George recalled him as energetic Munitions Minister 17 July 1917. Published *The World Crisis* (6 vols 1923-31). '

CLEMENCEAU, Georges   French Prime Minister 'The Tiger', 'Father of Victory"

b Mouillerons-en-Pareds, Vendée 28 Sept 1841 son of atheist republican doctor; d Paris 24 Nov 1929 aged 88

Studied medicine at Nantes and Paris 1858-65; became journalist; US stay 1865-70; Mayor of Montmartre 1870; opposed 1871 Peace; Radical Party Deputy 1876; lost seat 1893 after Panama Canal financial scandal; championed Dreyfus; re-elected 1902; Interior Minister 1906 and Prime Minister till 1909; founded *L'Homme Libre* newspaper 1910.

Declined Justice Ministry in first wartime cabinet. Main critic of French govts especially in Senate. Villified 'botched' medical services and munitions shortages. Blamed Joffre and Millerand. Singled out Interior Minister Malvy as treasonable. Invited to form 5th wartime ministry Nov 1917. Policy 'I wage war'. Rallied domestic front and brought generals under political control. Employed able military adviser Gen Mordacq. Americanophile Churchillian oratory made him symbol of victory. Unable to get security for France he wanted at Versailles Conference. Defeated for presidency and retired 1920. Prolific writer, published *Grandeur and Misery of Victory* (1930).

CONRAD, Franz Count von Hötzendorf   Austrian Field Marshal

b Penzing nr Vienna 11 Nov 1852 son of colonel; d Bad Mergentheim, Württemberg 25 Aug 1925 aged 72

Austria's Chief of Staff and effective C-in-C for 60% of war, his imaginative paper plans cruelly overtaxed a polyglot Army. Visited Front only 3 times.

Graduated Maria Theresa Military Academy into *Jäger* regt 1871; Lt on Gen Staff 1876; Bosnia/Herzegovina Palmatra campaigns 1878-9, 1882; Major, War Academy Instructor 1886-92. CO 1st Inf Regt 1895-9, Bde (Trieste) 1899, Div (Innsbruck) 1903; Chief of Gen Staff 1906-11 (ennobled Aug 1910). Aided by heir-apparent Archduke Ferdinand, Conrad did modernize prewar Army especially in artillery and aircraft but eagerness for preventive war v Serbia forced temporary resignation (1911). CoS again 1912 - 1 Mar 1917.

Conrad's 1914-15 Galician, Serbian and Carpathian Campaigns proved bloodiest and most disastrous in Habsburg history. One success at Limanowa-Lapanow (1-17 Dec 1914) v Russia could not disguise a loathed but growing dependence on Germany. Mackensen executed Conrad's Gorlice breakthrough idea and Serbia's crushing. A pet 1916 Trentino offensive against Italy merely weakened the Eastern Front for Brusilov. Promoted FM 11 Nov 1916.

The new Emperor Charles eventually replaced Conrad and insisted he command S Tyrol Army Group, till complete dismissal 15 July 1918. Retired 1 Dec and wrote unfinished *From My Note-book* (5 vols 1921-5).

CONSTANTINE I, King of Greece 'Tino'

b Athens 2 Aug 1868 son of reigning K George I; d Palermo 11 Jan 1923 aged 54

Educated Heidelberg Univ, Germany and War Academy, Berlin 1886; served as Imperial Guard officer in Prussian Army; married Kaiser's sister Sophia 1889; failed disastrously as Greek C-in-C in 1897 war with Turkey; exiled 1909; returned under Venizelos 1910; Insp-Gen of Army 1910-12 leading it in First Balkan War, capturing Salonika, succeeded to throne 18 Mar 1913 after father's murder.

Pro-German by education and marriage, yet torn between belief in German victory and fear of Allied seapower. Rejected Kaiser's invitation to join Central Powers 2 Aug 1914 but twice thwarted Venizelos' 1915 attempts to join Allies, ruling through more pliant prime ministers. With military adviser & deputy CoS Col John Metaxas, the future dictator, urged Berlin to throw Allied Salonika troops into the sea. Allowed Bulgars to seize Fort Rupel (27 May 1916) and Greek IV Corps to surrender (12 Sept 1916) triggering Venizelos' open revolt from Crete. Uncertain role in 1 Dec 1916 'Battle of Athens' where his troops attacked Allied naval landing parties, but twice declined Metaxas' appeals to lead Greek Army on German side in N Greece. Forced into Swiss exile 6 months later.

Returned to Athens 19 Dec 1920 after Venizelos' electoral humiliation and, unrecognized by Allies, succeeded his dead son Alexander. C-in-C a third time in the last calamitous Greco-Turkish War that forced a second final abdication Sept 1922.

DANKL, Viktor (1854-1941) (*see* AUSTRIAN GENERALS)

DENIKIN, Anton I (1872-1947) (*see* RUSSIAN GENERALS)

D'ESPEREY, Franchet, Louis (*see* SALONIKA GENERALS)

DIAZ, Armando   Italian General

b Naples 6 Dec 1861; d Rome 29 Feb 1928 aged 66

Italian Chief of Staff for the last year.

Educated at Naples & Turin military school; entered Arty 1881. Fought in Ethiopia 1896 when Major changed to inf. As Regt CO w at Zanzur, Libya Sept 1912 in Italo-Turk War. Junior Maj-Gen 1914 & i/c *Siena* Bde.

DMO at *Comando Supremo* till promoted Lt-Gen to cmd 49th Div June 1916; captured Volkovniak on N Carso 3 Nov. Visited W Front Jan-Feb 1917. OC XXIII Corps on the Carso Apr-Nov 1917 winning success Aug. Succeeded Cadorna 9 Nov 1917. Halted Austro-Germans on the Piave & in the mtns & rebuilt shattered Italian morale much as Pétain had nursed the French Army earlier that year. With Anglo-French support cautiously repulsed final Austrian Piave offensive 14-25 June 1918. At eleventh hour

severely defeated Austrians along their whole front & advanced to Trent & Trieste (Battle of Vittorio Veneto). Dictated armistice terms signed by Austrian delegates 4 Nov 1918.

Promoted Gen & Insp-Gen 1919. Created Duca della Vittoria (Duke of Victory) 1921; War Minister under Mussolini 1922-4 until ill-health forced retirement.

DJEMAL PASHA, Ahmed (*see* YOUNG TURKS)

EBERHARDT, Admiral Andrei Augustovich (1856-1919) (*see* RUSSIANS ADMIRALS)

ENVER PASHA (*see* YOUNG TURKS)

EUGENE, FM of Austria (1863-1954) (*see* AUSTRIAN GENERALS)

FALKENHAYN, Erich von   German Chief of Staff &'The Butcher of Verdun'

b Burg Belchau nr Thorn 11 Sept 1861; d Lindstadt nr Potsdam 8 Apr 1922 aged 60

Germany's top strategist for nearly 2 years and then an army cdr in Rumania & Palestine.

Entered German Army 1880. Attended War Academy, Berlin 1880-90; joined gen staff. On staff of Count Waldersee whose multinational force suppressed Boxer Rebellion in China 1900; stayed with occupation bde till 1903, his reports reaching Kaiser. Col 4th Gds Regt 1911. CoS IV Corps 1912. Prussian Minister of War & Lt-Gen 1913-14.

De facto CoS 14 Sept 1914 (formally announced & promoted Gen of Inf Dec 1914). Foiled in autumn bid for Channel ports but in 1915 crippled Russia & crushed Serbia. Then conceived a novel & brutal strategy of attrition at Verdun that actually discouraged the fortress' early capture and became a self-defeating calvary. Dismissed 29 Aug 1916 following Verdun failure & Rumania's intervention. Major part in Rumania's overthrow as Ninth Army cdr. Sent to retrieve Turkey's fortunes in Palestine & Mesopotamia 1917-18 after the fall of Baghdad. His Germanic staff training achieved little in managing erratic & dilatory Turks, replaced by Liman von Sanders after failing to retake Jerusalem from Allenby. Tenth Army garrison cdr in Lithuania & Belorussia with HQ at Minsk Mar-Nov 1918.

Published *General Headquarters 1914-16, and its Critical Decisions*, (Eng translation 1919) & *The Campaign of Ninth Army against Rumania and Russia* (2 vols in German, 1921).

FEISAL ibn Hussein   C-in-C Arab Northern Army (*see* ARAB LEADERS)

FERDINAND I King of Rumania

b Sigmaringen, Germany 24 Aug 1865, nephew of childless King Carol of Rumania; d Sinaia, Rumania 20 July 1927 aged 61

From Hohenzollern Swabian Catholic branch, cousin to Kaiser; educated Tübingen & Leipzig Universities; German military service at Kassel; Heir presumptive to Rumanian throne from 1889; married 17-year-old British Princess Marie, grand-daughter of Queen Victoria, 1893; nominal Rumanian C-in-C Second Balkan War 1913.

Described by his forceful wife as 'modest, timid, doubting , but honest and unselfish'. Personal sympathies with Central Powers (2 brothers in German Army) & like Constantine of Greece convinced Germany would win, but followed PM Ion Bratianu's neutrality policy on succeeding his uncle 10 Oct 1914. A pro-Allied consort and Rumanian Transylvanian ambitions led him by mid-1916 to back Bratianu on entering war at opportune moment.

Within 4 months had lost capital and most of kingdom. Remained with battered Army in Moldavia, pledged both lands & electoral reform (5 Apr 1917). Constitution amended to allow splitting up of large estates (June 1917). This, French guidance & Allied supply revived the Army & kept it effective even during the Russian collapse that forced Rumania to armistice (9 Dec 1917). Avoided signing Peace of Bucharest thus helping Bratianu to claim Rumania had never left Allied coalition & to share spoils of Nov 1918.

Returned in triumph to Bucharest 1 Dec 1918. Attended Versailles which doubled kingdom. Crowned with Marie, Monarch of Greater Rumania at Alba Julia (Transylvania) 15 Oct 1922. Land reform only limited & Bratianu PM when he died at royal retreat.

FERDINAND, Tsar of Bulgaria 'Foxy Ferdinand', 'The Balkan Richelieu'

b Vienna 26 Feb 1861 son of Prince Augustus of Saxe-Coburg and Louis Philippe's daughter; d Berlin 10 Sept 1948 aged 87

Served in Austrian Army; chosen as Prince by Bulgar National Assembly 1887; married Princess Marie-Louise of Bourbon-Parma 1893 (†1899); dominated politics from 1905; declared independence from Turkey and himself Tsar 1908; entered First Balkan War but dream of Constantinople not realized 1912; attacked Serbia and lost gains to her, Greece and Rumania in Second Balkan War 1913; shifted from Russian alliance to Central Powers. Bulgaria's disproportionately large army earned his kingdom the title of 'Prussia of the Balkans'.

Cunning, eccentric and widely distrusted homosexual ruler who played waiting game for first year of war to revenge himself on Serbia and regain Macedonia. Apparently gained all aims with capture of Rumanian Dobruja (3 Sept 1916 - 6 Jan 1917). Unable to wriggle out of Central Powers' alliance as Germans ransacked Bulgaria for food. Vainly changed govt 18 June 1918. Eventually Macedonian front v Salonika collapsed and brought abdication in his son Boris' favour. Retired to old hobbies of ornithology and entomology.

FISHER, John Arbuthnot   British First Sea Lord 'Jacky'

b Rambodde, Ceylon (Sri Lanka) 25 Jan 1841, son of army capt; d London 20 July 1920 aged 79

Known as 'The Maker of the Modern Navy' but also opinionated, fiery & controversial.

Entered the Navy at age 13, 1854. Fought in Crimean War, China War 1859-60 & commanded battleship *Inflexible* at Alexandria bombardment 1882. Controller of the Navy, C-in-C N America & W Indies Stn 1897. British rep at Hague Conference 1899. C-in-C Med Fleet 1901. Second Sea Lord i/c personnel 1901; introduced new training scheme, established Dartmouth & Osborne naval colleges. First Sea Lord 1904-10 giving priority to Home Fleet. Ordered world's first 'all big gun' turbine-driven battleship, *Dreadnought* 1905. Naval ADC to K Edward VII 1904-10. Conceived the battlecruiser 1908; pushed order through Parlt for 8 dreadnoughts to be laid down in single yr 1909-10. Raised to peerage as First Baron of Kilverstone 1909. Chmn Royal Commission on Oil Fuel 1912.

Reinstated as First Sea Lord by Churchill 30 Oct 1914 & together

they contrived the Falklands victory. Initiated unprecedented warship building programme, using US shipyards as well, that sustained RN in the years ahead. Backed Churchill's rash plan for naval attempt to force passage of Turk Dardanelles. Resigned in high dudgeon on its disastrous failure (which he ought to have foreseen) 15 May 1915. Chmn of Admiralty Inventions Board; gave evidence to Dardanelles Commission 1917. See his idiosyncratic *Memories* (London 1919) & *Records* (London 1919) & his correspondence ed by A J Marder (London, 1953-59).

FOCH, Ferdinand   French Marshal and Allied Generalissimo

b Tarbes 2 Oct 1851 son of Catholic solicitor; d Paris 20 Mar 1929 aged 77

Outstanding prewar French military thinker who, from the age of 62, without previous combat experience, proved himself as a 1914-18 leader at the highest Allied level.

Served but did not fight in Franco-Prussian War. Commissioned 1873 & posted to Arty; Capt 1878; appointed to Gen Staff 1885; Major 1891; Professor at *École de Guerre* 1895 (Cmndt 1908-11); Col 1903; Gen of Bde 1907; attended 1910 Russian maneouvres; Gen of Div i/c 14th Div 1911; Cdr XX Corps (Nancy) Aug 1913.

Defended Nancy & made major contribution to 'Miracle of the Marne'. Commanded on NW section of W Front 8 Oct 1914-12 Dec 1916 working well with BEF and Belgians; demoted when his patron Joffre fell. Became peripatetic 'troubleshooter' charged with preparing contingency plans; appointed CoS 15 May 1917. Injured in motor accident. Successful morale-boosting tour of Italian Front after 'Caporetto Catastrophe'. Coordinator of Allied armies on W Front 26 Mar 1918; Generalisssimo 14 Apr 1918, supreme cdr of Allied Forces on all fronts.

Failed to persuade Clemenceau to a harsher, securer Versailles & grimly predicted a second world war. Remained adviser to French Govt and Pres Inter-Allied Military Commission. Visited USA 1921. Attended Haig's funeral. Published *The Principles of War* (1903, Eng trans 1918), *The Conduct of War* (1904) & *Memoirs* (trans 1931).

FRANCIS JOSEPH I, Emperor of Austria, King of Hungary

b Schönbrunn Palace 18 Aug 1830 son of Archduke Francis Charles; d Schönbrunn Palace 21 Nov 1916 aged 86. Venerable symbol of a paradoxical empire.

Served 1848 Italian campaign; succeeded mentally unstable uncle Ferdinand 12 Dec 1848; quelled Hungarian Revolt 1848-9; ruled as absolute monarch till losing Lombardy to Napoleon III 1859; defeat by Prussia 1866 forced *Ausgleich* (compromise) with Hungary — the Dual Monarchy in which crowned King of Hungary; *Dreikaiserbund* 1873; Triple Alliance with Germany 1879, Italy 1882; only son Rudolf committed suicide at Mayerling 1889; wife Empress Elizabeth murdered 1898; agreed to universal suffrage 1907; annexed Bosnia-Herzogivina 1908; 3 times rejected preventive war v Serbia 1908-12.

Followed rather than led post-Sarajevo policy, 'put my faith in the Austro-Hungarian Army, in its bravery and dedicated loyalty'. Resisted 1915 concessions to Italy and continued spartan routine of daily desk work. Tutored great nephew Charles. By Nov 1916 had lost hope of victory and contemplating separate peace. Knew that his cherished Dual Monarchy in dire peril. Much-loved figurehead whose death weakened already strained ethnic loyalties. Longest reigning European monarch after Louis XIV.

FREDERICK, FM (1856-1936) (*see* AUSTRIAN GENERALS)

FRENCH, Sir John Denton Pinkstone, First Earl of Ypres
British C-in-C BEF and C-in-C Home Forces

b Ripple, Kent 28 Sept 1852 only son of Irish-born RN capt; d London 22 May 1925 aged 72

Underwent 4 yrs' naval training, then left to join militia. Commissioned into 8th Hussars 1874; fought in the Sudan 1884-5; CO 19th Hussars 1889; Asst Adj-Gen of Cav 1892; OC cav bdes 1897-9; GOC Natal Cav Div with rank of Maj-Gen 1899; stormed Viljoen's camp at Elandslaagte 21 Oct 1899 & trapped Cronje's Boer army at Paardeberg 17 Feb 1900. Relieved Kimberley & thwarted all Boer attempts to invade Cape Colony. GOC Aldershot 1902-7; Insp-Gen 1907; ADC to K George V 1911. CIGS Mar 1912 appointment criticized as not a staff college graduate, but had extensively studied military ops & concepts in Europe. Resigned 30 Mar 1914 during furore surrounding Curragh Mutiny.

Led the original BEF ('Old Contemptibles') 4 Aug 1914 - 15 Dec 1915 & bore brunt of first German onslaught at Mons, during retreat to the Marne & at Ypres. Despite Joffre's emotional appeal failed to hurry pursuit to the Aisne during decisive First Battle of the Marne (allegedly inhibited by British Govt strictures). Was first senior British officer to urge large-scale HE shell production & 'the organization of the nation's industrial resources upon a stupendous scale'. Mistakes at Loos (Sept 1915) led to his recall.

FM & C-in-C Home Forces 19 Dec 1915-5 May 1918; Lord-Lt of Ireland 1918-21; created Earl of Ypres 1921. See his fallible *1914* (London 1919) & Richard Holmes' *The Little Field-Marshal* (Cape, London 1981) as the most recent & rounded biography.

GOUGH, Sir Hubert de la Poer   British General, 'Goughie'
(*see* BEF ARMY CDRS)

GREY, Sir Edward (Viscount Fallodon 7 July 1916)   British Foreign Secretary

b London 25 Apr 1862 son of baronet & Army officer; d Fallodon Scotland 7 Sept 1933 aged 71

Winchester & Balliol College, Oxford; Liberal MP Berwick-on-Tweed 1885; Foreign Office Under-Sec 1892-5; supported Boer War and *Entente Cordiale*; Foreign Secretary 1905; upheld French claim to Morocco 1906; main author of 1907 Anglo-Russian Agreement; failed to mediate Austro-Russian Bosnian Dispute; renewed Anglo-Japanese Treaty & obtained German recognition of French Morocco protectorate 1911; contributed to Balkans London peace conference 1913.

Commented on 3 Aug 1914 looking across Green Park 'The lamps are going out all over Europe. We shall not see them lit again in our lifetime', reflected pessimism at his eleventh hour failure to mediate after Sarajevo. Bungled efforts to gain Greece for Allies due to pursuit of Bulgaria and thus fatally handicapped Gallipoli Campaign. Signed secret Treaty of London with Italy but for heavy concessions. Not included in 11 Nov 1915 War Committee.

Signed Grey-House Agreement 22 Feb 1916 to get US mediation, but policy out of tune with Lloyd George's total victory aims. Worsening health and especially eyesight necessitated elevation to House of Lords. Replaced by Balfour after 11 yrs at Foreign Office. Ambassador to Washington 1919-20. Published *Twenty-Five Years 1892-1916* (2 vols 1928).

HAIG, Sir Douglas   BEF C-in-C & British Field-Marshal

b Edinburgh 19 June 1861, youngest child of a laird and whisky distiller; d London 29/30 Jan 1929 aged 67

Enigmatic & laconic British W Front C-in-C who saw in final victory but whose command methods, choice of subordinates, and earlier battles of attrition will always be debated.

Educated Clifton & Brasenose College, Oxford; entered 7th Hussars 1885; Capt 1891. Made daring cav recon missions during Kitchener's reconquest of Sudan 1898; commanded anti-guerrilla columns during S African (Boer) War which he began as Maj-Gen French's CoS; CO 17th Lancers 1903; Insp-Gen of Cav, India 1903-6; Maj-Gen 1905; War Office director 1906-9; CoS India 1909-12; Lt-Gen 1910; GOC Aldershot (I Corps) 1912; KCB 1913.

Led I Corps 1914-15 particularly ably at First Ypres & First Army through 1915. After intrigues, succeeded French as BEF C-in-C 18 Dec 1915 for duration. Summer 1916 Somme offensive made advances but at heavy cost. Prolonged Third Yres (Passchendaele) offensive of 1917 aroused vehement dissent, not least from Lloyd George. Clung on to cmnd, confident in the King's support & lack of rivals, with all his Scottish obstinacy. Rendered great service to Allied cause by warmly urging Foch's elevation to supreme cmnd during the great Mar 1918 crisis. Loyally supported Foch during the fierce defensive battles of Apr-July. His troops spearheaded the victorious Allied counteroffensives July-Nov 1918 achieving great victories largely masked in public memory by the trench warfare horrors of 1915-17. Resigned as C-in-C Home Forces Jan 1920.

Spent last years tirelessly fundraising ('Poppy Appeal') for disabled and disadvantaged ex-servicemen as first pres of the (Royal) British Legion; rewarded with OM, an earldom (of Bermersyde) & a grant of £100,000. Married daughter of 3rd Lord Vivian 1905. Laid to rest beside Sir Walter Scott in Dryburgh Abbey, Scottish Borders. Published *Cavalry Studies* (1907). See *Despatches 1915-1919* (1919 & 1979), *Private Papers 1914-1919,* ed Robert Blake (1952).

HAMILTON, Sir Ian Standish Monteith   British General

b Corfu 16 Jan 1853 son of army officer, d London 12 Oct 1947 aged 94

Gifted but unlucky Allied C-in-C at Gallipoli.

Joined 12th Foot from Wellington College & Sandhurst 1872; first action, Afghanistan 1879; wounded & disabled in arm, Majuba Hill 1881; ADC to Lord Roberts in India 1882-93; Maj 1885; served in Nile & Burma campaigns 1884-7; Col 1891; i/c Hythe Musketry School 1898; Boer War 1899-1902, led bde before and in Siege of Ladysmith, on Roberts' & Kitchener's staff, i/c 17,000 men at end as Lt-Gen; Chief of Military Mission to Japanese Army 1904-5; published *A Staff Officer's Scrap Book* (2 vols 1906-7); GOC S Cmd 1905-9; Gen 1907; supported Roberts with book on *Compulsory Service* 1910; GOC Mediterranean Cmd 1910-14.

GOC Central Force, England 5 Aug 1914-12 Mar 1915 & Kitchener's choice for land command of makeshift Gallipoli expedition. Protégé of Roberts & Kitchener, once recommended for VC, most experienced & talented general of his generation. Did well to inspire his force ashore at all. Unfortunately over-optimism and failure to supervise subordinates cost him dear, especially at Suvla Bay. Loved music, painting & poetry. Perhaps lacked necessary singlemindedness & ruthlessness to transform a campaign starved of all resources & deficient in staff work. Believed that evacuation meant 50% losses so lost his command; never to be re-employed. Published *Gallipoli Diary* (2 vols 1920).

HINDENBURG, Paul Ludwig von Beneckendorf und von
German Field Marshal 'The Wooden Titan'

b Posen 2 Oct 1847 son of officer; d Neudeck, E Prussia 2 Aug 1934 aged 86

Cadet Corps 1859; fought in 3rd Foot Guards & decorated at Battle of Königgrätz v Austria 1866 and v France 1870-1; War Academy 1873-6; Colonel & Regt CO 1894; Maj-Gen 1897; Lt-Gen i/c Division 1900; CO IV Corps (Magdeburg 1903-11); retired 9 Jan 1911. (*see* LUDENDORFF for 1914-18).

HOEPPNER, Ernst Wilhelm von   German Army Air Service Commander

b Tonnin auf Wollin, Prussia 14 Jan 1860; d 27 Sept 1922 aged 62

Cavalryman who was CoS Second & Third Armies (1914); res div cdr on E Front; served in First Battle of the Somme; made *Kommandiererden General der Luftstreitkrafte* ('Kogenluft') 15 Nov 1916. Awarded *Pour le Mérite* 8 Apr 1917 for administrative & operational achievements. Realizing German inferiority over Somme, hastened large-scale production, disbanded Army airship service and expedited development of long-range heavy bombers & all-metal cantilever monoplanes. Encouraged new tactics, training & instituted rewards. Developed large-scale ground attack methods for the 1918 Ludendorff Offensives. Retired 30 Sept 1919.

HOOVER, Herbert Clark   US War Relief & Food Administrator

b West Branch, Iowa 10 Aug 1874 son of Quaker village blacksmith; d New York City 20 Oct 1964 aged 90

Remarkable American businessman who headed international relief efforts during and after the war.

Graduated Stanford Univ as mining engineer 1895; worked worldwide in mining, railways & metallurgy beginning with finding gold in W Australia 1897; Chief Engineer Dept of Mines, Peking, China 1899-1900 helping foreigners during Boxer Rebellion; by 1914 London-based directing engineer for companies totalling 175,000 workers.

European War found him in London representing the Panama-Pacific International Exposition. Chm of American Relief Ctee 1914-15 funding & facilitating return home of over 100,000 Americans. Chm of neutral & international Commission for Relief of Belgium 22 Oct 1914; first 2300t of food reached Brussels 1 Nov. Organized food supplies for over 10m civilians (incl 2m in N France from spring 1915) using about 200 ships under special flag & over $950m in voluntary contributions. Shrewd appeals to public opinion overcame friction with German, British & Belgian authorities. By May 1919 Commission had imported over 5m t of supplies in 1213 vessels, employed over 55,000 volunteers, acquired $1.3bn worth of goods. Funding was 47% US, 37% Anglo-French & 16% elsewhere. Staple relief food prices remained 15-20% below those in Allied countries.

Summoned home by Pres Wilson to be US Food Administrator June 1917-1 July 1919; tripled prewar food exports to 20m t pa. Formed US Grain Corp and Sugar Equalization Board. Chm Inter-Allied Food Council. Argued successfully for temporary blockade lifting 14 Mar 1919 & sent in food to Germany without prior payment. Formed American Relief Admin & ran European communications to make it effective. Helped combat typhus epidemic in Rumania & Poland plus feeding 6m children & clothing 2m in Europe amid aid totalling $100m to 30 countries. As Sec of Commerce sent 1m t of food to 12m people in famine-stricken Volga region of the USSR, $60m aid without political strings Sept 1921-July 1923. Published *American Individualism* (1922). Career as 31st President (1929-33) forms a sad contrast to this unprecedented humanitarian record.

HORNE, Henry Sinclair, 1st Baron   British General & artillery expert (*see* BEF ARMY CDRS)

HOUSE, Edward Mandell   US Presidential Adviser

b Houston, Texas 26 July 1858 7th & youngest son of rich English-born planter & trader; d New York City 28 Mar 1938 aged 79

Eminence grise of American wartime diplomacy.

Educated Bath, England; New Haven, Conn & Cornell Univ to 1879. Managed cotton plantation inheritance for 10 yrs before selling up, gaining financial independence thereafter; campaign manager for 3 Texas Democrat governor candidates 1892-1902 when given honorary title of 'Colonel' which stuck ever after; met Woodrow Wilson Nov 1911 & helped secure him Texas & Bryan's support; met British Foreign Sec Sir Edward Grey 1913 beginning lasting friendship.

In some respects foreshadowed post-1947 National Security Advisers except chosen unofficial position as Pres Wilson's 'silent partner' much more wide-ranging. Loyally supported Wilson's neutrality policy but advocated 'preparedness' much sooner. Visited London, Berlin & Paris for 'peace without victory' mediation attempts 1914, 1915 & 1916 culminating in the Grey-House Memorandum.

Formed the Inquiry agency to collect data for peace conference from Sept 1917; Chief of US Mission to London & Paris becoming Supreme War Council US rep 1 Dec 1917. In spring 1918 drafted League of Nations convenant for Wilson; US rep in Armistice negotiations from 17 Oct 1918. Firmness & threat of US separate peace persuaded Allies to accept Fourteen Points as basis & smoothed over Pershing's 'unconditional surrender' demand.

Deputized for Wilson at Paris Feb-Apr 1919. More realistic than Pres & vainly urged him to conciliate Senate. Never saw Wilson after 28 June 1919, friendship just lapsed & both fell seriously ill (Oct). Continued annual visits to Europe & high-level contacts. Discreet, laconic but a brilliant sympathetic listener. Co-edited American peace conference delegates' essays in *What Really Happened at Paris* (1921).

HUSSEIN, ibn Ali ibn Mohammed   Sherif of Mecca, King of Hejaz (*see* ARAB LEADERS)

JELLICOE, John Rushworth, 1st Earl Jellicoe   C-in-C British Grand Fleet & First Sea Lord

b Southampton 5 Dec 1859 son of merchant navy capt; d London 20 Nov 1935 aged 75

Conscientious but cautious commander of the main Allied battlefleet.

Educated at Rottingdean & RNC Greenwich (entered Navy 1872); Sub-Lt 1878; Gunnery Lt 1880; bombardment of Alexandria & naval bde to Cairo 1882; Cdr 1893; Capt 1897; led naval bde during Boxer Rebellion 1900 (wia); mainly Admiralty shore service 1902-10, Capt of cruiser *Drake* 1903-4 Rear-Adm; 2 i/c Atlantic Fleet 1907-8; Third Sea Lord & Controller (construction of ships) under Fisher 1908-10; as Vice-Adm commanded Atlantic Fleet 1910-11 & 2nd Sqn Home Fleet 1911-12; Second Sea Lord 1912-14.

C-in-C Grand Fleet 4 Aug 1914 - 29 Nov 1916; full Adm 5 Mar 1915; Adm of the Fleet 2 Apr 1919. Devised controversial & rigid tactics later followed at Jutland, Oct 1914 & predicted that, if misunderstood, they 'may bring odium upon me, and might be deemed a refusal of battle'. Popular in Fleet but overworked &

reluctant to delegate. Must bear ultimate responsibility for *Hampshire* disaster of 5 June 1916 in which Lord Kitchener drowned within sight of land, a few miles N of the Grand Fleet's main anchorage. No lifeboat on standby & search & rescue procedures totally inadequate.

As First Sea Lord from 4 Dec 1916 initially opposed convoys during the unrestricted U-boat campaign, telling Lloyd George that they offered too big a target & that RN 'would never be able to keep merchant ships sufficiently together to enable a few destroyers to screen them'. Such objections soon proved groundless. Forced to resign 24 Dec 1917.

Published *The Grand Fleet* (1919), *The Crisis of the Naval War* (1920) & *The Submarine Peril* (1934). Gov-Gen of NZ 1920-4. Made Viscount 1918, Earl 1925.

JOFFRE, Joseph Jacques Cesaire   French C-in-C-'Victor of the Marne'

b Rivesaltes, E Pyrenees 12 Jan 1852 eldest of a master cooper's 11 children; d Paris 3 Jan 1931 aged 77

Known as *Pére Joffre* . 'Silent, patient, mathematical' (Thorne & Collocott).

Educated at College de Perpignan & École Polytechnique, Paris; Engineer Sub-Lt & bty cdr during Siege of Paris 1870-1. Distinctions in maths, military engineering & German. Eng-Lt in refortifying of Paris, Versailles, Montpellier & Pontarlier; Capt 1876; extensive colonial service 1885-1900: Formosa (Taiwan), Indo-China, Senegal, French Sudan, Madagascar (he & Galliéni fortified Diego Suarez). Major 1889; studied military railway ops; fortification lecturer at Fontainebleau arty school (recommended by Galliéni); led relief column 500 miles to Tuareg stronghold of Timbuktu 1894 (see his *March to Timbuctoo* 1915); Col 1897; Gen of Bde i/c 19th Arty Bde 1903; DG of Engineers 1904, Gen of Div 1905, i/c inf div (1906) & II Corps 1908; promoted to Gen Staff 1910; CoS July 1911. Drew up notorious Plan 17 entailing risky counter-stroke into Alsace-Lorraine in event of German declaration of war; attended Russian manoeuvres & decorated by Tsar 1913; drew up mobilization plan Apr 1914.

'His methods are well illustrated by ...the [First] Battle of the Marne. All the orders written by himself were already drawn up on August 27 [1914] for the action which began on September 5. He pondered them all out and then pieced the whole battle together bit by bit, like a delicate piece of mechanism which, when the time came, ran like clockwork.' (Lord Northcliffe 1915). After 'First Marne' partisans of Galliéni & Sarrail accused Joffre of treating the Gen Staff & Govt with contempt & organizing a military junta at *GQG* Chantilly. Galliéni, War Minister from 30 Oct 1915, questioned policy of disarming Verdun's forts & other frontier bastions. Bloody 1915 attrition (J's 'nibbling') tactics in Artois & the Champagne also drew protests. Tendered resignation but Govt would not release him (Oct 1915). Named C-in-C French Armies 3 Dec 1915 but character-assassination campaign continued with surprise of Verdun although it was ultimately Joffre's decision to hold it. Eventually (13 Dec 1916) a face-saving formula named him 'Technical Adviser to the Matters Appertaining to the Direction of War' with courtesy title of C-in-C while operational W Front cmnd went to Nivelle. Premier Briand & the French Senate objected. When Briand's nominee Lyautey became War Minister (25 Dec 1916) Joffre's 2 offices were suppressed.

Created Marshal of France 26 Dec 1916 (first since 1870). Accompanied French military mission to USA Apr 1917. Spent 1922-28 assembling detailed (if selective) *Mémoires 1910 -1917* (Paris 1932).

JOSEPH, Archduke (1872-1962) (*see* AUSTRIAN GENERALS)

JOSEPH FERDINAND (1872-1942) (*see* AUSTRIAN GENERALS)

KALEDIN, Alexei M (1861-1918) (*see* RUSSIAN GENERALS)

KEMAL, Mustapha, Pasha   Turk General

b Salonika 1881 son of Ottoman clerk; d Istanbul 10 Nov 1938 aged 57

Turkey's Great War military hero and founder of her modern state.

Educated Salonika & Monastir Military Schools 1893-99; Constantinople Military Academy Infantry class 1899-1902; War Academy, graduated as Capt 1905, Adjt-Major 1907; active in 'Young Turk Revolution 1908-9; CO 38th Inf Regt 1909; active service in Albania & Military Mission to Paris 1910; defended Tobruk & Derna v Italy and promoted Major 1911-12; Military Attaché Sofia 1913-14; promoted Lt-Col.

Opposed Turkey's Central Powers' alliance, yet more than anyone ensured its survival by decisive leadership at 3 critical moments in Gallipoli Campaign. Checked Anzacs in landing he predicted and again at Suvla. Promoted Brig-Gen & Pasha aged 35. Led XVI Corps in sole 1916 successes v Russians. Army Commander 18 Mar 1917 but protest letter on country's plight to Enver Pasha cost command. Accompanied Crown Prince Vahid-ed-Din's visit to Germany 15 Dec-5 Jan 1918. Reappointed to Seventh Army 7 Aug & rallied *Yilderim* remnants N of Aleppo Oct 1918.

Left Constantinople for interior and led nationalists to win Greco-Turk War 1919-22 saving Anatolia from partition. Abolished Sultanate. Proclaimed Turk Republic as President 1923. Took Western-style surname Atatürk ('father of Turks') 1934.

KERENSKY, Alexander Fedorovich   Russian Prime Minister 'First Love of the Revolution', 'Supreme Persuader-in-Chief'

b Simbirsk (on Volga) 4 May 1881 son of headmaster; d New York City 11 June 1970 aged 89

Father taught Lenin brothers; read history and law at St Petersburg Univ 1900-4; married Olga Baranovskaya daughter of Gen Staff colonel and cousin of several social revolutionaries; joined PSR and edited social revolutionary newspaper 1905; jailed briefly for joining plot to murder Tsar 1906; defence lawyer in political cases including for Dashnak Party before Senate 1912; elected to 4th Duma 1912 as deputy for Volsk (Saratov Prov) at request of Trudovik Peasant party; brilliant orator whose speeches gained working class following.

Duma immunity prevented 1914 exile after leading St Petersburg Bar protest v anti-semitism. Abstained from voting war credits (26 July 1914) but called war effort the 'great elemental force of Russian democracy' (7 Aug). Opposed Duma's prorogation (3 Sept 1915) calling for constituent assembly à la 1789. Tubercular kidney operation in Finland. Investigated Central Asia rising 1916. Secretary of the Political Freemasonry.

Central figure of March Revolution. As Justice Minister abolished ethnic and religious discrimination and death penalty. Co-builder of 18 May coalition in which became charismatic War Minister inspiring disastrous July offensive that nevertheless made him Prime Minister. Moved into Alexander III's Winter Palace suite and used Tsar's Rolls-Royce. New coalition wrecked by complex Kornilov Affair. Ordered commission of inquiry but leaks enabled Lenin to suggest he and Kornilov conniving for 'dictatorship'.

Petrograd's population and garrison withdrew support. Even so tried to retake the capital with unreliable Cossacks after the Winter Palace fell. Eluded Bolshevik pursuit reaching Helsinki 23 Jan 1918 to begin rest of his life as émigré activist and writer. Works include *Memoirs: Russia at History's Turning Point* (1965).

KITCHENER, Horatio Herbert 1st Earl of Khartoum & Broome British War Minister 'Lord K' or 'K of K'

b Ballylongford, Co Kerry (Ireland) 24 June 1850 son of Lt-Col; drowned off Orkneys 5 June 1916 aged 65

Imperial soldier par excellence & recruiter of Britain's mass armies.

Graduated RMA Woolwich 1870; Franco-Prussian War ambulance driver; Royal Engineers 1871; Palestine & Cyrpus surveys 1874-82; Egyptian Cavalry CO & Nile Expedition 1882-5; Gov of Suakin 1886-8; Sirdar (C-in-C) Egyptian Army 1890; Maj-Gen & KCB 1896; won Battle of Omdurman & retook Khartoum 1898; CoS to Roberts in S Africa 1899-1900, then C-in-C 1900-2 ending Boer War; C-in-C India 1902-9; FM 1909; HM Agent & Consul-Gen Egypt 1911-14.

On leave from Egypt & recalled from Channel boat to be Asquith's soldier War Minister. Foresaw long 3yr war requiring million-plus New Armies. Less gifted administrator, blamed May 1915 for shell shortage. Belated convert to Gallipoli campaign which stubbornly persisted in until personal visit finally converted him to evacuation. Offered resignation refused. Many responsibilities shouldered by new CIGS Robertson. Encouraged Arab Revolt that began day he perished en route to Russia on urgent supply mission. Unpopular with politicians but national hero whose death recalled like Pres Kennedy's.

KOLCHAK, Vice-Admiral Alexander Vasilevich (1874-1920) (*see* **RUSSIAN ADMIRALS**)

KORNILOV, Lavr G (1870-1918) (*see* **RUSSIAN GENERALS**)

KÖVESS, FM Baron von Kövessháza (1854-1924) (*see* **AUSTRIAN GENERALS**)

KUROPATKIN, Alexei N (1848-1925) (*see* **RUSSIAN GENERALS**)

LAWRENCE, Thomas Edward   'Lawrence of Arabia'

b Tremadoc, N Wales 15 Aug 1888 illegitimate 2nd son of landowner; d Bovington Camp Hospital, Devon 19 May 1935 after motorcycle accident aged 46

Complex British popular hero of 1916-18 Arab Revolt.

Educated Jesus College, Oxford University 1907-10; travelled in Syria, Mesopotamia, Palestine & Turkey from 1909; joined British Museum expedition to excavate Hittite Carchemish on Euphrates 1911-14.

Too small for Army proper (5ft 5in min height), assigned War Office Geographical Section. Commissioned 2/Lt 26 Oct 1914. Sent to Cairo to join military intelligence (later Arab Bureau).

Briefly involved in negotiations before Kut's fall 19-30 Apr 1916. As Capt landed at Jeddah 16 Oct 1916. Adviser to Emir Feisal whose army he got transferred N to Wejh (Jan-Feb 1917) for ops v Hejaz Railway. Secret Recruiting Mission to Syria (9 May-16 June) earned CB. Captured Aqaba 6 July after destroying Turk bn.

Gained increased support from Allenby 10 July. Promoted Major Aug 1917. Raided Hejaz Railway Sept-Nov, captured but not recognized by Turks before 23 Nov. Won action at Tafila 25 Jan 1918, DSO & Lt-Col. Persuaded Feisal to join advance on Damascus Aug-Oct, paralyzing 15,000 Turks with under 3000 Arabs.

Disillusioned by Arabs' treatment at peace, but mitigated it as Churchill's Colonial Office adviser 1921-2. Served incognito RAF & Royal Tank Corps 1922-35. Published *The Revolt in the Desert* (1927), *Seven Pillars of Wisdom* (1935), *Crusader Castles* (1936). Subject of over 30 biographies to date and a vast bibliography (1988).

LECHITSKI, Platon A (1856-1923) (*see* **RUSSIAN GENERALS**)

LENIN, Vladimir Ilyich   Russian Communist leader

b Simbirsk (on Volga) 22 Apr 1870, 3rd child of provincial schools inspector; d Moscow of heart attack 21 Jan 1924 aged 54

Elder brother hanged for complicity in Tsar Alexander III's murder 1887; graduated in law from St Petersburg Univ by correspondence 1891 after expulsion from Kazan Univ for student demo; joined Marxist group at St Petersburg 1893; visited Switzerland 1895; arrested soon after return; exiled to Siberia 1897-1900 where married Nadezhda K Krupskaya and wrote *The Development of Capitalism in Russia*; went abroad and split RSDRP into Bolsheviks (the majority) and Mensheviks at 2nd Party Congress 1903; returned to Russia Oct 1905 but had little impact; escaped via Finland; returned to Switzerland 1907; declared Bolsheviks true Marxist party 1912. (*see* **TROTSKY** for 1914-18).

LETTOW-VORBECK, Paul von   German General 'The African Hindenburg'

b Saarlouis 20 Mar 1870 son of Prussian (Pomeranian) general; d Hamburg 9 Mar 1964 aged 93

Colonial guerrilla warfare genius who only surrendered after Armistice.

Educated Potsdam Cadet Corps 1881; Cadet High School 1888; War Academy 1894. Capt 1901 while adjutant to FM Waldersee during Chinese Boxer Rebellion; helped Gen Trotha suppress SW Africa Herrero-Hottentot Uprising 1904-7 & promoted Maj; CO 2nd Sea Bn, Wilhelmshaven 1909; Lt-Col Apr 1913; i/c German troops E Africa Apr 1914.

Rare and unorthodox German colonial soldier who defended German E Africa with masterly skill & improvision using able subordinates & loyal well-trained black African troops. Twice wounded. Continued resistance despite misgivings of Gov Schnee after expulsion from colony 25 Nov 1917. With under 3000 men rampaged across Portuguese E Africa (Mozambique). Returned to colony & invaded N Rhodesia before surrender. Succeeded in main aim of tying down Allied resources away from main fronts. Admired by British, like Rommel in next war.

Returned home Mar 1919 & led *Freikorps* to crush Hamburg Spartacists. Had to resign from Army after Kapp Putsch involvement. *Reichstag* Deputy 1928-30. Opposed Hitler. Revisited E Africa 1953. Published *My Reminiscences of East Africa* (1920) & *My Life* (1957).

LIGGETT, Hunter   US First Army Commander

b Reading, Pa 21 Mar 1857 son of a tailor-politician; d San Francisco 30 Dec 1935 aged 78

Most prominent & successful 1918 American field cdr.

Graduated West Point 1879 as 2nd Lt 5th US Inf; 1880s frontier post service; Capt 1897; Philippines Campaign 1899-1901; Major 1902; Army War College 1909-10 as Lt-Col & its Pres as Col 1912; Brig-Gen 1913; Philippines 1915-17 i/c for a year; Maj-Gen 6 Mar 1917 & i/c W Dept.

Arrived in France ahead of his command, 41st (Sunset) Div, Oct 1917. Given I Corps 20 Jan 1918 despite Pershing's scorn for over-age fat senior officers. The walrus-mustached Liggett replied that this 'the more serious if the fat is above the collar'. Led I Corps in Champagne-Marne defensive/offensive ops of July as part of French Sixth Army & in Second Battle of Marne. Part of US First Army 10 Aug, his 4 divs formed right wing of St Mihiel offensive (12-16 Sept). I Corps advanced 10 miles through the Argonne Forest 26 Sept-12 Oct before given (as Lt-Gen) the whole First Army (16 Oct) of a million men & 4000 guns. Rested & rebuilt it On 1 Nov finally broke through Hindenburg Line & by 11 Nov forced Germans beyond the Meuse.

Held Germany occupation commands incl Third Army till July 1919, i/c IX Corps Area (San Francisco) until 21 Mar 1921 retirement. Wrote *AEF: Ten Years Ago in France* (New York, 1928). Attributed as saying "War provokes more muddled thinking than any human activity I know of.' British military historian Sir Basil Liddell Hart assessed him as 'the soundest reasoner and strongest realist in the American Army'.

LIMAN von Sanders, Otto   German General & Turk Marshal

b Schwessin nr Stolp, Prussia 18 Feb 1855 son of landowner; d Munich 22 Aug 1929 aged 74

Victor of Gallipoli and Palestine's 1918 defender.

Joined Army 1874; Cavalry 1879; Gen Staff 1887; Maj-Gen & Bde CO 1906; Lt-Gen i/c 22nd Div (Kassel) 1911; ennobled July 1913 (adding wife's Scottish name); Chief of 70-officer Military Mission to Turkey Dec 1913. Turk Marshal & Insp-Gen Jan 1914.

Bitter rival of Field Marshal Baron Colmar von der Goltz (1843-1916) who returned to Constantinople a third time (14 Dec 1914). Yielded First Army (Bosphorus) to Goltz for Fifth Army Gallipoli command (25 Mar 1915). Tactfully always had Turk staff. Toughness and ability to delegate scored defensive triumph. Tried to halt Armenian deportations to Smyrna Nov 1916. Sidelined training at Smyrna (Fifth Army). Replaced Falkenhayn as C-in-C *Yilderim* in Palestine. Repelled 2 Allenby attacks E of Jordan but only narrowly escaped capture at Nazareth in final collapse. Repatriated German contingent. Interned at Malta Feb-Aug 1919.

Retired Oct 1919 and published *Five Years in Turkey* (1919). Bavarian Col Kress von Kressentein (1870-1948), ablest member of Liman's Mission; led 3 attacks towards Suez Canal; defended Gaza 3 times; Caucasus mission 1918.

LLOYD GEORGE, David   British Chancellor of Exchequer & Prime Minister 'The Welsh Wizard'

b Manchester 17 Jan 1863 son of schoolmaster; d Ty Newydd 26 Mar 1945 aged 82

Barrister 1884; Liberal MP for Caernarvon Boroughs 1890; bitterly opposed Boer War; President, Board of Trade 1905; Chancellor of Exchequer 1908-15, introduced old age pensions and national health insurance.

Brilliant platform speaker with ability to sway and sense popular mood. Champion of small nations like Serbia and Belgium. Drew up 1st War Budget and crusaded v evils of drink. Favoured non-

W Front 'Easterner' strategy 'to knock away the props' of Germany. Became new Munitions Minister massively increasing war production and enthusiastically employing women.

Meant to accompany Kitchener to Russia but Irish troubles kept in London so replaced 'K' at War Office. Reluctantly witnessed Somme Offensive. Intrigued with press, Tories and BEF GHQ to bring down Asquith. Reduced Cabinet of 23 to 5. Loathed Haig but dared not replace him. Urged convoy system on Admiralty and picked Allenby for Palestine, but unable to prevent 1917 W Front offensive.

Autumn 1917 holiday restored morale. Main creator of Allied Supreme War Council. Wilson endorsed 5 Jan 1918 War Aims speech. Undaunted in spring 1918 crisis and supported Foch's elevation. Won Dec 1918 'Khaki' election. Compromise Versailles role between Wilson and Clemenceau. Had Danzig put under League of Nations and plebiscites held in Saar basin and Upper Silesia. Published *War Memoirs* (6 vols 1933-6).

LUDENDORFF, Erich   German General 'The Robot Napoleon'

b Kruszevnia nr Posen 9 Apr 1865 son of rural estate agent; d Tutzing, Bavaria 20 Dec 1937 aged 72

Joined Army 1883; Capt, Gen Staff 1895; Head of General Staff Mobilization Section 1908-13; Colonel i/c 39th Fusilier Regt (Düsseldorf) 1913; Maj-Gen & CO 85th Inf Regt (Strassburg) 1914.

With Hidenburg, one of military history's most famous pairings. Ran much of Germany's E Front for war's first half and whole war effort for the second.

Ludendorff boldly stormed Belgium's Liège fortress and was teamed with Hindenburg to avert disaster in E Prussia. Tannenberg made their names, enabling them to compete with Falkenhayn's W Front priorities. Hindenburg's (promoted Col-Gen 27 Aug 1914) imperturbability complemented his workaholic chief of staff's energetic mind. Masurian Lakes, Warsaw, Lodz and the winter Battle of Masuria all blunted the Russian steamroller, but Ludendorff's Vilna 1915 grand envelopment scheme was delayed too long by Falkenhayn to score decisive success.

The 'Siamese Twins' were elevated to supreme command 29 Aug 1916. Ludendorff promoted Gen of Inf. Immediately recognized need to retreat in West to new Siegfried Line (March 1917) and rapidly crushed Rumania. Hindenburg Laws passed on Home Front but Ludendorff's support for unrestricted U-boat warfare and Lenin's return to Russia proved disastrous in long run. By July 1917 the 'silent dictatorship' was powerful enough to overturn Chancellor Bethmann. Only clearcut military defeat in the West after Ludendorff's tactically brilliant but strategically bankrupt offensives dissolved the partnership 26 Oct 1918. Ludendorff lost 2 pilot stepsons to British action 1917-18. Hindenburg's son was a serving army officer.

Hindenburg remained an Army idol and a national one being elected 2nd Weimar President 26 Apr 1925. Lived long enough to appoint Hitler Chancellor whose early bids for power had attracted Ludendorff's support. Hindenburg wrote *From My Life* (1927), Ludendorff *My War Memoirs* (1919).

MACKENSEN, August von   German Field Marshal

b Schmiedeberg, Saxony 6 Dec 1849 son of landowner; d Burghorn nr Celle 8 Nov 1945 aged 96

Successive victor on Russian, Serb & Rumanian fronts; most successful German general outside Western Front.

Joined Cavalry 1869: Franco-Prussian War 1870-1; Gen Staff 1880;

Major 1888; Count Schlieffen's Adjutant 1891; CO 1st 'Death's Head' Hussars 1893; Colonel & ennobled 1899; Kaiser's Adjutant; Maj-Gen 1901; Lt-Gen i/c 36th Div 1903; General i/c XVII Corps 1908 (Danzig).

Led XVII Corps in E Prussia & Poland almost to Warsaw. Given new Ninth Army 1 Nov 1914. Took Lodz (6 Dec) & made Germany's E border secure, promoted Col-Gen and given *Pour le Mérite*. After being first to use gas (Bolimow - 31 Jan 1915), given new Eleventh Army 16 Apr to make decisive breakthrough at Gorlice-Tarnow (2 May). Aided by brilliant CoS Col Hans von Seeckt (1866-1936). Promoted FM on Lemberg's recapture (22 June) & given Army Group Mackensen 6 July.

Given new Army Group (+Seeckt) to knock Serbia out 16 Sept, achieved in 4 weeks. Led Army of Dobruja into S Rumania, crossed Danube & took Bucharest remaining occupation chief till 10 Nov 1918. Awarded Grand Cross of the 1914 Iron Cross Jan 1917. Interned by French at Neusatz till Dec 1919. Retired from Army Jan 1920 but in hussar uniform became respectable totem for Nazis. Published *Briefe und Aufzeichnungen* 1938. Attended Kaiser's funeral 1941.

MAHON, Sir Bryan Thomas (*see* SALONIKA GENERALS)

MANNERHEIM, Baron Carl GE (1867-1951) (*see* RUSSIAN GENERALS)

MARSHALL, Sir William Raine   British Lt-General

b Stranton nr Hartlepool 29 Oct 1865, son of solicitor; d Bagnoles de l'Orne, France 29 May 1939 aged 73

Educated Repton & Sandhurst; Sherwood Foresters 1885; Capt, India 1893; Malakand Campaig 1897; fought notably at Bothaville 1900; Maj 1908; CO 1st Sherwood Foresters, India 1912.

Successive victorious C-in-Cs in Mesopotamia 1916-18. Colonels in Aug 1914, both men rose fast; Maude from BEF III Corps Staff to GOC 14th Bde (5th Div) 23 Oct, (not far from Marshall's regt, soon in 8th Div), being wounded 12 Apr 1915 nr St Eloi. Marshall led 87th Bde across X Beach, Gallipoli (promoted Maj-Gen June), where Maude arrived in Aug as GOC 13th Div. Both shone in the evacuation.

Maude took 13th Div to Mesopotamia while Marshall commanded 27th Div at Salonika (Jan-Sept 1916). Maude, a precise non-delegating staff officer, restored morale, medical care and communications first as GOC Tigris Corps then as C-in-C. Marshall led III Indian Corps, making a personal air recce before Maude's deliberate ops recovered Kut and gained Baghdad.

Marshall was Maude's natural successor, scoring many victories before the armistice gave him Mosul. Lt-Gen Jan 1919, GOC India S Cmd 1919-23. Retired 1924. Published *Memories of Four Fronts* (1929).

MAUDE, Sir Frederick Stanley   British Lt-General 'Systematic Joe'

b Gibraltar 24 June 1864 son of general and VC; d Baghdad, of cholera, 18 Nov 1917 aged 53

Educated Eton & Sandhurst; 2nd Coldstream Guards 1884; first action, Sudan 1885; Staff College 1895-7; Boer War Guards Bde-Major, won DSO; Military Sec to Canada's Gov-Gen 1901-5; War Office & staff posts 1906-14.

MILNE, George Francis, 1st Baron of Salonika & Rubislaw (*see* SALONIKA GENERALS)

MISIC, Zivojin (*see* SERB GENERALS)

MITCHELL, William   American air commander & pioneer 'Billy Mitchell'

b Nice, France 29 Dec 1879 son of a US senator; d NY City 19 Feb 1936 aged 56

Leading US exponent of air power in practice & theory.

Inf Pte in Spanish-American War 1898; commissioned as Signal Corps 2/Lt; served in Cuba, Philippines Insurrection & Alaska; Army's youngest capt 1903. Graduated from Staff College 1909; joined Signal Corps aviation section 1915; learnt to fly 1916; sent to Spain as military observer & Major early 1917.

Framed AEF aviation programme for Pershing June 1917; put i/c first US air units in France. CO First Army Air Service & Brig-Gen Aug 1918 with 49 sqns; personally led 1481 Allied aircraft over St Mihiel from 12 Sept. Bad weather, shortening days & lack of time thwarted his ambitious plans for mass bombing of Germany but still used 200-strong bomber formations deep behind the Meuse-Argonne fighting. Awarded DFC.

Asst Air Service Chief, Washington 1919-25. Personally flew with his chosen Martin MB-2 bombers to sink stationary target of the ex-German dreadnought *Ostfriesland* (12in armour) with 16 hits from 67 bombs in Chesapeake Bay 21 July 1921. Outspoken advocacy of & writing for separate air force culminated in 1925 court martial & resignation (1 Feb 1926). Warned of air threat to Pearl Harbor. Posthumously awarded CMH. See *My Brother Bill: The Life of General 'Billy' Mitchell* by Ruth Mitchell (1953) & the posthumously published *Memories of World War I* : 'From Start to Finish of our Greatest War' (NY 1960).

MOLTKE, Helmuth Johannes Ludwig von   German Chief of Staff 1914

b Gersdorf, Mecklenburg-Schwerin 23 May 1848; d Berlin 18 June 1916 aged 68

Nephew of Helmuth Count von Moltke, great strategist & Chief of Staff to the victorious Prussian armies of 1864-71.

Entered Prussian Army as Inf Lt; fought throughout Franco-Prussian War. Lecturer at Berlin War Academy. ADC to Kaiser 1891; Lt-Gen & CO 1st Gds Div 1902-4; Gen of Inf & CoS succeeding Count Schlieffen 1906.

His 'improvements' to Schlieffen's master plan for a 40-day campaign v France followed by an equally rapid settling of accounts with Russia proved disastrous in Sept 1914. Chose to isolate himself first at Koblenz & later at Luxembourg, far behind the fluid W Front, proved quite unable to coordinate the immense ops of his 2 ambitious & antagonistic spearhead gens, Bülow & Kluck. Superseded by Falkenhayn & given indefinite sick leave. Posthumously published *Memories, Notes and Documents* (in German, 1922 & 1923).

NICHOLAS, Grand Duke (1856-1929) (*see* RUSSIAN GENERALS)

NICHOLAS PETROVIC-NJEGOS, King of Montenegro 'Nikita'

b Njegos, SW Montenegro 7 Oct 1841 nephew of reigning Prince

Danilo II; d Antibes 1 Mar 1921 aged 79

Ruler of the smallest Allied country (under half the size of Wales or 2/3 of Connecticut) with 250,000 highlanders in clans.

Educated Trieste & Paris before returning 1860 to claim the Prince's throne after his uncle's murder. Led Montenegrin Army v Turks 1862 (defeated); had 9 children by Princess Milena 1864-87; made Russian alliance 1868 and hoped to free fellow Serbs from Ottoman rule. Russian intervention offset 1876 defeats by Turks and doubled mountain kingdom's size, giving it Adriatic coastline. Eldest daughter Zorka married Prince Peter of Serbia 1883; daughter Elena married K of Italy 1896. Took title of King 1910 on golden jubilee, but Montenegrin exiles used larger neighbour, Serbia, to plot against Nicholas. Poor military showing in Balkan Wars.

National Assembly at Cetinje forced avaricious old Nicholas into war despite tempting Austrian territorial offers. Early offensive N failed Oct 1914; besieged Albanian Scutari to S instead. Faced Austrians alone after Serbia's fall and left for Italian exile rather than negotiate, as widely rumoured. From mid-1916 Serb Crown Prince and PM encouraged Montenegrin politicians to call for Nicholas' abdication. Serb Army entered Montenegro and France ordered Nicholas to leave Bordeaux late 1918.

Supporters defeated in first postwar election and deposed 26 Nov 1918. Died in second exile, maintaining govt-in-exile. Tall and powerfully-built, often in national dress, to quote an English writer 'carried well into the twentieth century the essence of Balkan medievalism at its best'. Body brought home & buried at Cetinje 1 Oct 1989.

NICHOLAS II Alexandrovich, Tsar of all the Russias ('cousin Nickie')

b Tsarskoe Selo Palace 18 May 1868 son of Alexander III; murdered Ekaterinburg 16 July 1918 aged 50

Personally attractive but politically inept ruler of Russia.

Private tuition; Imperial Guards; Far East tour 1891, just escaped murder by Japanese student; succeeded autocratic father 1 Nov 1894 & married Princess Alexandra (Alix) of Hesse-Darmstadt (Q Victoria's grand-daughter); had 4 daughters; then haemophiliac son Alexis 1904; reluctantly conceded Duma (Parliament) in 1905 Revolution after disastrous Russo-Japanese War.

Cousin to Kaiser & K George V, reluctantly signed July 1914 mobilization order. Chose uncle Grand Duke Nicholas as C-in-C. Stayed at Petrograd for first year apart from frequent visits to fronts & hospitals. Resisted Cabinet changes & widening political base. Took supreme command 2 Sept 1915 despite Cabinet's advice. Left domestic affairs mainly to his unpopular German-born wife with whom he exchanged loving letters in English. She followed Rasputin's disastrous advice because of the holy man's healing gift with their son. Appeared at Feb 1916 Duma but rejected its Pres Rodzianko's pleas for constitutional reforms then & year later. Abdicated en route from Mogilev HQ to capital at Pskov when told Army's front commanders would not support continuance on throne. Arrested with family by Prov Govt.

NIVELLE, Robert Georges   French W Front C-in-C 1916/7

b Tulle (Correze) 15 Oct 1856 of French father, English mother; d Paris 23 Mar 1924 aged 67

Gifted gunner unable to repeat his limited Verdun successes in a large-scale, broad front offensive. Instead it nearly crippled France.

Arty Sub-Lt 1878; Lt 1880; Capt 1887; active service in Tunisia, Algeria & China (1900-1); Lt-Col 1908; Col & CoS Algiers Div 1911; Col of 5th Arty Regt Dec 1913.

Invasion of Alsace, First Battles of the Marne & Aisne; in each his massed guns checked German attacks. Gen of Bde 27 Oct 1914 i/c 44th & 60th Inf Bdes, then 61st Inf Div (19 Feb 1915) on the Aisne. Gen of Div i/c III Corps 23 Dec 1915; Second Army cdr 27 Apr 1916. His arty work (long preparation & creeping barrages) was crucial in halting the German May-July Verdun offensive & recapturing Ft Douaumont 24 Oct 1916. Replaced Joffre as C-in-C French armies of the N & NE 12 Dec 1916. Radiating apparently boundless self-confidence, made extravagant claims for his 'method' in a poorly disguised spring 1917 offensive ('Victory is certain!').

This Second Battle of the Aisne proved disastrous (10 times predicted cas toll) for French Army morale raised to fever pitch by America's entry, their first use of tanks & Nivelle's grandiloquent promises. Within 4 days resorted to his predecessor's familiar attrition tactics. Pétain was speedily appointed CoS to restrain him; on 15 May handed over to the other 'Victor of Verdun'. Even now many powerful friends blamed War Minister Painlevé for Aisne disaster & he emerged unscathed from military court of inquiry (Oct 1917). In Dec C-in-C N Africa; returned home 1919.

Represented France at 1920 *Mayflower* tercentenary; retired 11 Oct 1921. Tragic & interesting figure who uniquely rose from regt CO to be his country's top soldier in 28 months & fell in 5. Charm & command of English captivated Lloyd George. His backing of tank development & creation (with Gen Buat) of the *Réserve Générale d'Artillerie* (lorryborne 75s, rail guns & tractor-drawn heavy guns) both bore fruit in 1918.

PERSHING, John Joseph   American C-in-C AEF 'Black Jack'

b nr Laclede, Linn Co, Missouri 13 Sept 1860 son of a merchant (Alsace, France ancestry); d Washington DC 15 July 1948 aged 87

With all the unbending, tight-lipped implacability of a Roman consul, stone-faced Pershing was 'a master of tactics with a rigid devotion to logistics, not a strategist' (Herwig & Heyman).

Passed entry exam to USMA West Point (graduated with hons 1886). With 6th Cav v Apaches & Sioux in Arizona, New Mexico & S Dakota 1886-91; prof of military science & tactics at Lincoln (Neb) 1891-2; First Lt 1892; tactical instructor at West Point 1897-8; Led 10th (Negro) Cav Regt at Santiago Cuba during 1898 Spanish-American War, winning Silver Star & his nickname; Regular Capt 1901. Suppressed Moro guerrillas in Mindanao, Philippines 1901-3 winning Pres Teddy Roosevelt's approbation. Married Wyoming senior senator's daughter 1905. Military attaché at Tokyo & US observer in Russo-Japanese War; controversially promoted from Capt to Brig-Gen 1906 (Roosevelt's recommendation) above 862 officers; Cdr Mindanao Dept Philippines 1906-13 again defeating Moros; Cdr 8th Cav Bde 1913. Wife & 3 daughters burned to death San Francisco Mar 1916 (son Warren survived). Led punitive expedition v Pancho Villa, N Mexico 15 Mar 1916-5 Feb 1917.

AEF C-in-C 10 May 1917; promoted full general Oct 1917; faithfully complied with orders to maintain independence of cmnd (except during W Front crises of spring 1918). Won Foch's assent to conduct all-US op v St Mihiel Salient (Aug 1918). This he triumphantly flattened out 12-13 Sept 1918. There & in subsequent 7-wk Meuse-Argonne AEF general offensive this punctilious & cautious C-in-C ruthlessly relieved ineffectual or half-hearted cdrs. Methodical approach censured in letter from Clemenceau to Pres Wilson (21 Oct 1918). Early Armistice dashed hopes of crossing the Rhine & marching on Berlin in spring 1919.

Uniquely promoted 'Gen of the Armies' 1 Sept 1919; CoS 20 Apr 1921-4; consulted by Marshall, Bradley & Eisenhower during

Second World War. Rests in Arlington National Cemetery. See *Final Report* (Govt Printing Office Washington DC, Dec 1919) & *My Experiences in the World War* (New York 1931, Pulitzer History prize 1932).

PÉTAIN, Henri Philippe   French C-in-C 1917/18 'Saviour of Verdun'

b Cauchy-la-Tour, Pas-de-Calais (nr Arras) 24 Apr 1856 of peasant stock; d Port Joinville, Ile d'Yeu, French Atlantic coast 23 May 1951 aged 95

Saved Verdun 1916 & the French Army 1917, policy 'victory at the smallest price'.

Educated St Cyr military school 1876-8; Lt in *Chasseurs d'Alpins* ; Capt 1890; Major 1900; Asst Inf instructor, *École de Guerre* 1901-7 (under Foch); favourite & unfashionable motto 'firepower kills'; Col 1912; CO 33rd Inf Regt at Arras.

Due to retire when war broke out, so slow had promotion been for an elderly Colonel who had served only at home. Rose from cmnd of a regt to an army in under 11 months. Combined appreciation of modern firepower in defence with the necessity of careful preparation for attacks & looking after the ordinary soldier. Imparted this lesson to important subordinates, especially Fayolle who took over from him both XXXIII Corps (20 June 1915) & Central Army Gp (28 Apr 1917). Broke German lines briefly to capture Vimy Ridge twice 9 May & 16 June 1915.

Masterminded Verdun's defence especially its heavy guns, tenuous supply route & regular rotation of divs (2-8 days) to share out the ordeal. Briefly eclipsed by a contemporary, & more aggressive & optimistic subordinate Nivelle. Promoted CoS (28 Apr 1917) to rein him in then replaced him as mutinies began to affect half the French Army. Indefatigable in visiting units & alleviating conditions while sparing with executions. Rebuilt morale with clearcut, limited & successful attacks at Verdun & Malmaison. Urged & obtained massive aircraft & tank production while waiting for US reinforcements.

Less impressive v Ludendorff's tremendous spring 1918 offensives; seconded Foch & Haig in victorious Allied advances. Finest hour of May-Dec 1917 amply deserved a marshal's baton 8 Dec 1918.

Long Hindenburg-like & ultimately tragic postwar career. Sentenced to death for Vichy years at a 1945 trial in which he said 'The French will not forget. They know that I defended them as I did at Verdun.' Sentence commuted to life imprisonment by his former officer De Gaulle. See *Thirty Years with Pétain* by Serrigny (Plon, Paris 1959).

PETER KARADJORDJEVIC   King of Serbia

b Belgrade 29 June 1844 son of reigning monarch Prince Alexander; d Belgrade 16 Aug 1921 aged 77

Shared in Karadjordjevic exile 1859; educated in Switzerland & France; fought for France in 1870-1; volunteer in Bosnian revolt v Turks 1876; married Montenegrin Princess Zovka 1883; younger son Alexander born 1888; returned home on K Alexander's murder 1903 & succeeded to throne; liberal constitutional ruler but seen as 'the Yugoslav King' as early as 1903; old & sick during June 1914 crisis over newly conquered Macedonian lands, compelled to step down for son Prince Regent Alexander (qv).

PFLANZER-BALTIN, Baron (1855-1925) (*see* AUSTRIAN GENERALS)

PLEHVE, Wenzel von (1850-1916) (*see* RUSSIAN GENERALS)

PLUMER, Herbert Charles Onslow, 1st Baron Plumer of Messines 'Daddy' or 'Plum', British General (*see* BEF ARMY CDRS)

POLIVANOV, Aleksei (1855-1920) (*see* RUSSIAN GENERALS)

PUTNIK, Radomir (*see* SERB GENERALS)

RAWLINSON, Henry Seymour, 2nd Baronet & 1st Baron Rawlinson of Trent, Dorset   British General 'Rawly' (*see* BEF ARMY CDRS)

RICHTHOFEN, Manfred Freiherr (Baron) von   German 'Ace of aces', 'Red Knight'

b Breslau 2 May 1892 son of a Silesian nobleman officer; d nr Villers-Brettoneux, Somme 21 Apr 1918 aged 25

Top-scoring 1914-18 fighter pilot (80 victories). Rescued from E Front obscurity by the visiting Boelcke, who very quickly detected remarkable qualities (*'That is the man!'*)

Educated military school & Royal Prussian Military Academy from 1903; Lt in 1st Uhlan (Lancer) Regt 1912; fought in cav on E & W Fronts Aug-Sept 1914, before transfer to inf; promoted Rittmeister (Capt). After much pleading accepted for 4wks flying training May 1915. Trained as observer & again posted to E Front; transfer to BAO bomber unit Aug 1915, survived first solo landing Oct; qualified as pilot 25 Dec 1915. First confirmed victory on first patrol with Boelcke over Somme 17 Sept 1916 after unconfirmed Nieuport over Verdun 16 Mar; shot down first RFC ace Hawker 23 Nov 1916. Given cmnd of *Jasta 11* & awarded *Pour le Mérite* 16 Jan 1917; now flying a blood-red Albatros. Shot down by British aircraft 9 March 1917 but again escaped injury. *Jagdgeschwader 1* alias 'Richthofen Circus' ('Flying Circus') formed 24 June 1917, with 4 subordinate units: *Jasta 4* (Doering); *Jasta 6* (Dostler), *Jasta 10* (Althaus) & *Jasta 11* (Wolff). Received head wound 6 July from Lt A W Woodbridge (FE2 of No 20 Sqn) & hospitalized at Courtrai for 3wks. Returned to duty: '... never quite the same again, but he continued to give inspiring leadership and did not spare himself' (Nowarra). Killed in his favourite Fokker Triplane.

Buried with military honours by the Australians at Bertangles. Younger brother Lothar, an able companion pilot, scored 40 victories. Body exhumed & taken to the Berlin Invalide 1935. See Floyd Gibbons' *The Red Air Fighter* (London 1918); *Von Richthofen and the 'Flying Circus'* by H J Nowarra & Kimbrough S Brown (Letchworth, Herts 1959).

ROBERTSON, Sir William Robert   British CIGS 'Wully'

b Welbourn, Lincs 29 Jan 1860 son of a village tailor; d London 12 Feb 1933 aged 73

Unyielding 'Westerner' who directed all British land strategy from Kitchener's death until own resignation.

First & only soldier in the British Army to rise from private to the highest rank. Enlisted as trooper in 16th Lancers 1877, saw cav service at home & in India; wounded & won DSO in Chitral Relief Force, NW Frontier 1895; first 'ranker' admitted to Staff College, Camberley 1897-8 (commissioned 1888); War Office Intelligence Div 1898-99, 1902-7; on staffs of Roberts & Kitchener in S Africa 1899-1902 rising to bvt Lt-Col; Col 1903; Staff College Cmdt & Maj-Gen 1910-13; Director Military Training, War Office 1913-14.

QMG BEF 4 Aug 1914 - 24 Jan 1915; CoS BEF 25 Jan - 22 Dec 1915, promoted Lt-Gen; CIGS 23 Dec 1915 - 18 Feb 1918; Gen 1916; GCB 1917; GOC- in-C Home Forces 30 May 1918. Worked well with Haig; made excellent choices of Milne (Salonika) & Maude (Mesopotamia) for the peripheral theatres; improved War Office admin. Resigned Feb 1918 after protracted debate with Lloyd George over W Front manpower demands. C-in-C British forces on the Rhine 22 Apr 1919-19 Mar 1920; FM 1920. See his *From Private to Field-Marshal* (London, 1921) & *Soldiers and Statesmen 1914 -18* (London, 1926); also *Papers 1915-18* (Army Record Society, 1990).

RUPPRECHT, ('Rupert'), Crown Prince of Bavaria & German W Front army group cdr

b Munich 18 May 1869 eldest son of Ludwig III, King of Bavaria & Archduchess Maria Theresa of Austria-Este, theoretical claimant to the British throne through descent from Prince Rupert of the Rhine, nephew of Charles I; d Leustetten, Bavaria 2 Aug 1955 aged 86

Perhaps the last major European royal figure to hold a lengthy, real & important military command successfully (Prince Leopold of Bavaria on the E Front 1915-18 apart).

Entered Imperial German Army as Lt in Bav regt 1886; visited India 1899; made round-the-world voyage 1902-3 (account published 1905); CO I Bav Corps 1906; Insp-Gen 1913.

Led Sixth Army (with able CoS Kraft von Dellmensingen) 2 Aug-23 Sept 1914, commanded on the Lys when switched to Flanders Oct 1914. Prominent in First Ypres; later held German line from Ypres to Arras & saw much action; Army Gp Cdr from 28 Aug 1916; commanded front from the Oise to the sea 1917.

Nov 1918 Revolution ended all prospects of succeeding to Bav throne, which he renounced. Head of the Wittelsbachs by death of Ludwig III Oct 1921. Declined to participate in 1923 Ludendorff-Hitler Munich *Putsch* or the 1933 Nazi seizure of power. Published revealing & wide-ranging war diary 1929. Left Germany for Italy, only returning at end of Second World War.

RUSSIAN ADMIRALS' PROFILES

Tsarist naval leadership lay under the shadow of the defeats and mutinies of the disastrous 1904-5 Russo-Japanese War. The many technical improvements and heavy expenditure since had not restored Russia to being the world's third naval power, nor had it eradicated the gulf between a majority factory-worker lower deck and an aristocratic, often Baltic-German officer corps which had too few regular petty officers to keep discipline.

Admiral Nikolai Ottovich **von Essen** (1860-1915) was probably the ablest Fleet commander and certainly fortunate in dying long before inactivity and revolution demoralized his Baltic Fleet. Commanded a battleship and fought ashore at Port Arthur (1904-5), promoted rear-admiral (1908) and, given Baltic Fleet in 1909, obtained control of Gulf of Finland Coast defences in Aug 1912, mining its entrance and within to thwart the superior German Navy.

Put under Sixth Army around Petrograd and compelled to keep his battleships at anchor, nevertheless sent well-trained cruisers and destroyers on long night minelaying offensive sorties to hinder German shipping between the Kiel Canal and Baltic ports. Failed to get permission to strike at iron ore traffic between Sweden and Germany. His only son Otto was awarded DSC for liaison work aboard the British submarine *E9* and lost as a Lt-Cdr commanding Russian submarine *AG14* in 1917.

Essen's senior, Admiral Andrei Augustovich **Eberhardt** (1856-

1919) born at Patras, Greece of Russo-Swedish birth, also captained a battleship in 1904-5. Headed new Naval General Staff by 1908, took over the Black Sea Fleet as a vice-admiral in 1911. Achieved training successes despite 1912 mutiny.

Forced by *Goeben* and *Breslau* to use limited mine stock defensively till mid-1915 when two new dreadnoughts ready, was able to bombard Turk coal mines at Zonguldak but then faced German U-boats and hostile Bulgaria. Efficiently assisted Yudenich's Caucasus Army's amphibious operations towards Trebizond in early 1916 until replaced by younger more dynamic Kolchak.

Vice-Admiral Alexander Vasilevich **Kolchak** (1874-1920), descended from a 1730s Turk PoW and son of a Crimean War military engineer, first achieved prominence as a Lt on 1900-4 North Pole expeditions. Commanded a destroyer and a shore battery at Port Arthur. Returned from Japanese captivity to serve on new Naval General Staff. At own request given a destroyer under Essen (1912).

As staff and sea-going captain enthusiastically implemented Essen's strategy of offensive minelaying. Led 4 destroyers to mine Danzig approaches 12-16 Feb 1915. Active in Gulf of Riga, Aug 1915. Promoted rear-admiral spring 1916 aged 41. Sent to command Black Sea Fleet 16 July 1916. Stepped up mining ops and mounted a World War II-presaging seaplane carrier strike on Bulgaria's port of Varna. Even envisaged early 1917 attack on Dardanelles. Kept control until well after March Revolution and resigned 19 June throwing sword and Cross of St George overboard in protest at increased fleet cttees. Sent to Washington to discuss future co-operation with US Navy. On way home via Japan his tragic career as a White Russian leader began.

RUSSIAN GENERALS' PROFILES

Brusilov apart, command on Russia's main front ranged from disastrous to barely competent. **Grand Duke Nicholas** (1856-1929) was a popular figurehead C-in-C when real power lay with the Front commanders (NW & SW pulling v Germany and Austria respectively). The Tsar replaced his uncle but left the work to his Chief of Staff Gen Mikhail V **Alexeiev** (1857-1918), a dedicated but uninspiring staff officer and son of a private soldier who later created the White Volunteer Army at the Civil War's start.

Army, front & corps commanders were reshuffled with alarming regularity up or down to new levels of mediocrity. Only Platon A **Lechitski** (1856-1923) of Ninth Army enjoyed continuity and success, mainly over the Austrians. Many commanders (eg Rennenkampf, Sievers, Evert) suffered from suspicion over their German names when in reality their elderly inefficiency did not need treachery as well.

Russia's shortage of talent was symbolized by the recall of Alexei N **Kuropatkin** (1848-1925), arch-bungler of the 1904-5 Russo-Japanese War, to corps, army and then N Front command (late 1915-July 1916). Shell shortage was the excuse that all too often disguised pessimism, lethargy and ill-health. Of others over 60, Wenzel von **Plehve** (1850-1916), heading Fifth Army in Poland, and Aleksei **Polivanov**(1855-1920), at the War Ministry (26 June 1915-29 Mar 1916), used brief opportunities to display some ability. The latter succeeded Vladimir A **Sukhomlinov** (1848-1926) whose prewar reform work was overshadowed by legendary corruption that received a life prison sentence from the Provisional Govt.

Fighting divisional commanders like the Cossack Alexei M **Kaledin** (1861-1918) and the Siberian Lavr G **Kornilov** (1870-1918) were promoted beyond their level of ability. Anton I **Denikin** (1872-1947) led a superb division in 1916-17, but as with his later cavalry subordinate and abler successor Baron Peter N **Wrangel** (1878-1928), 1916 CO of the Tsarevich's Nerchinsk Cossack Regt, larger military opportunities came with the Civil War. In the long run the outstanding figure was not Russian at all but the Finn Baron Carl GE **Mannerheim** (1867-1951). From being a 1917 Tsarist cavalry corps cdr he won the 1918 Civil War in his country, and rose to become Marshal and President of Finland. He alone of the White generals surmounted the unprecedented political maelstroms unleashed by the 1917 revolutions.

SALONIKA GENERALS' PROFILES

Franchet **d'Esperey**, Louis   French W Front General & Allied C-in-C in Macedonia 'Desperate Frankie'

b Mostaganem, Algeria 25 May 1856; d Amancet, Tarn (S France) 8 July 1942 aged 86

Vigorous, long-serving W Front cdr who, like Allenby, found his moment in an overseas theatre.

Educated privately & at St Cyr Military Academy; entered Army 1876; fought in Tunisia, Indo-China, China & Morocco 1881-1913

Led I Corps in 1914 Fifth Army which he soon took over; won victories at Guise & Montmirail (Marne) 29 Aug/4 Sept 1914; C-in-C E Army Gp 4 Apr 1916; N Army Gp 27 Dec 1916. Consolidated last-ditch French positions on Reims-Villers-Cotterêts line after 27 May 1918 loss of the Chemin des Dames. C-in-C Army of the Orient 18 June 1918; launched general offensive Sept which speedily routed Bulgar armies & drove Bulgaria out of the war, freed Belgrade, then drove Austro-Germans from Serbia.

Led Allied occupation forces in Turkey-in-Europe until Nov 1920; received marshal's baton 1921; Insp-Gen of N Africa troops 1923-31; injured in Tunisia car accident 1933. Supported early 1930s French Fascist 'Leagues'; in 1937, now an invalid, actively associated with notorious Fascist murder gang the CSAR (or 'Cagoulards') which received arms from the Axis. Died in Vichy France keeping a revolver against German occupation. Many English works erroneously give his name an accent. See *Avec Franchet d'Esperey en 1914* by Gen de Marmies (Sabretache 1960).

Mahon, Sir Bryan Thomas   British General

b Co Galway, Ireland 1862 of Anglo-Irish family; d Dublin 24 Sept 1930 aged 68

Cav leader with long colonial service.

Entered 8th Hussars 1883; fought in Sudan & S African Wars (relieved Mafeking); Gov of Kordofan 1901-4; GOC Belgaum & then Lucknow Div, India 1904-13; Lt-Gen 1913.

Trained 10th (Irish) New Army Div & led it at Gallipoli & in Greece; C-in-C British forces at Salonika 28 Oct 1915 - 9 May 1916: C-in-C Ireland 9 Nov 1916 - 9 May 1918 for difficult period after the Easter Rising. Military cdr Lille 1918-19; KCB 1922. Irish Free State senator 1922.

Milne, George Francis, 1st Baron of Salonika & Rubislaw.   British General 'Uncle George'

b Aberdeen 5 Nov 1866; d London 23 Mar 1948 aged 81

Educated Gymnasium, Aberdeen & RMA Woolwich. Entered RA 1885; served in India; fought at Battle of Omdurman & S African War (bvt Lt Col & DSO 1902); Staff appointments 1901-13 (Col 1905).

Brig-Gen & CRA 4th Div 1913-15; Chief staff officer to Second Army (Second Ypres) 1915; GOC 27th Div July 1915; C-in-C British forces at Salonika 9 May 1916-26 Nov 1918 conscientiously holding the ring, keeping up morale and humouring allies in a thankless cmnd; twice had to launch costly pinning attacks v

strongest Bulgar defences around L Doiran.

C-in-C Army of the Black Sea (1 div + other troops = 34,125 all ranks 3 Apr 1920) 1919-21; Col Cmdt, RA 1918-48; CIGS & FM 1926-33; Air Raid Precautions Warden, London 1939-45. Founded Salonika Assoc.

Sarrail, Maurice Paul Emmanuel   French General, Allied C-in-C Salonika

b Carcassone 6 Apr 1856; d Paris 23 Mar 1929 aged 73

A flamboyant political general of inconsistent military achievement, called 'the only Republican general' because of his anti-clericalism.

Educated St Cyr Military Academy; joined Army 1875 as Lt in *Chasseurs-a-Pied*; in Algeria 1877-8; as Lt in Foreign Legion 1882 fought in Tunisia & Algeria; Capt 1887; Major 1897; Cmdt Inf School 1901; Lt-Col 1902; Col & CO 39th Inf Regt 1905; Director of Inf 1907-11; Gen of Div (12th) 1911; OC VIII & VI Corps 1913-14.

Commanded Third Army 2 Sept 1914 (First Battle of the Marne) - 22 July 1915; C-in-C French 'Army of the Orient' at Salonika 5 Aug 1915; C-in-C Allied forces at Salonika Jan 1916; *Médaille Militaire* Sept 1917; recalled 10-22 Dec 1917; placed on reserve (age limit 62) 6 Apr 1918.

High Commissioner in Syria v Druze rising 1923-5, recalled after bombarding Damascus. See his *Mon Commandement en Orient* (Paris 1920).

SARRAIL, Maurice Paul Emmanuel (*see* SALONIKA GENERALS)

SCHEER, Reinhard von   German High Seas Fleet Cdr 'The Man with the Iron Mask'

b Obernkirchen, nr Kassel 30 Sept 1863 son of teacher; d Marktredwitz 26 Nov 1928 aged 65

A protégé of Tirpitz. Able, energetic & more ruthless than predecessor Pohl. Advocated unrestricted U-boat warfare & battlecruiser/Zeppelin raids on English coast to tempt British Fleet to action under conditions of German local superiority.

Entered Navy 1879; active service in Cameroons & E Africa 1884 & 1889; torpedo service 1889-1900; Navy Office 1903. Capt of battleship *Elsass* 1907-8; High Seas Fleet CoS to Holtzendorf 1909; Head, Gen Dept Navy Office 1911-13; Vice-Adm i/c 2nd Battleship (pre-dreadnought) Sqn 1913.

CO 3rd Battleship (dreadnought) Sqn 25 Dec 1914; Chief of High Seas Fleet 24 Jan 1916-11 Aug 1918. Suppressed but could not remove its mutinous tendencies June-Sept 1917; Chief of Supreme Navy Cmnd 11 Aug-9 Nov until dismissed by Kaiser. Official retirement date 17 Dec 1918. See his *Germany's High Sea Fleet in the World War* (London, 1920) claiming Jutland as a victory.

SERB GENERALS' PROFILE

Mišić, Zivojin   Serb Voivode (Field Marshal)

b Stuganik nr Valjevo W Serbia July 1855 of peasant stock; d Belgrade 20 Jan 1921 aged 65

Trained as gunner; fought Turks as cadet 1876-8; Bn CO in war with Bulgaria 1885; studied in Austria 1887; Gen Staff 1891, succeeded Putnik as Deputy CoS; pensioned off by 1903 military revolt; 1909 Bosnian Crisis & Putnik recalled him to old post;

helped Putnik modernize Army and in Kumanovo victory (23 Oct 1912); shone at Battle of Bregalnitsa v Bulgars (2-27 July 1913); retired list Sept 1913.

Recalled by Putnik to be his deputy. Led First Army in month-long Nov 1914 retreat & spearheaded Dec counter-stroke, for which promoted field marshal (*voivode*). Twice outvoted trying to launch offensive v Central Powers in autumn 1915. Fell ill during retreat to sea, convalesced in France. Reassumed First Army command Sept 1916, regaining first Serb soil (heights of Kaj-mak-Calan) from Bulgars (19 Sept). Promoted CoS 1 July 1918. Convinced Crown Prince Alexander and kindred spirit Franchet d'Esperey that Balkans stalemate could be broken. Planned & directed 14 Sept-11 Nov victorious advance back to Belgrade. Cyril Falls called him 'the ablest soldier of the Balkan countries'.

Putnik, Radomir   Serb Voivode (Field Marshal)

b Kragujevac SE of Belgrade 1847; d Nice 17 May 1917 aged 70

Trained as gunner; fought Turks 1876-8; studied in Russia; Gen Staff 1884; fought in 1885 Serb-Bulgar War; Col 1889; Deputy CoS 1890; taught at Belgrade Military Academy; Radical Party links led to pensioning off 1895-1903; military revolt of 1903 made him CoS & general; 3 times War Minister 1904-14, modernizing Army; won Battles of Kumanovo and Monastir in First Balkan War 1912, promoted field marshal; defeated Bulgaria in Second Balkan War.

At Austrian Bad Gleichenberg health resort July 1914, owed return home and 5th war to Francis Joseph's personal intervention. Shattered two 1914 Austrian invasions by masterly retirements that culminated in carefully-timed counter-offensives. Faced by 3 enemies and hopeless odds from 6 Oct 1915 yet denied Mackensen battle of annihilation with well-timed series of retreats. Ordered final one to Adriatic 25 Nov when too ill to walk. Carried in sedan chair through Albanian mts to Scutari (arrived 7 Dec). Evacuated, and died during Nice convalescence.

SIMS, William Sowden   American Vice-Adm i/c European Waters

b Port Hope, Ontario Canada 15 Oct 1858; d Boston, Mass 28 Sept 1936 aged 77

Vigorous Anglophile, advocate of relentless A/S warfare & convoy system with literally global experience.

Graduated from USNA Annapolis & entered USN 1879; joining screw frigate *Tennessee* 1880-2; Ensign 1883; Lt & naval attaché Madrid, Paris & St Petersburg 1897-1900. Served in battleship *Kentucky* 1900; fleet intelligence officer to C-in-C US Asiatic Stn 1900; reforming inspector of gunnery target practice from 1902; Cdr & Naval ADC to Pres T Roosevelt 1907; Capt of battleship *Minnesota*, US Atlantic Fleet 1909-11. Publicly reprimanded by Pres Taft for his exuberant Anglophilia in London Guildhall dinner speech 1910. Capt 1911; CO destroyer flotilla, Atlantic Fleet 1913; Mexican intervention 1914; CO new battleship *Nevada* from Nov 1915; Pres Naval War College & Rear-Adm Jan-Mar 1917.

Cdr USN forces in European Waters (flagship tender *Melville*) June 1917-Mar 1919; (Vice-Adm May 1917). Member of Allied Naval Council 30 Nov 1917; promoted Adm Dec 1918; secured Congressional inquiry into Navy Dept maladministration that he claimed delayed victory by a yr; retired from Navy 1922. See his Pulitzer prize-winning (with B J Hendrick) *The Victory at Sea* (NY, 1920); *Admiral Sims and the Modern American Navy* (1942) by Samuel Eliot Morison.

SMUTS, Jan Christian   S African General & Statesman

b nr Riebeck, Cape Colony 24 May 1870 son of farmer; d Irene nr Pretoria 11 Sept 1950 aged 80

Educated Victoria College, Stellenbosch & Christ's College, Cambridge 1886-94; Barrister 1895; Transvaal State Attorney 1898; led daring commando raid on Cape Colony 1901-2; Transvaal Colonial Sec & Education Minister 1906; Union of S Africa Minister of Mines, Defence & Interior 1910.

He and Botha were Boer War leaders who became fervent supporters of British Empire.

Pillars of the new Union of S Africa & political associates since 1902, this pair suppressed their former comrades-in-arms' rebellion (Sept 1914-Feb 1915) & then speedily overran German SW Africa (future Namibia).

Smuts, newly appointed Britain's 2nd youngest Lt-Gen, overran most of German E Africa at heavy cost without decisively defeating Lettow (Mar-Dec 1916) but this earned seat in Imperial War Cabinet. Report backed Haig's Ypres offensive, refused Palestine command, & helped quell Welsh coalstrikes (Oct 1917). Secret negotiator with Austria in Switzerland 1918. Helped found RAF. Warned Lloyd George of US dominance (Oct 1918). He and Botha reluctantly signed 'Carthaginian' Peace of Versailles before latter died and Smuts became PM beginning another 30yrs of prominence.

SOPWITH, Sir Thomas Octave Murdoch   British pioneer aviator, inventor & constructor

b London 17 Jan 1888, 8th child of a Scottish civil engineer; d Compton Manor, King's Somborne, Hants 27 Jan 1989 aged 101

One of the first men in Britain to be granted a pilot's licence (self-taught). In a primitive Howard-Wright biplane won £4000 Baron de Forest Prize for longest flight by a British pilot to a continental destination during 1910 (169 miles). Founded Sopwith Aviation Co Ltd & Flying School at Kingston-on-Thames, & Brooklands 1912. Delivered 45 aircraft to RNAS by Aug 1914.

Built & often test-flew the agile Pup, Camel, Dolphin & Triplane (first such) Snipe (Bentley engine) 1914-18 fighter biplanes. Over 16,000 aircraft supplied to RFC, RNAS & RAF. Other types (total 31) were the multi-role 11/2-strutter (first British 2-seater fighter), used by France (4000 Sopwith aircraft), Russia, Belgium & USA; the single-seat Baby seaplane and the Cuckoo, first carrier torpedo plane. See *Sopwith : The Man & his Aircraft* by B Robertson, *Sopwith Aircraft 1912-1920* by H F King (London, 1980); *Pure Luck: The Authorised Biography of Sir Thomas Sopwith* by Alan Bramson (Patrick Stephens, Wellingborough, 1990).

SUKHOMLINOV, Vladimir A (1848-1926) (*see* RUSSIAN GENERALS)

TALAAT PASHA, Mehmed (*see* YOUNG TURKS)

TIRPITZ, Alfred Peter Friedrich von   German Grand Admiral & Sec of State Imperial Navy

b Kustrin 19 Mar 1849 son of a county court judge; d Ebenhausen, nr Munich 6 Mar 1930 aged 80

'Father of the German Navy', now re-assessed as 'Architect of the Battlefleet'. Unscrupulous instigator of Edwardian era Anglo-German 'Naval Race' & incorrigible advocate of 'total' submarine & air warfare against 'English warmongers' & their 'hate-envenomed' Press. In private life addicted to blood-sports.

Educated Frankfurt-am-Main *Realschule* ; entered then insignificant Prussian coast defence navy 1865; commissioned 1869; 1870s memo on torpedoes led to creation of Torpedo Section 1885; Inspector of torpedo boats 1880s; CoS Baltic 1890; CoS High Cmnd 1892-6; Rear-Adm 1895. In last sea-going duty led E Asiatic Sqn & selected Tsingtao as China naval base 1896-7. Sec of State 1897; Vice-Adm 1899; ennobled 1900. Drafted Navy Laws 1898 & 1900; Adm 1903 vigorously & shrewdly lobbied *Reichstag* & orchestrated nationwide propaganda for his projected hugely expensive battlefleet. Supplementary Navy Laws, 1906, 1908, 1912; Grand Admiral 1911; ultimate target was 60-battleship fleet by 1920.

Failed to become *de facto* C-in-C Navy Aug 1914, neither would Kaiser sanction him a compliant naval war staff. Hated Bethmann & wanted peace with Russia to concentrate v England. Announced first unrestricted U-boat campaign, but interminable wrangling & much vacillation over its real value (& fear of US intervention) brought Tirpitz's resignation 12 Mar 1916. Headed reactionary, xenophobic Fatherland Front 1917-18; took refuge in Switzerland till Weimar Republic secure; *Reichstag* member 1924-30. See *My Memories* (London 1919); 'The German Navy in the World War', in *These Eventful Years* (New York 1924), a torrent of bombast, anti-British abuse, distortions & downright lies.

TOWNSHEND, Sir Charles Vere Ferrers   British General

b Southwark 21 Feb 1861 son of minor railway official (cousin to 3rd Marquis); d Paris 18 May 1924 aged 63

Controversial defender of Kut in Mesopotamia.

Joined RMLI 1881; Gordon Relief Expedition 1884-5; joined Indian Army 1886, Capt 1892; successfully defended Chitral Fort 1895; Sudan Campaigns 1896-8, DSO; Military Attaché Paris as brevet Col 1905; Col 1908, Brig-Gen 1909 in S Africa & Maj-Gen 1911; i/c Rawalpindi Bde 1913.

'Charlie' Townshend, an ambitious and theatrical soldier, made his name at Chitral on NW Frontier. In Apr 1915 secured command of 6th Indian Div in Mesopotamia. Led it in his Tigris 'regatta' beyond Qurna to Amara 90 miles upriver. Failed to protest over Nixon's wish to advance on Kut, which he ably took 29 Sept. Objected only moderately to further reckless advance on Baghdad. Pyrrhic victory at Ctesiphon, forced retreat to and Siege of Kut. Initially underestimated supplies, issued bombastic communiqués and twice requested promotion to Lt-Gen, but held out 146 days.

Did little to discover his men's fate while in VIP Turk captivity. Asquith refused to help his wife join him 1 Aug 1916. 'Intermediary' for Mudros armistice Oct 1918. KCB but not re-employed. Published *My Campaign in Mesopotamia* (1920).

TRENCHARD, Hugh Montague, 1st Viscount   British RFC & RAF leader 'Boom'

b Taunton, Somerset 3 Feb 1873; d London 10 Feb 1956 aged 83

'Father of the RAF'. Nicknamed 'Boom' for his stentorian voice, temper & intimidatory presence.

Joined Army 1893 at third exam attempt; served in India with R Scots Fusiliers; fought in S African War (w, bvt Major) & with WAFF (3 campaigns, DSO 1906). Joined RFC 1910, obtained pilot's cert at Sopwith's Flying School 1912; Central Flying School instructor 2 months later.

CO 1st Wing, BEF, 18 Nov 1914 forging lasting links with Haig; CO Military Wing RFC 19 Aug 1915-17 succeeding the able & more cerebral Henderson. Promoted from Bvt Lt-Col (1915) to Maj-Gen (1917); first Chief of Air Staff 3 Jan-15 Apr 1918; C-in-C Independent Air Force 5 June-11 Nov 1918 laying foundations of strategic bombing.

His 1919 'White Paper' (CAS again as Air Marshal 1919-29) laid training groundwork for the mighty RAF of 1939-45. Commissioner of London's Metropolitan Police 1931-5; awarded OM 1959. Buried in Westminster Abbey.

TROTSKY, Lev Davidovich (Bronstein)   Russian Communist leader

b Yanovka village (Kherson Prov, N of Black Sea) 7 Nov 1879, son of wealthy Jewish peasant farmer; d Mexico City by Stalinist agent 21 Aug 1940 aged 60

Promising mathematician who abandoned higher education for Marxism and organizing Nikolayev factory workers; exiled to Siberia 1898; adopted name Trotsky from Odessa gaoler and first met Lenin (in London) 1902; brilliantly led first St Petersburg Soviet in 1905 Russian Revolution until again imprisoned; escaped abroad from 2nd Siberian exile; war correspondent to Serb and Bulgar Armies in Balkan Wars 1912-13.

By 1914 both veteran revolutionary exiles and wary,if respectful, rivals, Trotsky in Vienna, Lenin in Galicia. Both moved to Switzerland but Trotsky, a more militarily inclined reporter, travelled on to Paris (20 Nov). They re-met and debated at Zimmerwald (5-8 Sept 1915) and Kienthal (24-30 Apr 1916). Trotsky deported to Spain 30 Oct 1916 and landed New York 13 Jan 1917. Sailed aboard Norwegian ship for Russia 27 Mar but interned at Halifax, Canada in a German U-boat PoW camp (3-29 Apr). Reached Petrograd 17 May soon to work hand in glove with Lenin as organizer of November Revolution. Joined Bolshevik Party July 1917.

As Foreign Affairs Commissar Trotsky tried to mitigate Brest-Litovsk but bowed to Lenin's acceptance. As War Commisar from 8 Mar 1918 Trotsky organized Red Army and ensured Soviet regime's survival in vast and bloody Civil War. His political demise followed as Lenin's health declined from early 1922 and Stalin intrigued upwards. Expelled from Party 1927 and forced into exile 1929. Wrote *History of the Revolution* and *My Life* (1930).

VENIZELOS, Eleutherios   Greek Prime Minister

b Mournies nr Canea, Crete 23 Aug 1864, son of merchant; d Paris 18 Mar 1936 aged 71

Most dynamic and controversial figure of early 20th century Greece.

Educated in Athens and as lawyer; returned to Crete 1888 to lead struggle for independence from Turks; Cretan Rising 1896; Foreign Minister 1904 and led 1904 Rising; announced union with Greece March 1905; first PM of independent Crete 1908; called by Officers' League back to mainland; Prime Minister of Greece from Oct 1910; leading architect of Balkan League; doubled Greece's area in the two Balkan Wars 1912-13.

Believed First World War offered Greece the chance to fight a final decisive war with Turkey and liberate Asia Minor's Greeks (the Great Idea), if she joined Allied coalition. Resigned when Constantine vetoed his plan to join Gallipoli campaign for which Britain also offered Cyprus. Re-elected overwhelmingly 13 June 1915 and began second term 16 Aug. Invited Allies to Salonika v Bulgaria but not in numbers wanted, forced from office at same time.

Made last appeal to King for constitutional govt 27 Aug 1916 before leaving for Crete and Salonika as head of Provisional Govt. Venizelist-Royalist civil war skirmishes began early Nov. Declared Constantine, but not dynasty, deposed. Returned to Athens as head of National Govt declaring war on Central Powers June-July 1917. Greek Army shared in Allied Macedonian victory over Bulgaria.

Versailles brought Greece Thrace and Aegean Is, but Venizelos also wanted Asia Minor gains around Smyrna. More Paris diplomacy and Lloyd George's help secured them at Treaty of Sèvres (10 Aug 1920) only for Venizelos to return home to a stunning election defeat (Nov). Thrice more Prime Minister (1924 & 1928-33) before final Paris exile. Venizelos' Great Idea had vanished in the flames of Smyrna.

VON ESSEN, Admiral Nikolai Ottovich (1860-1915) (see RUSSIAN ADMIRALS)

WAR POETS

This profile will not list familiar names but attempt to assess war poets internationally.

In 1918 a St John Adcock published a book of remembrance for 44 British soldier poets killed in action. Two years later the number became 57. Catherine Reilly's definitive *English Poetry of the First World War: A Bibliography* (1978) identifies 2225 English poets of whom only 417 wore uniform and 532 were women. They published 3104 works between 1914 and 1970, apart from 131 anthologies. Even so these figures exclude newspaper or periodical and derivative poems as well as the Irish Easter Rising. Reilly's Second World War companion volume (1986) records 2679 poets (831 in uniform), a perhaps surprisingly larger number. Interestingly 88 were Great War veterans and 135 poets wrote about both world wars. Reilly concludes that 1939-45 (a longer more global conflict) produced more good poetry overall, but the minority of 1914-18 young soldier trench poets wrote the highest quality verse of all.

Paradoxically then most 'war poetry', if defined as wartime poetry about war, is written by civilians. The vast bulk was either patriotic and individually or institutionally commemorative rather than a searing exposure of Western Front horrors. Nor should the latter's dominance in the English- speaking world's memory of 1914-18 lead us to ignore poets who wrote in other languages.

Patrick Bridgwater's *The German Poets of the First World War* (1985) selects only 20 German-language poets from hundreds but points out that 50,000 German poems *a day* were written in August 1914.

France's great wartime poet Guillaume Apollinaire was just one of 419 writers killed. At least one anthology of war poems was published at Paris and Nancy as early as 1915.

Italy already had a great poet and dramatist in Gabriele d'Annunzio who spectacularly fought and wrote by land, sea and air.

Russia, between revolutions, produced little specifically world war trench poetry. Bulgaria and Serbia had poets for whom 1914-18 was the sequel to the patriotic 1912-13 Balkan Wars. The impressively international anthology *The Lost Voices of World War I* by Tim Cross (1988) lists 781 fallen artists and writers but they include just one Finn and a Belorussian from the Tsarist Empire and not a single Rumanian.

Turkey is not usually seen as a source of war poetry but the Ottoman Sultan Mohammed V's main personal contribution to the war was verses in praise of his Gallipoli soldiers. His rebellious Arab subjects too composed in the tradition of their warrior ancestors.

The best known American war poet Alan Seeger was killed in action with the Foreign Legion ('*I have a rendezvous with death at some disputed barricade*'). The most profound American literature (Hemingway, E E Cummings, Dos Passos and Faulkner) came from mainly prose writers serving with European armies, rather than in the AEF, but nevertheless Reilly identifies about 267 likely American poets, or pseudonymns, of whom 74 were women.

The Canadian Lt-Col John McCrae (1872-1918) wrote perhaps the most poignant poem of all '*In Flanders Fields*'.

WILLIAM II, Emperor of Germany, King of Prussia 'Kaiser Bill', Supreme War Lord, All Highest

b Potsdam 27 Jan 1859 eldest son of Prince Frederick William of Prussia and Princess Victoria of England; d Doorn, Holland 4 June 1941 aged 82

Lt 1st Foot Guards 1869; educated Kassel High School & Bonn Univ 1874-9; married Princess Augusta Victoria of Schleswig-Holstein 1881; had 6 sons & 1 daughter; CO Guard Hussar Regt 1885 and Guard Inf Bde 1886; succeeded to throne 15 June 1888; dropped Bismarck 1890, detested democracy but favoured industrial growth; enthusiastically backed Tirpitz's creation of Navy to rival Britain's from 1897; offered Kruger help during Boer War; failed in diplomatic coups at Tangier and Björko 1905; censored by *Reichstag* and considered abdication 1907; acquiesced in Second Moroccan Crisis 1911.

'In peace the Kaiser was a warlord, in war he avoided taking decisions, and in defeat he fled', summarized his 1897-1909 Chancellor Prince Bülow in 1930. A mixture of bombastic naivete and shrewdness, not a hard consistent worker. Love-hate relationship with Britain. Tried belatedly to avert world war by telegrams to his royal cousins. Became spectator of war from GHQ, neglecting Berlin and home front. Never visited a factory till 10 Sept 1918. Kept beloved Fleet out of harm but changed mind over U-boat warfare. Dismissed Chancellor Bethmann at Hindenburg and Ludendorff's bidding and became victim of their 1918 military bankruptcy. Declined death in battle and fled to neutral Holland for comfortable exile, renouncing 504-year-old Hohenzollern throne. Wrote *Memoirs* (1922).

WILLIAM, Crown Prince of Prussia and Germany, General 'Little Willie'

b Potsdam 6 May 1882 eldest son of William II; d Castle Hohenzollern nr Hechingen 20 July 1951 aged 69

Lt 1st Foot Guards 1892; educated Bonn Univ 1901-3; married Princess Cecilia of Mecklenburg-Schwerin 1905, had 4 sons & 2 daughters; toured Turkey and India; CO 1st Guards Cav Regt, Danzig 1911; wrote *My Hunting Diary* 1912; defended Army officers in Zabern (Saverne) affair 1913.

Arrogant and haughty, promoted Fifth Army commander 1 Aug 1914 though unqualified. Ignored Schlieffen Plan and attacked to gates of Verdun for which 1916 slaughterhouse titular German commander. Given Army Group Crown Prince with able CoS 26 Sept 1915, held sector 1917. Willing annexationist and Pan-German spokesman. Called Bethmann's removal 'the happiest day of my life'. Army Group made greatest 1918 advances. Opposed renunciation of throne but followed in father's path to Holland. Returned to Silesian Oels estate 1923. Kaiser forbad him to stand for 1932 Weimar presidency so backed Hitler. Joined Nazi Motorized Corps. Left Oels ahead of Red Army but seized by French 1944-5. Wrote *Memoirs* (1922).

WILSON, Sir Henry Hughes, Baronet   British CIGS

b Edgeworthstown, Ulster 5 May 1864; d 22 June 1922 aged 58 murdered by Irish terrorist gunmen on steps of his Belgrave Sq home, London

A pronounced Francophile who forged valuable prewar links with Foch & the French Army but notorious for behind-the-scenes politicking & scurrilous diaries. Principal military adviser to Lloyd George 1917-18.

Educated Marlborough College; entered Rifle Bde 1884. Fought in Third Burmese (w) & S African Wars; Col & War Office posts 1904-6; Brig-Gen & Cmdt Staff College 1907-10; DMO 1910-14; Maj-Gen 1913.

Asst CoS to Sir J French Aug 1914; chief liaison officer with French *GQG* ; GOC IV Corps, Arras sector 1915-16, then with Lord Milner's mission to Russia 1916-17. Lt-Gen & GOC E Command (England); British rep on Allied Supreme War Council 27 Nov 1917-18 Feb 1918; CIGS & Gen 18 Feb 1918-Feb 1922; FM 1919. See *Life and Diaries* by Maj-Gen Sir C E Callwell (London 1927), *Brasshat* by Basil Collier (London 1961) and *Military Correspondence 1918-22* , ed Keith Jeffery (Bodley Head for Army Records Society, London 1985).

WILSON, Woodrow   US President

b Staunton, Va 28 Dec 1856 son of Presbyterian minister; d Washington DC 3 Feb 1924 aged 67

Reluctant war leader whose idealistic plans for postwar Europe were defeated at home.

Graduated College of New Jersey (Princeton) 1879; read law at Virginia Univ; PhD at John Hopkins Univ 1903-6; Princeton Univ professor 1890; President, Princeton Univ 1902; Governor of New Jersey 1910; won Democrat presidential nomination and elected President 5 Nov 1912 thanks to Republican split.

Cautious, conservative anti-imperialist high-minded president, first since Jefferson to address both Houses of Congress. Interventionist in Mexico and Caribbean but strict neutral in European War though favouring Allies. Won some alleviation of U-boat war after *Lusitania* sinking. Narrowly won 1916 re-election on neutrality record. Forced by unrestricted U-boat campaign and Zimmermann Telegram into war as Associated (ie able to make separate peace) rather than Allied power. Achieved national war mobilization. Famous 'Fourteen Points' speech boosted Allied morale and basis of German armistice request, but also encouraged Austria's disintegration. Browbeat Paris Conference into approving League of Nations but offended Japan & Italy. Unable to persuade Republican Senate to ratify treaty or league and incapacitated by Oct 1919 paralysis for rest of term.

WRANGEL, Baron Peter N (1878-1928) (*see* RUSSIAN GENERALS)

YOUNG TURKS PROFILES

Djemal Pasha, Ahmed   Turk Navy Minister & General 'The Butcher'

b Constantinople 1872; assassinated by Armenian gunman Tiflis 21 July 1922 aged c50

Capt from Constantinople War Academy 1895; joined Young Turks at Third Army (Salonika) 1906; Inspector of Macedonian Railways; Young Turk Exec Ctee as Col helped suppress Constantinople counter-revolution 1909; Military Gov of Asiatic Constantinople, Adana & Baghdad 1909-11; led Konya Res Div in First Balkan War, secured capital & rose to Lt -Gen; Minister of Works Dec 1913; Navy Minister Feb 1914.

Enver Pasha   Turk War Minister & General

b Constantinople 22 Nov 1881 son of civil servant, d 4 Aug 1922 k by Red Army in Uzbekistan aged 40

Capt from Constantinople Military Academy, graduated 2nd 1902; Macedonian anti-guerilla ops 1902-5; Major HQ Third Army

(Monastir) & joined Young Turks 1906; engineered 1908 Revolution; Berlin military attaché 1909-11; defended Benghazi & interior v Italians 1911-12; shot War Minister & toppled Govt Jan 1913 to resume Balkan War & re-entered evacuated Adrianople July; Brig-Gen & War Minister 4 Jan 1914; married Sultan's niece Princess Nadjie 5 Mar.

Talaat Pasha, Mehmed   Turk Interior Minister & Grand Vizier

b nr Adrianople 1874 son of poor farmer; assassinated by Armenian in Berlin 16 Mar 1921 aged c46

Too poor for Army career, telegraph operator in local postal service; Young Turk founder member 1906; major role in 1908 Revolution; elected Deputy for Adrianople; Interior Minister 1909-11 & since 1913.

Not now seen as a simple dictatorial triumvirate, this modernizing Young Turk trio in Daimler cars nevertheless predominated from 1913. Most pro-German, Enver saw himself as an oriental Napoleon (sacked over 1200 officers early 1913), designed a new military hat and popularity survived even his Sarakamish winter 1914-15 catastrophe. Using German officers & strategy nevertheless pursued chimerical Persian & Baghdad ventures 1916-17 after Gallipoli. Resumed Pan-Turanian drive into Armenia and to Baku from Feb 1918 even though it meant clashes with German ally and ruin for Palestine & Mesopotamian armies. Responsible with Talaat for 1915 & 1918 Armenian Massacres.

Astute Talaat became Grand Vizier 4 Feb 1917 and vainly tried to improve food supplies.

Djemal governed Syria, Palestine & Arabia for 3 years. Undertook Suez Canal expeditions and public works in Syria but brutal treatment of Arabs helped provoke 1916 revolt. By 1918 back in capital as Navy Minister.

All 3 resigned and fled together, Talaat admitting mistakes, but Armenian vengeance caught him and Djemal who published apologia *Memories of a Turkish Statesman 1913-1919* (1922).

YUDENICH, Nikolai Nikolaevich   Russian General

b Minsk Province 30 July 1862 son of nobleman; d Nice 5 Oct 1933 aged 70

Only undefeated Russian general of 1914-18 thanks to his smashing victories against the Turks.

Joined Litovsky Guards Regt from Alexandrovsky Military College 1881; Gen Staff Academy graduate 1887 going to Poland and Turkestan till 1904; Infantry Col who displayed coolness and initiative in Russo-Japanese War 1904-5; Maj-Gen; Caucasus Army Deputy Chief of Staff 1907, Chief of Staff 1912.

Young and energetic by Russian standards (only 5ft 2in), turned Battle of Sarikamish (26 Dec 1914-4 Jan 1915) from potential disaster into annihilating triumph, in spite of superiors, and earned Caucasus Army's command (6 Jan 1915).

On secondary front in appalling terrain and weather nurtured his army with supplies and adequate winter clothing. Pre-empted Turk reinforcement to capture Eastern fortress of Erzerum (16 Feb 1916). Occupied Trebizond (18 Apr) after series of well-planned amphibious operations, destroyed Third Army (July 1916) and fought new Second Army to standstill by 15 Sept and early winter.

Briefly Gov-Gen of Caucasus c20 March - 12 June 1917. Recalled to Petrograd, leaving for Finland Nov 1918 to join Whites. Nominally but now physically slack 20-stone leader of NW Army to Petrograd suburbs (12-23 Oct 1919) before Red Army compelled retreat to Estonia. French exile 1920-33.

MAPS

Western Front: 1914-18

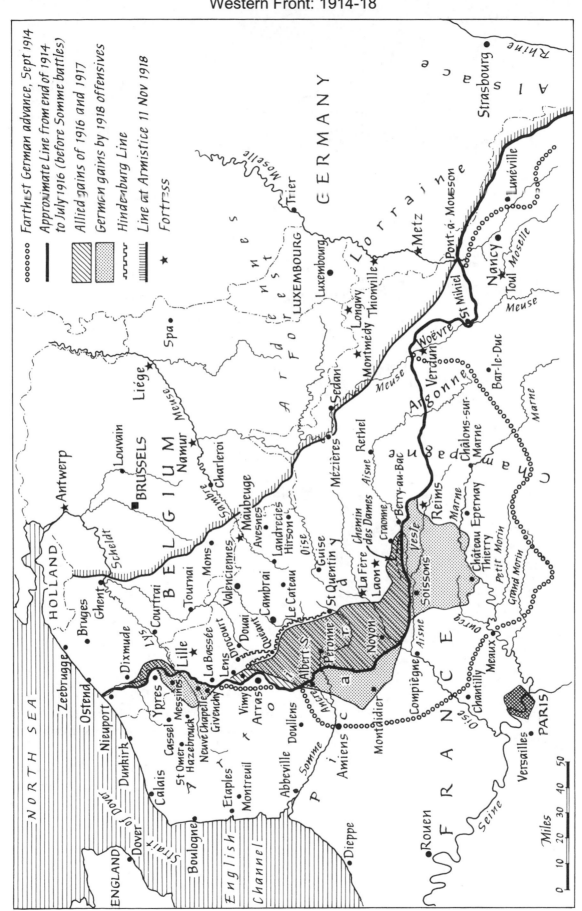

Legend:
- ○○○○○○ Farthest German advance, Sept 1914
- ——— Approximate Line from end of 1914 to July 1916 (before Somme battles)
- ▨ Allied gains of 1916 and 1917
- ▨ German gains by 1918 offensives
- ---- Hindenburg Line
- |||| Line at Armistice 11 Nov 1918
- ★ Fortress

Western Front: Ypres Salient 1914-18

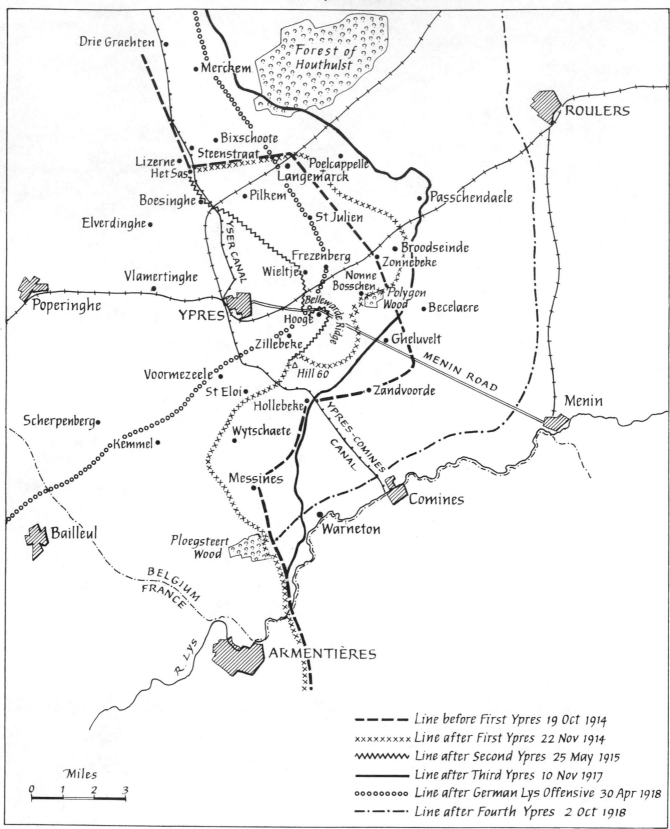

Drie Graehten

Merckem

Forest of Houthulst

ROULERS

Bixschoote

Lizerne • Steenstraat

Het Sas

Poelcappelle

Langemarck

Boesinghe

Pilkem

St Julien

Passchendaele

Elverdinghe

Frezenberg

Broodseinde

Zonnebeke

Vlamertinghe

Wieltje

Nonne Bosschen

Polygon Wood

YSER CANAL

YPRES

Bellewarde Ridge

Hooge

Becelaere

Poperinghe

Zillebeke

Gheluvelt

MENIN ROAD

Voormezeele

Hill 60

Zandvoorde

Menin

St Eloi

Hollebeke

YPRES-COMINES CANAL

Scherpenberg

Wytschaete

Kemmel

Messines

Comines

Bailleul

Warneton

Ploegsteert Wood

BELGIUM
FRANCE

R. LYS

ARMENTIÈRES

Miles

0   1   2   3

– – – – – Line before First Ypres 19 Oct 1914
xxxxxxxxx Line after First Ypres 22 Nov 1914
wwwwwwww Line after Second Ypres 25 May 1915
———— Line after Third Ypres 10 Nov 1917
oooooooooo Line after German Lys Offensive 30 Apr 1918
–·–·–·–· Line after Fourth Ypres 2 Oct 1918

Western Front: Verdun 1916-17

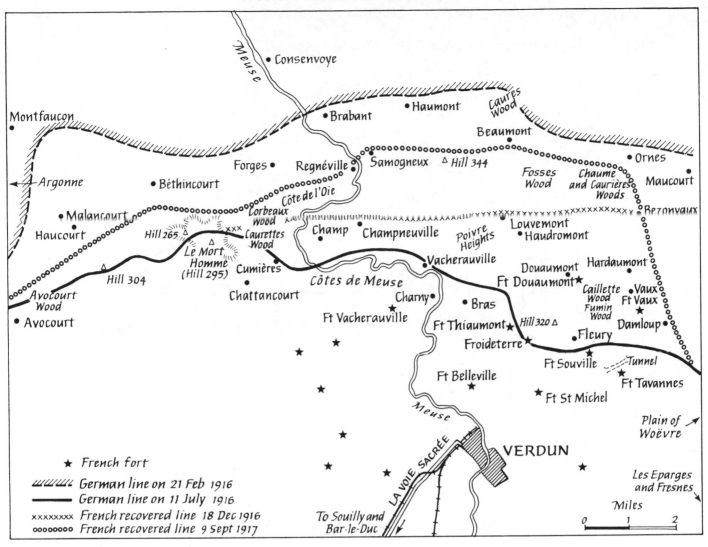

Meuse
• Consenvoye
Montfaucon
•
← Argonne
• Béthincourt
• Malancourt
Haucourt •
Hill 265 △
Avocourt
Wood
• Avocourt
Hill 304 △
Le Mort
Homme
(Hill 295)
Corbeaux
Wood
Caurettes
Wood
Cumières •
Chattancourt •
Brabant
•
Forges •
Regnéville •
Côte de l'Oie
Champ
•
Côtes de Meuse
Ft Vacherauville
• Haumont
Caures
Wood
Beaumont
•
Samogneux △ Hill 344
• Ornes
Fosses
Wood
Chaume
and Caurières
Woods
Maucourt
•
Louvemont
•
Champneuville
Poivre
Heights
Haudromont
•
Bezonvaux
Vacherauville •
Charny •
• Bras
Ft Douaumont ★
Douaumont
•
Hardaumont
•
Caillette
Wood
Fumin
Wood
Vaux
•
★ Ft Vaux
Damloup
•
Ft Thiaumont ★
Froideterre ★
Hill 320 △
★ Fleury
Ft Souville ★
Tunnel
★ Ft Tavannes
Ft Belleville ★
★ Ft St Michel
Meuse
Plain of
Woëvre →
★ French fort
////// German line on 21 Feb 1916
—— German line on 11 July 1916
xxxxxxx French recovered line 18 Dec 1916
ooooooo French recovered line 9 Sept 1917
To Souilly and
Bar-le-Duc
LA VOIE SACRÉE
VERDUN
Les Eparges
and Fresnes
Miles
0   1   2

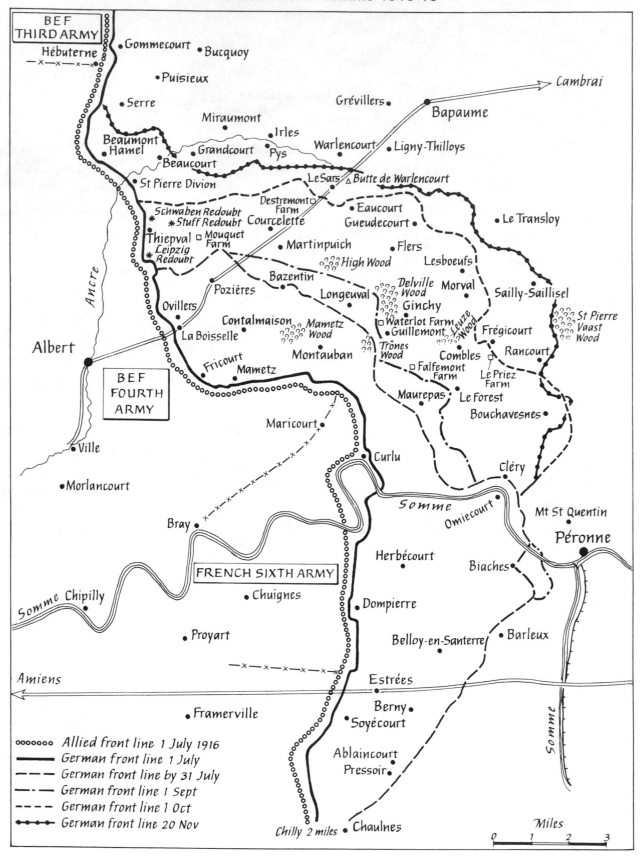

BEF
THIRD ARMY

Hébuterne
—x—x—x—

• Gommecourt   • Bucquoy
• Puisieux
• Serre
Miraumont
• Irles
Beaumont   • Grandcourt   Pys
Hamel   • Beaucourt
• St Pierre Divion
Schwaben Redoubt ✱
✱ Stuff Redoubt
Thiepval □ Mouquet
✱ Farm
Leipzig
Redoubt
Pozières
Ovillers
Contalmaison
La Boiselle
Fricourt   Mametz
Montauban
Albert ●

BEF
FOURTH
ARMY

• Ville
• Morlancourt

Ancre

Maricourt +

Bray •

Chipilly

Somme

FRENCH SIXTH ARMY

• Chuignes

• Proyart

Amiens

• Framerville

Grévillers •   ● Bapaume   → Cambrai
Warlencourt • • Ligny-Thilloys
Le Sars △ Butte de Warlencourt
Destremont
Farm □
• Eaucourt   • Le Transloy
Courcelette   Gueudecourt
• Martinpuich   • Flers
High Wood   Lesboeufs •
Bazentin   Delville   Morval
Longueval   Wood   Sailly-Saillisel
Ginchy   St Pierre
Mametz   Waterlot Farm   Vaast
Wood   • Guillemont   Leuze   Wood
Trônes   Wood   Frégicourt
Wood   Combles   Rancourt
□ Falfemont   Le Priez
Farm   Farm □
Maurepas   Le Forest
Bouchavesnes •

Curlu
Cléry
Somme
Omiecourt
Mt St Quentin
Péronne ●
• Herbécourt   Biaches •
• Dompierre
Belloy-en-Santerre • • Barleux
Estrées
Berny •
• Soyécourt   Somme
Ablaincourt •
Pressoir •
Chilly 2 miles • Chaulnes

Miles
0   1   2   3

ooooooo Allied front line 1 July 1916
———— German front line 1 July
– – – – German front line by 31 July
–·–·– German front line 1 Sept
– – – German front line 1 Oct
•–•–•– German front line 20 Nov

Eastern Front: 1914-18

Fortress ★

Limit of Russian advances 1914-15

Limit of Austro-German advances 1915-16

Regained by Brusilov, June-Aug 1916

German gains in Sept-Oct 1917

German penetration into Russia by 3 Mar 1918 (Treaty of Brest-Litovsk)

After 3 March 1918

Miles
0   50   100   150   200

German landings 1917-18

FINLAND

Viipuri

Lovisa

Lake Ladoga

Helsinki

Bjorko

Gulf of Finland

Kronstadt

Hangö

Reval

ST PETERSBURG (Petrograd)

Tsarskoe Selo

Estonia

Narva

Gatchina

Dagö

Moon I.

Yamburg

Osel

Pernau

Dorpat

Gulf of Riga

Pskov

Windau

Baltic Sea

Riga

Libau

Courland

Latvia

Jakobstadt

Mitau

Dvinsk

Shavli

Dvina

Memel

Lithuania

Königsberg

Kovno

Smolensk

Danzig

Gumbinnen

Vilna

L. Naroch

Dnieper

Mogilev (Stavka 1915-17)

Tula (main state arsenal)

E. Prussia

Masuria

Osovyets

Grodno

Minsk

Beresina

Tannenberg

Thorn

Narew

Baranovichi

R   U   S   S   I   A

Orel

Novo Georgievsk

Prasnysz

Vistula

Warsaw

Bug

Brest-Litovsk

Pinsk

Pripet

Kursk

Voronezh

Kalish

Poland

Lodz

Pilitsa

Ivangorod

Pripet Marshes

Desna

Silesia

Radom

Vistula

Lublin

Lutsk

Zhitomir

Don

G E R M A N Y

Cracow

San

Jaroslav

Lemberg

Rovno

Berdichev

Kiev

Belgorod

Vorskha

Kharkov

Brody

Przemysl

Ukraine

Poltava

DON COSSACKS

G a l i c i a

Tarnopol

Donetz

Carpathian Mountains

Stanislau

Dniester

Dnieper

Ekaterinoslav

Donbas Coalfields

A U S T R I A

Czernowitz

Bug

Nikolayev

Rostov

Budapest

Bukovina

Pruth

Kishinev

Taganrog

H U N G A R Y

Moldavia

Bessarabia

Odessa

Kherson

Sea of Azov

Danube

Transylvania

Kuban

Tisza

Crimea

R U M A N I A

Dobruja

Sevastopol

Belgrade

SERBIA

Black   Sea

• Moscow

Eastern Front (Southern Sector): Galicia, Bukovina and the Carpathians 1914-17

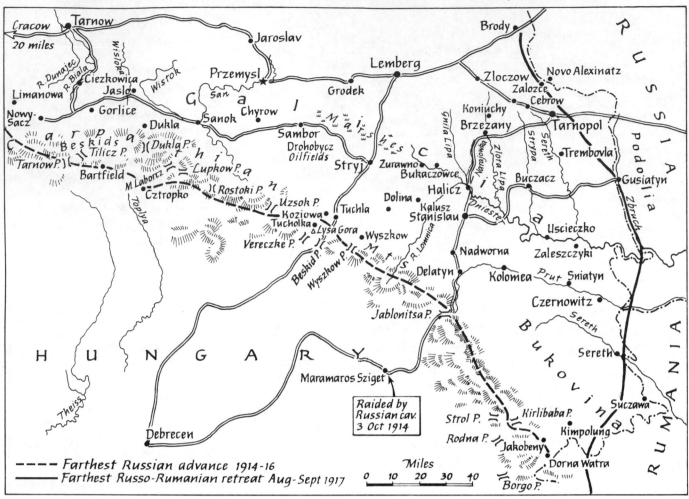

Raided by Russian cav. 3 Oct 1914

- - - - Farthest Russian advance 1914-16
——— Farthest Russo-Rumanian retreat Aug-Sept 1917

Miles
0 10 20 30 40

Eastern Front: Rumanian Campaign 1916-17

.... Farthest Rumanian
advance into Transylvania

~~~~~~ Russian Ninth Army

⬭ Rumanian armies

★ Important Rumanian
fortresses

Main passes
① Vulcan 24 Oct
② Rotenturm 26 Sept
③ Törzburg 9 Oct
④ Predeal 13 Oct
⑤ Bodza 21 Oct

ARCHDUKE
CHARLES

Austrian
Sixth Army
(Arz)

NINTH ARMY
(FALKENHAYN)

AUSTRIA-
HUNGARY

DANUBE ARMY
(MACKENSEN)

BULGARIA

RUSSIA

Moldavia

Dorna Watra Pass

Tolgyes Pass

Bekas Pass

Gyimes Pass

Jassy

Bender

Odessa

Fourth

Okna
16 Oct

Casin

Trotus

Oituz
Pass

Putna

Marasesti
23 July–3 Sept 1917

RUMANIANS

Ismail

Hatszeg

Hermannstadt

Petrosany

6-29
Sept

19 Sept   26 Sept

Fogaras

Kronstadt

29 Aug–
7 Oct

Sereth

Focsani
8 Jan 1917

27 Dec

Rimnicu

Galatz

Braila

Macin

Tulcea

2 Jan 1917

Transylvanian Alps

①   ②   ③   ④   ⑤

1 Nov

SECOND

14 Dec

Buzeu

Kimpulung

Rimnik

25 Nov

Ploesti

6 Dec

Hirsova

L. Babadagh

Russian
Dobruja Army

FIRST

Tirgu Jiu

15 Nov

Orsova

Iron Gates

5 Sept

Turnu
Severin

22 Nov

Filiasi

Wallachia

Alata

Pitesti

29 Nov

Arges

Jalomitsa

Bucharest
6 Dec

Cernavoda

Rasova

22 Oct

19 Oct

Constanza

Tuzla

Craiova

21 Nov

Slatina

Calugarino
6 Dec

THIRD

16 Sept

Black

Sea

Alexandria

26 Nov

23 Nov

Danube

Giurgevo
9 Sept

Tutracaia

Ruschuk

Silistria

3 Sept

Sistova

Varna

Miles

0   50   100

Southern Fronts: Serbia and Salonika 1914-18

Southern Fronts: Italian Front 1915-18

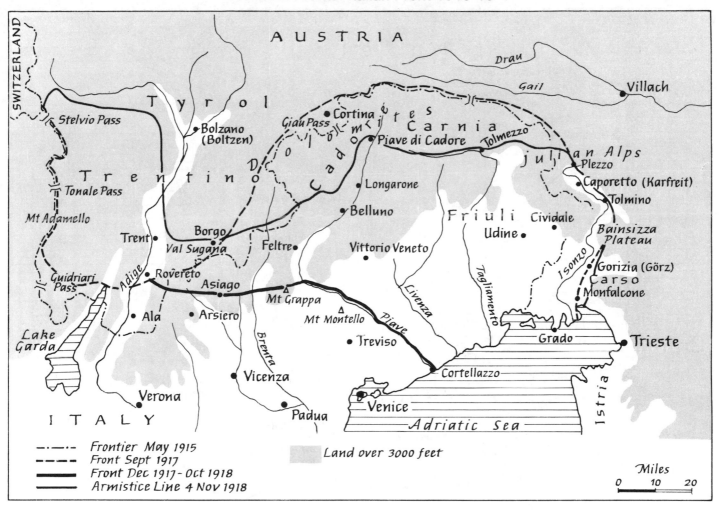

SWITZERLAND

AUSTRIA

Drau

Gail • Villach

T y r o l

• Stelvio Pass

• Bolzano (Boltzen)

Giau Pass • Cortina

D o l o m i t e s

C a r n i a

Piave di Cadore • Tolmezzo

j u l i a n Alps

• Plezzo

T r e n t i n o

D

C a d o r e

• Longarone

• Caporetto (Karfreit)

• Tolmino

• Tonale Pass

Mt Adamello

• Belluno

F r i u l i • Cividale

Udine •

Bainsizza Plateau

• Trent

Borgo •

Val Sugana

Feltre •

Vittorio Veneto •

Tagliamento

Isonzo

• Gorizia (Görz)

C a r s o

Guidriari Pass

Adige

• Rovereto

Asiago •

Mt Grappa

Mt Montello △

Livenza

Piave

• Monfalcone

• Ala

• Arsiero

• Treviso

Brenta

Grado •

• Trieste

Lake Garda

• Cortellazzo

Istria

Vicenza •

• Venice

• Verona

Padua •

Adriatic Sea

I T A L Y

Land over 3000 feet

— · — · — Frontier May 1915
— — — — Front Sept 1917
———————— Front Dec 1917 – Oct 1918
———————— Armistice Line 4 Nov 1918

Miles
0   10   20

Turkish Fronts: Armenia and the Caucasus 1914-18

Turkish Fronts: Mesopotamia and West Persia 1914-18

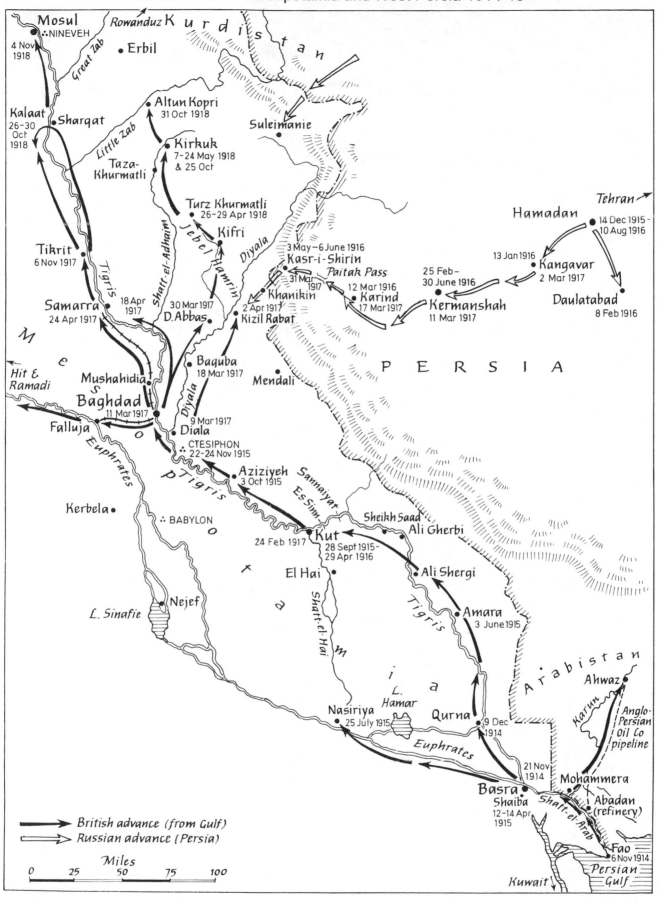

Mosul
∴ NINEVEH
Rowanduz K u r d i s t a n
4 Nov 1918
Great Zab
• Erbil
Kalaat 26–30 Oct 1918
• Sharqat
Little Zab
• Altun Kopri 31 Oct 1918
• Suleimanie
• Kirkuk 7–24 May 1918 & 25 Oct
Taza-Khurmatli
Shatt-el-Adhaim
Jebel Hamrin
• Turz Khurmatli 26–29 Apr 1918
Tehran
Hamadan
14 Dec 1915 – 10 Aug 1916
• Kifri
• Tikrit 6 Nov 1917
3 May–6 June 1916
Kasr-i-Shirin
13 Jan 1916
• Kangavar 2 Mar 1917
Paitak Pass
31 Mar 1917
25 Feb – 30 June 1916
• Daulatabad 8 Feb 1916
Tigris
Samarra 24 Apr 1917
18 Apr 1917
30 Mar 1917
• Khanikin
2 Apr 1917
12 Mar 1916
• Karind 17 Mar 1917
• Kermanshah 11 Mar 1917
• D. Abbas
• Kizil Rabat
M e
• Baquba 18 Mar 1917
P E R S I A
Hit & Ramadi
• Mushahidia
s
Diyala
• Mendali
Baghdad 11 Mar 1917
9 Mar 1917
o
Falluja
Euphrates
• Diala
∴ CTESIPHON 22–24 Nov 1915
p
• Aziziyeh 3 Oct 1915
Tigris
• Kerbela
∴ BABYLON
Sannaiyat
Es Sinn
• Sheikh Saad
• Ali Gherbi
L. Sinafie
• Nejef
t
El Hai •
Kut 24 Feb 1917
28 Sept 1915 – 29 Apr 1916
• Ali Shergi
a
Shatt-el-Hai
Ahwaz
A r a b i s t a n
• Amara 3 June 1915
Karun
Anglo-Persian Oil Co pipeline
L. Hamar
i a
• Qurna
9 Dec 1914
Nasiriya 25 July 1915
Euphrates
21 Nov 1914
• Mohammera
Basra
Shaiba 12–14 Apr 1915
Shatt-el-Arab
• Abadan (refinery)
Fao 6 Nov 1914
Kuwait
Persian Gulf

→ British advance (from Gulf)
⇒ Russian advance (Persia)

Miles
0   25   50   75   100

329

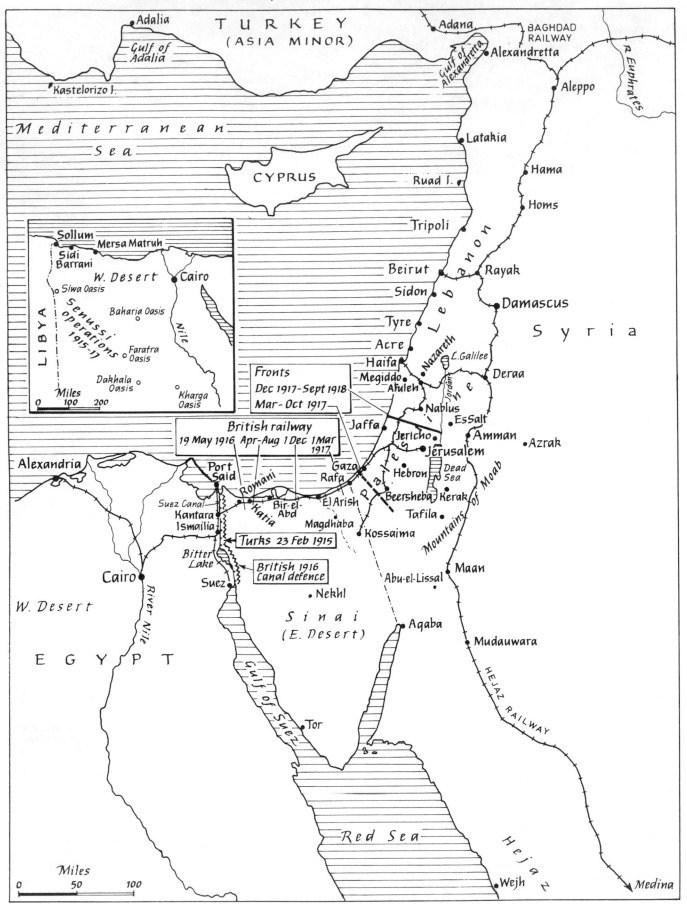

Turkish Fronts: Sinai, Western Desert and Palestine 1914-18

Adalia

T U R K E Y
(ASIA MINOR)

Adana

Gulf of Adalia

BAGHDAD
RAILWAY

Gulf of
Alexandretta

Alexandretta

R. Euphrates

Kastelorizo I.

Aleppo

M e d i t e r r a n e a n
S e a

Latakia

Hama

CYPRUS

Ruad I.

Homs

Tripoli

L e b a n o n

Sollum
Mersa Matruh
Sidi
Barrani
W. Desert
Cairo
Siwa Oasis
Baharia Oasis
Senussi operations 1915-17
Farafra Oasis
Dakhala Oasis
Kharga Oasis

L I B Y A

Miles
0   100   200

Beirut

Rayak

Sidon

Damascus

Tyre

S y r i a

Acre

Nazareth

L. Galilee

Haifa

Megiddo

Deraa

Afuleh

Fronts
Dec 1917-Sept 1918
Mar- Oct 1917

J o r d a n

P a l e s t i n e

Nablus

EsSalt

British railway
19 May 1916 Apr-Aug 1 Dec 1 Mar
1917

Jaffa

Jericho

Amman

Azrak

Jerusalem

Alexandria

Port
Said

Gaza
Rafa

Hebron

Dead
Sea

Suez Canal

Romani

El Arish

Beersheba

Kerak

Kantara
Ismailia

Katia

Bir-el-
Abd

Magdhaba

Tafila

M o u n t a i n s   o f   M o a b

Turks 23 Feb 1915

Kossaima

*Bitter
Lake*

**British 1916
Canal defence**

Abu-el-Lissal

Maan

Cairo

Suez

Nekhl

River Nile

S i n a i
(E. Desert)

Aqaba

Mudauwara

W. Desert

E G Y P T

Gulf of Suez

HEJAZ RAILWAY

Tor

Red Sea

H e j a z

Miles
0   50   100

Wejh

Medina

African Operations: East Africa 1914-18

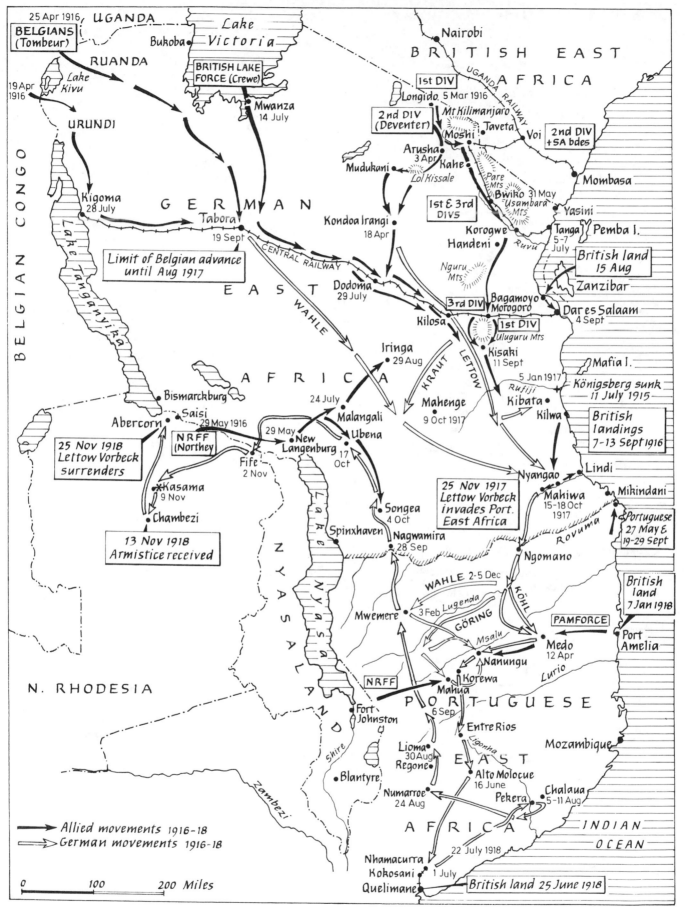

UGANDA

25 Apr 1916
BELGIANS (Tombeur)

RUANDA

19 Apr 1916 *Lake Kivu*

URUNDI

Lake Victoria Bukoba

BRITISH LAKE FORCE (Crewe)

Mwanza 14 July

BELGIAN CONGO

Kigoma 28 July

Lake Tanganyika

G E R M A N

Tabora 19 Sept

Limit of Belgian advance until Aug 1917

CENTRAL RAILWAY

E A S T

Nairobi

B R I T I S H   E A S T

A F R I C A

UGANDA RAILWAY

1st DIV
Longido 5 Mar 1916

2nd DIV (Deventer)
Mt Kilimanjaro Moshi Taveta Voi

2nd DIV + SA bdes

Arusha 3 Apr Kahe

Mudukani *Lol Kissale* *Pare Mts*

Kondoa Irangi 18 Apr

Bwiko 31 May
Usambara Mts

1st & 3rd DIVS

Korogwe Handeni

Mombasa

Yasini

Tanga 5-7 July Pemba I.

British land 15 Aug
Zanzibar

WAHLE

A F R I C A

Dodoma 29 July

Kilosa

Nguru Mts

3rd DIV Bagamoyo Morogoro

1st DIV *Uluguru Mts*

Dar es Salaam 4 Sept

Iringa 29 Aug

24 July

KRAUT LETTOW

Kisaki 11 Sept

Mahenge 9 Oct 1917

Rufiji

5 Jan 1917

Kibata

Mafia I.

Königsberg sunk 11 July 1915

Kilwa

British landings 7-13 Sept 1916

Bismarckburg

Saisi 29 May 1916
Abercorn

NRFF (Northey)

29 May New Langenburg

Fife 2 Nov

Malangali Ubena

17 Oct

25 Nov 1918 Lettow Vorbeck surrenders

×Kasama 9 Nov

Chambezi

13 Nov 1918 Armistice received

N. RHODESIA

Lake Nyasa

NYASALAND

Spinxhaven

Songea 4 Oct

Nagwamira 28 Sep

25 Nov 1917 Lettow Vorbeck invades Port. East Africa

Nyangao Lindi

Mahiwa 15-18 Oct 1917

Mikindani

Rovuma

Portuguese 27 May & 19-29 Sept

Ngomano

British land 7 Jan 1918

WAHLE 2-5 Dec
3 Feb *Lugenda*

KÖHL

Mwemere GÖRING *Msalu*

PAMFORCE

Medo 12 Apr

Port Amelia

Lurio

NRFF

Nanungu Korewa

Mahua 6 Sep

Fort Johnston

Shire

Entre Rios *Ligonha*

Mozambique

Lioma 30 Aug Regone

Alto Molocue 16 June

Chalaua 5-11 Aug

Blantyre

Numarroe 24 Aug

Pekera

E A S T

Zambezi

Nhamacurra
Kokosani 1 July

Quelimane

22 July 1918

A F R I C A

INDIAN OCEAN

British land 25 June 1918

→ Allied movements 1916-18
⇨ German movements 1916-18

0   100   200 Miles

Sea War: North Sea and British Home Waters 1914-18

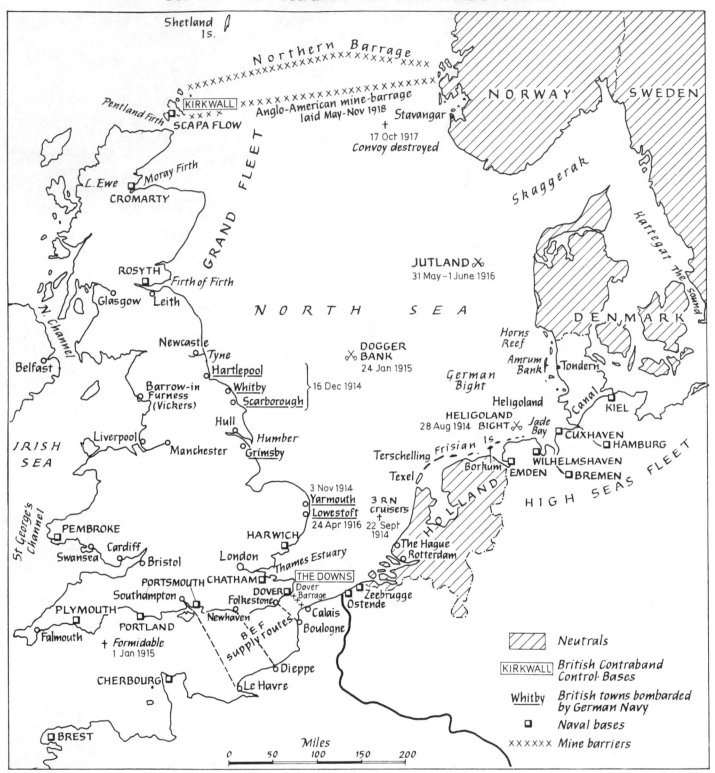

Shetland Is.

Northern Barrage

KIRKWALL
Pentland Firth
SCAPA FLOW

Anglo-American mine-barrage
laid May-Nov 1918

NORWAY   SWEDEN

Stavangar
+
17 Oct 1917
Convoy destroyed

Skaggerak

L. Ewe
Moray Firth
CROMARTY

Kattegat The Sound

GRAND FLEET

ROSYTH
Firth of Firth
Glasgow   Leith

DENMARK

N O R T H   S E A

JUTLAND ⚓
31 May – 1 June 1916

Horns Reef

N. Channel

Belfast

Newcastle
Tyne
Hartlepool
Barrow-in Furness
(Vickers)
Whitby
Scarborough

16 Dec 1914

DOGGER BANK
24 Jan 1915

German Bight

Amrum Bank
Tondern

Heligoland

HELIGOLAND
28 Aug 1914   BIGHT ⚓
Jade Bay

Kiel

Canal

Hull

IRISH SEA

Liverpool
Manchester

Humber
Grimsby

Terschelling   Frisian Is.

CUXHAVEN
HAMBURG

WILHELMSHAVEN
Borkum
EMDEN   BREMEN

Texel

HOLLAND

HIGH SEAS FLEET

St George's Channel

3 Nov 1914
Yarmouth
Lowestoft
24 Apr 1916

3 R N cruisers
+
22 Sept 1914

PEMBROKE
Swansea   Cardiff
Bristol

HARWICH

London

Thames Estuary

The Hague
Rotterdam

PORTSMOUTH   CHATHAM

THE DOWNS

Southampton
PLYMOUTH
Newhaven
PORTLAND
Folkestone
DOVER
Dover Barrage

Zeebrugge
Ostende

Falmouth
+ Formidable
1 Jan 1915

B E F supply routes

Calais
Boulogne

Dieppe

CHERBOURG

Le Havre

BREST

Miles

0   50   100   150   200

///// Neutrals

KIRKWALL British Contraband Control Bases

Whitby British towns bombarded by German Navy

□ Naval bases

xxxxxx Mine barriers

International Events: Europe 1923

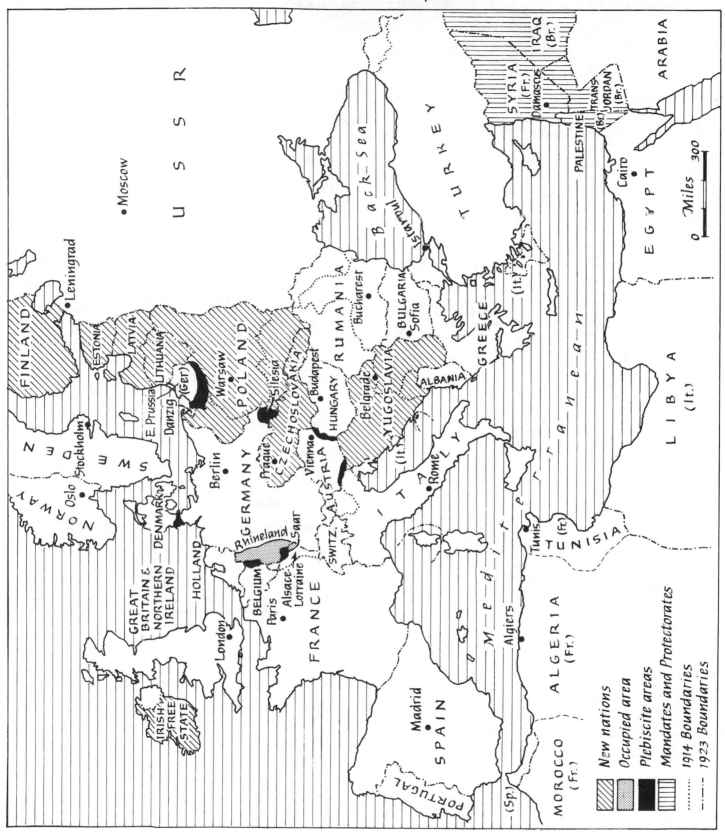

U S S R

• Moscow

• Leningrad

FINLAND

ESTONIA

LATVIA

LITHUANIA

E. Prussia (Ger.)

Danzig

• Warsaw

POLAND

Silesia

CZECHOSLOVAKIA

Prague

• Budapest

HUNGARY

Vienna

AUSTRIA

RUMANIA

• Bucharest

Dniester

BULGARIA

• Sofia

YUGOSLAVIA

Belgrade •

ALBANIA

GREECE

Bosporus

TURKEY

B l a c k   S e a

ARABIA

SYRIA (Fr.)

• Damascus

IRAQ (Br.)

PALESTINE

TRANS JORDAN (Br.)

• Cairo

E G Y P T

0   Miles   300

NORWAY

Oslo •

SWEDEN

Stockholm •

DENMARK

HOLLAND

GREAT BRITAIN & NORTHERN IRELAND

London •

IRISH FREE STATE

Berlin •

GERMANY

Rhineland

Saar

BELGIUM

Paris •

Alsace Lorraine

SWITZ.

FRANCE

ITALY

Rome •

M e d i t e r r a n e a n

(It.)

(It.)

Tunis •

TUNISIA

ALGERIA (Fr.)

Algiers •

MOROCCO (Fr.)

SPAIN

Madrid •

PORTUGAL

(Sp.)

L I B Y A (It.)

New nations

Occupied area

Plebiscite areas

Mandates and Protectorates

.... 1914 Boundaries

– – – 1923 Boundaries

SOURCES

CHRONOLOGIES 1914-18

Committee of Imperial Defence *Principal Events* (Official History of the War) (HMSO, London 1922 reprinted by London Stamp Exchange 1987)

Daily Telegraph History of World War I Wall Chart, Keith Simpson (1981)

Dearle, N B, *An Economic Chronicle of the Great War for Great Britain & Ireland 1914-1919* (Economic and Social History of the World War, Carnegie Endowment for World Peace, Humphry Milford/OUP, London 1929) [Supplement on 1920-1922]

Debyser, Felix *Chronologie de la Guerre Mondiale de Serajevo à Versailles* (28 Juin 1914-28 Juin 1919) (Payot, Paris 1938)

Gleichen, Maj-Gen Edward, Lord (ed) *Chronology of the War* Vol 1 1914-1915, Vol 2 1916-1917, Vol 3 1918-1919 plus small atlas vol (Ministry of Information/Constable, London 1918-1920); reprinted without atlas by Greenhill Books, London as one vol *Chronology of the Great War* (1988)

Mudd, Thomas B R *The Yanks were there: A Chronological and Documentary Review of World War I* (Vantage Press, New York 1958)

Official History of the Canadian Forces in the Great War 1914-1919 Gen Series Vol I Chronology, Appendices and Maps (Patenaude, Ottawa 1938)

Rowe, R P P *A Concise Chronicle of Events of the Great War* [to 10 Jan 1920] (Philip Allan, London 1920)

The Times Diary and Index of the War 1914-1918 [to 10 Aug 1920] (Hodder, London 1921, reprinted by Hayward 1985)

OTHER CHRONOLOGIES

Bowman, John S (exec ed) *The Twentieth Century: An Almanac* (Harrap, London 1986)

Carruth, Gorton & Associates (ed) *The Encyclopedia of American Facts and Dates* 6th ed (Crowell Co, New York 1972)

Chronicle of the 20th Century, ed Derrick Mercer (Longman, 1988)

Freeman-Grenville, G S P *Chronology of African History* (OUP 1973)

Irving S and Kull, Nell M *A Short Chronology of American History*, (Rutgers UP, New Brunswick NJ 1952)

Keller, Helen Rex *The Dictionary of Dates* 2 vols (Macmillan, New York 1934)

Matei, Horia C et al *Chronological History of Romania* 2nd ed (Editura Enciclopedica Romana, Bucharest 1974)

Moody, T W, Martin, F X, and Byrne, F J A *A Chronology of Irish History to 1976: A New History of Ireland Vol VIII* (Clarendon Press, Oxford 1982)

Trager, James (ed) *The People's Chronology: A Year-by-Year Record of Human Events from Prehistory to the Present* (Heinemann, London 1980)

Williams, Neville *Chronology of the Modern World* (Barrie and Rockliff, London 1966)

OTHER REFERENCE AND GENERAL HISTORIES

Banks, Arthur *Military Atlas of the First World War* (Heinemann, London 1975 reprinted 1989 by Leo Cooper)

Bayliss, Gwyn M *Bibliographic Guide to the two World Wars: An annotated survey of English language reference materials.* (Bowker, London & New York 1977)

Bell, A C *The Blockade of the Central Powers 1914-1918** (1937, HMSO, London 1961)

Bruce, Anthony *An Illustrated Companion to the First World War* * (Michael Joseph, London 1989)

Dupuy, R Ernest & Dupuy, Trevor N *The Encyclopedia of Military History from 3500BC to the Present** (Book Club ed 1970)

Edmonds, Brig-Gen Sir James E *A Short History of World War 1* (OUP, London 1959)

Encyclopedia Britannica, especially 12th edition (1922)

Encyclopaedia of Islam

Enser, A G S , *A Subject Bibliography of the First World War 1914-1978* (Deutsch, London 1979)

Esposito, Vincent J (ed) *A Concise History of World War 1* (Pall Mall Press, London 1964)

Falls, Cyril *The First World War* (Longman, London 1960)

Gilbert, Martin *First World War Atlas* (Weidenfeld, London 1970 reprinted 1985)

Gliddon, Gerald (ed) *First World War: List of 700 Books in Print* (Gliddon Books, Norwich 1990)

Hammerton, John *The War Illustrated* 9 vols (Amalgamated Press, London 1914-19)

Hammerton, J & Wilson, H W *The Great War* 13 vols (Amalgamated Press, London 1914-19)

Heinl Jr , Col Robert Debs *Dictionary of Military and Naval Quotations* (US Naval Institute, Annapolis, Maryland 1966)

Herwig, Holger H, & Heyman, Neil M *Biographical Dictionary of World War I**(Greenwood Press, London 1982)

Mitchell B R *European Historical Statistics 1750-1975* 2nd rev ed (Macmillan, London 1981)

Morris, B (ed) *Encyclopedia of American History* 6th ed (Harper & Row, New York 1982)

Mourre, Michel *Dictionnaire des Personnages Historiques de Tous Les Temps* (Bordas, Paris, Brussels & Montreal 1972)

Nash, D B *Imperial German Army Handbook 1914-1918* (Ian Allan, London 1980)

Palmer, A W *A Dictionary of Modern History 1789-1945* (Penguin ed 1964)

Purnell's History of the First World War 6 vols (BPC, London 1969-71) updated as *Marshall Cavendish Illustrated Encyclopedia of World War 1* * 13 vols (USA 1984-86)

*Statistics of the Military Effort of the British Empire during the Great War** (War Office, HMSO, London 1922)

Terraine, John *The Great War: A Pictorial History* (Hutchinson, London 1965)

Terraine, John *White Heat: The New Warfare 1914-1918** (Sidgwick, London (1982)

The Great War 1914-18 Bertram Rota Book Catalogue 245 (London 1988)

The Illustrated War Record 5th ed (Headley Bros, London nd but 1919)*

The Times History of the War 22 vols (London 1914-19)

Thoumin, Richard *The First World War* [eyewitness anthology] (Secker ed, London 1963)

Tuchman, Barbara W *The Guns of August — August 1914* (Four Square paperback edition 1964)

Valluy, Gen J E (with Pierre Dufourcq) *La Première Guerre Mondiale* 2 vols (Larousse, Paris 1968)

Vansittart, Peter *Voices from the Great War* (Cape, London 1981)

Webster's Biographical Dictionary (G & C Merriam Co, Springfield, USA 1969)

Wilson, Trevor *The Myriad Faces of War: Britain and the Great War 1914-1918* (Polity Press, Cambridge 1986)

Winter, J M, *The Great War and the British People* (Macmillan, London (1985)

Woodward, David R & Maddox, Robert Franken *America and World War 1: A Selected Annotated Bibliography of English-Language Sources** Wars of the United States vol 6 (Garland, New York & London 1985)

* = contains chronology

SARAJEVO TO OUTBREAK

Cassels, Lavender, *The Archduke and the Assassin* (Frederick Muller, London 1984)

Thomson, George Malcolm *The Twelve Days 24 July - 4 August 1914* (History Book Club, London 1964)

WESTERN FRONT

See also Chronologies & Other Reference and General Histories

General

Edmonds, Brig-Gen Sir James *Military Operations: France and Belgium* 13 vols (HMSO, London 1922-1948) and *The Occupation of the Rhineland 1918-1929* (IWM/HMSO, London 1987)

Lupfer, Timothy T 'The Dynamics of Doctrine: The Changes in German Tactical Doctrine During the First World War' Leavensworth Papers No 4 (US Army, July 1981)

Overstraeten, Gen R Van (ed) *The War Diaries of Albert I, King of the Belgians* (Kimber, London 1954)

1914

Owen, Edward *1914 Glory Departing* (Buchan & Enright, London 1986)

Spears, Brig-Gen E L *Liaison, 1914: A Narrative of the Great Retreat* (Heinemann, London 1930)

Terraine, John *Mons: The Retreat to Victory* (Pan Books ed, London 1972)
Van Creveld, Martin *Supplying War: Logistics from Wallenstein to Patton* (CUP 1977)

1915
Clark, Alan *The Donkeys* (Mayflower-Dell paperback ed, London 1967)

1916
Blond, Georges *Verdun* (Mayflower-Dell, London 1976)
Farrar-Hockley, A H *The Somme* (Pan Books ed, London 1966)
Horne, Alistair *The Price of Glory: Verdun 1916* (Macmillan, London 1962)

1917
Spears, Brig-Gen E L *Prelude to Victory* (Cape, London 1939)

1918
Barnett, Correlli 'A Successful Counter-Stroke: 18 July 1918' from *Old Battles and New Defences: Can We Learn from Military History?* (Brassey's, London/Oxford 1986)
Middlebrook, Martin *The Kaiser's Battle 21 March 1918: The First Day of the German Spring Offensive* (Allen Lane, London 1978)
Moore, William *See How They Ran: The British Retreat of 1918* (Sphere Books paperback ed, London 1975)
Rudin, Harry R *Armistice 1918* (Yale UP, New Haven 1944)
Terraine, John *To Win a War 1918 The Year of Victory* (Sidgwick & Jackson, London 1978 and Macmillan paperback 1986)

Armies, Formations and Units
AEF Intelligence Staff *Histories of 251 Divisions of the German Army which Participated in the War (1914-18)* (Washington 1920, repr London Stamp Exchange 1989)
American Battle Monuments Commission *American Armies and Battles in Europe : A History, Guide & Reference Book* (US Govt Printing Office, Washington 1938)
Becke, Maj A F *Order of Battle Part 4 (GHQs, Armies and Corps) 1914-1918* (HMSO, London 1945)
Bergot, Erwan *The French Foreign Legion* (Tatoo paperback, Wyndham, London 1976)
Merewether, Lt-Col J W B, and Smith, Sir F *The Indian Corps in France* 2nd ed (Murray, London 1919)
Nicholson, Col GWL *Canadian Expeditionary Force 1914-1919* [Official History] (Queen's Printer, Ottawa, 1962)
Stallings, Laurence *The Doughboys: The Story of the AEF, 1917-1918* (Harper & Row, New York 1963)
Turnbull, Patrick *The Foreign Legion* (Mayflower paperback ed, London 1966)
US War Department *Order of Battle of the United States Land Forces in the World War: AEF* (US Govt Printing Office, Washington, 1937)

Tanks
Cooper, Bryan *Tank Battles of World War I* (Ian Allan, 1973)
Liddell Hart, Capt B H *The Tanks: The History of the Royal Tank Regiment* Vol I (Cassell, London 1959)
Royal Tank Regiment, 50th Anniversary Souvenir 1917-1967 (London 1967)

Biographies
Barnett, Correlli *The Swordbearers: Studies in Supreme Command in the First World War* (Eyre & Spottiswoode, London 1963/Penguin 1966 & 1986)
Blumenson, Martin *The Patton Papers 1885-1940* Vol I (Houghton Mifflin, Boston 1972)
Falls, Cyril *Marshal Foch* (Blackie & Son, London/Glasgow 1939)
Farago, Ladislas *Patton: Ordeal and Triumph* (Arthur Barker, London 1966)
Griffiths, Richard *Marshal Pétain* (Constable, London 1970)
Hart, Capt Basil Liddell *Foch: Man of Orleans* (London 1931)
Holmes, Richard *The Little Field-Marshal, Sir John French* (Cape, London 1981)
Manchester, William *American Caesar: Douglas MacArthur 1880-1964* (Arrow paperback ed, London 1979)
Salisbury-Jones, Maj-Gen Sir Guy *So Full a Glory: A Life of Marshal de Lattre de Tassigny* (Weidenfeld, London 1954)
Vandiver, Frank E *Black Jack: The Life and Times of John J Pershing* 2 vols (Texas A & M UP 1977)

Weaponry
Hogg, Ian V *The Guns 1914-18* (Pan/Ballantine ed, London 1973)

EASTERN FRONT

Brusilov, Gen A A *A Soldier's Note Book 1914-1918* (Macmillan, London 1930)
Churchill, Winston S *The World Crisis: The Eastern Front* (Butterworth, London 1931)
Lt-Gen Nicholas N Golovine, *The Russian Army in the World War* (Yale UP, New Haven, 1931)
Gourko, Gen Basil *Memories & Impressions of War and Revolution 1914-1917* (Murray, London 1918)
Hoffmann, Maj Gen Max *War Diaries and other Papers* Vol I (Secker, London 1929)
Jukes, Geoffrey *Carpathian Disaster: Death of an Army* (Ballantine, London 1971)
Kettle, Michael *Russia and the Allies 1917-1920: Vol I The Allies and the Russian Collapse March 1917-March 1918* (Deutsch, London 1981)
Knox, Maj-Gen Sir Alfred *With the Russian Army 1914-1917,* 2 vols (Hutchinson, London 1921)
Littawer, Vladimir S *Russian Hussar* (J A Allen, London 1965)
Perrett, Bryan & Lord, Anthony *The Czar's British Squadron* (Kimber, London 1981)
Stone, Norman *The Eastern Front 1914-1917* (Hodder, London 1975)
Wildman, A *The End of the Russian Imperial Army* 2 vols (Princeton UP, 1980 & 1987)
Wrangel, Alexis *The End of Chivalry: The Last Great Cavalry Battles 1914-1918* (Hippocrene Books, New York 1982)

Russian Revolution and Civil War
Bradley, J F N *Civil War in Russia 1917-1920* (Batsford, London 1975)
Bunyan, James & Fisher, H H *The Bolshevik Revolution 1917-1918: Documents and Materials** (Hoover War Library Publications No 3, (Stanford UP, Stanford, California 1965)
Bunyan, James *Intervention, Civil War, and Communism in Russia April-December 1918* (John Hopkins University, Baltimore 1936)
Footman, David *Civil War in Russia* *(Faber, London 1961)
Jackson, Robert *At War with the Bolsheviks: The Allied Intervention into Russia 1917-1920* (Stacey, London 1972)
Luckett, Richard *The White Generals: The White Movement and the Russian Civil War* (Longman, Harlow 1971 & 1988)
McCauley, Martin *Octobrists to Bolsheviks: Imperial Russia 1905-1917** (Documents of Modern History, Edward Arnold, London 1984)
Mawdsley, Evan *The Russian Civil War* (Allen & Unwin, Boston 1987)
Seaton, Albert *Stalin as Warlord* (Batsford, London 1976)
Shukman, Harold (ed) *The Blackwell Encyclopedia of the Russian Revolution* (Oxford 1988)
Trotsky, Leon *How the Revolution Armed: The Military Writings and Speeches* Vol 1 *The Year 1918** (1923: New Park Publ, Britain 1979)
Weber, Gerda & Hermann *Lenin Life and Works* (Macmillan Chronology Series, London 1980)
Zeman, Z A B (ed) *Germany and the Revolution in Russia 1915-1918* (Documents: OUP, London 1958)

Finland
Hannula, Lt-Col J O *Finland's War of Independence* (Faber, London 1939)
Jagerskiold, Stig *Mannerheim Marshal of Finland* (C Hurst, London 1986)
Upton, Anthony F *The Finnish Revolution 1917-1918* (Univ of Minnesota Press, Minneapolis, 1980)
Mannerheim, K G, *The Memoirs of Marshal Mannerheim* (Cassell, London 1953)

* = chronology included

SOUTHERN FRONTS

Italian Front
Bertoldi, Silvio *Badoglio* (Rizzoli, Milan 1982)
Bovio, Col Oreste 'The Italian Army in World War I' *Revue Internationale d'Histoire Militaire* No 39 (Rome 1978)
Edmonds, Brig-Gen Sir James and Davies, H R *Military Operations: Italy 1915-1919* (HMSO, London 1949)
Falls, Cyril *Caporetto 1917* (Weidenfeld, London 1966)
Gooch, John *Army, State and Society in Italy 1870-1915* (Macmillan, Basingstoke & London 1989)
McClure, William 'Italian Campaigns', 'Caporetto' & 'Asiago' from *Encyclopedia Britannica* 12th ed (1922)
Prichard-Agnetti, Mary (trans) *The Battle of the Piave June 15-23, 1918* issued by the Supreme Command of the Royal Italian Army (Hodder, London 1921)
Rothenberg, Gunther E *The Army of Francis Joseph* (Purdue UP, W Lafayette, Indiana 1976)
Villari, Luigi *The War on the Italian Front* (Cobden-Sanderson, London 1932)

Serbia & Salonika
Anon "Salonika Campaigns' from *Encyclopedia Britannica* 12th ed (1922)
Atkinson, Maj Charles 'Serbian Campaigns' from *Encyclopedia Britannica* 12th ed (1922)

Falls, Capt Cyril *Military Operations: Macedonia* 2 vols (HMSO, London 1933 & 1935)
Fryer, Charles 'The Watch on the Danube: The British Naval Mission in Serbia 1914-1916' from *The Mariner's Mirror* vol 73 No 3 (Greenwich 1987)
Ministère de la Guerre *Les Armées Françaises dans la Grande Guerre* Tome VIII (Paris 1925-34)
Nicol, Graham *Uncle George: Field-Marshal Lord Milne of Salonika and Rubislaw* (Reedminster Publications, London 1976)
Palmer, Alan *The Gardeners of Salonika: The Macedonian Campaign 1915-1918* (André Deutsch, London 1965)
Villari, Luigi *The Macedonian Campaign* (Fisher Unwin, London 1922)

TURKISH FRONTS

General

A Brief Record of the Advance of the Egyptian Expeditionary Force July 1917 to October 1918 2nd ed (HMSO, 1919)
Celiker, Brig Gen F (Retd) 'Turkey in the First World War' from *Revue Internationale d'Histoire Militaire* No 46 (Ankara 1980)
Emin, Ahmed *Turkey in the World War* (Yale UP, New Haven 1930)
Larcheur, Commandant M *La guerre turque dans la guerre mondiale* (Chiron, Berger-Levrault, Paris 1926)
Trumpener, Ulrich 'Suez, Baku, Gallipoli: The Military Dimensions of the German-Ottoman Coalition 1914-18' from Neilson, Keith & Prete, Roy A *Coalition Warfare: An Uneasy Accord* (Wilfred Laurier UP, Waterloo, Canada 1983)
Winstone, H V F *The Illicit Adventure: The Story of Political and Military Intelligence in the Middle East from 1898 to 1926* (Cape, London 1982)

Arabia

Liddell Hart, B H ' *T.E.Lawrence' In Arabia and After* (Cape, London 1935)
Macro, Eric *Yemen and the Western World* (C Hurst, London 1968)
Tabachnick, Stephen E & Matheson, Christopher *Images of Lawrence* (Cape, London 1988)
Yardley, Michael *Backing into the Limelight: A Biography of T.E. Lawrence* (Harrap, London 1985)

Armenia

Allen, W E D & Muratoff, Paul *Caucasian Battlefields: A History of the Wars on the Turco-Caucasian Border 1828-1921* (CUP 1953)

Egypt and Palestine

Falls, Capt Cyril *Military Operations: Egypt and Palestine Part II from June 1917 to the End of the War* (HMSO, London 1930)
Falls, Cyril *Armageddon 1918* (Weidenfeld, London 1964)
Macmunn, Lt-Gen Sir George, & Falls, Capt Cyril *Military Operations: Egypt and Palestine to June 1917** (HMSO, London 1928)
Wavell, Col A P *The Palestine Campaigns* * 3rd ed (Constable, London 1932)

Gallipoli

Aspinall-Oglander, Brig-Gen C F *Military Operations Gallipoli* Vol II (Heinemann, London 1932)
Denham, H M *Dardanelles: A Midshipman's Diary* (Murray, London 1981)
James, Robert Rhodes *Gallipoli* (Batsford, London 1965)
Pugsley, Christopher *Gallipoli: The New Zealand Story** (Hodder, Auckland 1984)

Kemal Ataturk

Kinross, Lord *Ataturk: The Rebirth of a Nation* (Weidenfeld, London 1964).
Revue Internationale d'Histoire Militaire No 50 (1981) on Ataturk by Turkish Commission of Military History
Volkan, Vamik D & Itzhowitz, Norman *The Immortal Ataturk: A Psychobiography* (Univ of Chicago Press, 1984)

Mesopotamia and Persia

Barker, A J *The Neglected War: Mesopotamia 1914-1918* (Faber, London 1967)
Barker, A J *Townshend of Kut* (Cassell, London 1967)
Braddon, Russell *The Siege* [Kut] (Cape, London 1969)
Burne, A H *Mesopotamia: The Last Phase* (Gale & Polden, London 1936)
Goodman, Susan *Gertrude Bell* (Berg, Leamington Spa/Dover 1985)
Moberly, Brig-Gen F J *The Campaign in Mesopotamia* * 4 vols (HMSO, London 1923-27)
Moberly, Brig-Gen F J *Military Operations in Persia 1914-1919* (1929; repr HMSO/IWM 1987)

AFRICAN OPERATIONS

Farwell, Byron *The Great War in Africa* (Viking, London 1987)
Lucas, Sir Charles *The Empire at War Vol IV Africa* (OUP 1924)

West Africa

Haywood, Col A & Clarke, Brig F A S *The History of the Royal West African Frontier Force* (Gale & Polden, Aldershot 1964)
Moberly, Brig-Gen F J *Military Operations Togoland and the Cameroons* * (HMSO, London 1931)

South and South West Africa

Buxton, Earl *General Botha* (Murray, London 1924)
Meinjtes, Johannes *General Louis Botha: A Biography* (Cassell, London 1970)
Wheeler, Douglas L & Pelissier, René *Angola* (Pall Mall Press, London 1971)

East Africa

Clifford, Sir Hugh *The Gold Coast Regiment in the East African Campaign* (Murray, London 1920)
Crowe, Brig-Gen J H V *General Smuts' Campaign in East Africa* (Murray, London 1918)
Downes, Capt W D *With the Nigerians in East Africa* (Methuen, London 1919)
Hodges, Geoffrey *The Carrier Corps: Military Labor in the East Africa Campaign 1914-1918* (Greenwood Press, Westport, Connecticut 1986)
Hordern, Lt-Col Charles & Stacke, Maj H *Military Operations:East Africa* (HMSO, London 1941)
Lettow-Vorbeck, Paul von *My Reminiscences of East Africa* (Hurst & Blackett, London 1920)
Mackenzie, John 'The Naval Campaigns on Lakes Victoria and Nyasa 1914-18' from *The Mariner's Mirror* Vol 71 No 2 (Greenwich, 1985)
Miller, Charles *Battle for the Bundu: The First World War in East Africa* (Macdonald & Jane's, London 1974)
Moyse-Bartlett, Lt-Col H *The King's African Rifles: A Study in the Military History of East and Central Africa 1890-1945* (Gale & Polden Aldershot 1956)
Shankland, Peter *The Phantom Flotilla: The Story of the Naval Africa Expedition 1915-16* (Mayflower Books ed, St Albans 1969)
Sibley, Maj J R *Tanganyikan guerrilla: East African campaign 1914-1918* (Pan Ballantine ed, London 1973)

French Africa

Howe, Sonia E *Lyautey of Morocco* (Hodder, London 1931)
Service historique de l'armée (Lt-Cols Weithas & Remy) *Les Armées Françaises pendant la Grande Guerre* Tome IX vol 2 (Paris 1930)
Usborne, Vice-Adm C V *The Conquest of Morocco* (Stanley Paul, London 1936)

Senussi Revolt and Italian Africa

Evans-Pritchard E E *The Senussi of Cyrenaica* (Clarendon Press, Oxford 1949)
Gaibi, Maj A *Manuale di Storia Politico-Militare delle Colonie Italiane* (War Ministry Official History, Rome 1928)

SEA WAR

General

British Vessels Lost at Sea 1914-18 (Patrick Stephens, Cambridge 1977 repr of 1919 Admiralty publication)
Coletta, Paola E *Seapower in the Atlantic and Mediterranean in World War I* (UP of America, Lanham, New York & London, 1989)
Conway's All the World's Fighting Ships 1906-1921 (Conway Maritime Press, London 1985)
Encyclopedia Britannica 12th ed (1922)
Frere Cook, Gervis and Macksey, Kenneth *The Guinness History of Sea Warfare* (Guinness, Enfield 1975)
Marder, Arthur J *From the Dreadnought to Scapa Flow* 5 vols (OUP 1961-70)
Pemsel, Helmut *Atlas of Naval Warfare* (Arms & Armour Press, 1977)
Winton, John *The Victoria Cross at Sea* (Michael Joseph, London 1978)

Arctic, Baltic and Black Seas

Greger, René *The Russian Fleet 1914-1917* * (Ian Allan, Shepperton 1972)
Mawdsley, Evan *The Russian Revolution and the Baltic Fleet:War and Politics February 1917-April 1918* (Macmillan, London 1978)
Wilson, Michael *Baltic Assignment: British Submarines in Russia 1914-1919* (Leo Cooper, London 1985)

Mediterranean

Denham, HM *Dardanelles: A Midshipman's Diary 1915-16* (John Murray, London 1981)
Elliott, Peter *The Cross and the Ensign: A naval history of Malta 1798-1979* (Patrick Stephens, 1979)
Halpern, Paul G *Naval War in the Mediterranean* (Allen & Unwin, London 1987)

336

The Italian Navy in the World War 1915-1918 Facts & Figures (Rome, 1927)

North Sea and Grand Fleet
Roskill, Stephen *Admiral of the Fleet Earl Beatty* (Collins, London 1980)
Temple Paterson, A *Tyrwhitt of the Harwich Force* (Macdonald, London, 1973)

Naval Intelligence
Beesly, Patrick *Room 40: British Naval Intelligence 1914-1918* (Hamish Hamilton, London 1982)

Cruiser Warfare
Bennett, Geoffrey *Coronel and the Falklands* (Pan ed, London 1967)
Fayle, C Ernest *Seaborne Trade* Vol 1 *The Cruiser Period* (John Murray, London 1920)

U-boat War
Ritchie, Carson *Q-Ships* (Terence Dalton, Lavenham, Suffolk 1985)
Tarrant, VE *The U-boat Offensive 1914-1945* (Arms & Armour Press, London 1989)

German Navy
Herwig, Holger H *Luxury Fleet: The Imperial German Navy 1888-1918* (Ashfield Press paperback ed, London 1987)

Pacific
Howarth, Stephen *Morning Glory: A History of the Imperial Japanese Navy* (Hamish Hamilton, London 1984)

AIR WAR

Books
Bickers, Richard Townshend *The First Great Air War* (Hodder, London 1988)
Bowen, Ezra (& Editors of Time-Life Books) *Knights of the Air* (Time-Life Books, Alexandria, Va 1980)
Brown, D, Shores, C and Macksey, K *The Guinness History of Air Warfare* (Guinness Superlatives, Enfield 1976)
Bruce, JM *British Aeroplanes 1914-1918* (Putnam, London 1957)
Cole, Christopher and Cheeseman, EF *The Air Defence of Britain 1914-1918* (Putnam, London 1984)
Cole, Christopher (ed) *Royal Flying Corps 1915-1916* [Communiqués] (Kimber, London 1969; repr 1990)
Cole, Christopher (ed) *Royal Air Force 1918* [Communiqués] (Kimber, London 1968; repr 1990)
Dollfuss, Charles and Bouché, Henri *Histoire de l'Aéronautique* (L'Illustration, Paris 1937)
Finne, R *Sikorsky: The Early Years* (Airlife, Shrewsbury 1987)
Fitzsimons, Bernard (ed) *Warplanes and Air Battles of World War I* (BPC, London 1973)
Fredette, Raymond H *The First Battle of Britain 1917/18* (Cassell, London 1966)
Gibbons, Floyd *The Red Knight of Germany* (Cassell, London 1933)
Gray, Peter L and Thetford, Owen *German Aircraft of the First World War* 2nd edition (Putnam, London 1970)
Grey, CG (ed) *Jane's All the World's Aircraft* (Sampson Low, Marston, London 1919)
Imrie, Alex *German Fighter Units June 1917-1918* (Osprey, London 1978)
Imrie, Alex *Pictorial History of the German Army Air Service* (Ian Allan, London 1971)
Jones, HA *War in the Air* Vols 2-6 & Appendices (Clarendon Press, Oxford 1928-37; repr Hutchinson 1969)
Mason, Francis K and Windrow, Martin *Battle Over Britain* (McWhirter, London 1969)
Middleton, Edgar *The Great War in the Air* 4 vols (Waverley Book Co, London 1920)
Morrow, John H Jr *German Air Power in World War I* (U of Nebraska P, Lincoln 1982)
Penrose, Harold *British Aviation: The Great War and Armistice, 1915-1919* (Putnam, London 1969)
Raleigh, Sir Walter *War in the Air* Vol 1 (Clarendon Press, Oxford 1922)
Rimmell, Raymond Laurence *Zeppelin! A Battle for Air Supremacy in World War I* (Conway Maritime Press, London 1984)
Robertson, Bruce (ed) *Air Aces of the 1914-1918 War* (Harleyford, Letchworth 1959)
Robinson, Douglas H *The Zeppelin in Combat* (Foulis, London 1961) and *Giants in the Sky* (Foulis, London 1973)
Sikorsky, Igor *The Winged S* (Hale, London 1939)
Supf, Peter *Das Buch der Deutschen Fluggeschichte* 2 vols (Drei Brunnen Verlag, Stüttgart 1956-58)
Taylor, John W R et al (ed) *The Guinness Book of Air Facts and Feats* 3rd ed (Guinness, Enfield 1977)
Weyl, AR *Fokker: The Creative Years* (Putnam, London 1972)
Whitehouse, Arch *The Zeppelin Fighters* (NEL ed, London 1972)
Woodhouse, Jack and Embleton, G A *The War in the Air 1914-1918* (Almark, London 1974)

Aircraft Profiles
(All published Profile Publications, Leatherhead/Windsor 1965/67)
No 9 Gray, Peter L *The Albatros DV*
No 17 Andrews, CF *The SPAD XIII C.1*
No 25 Gray, Peter L *The Fokker D. VII*
No 26 Bruce, JM *The de Havilland D.H. 4*
No 31 Bruce, JM *The Sopwith Camel*
No 37 Bowers, Peter N *The Curtiss JN-4*
No 38 Bruce, JM *The Fokker Monoplanes*
No 43 Gray, Peter L *The Pfalz D. III*
No 49 Andrews, CF *The Nieuport 17*
No 61 Cattaneo, Gianni *The S.V.A. Ansaldo Scouts*
No 62 Bruce, JM *The de Havilland, D.H. 9*
No 68 Strnad, Frank *The Thomas-Morse Scout*
No 73 Bruce, JM *The Sopwith Triplane*
No 74 Bruce, JM *The Short 184*
No 79 Bowers, Peter M *The Nieuport N.28C-1*
No 85 Bruce, JM *The R.E. 8*
No 86 Gray, Peter L *The Siemens-Schuckert D III & IV*
No 103 Bruce, JM *The S.E. 5*
No 109 Bruce, JM *The Hanriot D.D. I*
No 115 Grosz, Peter M *The Gotha GI-V*
No 121 Bruce, JM *The Sopwith 1^1/2-Strutter*
No 127 Gray, Peter L *The Albatros DI-DIII*
No 145 Bruce, JM *The de Havilland D. 10*
No 151 Haddow, George *The O. Aviatik (Berg) DI*
No 157 Bruce, JM and Noël, Jean *The Breguet 14*
No 163 Grosz, Peter M *The Roland CII*
No 169 Bruce, JM *The Sopwith Dolphin*
No 175 Haddow, George *The Phönix Scouts*
No 181 Bruce, JM *The de Havilland D.H. 5*
No 187 Cowin, Hugh *The Junkers Monoplanes*
No 193 Bruce, JM *The Bristol M.1*
No 199 Grosz, Peter M *The Pfalz D XII*
No 200 Bruce, JM *The Martinsyde Elephant*

INTERNATIONAL EVENTS

Luebke, Frederick C *Bonds of Loyalty: German-Americans and World War I* (N Illinois UP, 1974)
Luebke, Frederick C *Germans in Brazil: A comparative history of cultural conflict during World War I* (Louisiana UP, Baton Rouge 1987)Ritter, Gerhard *The Sword and the Sceptre: The Problem of Militarism in Germany* Vols 3 & 4 (Allen Lane, London 1973)
Shanafelt, Gary W *The Secret Enemy: Austria-Hungary and the German Alliance 1914-1918* (Columbia UP, NY 1985)

Espionage and Intelligence
Andrew, Christopher *Secret Service: The Making of the British Intelligence Community* (Heinemann, London 1985)
Busch, Tristan *Secret Service Unmasked* (Hutchinson, London 1950)
Haswell, Jock *British Military Intelligence* (Weidenfeld, London 1973)
Kahn, David *The Codebreakers: The Story of Secret Writing* (Weidenfeld, London 1968)
Kahn, David *Hitler's Spies* (Arrow Books ed, London 1980)
Keay, Julia *The Spy who Never Was: The Life and Loves of Mata Hari* (Michael Joseph, London 1987)
Seth, Ronald *Encyclopedia of Espionage* (New English Library, 1972)

Prisoners of War
Garrett, Richard *P.O.W.* (David & Charles, Newton Abbot/London 1981)
Moynihan, Michael (ed) *Black Bread and Barbed Wire: Prisoners in the First World War* (Leo Cooper, London 1978)
Reid, Maj Pat & Michael, Maurice *Prisoner of War* (Hamlyn, London 1984)

HOME FRONTS

Rickards, Maurice & Moody, Michael *The First World War: ephemera, mementoes, documents* (Jupiter Books, London 1975)

Propaganda and Films
Haste, Cate *Keep the Home Fires Burning: Propaganda in the First World War*

(Allen Lane, London 1977)

Isenberg, Michael T *War on Film: The American Cinema and World War I 1914-1941* (Fairleigh Assoc Dickinson UPs, Rutherford NJ 1981)

Reeves, Nicholas *Official British Film Propaganda During the First World War* (Croom Helm, London 1986)

Sanders, Michael L & Taylor, Philip M *British Propaganda during the First World War 1914-18* (Macmillan, London 1982)

Austria

Brook-Shepherd, Gordon *The Last Habsburg* (Weidenfeld, London 1968)

McGarvie, Michael *Francis Joseph I: A Study in Monarchy* (Monarchist Press Assoc, London 1966)

Redlich, Joseph *Austrian War Government* (Yale UP, New Haven 1929)

Britain

Gilbert, Martin *Winston S Churchill Vols 3 & 4 1914-1922* (Heinemann, London 1971-72)

Hamilton, J A B *Britain's Railways in World War I* (Allen & Unwin, London 1967)

Lloyd George, David *War Memoirs* 2 vols (Oldhams, London 1938)

Bulgaria

Constant, Stephen *Foxy Ferdinand 1861-1948 Tsar of Bulgaria* (Sidgwick, London 1979)

France

Becker, Jean-Jacques *The Great War and the French People* (Berg, Leamington Spa 1985)

Fontaine, Arthur *French Industry During the War* (Yale UP, New Haven, 1926)

Saint Loup *Renault* (Bodley Head, London 1957)

Germany

Feldmann, Gerald D *Army, Industry and Labor in Germany 1914-1918* (Princeton 1966)

Hull, Isabel V *The Entourage of Kaiser William II 1888-1918* (CUP, London 1982)

Manchester, William *The Arms of Krupp 1587-1968* (Bantam Books ed, New York 1970)

Palmer, Alan *The Last Kaiser: Warlord of the Second Reich* (Weidenfeld, London 1978)

Whittle, Tyler *The Last Kaiser: A biography of William II German Emperor and King of Prussia* (Heinemann, London 1977)

Williamson, Gordon *The Iron Cross: A history 1813-1957* (Blandford, Poole 1984)

Wrisberg, Maj-Gen Ernest von *Wehr und Waffen 1914-1918* (Koehler, Leipzig 1922)

Hungary

Galántai, József *Hungary in the First World War* (Akadémiai Kiadó, Budapest, 1989)

Italy

Seton-Watson, Christopher *Italy from Literalism to Fascism 1870-1925* (Methuen, London 1967)

Portugal

Wheeler, Douglas L *Republican Portugal: A Political History 1910-1926* (Univ of Wisconsin Press 1978)

Rumania

Seicaru, Pamfil *La Roumanie dans la Grande Guerre* (Minard, Paris 1968)

Science and Technology

Crow, Duncan (ed) *Armoured Fighting Vehicles of World War One* (Profile Publications, Windsor 1970)

Haber, L F *The Poisonous Cloud: Chemical Warfare in the First World War* (Clarendon Press, Oxford 1986)

Hartcup, Guy *The War of Invention: Scientific Developments 1914-18* (Brassey's, London 1988)

Turkey and the Armenian Massacres

Gurun, Kamaran *The Armenian File: The Myth of Innocence Exposed* (Rustem/Weidenfeld, London/Istanbul 1984)

Lang, David Marshall *The Armenians: A People in Exile* (Allen & Unwin, London 1981)

Nassibian, Akaby *Britain and the Armenian Question 1915-1923* (Croom Helm, London 1984)

Walker, Christopher J *Armenia: The Survival of a Nation* (Croom Helm, London 1980)

Women

Ewing, Elizabeth *Women in Uniform through the centuries* (Batsford, London 1975).

Marwick, Arthur *Women at War 1914-1918* (London 1977)

Peace Movement

Moorehead, Caroline *Troublesome People: Enemies of War 1916-1986* (Hamish Hamilton, London 1987)

Poets

Bridgwater, Patrick *The German Poets of the First World War* (Croom Helm, London & Sydney 1985)

Cross, Tim *The Lost Voices of World War 1* (Bloomsbury, London 1988)

Reilly, Catherine W *English Poetry of the First World War: A Bibliography* (George Prior, London 1978)

Stallworthy, Jon (ed) *The Oxford Book of War Poetry* (OUP 1984)

Symons, Julian *An Anthology of War Poetry* (Penguin, 1942)

Periodicals & Newspapers

Stand To! The Journal of the Western Front Association 1980-
The Times (London) Aug 1914-Dec 1918
War Monthly 1974-82 (as *Military History* 1982-84)
Warship Journal 1983-85

GLOSSARY

Note: This alphabetical list includes not only abbreviations and terms used in the Chronicle, but also ones that readers might encounter in First World War literature. Usually it is restricted to terminology originating in the war itself. For a fuller and fascinating treatment of language used but often long pre-dating 1914-18, such as most regimental nicknames, see *Soldier and Sailor Words and Phrases* by Edward Fraser & John Gibbons (Routledge, London 1925), and *The Long Trail, What the British Soldier Sang and Said in the War of 1914-18* by Eric Partridge with John Brophy (Revised edition 1969, Sphere).

A

AA	Anti-aircraft guns or gunfire
Abdul	British slang for Turk
About turn	BEF slang for Hébuterne, France
Ace	Airman who has shot down at least 5 aircraft, originally a French 1915 definition
AChD	Army Chaplains' Dept (British), made Royal 22 Feb 1919 for war work. Grew from 117 to 3416 (Aug 1918)
ACM	Air Chief Marshal
Ack-Ack	(from Signallers code for 'A') anti-aircraft guns or fire
ADC	Aide-de-camp, officer on monarch's, general's or governor's staff
AD Corps	Army Dental Corps (British)
Adj	Adjutant
Adm	Admiral
admin	administration
AEC	Army Educational Corps (British)
AEF	American Expeditionary Forces (in France). Cynics said it stood for 'After England Failed'. Irreverent members called it 'Arse End First'.
AFSR	Armed Forces of South Russia, united White Volunteer Army and southern Cossacks 1919-20
Ah wee	British rendition of French *Ah oui*
AIF	Australian Imperial Force (Australian troops overseas)
Air pill	Bomb dropped by aircraft
'Alf a mo, Kaiser!'	British expression from a popular 1914 recruiting poster
ALH	Australian Light Horse (mounted infantry)
Alleyman	A German from French *Allemand*, gave way to Jerry
All Highest	Prussian title of the Kaiser's, from the German *Aller Hochst*
Alpini	Italian mountain troops (founded 1876), the 52 bns (8 regts) of 1915 expanded to 78 bns in 1916.
am [of 12]	morning [of the 12th]
AMC	Armed Merchant Cruiser
Antwerp Expresses	German Army term for large HE shells from their success on that city
ANZAC	Australia New Zealand Army Corps
Anzac	Australia/New Zealand beach and sector at Gallipoli. Originally suggested as simpler telegraphic code by British Lt A T White at ANZAC HQ, Cairo
AOC	Army Ordnance Corps (British), awarded title Royal for war work Nov 1918
APM	Assistant Provost Marshal (British Military Police), unofficially 'A Permanent Malingerer'
appt	appointed
approx	approximately
Apres la gare	Never, from the French *Après la guerre*
Archie	Anti-aircraft gun or its shell after music hall performer or song
Arditi	Italian picked assault troops formed 1917. Each corps (26 maximum) had a battalion-strength group of these specially trained young men with a higher issue of automatic weapons & grenades, & some flame-throwers *see Stosstruppen*
Arminteers	British slang for the French border town of Armentières and its famous mademoiselle
Armstrong hut	British small collapsible wood & canvas building
Army	Formation of several corps (qv) & their component divs
Army Council	Five military members, civil and finance members administering British Army since 1904

Arty	Artillery	Bangalore torpedo	A 6ft -long pipe-like explosive device (several could be jointed together) for destroying barbed wire and mines invented by Maj RL McClintock RE (1908-14) in India, hence name
ASC	Army Service Corps (British), also known as 'Ally Slopers' Cavalry' or unfairly 'Army Safety Corps'. Grew from 14,491 men with 246 motor vehicles to 327,603 (Sept 1918) with 125,149 motor vehicles (1 Mar 1919). Awarded title Royal Nov 1918.	Bankers' Battalion	British 26th Royal Fusiliers
		Bantam	British soldier under minimum Army height of 5ft 3in (35th Div once all Bantam)
Ash can	US Navy term for depth charge		
Asiatic Annie	Turk heavy gun at the Dardanelles	BAR	Browning Automatic Rifle, US light machine-gun first produced Feb 1918, 52,000 by Armistice
Askari	African native soldier		
Asquiths	British term for French matches, user had to 'wait and see' if they lighted	Barbette	Fixed armoured shelter in a warship behind which a gun revolves on a turntable (part of a turret from French *barbe* for beard)
Assoc	Association		
Asst	Assistant	Barishnya	British N Russia troops' term for unmarried Russian girl
A/S	Anti-submarine		
ASW	Anti-Submarine warfare	Baron	An Army commander (British slang)
Ataman	Chief of Cossack host	Barrage	Continuous artillery fire along a selected sector, and derived from the French (*see* creeping barrage). Also a large sea minefield
Attaboy	American baseball slang, became popular in England 1917-18		
Aus	Australian	Bat boat	Sopwith flying boat
av	average	Batman	An officer's servant
AVC	Army Veterinary Corps (British), jestingly rendered as 'All Very Cushy'. Grew from 519 men to 29,452. Awarded title Royal 1920 for war work (*see* RAVC).	Battalion	Basic unit of infantry formed of several companies (usually 4). Several battalions (usually 3) formed a regiment (all armies except British). 1914 full establishment strengths seldom thereafter ever achieved: Austrian 1064 all ranks; Belgian 1000+; British 30 officers & 992 other ranks; French 22 officers & 1030 ranks (750, 1918); German 26 officers & 1050 other ranks (reduced to 980 men then 880 on 1 July 1918); Russian 18 officers & 958 ranks; Italian 1000 (1915); American (1917) 27 officers & 1026 enlisted men
Avec	Spirits, as in *Café avec* (request for liquor)		

B

b	born		
BA	*Brieftauben-Abteilung* ('carrier pigeon unit', ie bomber unit)	Battery	Basic unit of artillery (4-8 guns). All powers except Britain, Germany, Austria & Russia began with 4-gun field batteries. Germany (from 6) and Russia (from 8) reduced to 4.
Baa lamb	Battleship HMS *Barham*		
BAB	Telephone code most commonly used in British trenches from 1916	Battle-bag	Naval airship (British slang)
		Battle bowler	Early name for British steel helmet
Baby Killers	Churchill's insult to the German Navy for bombarding Scarborough 16 Dec 1914. Soon applied to Zeppelins	Battlecruiser	Fast but lighter armoured (than battleship) capital ship since 1908 in British, Japanese and German navies (*Goeben* in Turkish)
Baby Monitors	British Dover Patrol term for M-class monitors		
Bags, the	Sandbags on trench parapet	Battle surplus	British personnel left out of an attack in order to rebuild the unit, also called the Lifeboat Party
Balb, to	Airman's jargon for getting an opponent in a bad position, of American origin		
Ballo, Ballyhooly	BEF nicknames for French border town of Bailleul, a haven till 1918	Battling Third	British destroyer flotilla (qv) with Harwich Force

Bav	Bavarian		used till after 1870-1 but may be contraction of *Alboche*, slang for *Allemand* (German), especially in Alsace.
Bde, bde	Brigade		
BE	Biplane Experimental (British). The BE8 was nick-named the Boater.	Bn, bns	Battalion(s)
		[5] bn	[5] billion
Beachy Bill	Large Turk gun at Gallipoli opposite Anzac	Boloism	Treason in high places, from French traitor Bolo Pasha executed 1918
Beaucoup	French word that became Allied term for 'plenty of'	Bombers	Grenade-throwing troops or bombing aircraft
Beetle off	British airmen slang for 'to fly straight'	Boob, the	A guardroom or military prison, of American origin
BEF	British Expeditionary Force (in France)		
Behemoths, the	Grand Fleet's 3rd Battle Squadron (8 *King Edward VII* class battleships)	Bond Street ribbon	Medal or decoration given for British Home Service
Belgeek	British slang for Belgium or a Belgian	Box barrage	Protective artillery fire put down on 3 sides of troops
Belly band	British flannel cholera belt	Box-respirator	British-made gas helmet of 1916
Belly flopping	British term for crouching rushes by attacking troops	Brass hat	A staff officer or senior officer from the gold lace on their cap. In Navy a Commander & higher
Bersaglieri	Elite Italian riflemen (founded 1836, *bersaglio* means target), 12 regts (68 bns incl 10 of cyclists) in 1915 became 21 by war's end	Brigade	Infantry, cavalry or artillery unit of 2-6 battalions, regiments or batteries; 2-4 brigades made a division. An American infantry brigade (1917) had 6 infantry battalions plus 1 MG battalion with 8469 all ranks, almost as big as many Allied and German divisions by then.
Bert	BEF slang for Albert, town N of the Somme		
Big Bertha	German gunners' nickname (after the Krupp owner) *'die dicke Bertha'* 'the fat Bertha' for the 2 Krupp-made 42cm (16.5-in) siege howitzers that smashed the Liége forts in 1914. Allies erroneously applied it to the 1918 Paris Gun (*see* Long Max).	Brig-Gen	Brigadier-General, most junior general officer (1-star general in Second World War parlance). British Army abolished rank 1920, replaced by one of Colonel-Commandant until rank of Brigadier introduced 1928
Big noise, a	American slang for VIP	Brigade-major	Principal staff officer of a British Brig-Gen, usually a captain
Birdcage	PoW barbed wire enclosure at the Front, also final Allied entrenched area N of Salonika	British warm	Short coat worn by British officers, not officially uniform till 1918
Black Maria	British slang for large German shell, emitting black smoke. German term was *Schwarz Maria*	Brownies, the	British Women's Land Army or Government girl messengers, from their uniform
Blighty	British slang for British Isles (from the prewar Army in India), hence Blighty one, a wound to ensure going home	BSA	British South Africa Police.
		Buck	A dapper private (US Army); too full of talk (British)
Blimp	A small non-rigid airship (Allied)		
Blue Cross	A 1917 German poison gas (from shell's colour coding)	Bully beef	Corned beef in a tin
		Bundesrat	Upper House of German Parliament. Set up 1871 to represent princes of the German States
Blue Cross, the	Auxiliary Veterinary Service (British civilian), first animal hospital in France before 16 Dec 1914 at Sequeux, 30 miles from Dieppe	Burglars	Bulgarians (British slang)
		Butterfly boat	Cross-Channel leave ferries, especially Le Havre-Southampton
Blue Devils	French *Chasseurs Alpins*		
BMA	British Medical Association	Butt-notcher	A sniper
Boche	French term of abuse for Germans with many derivatives. Origin disputed, not	Byng Boys	Canadian troops (from their GOC 1916-17)

C

c — circa, approximately

C3 — Men unfit for active service overseas (British Military Service Act 1916)

Cafard, le — French Army term for nervous debility after long duty in the trenches

Cagnas — French Army word for barracks, used by some Canadian units

Caimani di Piave — Italian Army unit of volunteer swimmers in that river 1917-18.

Calm-laylas, the — British nickname for Egyptian Labour Corps, from its chants to camels

Camouflage — Deception of the enemy by artifical scenery and dummy guns, etc or dazzle paint schemes at sea, from the French *camoufler* to bind or veil. Adopted into English 1914-15

Canteen eggs — Gas attack (British)

Capital ship — Battleship or battlecruiser, yardstick of naval strength

Capt — Captain

'Carl the Caretaker's in charge!' — Anglo-American W Front phrase for finding a quiet German sector opposite

cas — casualties

Catsood — Drunk, from the initial French price (*quatre sous*) of a drink at an *estaminet* or village café

Catwalk — Brick pathway across sodden fields, usually 1 brick (9 in) wide

Cav, cav — Cavalry

CB — confined to barracks - a punishment

Cdn — Canadian

Cdr, cdrs — Commander, rank and position

Cdt — Commandant

CEC — Central Executive Committee of Bolshevik (Communist) Party

CEF — Canadian Expeditionary Force (overseas)

Central Powers — Germany and Austria-Hungary due to their central position in Europe between France and Russia. Bulgaria and Turkey added 1914-15

CFS — Central Flying School (Britain)

CGT — *Comité Général du Travail* (French trade union founded 1895)

Chauchat — French 1915 LMG. Despite its legendary faults US Army accepted 37,000 as its main weapon until the Browning.

Challenge ships — American term for the ships *Orleans* & *Rochester* sent to France (May 1916) to test the U-boat blockade

Char d'assaut — A tank (French)

Cheka — Soviet political police, original KGB

Cherry Nobs — British Military Police, from their cap colour

Chicken, the — US Army slang for the national eagle badge

Chinese attack — A trick or feint

Chinese Rolls-Royce — A Ford van (RASC)

Chink, a — Chinese Labour Corps member in France

Chm — Chairman

Chit — Army official form or anything written

C-in-C — Commander-in-Chief

CID — Committee of Imperial Defence (British, founded 1906)

CIGS — Chief of the Imperial General Staff (British)

circ — circulation (of publications)

Civvies — Plain clothes as opposed to uniform

Click — To get what you want; especially to get home

CMAR — 'Can't manage a rifle', RAMC spelt backwards

CMB — Coastal Motor Boat (British), *see* Scooter

Cmdre — Commodore

CMH — Congressional Medal of Honor (US)

Cmndt — Commandant

CNS — Chief of Naval Staff

CO — Commanding Officer

Co — Company (business)

Coffee cooler, a — A shirker (US Army)

Coal-box — British slang for a heavy German shell. German word was *Kohlenkasten*. French phrase was *Gros Noir*.

Col — Colonel

col — column

Colco-Pari — Salonika Front term for how much, from the Bulgarian and used of illicit bargaining

Comb-out — to clear out men of military age from civilian work

Comic cuts	BEF term for intelligence summaries at brigade level & above		of advancing troops
Commo	Communication trench	Cricket ball, a	Type of British hand grenade
Compo	Pay	crimed	Entered on British Army 'crime sheet' as an offender
'Comrades of the Mist'	US Navy phrase for the Grand Fleet	Crown, the	British slang for Sergeant-Major, from the sleeve badge
Conchy	conscientious objector	Crucifix corner	Calvary cross on a French roadside or crossroads
Cons-Gen	Consul-General (diplomatic official)	Crucifixion	*See* FP1
contd	continued	Crump	Sound of the explosion of a large shell
Contour chasing	Low flying	Crystal Palace Army	Nickname for RND (qv) from their S London depot, hence glasshouse sailors. Also site of Imperial War Museum 1920-4, visited by 3m people. Crystal Palace also christened twin-tall pithead structures at Loos, France (1915).
Cordite	smokeless explosive introduced in 1889, so-called from its cord-like appearance		
Cook's tour, a	British term for a new unit's look at the trenches or a VIP visit to them		
Cookhouse official	Any baseless rumour (British)	CSM	Company Sergeant-Major (British)
Cooshu, a	A sleep, from the French *coucher*	Ctee	Committee
Corned dog	Canned beef	CUP	Committee of Union and Progress, Young Turks' political party 1908-18
Corp	Corporation	Cup and wad	British slang for tea and a bun in the canteen or YMCA hut
Corps, Army	In full *corps d'armée* from the French all-arms formations first developed in 1800 to be miniature armies. Comprised 2-3 divisions with supporting units. (1914: German c44,000 men & 160 guns; French c38,000 & 120 guns; Russian c35,000 & 144 guns; British c36,000 & 152 guns) Italian (1915) 40,250 men & c104 guns.	Curtain fire	A continuous wall of artillery fire to seal off an area
		Cushy	Comfortable, also La Cauchie, nr Arras, France
		Cuthbert	British term for one who avoided military service as being indispensable elsewhere. First coined by *Evening News* cartoonist 'Poy' who drew frightened looking rabbits.
Corpse ticket	Identity disc. In the British Army a green one was buried with the owner and a red one retained for record purposes.		
CoS	Chief of Staff, either to a commander or as head of an armed force.		
Coy, coy	Company, sub-unit of a battalion. Infantry ones all had 4. 1914 establishments: German 5 officers & 259 other ranks; Austrian 4 officers & 260 other ranks; Russian 4 officers & 240 other ranks; British 6 officers & 232 other ranks; American 1917 6 officers & 250 enlisted men.	**D**	
		d	died
		[3]d	[three] pence
Cp	Corporal	DADOS	Deputy Assistant Director of Ordnance Services (British). One for each division, supervised issue of over 20,000 items from guns to toothpaste. Hence Dado nickname for cholera belt.
CP	Command Post		
CPI	Committee on Public Information (US)		
CRA	Commander Royal Artillery (for a British div or higher)	Dandy	Fine, excellent. American term adopted by British from Canadian & US troops.
Crab grenade	British name for a type of German grenade	Darts	(French *flechettes*, German *Stahlpfeil* .) Early air-dropped anti-personnel weapon used in clusters
Crappo, a	French trench mortar, from *crapaud*	Dazzle	Striped naval camouflage (Allied) invented 1917 by the marine artist Cdr Norman Wilkinson RNVR
Creeping barrage	A barrage lifted at regular intervals (usually 50 yds every 90 seconds) ahead	DBR	Damaged beyond repair

DCM	Distinguished Conduct Medal (British, 1862) for Army NCOs and men for gallantry in field (24,620 with 481 bars awarded with 4957 and 1 bar to Allied armies 1914-20)
DCNS	Deputy Chief of Naval Staff
De-bus, to	Official British Army term coined for troops getting off motor transport
Decoy ships	*See* Q-ships
Depot ship	Mobile supply base for warships, especially submarines and destroyers
Dept	Department
Derby, a	British volunteer enlisted under the Derby scheme of October 1915
Der Tag	The Day, specifically the belief that it was a German Navy toast to victory over the British Fleet
Desert, to swing it across the	British EEF phrase for contriving one's way to hospital
Destroyer	In full torpedo boat destroyer (TBD), small gun & torpedo-armed warship for screening battlefleets against other destroyers and submarines
Det	Detachment
Devil's Wood	Delville Wood on the Somme, originally 160 acres dense woodland & under-growth
D/F	Direction-finding
DFC	Distinguished Flying Cross
DFM	Distinguished Flying Medal
DG	Director-General
DH	De Havilland, British aircraft make
Digger	An Australian or New Zealand soldier. Originally used of goldminers from the mid-1850s & revived by New Zealand troops in France 1916. Australian troops adopted it 1917 (Official History).
Dimback	A louse
Dingbat	Australian slang for batman
Dinky	Mule
Dir	Director
Dirigible	Balloon or airship directed by steering gear
dismtd	dismounted
Div, div(s)	Division(s)
Division	Infantry. Basic formation of combatant armies. German 17,500 men, 4000 horses, 72 guns & 24 MGs (1914) became 12,300

	men, 3000 horses, 48 guns, 120 mortars, 222 MGs, 6-12 lorries (1918). Austrian (1914) c15,000 men, 42 guns, 28 MGS. British 18,073 men, 5592 horses, 76 guns, 24 MGs became 13,035 men, 3673 horses, 48 guns, 36 mortars, 208 MGs, 14 cars & lorries (1918). French c15,000 men, 36 guns, 24 MGs (1914) became 11,400 men, 48 guns, 18 mortars, 324 MGs (1918). Russian 14,140 men, 48 guns, 32 MGs (1914). Belgian c22,000 men, 72 guns (1914). Serb (1914) 13,000-16,000 men, 26-44 guns. Bulgar (1915) 24,000 men, 44-66 guns. Italian (1915) 16,393 men, 2693 horses, 32 guns, 24 MGs. American (1917) 28,061 men, 72 guns, 260 MGs.
Division	Cavalry. (1914 establishments) German 5278 men, 5590 horses, 12 guns, 6 MGs (1914). British (BEF 1914) 9269 men, 9815 horses, 24 guns, 24 MGs. Belgian + French (+12 MGs) 5000/5250 men, 12 guns. Austrian c4500 men, 12 guns, 16 MGs. Russian 3466 men, 12 guns, 8 MGs.
Dixie	A camp cauldron
DH	De Havilland, British aircraft make
DMC	Desert Mounted Corps (British)
DMI	Director of Military Intelligence
DMO	Director of Military Operations
DNC	Director of Naval Construction (British)
DNI	Director of Naval Intelligence
Do an alley	To go off, from the French *aller*
Dock	A military hospital (British slang)
docs	documents
Doing it	BEF slang for Doingt, nr Péronne (Somme)
DORA	Defence of the Realm Act (British)
Doughboy	American soldier nickname, particularly infantrymen, dating from the Mexican or Civil Wars and derived from adobe huts or large buttons respectively. Much preferred to 'Sammies' (qv) or 'Teddies' (after Roosevelt), the original British nicknames & apparently chosen when US 1st Div CO asked for alternatives.
Dough nuts	Royal Navy term for the 8-man Carley float (life-saving raft)
Dover Patrol	Royal Navy force in the Channel to protect crossings & attack the occupied Belgian coast
dow	died of wounds
Dreadnought	Battleship built since 1906
DSC	Distinguished Service Cross, British naval decoration (1914) for officers below rank of Lt-Cdr. Also stood for 'Decent

	Suit of Civvies' to those awaiting demo-bilisation.		too much publicity after HMAS *Sydney 's* lauded victory
DRLS	Dispatch Rider Letter Service (British)	Emma	British signaller's code letter 'M'
Drowning Flotilla	Dover Patrol nickname for the German Flanders U-boat flotilla due to its heavy losses	Empire Battalion	17th Royal Fusiliers, wealthy unit raised in 10 days of August 1914
DSM	Distinguished Service Medal, British naval decoration (1914) for all non-commissioned ranks	EMSIB	Acronym for E Mediterranean Special Service Intelligence Bureau, a British Cairo-based counter-espionage body
DSO	Distinguished Service Order, British decoration (1886) for officers (9003 with 787 bars, 1916-on, conferred plus 1491 and 9 bars to 12 Allied armies 1914-20)	Entente	Name for Allied nations, from the Anglo-French *Entente Cordiale* of 1904
		eqpt	equipment
		eqvt	equivalent
Duay	My own, wartime slang apparently from the British Royal motto *Dieu et Mon Droit*	Erfs	Eggs, British rendering of *oeufs*
Duckboard	Slatted timber path or walk in trenches & camps, so-named from the sloping boards for duckhouses. Hence duckboard glide for stealthy night movement & duckboard harrier for a messenger.	*Ersatz*	German official word for reserve troops, soon applied to reliefs & substitutes of all kinds
		Esc	*Escadrille* , French air squadron
		ESMA	Listen! Arabic used by British EEF
Dug-out	Underground shelter in the trenches, British slang for retired officer recalled to service	est	estimated
		estab	established
Dullmajor	Interpreter for British PoW camps in Germany, from German *Dolmetsher* (interpreter)	excl	excluding
Dumdum bullet	From Dumdum arsenal nr Calcutta in India. A soft-nosed bullet which expands & lacerates on impact. Both sides accused the other of using such illegal ammunition.	**F**	
		FA	Field Artillery
Duncars	Armoured cars attached to British Dunsterforce in NW Persia and Baku 1918	Fairy light	Very pistol flare (BEF)
		Fan Tan	Name of British tank paid for (£6000) by En Tong Sen of the Malay States
Dun Cow	SS *River Clyde* at Gallipoli	FANY	First Aid Nursing Yeomanry Corps, British female Territorial unit founded 1909. Worked for Belgian Army from Oct 1914. Allowed to drive British ambulances in France from 1 Jan 1916. Staffed 3 French ambulance units from 1917.
Dunsterforce	Special British force equivalent to a reinforced brigade for operations in N Persia & at Baku, 1918		
		Fashy	Angry, from the French *fâché*
E		Fernleaves, the	New Zealander troops, from their badge
		FIDAC	*Fédération Inter-Alliée Des Anciens Combattants*, Allied veterans organization; 1st London Congress 1924
E	East/Eastern		
Earthed	An aircraft brought down (British term)	Field officers	Colonels, Lieutenant-Colonels, Majors (ie not company or general officers)
Eatables	BEF slang for Étaples, Pas-de-Calais town		
EEF	Egyptian Expeditionary Force (British, 1916-19)	Field rats	Prussian Guard scorn for ordinary line troops
EFC	Expeditionary Force Canteens, British supply organization on all fronts	Finee	No more, all gone! From the French *fini*
Egg shells	Cruiser HMS *Achilles*	Fivepence halfpenny	Derisive British Army term for something not there ie the supplementary Government daily rations allowance never seen by the soldier
Elephant, the	British Martinsyde aircraft		
Emden, sank the	Sarcastic British phrase for units getting		

Flaming onions	British slang for a German AA shell, apparently suggested by its similarity to Bretons selling street onions	FTR	Failed to return (aircraft or airships on operation)
Flapper's delight	British subaltern on leave in female company	Fuller phone	British Army tap-proof field telephone, replaced the Buzzer model from 1916
Flight	Aircraft unit of 5-6 aircraft (RFC/RAF)	Funk-hole	Colloquial term for small shelter or dugout, any safe refuge or job. Current in BEF by 29 Nov 1914.
Floating Ls, (or ELLS)	Royal Navy Harwich Force destroyer flotilla with L names, also known as Battling Ls	Funky Villas	BEF term for Fonquevillers village nr Hébuterne, France
Florrie Ford	Motor car or lorry, linked to Florrie Ford the actress	Furphy	Australian for rumour, originated at Melbourne on speculation as to their destination
Flotilla	Naval unit of destroyers etc or on inland waters		

G

Flt [Lt]	Flight [Lieutenant]	G	Gulf
Fly boys	Contemptuous Dublin term for English evading conscription by crossing to Ireland	Galloping Lockharts	British term for mobile field kitchens
FM	Field-Marshal	gals	gallons
FPI	Field Punishment No 1 (British offender lashed to gunwheel for given period)	Gas bag	Airship
		Gas guard	Night sentry duty to detect gas & strike a warning gong
Franc-tireur	French, literally 'free shooter' from the Franco-Prussian War of 1870-1. The spectre (largely) of these irregular guerilla marksmen haunted the Germans in 1914.	Gas patrols	British RAMC parties sent to detect mustard gas concentrations & warn passing troops
Fred Karno's Army	British New Army song-line after the period's popular comedian	Gaspirator	British slang for gas mask
Fred Karno's Navy	Dover Patrol, due to its variety of vessels (24 types)	Gassed at Mons	Whereabouts unknown. British joke reply perhaps precisely because no gas was used at Mons 1914.
Ft	Fort	Gat	Revolver (Canadian)
[360] ft	[360] feet	GCR	Gold Coast Regiment (British West African troops)
[10]-ft	[10]-foot (cliff, etc)	Gd(s)	Guard(s)
Freikorps	German irregular volunteer armed units of varying status that existed from the Armistice until 1922. About 120 of these 'free corps' formed, totalling 250,000 men. Most were of brigade or battalion strength with their equally-paid right wing veterans (especially officers) foreshadowing the Nazis.	Geddesburg	BEF name for Montreuil, site of GHQ, after Sir E Geddes became DG of Transportation there. Probably suggested by Gettysburg.
		Gentle Annie	Turk gun at the Dardanelles
Frightfulness	German war policy (Shrecklichkeit) of inspiring terror by wanton ruthlessness. Allied press term that became a Services joke.	George	British term for airman, equivalent to Jack and Tommy for the two older Services
		GER	Great Eastern Railway (British)
Frigo	Frozen or chilled meat	GHQ	General Headquarters
Fritz	A German, particularly in 1914-15. Also Royal Navy word for U-boat	Gin Palace	Battleship HMS Agincourt, perhaps because originally built for Turkey
Front	Russian and Soviet term for army group (several armies)	Glory hole	Any small billet or dugout, also German position nr Festubert captured at heavy cost
Frontiersmen, Legion of	25th (Service) Battalion, Royal Fusiliers, served E Africa. Derived from an Empire body founded 1906.	GOC	General Officer Commanding (British)

GOC-in-C	General Officer Commanding-in-Chief (British)	Gumboots	Trench waders, introduced to BEF from 1915
Gold stripe	British sleeve marking denoting a man wounded badly enough for removal to base hospital or home	Gwennie	Royal Navy equivalent of Archie (qv)

H

Go one better	Motto of British 42nd (E Lancs) Territorial Div	Hairbrush grenade	Early British trench weapon
Gong	Medal (old British Army term)	Hairy, a	Large British draught horse for medium or heavy artillery
Gooseberry	Small ball of barbed wire	Half Crown Battalion	Any 2/6th Bn, from the official designation
Gorgeous wrecks	Unflattering name for British Volunteer Defence Corps from their GR brassards. 'Govt rejects' was alternative usage	Hammer blows	German term first used to describe Verdun Offensive
Gotha	Name used for almost all German heavy bombers, from the type's town of manufacture	Handcart Cavalry	Nickname for British Stokes mortar units
		Hans Wurst	German term for an infantryman
Got me?	Do you understand? Phrase from a wartime American film in which the hero interrogates with a revolver.	Hard tack	Biscuit
		Hard tails	Mule
Gott Strafe England !	God punish England. German slogan spoken, published & inscribed everywhere.	Harkers	Men sent out on listening patrol
		Harry Tate's Cavalry	Nickname for British Yeomanry, after the well-known comedian
Gov-Gen	Governor-General	Harry Tate's Navy	RNVR (qv)
Govt	Government	Harwich Force	British cruisers & destroyers based at that E Coast port
GQG	*Grand Quartier Général* (French GHQ)		
Grabenkameradschaft	German for comradeship of the trenches, a feeling that separated 1914-18 front-line soldiers from all other participants	Hate	Artillery bombardment (British slang) from Ernst Lissauer's Sept 1914 'Hymn of Hate'
Grand Fleet	Main British force of capital ships & their escorts based at Scapa Flow & Rosyth. So dubbed by its commander Jellicoe; did not officially replace Home Fleet till May 1916.	Hazy Brook	BEF slang for Hazebrouck, French Flanders
		HE	High explosive
		Heine (Hiney)	A German, in US & Canadian Army parlance, from Heinz
Granny	Any large howitzer, originally the first British 15-in weapon of April 1915	Hellfire Corner	Lethal spot nr Menin Gate, Ypres & many other dangerous W Front places
Grasshopper	Military Policeman (British)	Herbaceous borders	Royal Navy's 'Flower class' sloops of 1915 on. (Names chosen by Admiralty's Acting Librarian).
Green Cross Shell	German type of poison gas shell		
Green Cross Society	Women's Reserve Ambulance Society (British) formed 1916 for hospital & nursing work, so-called from their badge	Heroine of Loos	Mlle Emilienne Moreau, a 17-yr-old French girl who won the MC protecting British wounded by killing 3 Germans at that battle
Green envelope	Ordinary British Army envelope for writing home and sent unsealed		
Greyback	British Army flannel shirt (from its colour)	HMG	His Majesty's Government (British)
		HMIMS	His Majesty's Indian Marine Ship (British)
Ground Hog Day	US Army slang for Armistice Day, ie everyone came out of cover		
Ground stunt	British air term for ground attack	HMS	His Majesty's Ship (British warship)
GSO	General Staff Officer	HMY	His Majesty's Yacht (British)
Guardian Angel	Parachute for escaping from a burning balloon	hols	holidays

Hommes forty	W Front term for a French railway van, from their capacity	IEF	Indian Expeditionary Force: 'A' for France, 'B' for E Africa, 'C' for Egypt and 'D' for Mesopotamia
Honved	Royal Hungarian *Landwehr* (qv) part of Austria's 5-part Army as renamed spring 1917. Organized in 32 infantry regts (96 bns) or 8 divs (increased by 17 regts to 12 divs), 10 hussar regts (2 cav divs) & 140 guns (9 regts or 35 btys became 24 regts).	Iggry	'Hurry up', British EEF term from the Arabic word
		IJN	Imperial Japanese Navy
		ILP	Independent Labour Party (British)
Hop out	BEF pronunciation of Hopoutre, suburb of Poperinghe, nr Ypres	Imperials, the	Dominion & Colonial troops' term for comrades from the Mother Country
Hop over	An attack, going over the top	[12-] in	[12-] inch
Horse of Troy	Nickname for SS *River Clyde* from her copying of the famous strategem enacted so near Gallipoli	incl	included/including
		indep	independent
Hostility Men	Royal Navy term for volunteers for the duration	Inf, inf	Infantry
		info	information
Howitzer	A short stubby gun firing heavy shells at low velocity & high angle. A dominant weapon in calibres from 75mm up to Big Bertha (qv).	Insp-Gen	Inspector-General
		int'l	international
HQ	headquarters	IRB	Irish Republican Brotherhood
Hun	Abusive term for a German, apparently derived from the Kaiser advising German troops sent to China in July 1900 to act like the Huns under Attila	Iron Cross	German gallantry award founded in 1813. Revived 1870 & 1914. Anything from 80,000 to c250,000 awarded.
Hunland	British airmen's term for any territory with German troops	Iron Division	Newspaper-coined compliment to British 13th Division (Gallipoli & Mesopotamia). Also Kaiser's prewar term for his 3rd Brandenburg Division. Also earned by the French XX Corps (11th & 39th Divs), French 20th & Russian 4th Divisions, Belgian 3rd (Liège) Div.
Hurrah Kanaille	Prussian cavalry's derogatory term for infantry, equivalent to 'cannon fodder'		
Hush Hush Army	Dunsterforce (qv)		
Hush Hush Crowd	British Tank Corps	Iron ration	Soldier's emergency ration not supposed to be eaten except by officer's permission but not uncommonly 'destroyed by shellfire' & replaced by fresh issue. Hence 'Jerry's iron ration' humorous British term for shells fired at Germans.
Hush Hush Operation	Projected British 1917 landing on Flanders coast		
Hush Hush Ships	Royal Navy expression for various unusual warship classes		
		ISP	Independent Socialist Party (German)
Hypo-helmet	Flannel bag with eye-pieces soaked in anti-gas solution, British equipment first made 10 May 1915	'It'	British nickname for phone-tapping apparatus used in trenches & No Man's Land
		Ivan	A Russian soldier
I		Ivory Cross	British dental organization giving free or low-cost treatment especially to demobilized soldiers
I	British abbreviation for Intelligence. Gen Staff Dept I(a) for enemy orders of battle; I(b) to prevent such information reaching the enemy & to examine civilians in newly-captured areas; I(c) counterespionage, maps & topography; I(d) the press and I(e) radio intercepts.	IWW	International Workers of the World (American Communist Party)
		J	
IB(s)	Incendiary bomb(s)	Jackies	US Navy term for seamen
i/c	in command or in charge	Jack Johnson	Anglo-Saxon slang (from negro heavyweight boxer) for large low-velocity German shell first used by Lt-Col
Iddy Umpties, the	Nickname for British signallers & the 17th Div, from its dot-dash sign		

	Swinton official eyewitness or war correspondent Sept 1914
Jacko, a	British EEF term for a Turk
Jam tin grenade	Home-made BEF weapon first used Nov 1914
'Japan'	From the French *du pain*, BEF word for bread
Jctn	Junction (railway)
Jericho Jane	Australian name for long-range Turk gun in Jordan Valley, eventually destroyed by RAF July 1918
Jerry	A German soldier
Jerry, to	To understand, hence Jerry over for 'Lights out!' when aircraft crossed British lines at night
Jewel of Asia	Nickname for Turk gun on that side of the Dardanelles
Jigger, up the	In the trenches
Johnny	A Turk, dating from Crimean War
Josephine	French Army nickname for its 75mm field gun
Joy Bag	British souvenir bag, usually a sandbag, from the trenches
Joy Spot	BEF officers' term for a good hotel or restaurant behind the line
Joy Waggon	Practice aircraft at a British flying school

K

K(1)	Popular press shorthand for Kitchener's first Hundred Thousand volunteers of Aug 1914
K	King
KG5	Battleship HMS *King George V*
k	killed
Kadet	Constitutional Democrat (liberal Russian party)
Kai	New Zealand troops' Maori word for food
Kamerad	German for comrade and used as a word of surrender, hence British 'to Kamerad'
'Kaiser's Own'	British derisive nickname for King's Royal Rifle Corps due to their Iron-cross resembling Maltese cross cap badge
Kapai	New Zealand troops' Maori word for very good, capital
Kaput	German for *kaputt*, finished

KAR	King's African Rifles (British East African native troops)
KCB	Knight Commander of the Bath
KG	Knight of the Garter
Khakis, the	German name for British troops
kia	killed in action
King's certificate	British 'Served with honour' discharge, designed by Bernard Partridge of *Punch*, etc
Kitch	Kitchener 'New Army' recruit
Kite balloon	Artillery observation balloon
Kiwi	New Zealand soldier, also British airmen's slang for ground crew (flightless bird)
Kiel whale	British PoW term for nauseous fish-meal
Knife rest	Spiked iron bar laid in barbed wire or wooden frame surrounded in barbed wire as quickly movable obstruction for roads etc
Knuts, the	British Dover Patrol term for VIPs on passage to France
Komuch	Ctee of Members of the Constituent Assembly, Russian SR anti-Bolshevik govt on the Volga 1918
Kosh	Trench raid club, from the London roughs' weapon
Kr	Kroner
kts	knots
Kultur	German education and Allied term of abuse for it.
KuK	*Kaiser und König*, appellation 'Imperial and Royal' for the Austrian armed forces (and other services) from Emperor Francis Joseph also being King of Hungary

L

L	Lake
LAMB	Light Armoured Motor Battery (British armoured car unit)
Land Girls	British female wartime farmworkers
Landowner, a	British description of a dead man on the W Front
Landship	Tank
Landsturm	German (men aged 20-45; untrained 9 yrs service) and Austrian 3rd line troops (extended to ages 18-55). Latter began as 210 bns with 10 Hussar half-regts. Expanded to 286 bns of 800 men or less (no artillery). Serbia also had a *Landsturm*

	of about 50,000 men	Lone Howitzer, the	British 4.5in howitzer in a Loos chalk-pit till knocked out Aug 1917. Barrel at the Imperial War Museum.
Landwehr	German (men aged 27$\frac{1}{2}$-38$\frac{1}{2}$; 11 yrs service) and Austrian 2nd line troops (*see Honved* for Hungarian *Landwehr*). Former mobilised 314 bns in 47 bdes as fortress and frontier guards, subsequently helped form 26 divs. Latter mustered 8 inf divs (120 bns), 5 mtn regts (16 bns), 9th Cav Div, 64 field howitzers (16 btys) doubled to 128 guns & howitzers (24 btys).	Lone Pine	Turk position at Gallipoli captured by the Australians and so-named because of its original landmark
		Lone Star	A 'one-pip' subaltern from his single badge
		Lonely Officers' Dances	British EEF phrase for Lady Allenby's Cairo dances for officers on leave
Lazy Eliza, a	Trench expression for long-range large shell	Long Bertha	A big Krupp gun
lb(s)	pound(s)	Long Horn	Early type of Maurice Farman biplane (MF7).
L/Cp	Lance-Corporal nicknamed Lance-Jack. Lowest NCO appointment	Long Jump, the	British airman's phrase for transferring from Home to overseas service
Ldg Mech	Leading Mechanic		
LEA	Local Education Authority (British)	'Long Max'	German gunners' nickname for the 15-in naval gun that shelled Dunkirk from Luegenboom
League of Remembrance	Princess Beatrice's organization for helping widows & daughters of dead British officers		
		Lord's Own, the	Battleship HMS *Vengeance*
Leaning Virgin	Damaged (Nov 1914) statue of the Virgin Mary on the spire of the Church of Notre Dame des Berbières at Albert, France. Its fall on 16 Apr 1918 was supposed to symbolize the war's imminent end.	Lorry hopping/ jumping	Catching a lift at the Front
		Lousy Wood	BEF pronunciation of Leuze Wood on the Somme
		Lt	Lieutenant
Leap-frogging	Trench warfare term for successive waves of troops leap-frogging through each other to capture objectives	lt	light
		Lt-Cdr	Lieutenant-Commander (naval)
Lebel Mam'selle	French Army nickname for its rifle	Lt-Col	Lieutenant-Colonel, usually a battalion CO
Lewis gun	Gas-operated, air-cooled machine gun (perfected by US Col Isaac N Lewis 1911) with 47-round circular drum magazine for ground use. 133,104 made in Britain (9434 sent to 7 Allies). Used in British, French & US aircraft (97-round ammunition pan) from Sept 1914 and by Belgian (known as 'Belgian Rattlesnake' to Germans) and British infantry (from Sept 1915).	Lt-Gen	Lieutenant-General, usually a corps commander
		Luger	German Army (1908) and Navy (1905) automatic 9mm pistol, officially called Parabellum Pistole '08
		Lyddite	British high-explosive named after Lydd in Kent where it was first made
Lid	Helmet		
Limpets	British newspaper term for civilians clinging to stay-at-home jobs	**M**	
'Liveliness, a certain'	Churchill's expression in a 19 Aug 1914 Admiralty communiqué that became a popular catch-phrase	[1.5]m	[1.5] million
Lizzie	Big shell or gun from HMS *Queen Elizabeth* at the Dardanelles Mar-May 1915	Maconochie	British tinned meat and vegetable ration, from the firm suppling it. Applied in jest to MC and MM, the stomach and the telephone
LMG	Light Machine-gun, a British platoon weapon from Feb 1917 (2 Lewis guns by Mar 1918). Each German company had 3 belt-fed slightly lighter Bergmann from Mar 1917 (afterwards doubled).	Madelon	French soldiers' tune, song and dance especially at Verdun
		Mafeesh	Arabic for dead, used by British on Turk fronts as much as Napoo (qv) on W Front
London Declaration	1909 international law (71 articles) on contraband and blockade. Not ratified by Britain.	Maggie	Nickname of battleship HMS *Magnificent*

Mainga	Zulu word for water used by S African troops	Mine-bumping, the	Grand Fleet 3rd Battle Sqn, sent ahead on a N Sea sweep (*see* Wobbly Eight)
Maj	Major	Minnie	Nickname for *minnenwerfer*, a large German trench mortar & its shell
Maj-Gen	Major-General, usually commanded a division	mins	minute(s)
Maleesh	Arabic for never mind, used on Turk fronts	ML	Motor launch
Mangle	To machine gun, especially British airmen's term	MM	Military Medal, British Army decoration from 1916 for all other ranks (115,577 awarded with 5989 bars 1916-20 plus 7389 with 6 bars to 11 Allied armies)
MAS	*Motobarca armata silurante* (torpedo-armed motor launch), Italian		
Maternity jacket	RFC double-breasted tunic	MMS	Military Message Service, British women's medical organization numbering 2000 by the Armistice
Mauser	German small arms manufacturer of standard pistols, rifles & automatic weapons	MO	Medical Officer/Orderly
		Mob store	Mobilization store
maximum	maximum	Mobile, to do a	British EEF terminology for a desert route march
Maxim	Machine gun, from its 1884 inventor Sir Hiram Maxim	Moo-Cow Farm	Mouquet Farm nr Thiepval on the Somme
MC	Military Cross, British Army decoration (1915) for Captains, Lieutenants & Warrant Officers (37,081 awarded with 3157 bars plus 3609 with 9 bars to 13 Allied armies)	Mopping up	Trench warfare term for troops following the initial waves, method first used by BEF at Arras Apr 1917. French called it *nettoyage*.
M & D	'Medicine and Duty', cure for British Army malingerers	*Morgenroth*	German forlorn home death song 'Morning bright'
MD	Military District (Russian)	Mossy Face	British air term for Bois d'Havrincourt (SW of Cambrai)
MEBU	Pillbox from the German *Machinengewehr-Eisenbeton-Unterstand* ('machine gun iron concrete emplacement')	Mother	Not only one of the first tanks but also the first British 9.2-in howitzer (Oct 1914-July 1916) & many subsequent weapons
MEF	Mediterranean or Mesopotamian Expeditionary Force (British)	Mournful Maria	Dunkirk air/sea raid siren
		Mouth organ	Stokes mortar bomb
Mermaid's visiting card	US Army identity disc, a wry allusion to an, in fact, unfounded danger of U-boat attack	Movies, the	Searchlights hence movie man for their operators
Mesop/Mespot	Mesopotamia	MP	Military Police, Member of Parliament (British)
Mesopolonica	Composite of above & Salonika to convey British troops' unresolved destination	MRAF	Marshal of the Royal Air Force
		[1¹/₂]mt	[1¹/₂] million tons
Methusilier	Austrian Remount Unit member, from his advanced years	Mt(s)	mount or mountains
MG(s)	Machine gun(s)	Mtd	Mounted
Micks	Irish Guards or any Irish troops	mths	months
MI1c	Literally Military Intelligence Section 1c, British Secret Service 1916-21	Mtn	Mountain, esp troops and artillery
		MTV	Motor Transport Volunteers
MI5	British internal security and counter-intelligence service, established 1909 (19 staff grew to 844 1914-18)	Muckle Flugga Hussars	British 10th Cruiser Sqn on blockade duty between the Orkneys and Greenland
Middx	Middlesex	Munitionette	British woman war worker

Mustard gas	Poison gas named after its pungent smell, otherwise Yellow Cross from its shell markings	NY	New York
		NZ	New Zealand
Mystery port	Richborough, Kent. Base of Channel Barge Service & train ferry, much enlarged Mar 1916 - Mar 1917	NZEF	New Zealand Expeditionary Force.

O

Mystery ships	*see* Q-ships

N

Oblt	*Oberleutnant*, German senior lieutenant
obs	observation
N	North/Northern
OC	Officer Commanding, more usually written than spoken *see* CO
NACB	Navy and Army Canteen Board (British) founded Apr 1916
OCAC	Officer Commanding Administration Centre (British New Army and Territorial depots from 1915)
'Nails in the Coffin of the Kaiser'	US minelayers' description of the 1918 Northern Mine Barrage
Office, the	Airmen's term for cockpit
Napoo	There is no more, from French *il n'y en a plus*, hence napooed 'killed'
Old Contemptible	Original regular BEF soldier from Kaiser's presumed 19 Aug 1914 sneer at 'General [*sic*] French's contemptible little army'
Narky	HM Sloop *Narcissus*
National Guard	US State troops and also British City of London Volunteer Corps of 2 bns
OHL	*Oberst Heeresleitung*, German Supreme Command
NCO	Non-Commissioned Officer
Newton pippin	A type of British rifle-grenade
Oil Can	German 250mm (10-in) trench mortar shell
Niet Dobra	Russian for no good used by British troops in N Russia
Old Bill, an	Old soldier, veteran (British) from Capt Bruce Bairnsfather's 1914 cartoon character. Nickname given to a London bus on W Front throughout
Niffy Jane	Cruiser HMS *Iphigenia*
Nissen hut	British corrugated iron roofed semi-cylindrical wooden building designed 1916 by Canadian mining engineer Lt-Col PN Nissen, DSO, RE, 47,000 soon ordered	Old one eye	Repair ship HMS *Cyclops*
Olive branch	British post-Armistice reinforcement
'Omms and Chevoos'	BEF vernacular for French railway truck capacity
nm	nautical mile
On the tapes	Ready to start, from the white tapes used to mark the 'lie out' positions for attacking infantry
Noah's doves	Australian description of reinforcements or comrades at sea on Armistice Day
No Man's Land	Ground between opposing trenches, belonging to neither side. Used in medieval land tenure 1328 and militarily by Engels 1870, but for Great War apparently first printed in a British official narrative of 15 Sept 1914.	Oofs	British slang for eggs (French *oeufs*)
OP	Observation Post, often called 'O Pip'
Ops	Operations (military)
ORs	Other ranks ie not officers
Nonstop	Trench expression for a long-range shell passing overhead	Out there	W Front
Outfit, an	Aircraft squadron
Norperforce	Unofficial acronym for British force in N Persia and Baku Nov 1918-1921	Over there	France (US) from the 1917 marching song
Not Forgotten Association	British organisation to support disabled veterans (30,000+ at end of 1923)	Over the top or the lid	To leave a trench for an attack
nr	near	Overseas men	British subjects abroad who came home to enlist
NRFF	Nyasaland-Rhodesia Field Force
NSW	New South Wales	Owl, the	Equivalent of Second World War's 'Careless talk costs lives'. Verses about the wise old silent owl were displayed at
NUR	National Union of Railwaymen (British)

	French railway stations & in Britain.	10pm	10 o'clock
Ox & Bucks	Oxfordshire & Buckinghamshire (Light Infantry)	*Poilu*	French soldier, from the French 'hairy' for his unshaven appearance, apparently first applied to elderly reservists. Word traceable back to Balzac's *Le Médecin de Campagne* (1833)

P

pa	per annum	Policeman's truncheon	Early British hand grenade with streamers attached
Parasol	Type of high-wing monoplane	Pop	BEF shortening of Poperinghe, 7 miles from Ypres
Parlt	Parliament	pop	population
PBI	Poor bloody infantry	Pork and beans	British nickname for Portuguese troops on W Front from tinned rations they were fond of
pd	per day		
[7] pdr	7-pounder (gun)	Potato-masher	German hand grenade (from shape)
Penguins, the	Nickname for the WRAF derived from the bird's inability to fly	*Pour le Mérite*	Germany's top gallantry medal (for officers only), 87 awarded of which 75 went to airmen (27 posthumous)
perf(s)	performance(s)	PoW	Prisoner(s)-of-War
Petrol Hussars, the	Duke of Westminster's armoured cars sent to Egypt 1916	PP's	Princess Patricia of Connaught's Light Infantry (Canadian)
PG	Battleship HMS *Prince George*	PR, the	Battlecruiser HMS *Princess Royal*
PH helmet	Early British gas helmet (late 1915, replaced Hypo-helmet), replaced by box-respirator (qv)	Pre-dreadnought	Battleship built before 1906, slow and usually bearing only 4 main guns
Pharaoh's Foot	Nickname for Volunteer companies of Europeans raised in Egypt 1915	prelim	preliminary
Pill-box	Small concrete blockhouse used by Germans from 1917	Princess Mary's gift box	Brass box of cigarettes or tobacco & pipe sent to every British soldier or sailor on active service after Oct 1914 appeal realised £131,000
Pimple	British slang for a hill. Noteworthy pimples were at Vimy, Gallipoli & Salonika.		
Pineapple	German 4lb grenade and a type of gas	prod	production
Pink	Secret, from the colour for HMG secret telegrams	Pronto	Spanish for 'hurry up', adopted from US troops who gained it in the Mexican War
Piou-piou	French soldier, prewar word soon replaced by *Poilu*	Prov	Province or Provisional
Pip-Emma	British signaller's code for pm	Provost-Sergeant	NCO policing a camp
Pip-squeak	Small German HE trench shell. Term officially banned in BEF	Pte	Private
Pirates, the	German U-boats	Pudding basin	British steel helmet
Platoon	Small sub-unit of infantry (58 estab, 50 av in British Army 1914, 31 by 1918) or other troops, 3-4 formed a company (2 sections in US Army (59 men, 1917) each of 3 squads, sections in British Army)	Pulpit, a	Artillery observation ladder (British)
		Pup tent	US Army 2-man infantry tent
		Pusher	Aircraft with rear-mounted engine
		PV	Paravane anti-sea mine device
		pw	per week
Plug Street	BEF rendering of Ploegsteert village nr Armentières	PZ	British Fleet tactical exercise battle from signal flags that announced it
PM	Prime Minister		
10 pm	10 per month		

Q

Q	Queen
QAIMNS	Queen Alexandra's Imperial Military Nursing Service (British). Founded 1902, grew from 463 members (1914) to 10,304 (1918); 112 died on service. Known as Red Capes from their uniform.
QARNNS	for Royal Navy branch
QE	Battleship HMS *Queen Elizabeth*
QF	Quick-firing
QM(G)	Quartermaster (General)
QMAAC	Queen Mary's Army Auxiliary Corps (British), title of WAAC (qv) from 9 Apr 1918
Q-ships	Allied anti-U-boat armed ship decoys, disguised as ordinary merchantmen. Royal Navy used 235 (39 lost from all causes). They sank up to 13 U-boats in over 70 duels. French, Italian & US Navies also operated some. The Germans fitted out 8 decoy vessels from Dec 1915, for the Baltic.
Quakers	Colloquial name for conscientious objectors, also old word for dummy gun
Quash	From Arabic *khwush* for good, used by British on Turk Fronts
Queenstown Navy	US destroyer flotilla based at Queenstown, Ireland 1917-18
Quick Dick	British gun on W Front
Quirk, a	Pilot learning to fly, or any unusual aircraft
qv	*Quod vide*, which see

R

R	River
RA	Royal Artillery. Grew from 132,920 all ranks & 1859 guns (1 Aug 1914) to 548,780 (1 Aug 1918) & 11,437 guns (11 Nov 1918). Lost 48,949 dead. *See* RFA, RGA, RHA.
RACD	Royal Army Clothing Dept
Race card, the	Morning Sick Report (British)
RAF	Royal Air Force
Raffish	RAF slang for any non-uniformed RAF or Royal Aircraft Factory personnel
Rag-Pickers	Field Salvage Corps (US Army)
Rainbow Division	US Army 42nd Div drawn from 27 states & all colours, hence also called All America Div
RAMC	Royal Army Medical Corps. Grew from 18,728 all ranks (Aug 1914) to 144,152 (Aug 1918)
RAN	Royal Australian Navy
Rapatrie	French term for those repatriated from German-occupied areas, adopted by British
'Rat Catcher Churchill'	German press abuse for Churchill after his 21 Sept 1914 speech
RAVC	Royal Army Veterinary Corps. Grew from 519 all ranks (4 Aug 1914) to 29,452 (Aug 1918) treating a maximum of 90,000 animals at any one time.
RC	Roman Catholic
RCAF	Royal Canadian Air Force
rd	road
RE	Royal Engineers. Grew from 11,689 all ranks (1 Aug 1914) to max 239,386 (1 Aug 1917). Also stands for Reconnaissance Experimental, British aircraft types.
Rear-Adm	Rear-Admiral
recce(s)	reconnaissance, reconnoitre(s)
recon	reconnaissance, reconnoitre(s) [in Air War]
Red Cap or Red Hat	Military Police (British)
Red Coats	British Women Inspectors of the Anti-Poison Gas Dept, from their uniform
Red Hussar	British Govt wartime brand of cigarette (*see also* Ruby Queen)
Red Lamp	British term for a French *Maison tolérée* (official brothel). Red Lamp Corner was a dangerous spot with a warning red light nr Festubert.
Red Triangle Man	British nickname for a YMCA member, from his badge
Regt	Regiment. Permanent unit of any arm under a colonel. Inf regts had 3 bns (Austrian 1914 estab 4356, Russian 1914 3535, US regt 1917 3832) and 2 regts made a bde in all armies except British. Cav regts (German 676+, Austrian 926+ & 4 MGs, Russian c866, French 683, British 551 & 2 MGs). Arty regts (German 36 field guns, 16 or 32 heavy guns, French 12 field guns & 554 men).
rep	representative
req'd	required
Res	Reserve
Rest Camp	British term for place of recuperation & light duties behind front, also port waiting point for going on leave

Ret	retired	Rooty	Old British Army word for bread
RFA	Royal Field Artillery. Grew from 51,228 all ranks (Aug 1914) to max 350,096 (Apr 1917)	Rouen, a client for	BEF VD hospital at Rouen
		rpd	rounds per day
RFC	Royal Flying Corps (formed 13 May 1912). Grew from 1200 (Aug 1914) to 144,078 (Mar 1918)	rpg	rounds per gun
		RSFSR	Russian Socialist Federative Soviet Republic, Soviet Russia's official title
RFP	Retail Food Price (British). 100 in July 1914, the working class cost of living was always at least 10% less	RSM	Regimental Sergeant-Major
		RTO	Railway Transport Officer (British)
RGA	Royal Garrison Artillery (British), responsible for siege, heavy, coast & mountain guns. Grew from 33,834 (1 Aug 1914) to max 210,554 (Aug 1918)	Ruby Queen	British Govt brand of ration-issue cigarettes. Occasional nickname for young nurse or Sister of fresh complexion
RHA	Royal Horse Artillery (British). Grew from 7538 all ranks (1 Aug 1914) to max 18,009 (May 1917)	Ruhleben Song	British PoW camp concert of May 1915, over 4000 British civilians were interned there
RIC	Royal Irish Constabulary	Rum jar	Type of German trench mortar shell
RIMS	Royal Indian Marine Ship	Rupert	British nickname for an observation balloon
RM	Royal Marines (British). Grew from 18,000 to 55,000, suffered 11,921 cas (-5 Apr 1919).		

S

RM [5 bn] [5 billion] *Reichsmark*	(German currency)	[10] s	[10] shillings
RMLE	*Régiment de Marche de la Légion Étrangère* (1915-18, 9 citations)	S	South
		SA	South African
RMLI	Royal Marine Light Infantry	SAA	Small-arms ammunition (for rifles, pistols & MGs)
RN	Royal Navy		
RNAS	Royal Naval Air Service (formed 23 June 1914). Jokingly rendered Really Not A Sailor.	Saida	Arabic for Good day! Used on Turk fronts
		Salient, the	The Ypres Salient
RND	Royal Navy Division. Became 63rd (Royal Naval) Div 19 July 1916 on W Front but kept naval terminology	Sally Booze	BEF vernacular for village of Sailly la Bourse
rnds	rounds	Salvo	Salvation Army Rest & Recreation hut
RNR	Royal Naval Reserve	Sam Browne	Officer's field service belt, named after its Indian Army designer
RNVR	Royal Naval Volunteer Reserve		
'Road of Remembrance'	Embarkation route to Folkestone harbour, England for troops going to & from France	Sammies	Unpopular British nickname for US Army troops suggested by *Punch* 13 June 1917. Soon replaced by Doughboys (qv).
Roger	British code term for poison gas cylinder June 1916, changed later	San Fairy Ann	No matter, British pet version of *Ça ne fait rien*
Roody Boy	BEF rendering of Rue du Bois nr Neuve Chapelle, Flanders	Sandstorm medals	Egyptian Army decorations
		Sang bon	Very good indeed (*cinq bon*)
Rosalie	French nickname for the bayonet from M Theodore Botrel's war song published in *Bulletin des Armées*, autumn 1914	Sankey, a	French five-franc note
		Sappers	Engineers
Room 40	Royal Navy's decrypting unit, part of Naval Intelligence and named after its first office in the Admiralty	Sausage	Observation balloon
		Sausage hill, to go to	To be taken prisoner by Germans

Scarlet runners	British bn dispatch carriers from their red arm brassard	SMS	*Seiner Majestät Schiff*, prefix to Imperial German warships
Scene shifter	Effective British heavy gun in 1917 Arras sector	SNO	Senior Naval Officer (British)
Scooters	Nickname for CMB (qv)	*Soixante-quinze*	75mm French QF field gun, from its calibre
Scrap of paper	A broken pledge from Chancellor Bethmann's 1914 remark to the British Ambassador	SOS course	BEF Sniping, Observation and Scouting Course, started 1916, one per Army
SDP	*Sozial-Demokratische Partei*	SOS signal	Rocket sent up to start British arty barrage v German attack; distress call from ship
Sec, sec	Secretary		
Section	Smallest military body or fire unit, 4 of about 12 men each led by NCO (7 men & NCO 1918) formed a British inf platoon or a cav troop; 2 guns in a battery. Squad in US Army (25 men). *Gruppe* of 8 men in German Army	Souvenir	A trophy from the front, hence to souvenir, to steal
		Sovnarkom	Council of People's Commissars, Soviet 'cabinet'
		Spad	French single-seater biplane (*Société Pour Aviation et Ses Dérivés*)
Senussi	North African Arab Islamic Sufi mystic brotherwood (estab 1837) opposed to European colonialism, especially strong in Cyrenaica	Sparks	Radio operator
		Sparks, to get the	To range an MG on the enemy barbed wire after dark
sgt	sergeant	Spartacus League	German revolutionary socialist party founded 27 Jan 1916 & led by Karl Liebknecht & Rosa Luxembourg. Named after the Thracian gladiator who led the third slave revolt against Rome (73-71BC).
Shell shock	Popular & official 1916 term for a neurosis contributed to by shellfire, one of 1914-18's medical discoveries. Later officially abolished & renamed Psycho-neurosis. Combat fatigue in modern US Army jargon.		
		Spit ball	Hand grenade (US Army)
Shock absorber	Air observer		
Shocks	French town of Choques nr Bethune (BEF)	Sports Ship, the	British SS *Borodino* , chartered Oct 1914 as officers' supply ship to Grand Fleet, Scapa Flow
Shooting Gallery, the	The front line		
Short horn, the	Type of Maurice Farman biplane	Sportsman's Battalion	British 23rd & 24th Bns of the Royal Fusiliers (France & E Africa). Composed of men up to 45 incl many ranchers, planters & farmers
Silent Deaths, the	Night patrol party on ambush in No Man's Land		
Silent Susan	Type of German high-velocity shell	Springboks, the	S African troops
Sim's Circus	US Navy nickname for its first destroyer flotilla in European waters, after the commanding admiral	*Spurlos Versenkt*	Gone entirely. Catchphrase from Count Luxemburg's infamous 1917 message 'Sunk without trace'.
		Sq	Square
Sister Susie, a	British woman doing Army work, especially Red Cross	sq [miles]	square [miles]
Skindles	Restaurant at Poperinghe named after the fashionable Maidenhead establishment	Squarehead	German, originally a seafarer's term but reinforced by German Army haircuts
Skolka, to	To sell, from the Russian how much or many. Used by British N Russia troops for illicit trafficking in Army food	Sqn, sqn(s)	Squadron (warships or cavalry). 1914 cav strengths: German 169; French & Austrian 150; Russian c145; British 160
		SR	Socialist Revolutionary (Russian peasant party)
Slacker, a	British press term for any man reluctant to enlist		
SM	Sergeant-Major	SS	Steamship
SMLE	Small-magazine Lee Enfield	St	Saint , Street
		Staff crawl	General's trench inspection tour (British)

Stand-to, the	Dawn to daylight alert for an attack (British) ended by Stand-down	TB	Tuberculosis
STAVKA	Tsarist and Red Army Supreme HQ	TBs	Torpedo boats
Stealth raid	Trench raid (British), generally without artillery support	TBD	Torpedo-boat destroyer
Stink bomb	Mustard gas shell	Teddy bear	Name for shaggy goatskin or fur coats issued to BEF, winter 1915
Stinks OC	Gas officer or instructor (British)	temp	temperature
Stn, stn(s)	Station(s)	Terrier	British Territorial Army volunteer (since 1909 foundation)
Stockbrokers' Battalion	British 10th Royal Fusiliers	TF	Territorial Force
Stokes mortar	Light British trench mortar, 3 in & 1 in models, 12,363 made	Theatre ship, the	Grand Fleet name for SS *Gourko* which also gave cinema showings
Stool pigeon	Informer, especially among PoWs	Ticket	Discharge from the British Army. Pilot's certificate (British)
Stosstruppen	German picked shock troops formed from 1916	Ticklers	Jam, from the British manufacturers since 1903. Plum & apple rather than strawberry always seemed to reach the ranks.
Strafe	Punish, attack (German) as in 'Gott strafe England'	Tiddly Chat	Cruiser HMS *Chatham*, tiddly meant smart
Strombos horn	Compressed air horn to give warning of German gas attack	Ti-ib	Very good, all right. From the Arabic *Tay-ib*, used on Turk fronts
Strs	Straits	Timbertown, HMS	RND name for Groningen Internment Camp, Holland
Subaltern	Second Lieutenant, most junior commissioned officer	'Tin, they've opened another'	Unflattering British reference to new arrival
Suicide Club	British term for any unit having risky duties	Tin hat	Steel anti-shrapnel helmet of early 1916
Suicide Corner	Lethal spot in Ypres Salient or elsewhere	Tin pirate	German U-boat
Sundenabwehrkanone	Anti-sin-gun, German Army slang for a padre	Tip and run raids	German naval coastal bombardments of Britain

T

		'Tipperary'	British popular song actually published a year before the war and written by Henry Williams of Birmingham. Became an international craze after the BEF sang it landing at Boulogne.
T [2m]	[2 million] Turkish pounds		
Tabloid, a	Small Sopwith biplane		
Tails up	In good spirits, keen fighting. Nickname of Sir John Salmond who used it to the Air Council.	*Tirailleur*	French for sharpshooter, 4 regiments (Algerians, Tunisians, Moroccans, or Senegalese) won 6 citations each
Tape, to	To get the artillery range of a target. To mark out the ground for a night assembly by troops before an attack, or the line for a new trench.	*Tir de barrage*	French for 'barring fire', same as curtain fire
Taps	'Last Post' bugle call (US Army)	Tirps	Royal Navy name for Admiral Tirpitz
Tattenham Corner	Grand Fleet term for narrow Firth of Forth entrance between May Island & Inchkeith where U-boats lurked	Tit-Bits	RFC weekly communiqué (began with 25-27 July 1915)
		TM	Trench mortar
		TNT	trinitrotoluene explosive
Taube	German monoplane (from the German for pigeon), used till 1916 (500 built)	Toad, a	Type of German hand grenade
		Toby	A steel helmet
Tavarish	Comrade (Russian). Also used by British N Russia EF troops	Toc-Emma	Signaller's code for trench mortar

Toc H	War name for Talbot House, a rest & social centre at Poperinghe nr Ypres opened 15 Dec 1915 by Rev P H Clayton	US	United States
Toffee-apple	British 2in trench-mortar stick bomb	USMC	US Marine Corps. Grew from 13,725 (6 Apr 1917) to 78,841 (authorized strength 1 July 1918, 31,824 served overseas during war, 11,500 cas in France, 12,371 total).
Tommy	British soldier, from Tommy Atkins (Thomas Atkins, the archetypal private on Army forms since the early 19th century). Thomasina Atkins or Tommy Waacks applied to the WAAC.	USN	US Navy. Grew to 599,051 (8106 cas)
Tony, a	A Portuguese	USNA	US Naval Academy (Annapolis, Maryland)
Toto	French Army word for vermin or lice	UXB	unexploded bomb

V

Tractor	Aircraft with front-mounted engine		
Trade, the	Royal Navy's term for its submarine service	v	versus, against
Trap ships	German Navy name for Q-ships	Va	Virginia
Trench fever	Infectious disease transmitted by vermin, prevalent from 1915	V & A	Victoria and Albert
Trench foot	Blood circulation illness resembling frostbite, caused by wet & cold, often ending in gangrene	VAD	Voluntary Aid Detachment. Territorial Women's nursing service founded 1909. Provided 122,766 male & female nurses of whom first 19 landed at Boulogne 21 Oct 1914 (142 died on service).
Trench ring, a	Finger ring made from any scrap of war material such as a German aluminium shell nose	Van blanc Anglais	Whisky
Tripe	Sopwith biplane (British)	VC	Victoria Cross, highest British award for valour (579 awarded with 2 bars, 173 posthumous 1914-20)
Troop	Cavalry sub-unit (British 1914 troop, 33 all ranks) 4 formed a squadron	VD	venereal diseases
TU	Trade union	Verst	Russian measurement of distance = 0.7 mile or 1.06 km
TUC	Trade Union Congress (British)	Vice-Adm	Vice-Admiral
Tutoring	British war term for attaching new battalions to ones with trench experience	Vickers	British armaments company. Delivered 4 battleships; 6 cruisers; 62 lighter war-ships; 53 submarines; 100,000+ MGs; 5500 aircraft.

U

		Vickers MG	British standard heavy machine gun for air & ground use, 71,355 made (10,336 sent to 6 Allies)
U-boat	A German submarine from German *Unterseeboot*	Victory Medal	Awarded after March 1919 to all Allied forces. Bronze, with reverse inscription 'The Great War for Civilisation'. Over 5m issued.
UB	Coastal U-boat, 155 built		
UC	Minelayer U-boat, 104 built	Vlam	BEF colloquial for Vlamertinghe, Flanders
Umpty poo	Just a little more (French *un petit peu*) especially exhortation to labour gangs	vols	volunteers
Undertaker's Squad	Stretcher bearers	Vrille	A spinning nose-dive, RFC from the French
Univ	University	VTC	Volunteer Training Corps (British). Title given Nov 1914 to *ad hoc* local home defence volunteers unfit for Army or not sparable. War Office took over as Volunteer Force May 1916. Men exempt from conscription were required to join. Peak recorded strength of the First World
UPS	Universities and Public Schools Battal-ions (British), ie 18th-21st Royal Fusiliers enrolled in 11 days Aug/Sept 1914). All but 20th (served to Apr 1918) disbanded Apr 1916, the men going to cadet schools or other Fusilier units.		
Unstick, to	Leaving the ground (airmen's jargon)		

War's Home Guard equivalent was 299,973 (May 1917) in 328 bns & units of which 46,559 under (min 17) & over (55+) military age. Tasks included trench digging, transport & ambulance driving, coast and AA defence

W

W	West
w	wounded
WAAC	Women's Army Auxiliary Corps (British), recruited 56,000 women for the duration from 13 Mar 1917. (Of over 9500 in France, 500 clerks served with AEF at Bourges & Tours). Transferred 7000 women to WRAF.
WAF	Women's Auxiliary Force (British) founded 1915 for part-time volunteer workers. Became Victory Corps 1920
WAFF	West African Field Force (British)
War baby	Any young officer or soldier, or a child born during hostilities
War bird, a	Any elderly man keen to enlist
Wavy Navy	RNVR because collar & sleeve markings were wavy not straight
W/Cdr	Wing Commander
WDRC	Women's Defence Relief Corps (British) formed Sept 1914 to free men for war service
Weary Willie, a	Long-range shell high overhead
WEC	Women's Emergency Corps (British), launched 6 Aug 1914 by suffragette Mrs Decima Moore & 5 peeresses (-Nov 1918) especially for food collection & relief, interpreters for Belgian refugees. Started canteens at Compiègne & Paris.
Wet Triangle, the	Royal Navy term for Heligoland Bight
WFC	Women's Forage Corps (British) formed Mar 1917. 4200 women served for a year or duration in khaki as part of RASC.
WFF	Western Frontier Force (British), Egypt
Whippet	Light tank (British), 14 tons, top speed 8mph, crew 3, with 4 Hotchkiss or Lewis MGs. First used 26 Mar 1918
Whistling Percy	A German naval gun captured at Cambrai, Nov 1917
White Sheet	BEF vernacular for Wytschaete, Flanders
Whizz-bang	German field-gun shell
WI	West Indian
wia	wounded in action
'Wilhelm's Gun'	German dubbing of the Paris Gun in the Kaiser's honour
Willie	(Big and Little) Kaiser and Crown Prince after *Daily Mirror* cartoons
Wind fight	False alarm
Windy Corner	Hazardous due to enemy fire, especially nr Menin Gate of Ypres
Winkle	To capture individual prisoners by stealth
'Winning the war, anyway it's'	Sarcastic comment for seemingly unnecessary task
Wipers	BEF name for Ypres, also called 'Eaps
Wipers' Express	German 420mm shell during Second Battle of Ypres
wk	week
WL	Women's Legion (British), founded July 1915 by Marchioness of Londonderry. Paid and wore khaki, over 40,000 enrolled including over 4000 full-time canteen workers.
WNLS	Women's National Land Service (British), founded early 1916, recruited 9022 farmworkers for Women's Land Army (qv)
Wobbly Eight	Grand Fleet's 3rd Battle Squadron of 8 *King Edward VII* -class battleships
Women's Forestry Service	Formed 1917 for timber felling & cutting, c3000 employed
Women's Land Army	Founded 26 March 1917 and employed 29,000 women at farmwork (- 30 Dec 1919). Popular uniform of overall, breeches & leggings. Scotland had 1816 women in its own organization.
Woodbine, a	Dominion & Colonial troops' name for a British soldier due to his partiality for that cigarette
Woodbines, The packet of	Five-funnelled Russian cruiser *Askold* at the Dardanelles 1915
Woolly-bear	Large German shrapnel shell releasing brownish-black smoke
Wound-stripe	Small strip of gold braid on left forearm (British Army), first sanctioned 1916
Wozzer, the	Australian for Haret el Wazza, Cairo's 1915 brothel street
WRAF	Women's Royal Air Force formed 1 Apr 1918. 32,230 served at home, in France & Germany (from Mar 1919) until 31 Mar 1920 demobilization.
WRAS	Women's Reserve Ambulance Service (Green Cross Corps) (British), formed June 1915 mainly for London area especially between main rail stations

Wrens	*See WRNS*	Yeo	Yeomanry, British volunteer cavalry
Write off	Air service expression for total aircraft crash	Y gun	Twin depth charge thrower aboard Allied anti-submarine vessels
WRNS	Women's Royal Naval Service, hence Wrens, founded 29 Nov 1917. Organized in 12 divs incl Mediterranean. Transferred 2033 ratings to WRAF. Max strength 6392 (21 Nov 1918). HQ Crystal Palace, London.	*Yilderim*	Turk Army Group in Palestine 1917-18, literally 'Lightning' from the sobriquet of the conquering Ottoman Sultan Bayazid I (c1354-1403)
		Yimkin	Arab for perhaps, used on Turk fronts
WSPU	Women's Social and Political Union (suffragette movement formed 1903)	Ypres Day	31 Oct, Anniversary Day observed by British Ypres League (founded by FMs French & Plumer 1920)
WVR	Women's Volunteer Reserve (British), branch of Women's Emergency Corps formed by Viscountess Castlereagh Mar 1915 especially for farming & gardening. Over 10,000 at Armistice in 40 County coys in Britain and 4 bns in Canada.	yr(s)	year(s)

X

X-ships	Twin-engined landing ships (6 knots) of shallow draft built for Fisher's projected invasion of N Germany, but used at Gallipoli	Z-day	Zero day, date fixed for major operation
		Zemstvo	Provincial or district council in Tsarist Russia, indirectly elected by electoral colleges for nobility, townsmen & peasantry. Functioned in 34 provinces from 1865-6 but did not apply to greater cities or non-Russian inhabited frontier provinces.
Xaroshie	Very good, quite right. British N Russia troops' term from the Russian		
		Zeppelin	German airship

Y

		Zeppelin in a cloud	Sausage & mash (mashed potato)
Yallah	Go on, get on with it. Arabic used on Turk fronts	Zero (Hour)	Time of an attack, made known to troops employed at latest possible moment
Yanks, the	Preferred British Army name for US troops on W Front	Zig-zag	Steering an erratic course to evade U-boat attack
yds	yards	Zouaves	French white North African troops in khaki service dress, 5 regiments each won 6 wartime citations

A comprehensive index would occupy as much space as the Chronicle itself. The present index concentrates on major events, particularly battles, actions and sieges strictly so called in official national battle nomenclature. Major references to leading generals, heads of state, important government ministers and significant developments in technology are also covered. In general the index excludes references to individual ships and military units, and to place names other than major battles, actions etc.

In keeping with the nature of a chronology, references to the main Chronicle are by date rather than by page, and sub-entries are arranged in date order, not alphabetical order.

Date references are followed by a number in brackets to identify the column in which the reference will be found, ranging from '0' for the 'Sarajevo to Outbreak' column, to '9' for the 'Home Fronts' column. Thus '12 Mar '17 (1)' refers the reader to the Chronicle at 12 March 1917 in column 1 (Western Front).

Cross-references to other index entries are printed in roman type. For example 'see also Gallipoli' refers the reader to the index entry for Gallipoli. Cross-references to other parts of the book, such as areas of the Chronicle itself, or to Maps or Tables, are printed in italics. For example 'see also E Front from 3 Jan '17' refers the reader to further references in the main Chronicle's Eastern Front column starting at 3 January 1917. A cross-reference such as 'see also Tables for W Front 1917' refers the reader to the tabulated matter which supplements the main Chronicle.

Boris, Prince Regent of Bulgaria, promoted General, 6 Oct '18 (3)
Boroevic,
  proposes to withdraw behind the Piave, 20 Jun '18 (3)
  tells Emperor position is untenable, 28 Oct '18 (3)
  see also Who's Who (Austrian generals)
Botha *see Who's Who*
Bothmer, Count, i/c new German Nineteenth Army, 4 Feb '18 (1)
Bourlon Wood,
  Battle of, begins, 23 Nov '17 (1)
  Battle of, ends, 4 Dec '17 (1)
Bratianu,
  cabinet resigns, 28 Jan '18 (9)
  replaced as Rumanian PM, 6 Feb '18 (2)
Brazil,
  breaks relations with Germany, 11 Apr '17 (8)
  anti-German riots, 15 Apr '17 (8)
  revokes neutrality in US-German war, 1 Jun '17 (8)
  seizes interned German merchant ships, 24 Oct '17 (6)
  declares war on Germany, 26 Oct '17 (8)
  conscription, 27 Dec '17 (9)
  sends sqn to Europe, 1 May '18 (6)
Brémond, Col, visits Feisal, 31 Jan '17 (4)
Breslau, in action off Imbros and sunk, 20 Jan '18 (6)
Brest-Litovsk,
  talks begin between Russia & Central Powers, 3 Dec '17 (2)
  28-day armistice signed, 15 Dec '17 (2)
  28-day armistice begins, 16 Dec '17 (2)
  peace negotiations begin, 22 Dec '17 (2)
  talks broken off, 26 Dec '17 (2)
  Bolsheviks denounce terms, 2 Jan '18 (2)
  Ukrainian delegation arrives, 3 Jan '18 (2)
  Bolsheviks resume talks under Trotsky, 8 Jan '18 (2)
  Trotsky breaks off talks, 18 Jan '18 (2)
  Trotsky suspends talks, 23 Jan '18 (2)
  talks resume, 30 Jan '18 (2)
  Kaiser orders talks to end, 7 Feb '18 (2)
  Trotsky leaves talks for 4th time, 10 Feb '18 (2)
  Germany resumes war, 18 Feb '18 (2)
  Soviets accept German terms, 24 Feb '18 (2)
  Soviet delegates return, 26 Feb '18 (2)
  Russo-German peace, 3 Mar '18 (2)
  strips Russian naval bases, 3 Mar '18 (6)
  Soviets ratify treaty, 14 Mar '18 (2)
  Allies refuse to recognize treaty, 18 Mar '18 (2)
  CEC repudiates treaty, 13 Nov '18 (2)
  see also E Front from 2 Jan '18
Briand,
  proposes French authority over BEF, 25 Feb '17 (1)
  and Calais Agreement, 27 Feb '17 (1)
Bridges, Lt-Gen TM, British rep with Franchet d'Esperey, 29 Oct '18 (3)
Britain,
  balance of payments 1914-18 *see 1914-1918 General Tables*
  British Army *see* British Expeditionary Force
  civilian dead 1914-18 *see 1914-1918 General Tables*
  financial & economic costs 1914-18 *see 1914-1918 General Tables*
  war expenditure/revenue *see 1914-1918 General Tables*
  Silvertown explosion, 19 Jan '17 (9)
  Admiralty warns of food crisis, 8 Mar '17 (9)
  Imperial War Cabinet first meets, 20 Mar '17 (8)
  wheat & grain stocks low, 31 Mar '17 (9)
  Food Hoarding Order, 9 Apr '17 (9)
  Food Ministry warns food may not last till harvest, 25 Apr '17 (9)
  Anglo-French Paris War Conference, 3 May '17 (8)
  first night aeroplane bombing raid on London, 6 May '17 (7)
  Gotha air bombing campaign begins, 25 May '17 (7)
  worst civ cas of war in Gotha raid, 13 Jun '17 (7)
  Royal Family changes name, 17 Jul '17 (8)
  Reconstruction Ministry formed, 21 Aug '17 (9)
  Gothas begin night raids on Britain, 2 Sep '17 (7)
  censorship of press accounts of air raids, 6 Sep '17 (9)
  sugar rationing begins, 15 Sep '17 (9)
  subsidized bread, 17 Sep '17 (9)
  first London balloon barrage, 1 Oct '17 (7)
  London air raid shelters, 16 Oct '17 (9)
  first Gotha incendiary raid, 31 Oct '17 (7)
  coal rationing, 1 Nov '17 (9)
  conscientious objectors disenfranchized, 20 Nov '17 (9)
  recalls Ambassador from Russia, 3 Jan '18 (2)
  women over 30 receive vote, 6 Feb '18 (9)
  Information Ministry founded under Beaverbrook, 10 Feb '18 (9)
  Resettlement Ctee formed, 12 Mar '18 (9)
  gas coal & electricity rationing, 20 Mar '18 (9)
  national meat rationing introduced, 7 Apr '18 (9)
  last successful Zeppelin raid on Britain, 12 Apr '18 (7)
  Military Services Bill, 16 Apr '18 (9), 18 Apr '18 (9)
  Milner replaces Derby as War Minister, 20 Apr '18 (9)
  record month's gun production, 1 May '18 (9)
  Maurice Affair, 7 May '18 (9)
  last & costliest raid on London, 19 May '18 (7)
  to send military mission to help White Russians, 23 May '18 (2)
  flu pandemic begins, 1 Jun '18 (9), 1 Jul '18 (9)
  non-interference declaration to Russian people, 6 Aug '18 (2)
  'Feed the Guns' campaign, 30 Sep '18 (9)
  Commons votes for women MPs, 23 Oct '18 (9)
  Turks sign Armistice with, 30 Oct '18 (4)
  hostilities cease v Turkey, 31 Oct '18 (4)
  ministers agree general election, 6 Nov '18 (9)
  King's Armistice message to Empire, 11 Nov '18 (9)
  Labour decides to leave coalition, 14 Nov '18 (9)
  election campaign opens, 16 Nov '18 (9)
  Govt announce war cas figures, 19 Nov '18 (9)
  Parlt dissolves, 25 Nov '18 (9)
  car restrictions relaxed, 1 Dec '18 (9)
  Army Demobilization begins, 4 Dec '18 (9)
  'Khaki' or 'Coupon' General Election, 14 Dec '18 (9)
  Information Ministry abolished, 18 Dec '18 (9)
  General Election results, 28 Dec '18 (9)
  new Coalition Govt, 10 Jan '19 (10)
  'Red Friday' dock strike riot, 31 Jan '19 (10)
  Liquor control relaxation, 17 Mar '19 (10)
  civil flying allowed, 1 May '19 (10)
  ration book issue ended, 3 May '19 (10)
  National Peace Thanksgiving Day, 6 Jul '19 (10)
  Empire Official Peace Day & Victory Parade, 19 Jul '19 (10)
  State of National Emergency declared, 27 Sep '19 (10)
  ratifies Versailles Treaty, 10 Oct '19 (10)
  first Armistice Remembrance Day, 11 Nov '19 (10)
  meat rationing ended, 15 Dec '19 (10)
  mandates over Palestine & Mesopotamia announced, 25 Apr '20 (10)
  abolishes conscription, 30 Apr '20 (10)
  Cenotaph unveiled, 11 Nov '20 (10)
  Unknown Soldier buried in Westminster Abbey, 11 Nov '20 (10)
  British Legion founded, 24 May '21 (10)
  termination of war in all aspects, 31 Aug '21 (10)
  see also Air War from 26 Jan '17; Conscription; *Home Fronts from 1 Jan '17*; *Int'l Events from 10 Feb '17*; Ireland; Rationing; *Sea War from 8 Jan '17*; Strikes; Women
British Expeditionary Force,
  statistics for final advance in 1918 *see Tables for W Front 1918*
  forms 1st Tank Bde, 1 Feb '17 (1)
  (proposed) French authority over, 25 Feb '17 (1), 27 Feb '17 (1)
  last TF formation joins, 1 Mar '17 (1)
  most divs 2000 men under strength, 1 Sep '17 (1)
  Second Army HQ moves to Italy, 9 Nov '17 (1)
  GHQ predicts German 1918 offensive, 7 Dec '17 (1)
  War Office recommends fewer bns per div, 10 Jan '18 (1)
  GHQ says German offensive imminent, 10 Mar '18 (1)
  Germans overrun most of BEF battle zone, 22 Mar '18 (1)
  possible retreat to Channel ports, 25 Mar '18 (8)
  Fifth Army reformed under Birdwood, 23 May '18 (1)
  Gater's Force formed, 30 May '18 (1)
  reformed Fifth Army takes over sector of line, 1 Jul '18 (1)
  relieves last French corps in Flanders, 7 Jul '18 (1)
  cas and successes since 21 Aug, 2 Sep '18 (1)
  attacks Hindenburg Line, 27 Sep '18 (1), 29 Sep '18 (1)
  fires record number of shells, 29 Sep '18 (1)
  first uses mustard gas, 30 Sep '18 (1)
  breaks through Hindenburg Line, 5 Oct '18 (1)
  begins advance to Armistice line, 8 Nov '18 (1)
  Foch names it 'decisive factor' in final victory, 17 Nov '18 (1)
  reaches German frontier, 24 Nov '18 (1)
British Forces, in Middle East *see* Mesopotamia; Palestine etc
British Somaliland, fighting at Endow Pass, 9 Oct '17 (5)
Broodseinde, Battle of, 4 Oct '17 (1)
Brooking, at Battle of Ramadi, 28 Sep '17 (4)
Brown, Capt A Roy, shoots down Richthofen, 21 Apr '18 (7)
Browning, Sir M, takes over 4th Battle Sqn from Sturdee, 31 Jan '18 (6)
Bruges, reoccupied by Belgians, 19 Oct '18 (1)
Brusilov,
  replaces Alexeiev, 22 May '17 (1)
  farewell to SW Front, 5 Jun '17 (2)
  second offensive begins, 1 Jul '17 (2)
  replaced as C-in-C, 1 Aug '17 (2)
  see also Who's Who
Brussels,
  reoccupied by Belgians, 18 Nov '18 (1)
  King Albert's procession into, 22 Nov '18 (1)
Buat, CoS to Pétain, 5 Jul '18 (1)
Buchan, John,
  Director of Dept of Information, 9 Feb '17 (9)
  Information Ministry liquidator, 13 Nov '18 (9)
Bucharest,
  Peace of, 7 May '18 (2)
  Treaty of, 5 Jul '18 (8)
Bukovina,
  National Ctee of Rumanians of Transylvania & Bukovina formed, 30 Apr '18 (8)
  Ukrainians seize Czernowitz, 3 Nov '18 (2)
  Congress decides for union with Rumania, 28 Nov '18 (8)
  Rumania ratifies Union, 29 Dec '19 (10)
  see also E Front from 3 Jan '17
Bulgaria,
  aid to Germany *see 1914-1918 General Tables*
  civilian dead 1914-18 *see 1914-1918 General Tables*
  financial & economic costs 1914-18 *see 1914-1918 General Tables*
  war expenditure/revenue *see 1914-1918 General Tables*
  Germany refuses to supply munitions & clothing, 1 Mar '18 (8)
  PM Radoslavov resigns, 18 Jun '18 (9)
  Tsar Ferdinand orders Lukov to stand, 16 Sep '18 (3)
  British troops cross frontier, 25 Sep '18 (3)
  Stambolski freed to calm mutineers, 25 Sep '18 (9)
  requests armistice, 26 Sep '18 (8)
  Republic proclaimed at Radomir, 27 Sep '18 (9)
  signs armistice, 29 Sep '18 (3)
  hostilities cease, 30 Sep '18 (3)
  Armistice with Allies, 30 Sep '18 (8)
  Tsar Ferdinand abdicates in favour of Boris, 3 Oct '18 (8)
  last Germans leave, 18 Oct '18 (3)
  French troops reach Danube, 19 Oct '18 (3)
  British div lands at Dedeagach, 28 Oct '18 (3)
  K Boris abdicates, 1 Nov '18 (8)
  Allies cross Danube, 10 Nov '18 (3)
  PM Malinov resigns & Todorov forms govt, 28 Nov '18 (9)
  blockade ends, 28 Feb '19 (10)
  new govt accepts peace terms, 13 Nov '19 (10)
  signs peace Treaty of Neuilly, 27 Nov '19 (10)
  Yugoslavia signs Austrian & Bulgar peace treaties, 5 Dec '19 (10)
  Rumania signs peace treaty, 9 Dec '19 (10)
  see also Air War from 11 Aug '17; S Fronts from 28 Jun '18
Bullecourt, Battle of, 3 May '17 (1)
Burges, Lt-Col, wins VC, 18 Sep '18 (3)
Burian, Baron,
  Austrian Foreign Minister again, 14 Apr '18 (8)
  succeeded by Andrassy, 24 Oct '18 (8)
Burney, replaced as Second Sea Lord, 7 Aug '17 (6)
Buxton's camelry,
  meet Lawrence, 30 Jul '18 (4)
  take a station, 8 Aug '18 (4)
  rejoin EEF, 6 Sep '18 (4)
Bweho Chini, Battle of, 22 Sep '17 (5)
Byng,
  replaces Allenby as GOC BEF Third Army, 9 Jun '17 (1)
  see also Who's Who (BEF Army cdrs)

C

Cadorna,
  cancels 12th Isonzo offensive, 18 Sep '17 (3)
  orders general retreat on Isonzo, 27 Oct '17 (3)
  issues final Order of the Day, 7 Nov '17 (3)
  replaced as C-in-C, 9 Nov '17 (3)
  on Allied Supreme War Council, 27 Nov '17 (8)
  recalled from Allied Supreme War Council, 1 Feb '18 (3)
  replaced on Supreme War Council, 8 Feb '18 (8)
  retires after Caporetto report, 24 Jul '19 (10)
  see also Who's Who
Caillaux, arrested for treason, 14 Jan '18 (9)
Calais Agreement, 27 Feb '17 (1)
Calthorpe *see* Gough-Calthorpe
Cambrai,
  Haig approves Byng's tank attack, 16 Sep '17 (1)
  Haig approves thrust, 13 Oct '17 (1)
  Battle of, RFC support, 20 Nov '17 (7)
  German surprise counter-attack, 30 Nov '17 (1)
  Battle of, inquiry ordered, 12 Dec '17 (9)
  Battle of, British tanks move to start line, 19 Nov '17 (1)
  Battle of, begins, 20 Nov '17 (1)
  Battle of Bourlon Wood, 23 Nov '17 (1)
  Battle of Bourlon Wood ends, 4 Dec '17 (1)
  Battle of, ends, 7 Dec '17 (1)
  Battle of, forces & losses *see Tables for W Front 1917*
  Bryce inquiry report, 15 Jan '18 (1)
  Battle of Havrincourt, 12 Sep '18 (1)
  Battles of the Hindenburg Line begin, 12 Sep '18 (1)
  British tanks at, 21 Sep '18 (1)
  Battle of Canal du Nord, 27 Sep '18 (1)
  Battle of Beaurevoir Line, 3 Oct '18 (1)
  Second Battle of, 8 Oct '18 (1), (7)
  entered by Canadians, 9 Oct '18 (1)
Cameroons, French forbid female slavery, 18 Aug '17 (5)
Campbell, Lt D, first US air ace, 31 May '18 (7)
Canada,
  RFC training begins at Toronto, 26 Jan '17 (7)
  PM visits France, 8 Mar '17 (1)
  Trotsky arrested, 3 Apr '17 (8)
  conscription introduced, 15 May '17 (9), 20 May '17 (9), 11 Jun '17 (9)
  Conscription Bill & Act, 6 Jul '17 (9), 29 Aug '17 (9)
  some women enfranchised, 14 Sep '17 (9), 20 Sep '17 (9)
  conscription in force, 26 Sep '17 (9)
  Bordern's Coalition Union Govt formed, 12 Oct '17 (9)
  progress of conscription, 10 Nov '17 (9)
  Halifax wrecked by munitions explosion, 6 Dec '17 (9)
  Unionists win election, 17 Dec '17 (9)
  Soldier Re-settlement Board founded, 1 Feb '18 (9)
  Women's Ottawa War Conference, 28 Feb '18 (9)
  anti-conscription riots in Quebec, 28 Mar '18 (9), 1 Apr '18 (9)
  Conscription Bill in Newfoundland, 23 Apr '18 (9)
  Canadian Pacific liner sunk by U-boat, 30 Apr '18 (6)
  farmers' sons refused conscription exemption, 14 May '18 (9)
  Dept of Public Instruction for propaganda, 12 Sep '18 (9)
  'Khaki University', 19 Sep '18 (9)
  strikes & lockouts forbidden, 11 Oct '18 (9)
  ratifies Versailles Treaty, 12 Sep '19 (10)
  see also Home Fronts from 18 Jan '17
Canadian forces,
  storm Vimy Ridge, 9 Apr '17 (1)
  clear Vimy Ridge, 10 Apr '17 (1)
  storm Pimple Hill, 12 Apr '17 (1)
  capture Vimy village & Petit Vimy, 13 Apr '17 (1)
  losses at Vimy, 14 Apr '17 (1)
  1st Div in Battle of Arleux, 28 Apr '17 (1), 11 May '17 (1)
  in Third Battle of the Scarpe, 3 May '17 (1)
  make powerful raid in Artois, 8 Jun '17 (1)
  Sir A Currie becomes GOC Cdn Corps, 9 Jun '17 (1)
  begin capture of Avion, 26 Jun '17 (1)

370

US troops fire first shot, 23 Oct '17 (1)
see also W Front from 2 Jan '17
Lossberg, CoS German Sixth Army, 22 Apr '17 (1)
Ludendorff,
hears belatedly of French mutinies, 30 Jun '17 (1)
cables resignation, 12 Jul '17 (9)
approves Caporetto offensive, 29 Aug '17 (3)
proposes great 1918 offensive at Mons conference, 11 Nov '17 (1)
interviewed on Russian revolution, 1 Dec '17 (8)
makes final decision to launch 1918 Spring Offensive, 21 Jan '18 (1)
promises Kaiser victory in Spring Offensive, 13 Feb '18 (1)
decides to abandon attack on Amiens for good, 5 Apr '18 (1)
begins Battle of the Lys, 9 Apr '18 (1)
suspends offensive, 29 Apr '18 (1)
suspends Op *Georgette*, 30 Apr '18 (1)
refuses to recognize Turk treaties with Armenia & Georgia, 8 Jun '18 (4)
calls off *Gneisenau* offensive, 12 Jun '18 (1)
launches *Friedensturm* offensive, 15 Jul '18 (1)
rows with Hindenburg over Marne battle, 18 Jul '18 (1)
orders retreat to *Blücher* position, 29 Jul '18 (1)
slights AEF, 2 Aug '18 (1)
promises tank offensive, 4 Aug '18 (1)
'Black day of the German Army', 8 Aug '18 (1)
says Germany cannot win but must not lose, 9 Aug '18 (8)
offers resignation, 11 Aug '18 (1)
sees U-boats as Germany's only hope, 11 Aug '18 (6)
recommends peace negotiations, 14 Aug '18 (1)
'another black day', 20 Aug '18 (1)
issues order for 2nd phased retirement, 2 Sep '18 (1)
decides Germany must seek armistice, 28 Sep '18 (1)
persuades Hindenburg to call for armistice, 28 Sep '18 (8)
severely depressed, 29 Sep '18 (1)
urges Germany to make peace offer, 1 Oct '18 (1)
demands a fight to the finish, 17 Oct '18 (1)
resigns, 26 Oct '18 (1), (8)
acquitted of war crimes, 10 Jan '21 (10)
see also Who's Who
Luke, Lt Frank, awarded posthumous CMH, 25 Sep '18 (7)
Lusitania, U-boat which sank her, sunk, 5 Sep '17 (6)
Luxemburg, Rosa, murdered, 15 Jan '19 (10)
Lyautey,
and Calais Agreement, 27 Feb '17 (1)
again Resident-General in Morocco, 5 Apr '17 (5)
Lys,
Battle of the, forces & losses Apr 1918 *see Tables for W Front 1918*
Battle of the, begins, 9 Apr '18 (1)
Battle of the, fog delays flying, 9 Apr '18 (7)
Battle of the, German offensive slackens, 12 Apr '18 (1)
Battle of the, ends, 29 Apr '18 (1)
German evacuation of Lys Salient complete, 6 Sep '18 (1)

M

McAndrew, Maj-Gen J, AEF CoS, 3 May '18 (1)
MacArthur,
meets Patton under fire, 12 Sep '18 (1)
i/c 42nd US 'Rainbow' Div in final battles, 5 Nov '18 (1)
Macedonia,
forces & losses *see Tables for S Fronts 1917, 1918*
Sarrail ends Allied spring offensive, 21 May '17 (3)
Combat of Skra di Legen, 30 May '18 (3)
Lloyd George approves offensive, 4 Sep '18 (3)
Allied final offensive, 14 Sep '18 (3)
Battle of the Vardar (or Dobropolje or Moglenitsa), 14 Sep '18 (3)
Franco-Serb breakthrough, 17 Sep '18 (3)
British troops cross Bulgar frontier, 25 Sep '18 (3)
Bulgaria signs Armistice, 29 Sep '18 (3)
Bulgarian hostilities cease, 30 Sep '18 (3)
see also Air War from 12 Feb '17; *S Fronts from 21 Feb '17*; Salonika
Mackensen,
ultimatum to Rumania, 6 Feb '18 (2)
C-in-C occupied Rumania, 7 May '18 (2)
forces surrender & he interned, 16 Dec '18 (8)
see also Who's Who
Mackenzie, Compton, 1 May '17 (4), 1 Aug '17 (8)
Maghiloman, becomes Rumanian PM, 20 Mar '18 (2)
Mahon,
succeeded by Shaw as GOC Ireland, 9 May '18 (9)
see also Who's Who (Salonika generals)
Maistre,
replaces Mangin, 29 Apr '17 (1)
replaced as French C-in-C Italy, 24 Mar '18 (3)
moved from Tenth Army to Centre Army Gp, 16 Jun '18 (1)
Maksimov, replaces Nepenin, 17 Mar '17 (6)
Malaria,
British troops in Salonika, 30 Jul '17 (3), 30 Dec '17 (3), 23 Mar '18 (3), 30 Sep '18 (3)
Italian troops in Albania, 6 Jul '18 (3)
Austrians on Piave, 1 Aug '18 (3)
Malleson, Maj-Gen,
Trans-Caspian Mission sets off, 28 Jun '18 (2)
reaches Meshed, 6 Jul '18 (2)
assists White Russians, 1 Aug '18 (2)
Malvy, trial, 21 Jan '18 (9), 16 Jul '18 (9), 6 Aug '18 (9)
Manchuria, 24 Apr '18 (2)
Mandate system, comes into effect, 10 Jan '20 (10)
Mangin,
abandoned by Nivelle & replaced by Maistre, 29 Apr '17 (1)
put on res list, 31 Jul '17 (1)
restored to duty as i/c French IX Corps, 15 Dec '17 (1)
i/c French Tenth Army, 16 Jun '18 (1)
Mann, replaces Behnke as German Navy Sec, 7 Oct '18 (6)
Mannerheim,
Finnish C-in-C, 18 Jan '18 (2)
'Karelian' order of the day, 23 Feb '18 (2)
offensive, 15 Mar '18 (2)
takes Tampere, 6 Apr '18 (2)
takes Viborg, 29 Apr '18 (2)
leads victory parade, 16 May '18 (2)
resigns as C-in-C, 27 May '18 (2)
elected Regent of Finland, 11 Dec '18 (2)
see also Who's Who (Russian generals)
Marasesti,
Battle of, begins, 23 Jul '17 (2)
Battle of, first phase ends, 1 Aug '17 (2)
Battle of, second phase begins, 6 Aug '17 (2)
Battle of, ends, 3 Sep '17 (2)
Markiewicz, Countess, elected to British Parlt, 28 Dec '18 (9)
Marne,
Second Battle of the, forces & losses *see Tables for W Front 1918*
Germans capture Soissons, 29 May '18 (1)
Germans reach the Marne, 30 May '18 (1)
reached by the Germans, 3 Jun '18 (1)
Second Battle of the, begins, 15 Jul '18 (1)
Second Battle of the, Allied counter-stroke, 18 Jul '18 (1)
Battle of Tardenois, 20 Jul '18 (1)
recrossed by the Germans, 20 Jul '18 (1)
crossed by Allies, 22 Jul '18 (1)
Second Battle of the, general retreat by Germans, 26 Jul '18 (1)
Second Battle of the, ends, 4 Aug '18 (1)
Marneschutz, Op, 14 Jun '18 (1)
Marshall,
succeeds Maude in Mesopotamia, 18 Nov '17 (4)
see also Who's Who
Marushevski, White Russian Gov-Gen & C-in-C at Archangel, 20 Nov '18 (2)
Marwitz, moved from Second to Fifth Army, 22 Sep '18 (1)
Masaryk, becomes Pres of Czechoslovakia, 10 Nov '18 (8), 14 Nov '18 (8)
Mata Hari *see* Espionage
Matz,
Fourth German offensive on R, begins, 9 Jun '18 (1)
Fourth German offensive on R, ends, 14 Jun '18 (1)
Maude,
lands at Baghdad, 11 Mar '17 (4)
promises Arab freedom at Baghdad, 19 Mar '17 (4)
discounts Arab help, 24 Jun '17 (4)
orders attack on Ramadi, 15 Sep '17 (4)
dies of cholera, 18 Nov '17 (4)
see also Who's Who
Maud'huy,
sacked by Clemenceau, 9 Jun '18 (1)
French Military Governor at Metz, 26 Nov '18 (1)
Maugham, Somerset,
accepts mission to Russia, 20 Jun '17 (8)
urges Allied propaganda in Russia, 16 Oct '17 (8)
sees Kerensky, 31 Oct '17 (8)
Max, Prince of Baden,
becomes German Chancellor & Foreign Minister, 3 Oct '18 (8)
becomes Regent, 9 Nov '18 (8)
hands Chancellorship to Ebert, 9 Nov '18 (9)
Maxwell, Sir R, resigns as BEF QMG, 22 Dec '17 (1)
'May Island, Battle of', 31 Jan '18 (6)
Maynard, Maj-Gen, arrives in North Russia, 23 Jun '18 (2)
Mazel, replaced at French Fifth Army, 6 May '17 (1)
Medals & decorations,
Rumania creates Michael the Brave War Order, 7 Jan '17 (9)
Russia abolishes most, 25 Mar '17 (9)
Order of the British Empire founded, 4 Jun '17 (9)
British 1914 Star announced, 9 Sep '17 (9)
Amundsen returns his German decorations, 25 Oct '17 (8)
US Army institutes DSC & DSM, 12 Jan '18 (9)
Italy institutes War Cross of Merit, 18 Jan '18 (9)
Finnish Order of the Cross of Liberty formed, 4 Mar '18 (2)
US DSM authorized, 7 Mar '18 (9)
British DFC instituted, 3 Jun '18 (7)
Order of the Red Banner instituted, 1 Sep '18 (2)
Allied Victory medal, 1 Mar '19 (10)
British War Medal issued, 19 Jul '19 (10)
Mediterranean,
US submarine chasers arrive, 7 Jun '18 (6)
Scheer orders all seaworthy U-boats home, 25 Oct '18 (6)
Allied blockade raised, 26 May '19 (10)
see also Sea War from 1 Jan '17
Medo, Action at, 12 Apr '18 (5)
Megiddo,
forces & losses *see Tables for Turk Fronts 1918*
Battles of, 19 Sep '18 (4)
Meinertzhagen, head of GHQ intelligence at Cairo, 24 May '17 (4)
Meinertzhagen, Col, successful ruse, 10 Oct '17 (4)
Memorials,
Gallipoli Chapel & Remembrance Service, 25 Apr '17 (9)
to first AEF man killed, 6 Apr '18 (9)
British war shrine in Hyde Park, 4 Aug '18 (9)
first British Armistice Remembrance Day, 11 Nov '19 (10)
British & French Unknown Soldiers buried, 11 Nov '20 (10)
British Cenotaph unveiled, 11 Nov '20 (10)
US Unknown Soldier buried, 24 Aug '21 (10)
Menin Road Ridge,
Battle of the, begins, 20 Sep '17 (1)
Battle of the, ends, 25 Sep '17 (1)
Mesopotamia,
losses in 1917, 1918 *see Tables for Turk Fronts 1917, 1918*
losses 1914-18 *see 1914-1918 General Tables*
Battle of Kut, 9 Jan '17 (4)
British armoured cars reach front, 20 Jan '17 (4)
main Tigris crossing, 23 Feb '17 (4)
Kut abandoned by Turks, 24 Feb '17 (4)
British War Cabinet approves advance on Baghdad, 28 Feb '17 (4)
Fall of Baghdad, 11 Mar '17 (4)
Battle of Mushahida Station, 14 Mar '17 (4)
Maude's Baghdad proclamation, 19 Mar '17 (4)
Battle of Jebel Hamrin, 25 Mar '17 (4)
Action of Duqma, 29 Mar '17 (4)
British & Russians meet up, 2 Apr '17 (4)
Battle of Istabulat, 21 Apr '17 (4)
Maude plans joint offensive with Russians, 22 Apr '17 (4)
possible co-operation with Russians, 22 Apr '17 (4), 2 Aug '17 (4), 21 Sep '17 (4)
Battle of Band-i-Adhaim, 30 Apr '17 (4)
Falkenhayn at Constantinople to discuss retaking of Baghdad, 7 May '17 (4)
Maude discounts Arab help, 24 Jun '17 (4)
Commission blames India for early setbacks, 26 Jun '17 (4)
India Sec Chamberlain resigns, 11 Jul '17 (9)
3 British railways completed, 31 Jul '17 (4)
Battle of Ramadi, 28 Sep '17 (4)
Battle of Daur, 2 Nov '17 (4)
Battle of Tikrit, 5 Nov '17 (4)
Maude dies of cholera, 18 Nov '17 (4)
Third Action of Jebel Hamrin, 3 Dec '17 (4)
British Baghdad-Falluja (Euphrates) railway completed, 21 Dec '17 (4)
Battle of Khan Baghdadi, 26 Mar '18 (4)
British occupy Kirkuk, 7 May '18 (4)
British Basra-Baghdad Euphrates railway approved, 18 Jul '18 (4)
Germans withdraw, 19 Oct '18 (4)
Battle of Sharqat, 28 Oct '18 (4)
Turk Tigris Group surrenders at Sharqat, 30 Oct '18 (4)
Turks sign armistice, 30 Oct '18 (4)
hostilities cease, 31 Oct '18 (4)
British enter Mosul, 4 Nov '18 (4)
Turks evacuate Mosul, 10 Nov '18 (4)
Abdulla elected King, 9 Mar '20 (10)
British Mandate announced, 25 Apr '20 (10)
insurrection v British, 3 Jun '20 (10)
see also Air War from 20 Jan '17; Dunsterville; Kut; *Turk Fronts from 7 Jan '17*
Messines Ridge,
forces & losses in Battle of *see Tables for W Front 1917*
Battle of, feint barrage begins, 3 Jun '17 (1)
Battle of, 7 Jun '17 (1)
Battle of, Haig's dispatch, 8 Jan '18 (1)
Germans recapture, 10 Apr '18 (1)
Metz, reoccupied by French, 19 Nov '18 (1)
Meuse,
Battle of St Mihiel, 12 Sep '18 (1)
Franco-US offensive, 1 Nov '18 (1)
AEF crosses, 10 Nov '18 (1)
French reach Mézières, 10 Nov '18 (1)
see also W Front from 9 Feb '17
Meuse-Argonne,
forces & losses Sept-Nov 1918 *see Tables for W Front 1918*
Battle of, 26 Sep '18 (1), (7)
Mexico,
German spy captured, 15 Jan '18 (8)
see also Int'l Events from 28 Jan '17
Michael, Op *see* Spring Offensive, German 1918
Michaelis,
succeeds Bethmann as Chancellor, 13 Jul '17 (8)
replaced as Chancellor, 30 Oct '17 (8)
Micheler,
takes over French Fifth Army, 6 May '17 (1)
replaced at Fifth Army, 5 Jul '18 (1)
Michelsen, Capt Andreas, replaces Bauer i/c U-boats, 5 Jun '17 (6)
Military service *see* Conscription
Miliukov,
Russian Foreign Minister, 15 Mar '17 (8)
'Russia will never agree to a separate peace', 5 May '17 (8)
resigns, 16 May '17 (8)
Milne,
promoted Lt-Gen, 1 Jan '17 (3)
on Salonika climate, 5 Mar '17 (3)
sails for Constantinople, 26 Nov '18 (3)
arrives in England on leave, 14 Dec '18 (3)
C-in-C at Constantinople, 8 Jan '19 (10)
i/c Trans-Caspia, 15 Jan '19 (10)
see also Who's Who (Salonika generals)
Mines, sea,
statistics 1914-18 *see Tables for Royal Navy losses 1918*
British minefield round Heligoland Bight, 1 Jan '17 (6)
Dover Strait minefield, 8 Feb '17 (6)
Dover Strait barrage relaid, 31 Jul '17 (6)
RN gets efficient H2 mine, 1 Sep '17 (6)
first air-dropped mining successes, 27 Sep '17 (6)
British mines off Flamborough Head, 1 Nov '17 (6)
Dover Straits deep minefield, 21 Nov '17 (6), 19 Dec '17 (6)
3 British destroyers sunk, 23 Dec '17 (6)
U-boat minelayers attempt to seal off Forth, 31 Jan '18 (6)
first mine of Northern Barrage laid, 3 Mar '18 (6)
US Navy helps lay Northern Barrage, 26 May '18 (6)
British E Coast Barrage, 1 Jun '18 (6)
areas A & C of Northern Barrage begun, 8 Jun '18 (6)
shore-controlled mines, 26 Jun '18 (6)
Northern Barrage begins to inhibit U-boats, 1 Jul '18 (6)
RN lays first magnetic mines, 8 Aug '18 (6)
British shore-controlled, 19 Aug '18 (6)
electrically controlled minefield, 28 Oct '18 (6)
Mining & counter-mining,
Messines mines produce largest non-nuclear explosion, 7 Jun '17 (1)
Italian on Trentino, 9 Jun '17 (3)
Minsk, Red Army reoccupies, 10 Dec '18 (2)
Mirabach, Count, murdered, 6 Jul '18 (2)
Mirbach, Count, appointed German Ambassador to Moscow, 9 Apr '18 (2)

378

379